WRITING
ARGUMENTS

Second Edition

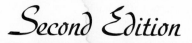

WRITING

A Rhetoric with Readings

ARGUMENTS

JOHN D. RAMAGE
ARIZONA STATE UNIVERSITY

JOHN C. BEAN
SEATTLE UNIVERSITY

MACMILLAN PUBLISHING COMPANY

NEW YORK

Editor: **Eben W. Ludlow**
Production Supervisor: **Linda Greenberg**
Production Manager: **Nick Sklitsis**
Text and Cover Designer: **Sheree L. Goodman**

This book was set in Palatino by Digitype, Inc., and was printed and bound by Book Press. The cover was printed by New England Book Components, Inc.

Acknowledgments begin on page 765, which constitutes an extension of the copyright page.

Macmillan Publishing Company
866 Third Avenue, New York, New York 10022

Macmillan Publishing Company is part of
the Maxwell Communication Group of Companies.

Library of Congress Cataloging-in-Publication Data
Ramage, John D.
 Writing arguments : a rhetoric with readings / John D. Ramage,
John C. Bean.
  p. cm.
 Includes index.
 ISBN 0-02-398120-2 (paper)
 1. English language—Rhetoric. 2. Persuasion (Rhetoric)
3. College readers. I. Bean, John C. II. Title.
PE1431.R33 1992
808'.0427—dc20   91-2650
                             CIP

Printing: 2 3 4 5 6 7   Year: 2 3 4 5 6 7 8

PREFACE

Overview

Encouraged by the enthusiastic reception of the first edition of *Writing Arguments: A Rhetoric with Readings*, we have attempted in this second edition to retain the text's original strengths while making extensive changes aimed at enhancing the text's clarity, comprehensiveness, and usefulness in the classroom.

Our primary purpose remains unchanged: to integrate a comprehensive study of argument with a process approach to writing. The text treats argument as a means of personal discovery and clarification as well as a means of persuading audiences. In both its treatment of argumentation and its approach to teaching writing, the text is rooted in current research and theory. *Writing Arguments* can be used successfully at the freshman level and in upper-division courses devoted solely to argument.

Improvements in the Second Edition

Based on recommendations from many users of the first edition at both four-year and two-year institutions, we have substantially strengthened the text through the following additions and changes:

- A new chapter on reading arguments (Chapter 2: "The Process of Reading Arguments"). Integrated into the first part of the text, this chapter helps teachers treat argumentation as a reciprocal process of reading and writing.

- A new chapter on evidence (Chapter 7: "A Detailed Look at the Uses of Evidence in Argumentation"). This chapter treats the problem of evidence in depth: what constitutes good evidence; how to find it; how to use it effectively; how to proceed when the evidence is ambiguous and inconclusive.

- A new collection of readings in the anthology section (Part VI). The anthology, focusing on 12 different issues, contains 47 arguments, carefully selected to insure student interest and to represent a wide variety of argumentative strategies and types. The anthology begins with four issues treated, for pedagogical purposes, as sharply contrasted pro/con pairs. The remaining issues are treated in greater depth through inclusion of a wide spectrum of views suggesting the subtlety and complexity of arguments in the real world. Throughout the rhetoric section of the text we have included several dozen additional arguments—both student and professional—that illustrate strategies and features under discussion.

- An expanded treatment of research writing in Part V including explanation of the APA documentation system as well as the MLA system. An additional student researched argument—using the APA system—now supplements the original student argument using the MLA system.

- An expanded treatment of the writing process, both in Chapter 3 ("The Process of Writing Your Own Arguments") and throughout the text. Chapter 3 now includes an improved treatment of argumentative heuristics and provides additional advice on improving the organization of drafts, including use of tree diagrams. A case study of a student writer shows one student's progress from the inception of an idea in response to readings, through early freewriting, to a final draft.

- Reconceived and reshaped explanations of *pathos* and *ethos*, as well as reorganized treatment of strategies for reaching audiences. Part III of this second edition, "The Rhetorical Structure of Arguments," represents a much improved treatment of this vital material.

- A substantially expanded treatment of informal fallacies ("Appendix 1"), now organized as fallacies of *pathos*, fallacies of *ethos*, and fallacies of *logos*.

- Numerous minor improvements and additions throughout the text, including a section on practical proposals in Chapter 15, improved "microtheme" writing assignments in Part II, a new collection of student arguments for classroom "norming sessions" in Appendix 3, and more extensive use of student arguments as illustrations throughout the text.

Theory of Argumentation in the Text

Our interest in argumentation grows out of our interest in the relationship between writing and thinking. When writing arguments, we are forced to "lay bare" our thinking processes in an unparalleled way. But as might be expected, there's no clear agreement among writing teachers on how best to approach the relationship between thinking and writing.

One approach links argument closely to formal logic. Typical of this approach is a classroom emphasis on the study of syllogisms, problems of valid and invalid syllogistic forms, patterns of inferences, Venn diagrams, and the traditional informal fallacies.

A second approach treats argument more rhetorically, taking its methods from debate, legal reasoning, and speech. Often this approach uses Stephen Toulmin's model of argument and finds additional philosophical grounding in the work of Chaim Perelman and others who see meaning as socially constructed rather than rooted in the changeless universal system of formal logic.

A third approach—represented in the important text *A Rhetoric of Argument* by Jeanne Fahnestock and Marie Secor—employs what is sometimes called a "stasis system." This approach attempts to classify arguments according to types of claims and teaches typical patterns of development for each claim type.

In *Writing Arguments* we draw on elements of all three approaches. Our text treats both syllogistic and Toulmin logic as heuristics to help students learn how to discover and support the premises of their arguments. Drawing on Aristotle's conception of the enthymeme as a structure for "rhetorical proofs"—which must be rooted not in a certain premise but in a probabilistic assumption granted by the audience—we teach an audience-centered invention system in which the writer appeals to values or beliefs held by the audience. Thus, during the composing process, emerging arguments need to be "unpacked," or laid out completely, so that the underlying assumptions are brought to the surface. The stasis approach that we use in Part IV gives students another view of the same territory, this time showing them how different kinds of claims demand different strategies for support.

Structure of the Text

The text has six main parts plus appendixes. Part I gives an overview of argumentation. These first three chapters present our philosophy of argument, showing how argument helps writers clarify their own thinking. Throughout we link the process of arguing—finding issue questions, formulating propositions, examining opposing arguments, and creating structures of supporting reasons and evidence — with the processes of reading and writing.

Part II examines the logical structure of arguments. These chapters show that the core of an argument is a claim with reasons; in arguments most likely to be successful these reasons will link the claim to values, beliefs, or other assumptions already held by the audience. Discussions of Toulmin logic show students how to discover both the stated and unstated premises of their arguments and to provide structures of reasons and evidence to support them.

Part III focuses on the rhetorical structure of arguments. These three chapters discuss the writer's relationship with an audience, particularly with finding audience-based reasons, with using *pathos* and *ethos* effectively and responsibly, and with accommodating or refuting opposing views.

Part IV discusses five different categories of argument: definitional arguments (X is/is not a Y), causal arguments (X causes/does not cause Y), resemblance arguments (X is/is not like Y), evaluation arguments (X is a good/bad Y), and proposal arguments (we should/should not do X). These chapters introduce students to two recurring strategies of argument that cut across the different category types: "criteria-match" arguing in which the writer establishes criteria for a Y and argues that X meets those criteria, and "causal " arguing in which the writer shows that X can be linked to Y in a causal chain. The last chapter of Part IV deals with the special complexities of moral arguments.

Part V shows students how to incorporate research into their arguments. It explains how writers use sources, with a special focus on the skills of summary, paraphrase, and judicious quotation. Unlike standard treatments of the research paper, our discussion explains to students how the writer's meaning and purpose control the selection and shaping of source materials. Part V explains both the MLA and the APA documentation systems and illustrates them with two student examples of researched arguments.

Part VI is an anthology of arguments by professional writers focusing on twelve different issues. Throughout the text are other shorter examples of professional arguments as well as student essays.

The appendixes provide important supplemental information useful for courses in argument. Appendix 1 gives an overview of informal fallacies; Appendix 2 discusses some uses and abuses of statistics in argument. Finally, Appendix 3, adapted from our textbook *Form and Surprise in Composition: Writing and Thinking Across the Curriculum* (Macmillan, 1986), shows students how to get the most out of collaborative groups in an argument class. It also provides a sequence of collaborative tasks that will help students learn to peer-critique their classmates' arguments in progress.

The numerous "For Class Discussion" exercises within the text provide additional tasks for group collaboration.

Writing Assignments

The text provides a variety of sequenced writing assignments, including expressive tasks for discovering and exploring arguments, "microthemes" for practicing basic argumentative moves (for example, supporting a reason with statistical evidence), cases, and numerous other assignments calling for complete arguments. Thus, the text provides instructors with a wealth of options for writing assignments on which to build a coherent course.

Acknowledgments

We are happy for this opportunity to give public thanks to a number of scholars and teachers who have influenced our approach to composition and argument. Our special thanks to Harvey Wiener, now Associate Dean of Academic Affairs at the City University of New York, who taught us how to design writing tasks; to Andrea Lunsford of Ohio State University, who introduced us to new connections between writing and thinking; to Jeanne Fahnestock of the University of Maryland and Marie Secor of Pennsylvania State University, who broke new ground in their treatment of argument; to George Hillocks of the University of Chicago, whose study of the "environmental mode" of composition teaching has helped us clarify what we are trying to do and whose research into the teaching of definition has influenced us in a number of ways; to Ann Berthoff of the University of Massachusetts, who persuaded us that writing can never be reduced to skills; and finally to Kenneth Bruffee of Brooklyn College, the City University of New York, who taught us about collaborative learning and whose text *A Short Course in Composition* (Boston: Little, Brown, 1985) has influenced our whole approach to the process of writing arguments.

In addition to the teachers and scholars named above, we would like to thank the following reviewers, who gave us unusually helpful and cogent advice: Betty Bamberg, University of Southern California; James P. Farrelly, University of Dayton; Michael C. Flanigan, University of Oklahoma; Jean F. Goodine, Northern Virginia Community College; Gary Layne Hatch, Arizona State University; June Hobbs, University of Oklahoma; Christine A. Hult, Utah State University; Renee H. Major, Louisiana State University; Christina Murphy, Texas Christian University; Linda K. Shamoon, University of Rhode Island; David W. Smit, Kansas State University; Stephen

Wilhoit, University of Dayton; Linda Woodson, The University of Texas at San Antonio; and Richard J. Zbaracki, Iowa State University.

We would also like to thank Eben Ludlow, Executive Editor at Macmillan Publishing Company, whose unflagging good humor and faith in our approach to both composition and argument have kept us writing and revising for the better part of five years. Eben called this book forth and kept it going. For that we are grateful.

We wish to give special thanks to our wives, Kathleen Ramage and Rosalie (Kit) Bean, for their professional help and encouragement. Kathy Ramage's many years' experience in teaching argumentation has shaped our ideas in numerous ways. And Kit Bean's background in library science has influenced our approach to research writing throughout Part V. Moeover, we are especially grateful for Kit's help in writing the section of Chapter 18 explaining the MLA and APA documentation systems.

Finally, we would like to thank our children, Laura and Chris Ramage and Matthew, Andrew, Stephen, and Sarah Bean, who have graciously put up with us. Any resemblance between these children and Young Person in Chapter 1 is purely coincidental.

J.D.R.   J.C.B.

BRIEF CONTENTS

Part IV Arguments in Depth: Five Categories of Claims   *205*

Part V Writing from Sources: The Argument as a Formal Research Paper   *375*

Part VI An Anthology of Arguments   *441*

Appendixes

DETAILED CONTENTS

Part IV   Arguments in Depth: Five Categories of Claims

205

Soviet Union, Soviet Premier Gorbachev took immediate
action to prevent secession, thereby maintaining the
Union of Soviet Socialist Republics. Many Americans
supported Gorbachev by drawing a parallel between
him and Lincoln, who moved swiftly to prevent the
secession of South Carolina. But is Lithuania like South
Carolina? Charles Krauthammer argues that it is not.

Sample Arguments

Annual state competition for high school dance and
drill teams in Washington, claims Karen Kartes, mixes
different talent levels and genres of teams, produces
animosity among participants, confuses viewers, and
places stress on judges. In this practical proposal, Kartes
offers two possible solutions.

By determining wages on the basis of level of education
needed, responsibility required, and other factors
related to a job's importance in our total economy,
comparable worth will bring to the society benefits that
outweigh its costs.

Sample Argument

Part V *Writing from Sources: The Argument as a Formal Research Paper* 375

Part VI   An Anthology of Arguments   **441**

between "conscientious disobedience"—in which one willingly accepts punishment in order to make a moral protest—and active group disobedience aimed at changing laws. "[C]ivil disobedience [e.g., the kind practiced by Martin Luther King, Jr.], whatever the ethical rationalization, is still an assault on our democratic society, an affront to our legal order and an attack on our constitutional government."

Socrates, who was himself ill-served by the state, here argues in favor of a citizen's absolute obligation to obey the rules of the state. He has been unjustly sentenced to die, and his friend Crito urges him to escape from prison. Socrates declines on ethical grounds.

Censorship and Pornography: Should a Democratic Society Suppress Pornographic or Obscene Works?   **526**

New York University Professor Irving Kristol argues that a liberal today "ought to favor a liberal form of censorship." Basing his arguments on the moral relevance of art, Kristol says bluntly: "If you care for the quality of life in our American democracy, then you have to be for censorship."

Responding directly to Kristol's argument, Oboler claims that Kristol "has clearly failed to consider the most basic of all issues in the censorship/noncensorship dispute."

Feminist author Susan Brownmiller argues against pornography insofar as its primary effect is to raise male self-esteem by degrading women and reducing them to "adult toys . . . to be used, abused, broken and discarded."

In this interview from *Playboy Magazine*, Canadian philosopher F. M. Christensen argues that "nothing is more human than sexual fantasies and feelings. . . . Emotional reactions against pornography tell more about the complainant's own sexual inhibitions than about pornography."

extremely narrow and technical rulings on affirmative
action cases and questions whether they understand the
spirit as well as the letter of civil rights law. Hertzberg
characterizes affirmative action as a sacrifice by this
generation for future generations but worries that it will
have little effect on the vast black "underclass."

Appendixes

I

AN OVERVIEW OF ARGUMENT

THE PROCESS OF ARGUMENT: AN INTRODUCTION

Consider the following scenario:

STAGE 1 You are the marketing manager of a hair products manufacturing firm, the makers of a successful bargain basement shampoo, Kurl-Kleen. Recently you have been toying with the idea of entering the expensive shampoo market with a new high-end product. You call a staff meeting to discuss the pros and cons of such a shift in manufacturing and marketing.

STAGE 2 As a result of numerous staff meetings, marketing analyses, and discussions with your technical department, your staff has concluded that your company should indeed enter the new market. In two weeks you will present your staff's proposal to the company board of directors. Your goal is to persuade these decision makers to support your staff's proposal.

STAGE 3 Your company has now decided to enter the expensive market, and your technical department has developed the formula for its new shampoo, which is essentially the old KurlKleen product with the addition of a strawberry scent, wheat germ oil, and some conditioners to create "softness." You are now meeting with your advertising department to create magazine and TV advertisements for your new Strawberry Fields Shampoo.

THE DIFFERENCE BETWEEN PERSUASION AND ARGUMENT

At the outset of this text, we need to distinguish between two important activities that are frequently mistaken for each other, *persuasion* and *argument*. "Persuasion" is primarily concerned with influencing the way people think or act, whereas "argument" is concerned with discovering and conveying our best judgments about the truth of things through an appeal to reason. All arguments involve persuasion, but all persuasive acts do not involve arguments.

In the above examples, Stages 1 and 2 illustrate argument. In Stage 1, you and your staff attempt through dialogue to arrive at the best decision for your company's welfare. You raise issues, look at evidence, make comparisons, ask questions, play devil's advocate, imagine different consequences. Rhetoricians sometimes call such a discussion a "heuristic dialogue," where *heuristic** means "discovering," "searching," or "finding out." In such a dialogue, participants proceed reasonably, contributing ideas and assessing the merits of different points of view. They locate and weigh evidence, examine values, question consequences, evaluate risks, and so forth — all with the aim of making the best decision possible. As we will see throughout this text, such heuristic dialogues provide a model for the kind of thinking good writers go through in the process of composing an argument.

Stage 1 can be seen as argument in process. In Stage 2, you must go before the board of directors to deliver a final product, your own written or oral argument that shows the directors "good reasons" for entering the expensive shampoo market. The argument you present to the board of directors is based on the ideas you and your staff developed during the previous process of discussion. If your presentation is effective, it will illustrate the close connection between *argument* (the best case based on reasons and evidence) and *persuasion* (effective use of language to win support for the proposal).

The third stage, however, probably represents persuasion disconnected from argument. There are probably no "good reasons" to support a claim that Strawberry Fields Shampoo is superior to its competitors. Without good reasons to support a case, a persuader must take a tack different from argument in order to influence the behavior of others. One choice would be to create a pseudo-argument with bogus reasons ("Buy Strawberry Fields Shampoo because it is made with an exclusive patented formula unlike any other on the market" [translation: "It smells like strawberries"]). Or you could abandon the appearance of argument altogether and appeal to the

---

Heuristic is derived from a classical Greek word related to our word *Eureka* — "I have found it!"

audience's unconscious motivations and fears: You could associate the shampoo, through skillful use of words and images, with upscale living, with erotic adventure, or with the naturalness of fields of strawberries. Our point, then, is that there are many other ways besides argument to persuade people to act in certain ways.

If we were to make a drawing, therefore, of the relationship between argument and persuasion, it might look like this:

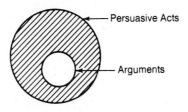

FIGURE 1-1. The Relationship of Argument to Persuasion

What this drawing tells us is that all arguments are concerned with persuasion, but that not all attempts at persuasion are arguments. The shaded area of the drawing would include all those persuasive acts that are not arguments, acts such as propaganda; mesmerizing speeches; psychologically sophisticated sales pitches; and numerous other attempts at influencing human behavior through subtle uses of force, subterfuge, or reward.

This book is concerned with the smaller circle in the above diagram. That is to say, this is a book primarily about acts of persuasion that are arguments. In our view, the value of argumentation lies in its power to deepen and complicate our understanding of the world and to defend ourselves against the many persuasive forces in our culture. In the rest of this chapter, we explore the conflict between argument and persuasion in more depth.

AN INITIAL DEFINITION
OF ARGUMENT

To help us define argument, let's look at a situation that is close to being universal in our culture, one often associated with the idea of arguing: the conflict between parents and children over rules. All of us have probably engaged in that occasional parent–child skirmish. Some of us have had the dubious pleasure of being on both sides of the issue. In what way and in what circumstances do these conflicts constitute arguments?

Consider the following dialogue:

YOUNG PERSON (racing for the front door while putting coat on): "Bye, guys. See you later."

PARENTS (in unison): "Whoa! What time are you planning on coming home?"

YOUNG PERSON (coolly, hand still on doorknob): "I'm sure we discussed this earlier. I'll be home around 2 A.M." (The second sentence, spoken very rapidly, is barely audible.)

PARENTS (with clenched jaws after exchange of puzzled looks): "We did *not* discuss this earlier and you're *not* staying out 'til two in the morning. You'll be home at twelve."

At this point in the exchange, we have a disagreement but not, we would claim, an argument. A disagreement involves the exchange of two or more antagonistic assertions without any attempt to provide reasons for them. The key to whether or not a disagreement can become an argument is how the participants go about defending their assertions. If the dialogue never gets past the "Yes-you-will/No-I-won't" stage, it either remains a disagreement or turns into a fight, depending on how much heat and volume the participants generate.

Let us say, however, that the dialogue takes the following turn:

YOUNG PERSON (tragically): "But I'm *sixteen years old!*"

Now we've got an argument. Not, to be sure, a particularly well-developed or cogent one, but an argument all the same. It's now an argument because one of the combatants has offered a reason for her assertion. Her choice of curfew is satisfactory, she says, *because* she is sixteen years old, an argument that depends on the unstated assumption that sixteen-year-olds are old enough to make decisions about such matters.

The parents can now respond in one of several ways that will either advance the argument or turn it back into a disagreement. They can simply invoke parental authority ("I don't care—you're still coming home at twelve"), in which case argument ceases, or they can provide a reason for their own position ("You will be home at twelve because we pay the bills around here"), in which case the argument takes a new turn. But enough is enough. We'll leave this little domestic tiff before Young Person has a chance to invoke her major piece of empirical evidence ("But all my friends are allowed to stay out 'til two") and the parents respond with theirs ("But we certainly never stayed out that late when we were your age").

So far we've established two necessary conditions that must be met before we're willing to call something an argument: (1) a set of two or more conflicting assertions and (2) the attempt to resolve the conflict through an appeal to reason.

But a good argument demands more. For the argument to be effective, an arguer is obligated to clarify and support the reasons presented. For example, "But I'm sixteen years old!" is not yet a clear support for the assertion "I should be allowed to set my own curfew." On the surface, Young Person's argument seems absurd. Her parents, of all people, know precisely how old she is. What makes it an argument is the unstated assumption behind her reason—all sixteen-year-olds are old enough to set their own curfews. What Young Person needs to do now is to defend that assumption. In doing so, she must anticipate the sorts of questions the assumption will raise in the minds of the parents: What is the legal status of sixteen-year-olds? How psychologically mature, as opposed to chronologically mature, is Young Person? What is the actual track record of Young Person in being responsible? and so forth. Each of these questions will force Young Person to reexamine and clarify her assumptions about the proper degree of autonomy for sixteen-year-olds. And her response to those questions should in turn force the parents to reexamine their assumptions about the dependence of sixteen-year-olds on parental guidance and wisdom. (Likewise, the parents will need to show why "paying the bills around here" automatically gives them the right to set Young Person's curfew.)

In arguing, then, we often find ourselves in the uncomfortable position of being forced to clarify our reasoning and thus of having to justify ideas we had always comfortably assumed. Doing so can be a frustrating and humbling experience. Here we are encountering one of the earliest senses of the term *to argue*, which is "to clarify." An argument, according to one of the first definitions of the word, was "the naked setting forth of ideas." We still see this sense of the term when people read through an essay and say, "As I understand it, your argument here is. . . ." The argument is the core of the essay, which can be abstracted out and "set forth nakedly." In addition, when philosophers translate complex statements into the formal code of logic, they do so to reveal the "argument" at the core. Thus, a logician might translate Young Person's justification into something like this:

All sixteen-year-olds are old enough to stay out until 2:00 A.M.

I am a sixteen-year-old.

Therefore, I am old enough to stay out until 2:00 A.M.

Likewise, they might show the parents' argument this way:

Whoever pays the bills in the household has a right to set the rules.

The parents do pay the bills in the household.

Therefore, the parents have the right to set the rules.

Setting forth the argument in this fashion (these three-sentence statements are called syllogisms, and we'll talk more about them later) allows us to focus on the logical structure of the arguments. To our way of thinking, neither Young Person nor the parents have yet created a strong argument for their positions since we would take issue with the first statement in both syllogisms.

Later, we'll suggest other ways besides syllogisms to clarify or nakedly set forth our ideas in argument. But in our view, any argument worth its salt should eventually lead toward clarification of the issue rather than increasing obscurity. Our emphasis on argument as clarification is an expression of our own assumptions about the function of argument. Although we are concerned with teaching people how to write persuasive arguments, we are more concerned with teaching them how to write arguments that advance understanding—their own understanding as much as their audience's or opponents' understanding. Thus, we think it may be more important for Young Person and the parents to work out a mutual understanding of the relationship between teenage maturity and parental responsibility than it is for either side to win the midnight versus 2 A.M. debate.

CLARIFICATION OR VICTORY? THE DEBATE BETWEEN SOCRATES AND CALLICLES

The issue we've just raised—whether the purpose of argument is clarification or victory—is one of the oldest in the field of argumentation. One of the first great debates on the subject occurs in Plato's dialogue *The Gorgias*, in which the philosopher Socrates takes on the rhetorician Callicles.

By way of background to the dispute, Socrates was a great philosopher known to us today primarily through the dialogues of his student Plato, who depicted Socrates in debates with various antagonists and friends. Socrates' goal in these debates was to try to rid the world of error. In dialogue after dialogue, Socrates vanquishes error by skillfully leading people through a series of questions that force them to recognize the inconsistency and implausibility of their beliefs. He was a sort of intellectual judo master who takes opponents' arguments the way they want to go until they suddenly fall over.

Callicles, on the other hand, is a shadowy figure in history. We know him only through his exchange with Socrates. But he's immediately recognizable to philosophers as a representative of the Sophists, a group of teachers who taught ancient Athenians how to be "successful," much as authors of contemporary self-help books offer to teach us how to make more money, be better looking, and look out for Number One. The Sophists were a favorite, if elusive, target of both Socrates and Plato. Indeed, opposition to the Sophists' self-centered, utilitarian approach to life is at the core of Platonic philosophy. Now let's look at the dialogue.

Early in the debate, Socrates is clearly in control. He easily — too easily as it turns out — wins a couple of preliminary rounds against some less-determined Sophists before confronting Callicles. But in the long and arduous debate that follows, it's not at all clear that Socrates wins. In fact, one of the points being made in *The Gorgias* seems to be that philosophers committed to discovering truth may occasionally have to sacrifice winning the debate. If Callicles doesn't necessarily win the argument, he certainly gives pause to idealists, who like to see the purpose of argument as truth for its own sake. Although Plato makes an eloquent case for enlightenment as the goal of argument, he may well contribute to the demise of this noble principle if he should happen to lose. Unfortunately, it appears that Socrates can't win the argument without sinning against the very principle he's defending.

The effectiveness of Callicles as a debater lies in his refusal to allow Socrates *any* assumptions. In response to Socrates' concern for virtue and justice, Callicles responds sneeringly that such concepts are mere conventions, invented by the weak to protect themselves from the strong. In Callicles' world, "might makes right." And the function of argument in such a world is to extend the freedom and power of the arguer, not to arrive at some arbitrary notion of truth or justice. Indeed, the power to decide what's "true and just" belongs to the winner of the debate. For Callicles, a truth that never wins is no truth at all because it will soon disappear. In sum, Callicles, like a modern-day pitchman, sees the ends (winning the argument) justifying the means (refusing to grant any assumptions, using ambiguous language, and so forth). Socrates, on the other hand, believes that no good end can come from questionable means.

As you can probably tell, our own sympathies are with Socrates and his view of argument as enlightenment and clarification. But Socrates lived in a much simpler world than we do, if by "simple" we mean a world where the True and the Good can be confidently known. For Socrates, there was one True Answer to any important question. Truth resided in the ideal world of forms, and through philosophic rigor humans could transcend the changing, shadow-like world of everyday reality to perceive the world of universals where Truth, Beauty, and Goodness resided. Even though our sympathies are with Socrates, we acknowledge that Callicles had a vision of truth closer to that of our modern world. Callicles forces us to confront the nature of truth itself. Is there only one possible truth at which all arguments will necessarily arrive? Can there be degrees of truth or different kinds of truths for different situations or cultures? How "true" is a truth if you can't get anybody to accept it? Before we can attempt to resolve the debate between Socrates and Callicles, therefore, it will be useful to look more closely at some notions of truth in the modern world.

WHAT IS TRUTH? THE PLACE OF ARGUMENT IN CONTEMPORARY LIFE

Although the debate between Socrates and Callicles appears to end inconclusively, many readers over the centuries conceded the victory to Socrates almost by default. Callicles was seen as cheating. Sophistry, for good reasons, was synonymous with trickery in argument. The moral relativism of the Sophists was so repugnant to most people that they refused to concede that the Sophists' position might have some merits or that their methodology might be turned to other ends. In our century, however, the Sophists have found a more sympathetic readership, one that takes some of the questions they raised quite seriously. Indeed, the fact that the Sophists are no longer dismissed out of hand is evidence of the shift away from a Platonic world where there was a single, knowable Truth attainable by rational means.

One way of tracing this shift in attitude toward truth is by looking at a significant shift in the definition of the verb *to argue* over the centuries. We have already mentioned that one early meaning of *to argue* was "to clarify." Another early meaning was "to prove." Argument was closely associated with demonstrations of the sort you see in math classes when you move from axioms to proofs through formulae. An argument of this sort is virtually irrefutable—unless we play Callicles and reject the axioms.

Today, on the other hand, *to argue* is usually taken to mean something like "to provide grounds for inferring." Instead of demonstrating some preexisting truth, an argument can hope only to make an audience more likely to agree with its conclusions. The better the argument, the better grounds one provides, the more likely the audience will infer what the arguer has inferred. One contemporary philosopher says that argument can hope only to "increase adherence" to ideas, not absolutely convince an audience of the necessary truth of ideas.

In the twentieth century, absolute, demonstrable truth is seen by many thinkers, from physicists to philosophers, as an illusion. Some would argue that truth is merely a product of human beings' talking and arguing with each other. These thinkers say that with regard to questions of interpretation, meaning, or value, one can never tell for certain whether an assertion is true—not by examining the physical universe more closely nor by reasoning one's way toward some Platonic form nor by receiving a mystical revelation. The closest one can come to truth is through the confirmation of one's views from others in a community of peers. "Truth" in any field of knowledge, say these thinkers, is simply an agreement of experts in that field.

As you can see, the world depicted by many twentieth-century thinkers, although it is certainly different from the world depicted by Callicles, has some important similarities to the Sophists' world view. Whatever else we may say about it, it is a world in which we look toward our social groups more than toward the world of objects to test our beliefs and ideas.

To illustrate the relevance of Callicles to contemporary society, suppose for the moment that we wanted to ask whether sexual fidelity is a virtue. A Socratic approach would assume a single, real Truth about the value of sexual fidelity, one that could be discovered through a gradual peeling away of wrong answers. Callicles' approach would assume that the value of sexual fidelity is culturally relative, so Callicles would point out all the societies in which monogomous fidelity for one or both sexes is not the norm. Clearly, our world is more like Callicles'. We are all exposed to multiple cultural perspectives directly and indirectly. Through TV, newspapers, travel, and education we experience ways of thinking and valuing that are different from our own. It is difficult to ignore the fact that our personal values are not universally shared or even respected. Thus, we're all faced with the need to justify our ideas in such a diverse society.

FOR CLASS DISCUSSION

On any given day, newspapers provide evidence of the complexity of living in a pluralistic culture. Issues that could be readily decided in a completely homogeneous culture raise many questions for us in a society that has so few shared assumptions. Consider the difficulties of sorting out the following value questions.

In the fall of 1985, a Japanese woman in California was charged with the first-degree murder of her two children. The woman allegedly walked into the surf with the youngsters in an attempt at "parent–child suicide." The children died; the mother lived. According to news accounts: "In Japan, parent–child suicide happens almost daily. They call it *Oyako Shinju*, and a parent who survives is rarely prosecuted." The mother had lived under the Japanese value system, where her life had been centered on her husband and children. She was a good Japanese mother, even an overprotective mother by American standards, worrying over the children's most minor colds and sniffles. The crisis arose when her husband abandoned the family, thereby taking away not only their material support but their honor. The parent–child suicide followed the dictates of Japanese values and tradition.

Working in small groups, try to create arguments for both the prosecution and the defense of the mother. If time permits, conduct a mock trial in class.

CALLICLES AND SOCRATES RECONSIDERED: SEEKING TRUTH IN A PLURALISTIC WORLD

As we have suggested, our sympathies are with Socrates, who regarded argument as a pursuit of truth. On the other hand, we acknowledge with the descendants of Callicles that the modern world contains many competing voices espousing different kinds of truth. Although some of these competitors believe themselves in possession of "the real truth," none has so far successfully convinced everyone else to yield to them.

Given, then, such disagreement about truth, what is the place of argument in a pluralistic world? In our view, argument is more important than ever because only through skilled and responsible argumentation can we as a society hope to make the important public decisions that will shape our lives. We have mentioned that an early meaning of *to argue* is "to clarify." This meaning is useful, for it reminds us that argument has two functions —not only to sway an audience toward the writer's point of view, but also to help the writer clarify his or her own thinking on an issue. Such clarification is a gradual process driven forward by the writer's continuing confrontation with the complexities of issues and with the competition of opposing views. Ideally, the "finished" essays that you turn in for grades should evolve gradually out of exploratory writing, rough drafts, discussion with classmates, role playing of opposing views, and more discussion; throughout this process, your own view of your subject will gradually become clarified.

What we are suggesting, then, is that argument is both a process and a product and that the quality of the product depends on the quality of the previous process. In the rest of this chapter we have two aims: first, to suggest that a good model for the arguing process is the deliberations of a well-functioning committee and second, to persuade you that a good product depends on a good process.

A SUCCESSFUL PROCESS OF ARGUMENTATION: THE WELL-FUNCTIONING COMMITTEE

Many people might not recognize committee deliberations as a form of argument. For many, an argument is a structured debate on the floor of Congress, an empassioned speech, or an angry newspaper editorial. The

give and take of group decision making, which freq
without rancor and is aimed at some common purpose, ᶜ
the term *argumentation*.* We believe, however, that these dᶜ
good model of argumentation because committee members, ᵍ
task, focus on clarification rather than on winning. Members ot
committee, like the bulk of people who engage in argumentation ₍
basis, are continually making tentative choices, justifying them, anᵅ
ing others to do the same. If two committee members disagree on a ₎
point, other members are likely to adopt the position supported by the ᵇ
reasons. Sometimes one of the speakers will recognize the cogency of thᵪ
other case and concede the point. Argumentation is not an end in itself;
rather, it is a means to achieving good decisions.

An example of a well-functioning committee is one observed by co-author John Ramage when we were writing the first draft of this text. The committee was the Montana Science and Technology Alliance Board, which Ramage observed over a period of several days shortly after the board was created by the state legislature. The board consists of ten people, appointed by the governor, to oversee the granting of 1.7 million state dollars as seed money to stimulate the growth of high-tech industry in Montana. Its mission is to award grant money to risk-taking businesses and researchers trying to commercialize technological innovations within the state. The purpose of the board's discussions during its first weeks of existence was to decide on the procedures they would follow in making awards and the criteria they would use in ranking applicants.

During the course of its initial meetings, all of the argument types examined in Part IV of this text (Chapters 11–15) surfaced in the committee conversations. They faced definition issues ("When does a business qualify as 'high tech'?"); causal issues ("What will be the short- and long-range consequences of giving a lot of money to a few businesses or less money to a lot of businesses?"); resemblance issues ("Will a decision process that worked in Indiana work in Montana?"); evaluation issues ("What criteria should we use to rank proposals?"); and proposal issues ("Should we hire a consultant to help us with some of these decisions?").

Although many people stereotype committees as unproductive, wrangling, time-wasting bodies, the Montana Science and Technology Alliance Board proved to be a remarkably productive group. One cause of their success was their willingness to observe certain courtesies of argument. For example, they regularly showed respect for each other's viewpoints — not

---

*Almost everyone, of course, has experienced bad committees. (You know the old joke: "A camel is a horse designed by a committee.") Perhaps only a few have had the pleasure of working on a productive, successful committee. A committee goes bad when it doesn't have a clearly specified task or when committee members don't put egos and private agendas aside in order to listen to each other. We use the term *committee* to designate any small group charged with an important task that must be accomplished through civic deliberation. The group that wrote the Declaration of Independence or hammered out various sections of the U.S. Constitution could be termed a "committee" in our usage. So could collaborative learning groups in an argument class.

ιterrupting another person, not ignoring one point and moving on to ₋nother, avoided loaded characterizations of each other's views, keeping one's remarks focused on the ideas being put forth by a person rather than on the person's personal motives, and so forth. What these practices have in common is that they indicate a sense of engagement with the ideas under discussion that is stronger than a concern for one's ego.

On the few occasions when board members failed to observe the courtesies of argumentation, the discussion invariably went astray. The result was wasted time, ruffled egos, and a general sense of being "off track." The group had to reexamine its processes, refocus the issue at hand, and begin afresh, sometimes backtracking extensively. Our point here is that it's not simply discourteous to ignore the social conventions of argumentation, it's unproductive.

Another cause of their success was that following the courtesies of argumentation allowed the board to consider various points of view in depth. Board members were able to develop an idea without interruption, and the chairperson kept discussion focused so that the significance and complexity of an idea could be understood.

An example of a sustained, focused discussion concerned the issue of the short-range versus long-range consequences of board decisions. Should the technology board award grants leading to immediate short-range benefits or should it sow seeds for long-term growth in the next decade? An unsuccessful committee might raise such an issue and then drop it. But the board examined it in depth, allowing time for members to make cases for both sides. Proponents of short-range benefits argued that the legislature wouldn't continue to support the board if the board couldn't show quick results and that the board could exert influence over the near future more predictably than over the distant future. Proponents of long-range goals argued that the state must take on the responsibility of planning for the future and that knee-jerk solutions to immediate problems cost taxpayers more money in the long run. Faced with both views, board members asked tough questions, challenged each other to provide more evidence, decided jointly that more research was needed, and looked again at the granting criteria developed by similar boards in other states. In short, the play of opposing views led to sharper focus of the issue and a greater understanding of its complexity. The deliberations thus illustrate how argument is a clarifying process.

Let us now see what a finished product might look like when this process of clarification has been short-circuited.

WHAT HAPPENS WHEN THE ARGUING PROCESS FAILS?—THE CRANK LETTER

The Letters to the Editor section of almost any newspaper will contain occasional examples of breakdowns in argumentation. The worst of these we label as "crank" letters, identifiable by their moral fervor, obscure allusions, and missing logical links. Here is one example, certainly not the worst of the lot, taken from a Montana newspaper.

> I do believe Wiesner overstepped the line a bit Sept. 1 in criticizing the recent letters on creationism and evolution. (He hit a nerve is what he did.) We discuss these things because they are significant and to acquire better knowledge and understanding. Whether it can be proven or not, it can lead to dispellation of ignorance and fallacy. Things don't get accomplished by "having faith" that perhaps God will see to it. Someone has to get out and do it and a certain amount of knowledge and understanding is necessary for proper direction.
>
> In regard to Dr. Freiburger's presentations, I'm reminded of a religious discussion on TV some years ago, what about I don't remember. One so-called clergyman could quote most anything from anywhere to stand on but actual thoughts of his own I couldn't discuss. Quoting studied sources is no doubt valuable but like quoting the Bible, if you can't put it in your own words, you haven't really shown an understanding of it. (I've probably hit some nerves now, myself.)
>
> On a trip to Billings Labor Day, I noticed that the left side parking strip of eastbound I-94 is 10 feet wide only in some places. It's rather misleading to be driving along expecting it to be wide enough to park on and then it isn't. Then it is, then it isn't. Not something for an unconcerned motorist to have to find out at the last minute. That strip should be wide enough so a person at least doesn't have to step out in the grass and weeds on top of a rattlesnake.

Often a crank letter will begin in the middle with insufficient background or summary of the issues ("I do believe Wiesner overstepped the line a bit . . ." "In regard to Dr. Freiberger's presentations . . ."). Who's Wiesner? Who's Dr. Freiburger? What did they say? The writer has assumed, somehow, that all newspaper readers have been following the debate with the same passion as he has. By way of contrast, imagine that you are a Technology Board member who had to miss several days of meetings because of illness. When you returned you would expect board members to fill you in on what you had missed, to bring you up to date on the discussions so that you could rejoin the conversation. This is the kind of courtesy the crank letter writer doesn't show.

In addition to starting in the middle, crank letters are often characterized by unclear pronoun references and vague nouns. In the opening paragraph of the above letter, it is difficult to tell what "these things," "they," and the four occurrences of "it" stand for. Such confusion is not simply a matter of being clear to readers. We suggest that the letter writer would be hard pressed to explain their precise meaning to himself.

Showing little concern for the clarity of his own thinking, the crank letter writer typically shows little respect for opposing views ("one so-called clergyman"). Because he doesn't take opposing views seriously or treat them with any thoroughness, the crank writer seldom sees the need to defend his own views reasonably. The result is a tendency to insult the opposition and to ignore the limitations of people and ideas friendly to the writer's own position. The ratio of assertions to evidence in a crank letter is roughly equal to the ratio of salt to pepper in the Dead Sea. And, finally, the logical leap from biblical argument to parking strip widths on I-94 is symptomatic of a writer so caught up in his own world that he can't imagine a need for transitions.

The chief difference between the crank's argument and the arguments created by the Montana Science and Technology Alliance Board is that the board used argument for clarification, whereas the crank uses it to express personal feelings toward people and ideas. Although individual board members argued forcefully for their own positions, they were willing to let their positions evolve in light of differing arguments. The writer of the crank letter, however, already knows the Truth and treats those who haven't seen the light as ignoramuses. Paradoxically, the best arguers don't know the truth but seek it.

FOR CLASS DISCUSSION

Working in small groups, compose a group crank letter about some topic currently at issue in your college newspaper. Have fun making the letter as cranky as possible. After the groups have finished their letters, they should be shared with the class as a whole. Then discuss why crank letters can be written so much more quickly than truly clarifying and persuasive arguments.

ADAPTING THE ARGUING PROCESS TO WRITING

How, then, can writers incorporate the arguing process into their written arguments? Let us suggest several ways.

Imagine Your Reader as an Absent Listener

A primary difference between spoken and written arguments is that speakers and writers have a very different relationship with their audiences. For example, committee members are all in direct contact with each other and hence can gauge with some precision when their points are being understood, accepted, or rejected by other members. Nods of agreement will keep a speaker moving ahead quickly, whereas a frown will slow her down, even cause the speaker to back up, making the point in a new way, going into more detail. But writers can't see their readers' nods and frowns. They need to role play the reader, anticipating where general agreement will keep the argument moving ahead, where potential confusion calls for clarification, and where potential disagreement calls for a summary of opposing views and either concession or refutation in response to the imagined frown.

Respect Your Audience's Humanity

Good writers have a number of choices on how they want to treat their audience. Usually, however, it is best to treat your audience with the kind of respect shown to each other by members of the Technology Board. Consider again the difference between the board members and the crank. Whereas the board members addressed each other respectfully, cranks distance themselves from anyone with different views by adopting an insulting tone. This insulting tone can often backfire. Our reading of their words may become hypercritical, unforgiving, and perversely counter to their intentions. Long ago the ancient rhetoricians recognized the importance of *ethos* in argument — that is, the hearer's faith that the speaker is a good and trustworthy person. A cranky tone can break down *ethos*. Just as respect tends to beget respect, so crankiness tends to beget crankiness. Unless writers appear to be open to other views, they cannot expect other people to be open to their own.

Respect Your Audience's Ideas

Not only do writers need to treat their audience courteously, they also need to respect their audience's ideas. This respect is evidenced in two ways: an openness toward opposing views during the writing process and a fair acknowledgment of opposing views in the finished product.

During the writing process writers seek clarity for themselves. In order to achieve this clarity, writers need to practice doubting their own ideas, to try seeing their position from differing perspectives. As we saw in the example of the Technology Board, such confrontation with opposing views can bring out the complexity of an issue. Considering contrary ideas will cause us either to create arguments countering the opposition or to concede key points, thereby demonstrating the kind of openness to opposing views that characterizes arguers seeking clarity. Argument becomes a cooperative search for the "best reasons" among people with differing views, as opposed to a pro/con debate between unyielding opponents.

Within the finished product itself, a writer will usually summarize one or more differing views, taking care to recreate differing arguments fairly and charitably. In addition, writers will anticipate places in the argument where opponents are apt to raise objections and will move to acknowledge and counter these objections at that point. Whereas the writer of crank letters seems to carry on a one-sided conversation with other believers, the skilled arguer is mentally carrying on a dialogue with doubters.

CONCLUSION

Our goal in this text is to help you learn skills of argumentation. If you choose, you can use these skills, like Callicles, to argue any side of any issue. And yet we hope you won't. We hope that, like Socrates, you will use argument for clarification and that you will consequently find yourselves, on at least some occasions, changing your position on an issue while writing a rough draft (a sure sign that the process of arguing has been a process of clarification). We believe that the skills of reason and inquiry developed through the writing of arguments can help you get a clearer sense of who you are. If our culture sets you adrift in pluralism, argument can help you take a stand, to say "These things I believe." In this text we will not pretend to tell you what position to take on any given issue. But as responsible beings, you will often need to take a stand, to define yourself, to say "Here are the reasons that choice A is better than choice B, not just for me but for you also." If this text helps you base your commitments on reasonable grounds, then it will be successful.

2

THE PROCESS OF READING ARGUMENTS

WHY READING ARGUMENTS IS IMPORTANT FOR WRITERS OF ARGUMENT

In the previous chapter we explained how argument is a social phenomenon. It grows out of people's search for the best answers to questions, the best choices among alternative courses of actions. Part of the social nature of argumentation is the requirement to read arguments as well as write them.

Although this chapter focuses on reading, much of its advice applies also to listening. In fact, it is often helpful to think of reading as a conversation. We like to tell students that a college library is not so much a repository of information as a discussion frozen in time until you as reader bring it to life. Those books and articles, stacked neatly on library shelves, are arguing with each other, carrying on a great extended conversation. As you read, you bring those conversations to life. And when you write, you enter those conversations.

So writing and speaking are only half of the arguing process. The other half is careful reading and listening.

SUGGESTIONS FOR IMPROVING YOUR READING PROCESS

Before we offer specific strategies for reading arguments, let's examine some general strategies that can improve your ability to read any kind of college-level material, from complex textbooks to primary sources in history.

1. Slow down: Advertisements for speedreading workshops can mislead us into believing that expert readers read rapidly. In fact, when experts read difficult texts, they read slowly and often reread. They struggle with the text. They hold confusing passages in mental suspension, having faith that later parts of the essay may clarify earlier parts. They "nutshell" passages as they proceed, often writing summarizing statements in the margins. They read a difficult text a second and third time, treating their first readings as approximations or rough drafts. They interact with the text by asking questions, expressing disagreements, linking the text with other readings or with personal experience. The more difficult the text, the greater their struggle in mastering it.

Our advice, then, is to slow down. Reading difficult texts effectively is a recursive process demanding reading and rereading.

2. Get the dictionary habit: Although you can often figure out word meanings from context, get in the habit of looking up words that you don't know. One strategy is to make a small tic mark next to words that you aren't sure of; when you come to a break in your reading, look them up in your dictionary. This method allows you to continue reading without having to break your concentration to consult a dictionary. As you look up the words later, reread the passages in which they occur as a means of review.

3. Throw away the yellow highlighter and make written marginal comments: A yellow highlighter allows you to be too passive as a reader. The next time you get the urge to highlight or underline a passage, write in the margin why you think the passage is important. Is it a major new point in the argument? A piece of supporting evidence? A summary of an opposing view? An important analogy? Imagine yourself having to restate the text's argument in your own words and to test its reasoning against your own experience. Some of your marginal commentary should summarize the argument. Other pieces of commentary should react to the argument, expressing your own views, entering into conversation with the author.

4. Set the stage for readings by reconstructing the rhetorical context: Train yourself to ask questions such as these: Who is this author? What audience is he or she writing for? What occasion prompted this writing? What is the author's purpose? Any piece of writing makes more sense if you think of its author as a real person writing for some real purpose out of a real historical context.

5. Whenever possible, join the text's conversation prior to reading by exploring your own views on the text's issue: You will often find yourself more interested in an argument if you have thought about the issue beforehand. You can create your own prereading activities by skimming the text quickly before your first careful reading. By looking at the text's title, by reading the opening paragraphs, and by looking quickly at the opening sentences of paragraphs, you can get a rough idea of what the text is going to be about and what questions it is going to address. You can then explore your own views on that question prior to reading.

6. Continue the conversation after completing your reading: After completing a reading, try taking an extra five minutes or so to respond in a journal or notebook to reflection questions such as these: "The most significant question this essay raised in my mind was. . . ." "The most important thing I learned from reading this essay was. . . ." "I agree with the author about . . . ; however, I disagree about. . . ." These questions help you remember the reading and urge you to respond actively to it.

7. Try writing "translations" of difficult passages: Whenever you encounter a difficult passage that doesn't make sense to you, try "translating" it into your own words. In writing the translation, you can often see more clearly where the difficulty arises. The act of close paraphrasing—of turning the passage into your own language—will force you to focus attention on precise meanings of words. Your translation of the passage may not be exactly what the original author intended, but you will be closer to an understanding than you would be by simply skipping over the passage.

STRATEGIES FOR READING ARGUMENTS: AN OVERVIEW

Whereas the above suggestions can be applied to all sorts of reading tasks, the rest of this chapter focuses on reading strategies specific to arguments. Because argument begins in disagreements within a social community, we recommend that you examine any argument as if it were only one voice in a larger conversation. We therefore recommend the following strategies in sequence:

1. Read as a believer.
2. Read as a doubter.

3. Seek out alternative or opposing views and analyze why participants in the conversation are disagreeing with each other.

4. Evaluate the various positions.

Let's now explore each of these strategies in turn.

Strategy 1: Reading as a Believer

When you read a text as a believer, you adopt the habit of what psychologist Carl Rogers calls "empathic listening," in which you walk in the author's shoes, mentally trying to join the author's culture, seeing the world through the author's eyes. Reading as a believer helps you guard against coloring the author's ideas with your own biases and beliefs.

Because empathic listening is such a vital skill, we ask you now to try reading a controversial article and seeing how well you can "listen" to the writer's argument. Please read "Let Our Police Take On the Drug Dealers" by attorney Charles Brandt (pp. 445–449). In this article, which appeared originally in *Readers' Digest*, Brandt attacks the "exclusionary rule," which severely limits the ways police can collect evidence. Prior to reading the article, take a few minutes to reflect on your own views about the rights of police versus the rights of criminal suspects. Do you think that the legal technicalities that sometimes get cases thrown out of court are ultimately good for our society or harmful to it?

Once you finish the article, ask yourself how well you listened to it empathically. The best way to demonstrate such listening is through your ability to restate the author's argument fairly and accurately in your own words—that is, to summarize it.

SUMMARY WRITING AS A WAY OF READING TO BELIEVE

A summary (also called an abstract or a precis) is a condensed version of an article in which the specific examples and details of the essay are eliminated, leaving only the major points. Summaries can vary in length from one or two sentences to several pages (if, say, you are summarizing a book). Typical lengths for summaries are from 100 to 250 words.

The following steps should help you learn to write summaries. With practice, you will do many of these steps automatically, making the process much quicker and easier than it may seem at first.

1. Plan to read the essay several times. The first time through, read the essay for its general meaning, paying attention to the flow of the argument and withholding judgment and criticism. Try to see the world the way the author of the article sees it. Any disagreements you have with the author's argument should *not* be expressed in a summary, which is aimed solely at careful listening.

2. After reading the essay once for a general overview, reread carefully, and in the margins next to each paragraph (or group of closely related paragraphs) try writing brief statements that sum up what the paragraph says and what it does. A "what it says" statement summarizes the paragraph's ideas. A "what it does" statement identifies the purposes or functions of the paragraph such as "gives examples for previous point," "states a new reason," "summarizes an opposing argument," "tells a story to illustrate a point," "provides statistical evidence to support a point," and so forth. Figure 2–1 shows a page from Brandt's article with marginal notations making "what it says" or "what it does" statements.

The first few times you summarize an article, you may find it helpful to write out your summarizing statements for each paragraph on a piece of scratch paper. Here are some example sentences from our own paragraph-by-paragraph condensation of the Brandt essay (numbers in boldface refer to original paragraph numbers):

> **Paragraphs 1–5:** Gives the example of Gary Most, whose drug conviction was overturned because the arresting officer handled a bag of drugs prematurely. **6:** Gives the example of a Denver SWAT team's losing a conviction because they battered down a defendant's door without knocking even though they had a search warrant. . . . **9:** Summarizes the examples and concludes that "legal hair-splitting" has left police powerless in the war on drugs. . . . **11:** Contrasts the freedom enjoyed by police during preexclusionary rule days to their present impotence, thus showing the negative effects of the rule. . . . **14:** Cites a Columbia University study showing that narcotics arrests were cut in half immediately after exclusionary rule and that convictions were harder to obtain. . . . **19:** Cites personal experience to show that the concern for citizens' rights has actually served to protect drug dealers. **20:** Gives an example of how police following a known drug dealer cannot search the dealer even when they know the dealer is carrying drugs. . . . **29:** Proposes congressional hearings and citizen input on the issue of the exclusionary rule. **30:** Assures readers that the author is all for protection of Constitutional rights and that the exclusionary rule is not a Constitutional right but a "judge-made" one. **31:** Defines the law as "dynamic" and thus necessarily responsive to social phenomena like the current drug epidemic.

3. After you have analyzed the argument paragraph by paragraph, try to locate the main divisions or parts. Sometimes writers forecast the shape of their essays in their introductions or use their conclusions to sum up main points. For example, paragraph 9 of Brandt's article gives some clues about the argument's structure. This paragraph states the argument's main point that current laws hamper law enforcement while protecting drug dealers. Closer examination of the article shows that the body of the essay has several main divisions:

This "exclusionary rule" had its most devastating impact on one area of law enforcement: drug arrests. Before the Mapp decision, a police officer could stop and search a drug dealer or user on suspicion. An anonymous tip from a neighbor was enough to justify a house search warrant. Today, because of the exclusionary rule, there is a barrage of court rulings on proper ways to gather evidence. Police practically *need* a search warrant to gather enough facts to *get* one.

Most devastating effect: drug arrests. Description of what it was like before & after.

On November 1, 1987, for example, a resident of an Atlantic Beach, Fla., apartment complex found a three-year-old boy wandering the parking lot. She called the police. When they questioned the boy, he ran to an apartment, saying, "Mama's in there." The door was ajar and swung open as police knocked. The officers announced their presence. Getting no response, they drew their weapons and entered. They could see marijuana and drug paraphernalia in the bedroom, where the boy's mother and one David Emory Eason were asleep.

Example supporting above point

Police then obtained a search warrant for the rest of the apartment, which held even more drugs. Eason was charged with drug possession. But not for long. On June 28, 1989, the District Court of Appeal of Florida dismissed the case because the police had not obtained a search warrant *before* their initial visit to the apartment.

Continued example. The police had to have a search warrant first.

A Columbia University study compared the number of narcotics-possession arrests during a six-month period just prior to the Mapp decision and the same period the following year. The study found that arrests were cut in half. Furthermore, it noted that "convictions have been harder to obtain since Mapp."

Further evidence showing effects of exclusionary rule on drug arrests. Convictions harder to get; no. of arrests cut in half.

Steven Schlesinger, former director of the Bureau of Justice Statistics, estimated in *Crime and Public Policy* that the exclusionary rule derailed 45,000 to 55,000 *serious* criminal cases in 1977–78 alone. And this didn't include arrests that never happened because, while the cop felt sure drugs were being dealt right under his nose, he knew he didn't have enough evidence to obtain a search warrant.

Further evidence; exclusionary rule derailed 45,000–55,000 serious criminal cases in 1977-78.

Balancing Act. The exclusionary rule has become the police officer's nightmare. The courts cranked out so many restrictions on police that the 1960s have been called the "criminal-law revolution." It wasn't enough to require a search warrant: the search also had to be limited to a narrowly specified crime, and the warrant had to list facts amounting to "probable cause" for arrest. If the police presented facts suggesting stolen television sets, for example, the warrant would not allow a search for drugs in a desk drawer. Then the courts began to pass judgment on the "reliability" of information that went into the "probable cause" argument.

Sums up previous argument. So many restrictions that 1960s are a "criminal-law revolution."

Exclusionary rule is "police officer's nightmare."

To do his job, a police officer now has to balance a 3342-page law book on his head. Prof. Wayne R. LaFave's standard treatise, *Search and Seizure*, cited by judges in many of the decisions described in this article, is based

Further describes effect on police.

FIGURE 2-1. Reading-to-Believe Annotations on Brandt Text

- a section showing how the exclusionary rule has reduced the number of arrests and convictions (paragraphs 10–15)
- a section showing that the rule has become a policeman's nightmare (paragraphs 16 and 17)
- a section about the citizens' rights issue showing that the rule's effect has been to protect the drug dealer more than society (paragraphs 19–24)
- a concluding part that calls for Congress to take action and assures readers that overturning the exclusionary rule doesn't mean violating the Constitution

4. Based on your awareness of the essay's main divisions and the functions of the paragraphs as the essay unfolds, make an outline, flowchart, or diagram of the article. Our diagram of the Brandt article is shown in Figure 2–2.

5. Write a first draft of your summary by turning your outline or diagram into prose. The key here is to summarize the main ideas of the article while leaving out the supporting details and examples. Some writers like to start off writing a long summary, following the essay paragraph by paragraph, and then gradually pruning it down. Others like to begin the essay with a one-sentence summary that captures only the argument's thesis and main reasons and then gradually to add more of the supporting ideas. If you try this second method, ask yourself, "If I had to summarize this whole argument in one sentence, what would it be?"

6. Take your summary through as many drafts as necessary to achieve the desired length. The criteria you are shooting for are clarity, conciseness, and completeness.

What follows are our summaries of the Brandt article, beginning with a one-sentence version and working up to a two-hundred-word summary.

ONE-SENTENCE SUMMARY

Congress should overturn the exclusionary rule because it has greatly hampered police officers' ability to enforce drug laws, because its complexity has become a police nightmare, and because its purpose of protecting citizens' rights has served mainly to protect drug dealers.

SEVENTY-WORD SUMMARY

Congress should abolish the senseless restrictions of the 1961 *Mapp v. Ohio* decision. The resulting exclusionary rule has hampered police officers' ability to make arrests and gain convictions; the rule's complexity has become a police nightmare; and in its intent to protect citizens' rights, it has given increased protection to drug dealers. Overturning the rule will not destroy society's freedoms because today we are threatened more by criminals than by police.

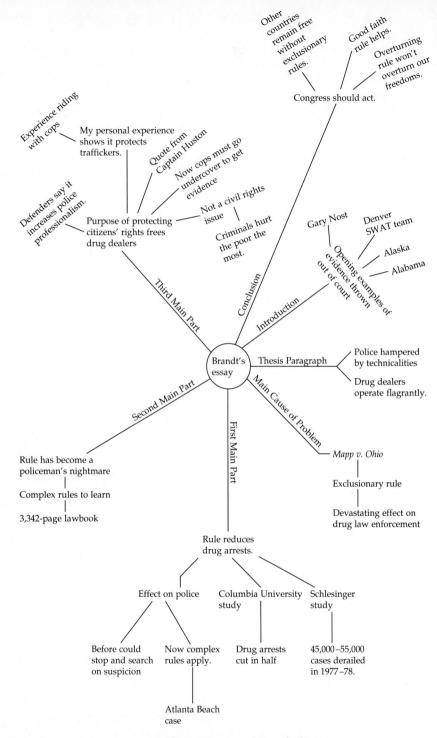

FIGURE 2-2. Diagram of Brandt Essay

TWO-HUNDRED-WORD SUMMARY

The exclusionary rule resulting from the 1961 Supreme Court decision in *Mapp v. Ohio* has had a devastating effect on the war against drugs. Before 1961 suspicion or anonymous tips were allowable grounds for searching suspects. But now legal searches require narrowly drawn search warrants. Studies show that drug arrests were cut in half immediately following *Mapp* and that the exclusionary rule "derailed" 45,000 to 55,000 criminal cases in one year. Additionally, the exclusionary rule is a police nightmare requiring knowledge of complex court decisions governing rules of evidence. Although its defenders claim that the rule has made police more professional, the rule's major effect has been to protect drug dealers. To get evidence for a search warrant, police must go through needlessly complex and dangerous undercover operations. Such restrictions may have been valuable in the 1960s, but today drug dealers are a greater threat than the police, especially in poorer neighborhoods, which are affected most by crime. Although the recent "good faith" exception is helpful, Congress should reassess the whole question of admissable evidence. Overturning the judge-made exclusionary rule won't violate our Constitution. The dynamics of our legal system will allow us to abolish laws that hamstring the police.

Not all arguments are equally easy to summarize. Brandt's argument on the exclusionary rule is actually quite difficult to summarize because his argument lacks explicit transitions between parts, forcing the reader to make decisions about the shape of the argument and about the relative importance of certain passages. For example, Brandt doesn't tell us explicitly that the body of the essay has three main parts. Other readers might find four parts in the body, or two, and might argue that our summary has left out important material while including less important material. Such differences are to be expected unless the author explicitly guides the reader by means of prominently stated reasons and transitions.

What is important is that you see summary writing as a means of reading to believe. When summarizing, you put aside your own criticisms, objections, and judgments in order to listen empathically to someone else's view on a given issue—a view that might seem unusual, strange, or troubling to you. As a believer, your job is to expand your view of the world by taking in new ways of seeing.

Strategy 2: Reading as a Doubter

But reading as a believer is only half your duty as an experienced reader of arguments. The other half is to raise objections, queries, and doubts—to remain skeptical of the view you are reading. Once you have listened empathically to an article, you can reread it with an eye to raising questions and doubts. In the margins, you now add a new layer of notations in which you demand more proof, doubt evidence, challenge the author's assumptions and values, and so forth. Figure 2–3 shows one reader's doubting commentary as she made marginal notations on a page from Brandt's article. (For purposes of illustration this reader's believing commentary— efforts to understand and summarize the argument—aren't shown. Marginal notations of a text usually intermingle both believing and doubting commentary.) What follows is a selective list of doubts and queries about Brandt's essay raised by students in our classes during practice sessions on doubting.

- How representative are Brandt's examples? He cites lots of cases, but what percentage of arrests and convictions are actually affected by the exclusionary rule?

- Paragraph 14 says that arrests were cut in half during the six months just after the *Mapp* decision. What has happened to arrests since then? Maybe police became more adept at understanding the new rules and got better at using them.

- The way Brandt summarizes his examples makes the exclusionary rule look pretty stupid. But does he give us a fair look at the whole story? In paragraph 12, for example, why do the police draw their guns before entering the apartment? Nothing in the story as Brandt tells it should require a gun. What is Brandt leaving out?

- Paragraph 18 concedes that police departments may have become more professional as a result of the exclusionary rule. Our group would like to hear more about this side of the story.

- Paragraph 5 ridicules the rule that kept the police from opening the bag left in the grocery story. But I'm not sure I would want police to have the right to open up something of mine that I left around.

It should be clear by now why both believing and doubting are important. Believing helps us expand our view of the world. Through believing we become open to new ideas, see the world through new perspectives. Without believing, we would never change. On the other hand, doubting protects us from being overpowered by someone else's argument. It helps us stand back, consider, and weigh carefully. Through doubting, we differentiate ourselves from others. By alternating back and forth between active believing and active doubting, we grow as readers of arguments.*

---

*For our use of the terms *believing* and *doubting* we thank Peter Elbow in *Writing without Teachers* (London: Oxford University Press, 1973). His discussion of the "believing and doubting game" introduced us to this powerful way of teaching thinking.

This "exclusionary rule" had its most devastating impact on one area of law enforcement: drug arrests. Before the Mapp decision, a police officer could stop and search a drug dealer or user on suspicion. An anonymous tip from a neighbor was enough to justify a house search warrant. Today, because of the exclusionary rule, there is a barrage of court rulings on proper ways to gather evidence. Police practically *need* a search warrant to gather enough facts to *get* one.

On November 1, 1987, for example, a resident of an Atlantic Beach, Fla., apartment complex found a three-year-old boy wandering the parking lot. She called the police. When they questioned the boy, he ran to an apartment, saying, "Mama's in there." The door was ajar and swung open as police knocked. The officers announced their presence. Getting no response, they drew their weapons and entered. They could see marijuana and drug paraphernalia in the bedroom, where the boy's mother and one David Emory Eason were asleep.

Why did the officers draw their weapons? Unclear why they expected any danger. Is Brandt telling us the whole story here?

Police then obtained a search warrant for the rest of the apartment, which held even more drugs. Eason was charged with drug possession. But not for long. On June 28, 1989, the District Court of Appeal of Florida dismissed the case because the police had not obtained a search warrant *before* their initial visit to the apartment.

A Columbia University study compared the number of narcotics-possession arrests during a six-month period just prior to the Mapp decision and the same period the following year. The study found that arrests were cut in half. Furthermore, it noted that "convictions have been harder to obtain since Mapp."

What happened later? Did patterns of arrests start going up?

Steven Schlesinger, former director of the Bureau of Justice Statistics, estimated in *Crime and Public Policy* that the exclusionary rule derailed 45,000 to 55,000 *serious* criminal cases in 1977–78 alone. And this didn't include arrests that never happened because, while the cop felt sure drugs were being dealt right under his nose, he knew he didn't have enough evidence to obtain a search warrant.

What percentage of all cases in this? What does he mean by "derailed" and "serious"? I'd like to see how he got these figures.

Balancing Act. The exclusionary rule has become the police officer's nightmare. The courts cranked out so many restrictions on police that the 1960s have been called the "criminal-law revolution." It wasn't enough to require a search warrant: the search also had to be limited to a narrowly specified crime, and the warrant had to list facts amounting to "probable cause" for arrest. If the police presented facts suggesting stolen television sets, for example, the warrant would not allow a search for drugs in a desk drawer. Then the courts began to pass judgment on the "reliability" of information that went into the "probable cause" argument.

Have there been any positive tradeoffs? What argument can be made in favor of the exclusionary rule?

To do his job, a police officer now has to balance a 3342-page law book on his head. Prof. Wayne R. LaFave's standard treatise, *Search and Seizure*, cited by judges in many of the decisions described in this article, is based

Probably misleading — police don't have to read & know 3342 pages! cheap trick.

FIGURE 2–3. Reading-to-Doubt Annotations on Brandt Text

Strategy 3: Analyzing Why Disputants Disagree

By simultaneously believing and doubting, you may well find yourself in a quandary of questions and mixed feelings. Your search for clarity logically leads you to seek out alternative or opposing points of view. If you were an arbitrator, you wouldn't think of settling a dispute between A and B on the basis of A's testimony only. You would also insist on hearing B's side of the story.

You can discover opposing views through class discussion, through interviews, or through library research (see Chapter 17 for advice on using a library). As this course progresses, your skill in analyzing and evaluating arguments will increase. But even at the outset of this course, you can depend on your own common sense and natural skills as an arguer to deepen your view of an issue through examination of opposing views. For the rest of this chapter, we provide a series of short pro/con arguments for you to consider. After you have read the alternative points of view, ask yourself why the disputants disagree. We suggest that you examine four primary causes of disagreement: (1) disagreement about the facts of the case; (2) disagreement about definitions; (3) disagreement about appropriate analogies; and (4) disagreements about beliefs, basic assumptions, or values. Let's look at each in turn.

DISAGREEMENTS ABOUT FACTS

Theoretically, a "fact" is a piece of empirical data that everyone agrees upon. But often arguments occur when one person accepts as a fact something that another person doubts. The result, therefore, is a disagreement about the facts of the case—a dispute about truth. Did X happen or not? Who saw whom when? Do these statistics come from a representative sample or not? Writer A supports her claim using one set of "facts." Writer B supports an opposing claim using a different set of "facts." As a reader, you won't know whom to believe without further research. Yet it is helpful to know that the disagreement stems primarily from dispute about facts because if you can find out the facts, or build a strong case for accepting a particular interpretation of the facts, you can help resolve the disagreement. Examples of disagreement about facts include the following:

- In arguing whether silver/mercury amalgam tooth fillings should be banned, dentists and dental researchers disagree on the amount of mercury vapor released by fillings that are five or more years old.

- In arguing about the legalization of drugs, writers disagree about the extent to which alcohol consumption in the United States was reduced during prohibition.

DISAGREEMENTS ABOUT DEFINITIONS

Sometimes disagreements between people are really disputes about definitions. For example, A and B may disagree about whether *Playboy Magazine* exploits women. But this disagreement may stem primarily from different definitions of *exploit*. Or to take another example, when arguing whether a therapy based on behavioral modification leads to improvement in a client's mental health, persons A and B might disagree on what is meant by *improvement*.

DISAGREEMENTS ABOUT
APPROPRIATE ANALOGIES

Other disagreements arise from the use of analogies, or comparisons. As we will see throughout this text, a powerful arguing strategy is to compare one thing to another. For example, in supporting a Texas law forbidding flag burning, Chief Justice William Rehnquist argued that desecration of a flag in the name of free speech is similar to desecrating the Washington Monument by posting leaflets all over it. Just as we would forbid desecration of a national monument, so should we forbid desecration of the flag. (See his argument on pages 631–632). Opposing justices did not think the analogy was valid.

Here is another example. Person A and Person B disagree on whether it is ethically acceptable to have Down's syndrome children undergo plastic surgery to correct some of the facial abnormalities associated with this genetic condition. Person A supports the surgery, arguing it is similar to any other cosmetic surgeries done to improve appearance. Person B argues against such surgery, comparing it to the racial self-hatred of some minority persons who have tried to change their ethnic appearance and become lily-white. (The latter analogy argues that Down's syndrome is nothing to be ashamed of and that persons should take pride in their difference.)

DISAGREEMENTS ABOUT VALUES,
BELIEFS, OR ASSUMPTIONS

A fourth source of disagreement concerns differences in values, beliefs, or assumptions. These are often the chief causes of disagreement and the least likely to be changed through argumentation. It is very helpful, however, to identify the conflicting values in order to clarify the debate and help you develop your own beliefs and values. Here are some examples:

> Persons A and B might agree that a huge tax on gasoline would cut down on the consumption of petroleum. They might agree further that the world's supply of petroleum will eventually run out. Thus A and B agree at the level of facts. But they might disagree about whether the United States should enact a huge gas tax. Person A might support the law in order to conserve oil while B might oppose it, perhaps because B believes that scientists will find alternative energy sources before the

petroleum runs out or because B believes the short-term harm of such a tax outweighs distant benefits.

Person A and Person B might agree that capital punishment deters potential murderers. Person A supports capital punishment for this reason, but person B opposes it, believing that the taking of a human life is always wrong in principle.

FOR CLASS DISCUSSION

Consider the following short pro/con articles expressing opposing positions on issues. Working as a whole class or in small groups, analyze why the authors disagree with each other on each of the issues. Try to answer each of these questions:

1. Do the two sides disagree about facts or interpretations of facts?
2. Do the two sides disagree about definitions of any key terms?
3. Do the two sides use different analogies or comparisons that suggest points of disagreement?
4. Do the two sides differ in values, beliefs, or basic assumptions about the world?

As an illustration, we will analyze the first pro/con pair for you.

SET ONE

The issue: A California surrogate mother, Anna Johnson, is carrying a fetus that is the product of a married couple's egg and sperm. She originally agreed to bear the child for them, but is now refusing to give it up and is suing the biological parents for custody. Should state laws be enacted to ban surrogate parenthood?

SHOULD STATE LAWS BE ENACTED TO BAN SURROGATE MOTHERHOOD?

Linda Chavez (YES)

The rent-a-womb industry may have few customers now, but unless legislators outlaw surrogate parenting, the practice is likely to become frighteningly common.

Never underestimate the desire of the Me Generation to avoid sacrifice and discomfort. Why go through the hassle of pregnancy and the pain of childbirth if you can pay someone to do it for you?

Already, there have been an estimated 4,000 traditional surrogate births in the United States, in which a "surrogate" mother is impregnated with sperm from the husband of the couple who hired her. But a new technique makes it possible to implant a couple's own embryo into the body of a surrogate who carries the baby to term.

So far, the technique has been used to allow couples who cannot have a 4
baby naturally to produce a child that is genetically theirs. But no matter how justified the end might seem, the means are clearly immoral.

The desire to have a child does not excuse the exploitation of another's 5
body. The usual payment to surrogate mothers is $10,000, or about $1.50 an hour for nine months of "work," 24 hours a day—never mind the physical and psychological toll of the whole process.

Make no mistake, only a desperate woman would allow herself to be used 6
this way.

Have we really become so blind to the moral dimensions of our actions that 7
we think infertile couples should have the right to"rent" bodies in this fashion?

Nor should surrogates have the right to turn over their bodies to serve as 8
human incubators. We prohibit persons from selling their bodies for sexual pleasure, arguably a less oppressive activity than using them to host fetuses. We would be horrified at the thought that anyone has the right to buy or sell spare body parts—kidneys, for example.

Surrogacy is no less barbaric a practice. Medical technology has ushered in 9
a Brave New World. It's time we begin to define its limits.

Bonnie Erbe (NO)

It's difficult to imagine why anyone would want to endure pregnancy, except 1
to have a child of her own. Morning sickness (which in many cases would more aptly be called all-day sickness), weight gain, the ridiculous distortion of one's body, and the incredible pain of childbirth are enough to drive me running furiously in the opposite direction.

But there are many women who sail through pregnancy, and some who 2
even enjoy it. Do we really want the government to step in and tell women who want to become surrogate mothers that they cannot use their bodies in this fashion, or deny would-be parents the right to their own biological progeny? I think not.

Oh, yes, we ban prostitution. That's been a crashing success. Local law- 3
enforcement officers have done a stunning job of putting hookers out of business. And they would be equally inept at banning surrogacy arrangements.

The fact that surrogacy has been outlawed in four states only creates a 4
booming business for doctors, lawyers, and surrogate mothers in states where the practice is legal.

And now that the medical technology is here, if it were banned on the 5 national level, infertile American couples would simply look to women of other nations to act as surrogates, as they now adopt foreign babies when American children can't be had.

Besides, in most cases, surrogacy arrangements work beautifully. The famous Baby M case and the more recent Johnson case are the vast exceptions. The Center for Surrogate Parenting in California reports that about 80 babies have been carried by women with no biological ties to them and handed over to their biological parents upon birth, with no legal tangles or emotional upheaval.

Surrogacy is not barbaric, as my colleagues would have you believe. Government is barbaric when it tries to control the most intimate decisions of life.

Our analysis: *Facts:* The two authors disagree about the kind of woman who would become a surrogate mother. Chavez feels that such women are desperate; they consent to exploitation solely out of need for money. On the other hand, Erbe implies that surrogate mothers are the kind of women "who sail through pregnancy . . . and even enjoy it." Thus Erbe portrays a woman who wants to become a surrogate mother, while Chavez portrays a woman forced into it by desperation. They also seem to disagree on the kind of couples who would seek to have a child by surrogacy. Erbe believes such couples are infertile and unable to have their own children. Chavez, however, implies they are apt to be Me Generation people who want to have a child without the hassles of pregnancy. *Definition:* Erbe seems to define "surrogacy" neutrally as the carrying of a fetus by a woman who has no biological ties to it. Chavez's implied definition, however, has an economic implication—the "renting" of a womb. *Analogy:* Chavez's argument depends on analogies. Chavez compares surrogate motherhood both to prostitution and to selling spare body parts, indicating her moral disapproval. Erbe doesn't have any such negative comparisons. She does say, however, that laws against surrogate motherhood would be ineffective just the way laws against prostitution are ineffective. She also says that couples would turn to surrogate mothers from other countries in the same way that adoptive parents now adopt children from other countries. *Beliefs, values, assumptions:* Chavez argues that the ends do not justify the means. She then criticizes the means as the exploitation of desperate females. The main value she focuses on is preventing the exploitation of women. She doesn't deny the value of couples being able to have biologically related children, but she doesn't believe the exploitation of the surrogate mother justifies this end. Additionally, Chavez believes that surrogate motherhood is wrong in principle, just as prostitution or selling of body parts is wrong. Erbe, on the other hand, values the freedom of the individual from government interference. She believes that infertile couples have a "right to their own biological progeny." She also implies that a surrogate mother has the right to do what she wants to with her body. She also believes there is no point enacting a law that can't be enforced. Couples will simply turn to other states or other countries to find a surrogate mother. Most of all, the two writers seem to disagree in their basic assumptions about the consequences of surrogate parenthood. Chavez seems to visualize a nightmare of lawsuits and irresponsible Me Generation parents. In contrast, Erbe cites some evidence that in most cases surrogacy works beautifully and that the Baby M case was an exception.

SET TWO

The issue: When a physician prescribes medication, he or she usually writes out a prescription, which the patient then takes to a pharmacy to be filled. Some physicians now believe that states ought to license physicians to sell prescription drugs themselves. Generally, pharmacists oppose such licensing. Should physicians be allowed to sell prescription drugs?

SHOULD PHYSICIANS BE LICENSED TO DISPENSE PRESCRIPTION DRUGS?

Richard A. Peters (YES)

Each year five times as many Americans die from failure to take their medicine   1
as prescribed than from drunken driving accidents — an estimated 125,000 —according to a report presented at the Rutgers University Pharmaceutical Conference in June.

This "noncompliance" not only costs 125,000 lives annually, but leads to   2
hundreds of thousands of unnecessary extra hospitalizations and a loss of 20 million work days, costing employers about $1.43 billion annually.

The problem of noncompliance does have a solution, however: physician   3
dispensing.

The report presented at Rutgers — by the director of pharmacy affairs at   4
Schering Laboratories — found that of 2,000 adults selected randomly across the country, 92 percent recalled their doctors' giving them detailed instructions on dosage at the time they received the prescription. Only 43 percent could recall a pharmacist's giving them instructions. The problem of noncompliance evidently comes after the patient leaves the doctor's office.

The study also found that: 5

- One hundred million prescriptions go unfilled annually.
- Fifteen percent of patients do not take their prescription for the full length of time.
- Thirty-two percent of patients do not have their prescriptions refilled, even though they need to do so.

If patients were presented the option to purchase their prepackaged, 6
sealed medication at the doctor's office at the time of their visit, wouldn't the
problem of noncompliance decrease?

As a doctor, I have found that this is the case. My patients are more likely 7
to have their prescription filled, understand the procedure, and take/finish
the medicine because I am more capable than a pharmacist of realizing
whether my patient understands and is following my directions.

This obviously reduces or eliminates noncompliance, ultimately saving 8
thousands of lives each year.

Today fewer than 5 percent of doctors dispense prescriptions to their 9
patients (often at lower prices than drugstores). This creates competition,
which is good for consumers but bad for the drugstores.

The last thing that drugstore chains want is competition. Rep. Ron 10
Wyden, D-Ore., has proposed federal legislation that would prohibit doctors
from profiting from drugs they dispense to their patients. His bill does not
limit the amount a drugstore can make from the sale of prescriptions. Yet last
year alone, according to a Drug Store News survey, drugstore prescription
prices increased an average of 20 percent.

Doctors charge patients for all their services, such as selling eyeglasses, 11
performing blood work, and taking X-rays and throat cultures. They make a
profit from each of these. These services we doctors provide in-house allow us
to have greater control over the well-being of our patients. Dispensing
medication is another service where our control will help patients get healthier faster and stay healthy.

Chain drugstores are waging an expensive fight to keep their monopoly. 12
This issue is causing a huge battle in Washington and state houses across
America between the well-funded drugstore lobby and doctors.

If the drugstores win, consumers — especially the elderly, who spend a lot 13
of their money on prescription drugs — will be the real losers. If doctors are
permitted to continue dispensing commonly prescribed drugs at lower prices,
then drugstores will be forced to lower their prices. That's what competition
does; it lowers prices.

If Wyden's legislation passes, however, consumers lose the option to 14
purchase medicine at lower prices.

Wyden and the chain-drugstore lobbyists say we physicians will "rip off" 15
patients with huge markups, misprescribe a drug that we have on hand, or
fail to inform a patient of an adverse reaction. These accusations are not only
ridiculous but incredibly naive.

I don't believe any doctor would risk losing a patient for a $3 markup, let 16
alone the risk of a malpractice suit for misprescribing. Furthermore, doctors
take a drug history of the patient "face to face" and are therefore more
qualified than pharmacists to prescribe and dispense the appropriate medication.

The Schering report found that one of the biggest problems with patient 17 noncompliance is the fact that pharmacists deal face-to-face with their customers only half the time.

It makes sense that the consumer is finally seeing changes in the medical   **18**
profession that will save lives, time and money.

As one whose profession is under fire by pharmacists who contend that   **19**
physicians dispense drugs solely for monetary gain, I find it ironic that the
drugstore-trade journal from which much of this information is taken, American Druggist, titles its article: "Noncompliance Costs Pharmacies Billions."

Druggists seem to think that $1.5 billion in lost revenues is far more   **20**
important than losing 125,000 American lives.

Uwe Reinhardt (NO)

At professional meetings of American physicians these days, one often finds   **1**
drug repackaging firms openly advertising the substantial profits (between
$30,000 and $50,000 a year) that physicians could earn by selling directly to
patients the drugs they prescribe.

Physicians are asked to list the dozen or so medicines they most frequently   **2**
prescribe. The repackager then purchases these drugs in bulk and resells
them to individual physicians in conveniently sized containers for patients,
leaving it to physicians to set their own retail markups.

According to the Federal Trade Commission, the practice not only adds   **3**
convenience for patients but also will lower drug prices. That assessment
rests on the theory that price competition among vendors always intensifies
as the number of vendors increases.

Pharmacists resent the new guests at their traditional corner of the   **4**
health-care dinner table. After all, why would normal human beings welcome
someone else's spoon in their soup bowls, especially when the new guests will
fish out only the most delicious (high volume) morsels from that bowl?

Presumably, social responsibility for stocking less frequently used but   **5**
essential drugs will remain with the pharmacist.

Leaving aside the obviously self-serving reservations of pharmacists, however, are there more objective grounds for looking askance at this practice? I   **6**
think there are.

- First, the practice cuts out the valuable second opinion that pharmacists render on the physician's prescriptions. Not even physicians argue that their clinical judgments are invariably infallible.

- Second, the Federal Trade Commission's theory strikes me as simplistic. An additional pharmacy may well enhance price competition in a market area. But do the commission's economists seriously believe that, to a sick and anxious patient, the physician's dispensary appears as just one more price-competing pharmacy? Have we ever observed that tendency in connection with laboratory tests?

The typical patient's reluctance to alienate his or her physician probably would give physicians a protected edge in the market for prescription drugs.

- Third, between 1970 and 1986 the average number of patients per practicing American physician has fallen from 700 to 430. That number, really the economic base for the physician's livelihood, will continue to fall for the next three decades or so. Is it socially wise to add ever more conflicts of economic interest to that already inherent in fee-for-service medicine?

Physicians naturally resent any legislative limits on their professional 7
activities, such as the recent proposal by Rep. Ron Wyden, D-Ore., to outlaw this practice.

But physicians have never hesitated to enlist the coercive power of govern- 8
ment in their lobbying for statutory limits on the professional freedom of optometrists, pediatric nurse practitioners, and other health professionals who might step onto their economic turf.

These turf battles usually are fought under the lofty banner of "quality." 9
But neither economists nor journalists nor, one suspects, the general public are unaware of the economic motives that drive our system of occupational licensing.

Although I do not regard the dispensing of drugs by physicians as a 10
wholesome development for either patient or physician, as an economist with libertarian leanings I would be loath to argue for legislative prohibition of that practice. Instead I would favor two legislative initiatives.

- First, for the sake of both fairness and economic efficiency, I would like to see other health professionals freed wherever possible from the statutory shackles that now limit their ability to compete head-on with physicians.

- Second, I favor the disclosure of information pertinent to the proper functioning of markets. I would endorse legislation compelling physicians to post in their waiting rooms their prices for drugs and any other sundries they may wish to sell, and any financial interest they have in health care facilities to which they refer patients.

As physicians derive an ever greater proportion of their income from 11
being capitalists and economic predators, they may lose the affection, trust and respect that society has traditionally accorded them for their intellect, knowledge, skill and compassion.

SET THREE

We have already looked at Charles Brandt's argument against the exclusionary rule. Now read George Kannar's defense of the exclusionary rule in "Liberals and Crime" (pages 450–454). Do laws protecting suspects' rights benefit society?

Strategy 4: Evaluating the Conflicting Positions

When we ask you to evaluate an argument or a set of arguments, we aren't asking you to choose a winner. Rather, we are asking you to take stock as you make your own journey toward clarity. Which lines of reasoning seem strong to you? Which seem weak? Before you could make up your mind on the issue, what additional research would you want to pursue? What value questions do you still need to resolve? As you will have noticed from reading the pro/con sets in the previous For Class Discussion exercise, writers don't always address neatly the questions you would like to see addressed. For example, in his argument supporting physicians' dispensing drugs, Richard Peters claims this proposal will save 125,000 American lives. In his opposing argument, Uwe Reinhardt never mentions the claim that lives will be saved. Instead, he implies that physicians' primary motivation is money. How are we to resolve such disagreements? For starters, we might locate and read the Schering Laboratory report presented at Rutgers in order to evaluate how likely it is that physicians' dispensing drugs would save patient lives. Then we would want to find out what profits doctors are apt to make by selling drugs. Peters downplays the profits by referring to a measly $3 markup without raising the question of how many drug sales are involved. Reinhardt emphasizes profits by citing advertisements that claim a physician might net $30,000 to $50,000 per year from drug sales. Are these realistic expectations or inflated advertising promises? Before we would take a side on this controversy, therefore, we would like to resolve several questions of fact or value:

- Will physicians' dispensing drugs save 125,000 American lives per year?
- How much money will the average physician make per year from selling drugs?
- Will increased competition reduce the price of drugs to consumers as the doctors claim or threaten to put pharmacists out of business as the pharmacists claim?
- What would be the long-term consequences to our health system if the pharmacists' predictions are true—that physicians would take

over the market for the most popular drugs, leaving pharmacists with the obligation of stocking the expensive, rarely used drugs?

- Is allowing physicians to dispense drugs the only solution to the problems raised by the Schering Laboratory report?

- Which do I value more: the 125,000 lives or the $1.5 billion in lost revenues to pharmacists? Is this really the choice?

What the evaluation of the pro/con articles does for us, in other words, is show us the lines of debate, the essential questions at issue, and the research remaining to be done.

FOR CLASS DISCUSSION
As a whole class or in small groups, make a list of unresolved questions of fact or value that you would want to pursue before you took a stand on the issues raised in Set 1 and Set 3 of the previous For Class Discussion exercise. Use as a model our list of unresolved questions for Set 2.

JOINING AN ARGUMENT: A BRIEF CASE STUDY

We will close this chapter by showing you how one of our students, Sandra Nelson, joined a conversation based on readings she did at the beginning of an argument course. Students were given the following case:

Situation: A middle-aged couple are in despair because their seventeen-year-old daughter is dying of leukemia. Doctors searched in vain for a genetically similar bone-marrow donor for a transplant, her only hope for life. The couple decided to conceive a child in hopes that the baby's bone marrow would be compatible with the daughter's. If so, a transplant could take place when the baby was six months old. The transplant operation would not be life-threatening to the baby. **Your problem:** Was the couple's decision morally justifiable? In other words, is it morally permissible to conceive a child in order to provide bone marrow for a dying sister?

FOR CLASS DISCUSSION
Working as a class or in small groups, try to resolve for yourselves this ethical dilemma. Try to reach a consensus on whether or not this couple's decision to conceive a baby was morally justified. Articulate your reasons for believing so. If consensus is impossible, articulate majority and minority views.

If your classroom is like ours, you will find your classmates about equally divided on this issue. Students supportive of the couple focused on the plight of the dying daughter, arguing that the bone marrow transplant might save the daughter's life and wouldn't harm the baby. Those opposed to the couple's decision focused on the life of the baby and imagined how that child would feel toward the parents if the baby were permanently injured by the transplant. They also wondered if the couple would love the baby for its own sake.

This dilemma is based on a real case reported in the news in the spring of 1990. After the above discussion, the instructor passed out the following article, which appeared in the weekly magazine *People*. The article was accompanied by several pictures of the couple and their ill daughter.

TO SAVE THEIR DAUGHTER FROM LEUKEMIA, ABE AND MARY AYALA CONCEIVED A PLAN — AND A BABY

Anissa Ayala had always hated hypodermic needles; even the thought of going to the doctor made her nervous. So when mysterious lumps appeared around her ankles two years ago and she began experiencing cramplike stomach pains, the athletic teenager from Walnut, Calif., decided not to tell her parents. "I was scared to go to a doctor," Anissa recalls. "My main fear was that I would have to get a blood test." 1

Soon afterward, Ayala discovered that having blood drawn would be the least of her worries. On Easter Sunday 1988, just a few days after she celebrated her 16th birthday, her agony reached the point where she realized she needed medical care. Hospital tests were performed, and the doctors came back with a grim diagnosis: Anissa was suffering from chronic myelogenous leukemia — a disease that would kill her in three to five years unless a donor could be found for a bone marrow transplant. 2

Testing of Anissa's extended family, including her mother, Mary, 43, her father, Abe, 45, and brother Airon, 19, failed to locate a suitable donor. A search by the National Bone Marrow Donor Registry for an unrelated transplant candidate — the odds against a successful match are 20,000 to 1 — also failed. So, in desperation, Mary and Abe Ayala, who own a speedometer-repair business, seized upon a final alternative. Told that the chances of a sibling marrow match were one in four, they decided to try to conceive another child. Little did they know that their gamble to save Anissa would catapult them into a heated medical-ethics controversy and raise troublesome questions about the rightful reason for having a baby. 3

Not that bringing another Ayala into the world would be easy. Aside from the couple's relatively advanced age, Abe first had to undergo surgery to reverse a vasectomy performed 16 years earlier. But he had the operation, and just six months later Mary became pregnant. Then came more good news: 4

The Ayalas learned from amniocentesis and tissue-typing tests that bone marrow cells of the baby — a girl to be born in April — will almost certainly be compatible with Anissa's.

"This is our miracle baby," a jubilant Abe Ayala told reporters last week. 5
"We are all very, very blessed," sobbed his wife. 6

Those who knew only that the Ayalas had conceived for the purpose of 7 finding a marrow match, however, were troubled by the implications of the pregnancy. "What they're doing is ethically very troubling," said Alexander M. Capron, a professor of law and medicine at USC. "The major objection," says Dr. Arthur Caplan, Director of Biomedical Ethics at the University of Minnesota in Minneapolis, "[is that] it's wrong to have a child just to have a donor."

For their part, the Ayalas insist that their baby was conceived in a spirit of 8 love. "She's my baby sister, and we're going to love her for who she is, not what she can give to me," says Anissa. Mary Ayala believes the baby has already proved her healing powers, regardless of the success of the transplant. "She has given Anissa more of a reason to live," she says. The special circumstances of her conception are underscored by the name the family has chosen for her: Marissa, a combination of Mary and Anissa.

From the outset, Anissa's illness has been a burden shared by her family. 9 Though Anissa herself remained remarkably calm — "I wanted to know everything," she says — her parents were panic-stricken. "The first thing you think is, 'She's going to die,'" says Abe Ayala. "I started getting flashbacks to when she was a little girl. I remember going into her room at home when she was in the hospital and thinking that maybe she'd never come back. It's really hard on the heart."

Luckily, Anissa responded well to initial chemotherapy treatments and was 10 able to leave the hospital after only nine days. Compared with many leukemia patients, Anissa has been fortunate so far. She has not had to undergo radiation treatments or massive chemotherapy. Still, the possibility of premature death has cast a shadow on her and her family. "At the beginning, the stress was really bad," says Mary. "I was trying to stay up for her, and she was trying to stay up for me. She would look at me, and I would start crying." Inevitably, there are moments of fear. When Anissa is plagued by nightmares, she sleeps with her parents in their king-size bed. "I'll sing to her," says Mary, "or read the Bible to her."

That kind of support was especially necessary after a heartbreaking epi- 11 sode last October, when the UCLA Medical Center contacted the Ayalas to tell them a perfect marrow match had been found for Anissa. But the donor backed out at the last moment. Apparently, he had been willing to give blood but not to go through the more complex and time-consuming procedure of donating bone marrow. "Anissa was devastated," says Mary. "She took it personally, and it was a good two weeks before she got over the trauma of it."

Fortunately, eight months earlier, Mary and Abe had considered having 12 another child — at an age when most of their friends were having grandchildren. "I had a dream," says Mary. "God told me everything was going to be okay. I woke up and told Abe, 'God told me to go ahead and have a baby.'"

Although the prognosis for Anissa is favorable now, she is hardly out of 13 jeopardy. Anissa's doctors hope to obtain stem cells from the baby's umbilical cord at the time of birth, a painless procedure for the infant. When Marissa is 6 months old, those stem cells will be combined with additional bone marrow cells that have been taken from the child. They will then be injected into Anissa's body, where the transplant has a 70 percent chance of success. Should the transplant fail, or if Anissa's condition deteriorates seriously between now and next fall, she will need to find another donor.

Meanwhile, Anissa has found another source of hope in the Life-Savers 14 Foundation of America (900-990-1414), a group that raises money and recruits donors for those in need of bone marrow transplants. "Anissa is a really effective spokesperson," says Mary. "She's not afraid to go up to people and say, 'I'm dying, and I need your help.'" Though she continues to project remarkable optimism, Anissa has been robbed of some of the simple pleasures of being a teenager. She broke up with her boyfriend recently and despairs of finding another. "I want a boyfriend, but I can't stand how immature a lot of the guys I meet can be," she says. "I have a totally different outlook on life now."

After graduating from Walnut High this spring, Anissa hopes to attend 15 Azusa Pacific University and study to become a psychologist or a social worker specializing in treating cancer patients. But even if a transplant from her new baby sister cures her leukemia, she is resigned to surrendering one childhood dream. "I've always wanted to get married early and have a baby," she says wistfully. "But now I figure this baby is enough. I mean, she could be like my own."

This article by itself, in its favorable treatment of the Ayalas, convinced a number of students that the couple made the right decision. That judgment was strengthened by the following editorial written by nationally syndicated columnist Ellen Goodman.

WE HAVE CHILDREN FOR ALL SORTS OF REASONS, AND NOW ONE IS MADE TO SAVE HER SIBLING

Ellen Goodman

Boston — When the Prince and Princess of Wales did their royal duty, and 1 begat two children, a British colleague of mine referred to their little boys in a poetic fashion. He called them "The Heir and The Spare."

It was a phrase that rang wildly off-key in the American ears of this second   2
child. A spare? In the unroyal Western world, we don't have children for the
sake of the crown. We don't set out to conceive a little regal understudy.

What then are we to think about the couple in California who conceived a   3
child in hopes of providing their older daughter with a bone-marrow donor? Is
this a new family designation: "The Heir and The Spare Part"?

Abe and Mary Ayala didn't plan to have a second child until their 17-year-   4
old daughter Anissa came down with leukemia, a cancer of the blood cells
that can sometimes be cured by transplanting bone-marrow cells from a
compatible donor. After a futile search for such a donor, the Ayalas decided to
create a child, taking a one-in-four chance that it would be compatible.

Abe had his vasectomy reversed, Mary was impregnated and seven months   5
later their gamble may be paying off. Testing has suggested that the female
fetus is compatible with the sister. At birth, they may be able to use the cells
from her umbilical cord. At six months, they may be able to use her bone
marrow.

This is a birthday tale that raises all sorts of ethical hackles. Is it right to   6
conceive one person to serve the needs of another? Can parents distribute one
child's bodily parts to save another child? Are there moral and immoral
motives for creating life?

Not long ago, when fetal tissue was first used in treating Parkinson's   7
disease, a woman considered deliberately conceiving and aborting a fetus
to donate the tissue to her father. The ethicists' response was unanimous
horror.

Last year, a medical journal reported the case of a couple prepared to   8
conceive and abort any fetuses that were incompatible, until they got what
they wanted: a marrow donor for their first child. The creation of human life
as a means to an end rather than an end in itself also was regarded as horrific.

The Ayala case isn't that simple. No, it is true, this couple wouldn't have   9
decided on a second child if Anissa hadn't needed a donor. But they also
determined to raise and love this child for itself whether it was compatible or
not. As the mother said, "If it's not a match we'll love our baby just the
same."

If we accept the parents' intentions, then, there are a variety of good   10
intentions in this act. The desire to save their older daughter. The decision to
lovingly raise another child. The hope that one can help the other.

Calculated carefully, these goods don't add up to a bad. The Ayalas have   11
skated across the thin ethical ice to safety. But the ice is indeed very thin. I
don't know how many other couples could negotiate the passage.

Bone-marrow transplants are relatively risk-free and pretty successful. The   12
decision might look quite different if this baby were created to be a kidney or
liver donor. Parents don't have an unfettered right to sacrifice one child for
another, or to give a piece of a child to another.

Even in this case, if Anissa goes into some medical crisis that could rush   13
the need for a transplant, there should be safeguards to make sure that the
baby's health is a matter of equal concern. I will leave it to the parents to
ensure the baby's mental health. How do you explain to a child that she was
created for her sister? What if that sister dies anyway?

The entire story raises a long-dormant set of questions about motives for   14
having children. Throughout human history, people had children for all sorts
of reasons. And mostly for no reason at all. We had children to be our farm
workers and children to take care of us in old age. We had one child as a
sibling for another or even, like the royals, as an insurance policy.

It's only since children began to survive longer, and since birth control,   15
and since the family as an economic unit was replaced by its role as an
emotional unit, that we have devised a list of right and wrong reasons to have
children. Today, the one reason we admit to in public is an altruistic desire to
raise and nourish and love human beings for themselves.

Now the new world of medical choices has offered us another entry onto   16
the wrong side of the ledger. It is wrong to create a child only for its spare
parts. Wrong to regard a person exclusively as something to be used.

But the Ayalas present us with a case of mixed motives, and mixed motives   17
are more common than we allow. It is possible to decide to have a child for
one reason and love it for other reasons. If this family is very, very, very
lucky, they will have reason to be grateful for two children.

————————————

Goodman asks the question "Is it right to conceive one person to serve
the needs of another?" and in this article gives her implied answer: In many
cases it is not right, but in this one case — the case of the Ayalas — it is right,
though just barely. The difficulty of the moral issue for Goodman is evident
in the very tentative conclusion she draws. Basically, she gives three reasons for believing the Ayalas were morally justified in their decision:

Reason 1: The Ayalas seem committed to raising and loving the baby
for its own sake. In contrast, Goodman wouldn't tolerate aborting the
fetus simply to use its tissues (as in the Parkinson's disease case) or
aborting and reconceiving until a correct match is found (as in an
earlier bone-marrow case).

Reason 2: The bone-marrow transplant is relatively risk-free to the
baby. In contrast, Goodman wouldn't tolerate conceiving a child for a
kidney or liver transplant, which is more threatening to the donor.

Reason 3: The family can probably ensure the baby's psychological
health. In giving this reason, Goodman shows her concern for the
child's psychological well-being — not growing up feeling "used" or
feeling value only in being a spare part for the older sister.

Goodman's article persuaded almost every person in our class, except for Sandra, who had doubts. In class discussion Sandra couldn't immediately articulate why she didn't agree with Goodman — she just felt something was the matter with the argument. Several days later she wrote about this issue in her idea-log (see next chapter) in order to explore her feelings. When the class was given one of its first formal assignments (assignment 6, page 139), Sandra chose this topic for her essay. The final version of her argument, which makes an excellent "con" to oppose Goodman's "pro," appears in the next chapter, "The Process of Writing Your Own Arguments."

3

THE PROCESS OF WRITING YOUR OWN ARGUMENTS

As the opening chapters have suggested, one goal of writing arguments is clarification—both for yourself as writer and for your readers. As you write about an issue, you begin seeing it more complexly and completely. By role playing opposing views and by examining more closely the logic and structure of your own position, you often begin discovering that what you have been saying seems doubtful or requires qualification or is simply an assertion of faith without persuasive supporting reasons. It follows, then, that writing is an act of discovering your argument, of developing and clarifying your thinking.

If you accept the notion presented in Chapters 1 and 2 that you learn about your ideas as you write, then you will accept the notion of writing as process. We like to tell our own students that a "C" essay is often an "A" essay turned in too soon. A lot of the "errors" teachers note in the margins of student essays—particularly problems of organization, development, or clarity—are normal features of a healthy rough draft. Like a growing seed or embryo, drafts evolve through stages, and for most writers it is impossible to achieve an effective product without going through some rambling, confusing drafts. Too often students stop the process short, turning in as a finished product something that is not yet "ready for strangers" but that is nonetheless a good draft on its way to becoming a good essay.

You should plan, then, to start your essays for this course early. We recommended finishing a first draft for most essays at least a week before the final product will be due. (Some writers don't need this much time for revision. There are even some who can write finished copy rapidly on the first try. These people are exceptions, though, even among professional writers.) Such a schedule will give you enough time to revise your essays substantially. You should think of revision as "re-vision"—"seeing again."

To be willing to "see again" is to be willing to make major changes in your draft, even to throw a draft out and recompose your ideas from beginning to end. The more your final product differs from your first draft, the more you will be engaging in deep revision as opposed to surface editing that merely cleans up problems with spelling, punctuation, or grammar. A brief description of the kinds of processes skilled writers go through will help us clarify our point.

A BRIEF DESCRIPTION OF WRITERS' PROCESSES

No two writers go through exactly the same process when composing an argument. In fact, your own writing processes will vary from essay to essay depending on circumstances. Although there are many paths to a good argument, most writers go through stages that are somewhat similar. Of course, writers do not approach each stage in the same way, nor do the stages occur in an orderly sequence. Instead, writers loop back through earlier stages whenever they encounter difficulties, and often parts of a draft will be in one stage of the process while other parts will be in different stages. Nevertheless, the stages can be described in a loose way as follows:

First Stage—Starting Point: Most writers begin with a sense of a problem. In the case of argumentative writing, writers usually begin with an issue, that is, with a sense of a conversation going on "out there" in which people are disagreeing about something. Their goal is to make a contribution to that conversation. Writers sometimes begin with their point of view already decided, sometimes not.

Second Stage—Exploration and Rehearsal: Writers try to find out as much as they can about the issue through reading, interviewing, and recalling personal experiences. They examine reasons and weigh evidence on all sides of the issue. Particularly, they try to understand the causes of disagreement among people on this issue, including disagreements about the facts of the case and conflicts about values, assumptions, and beliefs. Many writers do exploratory writing at this stage, either in notes or in journals, jotting down ideas or rehearsing parts of their argument through rapid drafting.

Third Stage—Writing a Discovery Draft: Stage 2 blends into Stage 3 when the writer's attention shifts from gathering data and exploring an issue to actually composing a draft. Writers at this stage often shut out their audiences temporarily and concentrate on getting their ideas clear for themselves. Discovery drafts are often messy, jumbled, and incoherent to others.

Fourth Stage—Revision, or "Seeing Again": The completion of a discovery draft often sends the writer back to earlier stages to get new ideas and to rethink the problem. At this stage, talking to others is particularly helpful. As their arguments become increasingly clarified to themselves, writers begin to reshape their essays for readers, worrying now about unity, coherence, emphasis, and all the traditional features of formal writing. Often several drafts are needed at the revision stage.

Fifth Stage—Editing: Writers now polish their drafts, worrying about the clarity of each sentence and the links between sentences. Often writers are still trying to clarify their meanings at the level of individual sentences and paragraphs. Thus, they try to make each sentence more precise—reworking structure to keep each sentence focused on intended meaning. They are also concerned about surface features such as spelling, punctuation, and grammar. Before they submit a finished product, writers proofread carefully and worry about the appearance and form of the final typed manuscript.

STRATEGIES FOR IMPROVING YOUR WRITING PROCESS

The stages of the writing process described above are based on observations of skilled writers actually composing. Unskilled writers, however, generally go through a quite different process, one that takes less time and is less rigorous in its demand for clarity. Many student writers, for example, compose rough drafts without sufficient exploration and rehearsal beforehand and revise without sufficient concern for the needs of readers. A good, long-range way for most college students to improve their writing, then, is to try to enrich their processes of composing. Here are some strategies you might try.

Talking about ideas in small groups: This is especially helpful in the very early stages of writing when you may have an issue in mind but not yet a claim to make or a sense of how to develop your argument. The greatest power of groups is their ability to generate ideas and present us with multiple perspectives. Listen to objections your classmates make to your arguments, trying to get a sense of what kinds of reasons and evidence succeed or fail. Appendix 3 in the back of this text suggests ways to make group work as successful as possible.

Using expressive writing for discovery and exploration: Expressive writing is writing you do for yourself rather than for others; it is like talking to yourself on paper. Its purpose is to help you think through ideas and get them recorded for later recall. At the end of this chapter we provide some expressive writing tasks that will help you discover and explore ideas for your argument essays.

Talking your draft: After you have written a draft, it's often helpful to talk through your argument with another person (classmate, roommate, tutor, instructor). Without reading from your draft or even looking at it, explain your argument orally to your listener. Be prepared for interruptions when your listener looks confused or unpersuaded. The act of talking through your argument forces you to formulate your ideas in new language. Often you will immediately see ways to improve your draft.

Inventing with research: Invention is a term used by the rhetoricians of ancient Greece and Rome. It is the art of finding "the best available means of persuasion" — that is, the art of generating ideas and finding arguments. One good way to do so is through reading in the library, where you can gather evidence related to your issue and examine the argumentative strategies used by others. Although most students know how to use a card catalog, few are experienced in using indexes to find articles appearing in magazines, journals, and newspapers. Yet these are often the best sources for arguers. If you don't know how to use a library or how to incorporate sources into your arguments, read Part V in this text, which deals with research writing.

Inventing with heuristic strategies: Another strategy for generating ideas for an argument is to use one or more structured processes called "heuristics" (derived from the Greek word *heuresis* meaning "to discover"). In the next section we will explain several heuristic strategies in more detail. You may find them helpful as ways to think of ideas for your arguments.

Using visual techniques for brainstorming and shaping: Cognitive psychologists have conducted extensive research on the way human beings think. One of their discoveries is that verbal modes of thinking can often be enhanced when supplemented with visual modes. In our own teaching, we have had good results emphasizing visual techniques such as idea-maps and tree diagrams as ways of helping writers imagine the content and shape of their emerging arguments. Later in this chapter we will explain idea-maps and tree diagrams in more detail.

Seeking out opposing views: Although you will often address your arguments to a neutral audience who will be weighing arguments on all sides of the issue, you can get excellent help by discussing your ideas directly with someone skeptical of your position or downright opposed to it. Unlike friendly audiences, who will usually tell you that your argument is excellent, skeptical audiences will challenge your thinking. Skeptics may find holes in your reasoning, argue from different values, surprise you by conceding points you thought had to be developed at length, and dismay you by demanding development of points you thought could be conceded. In short, opponents will urge you to "re-see" your draft.

Extensive revision: Don't manicure your drafts, rebuild them. Make sure you leave lots of white space between lines and in the margins for rewriting. And be sure to apply some of the systematic strategies described later in this text for testing the logic and evidence of an argument. Apply these tests to your own drafts as well as to opposing arguments as a means of being more objective about the substance of your argument.

Exchanging drafts: Get other people's reactions to your work in exchange for your reactions to theirs. Exchanging drafts is a different process from conversing with an opponent. Conversation with an opponent is aimed at invention and clarification of ideas; it focuses on content. An exchange of drafts, however, is aimed at the creation of well-written arguments. In addition to content, partners in a draft exchange focus on organization, development, and style. Their concern is on the quality of the draft as product.

Saving "correctness" for last: Save your concern for sentence correctness, spelling, and punctuation for last. Focusing on it at the early stages of writing can shut down your creative processes.

USING EXPRESSIVE WRITING FOR DISCOVERY AND EXPLORATION: KEEPING AN "IDEA-LOG"

We have already suggested the usefulness of expressive writing as a way to talk to yourself on paper. We recommend that you keep all your expressive writings for this course in a notebook or portfolio called an "idea-log," where you will have them as a permanent record of your exploratory thinking.

An idea-log is like a journal for discovering and exploring ideas. Unlike journal writing, however, you don't need to write in your idea-log every day. Rather, you write in it occasionally, whenever ideas for a potential or emerging argument strike you. Entries can be short (a sentence or two about an idea) or extended (a half-hour or longer rehearsal of one part of an argument in progress). It is like a scrapbook for your ideas, a place for thinking, planning, and rehearsing.

There are some occasions, however, when we suggest that you write regularly in your idea-log. The first occasion is at the start of this course when you need to build up a repertory of possible issues and ideas to write about. The set of tasks called "Starting Points" (pages 68–73) will help you develop this storehouse of ideas. The other occasions for regular expressive writing occur during the exploration and rehearsal stages of writing prior to composing your first draft. Doing so will help you develop your ideas, avoid writer's block, and eliminate some of the distress that all writers feel when facing a blank page. The set of tasks called "Exploration and Rehearsal" (pages 73–75) will help you think through each of your arguments at the exploration stage.

What is important is that you discover how expressive writing can help you clarify, elaborate, and deepen your thinking. Similar benefits can occur through expressive talking—when you and others explore ideas through group brainstorming or other kinds of productive discussion. How to use language for exploration and discovery, along with an explanation of some systematic searching procedures, is the subject of the next section.

HEURISTIC STRATEGIES FOR DISCOVERING AND EXPLORING IDEAS

What follows is a compendium of strategies to help you discover and explore ideas. Some of these strategies may not work very well for you, but many of them might work and all of them are worth trying. Each of them takes practice before you get good, so don't give up too soon if the strategy doesn't seem to work for you when you first try it.

Freewriting

Freewriting is a brainstorming activity useful at almost any stage of the writing process. When you freewrite, you put pen to paper and write rapidly *nonstop*, usually 10 to 15 minutes at a stretch. Don't worry about grammar, spelling, organization, transitions, or other features of edited writing. The object is to think of as many ideas as possible. Some freewriters achieve almost a stream-of-consciousness style: Their ideas flow directly onto the paper, stutters and stammers and all, without editing or rearrangement. Other freewriters record their thinking in more organized and focused chunks, but nevertheless they keep pushing ahead without worrying whether or not the chunks connect clearly to each other or whether they fully make sense to a strange reader. Many freewriters, perhaps most, find that their initial reservoir of ideas runs out in 3 to 5 minutes. When this happens, force yourself to keep your pen moving. If you can't think of anything to say, write "relax" over and over (or "this is stupid," or "I'm stuck," or whatever) until new ideas emerge.

Here is an example of a student's freewrite on the trigger question "When people discuss rock music, what do they disagree about?'

Lets see, rock music is a real issue of arguing. When people argue about rock-n-roll, they argue about whether or not it is harmful or helpful to young people. Older people seem to think that the lyrics have too much violence, sex, and other bad stuff that porn movies show but are restricted from general viewing. They think that certain explicit records should be labeled and restricted from younger listeners. Young people, on the other hand, tend to think that the music is a way of expressing themselves and provides a release for tension that is a result of the pressure our society places on the younger generation. They also tend to disclaim the notion that the explicit words in some songs gives them "ideas" for future actions. Let's see. Relax, relax, I got into an argument with a teacher once about classical music. She said classical music was a higher form of art than rock music. But I sometimes think that this distinction is just a class difference or a generation difference. I think I could argue that rock music is serious art. That would make a good topic or issue. "Is rock music serious art?" I wonder how I would argue that. Let's see. Relax. Relax. What else do people argue about, I know, they argue about what kind of equipment to play rock music on. What is the best kind of speaker, should a person buy records or get a compact disk. Is it ethical to copy someone else's album on your cassette deck. Is that stealing? That is a good issue. Almost everyone does it though so if it is stealing we are robbers. Let's see, what else. I am supposed to go 15 minutes. I've got three minutes left. Let's see. Relax. Sony Walkman. In some of my classes there are students who listen to their walkman during class and this seems really rude to me. A lot of people are always plugged into their portable stereos. I like these portable stereos a lot better than the old ghetto blasters. For some reason I hate loud music played outside. I think it is awful for people to blare their ghetto blasters while they are washing their cars in front of the house or are at the beach. So I guess walkmen are a real advantage. But when you see people always plugged in you wonder if those people are actually aware of their surroundings. Do they become like the rat in our psychology book that has electrodes placed in its pleasure center?

Idea-mapping

Another good technique for exploring ideas is idea-mapping, which is more visual than freewriting and which causes you to generate ideas in a different way. When you make an idea-map, you draw a circle in the center of the page and write out some trigger idea (usually a broad topic area if you are searching for an issue, or your working thesis statement if you are exploring an argument in progress) inside the circle. Then you record your ideas on branches and subbranches that extend off from the center circle. As long as you pursue one train of thought, you keep recording your ideas on subbranches off the main branch. But as soon as that chain of ideas runs dry, you can go back and start a new branch. Often your thoughts will jump back and forth between one branch and another. That's a major advantage of picturing your thoughts. You can see them as part of an emerging design rather than as strings of unrelated ideas.

An idea-map usually records more ideas than a freewrite, but the ideas are not so fully developed. Writers who practice both techniques report that they think of ideas in quite different ways, depending on which strategy they are using. Figure 3–1 is an idea-map created by a student assigned to evaluate the controversy between Peter Singer and Carl Cohen over animal rights. (Singer's and Cohen's arguments can be found on pages 480–497 of this text.) At this stage, the student is exploring the strengths and weaknesses of each argument.

Playing the Believing and Doubting Game

In order to argue effectively, you must appreciate that positions different from your own can be reasonably defended. An excellent way to imagine opposing views is to play the "believing and doubting" game.*

When you play the believing side of this game, you try to become sympathetic to an idea or point of view; you listen carefully to it, opening yourself up to the possibility of its being true. You try to appreciate why the idea has force for so many people; you try to accept the idea by discovering as many reasons as you can for believing it. It is easy to play the believing game with ideas you already believe in, but the game becomes more difficult, sometimes even frightening and dangerous, when you try believing ideas that seem untrue or disturbing to you.

The doubting game is the opposite of the believing game. It calls for you to be judgmental and critical, to find faults with an idea rather than to accept it. When you doubt a new idea, you try your best to falsify it, to find counterexamples that disprove it, to find flaws in its logic. Again, it is easy to play the doubting game with ideas you don't like, but it too can be threatening when you try to doubt ideas that are dear to your heart or central to your own world view.

Here is how one student played the believing and doubting game with the assertion "Pornography serves a useful function in society."

DOUBT

Pornography is smutty, indecent, outlandish usage of the human body. People who look at that have to be indecent nonmoralistic sexists with nothing better to do. Pornography uses the human body to gain pleasure

*A term coined by Peter Elbow, *Writing without Teachers* (Oxford University Press, 1973), pp. 147–190.

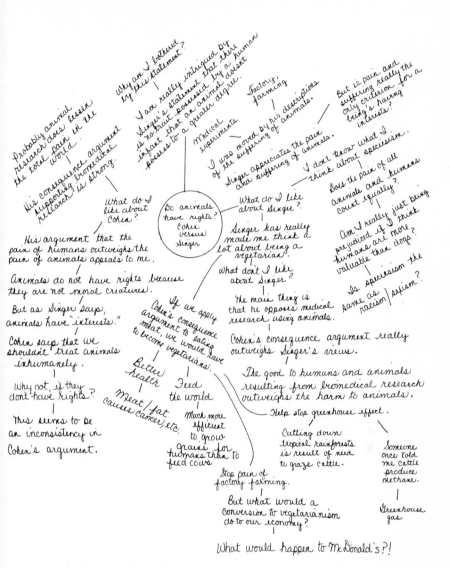

FIGURE 3-1. Idea-map Exploring Student's Reactions to Animal Rights Arguments (Arguments discussed appear on pages 480–497.)

when the human body is supposed to be like a temple that you take care of. I feel very strongly against pornography especially when they use it with young children and pets, etc. I just don't understand how people can get such a big kick out of it. It really surprised me how Dr. Jones [a guest speaker in this student's psychology course] admitted that he had bought pornographic materials, etc. I would think that it would be something that someone wouldn't readily admit to. It seems socially unacceptable to me.

BELIEVE

Pornography is something that people look at when they are feeling sexually frustrated or lonely. It is a form of escape that everyone needs at one time or another. There is always a time where one is unhappy with their sexual relationships and looking at pornography helps. Pornography is an art form. The human body is a beautiful thing and these pictures are for everyone to see the beauty of it all. People should not be afraid to be open about sex and their bodies. Everyone feels the same things. Why not share the experience with others? There is nothing dirty or smutty about being open. It is so individualistic, another way of getting out of the rut of conformity. Sex is beautiful and pornography helps share it with others that aren't quite so lucky to share these moments. (I feel this doubting game with this topic for me opens no new ideas because my mind is so set against pornography but I guess it is good to open up the new avenues of thinking.)

It is easy to see from this entry how the believing game threatens this student's moral views. Yet she does a good job of starting to get inside the head of someone who believes that pornography serves a useful purpose. Although she denies at the end of her entry that playing this game opened up new ideas, the game certainly helped her to see what the issue is and to appreciate that not all people share her values.

When you play the believing and doubting game with an assertion, simply write two different chunks, one chunk arguing for the assertion (the believing game) and one chunk opposing it (the doubting game). Freewrite both chunks, letting your ideas flow without censoring. Or, alternatively, make an idea-map with believing and doubting branches.

Brainstorming for Pro and Con "Because Clauses"

This activity is similar to the believing and doubting game in that it asks you to brainstorm ideas for and against a controversial assertion. In the believing and doubting game, however, you simply freewrite on both sides of the issue. In this activity, you try to state your reasons for and against the proposition as "because clauses." The value of doing so is discussed in depth in Chapter 4, which shows how a claim with reasons forms the core of an argument.

Here is an example of how you might create because clauses for and against the assertion "Pornography serves a useful function in society."

PRO

Pornography serves a useful function in society

- because it provides a sexual outlet for lonely men.
- because it helps society overcome Victorian repression.
- because many people obviously enjoy it.
- because it may relieve the sexual frustration of a person who would otherwise turn to rape or child molestation.
- because what some people call pornography might really be an art form.

CON

Pornography is harmful to society

- because it is degrading and oppressive to women.
- because it depersonalizes and dehumanizes sexuality.
- because it gives teenagers many wrong concepts about loving sexuality.
- because it is linked with racketeering and crime and destroys neighborhoods.
- because it often exploits children.
- because it might incite some people to commit rape and violence (serial murderer Ted Bundy's claim).

Generating because clauses like these is an especially productive discussion activity for groups. Chapter 4 takes up because clauses in greater detail.

Using the Stock Issues Strategy

This exploration strategy is particularly useful for proposal arguments, a frequently encountered argument type in which the writer identifies a problem, offers a solution, and gives reasons justifying the solution. Often a proposal argument has a claim of the type "We should/should not do X." A typical example might be the following: "In order to solve the problem of students who won't take risks with their writing, the faculty at Weasel College should adopt a pass/fail method of grading in all writing courses."

The stock issues strategy invites the writer to consider "stock" ways (that is, common, usual, frequently repeated ways) that such arguments can be conducted.

Stock issue 1: *Is there really a problem here that needs to be solved?* Is it really true that a large number of student writers won't take risks in their writing? Is this problem more serious than other writing problems such as undeveloped ideas, lack of organization, poor sentence structure, and so forth? This stock issue invites the writer to convince her audience that a true problem exists. Conversely, an opponent to the proposal might argue that a true problem does not exist.

Stock issue 2: *Will the proposed solution really solve this problem?* Is it true that a pass/fail grading system will cause students to take more risks with their writing? Will more interesting, surprising, and creative essays result from pass/fail grading? Or will students simply put less effort into their writing? This stock issue prompts a supporter to demonstrate that the proposal will solve the problem; in contrast, it prompts the opponent to show that the proposal won't work.

Stock issue 3: *Can the problem be solved more simply without disturbing the status quo?* An opponent of the proposal might agree that a problem exists and that the proposed solution might solve it. However, the opponent might say, "Are there not less radical ways to solve this problem? If we want more creative and risk-taking student essays, can't we just change our grading criteria so that we reward risky papers and penalize conventional ones?" This stock issue prompts supporters to show that *only* the proposed solution will solve the problem and that no minor tinkering with the status quo will be adequate. Conversely, opponents will argue that the problem can be solved without acting on the proposal.

Stock issue 4: *Is the proposed solution really practical? Does it stand a chance of actually being enacted?* Here an opponent to the proposal might agree that the proposal would work but that it involves pie-in-the-sky idealism. Nobody will vote to change the existing system so radically; therefore, it is a waste of our time to debate it. Following this prompt, supporters would have to argue that pass/fail grading is workable and that enough faculty are disposed to it that the proposal is worth debating. Opponents might argue that the faculty at Weasel College are so traditional that pass/fail has utterly no chance of being accepted, despite its merits.

Stock issue 5: *What will be the unforeseen positive and negative consequences of the proposal?* Suppose we do adopt a pass/fail system. What positive or negative consequences might occur that are different from what we at first predicted? Using this prompt, an opponent might argue that pass/fail grading will reduce the effort put forth by students and that the long-range effect will be writing of even lower quality than we have now. Supporters would try to find positive consequences — perhaps a new love of writing for its own sake rather than the sake of a grade.

Proposal arguments, along with the stock issues strategy, are discussed at length in Chapter 15.

Using Toulmin's System of Argument Analysis

Among the most powerful of heuristics is a method of argument analysis developed by the philosopher Stephen Toulmin. This system helps the writer convert a claim with reasons into a persuasive, developed argument. Because Toulmin's system is so important for arguers, we devote most of Chapter 5 to a detailed explanation of it, and we use it subsequently throughout the text. We mention it here so that readers can see its relationship to other heuristics.

Using the "Three Approaches" Heuristic: Arguing from Principle, from Consequences, and from Analogy

A final invention strategy is the "three approaches" heuristic. Using this strategy, you try to think of reasons based on principles, on consequences, and on analogies. Like the stock issues strategy, this method is particularly valuable for proposal arguments of the type "We should/should not do X," but it can also be applied to other arguments. This is an advanced argumentative strategy, which we discuss at length in Chapter 8, after you have had more instruction on the logical structure of arguments in Chapters 4 through 7.

SHAPING YOUR ARGUMENT: THE POWER OF TREE DIAGRAMS

We turn now from a discussion of heuristics to a discussion of strategies for organizing and shaping your argument. When you begin writing the first draft of an argument, you probably need some sort of plan, but how elaborate or detailed that plan is varies considerably from writer to writer. Some writers need to plan extensively before they can write; others need to write extensively before they can plan. But somewhere along the way, whether at the first draft stage or much later in the process, you need to concentrate on the shape of your argument. At that point, we recommend the power of tree diagrams over traditional outlines.

A tree diagram differs from an outline in that headings and subheadings are indicated through spatial locations rather than through a system of letters and numerals. An example of a simple tree diagram is shown in Figure 3–2. It reveals the plan for a three-reason argument opposing the installation of university-purchased carpets in dorm rooms. The writer's introduction is represented by the inverted triangle at the top of the tree above her claim. Her three main reasons appear as because clauses beneath the claim, and the supporting evidence and argumentation for each reason are displayed vertically underneath each reason.

This same argument displayed in outline form would look like this:

THESIS: The university should not provide carpets for the dorms.

I. Many students want the freedom to decorate their rooms in their own way.
A. University carpets would be ugly.
B. Many students have their own carpets and their own decorating style.
C. Many students don't want the responsibility of carpets.

II. Carpeting the dorms would be too expensive.
A. Initial cost would be high.
B. Cost of upkeep would be high.

III. Students might incur hefty damage costs.
A. Shaving cream fights, pizza parties, etc., could lead to major expenses.
B. Carpet is very expensive to replace once it is damaged.
1. Carpet is hard to patch.
2. Whole room must be recarpeted.

Although the traditional outline may be the more familiar way to plan an argument, tree diagrams have distinct advantages. First, they are visual. The main points of an argument are laid out horizontally, while the evidence and details supporting each point are displayed vertically. In planning the argument, a writer can move back and forth between both dimensions, working horizontally to develop the main reasons of the argument and then working vertically to find supporting data and evidence. Our own teaching experience suggests that this visual/spatial nature of tree diagrams leads writers to produce fuller, more detailed, and more logical arguments than does traditional outlining.

A related advantage of tree diagrams is their flexibility in representing different mental operations. Traditional outlines represent the division of a whole into parts and of parts into subparts. Consequently, a rule of outlining is that you can't divide a whole into just one part (that is, if you divide something, you must have at least two pieces). Thus every A must have a B, every 1 must have a 2, and so forth. Tree diagrams can easily represent this mental operation by showing two or more lines branching off a single point. But tree diagrams can also show a single line descending vertically from a

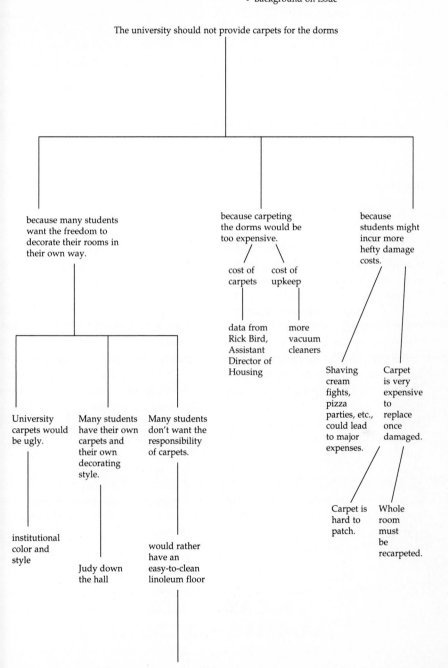

- Example of Susan spilling pie on a carpet and having to pay for carpet cleaning.
- Background on issue

The university should not provide carpets for the dorms

because many students want the freedom to decorate their rooms in their own way.

because carpeting the dorms would be too expensive.

cost of carpets   cost of upkeep

data from Rick Bird, Assistant Director of Housing

more vacuum cleaners

because students might incur more hefty damage costs.

University carpets would be ugly.

Many students have their own carpets and their own decorating style.

Many students don't want the responsibility of carpets.

Shaving cream fights, pizza parties, etc., could lead to major expenses.

Carpet is very expensive to replace once damaged.

institutional color and style

Judy down the hall

would rather have an easy-to-clean linoleum floor

Carpet is hard to patch.

Whole room must be recarpeted.

no muss, no fuss

FIGURE 3-2. Tree Diagram of Argument on Carpets

higher-level point. Such a line might represent a sequence of step-by-step ideas as in a flowchart (in Figure 3–2, see the branch ending "no muss, no fuss"). Such a line might also represent a movement from a generalization to a specific, as when you choose to support a point with a single example. Thus you could logically have the following structure on a tree diagram:

generalization

example

If you tried to put that same structure on an outline, however, it would look like this:

A. Generalization
   1. example

and some stuffy traditionalist might tell you you were being illogical. To put it another way, traditional outlines are effective in representing a division of parts into subparts, but they are less effective in representing a flowchart of ideas or a movement from generalizations to specifics. Note the amount of information on the tree diagram that could not easily be represented on the traditional outline and was hence omitted (for example, the entries "Judy down the hall," "more vacuum cleaners," and so forth).

Finally, tree diagrams can be powerful aids to invention because you can put question marks anywhere on a tree to "hold a space open" for ideas that you haven't thought of yet. Consider the value of tree diagramming for the student writer who produced the idea-map on animal rights (Figure 3–1). The student's assignment was to show which of the two animal rights arguments was stronger. His first tree diagram is shown in the dark continuous lines of Figure 3–3. As he wrote his first draft, he returned to his idea-map for ideas, which he added to the tree (shown in the broken, dotted lines on Figure 3–3). Note his use of question marks at places where he needs to add more ideas. His final tree diagram, produced after another draft, is shown in Figure 3–4. The fluid, evolving nature of tree diagrams, where branches can be added or moved around, makes them particularly valuable planning tools for writers.

A CASE STUDY:
SANDRA'S ARGUMENT

To conclude this chapter, let's return briefly to our case study of Sandra, whom we left in Chapter 2 contemplating an argument that Abe and Mary Ayala were not justified morally in conceiving a child to provide bone

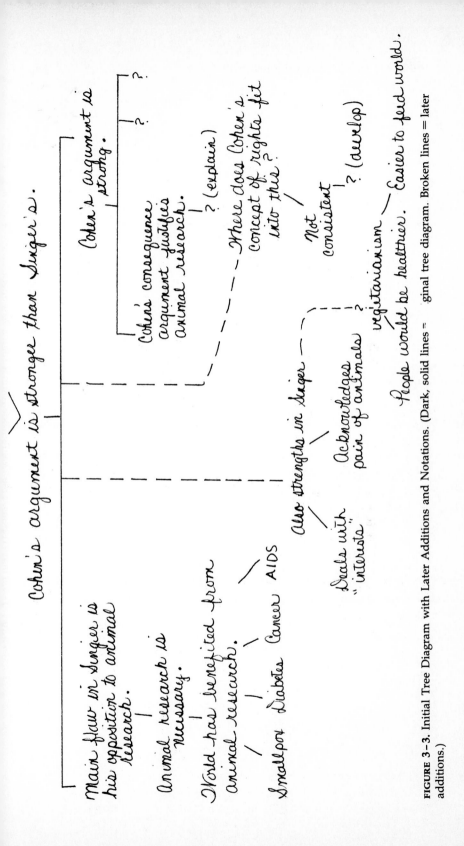

FIGURE 3–3. Initial Tree Diagram with Later Additions and Notations. (Dark, solid lines = ⸳ginal tree diagram. Broken lines = later additions.)

✓ Introduction background

Thesis: Cohen's argument is stronger than Singer's.

Despite its attractiveness, Singer's argument has a major flaw.

Although Cohen doesn't take adequate account of the suffering of animals, his argument justifies use of animals for biomedical research.

Singer's argument has major strengths.

Singer's major flaw is that his argument forces us to condemn use of animals for biomedical research.

The major weakness of Cohen is that he argues we should treat animals humanely even though he says they have no rights.

Inconsistent

Saying they have no rights doesn't address what they do have that makes it necessary for us to treat them humanely.

Singer's notion of interests not dealt with in Cohen.

(Cohen's argument does provide a consistent justification for use of animals in biomedical research.)

Argument from rights shows why human interests more than animal suffering.

Argument from consequences justifies animal research.

Criterion of pain is consistent and easy to apply.

(Argument that animals have interests is a more useful idea than Cohen's argument that animals have no rights.)

His argument against vegetarianism is hard to deny.

His argument against speciesism depends on his assumption that humans and animals have equal worth.

I can't buy that.

The world has benefited greatly from biomedical research.

Singer is sensitive to animals' interests.

Speciesism - treating animals' suffering as powerful.

Our moral nature surely requires us to respect animals' interests.

(Cohen's focus on rights embroils issue of what to do about animal's pain.)

Smallpox

Search for diabetes cure

(Current AIDS research)

Medical research

Factory farming

World would be better off if we converted to vegetarianism.

Matthew people

Easier to feed the world

Cut down on destruction of tropical rainforest

Land needed to graze cattle

FIGURE 3–4. Final Working Tree Diagram for Animal Rights Argument

marrow for their sixteen-year-old daughter dying of leukemia. Something about the Alayas's decision troubled Sandra. Early in the course, she explored what was bothering her in the following freewrite.

> OK I read Ellen Goodman and I read the *People* magazine article, but I am not convinced. What sways me in an argument is: when the verbals match the visuals. In other words, when what is being claimed as a future reality is supported by past history or personal performance. This to me supplies credence of intent. And it is precisely this that bothers me in the leukemia case: Vasectomy after two children, as opposed to 3 does not say to me that they just wanted another child. Daughter's statement. "I've always wanted a baby sister. Whatever happens she will be loved." On the surface it would seem that this statement clearly supports the notion that the child will be loved. But underneath the surface, why haven't the parents given her a baby sister before. Therefore, I have to ask "Loved by who, the parents or the daughter?"

Sandra's argument went through several drafts before it reached the stage printed below. Although we will not ask you to observe all the changes she made from draft to draft, we think it is instructive to look at her initial tree diagram (Figure 3–5), made after she had written her first draft. As is readily apparent, her thinking processes seem fluid, even chaotic, but her plan eventually solidified into the well-designed shape shown in her final draft. We show you this tree to convince you that the unseen processes behind a polished product are fascinating for a reader to observe and fatal for a writer to omit.

WAS IT MORALLY WRONG FOR THE AYALAS TO CONCEIVE A CHILD TO ACT AS A BONE-MARROW DONOR FOR THEIR OLDER DAUGHTER?

Sandra Nelson (student)

How far should the love for a child take parents? A California couple, Abe and 1 Mary Ayala, believed that their love for their sixteen-year-old daughter, Anissa, who was dying of leukemia, warranted the conception of another child to act as a bone-marrow donor. Was this morally wrong? Some believe it wasn't, that the parents' love obligated them to any means open. Columnist Ellen Goodman pointed out that the medical procedure would cause no harm to the child and that, should the older daughter die anyway, the parents would have the new baby to love.

The decision to have another child is one that grieving parents often make, 2 but usually after the death of the other child. In the February 1990 issue of *People Weekly*, the Ayalas gave a family interview and, if one is not reading

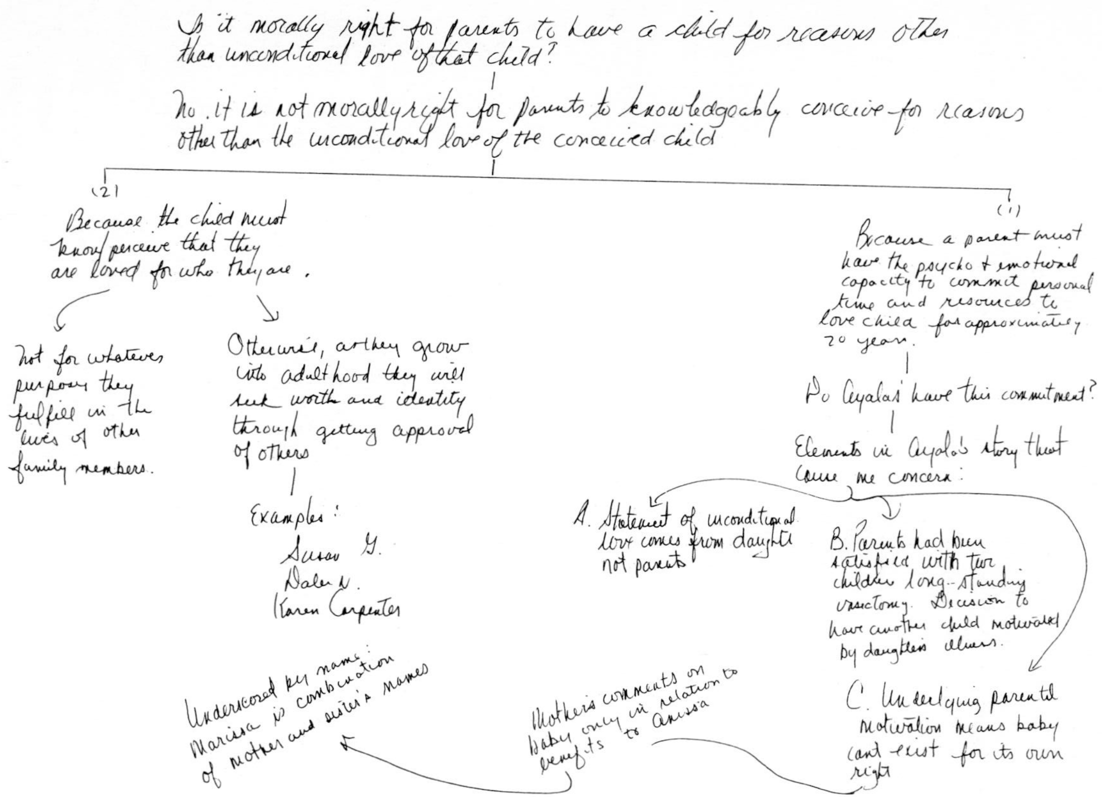

Is it morally right for parents to have a child for reasons other than unconditional love of that child?

No. It is not morally right for parents to knowledgeably conceive for reasons other than the unconditional love of the conceived child

(2)

Because the child must know/perceive that they are loved for who they are.

Not for whatever purpose they fulfill in the lives of other family members.

Otherwise, or they grow into adulthood they will not worth and identity through getting approval of others.

Examples:
Susan V.
Duke V.
Karen Carpenter

Underscored by mention
Marion is emphasized
of mother as victim

Mother's comments on
relationship with Anna
baby only for baby's
benefits

(1)

Because a parent must have the psycho + emotional capacity to commit personal time and resources to love child for approximately 20 years.

Do Ayala's have this commitment?

Elements in Ayala's story that cause me concern:

A. Statement of unconditional love comes from daughter not parents

B. Parents had been satisfied with their children long-standing reaction to have another child motivated by daughter's illness

C. Unless giving parental motivation means baby had exist for its own sight

FIGURE 3-5. Sandra's Working Tree Diagram

carefully, it would appear that they offer a secure, well-adjusted, and loving home. However, several statements made by the family members themselves convinced me that the Ayalas did indeed decide to have this child to save their daughter rather than to have another child to love. It is for this reason that I believe that their decision to give birth was morally wrong.

Both those in favor of the birth and those opposed to it agree that the 3 unconditional love of the parents for the child is prerequisite to a child's developing a strong sense of self-worth and identity. It is the lack of evidence of this vital component of parenting that first raises my concern. It is the daughter, not the parents, who makes this statement:

> I've always wanted a baby sister. . . . Whatever happens she will be loved. . . . She's my baby sister and we're going to love her for who she is, not what she can give to me.

While there is obviously a pledge to unconditional love, the only references to it come from the daughter and not the parents. Mary Ayala relates her fear and concern for her older daughter and calls the baby a "miracle that has given Anissa more of a reason to live." Abe Ayala, too, speaks only of his grief and fear that he will lose Anissa.

The second vital component of parenting is the commitment to meet all the 4 psychological and emotional needs of a child for fifteen to twenty years. To remain consistent in this regard requires purposeful intent on the part of the parents. Having had a son and a daughter, the Ayalas apparently assessed their parenting desires sixteen years ago and chose to prevent further conception through a vasectomy. I see no evidence of a reassessment, change of heart, or reversal of their decision until the daughter's illness threatened to take her life. Therefore, I must ask, who is prepared to raise this child? The only clear pledge that is made toward this responsibility, once again, comes from the daughter, who says, "I've always wanted to get married early and have a baby . . . but now, I figure this baby is enough. I mean, she could be like my own."

My third concern centers on the many family attitudes voiced by the family 5 that could conceivably prevent the child from perceiving herself to be loved in her own right. Abe Ayala is clearly focused on this baby's usefulness to his older daughter as he speaks about his belief that Anissa is going to die, his panic, and his desire to stop the wear and tear on his heart. Mary Ayala states that she conceived to save her daughter at divine direction and that proof of the child's healing powers is already evident in her older daughter's enthusiasm. Anissa herself is unabashedly elated that, should she live, the disease will not have robbed her of the opportunity to be a parent. Most symbolic of the many expectations this child will have to fill before she will be viewed and valued simply because she has arrived is the name chosen for the baby by the mother and daughter. When the new Ayala arrives, she will be christened Marissa — a combination of their own two names.

To my way of thinking, these underlying motivations and overlying 6 agendas cannot help but create confusion for the child and all but obscure the sacred trust of personhood through birth. Although the Ayalas are well intended, the decision to conceive does not reflect the same level of responsible commitment that they have made toward their other two children. It was, therefore, morally incorrect.

USING EXPRESSIVE WRITING TO DISCOVER AND EXPLORE IDEAS: TWO SETS OF IDEA-LOG TASKS

The tasks that follow are intended to help you use expressive writing to generate ideas and to expand and deepen your thinking. The first set of tasks — designed to take approximately three hours — helps you build up a repertory of ideas to write about early in the course. The second set of tasks — to be completed prior to writing the first draft of each of your formal assignments throughout the course — takes between one and two hours each time. But these hours are well spent since, in doing the tasks, you are getting on paper most of the ideas you will need for your argument.

Idea-Log, Set One: Starting Points

The first three tasks in Starting Points will help you take an inventory of issues that already interest you and about which you may have had personal experiences.

TASK 1 (15 MINUTES)

Jot down your responses to the following "idea-starters." Use the idea-starters to take an inventory of issues that interest you and to help you identify some of your beliefs or opinions that might serve as an entry into an argumentative conversation.

- My friends and I like to argue about . . .
- I think it is wrong when . . .
- I wish I could convince [someone] that . . .
- I am definitely opposed to . . .
- X [someone] believes . . . ; however, I believe . . .

- I wish my college would solve the problem of . . .
- I think we should pass a law so that . . .

EXPLANATION   These idea-starters are intended to stimulate thinking. In your idea-log make lists of thoughts that come to mind in response to each starter. Spend fifteen minutes brainstorming for this task. Try to fill a whole page with ideas. If possible, share your list with other persons in your class. Start some argumentative conversations.

TASK 2 (5 MINUTES)

Make a list in response to the following idea-starter:

I am not sure where I stand on the issue of . . .

EXPLANATION   The first task helped you identify strong opinions and beliefs. This task has the opposite aim. It asks you to identify issues that you have not been able to take a stand on. Perhaps you haven't studied the issue enough to know where you stand (for example, what to do about the greenhouse effect, Contra aid, tariffs to protect threatened industries). Or perhaps you can't take a stand because an issue involves you in an uncomfortable conflict of values (for example, abortion, mandatory testing for AIDS). Sometimes the best experience you can have in an argument course is to think through such an issue for the first time, using the arguing process to help you clarify your views and take a stand. Your goal for this task is to identify a number of issues that you would like to be able to take a stand on but that currently leave you confused and bewildered.

TASK 3 (10 MINUTES)

Freewrite for ten minutes on the following trigger question:

"When people discuss X, what do they disagree about?"

Substitute for X any topic area of your choice such as "home economics," "Moby Dick," "sex," "justice," or some off-the-wall topic such as "hamburgers." Write steadily for fifteen minutes, switching to a different X if you run out of ideas.

EXPLANATION   The first two tasks skimmed off ideas close to the surface of your consciousness. The next two tasks will help you probe for ideas in unsuspected places.

The strategy you will use in this task is freewriting. For an example of a freewrite in response to this task, see the freewrite on "rock music" on page 53.

TASK 4 (30 MINUTES, EXCLUDING READING TIME)

Join a conversation going on in print. Read the set of essays on one of the issues in Part VI of this text (the exclusionary rule, birth control clinics in the schools, the Hiroshima bombing, animal rights, censorship, civil disobedience, and so forth; choose any set that interests you). After you have finished the essays, make a full, detailed idea-map exploring your reactions to your readings. Use as a model the student's idea-map exploring the Cohen/Singer animal rights debate (Figure 3–1, page 55).

EXPLANATION   This task will help you see that there are many ways to join an ongoing conversation. For this task, explore all the ways you might raise questions about the arguments you have selected. Raise questions about facts, about definitions, about analogies, or about values, beliefs, and assumptions (see Chapter 2). You can either explore your views on the main issue under discussion or say "yes, but . . ." to any of the sub-issues or side-issues that occur during the course of your reading. By participating in a conversation already in progress, you will appreciate the social nature of argument and experience the intertwining of issues that all arguments entail.

TASK 5 (30 MINUTES)

Make several idea-maps of issue questions.

EXPLANATION   The purpose of this task is to use idea-maps to think of issue questions. As we explain in more detail in Chapter 4, an issue question is any question that can be reasonably answered in two or more opposing ways. A good way to begin thinking about arguments, therefore, is to try writing issue questions themselves. Ideally, each question will help you recall actual disagreements you have experienced, either in person or through your reading.

For this task make two or three idea-maps, each focusing on a different topic area, which can range from your own personal life to public policy or controversies in academic fields. Inside the circle of each map, write a trigger word signifying a broad topic area (for example, "children," "music," "athletics," "Intro to Psychology," "student government," "food"). Then make several branches off each circle, letting each branch represent a narrower subdivision of the general topic. (For example, if your circle was labeled "athletics," you might label your branches "baseball," "football, "coaches," "game plans," "women's athletics," and so forth.) Then ask issue questions stemming off each branch. Examples of issue questions related to football might be "Are midget football leagues good for young children?" "Should NFL professional football players have free agency?" "Does a winning football team improve the quality of life on a college campus?" "Should Coach Jones switch to a quarterback option offense?"

TASK 6 (15 MINUTES)

Start an issue list.

EXPLANATION For this task, reexamine your entries from the first five tasks and select a half-dozen or so issue questions that you might like to choose as issues for a written argument. Write these issue questions in a list. Then leave a blank page in your idea-log so that you can add to your list whenever new ideas occur to you. Whenever you are given an assignment with optional issues, you can turn to this list for ideas. Exchange issue lists with other members of your class and add interesting ideas from their lists to your own.

In the last three tasks in Starting Points we are going to give you some controversial issues and ask you to start exploring what you feel about them. In earlier tasks you tried to recall arguments you had already engaged in or had strong personal feelings about. In these next tasks we will try to stimulate new arguments.

TASK 7 (30 MINUTES)

Play the believing and doubting game with two assertions from the following list. Try to choose assertions that will disturb you when you play either the believing or the doubting side.

- A student should report a fellow student who is cheating on an exam or plagiarizing an essay.
- States should legalize marriages between homosexuals.
- Indian reservations should be abolished.
- The federal government should eliminate guaranteed student loans.
- It is healthier to be a punk rocker than an Eagle Scout.
- Colleges should place primary emphasis on career-preparation courses rather than on the liberal arts.
- The federal government should mandate universal AIDS testing every six months.

EXPLANATION At least a few of the above claims should stimulate disagreement among your friends or classmates. Choose two for exploration, spending approximately fifteen minutes believing and doubting each assertion (seven to eight minutes believing, seven to eight minutes doubting). For an example, see pages 54–56.

TASK 8 (15 MINUTES)

Play the believing and doubting game with one of your own assertions.

EXPLANATION For this task choose an issue from your issue list (Task 6) and develop a single, strong assertion in response to your issue. After you have made an assertion, play the believing and doubting game with it.

TASK 9 (30 MINUTES)

Use the stock issues heuristic to explore ideas either for or against one of the following proposals. Reread pages 57–58 for an explanation of the stock issues heuristic.

- In order to solve the problem of dependence on foreign oil, the U.S. Congress should impose a gasoline tax of $2.00 per gallon.
- In order to make it possible for small men to play varsity college basketball, colleges should institute two divisions based on height. One division ought to be limited to persons six feet tall and smaller.
- In order to eliminate the perpetuation of sexual stereotypes, colleges ought to abolish cheerleaders.
- In order to eliminate the high social cost of crime and gangsterism associated with drugs, the United States ought to legalize all drugs.
- In order to reduce teenage pregnancy and disease, high schools should pass out free condoms to students.
- [any equivalent problem/proposal statement of your own]

EXPLANATION The purpose of this task is to give you an opportunity to practice asking the questions (and exploring answers to them), prompted by the stock issues heuristic.

FOR CLASS DISCUSSION

1. Divide into small groups. Your instructor will distribute large sheets of butcher paper and marking pens (or you can use the blackboard). Each group should make a master list of issue questions compiled from each person's individual log of issues (Task 6). When your group finishes its master list (fifteen to twenty issues), group members should rate each issue question for the "degree of controversy" it stimulates (4 = highly controversial; 1 = noncontroversial). Place a star next to highly controversial issues. When you are finished, tape your list to the wall and then observe other groups' lists. Each person's goals should be to find several people in the class who disagree with his or her views on some issues. Try to get together after class with some of these "opponents" for further discussion of issues.

2. Again divide into small groups. Your instructor will ask your group to "believe" and "doubt" a proposition that he or she will provide (perhaps one of the propositions in Task 7). Elect a spokesperson for your group and spend fifteen minutes helping your spokesperson think of believing and doubting arguments. Then the spokespersons should represent their groups in a panel discussion or debate in front of the class. At this time the instructor will assign each panel member a role as a supporter or opponent of the assertion.

Idea-log, Set Two: Exploration and Rehearsal

The first set of idea-log tasks was designed to help you think of topics for your formal essays in this course. The following set of tasks is designed to help you with the exploration and rehearsal stage of writing, after you have chosen a topic for an essay. It takes most students about two hours to do all eight of the freewriting tasks, but the payoff is that you will get down on paper plenty of ideas for your essay. We recommend that you go through this second set of tasks each time you are given a formal essay assignment for this course.

TASK 1

Write out the issue question you think you would like to focus on in this essay. Then try wording your question in several different ways. Sometimes slight changes in the way you word the question—for example, making it somewhat broader or somewhat narrower—will help you clarify the way your argument will proceed. Finally, write the question in the way that currently seems best. Put a box around it.

TASK 2

Look back at the issue question you placed in the box in Task 1. Now write out your own tentative answer to the question. This will be your beginning thesis statement or claim—the position you will try to defend in your essay. Put a box around this answer. Next write out one or more different answers to your question. These will be the possible alternative claims that a neutral audience will be considering—summaries of the equally plausible opposing positions you will be arguing against. Finally, explore whether or not your issue question seems to be a two-sided issue—one on which people in the conversation will divide neatly into pro and con sides—or whether it is a multi-sided issue with many different points of view. Your exploration here can make a difference later when you try to achieve a final focus for your argument.

TASK 3

For this task, explain why you think people disagree on your issue. In other words, why is this issue controversial? Is there not yet enough evidence to resolve the issue? Is the evidence controversial? Is there disagreement about the definition of key terms? Do different parties in the controversy hold different values, assumptions, or beliefs?

TASK 4

What personal interests or personal experiences do you have with this issue? (By "personal experiences" we mean not only firsthand experiences but also memories from things you've read, TV news stories you've seen, lectures you've heard, and so forth.) Exploring these questions should help you clarify your personal interest in this topic, as well as its relationship to concerns and values in your own life.

TASK 5

What reasons and evidence can you think of to support your position on this issue? Brainstorm for every possible point you can think of in support of your position. You might want to use an idea-map here instead of freewriting. Get as many ideas as possible on paper. In this task, you will be "rehearsing" the main body of your paper, which will set forth reasons and then support them with evidence or chains of other reasons.

As you generate ideas for reasons and evidence, you are likely to find gaps in your knowledge where you need to do further research either in the library or through interviews. If your claim could be strengthened through the use of statistics, testimony of experts, and so forth, develop a plan for conducting your research.

TASK 6

In this task, begin by rereading what you wrote in Task 5 and then reconsider your argument from the perspective of a neutral or opposing audience. What values, beliefs, or assumptions would your audience have to hold in order to accept your argument? Do you think your audience holds these values, assumptions, or beliefs?

TASK 7

Continue your exploration of audience by assuming the role of someone who opposes your position. Writing from that person's perspective, try to construct a counterargument that opposes your own views. (In other words, play the doubting game with the argument you created in Task 5.)

TASK 8

Why is this an important issue? What are its broader implications and consequences? What other issues does it relate to? Thinking of possible answers to these questions may prove useful when you write your introduction or conclusion.

WRITING ASSIGNMENTS FOR PART I

OPTION 1: **A Letter to Your Instructor about Yourself as a Writer** Write a letter to your instructor about yourself as a writer. In the first part of your letter, give your instructor a complete picture of how you go about writing. Describe the process you normally go through, using examples from recent writing experiences. Address questions such as the following:

Mechanical procedures: When and where do you like to do your writing? Do you compose your drafts by hand, by typewriter, or by word processor? If by hand, what kind of paper and pens do you use for your first drafts? Subsequent drafts? Do you single-space or double-space your early drafts? One side of the page or two? If you handwrite, do you write large or small? Big margins or little margins? Do you write rapidly or slowly? Do you use the same procedures for second and later drafts? If you use a word processor, do you compose directly at the terminal or do you write out a draft and then type it in? Do you revise at the terminal or make changes on hard copy?

Mental procedures: Do you procrastinate when you need to write? Do you suffer writer's block or anxiety? Do you write a paper the night before it is due or spread your writing time out over several days? Do you normally do exploratory writing such as freewriting and idea-mapping? Do you organize your ideas before drafting or draft first and then organize? How many drafts do you typically make? What kinds of changes do you typically make as you revise? Do you discuss your ideas with friends before you write or between drafts? Do you exchange drafts with friends?

Writing preferences: Do you like to write? What kind of writing do you most like to do? Least like to do? Do you like to choose your own topics or have the teacher choose topics for you? Do you like open-ended assignments or assignments with clear guidelines and constraints? How much time are you willing to put into a paper?

In the second part of your letter, analyze your strengths and weaknesses as a writer. Address questions such as these:

Strengths and weaknesses in final products: What have you been praised for or criticized for in the past as a writer? How consistent are you in coming up with good ideas for your papers? In general, do you have trouble organizing your papers or is organization a strength? Are your sentences usually clear and grammatically correct? Do you have trouble with punctuation? Are you a good speller?

Strengths and weaknesses in writing process: How does your writing process compare with the typical writing processes of experienced writers as described in Chapter 3? If you were to improve your writing process, what would you work on most?

These questions are meant to be representative only. Use them as suggestions for the kinds of information your instructor needs to get to know you as a writer. Your goal is to give your instructor as much helpful information as possible.

OPTION 2: **AN ARGUMENT SUMMARY**   Write a two-hundred-word summary of an argument selected by your instructor. Then write a one-sentence summary of the same argument. Use as models the summaries of Charles Brandt's "Let Our Police Take On the Drug Dealers" in Chapter 2 (pages 25, 27).

OPTION 3: **AN ANALYSIS AND EVALUATION OF OPPOSING ARGUMENTS**   Using as a model the analysis and evaluation in Chapter 2 of the Erbe/Chavez discussion of surrogate motherhood, write an analysis and evaluation of any two pro/con articles selected by your instructor.

OPTION 4: **A DEBATE ESSAY**   Write a debate essay on an issue of your own choosing. Write your essay as a mini-play in which two or more characters argue about an issue. Create any kind of fictional setting that you like: a group of students having beers at a local tavern, two people on a date, a late-night dorm room bull session. Have the characters disagree with each other on the issue, but make your characters reasonable people who are trying to argue logically and intelligently.

The purpose of such an assignment is to free you from strict demands of organization in order to let you explore an issue from all sides. Try to have characters find weaknesses in each other's arguments as well as present their own side of the issue.

Here is a brief example of the format. Imagine that you are looking in on the middle of a debate essay on whether writing courses should be pass/fail:

JOE: Here's another thing. Pass/fail would make students a lot more creative. They wouldn't worry so much about pleasing the teacher.

ANN: Hogwash, Joe. Pass/fail would make them less creative.

JOE: Why?

ANN: They'd put less time into the course. If a course is pass/fail students won't work as hard. They'll put their energy into the courses that will be graded. That's what happened to me when I took an art class pass/fail my freshman year. I started out really interested in it and vowed to spend a lot of time. But by midterms I was getting behind in my other classes, so I neglected art in order to get good grades where they would show up on my transcripts.

JOE: But pass/fail will make you examine your values. Maybe you would quit working just for grades. Besides, in a writing class you would have a different motivation. In a writing class you would have the motivation of knowing that your writing skills will make a big difference in other classes and in your future careers.

ANN: Yes, but students don't worry about long-range benefits. They always take the short-range benefit.

JOE: But maybe you would really get into writing for its own sake. If you don't have to follow a teacher's silly rules, writing can be really creative, like doing art. Remember how much time you spent drawing pictures when you were a little girl? You weren't motivated by grades then. You liked to draw because people are naturally creative. We would still be creative if we weren't afraid. A pass/fail course would take away the fear of failure. How long would you have painted those little kid pictures if some teacher came along and marked up your painting with red ink and said, "Shame, look at all the mistakes you made." You'd quit drawing right away. That is what has happened to writing. Students hate to write because all they get for it is criticism. A pass/fail course would allow us to get praise and to explore writing in new ways.

ANN: You have too much faith, Joe, in the natural creativity of students. You can't overcome twelve years of schooling in one pass/fail course. Look at some other consequences of a pass/fail system. First . . .

OPTION 5: **BEGIN A MAJOR COURSE PROJECT** An excellent major project for an argument course is to research an issue about which you are initially undecided. Your final essay for the course could be an argument in which you take a stand on this issue. Choose one of the issues you listed in Starting Points, Task Three, "I am unable to take a stand on the issue of . . ." and make this issue a major research project for the course. During the term keep a log of your research activities and be ready, in class discussion or in writing, to explain what kinds of arguments or evidence turned out to be most persuasive in helping you take a stand.

For this assignment, write a short letter to your instructor identifying the issue you have chosen and explain why you are interested in it and why you can't make up your mind at this time.

II

THE LOGICAL STRUCTURE OF ARGUMENTS: CLAIMS, REASONS, AND EVIDENCE

4

THE CORE OF AN ARGUMENT: A CLAIM WITH REASONS

THE RHETORICAL TRIANGLE

Before looking at how arguments are structured, we should recognize that arguments occur within a social context. They are produced by writers or speakers who are addressing an audience—a relationship that can be diagrammed as follows:

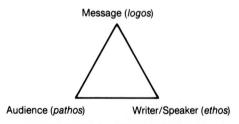

FIGURE 4-1. The Rhetorical Triangle

In composing an effective argument, writers must concern themselves with all three elements in this "rhetorical triangle." By a long-standing tradition, the terms for the relationships in the rhetorical triangle are called *logos*, *ethos*, and *pathos*.

Logos (Greek for "word") refers to the internal consistency of the message — the clarity of its claim, the logic of its reasons, and the effectiveness of its supporting evidence. The impact of *logos* on an audience is sometimes called the argument's "logical appeal."

Ethos (Greek for "character") refers to the trustworthiness or credibility of the writer or speaker. *Ethos* is often conveyed through the tone and style of the message and through the way the writer or speaker refers to opposing views. It can also be affected by the writer's reputation as it exists independently from the message — his or her expertise in the field, his or her previous record of integrity, and so forth. The impact of *ethos* is often called the argument's "ethical appeal" or the "appeal from credibility."

Our third term, *pathos* (Greek for "emotion"), is perhaps the most difficult to define. It refers to the impact of the message on the audience, the power with which the writer's message moves the audience to decision or action. Although *pathos* refers primarily to the emotional appeal of an argument, it is difficult to disentangle such appeals from the logical structure of an argument. As we show in the following chapters, a successful logical structure is rooted in assumptions, values, or beliefs shared by the audience so that an effective logical appeal necessarily evokes a reader's or listener's emotions. Whereas *logos* engages our rational faculties, *logos* and *pathos* together engage our imaginations. The impact of *pathos* on an audience is often called the "appeal to emotions" or the "motivational appeal."

Using the rhetorical triangle, we can create a checklist of questions that can help a writer plan, draft, and revise an argument (see Figure 4–2). As the checklist suggests, writers should consider ways to make their messages as logically sound and well developed as possible, but they should also take care to link their arguments to the values and beliefs of the audience and to convey an image of themselves as credible and trustworthy.

The chapters in Parts II and III of this text treat all three elements in the rhetorical triangle. Part II (Chapters 4–7) is concerned primarily with *logos*, whereas Part III, especially Chapter 9, is concerned with *pathos* and *ethos*. However, all these terms overlap so that it is impossible to make neat separations among them.

Given this background on the rhetorical triangle, we are ready now to turn to *logos* — the logic and structure of arguments.

ISSUE QUESTIONS AS THE ORIGINS OF ARGUMENT

At the heart of any argument is an issue, which we can define as a topic area such as "criminal rights" or "the minimum wage," that gives rise to a dispute or controversy. A writer can usually focus an issue by asking an

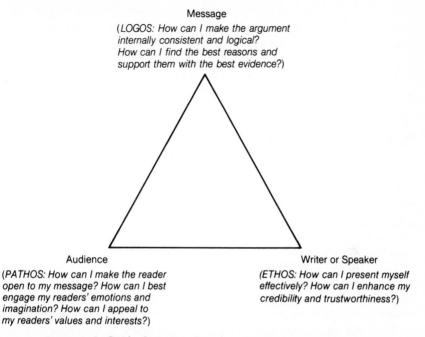

Message
(*LOGOS: How can I make the argument internally consistent and logical? How can I find the best reasons and support them with the best evidence?*)

Audience
(*PATHOS: How can I make the reader open to my message? How can I best engage my readers' emotions and imagination? How can I appeal to my readers' values and interests?*)

Writer or Speaker
(*ETHOS: How can I present myself effectively? How can I enhance my credibility and trustworthiness?*)

FIGURE 4-2. Guide Questions Based on the Rhetorical Triangle

issue question that invites at least two opposing answers. Within any complex issue — for example, the issue of abortion — there are usually a number of separate issue questions: Should abortions be legal? Should the federal government authorize Medicare payments for abortions? When does a fetus become a human being (at conception? at three months? at quickening? at birth?)? What are the effects of legalizing abortion? (One person might stress that legalized abortion leads to greater freedom for women; another person might respond that it lessens a society's respect for human life.)

The Difference between an Issue Question and an Information Question

Of course, not all questions are issue questions that can be answered reasonably in two or more opposing ways; thus, not all questions can lead to effective argument essays. Rhetoricians have traditionally distinguished between "explication," which is writing that sets out to inform or explain, and "argumentation," which sets out to change a reader's mind. On the surface, at least, this seems like a useful distinction. If a reader is interested in a writer's question mainly to gain new knowledge about a subject, then the writer's essay could be considered explication rather than argument. According to this view, the following questions about abortion might be called information questions rather than issue questions:

How does the abortion rate in the United States compare with the rate in Sweden?

If the rates are different, why?

Although both questions seem to call for information rather than for argument, we believe the latter one would be an issue question if reasonable people disagreed on the answer. Thus, two writers might agree that abortion rates in the United States and Sweden differ significantly, but they might disagree in their explanations of why. One might say that Sweden has a higher abortion rate because of the absence of a large Catholic or conservative Protestant population in the country. The other might say, "No, the real reasons are linked to the country's economic structure." Thus, underneath the surface of what looks like a simple explication of the "truth" is really a controversy.

You can generally tell whether a question is an issue question or an information question by examining your purpose in relationship to your audience. If your relationship to your audience is that of teacher to learner, so that your audience hopes to gain new information, knowledge, or understanding that you possess, then your question is probably an information question. But if your relationship to your audience is that of advocate to decision maker or jury, so that your audience needs to make up its mind on something and is weighing different points of view, then the question you address is an issue question. Often the same question can be an information question in one context and an issue question in another. Let's look at the following examples:

- How does a diesel engine work? (This is probably an information question since reasonable people who know about diesel engines will probably agree on how they work. This question would be posed by an audience of new learners.)

- Why is a diesel engine more fuel-efficient than a gasoline engine? (This also seems to be an information question since all experts will probably agree on the answer. Once again, the audience seems to be new learners, perhaps students in an automotive class.)

- What is the most cost-effective way to produce diesel fuel from crude oil? (This could be an information question if experts agree and you are addressing new learners. But if you are addressing engineers and one engineer says process X is the most cost-effective and another argues for process Y, then the question is an issue question.)

- Should the present highway tax on diesel fuel be abolished? (This is certainly an issue question. One person says yes; another says no; another offers a compromise.)

FOR CLASS DISCUSSION
Working as a class or in small groups, try to decide which of the following questions are information questions and which are issue questions. Many of them could be either, depending on the rhetorical context. For such questions, create hypothetical contexts to show your reasoning.

1. What is the definition of a "fiscal conservative" in the article by Rudolph Jones?
2. During his first term of office, was Ronald Reagan a fiscal conservative?
3. Is fiscal conservatism the best fiscal policy for the United States at this time?
4. What percentage of TV shows during prime-time hours depict violence?
5. What is the effect of violent TV shows on children?
6. Are chiropractors legitimate health professionals?
7. How does chiropractic treatment of illness differ from a medical doctor's treatment?
8. Are extended-wear contact lenses safe?
9. Should a woman with a newly detected breast cancer opt for a radical mastectomy (complete removal of the breast and surrounding lymph tissue) or a lumpectomy (removal of the malignant lump without removal of the whole breast)?
10. Is Simone de Beauvoir correct in calling marriage an outdated, oppressive, capitalist institution?

THE DIFFERENCE BETWEEN A GENUINE ARGUMENT AND A PSEUDO-ARGUMENT

We have said that the heart of an argument is an issue question that invites two or more competing answers. This does not mean, however, that every disagreement between people can lead to a rational argument. Rational arguments depend also on two additional factors: (1) reasonable participants, that is, participants who agree to operate within the conventions of reasonable behavior, and (2) potentially shareable assumptions that can serve as a starting place or foundation for the argument. You should learn to recognize the difference between genuine arguments, which proceed reasonably, and pseudo-arguments, which generate a lot of heat but are as irresolvable as a game of chess in which the players do not agree on how the pieces move.

Pseudo-arguments: Fanatics and Skeptics

As you know, many arguments that at first seem like reasonable disputes are really shouting matches masquerading as arguments. Without really listening to each other, these disputants carry on into the night asserting as facts statements they are unsure of, citing vague authorities, moving illogically into tangential issues, and trying, in general, to rationalize a position based more on feeling and opinion than on careful thought.

Often such disputants belong to one of two classes, Fanatics and Skeptics. Fanatics are people who believe their claims are true because they say so, period. Oh, they may assure us that their claims rest on some authoritative text—the Bible, the *Communist Manifesto*, Benjamin Spock's books on child raising—but in the end it's their narrow and quirky reading of the text, a reading claiming to be fact, that underlies their argument. When you disagree with a Fanatic, therefore, you'll get a desk-thumping rehash of the Fanatic's preconceived convictions.

The Skeptic, on the other hand, dismisses the possibility that anything could be proven right. Because the sun has risen every day in recorded history is inadequate reason for the Skeptic to claim that it will rise tomorrow. Short of absolute proof, which never exists, Skeptics accept no proof. Skeptics, in short, do not understand that an argument cannot be a proof. We can hope that a good argument will increase its readers' "adherence" to a claim by making the claim more plausible, more worthy of consideration, but only rarely will it eliminate doubt or overcome the influence of opposing views. In the presence of Fanatics or Skeptics, then, genuine argument becomes impossible.

Although few of us encounter extreme forms of fanaticism or skepticism in our daily rounds, we are all capable of slipping into habits of mind that distressingly resemble those of the Fanatic or Skeptic. On some topics that are very emotionally charged for us, in which we have a powerful personal stake, we may indeed retreat into irrationality. Even the reasonable souls who authored this textbook have been known to stray from the paths of good sense and sound argumentation on occasion. Ramage, for example, continues to argue loudly and tirelessly that the 1987 National League champion St. Louis Cardinals were a lousy baseball team, completely ignoring every accepted standard for measuring baseball excellence. Bean, meanwhile, believes fervently that by cutting his own firewood he is saving a bundle, even though he's yet to recover a not-inconsiderable initial investment in a chainsaw to cut the wood, a trailer to put the wood in, and a car large enough to pull trailer and wood. Neither will listen to reason on these topics, so friends and loved ones carefully avoid bringing them up in public to avoid the invariably embarrassing speeches that ensue.

Another Source of Pseudo-arguments: Lack of Shared Assumptions

A reasonable argument is difficult to conduct unless the participants share common assumptions on which the argument can be grounded. These assumptions are like axioms in geometry or the self-evident truths in the Declaration of Independence — starting points or foundations for the argument. Consider the following conversation in which Randall refuses to accept Rhonda's assumptions.

RHONDA: Smoking is bad because it causes cancer. (Rhonda assumes that Randall will agree with her that cancer is bad. This is the assumption that lets her say that smoking is bad.)

RANDALL: I agree that smoking causes cancer, but what's so bad about that? I like cancer. (Rhonda looks at him in amazement.)

RHONDA: Come on, Randy! Cancer is bad because it causes suffering and death. (Now she hopes Randall will accept her new assumption that suffering and death are bad.)

RANDALL: What's so bad about suffering and death?

RHONDA: Suffering reduces pleasure, while death is a total absence of being. That's awful!

RANDALL: No way. I am a masochist, so I like suffering. And if you don't have any being, you can't feel anything anyway.

RHONDA: O.K., wise guy. Let's assume that instead of absence of being you are dropped head-first into an everlasting lake of boiling oil where you must stay for eternity.

RANDALL: Hey, I said I was a masochist.

As you can see, the conversation becomes ludicrous because Randall refuses to share Rhonda's assumptions. Rhonda's self-evident "truths" (cancer is bad, suffering is bad, an everlasting lake of boiling oil is bad) seem to have no force for Randall. Without assumptions held in common, an argument degenerates into an endless regress of reasons that are based on more reasons that are based on still more reasons, and so forth. Randall's technique here is a bit like Callicles' rebuttals of Socrates — a refusal to accept the starting points of Socrates' argument. Attacking an argument's assumptions is, in fact, a legitimate way of deepening and complicating our understanding of an issue. But taken to an extreme, this technique makes argument impossible.

Perhaps you think the above argument about smoking is a cornball case that would never crop up in real situations. In fact, however, a slight variation of it is extremely common. We encounter the problem every time we argue about purely personal opinions: opera is boring, New York City is too big, pizza tastes better than nachos, baseball is more fun than soccer. The problem with these disputes is that they rest on personal preferences rather than on shared assumptions. In other words, there are no common criteria for "boring" or "too big" or "tastes better" that writer and reader can share.

Of course, reasonable arguments about these disputes become possible once common assumptions are established. For example, a nutritionist could argue that pizza is better than nachos because it provides more balanced nutrients per calorie. Such an argument can succeed if the disputants accept the nutritionist's assumption that "more balanced nutrients per calorie" is a criterion for "better." But if one of the disputants responds, "Nah, nachos are better than pizza because nachos taste better," then he makes a different assumption — "My sense of taste is better than your sense of taste." This is a wholly personal standard, an assumption that others are unable to share.

FOR CLASS DISCUSSION
The following questions can all be answered in competing ways. However, not all of them will lead to reasonable arguments. Try to decide which questions will lead to reasonable arguments and which will lead only to pseudo-arguments:

1. Is Roman Polanski a good film director?
2. Are science fiction films better than westerns?
3. Should our city subsidize the development of a convention center?
4. Is this abstract oil painting by Bozo, the ape from the local zoo, a true work of art?
5. Is Danish Modern furniture attractive?
6. Is football a fun sport to play?
7. Does extrasensory perception (ESP) exist?
8. Which would look more attractive in this particular living room, Early American furniture or Danish Modern furniture?
9. Which are better, argumentation essays or short stories?
10. Which is better, Pete's argumentation essay or Jaynee's?

THE FRAME OF AN ARGUMENT: A CLAIM SUPPORTED BY REASONS

We have said earlier that an argument originates in an issue question, which by definition is any question that can be answered in two or more competing ways. When you write an argumentation essay, your task is to commit yourself to one of the answers and to support it with reasons and evidence. The claim of your essay is the position you are trying to defend. To put it another way, your position on the issue is your essay's thesis statement, a one-sentence summary answer to your issue question. Your task, then, is to make a claim and defend it with reasons.

What Is a Reason?

A reason (also called a premise) is a claim used to support another claim. In speaking or writing, a reason is usually linked to the claim with such connecting words as *because, since, for, so, thus, consequently,* and *therefore,* indicating that the claim follows logically from the reason.

Let's take an example. Suppose you were interested in the issue question "Are after-school jobs beneficial for teenagers?" Here are frameworks for two possible arguments on this issue:

PRO

Claim: Holding an after-school job can be beneficial for teenagers (aimed, say, at parents who forbid their teenager to get a job).

Reason 1: An after-school job provides extra spending money.

Reason 2: It develops responsibility.

Reason 3: It teaches time management.

Reason 4: It establishes a record of employment experience useful for later job hunting.

CON

Claim: An after-school job can often be harmful to teenagers (aimed, say, at teenagers seeking an after-school job).

Reason 1: An after-school job takes time away from schoolwork, thus sacrificing long-range career success for short-range pocket money.

Reason 2: It reduces opportunities for valuable social and recreational time during high school years.

Reason 3: Too often it encourages materialism and conspicuous consumption (if extra money is spent on cars, clothes, etc.).

Formulating a list of reasons in this way breaks your argumentative task into a series of smaller parts. It gives you a frame, in other words, on which to build your essay. The preceding "pro" argument could consist of four main parts. In the first part you would support the first reason—an after-school job provides extra spending money. You might give some examples ("My friend Matt made $50 a week washing dishes at George's Grease Heaven") and show how your making extra spending money would help out the family or improve the quality of your life. In each of the other parts you would proceed the same way, trying to convince the reader that each reason is both true and significant—in other words, you would try to show not only that it is true that a job teaches time management but also that learning time management is valuable. If your argument is to be persuasive to your intended audience, each reason should link your claim to an assumption or belief held by the audience.* How a reason is linked to a claim by the rules of logic and how reasons themselves are supported with facts, examples, statistics, testimony, or further reasons are the subject of Chapters 5, 6, and 7. How arguments must be linked to the audience's values gets additional treatment in Chapter 8.

To summarize our point in this section, the frame of an argument consists of a claim (the thesis statement of the essay), which is supported by one or more reasons (other claims linked logically to the main claim), which are in turn supported by evidence or chains of further reasons.

The Advantages of Expressing Reasons in "Because" Statements

Chances are that when you were a child the word *because* contained magical explanatory powers:

DOROTHY: I want to go home now.

TOMMY: Why?

DOROTHY: Because.

TOMMY: Because why?

DOROTHY: Just because.

Somehow *because* seemed decisive. It persuaded people to accept your view of the world; it changed people's minds. Later, as you got older, you

---

*The values appealed to in the "pro" argument are these: It is good to have extra spending money, to develop responsibility, to learn time management, and to have greater potential for job success. These values are likely to be granted by parents, who are the intended audience. What values are appealed to in the "con" argument? Are the intended readers in the con argument—teenagers—likely to share these values?

discovered that *because* only introduced your arguments and that it was the reasons following *because* that made the difference. Still, the word *because* introduced you to the powers potentially residing in the adult world of logic.

Of course, there are many additional ways to express the same connection between reasons and claim. Our language is rich in ways of stating "because" relationships:

- An after-school job is valuable for teenagers because it teaches time management.

- An after-school job teaches time management. Therefore, it is valuable for teenagers.

- An after-school job teaches time management, so it is valuable for teenagers.

- One reason after-school jobs are valuable for teenagers is that they teach time management.

- My argument favoring an after-school job for teenagers is grounded partly on the fact that such jobs teach time management.

Even though logical relationships can be stated in various ways, writing out one or more "because" clauses seems to be the most succinct and manageable way to clarify an argument for oneself. We therefore suggest that sometime in the writing process you create a "working thesis statement" that summarizes your main reasons as because clauses attached to your claim.* Just when you compose your own working thesis statement depends largely on your writing process. Some writers like to plan out their whole argument from the start and often compose their working thesis statements with because clauses before they write their rough drafts. Others discover their arguments as they write. And sometimes it is a combination of both. For these writers an extended working thesis statement is something they might write halfway through the composing process, as a way of ordering their argument when various branches seem to be growing out of control. Or they might compose a working thesis statement at the very end as a way of checking the unity of the final product.

Whenever you write your extended thesis statement, the act of doing so can be simultaneously frustrating and thought-provoking. Composing because clauses can be a powerful discovery tool, causing you to think of many different kinds of arguments to support your claim. But it is often difficult to wrestle your ideas into the because clause shape, which some-

---

*The working thesis statement for the essay supporting after-school jobs would look like this: "Holding an after-school job can be beneficial for teenagers because it provides extra spending money, because it helps develop responsibility, because it helps teenagers learn time management, and because it helps them establish a record of employment experience useful for later job hunting." You probably wouldn't put such a statement into your essay itself; rather, it is a way of summarizing your argument for yourself so that you can see it whole and clear.

times seems to be overly tidy for the complex network of ideas you are trying to work with. Nevertheless, trying to summarize your argument as a single claim with reasons should help you see more clearly what you have to do.

FOR CLASS DISCUSSION

Try the following group exercise to help you see how writing because clauses can be a discovery procedure.

Divide into small groups. Each group member should contribute an issue from his or her issue list (Starting Points, Task 6). Discussing one person's issue at a time, help each member write a working thesis statement by creating several because clauses in support of the person's claim. Then try to create because clauses in support of an opposing claim for each issue. Recorders should select two or three working thesis statements from the group to present to the class as a whole. Report in twenty-five minutes.

APPLICATION OF THIS CHAPTER'S PRINCIPLES TO YOUR OWN WRITING

In Chapter 2, during our discussion of summary writing, we mentioned that not all arguments are equally easy to summarize. Generally, an argument is easiest to summarize when the writer places her thesis or claim in the essay's introduction and highlights each reason with explicit transitions as the argument progresses. We say that such arguments have a "self-announcing structure," in that the essay announces its thesis (and sometimes its supporting reasons) and forecasts its shape before the body of the argument begins. Such arguments aim at maximum clarity for readers by focusing attention on the content and structure of the writer's ideas.

Arguments with self-announcing structures can be distinguished from those with "unfolding structures." An argument with an unfolding structure often delays its thesis until the end or entwines the argument into a personal narrative, story, or analysis without an explicitly argumentative shape. Often the reader must tease out the writer's thesis and supporting reasons, which remain implied only. Unfolding arguments are often stylistically complex and subtle.

The strategy for generating ideas set forth in this chapter—thinking of parallel because clauses and combining them into a working thesis statement that nutshells your argument—leads naturally to an argument with a self-announcing structure. Each because clause, together with its supporting evidence, becomes a separate building block of your argument. The building blocks, which can vary in length from a single paragraph to a whole series of paragraphs, are linked back to the thesis through appropriate transitions.

In our own classes we ask students early in the course to write arguments with self-announcing structures because such structures force writers to articulate their arguments clearly to themselves and because such structures help students master the art of organizing for readers. Later on in the course we encourage students to experiment with structures that unfold their meanings rather than announce them in the introduction.

In writing self-announcing arguments, students often ask how much of the argument to summarize in the introduction. Consider the following options. Within the introduction you could choose to announce only your claim:

> After-school jobs are beneficial for teenagers.

Or you could also predict a series of parallel reasons:

> After-school jobs are beneficial for teenagers for several reasons.

Or you could forecast the actual number of reasons:

> After-school jobs are beneficial for teenagers for four reasons.

Or you could forecast the whole argument:

> After-school jobs are beneficial for teenagers because they provide extra spending money, because they help develop responsibility, because they help teenagers learn time management, and because they help teenagers establish a record of employment experience useful for later job hunting.

These, of course, are not your only options. If you choose to delay your thesis until the end (a simple kind of unfolding argument), you might place the issue-question in the introduction but not give away your own position:

> Are after-school jobs beneficial for teenagers or not?

There are no hardbound rules to help you decide how much of your argument to forecast in the introduction. In Chapter 9 we discuss the different *ethos* projected when the writer places the claim in the introduction versus withholding it until later in the essay. It is clear at this point, though, that in making this decision a writer trades off clarity for surprise. The more you forecast, the clearer your argument is and the easier it is to read quickly. The less you forecast, the more surprising the argument is because the reader doesn't know what is coming. The only general rule is this: Readers sometimes feel insulted by too much forecasting. In writing a self-announcing argument, announce at the beginning only what is needed for clarity. In a short argument readers usually don't need all the because clauses stated explicitly in the introduction. In longer arguments, however, or in especially complex ones, readers appreciate having the whole argument forecast at the outset.

Of course, stating your reasons in because clauses is only one part of generating, organizing, and developing an argument. In the next chapter we will see how to support a reason by examining its logical structure, uncovering its unstated assumptions, and planning a strategy of development.

5

THE LOGICAL STRUCTURE OF ARGUMENTS

In Chapter 4 you learned that the core of an argument is a claim supported by reasons and that these reasons can often be stated as because clauses attached to a claim. In the present chapter we examine the logical structure of arguments in more depth.

OVERVIEW TO *LOGOS:* WHAT DO WE MEAN BY THE "LOGICAL STRUCTURE" OF AN ARGUMENT?

As you will recall from our discussion of the rhetorical triangle in Chapter 4 (pages 81–82), *logos* refers to the internal consistency of an argument. It is the argument's logical structure, the way the claim is supported by reasons and evidence. But what do we mean by "logical structure"? Unlike formal logic of the kind you would study in a philosophy course, which has mathematical precision and clarity, arguments in the real world cannot provide "proofs." Formal logic deals with symbolic assertions that are certain and unchanging, such as "All *p*'s are *q*'s." Real-world arguments, on the other hand, deal with assertions that are often debatable or probabilistic. Thus, real-world arguments cannot begin from principles or axioms that are certain. What they must begin from, instead, are assumptions, values, or beliefs granted by the audience. Thus, if an audience will grant you this assumption (taken from the issue of after-school jobs in Chapter 4):

Activities that take time away from studying are bad for teenagers.

then you can construct the following argument:

After-school jobs are bad for teenagers because they take time away from studying.

The Greek philosopher Aristotle would have called the argument put forward in this last sentence an *enthymeme*. An enthymeme is an incomplete logical structure that depends, for its completeness, on one or more unstated premises. These unstated premises serve as the starting point of the argument and therefore should be assumptions, values, or beliefs granted by the audience.

To clarify the concept of "enthymeme" further, let's look at the after-school job argument more closely. The working thesis — "After-school jobs are bad for teenagers because they take time away from studying" — is an enthymeme. It is a logical structure since it combines a claim ("After-school jobs are bad for teenagers") with a reason ("because they take time away from studying"). But the structure of this argument is incomplete as stated. For its completeness, the structure depends on the unstated premise "Activities that take time away from studying are bad for teenagers." If the audience grants that premise, then the structure is valid and can serve as the skeleton for an argument.

WHY IT IS USEFUL TO EXAMINE THE STRUCTURE OF AN ARGUMENT

As we have just seen, a claim with a because clause is an enthymeme. To see if the enthymeme will be effective, you need to formulate the unstated premises on which the enthymeme depends and decide whether your audience will grant them. The value of this process is that it causes you to discover and make explicit the unstated assumptions or premises on which your argument is based.

One way to discover assumed premises is to convert each of your enthymemic because clauses into a three-part structure called a syllogism. The syllogism for the enthymeme we have been examining is as follows:

Activities that take time away from studying are bad for teenagers.

An after-school job takes time away from studying.

Therefore, an after-school job is bad for teenagers.

Note that the first statement in this syllogism ("Activities that take time away from studying are bad for teenagers") was not present in the original enthymemic because clause. We have had to spell out this originally unstated premise in order to show the complete structure of the argument. Note also that the statement about the value of studying says nothing about after-school jobs; it focuses our attention instead on the general principle that teenagers are harmed by activities that take time away from studying. If the first statement of this syllogism is granted by the audience, then the second statement in the syllogism could designate any activity that takes time away from studying—for example, after-school athletics or band—and we would be forced to conclude that these activities are also bad for teenagers.

The value of writing out the unstated premise is that it forces you to look at your argument from the perspective of your audience. Perhaps your audience does not believe in the value of study time the same way you do. Perhaps they believe that job experience is so important that a C average with good job experience has greater future value than a B average without job experience. To argue persuasively to such an audience, you would need to show why you believe that ample study time is more important than a job. In other words, you would have to create an explicit argument for the value of study time, instead of leaving this premise unstated. Our point is that writing out the unstated premises within an enthymeme can help you see what your argument needs to cover.

If we look at another of the arguments opposing after-school jobs— "After school jobs are bad for teenagers because they promote materialism" (Chapter 4, page 90)—we discover that supporting the unstated premise may be the most crucial part of the argument. Here is the syllogism that shows the complete argument underlying the enthymeme:

An activity that promotes materialism is bad for teenagers.

An after-school job promotes materialism.

Therefore, an after-school job is bad for teenagers.

If this were your argument, it would need further clarification because readers can't be sure what you mean by "materialism." Moreover, what to you is "bad" about materialism might be for others the "good old American way." An argument supporting this reason must therefore answer three questions:

What do you mean by "materialism"?

Why do you think materialism is bad?

Why do you think an after-school job promotes this sort of materialism?

In the act of writing this argument, you might find that your reasoning is less persuasive than you originally thought. The more you try to define *materialism*, the more it might seem favorable rather than unfavorable to your audience. Whenever you discover that you can't base your argument on values or assumptions granted by your audience, you have several options: (1) to find different reasons to support your claim, (2) to change or modify your claim, or (3) to stick to your argument but to concede that you and your audience don't agree on this value or belief, thus clarifying the places where differences between you and your audience seem irreconcilable. Turning an enthymeme into a syllogism thus helps the writer see the questions that an argument should address. Bringing unstated premises to the surface is a discovery procedure that helps you plan the content of your essay and often causes you to modify your ideas.

THE STRUCTURE OF ARGUMENTS: WHAT WE CAN LEARN THROUGH FORMAL LOGIC

What Is a Syllogism?

The main value of formal logic for real-world argumentation is that familiarity with syllogisms can help you formulate the unstated premises in enthymemes. As we saw earlier, a syllogism consists of three statements, which we will now call a major premise, a minor premise, and a conclusion. The most common form of syllogism links three terms. The major premise, which is usually a general statement, principle, or rule, links together terms A and B. The minor premise, which is a specific kind of statement that is usually verifiable by fact or evidence, introduces a new term C and links it to A. The conclusion or claim then links B to C. Here are two examples:

       A   B

MAJOR PREMISE: All dogs are mammals.

       C   A

MINOR PREMISE: Cecil is a dog.

       C   A

CLAIM: Cecil is a mammal.

       A

MAJOR PREMISE: Actvities that take time away from studying are

       B

bad for teenagers.

       C   A

MINOR PREMISE: An after-school job is an actitivy that takes time away from studying.

       C   B

CLAIM: An after-school job is bad for teenagers.

Such syllogisms can be rewritten as "if–then" structures, which are sometimes easier to formulate when you are composing your own arguments.

            A   B
If something is a dog, then it is a mammal.

    C   A
Cecil is a dog.

          C   B
Therefore, Cecil is a mammal.

If you were to take a course in formal logic, you would study various kinds of syllogisms as well as valid and invalid ways of structuring them. In a writing course, however, the purpose of studying syllogisms is simply to see that most because clauses imply an unstated premise—usually the major premise—that often needs to be supported in your argument. Formulating the major premise of each because clause is a way of reminding yourself of the assumptions your audience must grant if your argument is to be persuasive.

FOR CLASS DISCUSSION

Working in small groups, identify the unstated major premise that completes each of the following enthymemic arguments. Write out a syllogism to show the complete argument. Recorders for each group should be ready to report the group's syllogisms to the class as a whole. (Reporting time: approximately twenty minutes.)

> EXAMPLE: Rabbits make good pets because they are gentle.
>   Gentle animals make good pets.
>   Rabbits are gentle animals.
>   Therefore, rabbits make good pets.

1. Joe is a bad leader because he is too bossy.
2. Buy this stereo system because it has a powerful amplifier.
3. Buy this stereo system because it will impress your friends.
4. Practicing the piano is good for kids because it teaches discipline.
5. A diesel-powered car is often cheaper to own than a gasoline-powered car because it is more durable.
6. *Ordinary People* is a great movie because its characters are psychologically complex.
7. Worldwide military disarmament is unwise because it will make world economies collapse.
8. Athletic scholarships are unfair because they are not based on academic performance.

9. Bill Jones is a great leader because he is open-minded yet decisive.

10. Abortion should be legal because a woman has the right to control her own body. (This enthymeme has several syllogisms behind it; see if you can recreate all the missing premises.)

The Limitations of Formal Logic for Writers

As we have hinted earlier, formal logic deals only with the structure of an argument, not with the truth of its premises. Unless a properly structured argument also has true premises, we can conclude nothing about the truth of its claim. Consider the following arguments.

Any loan that can be paid back with funny money is a free gift.

Guaranteed Student Loans can be paid back with funny money.

Therefore, guaranteed Student Loans are free gifts.

The blood of insects can be used to lubricate lawn-mower engines.

Vampires are insects.

Therefore, the blood of vampires can be used to lubricate lawn-mower engines.

Because their premises are untrue, these arguments are ludicrous; nevertheless, in a logic class they would be considered validly structured. The limitation of formal logic for writers, then, is that it deals solely with the validity of an argument's structure and not with the truth of its premises. Since the main concern of writers is to show the truth of the premises, formal logic is of limited value. For this reason, teachers of argument have looked for different ways of representing an argument's structure — ways that would more directly meet the needs of writers. We next examine one of the most popular of these systems, developed by philosopher Stephen Toulmin.

THE STRUCTURE OF ARGUMENTS: WHAT WE CAN LEARN THROUGH TOULMIN'S INFORMAL LOGIC

Toulmin logic highlights different features of an argument's structure than does formal logic. Toulmin's method is based on a legal model of argumentation in which you imagine an adversary whose duty it is to question your reasoning whenever appropriate. You also imagine a judge or jury who will weigh your argument and your adversary's argument fairly and reasonably. If you speak only to your adversary, ignoring the jury, you are apt to become lost in a maze of nitpicking fine points; if you speak only to the jury, ignoring your adversary, you are unlikely to anticipate weaknesses in your own argument or possible counterarguments. Toulmin's model, then, involves a dramatic conflict between adversaries, as opposed to the non-dramatic world of uncontested propositions confidently assumed by formal logic.

According to Toulmin, there are six elements in an argument. The first three correspond roughly to the major and minor premises and the conclusion of a syllogism. Toulmin refers to these three elements as the warrant (W), the grounds (G), and the claim (C). The grounds (sometimes referred to as the data) are all the facts and information at your disposal. For example, if you wanted to argue that Polly Smith is a good trial lawyer, you could use as grounds the fact that she won three recent trials on the basis of her skillful argumentation in the courtroom. Toulmin calls the grounds "what you have to go on." It approximates the minor premise of a syllogism together with the evidence you would use to support the minor premise.

A warrant, on the other hand, is a general sort of statement that licenses you to draw an inference from your grounds (just as a search warrant licenses someone to search your house). Toulmin says that a warrant is "how you get from your grounds to your claim." It approximates a major premise in a syllogism. To continue with the Polly Smith example, your justification for calling Polly Smith a good trial lawyer is the warrant that effective argumentation skills are a criterion for excellence as a trial lawyer. Finally, your claim is the inference that you have drawn and must justify. It is like the conclusion in a syllogism. In the Polly Smith example, your claim is that Polly Smith is a good trial lawyer.

But Toulmin recognizes that in the real world an argument's warrant — the general statement that licenses the arguer to make a particular claim — is often open to question. You may therefore be required to provide a fourth element of an argument, backing (B), to substantiate your warrant. Thus Toulmin's system requires you not only to have evidence for your grounds (that is, some evidence that would make us admit that Polly Smith argues effectively), but also arguments backing your warrant. For example, you might back your warrant by polling judges on which qualities are most important in distinguishing excellent trial lawyers from run-of-the-mill lawyers. If effective argumentation is the most frequently cited quality, that constitutes backing for your warrant.

The final two elements of Toulmin's logical model are ways of limiting your claims. Toulmin calls these qualifiers (Q) and conditions of rebuttal (R). With a qualifier, we limit the force of our claim to indicate the degree of its probable truth. We may say things like "very likely," "probably," or "maybe" to indicate the strength of the claim we are willing to draw from our grounds and warrant. Thus, if there are exceptions to your warrant or if your grounds are not very strong, you will have to qualify your claim. For example, you might modify your claim about Ms. Smith by saying that she is *generally* a good trial lawyer, especially in medical liability cases.

A condition of rebuttal differs somewhat from a qualifier. It points out specific instances not covered by your warrant (exceptions to the rule) or other ways that your argument could be rebutted. Thus you might say that Polly Smith argues effectively in the courtroom so long as she has adequate time to prepare her case. She becomes less effective, however, if she doesn't have her facts immediately at hand.

We can diagram Toulmin's model as follows:

ORIGINAL BECAUSE CLAUSE: Ms. Smith is a good trial lawyer because she is an effective arguer.

GROUNDS	CLAIM
Polly Smith has won three recent cases as a result of her courtroom arguing techniques.	Ms. Smith is a good trial lawyer.

WARRANT	QUALIFIER
Since effective argumentation is a criterion for being a good trial lawyer.	For most kinds of cases.

BACKING	CONDITIONS OF REBUTTAL
Because the judges we polled cited effective argumentation as being what distinguishes good trial lawyers from mediocre ones.	Unless she doesn't have time to prepare extensively.

ORIGINAL BECAUSE CLAUSE: The Oakland Athletics will win the pennant because they have the best pitching staff in baseball.

G	C
The A's have the best pitching staff in baseball based on records of starters and relievers.	The A's will win the pennant.

W	Q
Since pitching is the key to winning baseball games.	Probably.

B	R
Because statistical evidence shows a correlation between strong pitching and winning.	Unless their defense collapses.

ORIGINAL BECAUSE CLAUSE: Professor Choplogic is a poor teacher because his courses are disorganized.

G	C
Professor Choplogic's courses are disorganized (no syllabus, rambling lectures, etc.).	Professor Choplogic is a poor teacher.

W	Q
Since organized courses are esssential for good teaching.	For most students.

B	R
Because studies show that disorganized courses don't provide the structure students need for effective learning.	Unless Choplogic is using "disorganization" intentionally to stimulate creative thinking.

As you can see, Toulmin's system places less emphasis than does formal logic on the structure of an argument and more emphasis on how the parts of an argument will be supported. Although Toulmin's "grounds" are like the minor premise of a syllogism, they cause us to think not simply of a general statement ("Polly Smith is an effective arguer") but of the empirical evidence that gives rise to the generalization ("Smith's winning of three recent cases"). Similarly, the need to think of backing, qualifiers, and conditions of rebuttal reminds us that our argument is aimed at doubters who are also weighing the merits of opposing views. In looking at Toulmin's model, we get a clearer sense of what's required of a convincing argument. Whereas a syllogism assumes the truth, relevance, and plausibility of its premises, Toulmin's model shows us that considerably more justification is required of us. In turn, his model shows how tentative our claim must be when so many particulars of the case are taken into account.

CONCLUSION

What is most important to see in this chapter is that the typical thesis statement of an argumentation essay (a claim with attached because clauses) is a series of enthymemes. By this term, we mean that for each because clause there are one or more unstated assumptions that must be "brought to the surface" to reveal the complete structure of its argument. Moreover, it is often crucial to defend these unstated assumptions if your argument is both to clarify and to persuade. If we examine an argument using the system of formal logic, we will pay particular attention to its internal validity and tend to neglect the truth of its premises. If we use Toulmin's legal model, we will place greater emphasis on how we are going to support the premises.

We don't need to make an either/or choice, however, between the two systems, both of which have their usefulness. Both systems remind us that arguments contain unstated assumptions (usually the major premise of a syllogism or the warrant of Toulmin's system) that must often be brought into the open and examined (Toulmin's backing). Both show us that sound arguments must have a valid internal structure (a formally correct linking of premises or, in Toulmin's terms, an acceptable warrant linking grounds to claim). And both systems remind us that the ultimate acceptability of an argument depends on the acceptability of its premises. In the next chapter we look more closely at how you go about supporting your premises. You will see how both the formal system and the Toulmin system can be combined to help you generate supporting ideas for your argument.

FOR CLASS DISCUSSION

Working either individually or in small groups, return to the ten enthymemes listed in the For Class Discussion exercise on pages 99–100 and analyze each using the Toulmin schema. Imagine that you have to write arguments that contain these enthymemes. Use the Toulmin schema to help you determine what you will need to consider when defending each enthymeme. As an example, we have applied the Toulmin schema to the first enthymeme.

Joe is a bad leader because he is too bossy.

G	C
Three or four examples of Joe's bossiness.	Joe is a bad leader.

W	R
Since bossy people make bad leaders.	Unless these examples aren't really representative — that is, Joe really isn't bossy (rebuts the grounds). Unless Joe has other traits of good leadership that outweigh his bossiness (rebuts the warrant).

B	Q
Because evidence suggests that other things being equal, bossy people tend to bring out the worst rather than the best in those around them.	Many people think he isn't a good leader. On some occasions, he isn't a good leader.

6

SUPPORTING AN ARGUMENT: EVIDENCE AND CHAINS OF REASONS

So far, we have seen that most arguments can be summarized as a claim with one or more attached reasons in the form of because clauses. Some writers develop their own claim and because clauses very early in the writing process, as a working thesis statement prior to writing a first draft. Others wait until later in the process to write such a statement, and, of course, many skilled writers never explicitly formulate because clauses at all. Our point isn't that all writers consciously write a claim with attached because clauses; our point, rather, is that almost all arguments *can* be summarized this way, and that doing so is a good way for writers to discover and organize material.

One value of writing because clauses is that doing so helps you identify the enthymemes that form the core of your argument's structure. You can then use the syllogism method or Toulmin's method to identify the unstated premises of your argument and to plan ways to support premises that your audience won't grant at the outset. In the syllogism method, the unstated premise behind a because clause is called the argument's major premise. In Toulmin's schema, which we mainly use from now on, the unstated premise is called the warrant. As Toulmin's system makes particularly clear, the warrant itself must often be supported with backing; moreover, even the most airtight arguments are subject to qualification (the qualifier) and to rebuttal (conditions of rebuttal).

OUR OWN SYSTEM FOR ANALYZING ARGUMENTS

The rest of this text relies primarily on Toulmin's terminology for arguments. However, we make a slight modification in Toulmin's terminology in order to make a clearer connection between Toulmin's schema and our own emphasis on a claim with because clauses as the core of an argument. In Toulmin's system, the "grounds" refer to all the information and material available to support the argument's minor premise. However, his system has no word for the minor premise itself. From now on, we call the minor premise of an argument its "stated reason" — the assertion set forth in a because clause. For example:

Enthymeme: Dr. Choplogic is a bad teacher because his courses are disorganized.

Claim: Dr. Choplogic is a bad teacher.

Stated Reason: Dr. Choplogic's courses are disorganized.

Grounds: no syllabi; confusion about the text; rambling lectures, etc.

Warrant: Disorganized courses are a sign of bad teaching.

Enthymeme: Buy this stereo because it has a powerful amplifier.

Claim: [You should] buy this stereo.

Stated Reason: It has a powerful amplifier.

Grounds: It delivers 100 watts per channel; it will drive speakers big enough to blast your ears off in a movie theater, etc.

Warrant: High power is the most important criterion for choosing an amplifier.

USING TOULMIN'S SCHEMA TO DETERMINE A STRATEGY OF SUPPORT

Having made this slight modification in Toulmin's terminology, we can turn directly to a discussion of how to develop your argument by supporting each of your reasons. The purpose of using the Toulmin schema is to help you see what parts of your argument need to be supported. Often, for example, you need to defend your unstated warrants as much as your stated reasons. (And if you find that you can't support your warrants in a way that your audience will find convincing, you may have to rethink both your reasons and your claim.) As a way of further clarifying this point, let's imagine that you wanted to defend the following enthymemic argument put forth by the woman president of a major corporation:

Women often make better managers than men because they are more people-conscious. They are better listeners and more aware of other people's feelings. They like to find out where people are coming from.

Figure 6-1 shows how one student used the Toulmin schema to examine this enthymeme. The warrant behind this argument is that persons who are "people-conscious" are better managers than those who aren't. In examining the stated reason and the warrant, the writer can see that the argument must be supported in two parts: The writer will have to show that women are more people-conscious than men (this is the original stated reason, the because clause); the writer will also have to show that being people-conscious is the key to being a good manager (this is the unstated warrant or major premise). For this particular argument, supporting the warrant with backing might be even more crucial than supporting the stated reason.

As Figure 6-1 shows, the writer complicated her sense of the issue by also considering Toulmin's conditions of rebuttal. In considering how her stated reason might be rebutted, the writer discovers that she has to define *people-consciousness* clearly and then find some way to demonstrate that women are more people-conscious than men. The writer decides to qualify the argument by saying "women are *frequently* more people-conscious than men"; this qualification helps defend the argument against the exceptions that a skeptical audience might raise. The writer also sees that she should explain what traits or actions characterize a "people-conscious" manager. Then, in order to support the stated reason that women are frequently more people-conscious than men, the writer can look for research studies that might support the claim, think of persuasive representative examples from personal experience, or develop a causal argument based on women's being socialized as nurturers, and so forth. These supporting examples and arguments would become the grounds for the stated reason.

Similarly, considering conditions for rebuttal helps the writer see how to qualify the warrant—what to concede to the opposition and what to support. Rather than make the sweeping generalization that people-consciousness is an essential aspect of good management, the writer might argue more narrowly that people-conscious managers build trust and cooperation in an organization. Once again, the writer may uncover some data about the effectiveness of different management styles or bring in personal examples from job experience. In sum, the purpose of brainstorming for opposing views under "conditions for rebuttal" is to sharpen your sense of the potential strengths and weaknesses of your argument.

Stated Reason:
Women are more people-conscious than men.

Claim:
Women are often better managers than men.

Grounds:
Let's see, how could I support this? Examples of people-conscious women: Mrs. Raybourne at church. Examples from books. I could talk about the way girls are raised differently from boys — emphasis on being listeners; earlier development of verbal skills. Maybe I could find some testimony. I'll brainstorm this with my group.

Conditions of Rebuttal:
How could I doubt the stated reason and grounds? Why not say men are more people-conscious than women? I know quite a few people-conscious men and bitchy women. What does it mean to be people-conscious anyway? How could you ever define that? Are you people-conscious just because you are a good listener?

Warrant:
Other things being equal, being people-conscious makes a person a better manager.

How could I doubt the warrant?

Maybe being too people-conscious means you are a weak manager who can't make hard economic decisions. Maybe in the list of criteria for excellence as a manager, being "people-conscious" is less important than being decisive, fair, creative, knowledgeable about marketing, etc. Lee Iacocca doesn't strike me as being too people-conscious.

Backing:
People trust you more; They realize you aren't just a number. People-conscious managers will be more supportive if you have a down time. They will recognize your need for family. They will look out for your welfare, not just company profits. Build a better team.

Qualifier:
"Other things being equal"

FIGURE 6-1. Toulmin Schema of Argument about Women Managers

SUPPORTING YOUR REASONS

As you become more practiced in argumentation, you will see that support for reasons generally takes one of two forms: Sometimes reasons can be supported by evidence such as facts, examples, case studies, statistics, testimony from experts, and so forth. At other times, a reason can be supported only by further conceptual argument—a chain of other reasons. Figure 6–2 shows this structure of support schematically. Let's look at each kind of support separately.

Evidence as Support

It's often easier for writers to use evidence rather than chains of reasons for support because using evidence entails moving from generalizations to specific details—a basic organizational strategy that most writers practice regularly. Consider the following hypothetical case. A student, Ramona, wants to write a complaint letter to the head of the Philosophy Department

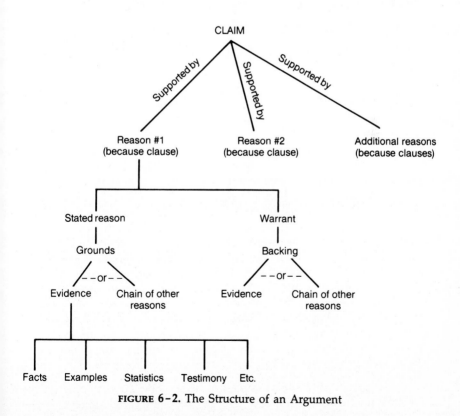

FIGURE 6–2. The Structure of an Argument

about a philosophy professor, Dr. Choplogic, whom Ramona considers incompetent. Ramona bases her complaint on two reasons: His courses are disorganized, and he's unconcerned about students.

Let's look briefly at how she can use evidence to support her first reason. Her warrant for the first reason is that teachers whose courses are disorganized are ineffective. Figure 6–3 shows Ramona's planning notes as she went through the Toulmin schema to examine her argument. Ramona began by identifying her stated reason, grounds, and warrant. She then turned to consider the conditions for rebuttal, asking herself whether readers might disagree with either her stated reason or her warrant or both. As her notes show, she decided that most readers would accept her warrant that disorganized courses are ineffective. However, she thought of one important exception to the warrant—some teachers put the burden of organizing a course onto the students as a way of teaching independent, creative thinking. Her argument would have to show that Dr. Choplogic isn't this kind of teacher. Except for this one problem, however, Ramona didn't believe she would have to provide backing for her warrant.

Using the Toulmin schema, Ramona decided that the main part of her argument would be in support of her stated reason that Dr. Choplogic's courses are disorganized. After all, her primary audience—the head of the Philosophy Department—has never suffered through Choplogic's courses and would have to be convinced of how bad he is. In support of this premise, Ramona has lots of evidence, which forms the main ammunition for the passage below:

> Dr. Choplogic is an ineffective teacher because his courses are poorly organized. I have had him for two courses—Introduction to Philosophy and Ethics—and both were disorganized. He never provided a syllabus or explained his grading system. At the beginning of the course he never announced how many papers he would require, and he never seemed to know how much of the textbook material he planned to cover. For Introduction to Philosophy he told us to read the whole text but covered only half of it in class. A week before the final I asked him how much of the text would be on the exam and he said he hadn't decided. The Ethics class was also disorganized. Dr. Choplogic told us to read the text, which provided one set of terms for ethical arguments, and then he told us he didn't like the text and presented us in lecture with a wholly different set of terms. The result was a whole class of confused, angry students. In Dr. Choplogic's defense, it might be thought that he is trying to make us see that philosophy doesn't have "right answers" and is full of controversy. Perhaps Dr. Choplogic is using "disorganization" to try to make us think for ourselves. If so, he is not helping us. We never work in groups in class or have any opportunity to get guidance. He teaches almost entirely through lecture and simply can't present his ideas coherently.

Most of this paragraph is devoted to supplying evidence in support of the stated reason. However, the last part of the paragraph anticipates the

Choplogic is not an effective teacher
because his courses are disorganized.

Stated reason: His courses are disorganized.

Claim: He is not an effective teacher.

Grounds – no syllabus in either Intro or Ethics
  – never announced how many papers we would have
  – didn't know what would be on tests
  – didn't like the textbook he had chosen
  – didn't follow any logical sequence in his lectures

Conditions for rebuttal: Grounds
  ↓
Will anyone attack these grounds?
No – everyone agrees that these are the facts about Choplogic's courses. Of course, audience might not know this. I will have to provide details.

Warrant: Teachers whose courses are disorganized are ineffective.

Backing: – Organization helps you learn.
  – gets material arranged in logical way.
  – Helps you take notes.
  – Gives you confidence in teacher.

Conditions for rebuttal: Warrant
Most people will accept my warrant and backing.
  ↓
Will anyone attack my warrant?
  ↓
Is it possible that a disorganized teacher might be effective?
  ↓
Some Teachers like to place burden of organizing on the students. Way to teach thinking skills. Stimulate Creativity.
  ↓
Choplogic isn't like this.

He just ✓   Not trying to teach
lectures.   thinking skills.

FIGURE 6-3. Ramona's Planning Notes

objection that Dr. Choplogic may be using disorganization creatively and tries to counter it by citing more evidence that Choplogic is not one of those creative teachers.

In general, evidence in support of your reasons can come either from your own personal experiences and observations or from library research. Although many arguments will depend on your skill at research, many can also be supported wholly or in part from your own personal experiences, so don't neglect the wealth of evidence from your own life when searching for data.

When evidence is incorporated into your essays, it can take several different forms. In the previous example of Ramona's complaint against Dr. Choplogic, it took the form of a series of relevant facts. Other common forms of evidence include examples, statistics, and testimony. Let's look at each in turn.

EXAMPLES

A great number of arguments can be supported by examples. If you want to argue that Joe is a bad leader because he is bossy, you could use some examples of his bossiness as grounds for your argument. Similarly, you might use the example of your grandparents to argue that welfare reforms have caused new hardships to the elderly in your community. The following quotation illustrates how one writer used examples to support his claim that the city of Seattle needs a stronger antidiscrimination law. His main argument is that current laws are not preventing discrimination, an argument he supports by piling up eight different examples (we quote only his first two examples as illustration of the strategy):

> If you don't think such an ordinance is necessary, possibly the following incidents will convince you:
> — Christmas Eve 1983 — Sewage began to back up at the residence of Steve Reiswig and Ray Woods. Because they couldn't find their landlord, they dialed 911 to contact the Seattle Fire Department for assistance. They say a member of the department answered and replied to their request, "You guys have hepatitis and AIDS," and refused assistance.
> — January 1984 — The owner of a downtown tavern placed a large hand-lettered sign in the window that said, "Cubans Keep Out." [Six more examples follow.]*

STATISTICS

Another common form of evidence is statistics. Since statistical data pose tricky problems in arguments — some people claim you can prove almost anything with statistics — we have devoted a special section of this text to arguing with numbers (Appendix 2). Here is how the writer of a *Newsweek*

*From Steven L. Kendall, "Why We Need New Anti-Discrimination Law," *Seattle Times*, September 12, 1987, p. A11.

article used statistical data to argue that the use of fluorocarbons is harming the earth's ozone layer:

> The ozone layer also blocks out harmful ultraviolet light, which causes skin cancer and other damage. The U.S. Environmental Protection Agency claims that a loss of 2.5 percent of the ozone layer would lead to 15,000 additional victims of the deadliest forms of skin cancer per year. Additionally, UV light kills plankton, a major food source for much of the ocean's fish, as well as the larva of some kinds of fish. A 20 percent increase in UV light, for example, could destroy 5 percent of the ocean's anchovie larvae, which is a major source of animal feed worldwide.*

TESTIMONY

Finally, much evidence comes in the form of testimony, whereby you cite an expert to help bolster your case. Testimony is often blended with other kinds of evidence, as in the above example where the U.S. Environmental Protection Agency is cited as the source of the skin cancer statistics. Citing authorities is particularly common in those arguments where lay persons cannot be expected to be experts—the technical feasibility of cold fusion, the effects of alcohol on fetal tissue development, and so forth. Often, a noteworthy quotation from an expert will have considerable persuasive power. The author of the *Newsweek* article from which we drew our previous example used such a quotation as the thesis statement of her essay:

> But the world may no longer have the luxury of further study. As Senator John Chafee put it last week, at a hearing of his Subcommittee on Environmental Pollution, "There is a very real possibility that man—through ignorance or indifference or both—is irreversibly altering the ability of our atmosphere to [support] life."

Later in the article, more authorities are cited:

> This greenhouse effect, according to a parade of witnesses at last week's hearings, is no longer a matter of scientific debate, but a frightening reality. "Global warming is inevitable—it's only a question of magnitude and time," concluded Robert Watson of the National Aeronautics and Space Administration, the agency whose satellites monitor the upper atmosphere.

Chain of Reasons as Support

So far we have been discussing how to support reasons with evidence. Many reasons, however, cannot be supported this way; rather, they must be supported with a chain of other reasons. Such passages are often more

---

*The information on fluorocarbons in this and the following examples is based on Sharon Begley, "Silent Summer: Ozone Loss and Global Warming," *Newsweek*, June 23, 1986, pp. 64–66.

difficult to write. Let's take as an example a student who wants to argue that the state should require the wearing of seatbelts. His claim, along with his main supporting reason, is as follows:

> The state should require the wearing of seatbelts in moving vehicles because seatbelts save lives.

In planning out the argument, the writer determines the unstated warrant, which in this case is that the state should enact any law that would save lives. Stated as a syllogism, the writer's argument looks like this:

> Laws that save lives should be enacted by the state.
> A mandatory seatbelt law will save lives.
> Therefore, the state should enact a mandatory seatbelt law.

The writer's next step is to consider the conditions for rebuttal for these premises. He realizes that he will have no trouble supporting the stated reason ("Seatbelts save lives") since he can use evidence in the form of examples, statistics, and testimony. But the warrant of the argument ("Laws that save lives should be enacted by the state") cannot be defended by an appeal to such data. Although this statement operates as a warrant in the original seatbelt argument, it is actually a new claim that must itself be supported by additional reasons. As this example illustrates, a statement serving as a reason in one argument can become a claim in another, setting off a potentially infinite regress of reasons.

Examining the conditions for rebuttal reveals to the writer how vulnerable the warrant is. If the state is supposed to enact any law that saves lives, should it then pass laws requiring you to take your vitamins, get your blood pressure checked, or put safety strips in your bathtub? How could the writer argue that the state has the right to require seatbelts without opening the way for dozens of other do-gooder laws? Unable to use evidence, the writer proceeded to think of chains of reasons that might add up to a convincing case.

The seatbelt law differs from other do-gooder laws:

* Because it mandates behavior only on public property.
* Because it concerns highway safety, and the state is clearly responsible for public highways.
* Because the connection between wearing seatbelts and safety is immediately clear.
* Because it is similar to already established laws requiring the wearing of motorcycle helmets.
* Because the law is easy to follow, is minimally disruptive, and costs relatively little so that the benefits outweigh the disadvantages.

Each of these arguments distinguishes seatbelt legislation from other, less acceptable laws government might enact in the name of citizen safety, and they thus become ways of qualifying the warrant that the state should enact *all* laws that save lives. Together they constitute some reasons for supporting seatbelt legislation and for arguing that such legislation is not an unreasonable infringement of citizens' rights.

Having worked out these differences between seatbelt laws and other do-gooder laws, the writer is ready to draft the argument in essay form. Here is a portion of the writer's essay, picking up his argument after he has shown that seatbelts do indeed save lives:

> But just because seatbelts save lives does not necessarily mean that the state has the right to make us wear them. Certainly we don't want the state to make us put non-slip safety strips in our bathtubs, to require annual blood-pressure checks, or to outlaw cigarettes, alcohol, and sugar. But seatbelt regulation governs our behavior on public roadways, not in the privacy of our homes, and the government is obviously responsible for making the highways as safe as possible. After all, we can sue the government for negligence if it disregards safety in highway construction. Forcing motor vehicle passengers to wear seatbelts can thus be seen as part of their general program to make the highways safe. Moreover, the use of seatbelts constitutes a minimal restriction of personal freedom. Seatbelts are already standard equipment in cars, it costs us nothing to wear them, and they are now designed for maximum comfort.
>
> There are also a number of precedents for seatbelt legislation. Indeed, there are already government regulations requiring the installation of seatbelts in cars. To require their installation but not their use is silly. It is to require people to be potentially, but not actually, safe. In addition, a number of states, following the same sort of rationale as the one I've followed above, require motorcyclists to wear helmets. Such helmets are often costly and uncomfortable and, according to some cyclists, hurt the biker's image. But because they protect lives and save millions of dollars in insurance and hospital costs, such objections have been overriden.

As you can tell, this section is considerably more complex than one that simply cites data as evidence in support of a reason. Here the writer must use an interlocking chain of other reasons, showing all the ways that a seatbelt law is different from a safety-strip-in-the-bathtub law. Certainly it's not a definitive argument, but it is considerably more compelling than saying that the state should pass any law that protects lives. Although chains of reasons are harder to construct than bodies of evidence, many arguments will require them.

CONCLUSION

Chapters 4, 5, and 6 have provided an anatomy of argument. They have shown that the core of an argument is a claim with reasons that usually can be summarized in one or more because clauses attached to the claim. Often, it is as important to support the unstated premises in your argument as it is to support the stated ones. In order to plan out an argument strategy, arguers can use the Toulmin schema, which helps writers discover grounds, warrants, and backings for their arguments and to test them through conditions for rebuttal. Finally, we saw how stated reasons and warrants are supported through the use of evidence or chains of other reasons. In the next chapter we will look more closely at the uses of evidence in argumentation.

FOR CLASS DISCUSSION

1. Working individually or in small groups, consider ways you could use evidence from personal experience to support the stated reason in each of the following partial arguments:
   a. Another reason to oppose a state sales tax is that it is so annoying.
   b. Professor X should be rated down on his (her) teaching because he (she) doesn't know how to use homework effectively to promote real learning.
   c. Professor X is an outstanding teacher because he (she) generously spends so much time outside of class counseling students with personal problems.

2. Now try to create a chain-of-reasons argument to support the warrants in each of the above partial arguments. The warrants for each of the arguments are stated below.
   a. Support this warrant: We should oppose taxes that are annoying.
   b. Support this warrant: The ability to use homework effectively to promote real learning is an important criterion for rating teachers.
   c. Support this warrant: Time spent counseling students with personal problems is an important criterion for rating teachers.

7

A DETAILED LOOK AT THE USES OF EVIDENCE IN ARGUMENTATION

In the previous chapter, we examined the two basic ways that writers support their arguments: through reasons supported by evidence and through reasons supported by chains of other reasons. In this chapter we return to a discussion of evidence. Our purpose in this chapter is to help you develop strategies for finding, using, and evaluating evidence. We focus first on the various ways you can use your own personal experiences to support an argument, including research data gathered from interviews, surveys, and questionnaires. Next we discuss evidence from library research and examine the knotty problem of what to do when the experts disagree. Finally, we discuss how you can evaluate evidence in order to use it fairly, responsibly, and persuasively.

USING EVIDENCE FROM PERSONAL EXPERIENCE

Your own life can be the source of supporting evidence in many arguments. Often a story from your own life can support an important point or show your readers the human significance of your issue. Whenever you include specific, vivid evidence from personal experience, you will be reaching out to your readers, who generally empathize with the personal experiences of others. A writer's credibility is often enhanced if the reader senses the writer's personal connection to an issue. Task 4 in Idea-Log 2, which we recommend that you use to explore ideas for your formal arguments, asks you to inventory personal experiences related to your topic (see Chapter 3, page 74).

Using Personal Experience Data

Many issues can make extensive, even exclusive, use of personal experience data. Here is how a student from a small Montana town used a personal experience to support her claim that "small rural schools provide a quality education for children."

> Another advantage of small rural schools is the way they create in students a sense of identity with their communities and a sense of community pride. When children see the active support of the community toward the school, they want to return this support with their best efforts. I remember our Fergus Grade School Christmas programs. Sure, every grade school in Montana has a Christmas program, but ours seemed to be small productions. We started work on our play and songs immediately after Thanksgiving. The Fergus Community Women's Club decorated the hall a few days before the program. When the big night arrived, the whole community turned out, even Mr. and Mrs. Schoenberger, an elderly couple. I and the eleven other students were properly nervous as we performed our play, "A Charlie Brown Christmas." As a finale, the whole community sang carols and exchanged gifts. One of the fathers even dressed up as Santa Claus. Everyone involved had a warm feeling down inside when they went home.

The community bonding described in this paragraph—the father playing Santa Claus, the attendance of the elderly couple, the communal singing of Christmas carols—supports the writer's stated reason that small rural schools help students feel an identity with their communities.

Using Personal Observations

For some arguments you can gather evidence through personal observations. For example, suppose you want to argue that your city should install a traffic light at a particularly dangerous pedestrian crossing. You could draw on your past experience by relating an accident you almost had at that crossing. But even more persuasive might be some facts and statistics you could gather by observing the crossing for an hour or so on several different days. You could count numbers of vehicles, observe pedestrian behavior, take note of dangerous situations, time how long it takes to cross the street, and so forth. These could then become persuasive data for an argument.

EXAMPLE ARGUMENT USING PERSONAL OBSERVATION DATA

The intersection at 5th and Montgomery is particularly dangerous. Traffic volume on Montgomery is so heavy that pedestrians almost never find a comfortable break in the flow of cars. On April 29, I watched fifty-seven pedestrians cross this intersection. Not once did cars stop in both directions before the pedestrian stepped off the sidewalk onto the street. Typically, the pedestrian had to move into the street, start tentatively to cross, and wait until a car finally stopped. On fifteen occasions, pedestrians had to stop halfway across the street, with cars speeding by in both directions, waiting for cars in the far lanes to stop before they could complete their crossing.

USING EVIDENCE FROM INTERVIEWS, SURVEYS, AND QUESTIONNAIRES

In addition to direct observations, you can gather evidence by conducting interviews, taking surveys, or passing out questionnaires.

Conducting Interviews

Of these methods, interviews are especially powerful sources of evidence, not only for gathering expert testimony and important data, but also for learning about opposing or alternative views. To conduct an effective interview, you need to have a clear purpose for the interview and to be professional, courteous, efficient, and prepared. Probably most interviews go wrong because the interviewer doesn't have a specific plan of questioning. Prior to the interview, write out the questions you intend to ask based on your purpose. (Of course, be ready to move in unexpected directions if the interview opens up new territory.) Find out as much as possible about the interviewee prior to the interview. Your knowledge of his or her background will help establish your credibility and build a bridge between you and your source. Be punctual, and remember that the interviewee is probably busy and hasn't time for small talk. Finally, in most cases it is best to present yourself as a listener seeking clarity on an issue, rather than as an advocate of a particular position. Except in rare cases, it is a mistake to enter into argument with your interviewee, or to indicate through body language or tone of voice an antagonism toward his or her position. During the interview, play the believing role. Save the doubting role for later, when you are looking over your notes.

While conducting the interview, plan either to tape it (in which case you must ask the interviewee's permission) or to take good notes. Immediately after the interview, while your memory is fresh, rewrite your notes more fully and completely.

When you use interview data in your own writing, put quotation marks around any direct quotations. Except when unusual circumstances might require anonymity, identify your source by name and indicate his or her title or credentials—whatever will convince the reader that this person's remarks are to be taken seriously. Here is how one student used interview data to support an argument against carpeting dorm rooms.

> Finally, university-provided carpets will be too expensive. According to Robert Bothell, Assistant Director of Housing Services, the cost will be $300 per room for the carpet and installation. The university would also have to purchase more vacuum cleaners for the students to use. Altogether, Bothell estimated the cost of carpets to be close to $100,000 for the whole campus. [Here the student writer uses interview data from Robert Bothell as evidence that university-provided carpets will be too expensive. As Assistant Director of Housing Services, Bothell has the credentials to be an authoritative source on these costs.]

Using Surveys or Questionnaires

Still another form of field research data can come from surveys or questionnaires. Sometimes an informal poll of your classmates can supply evidence persuasive to a reader. One of our students, in an argument supporting public transportation, asked every rider on her bus one morning the following two questions:

> Do you enjoy riding the bus more than commuting by car? If so, why?

She was able to use her data in the following paragraph:

> Last week I polled forty-eight people riding the bus between Bellevue and Seattle. Eighty percent said they enjoyed riding the bus more than commuting by car, while 20 percent preferred the car. Those who enjoyed the bus cited the following reasons in this order of preference: It saved them the hassle of driving in traffic; it gave them time to relax and unwind; it was cheaper than paying for gas and parking; it saved them time.

More formal research can be done through developing and distributing questionnaires. Developing a good questionnaire is a complex task, so much so that social science or education majors often have to take special courses devoted to the topic. In general, problems with questionnaires arise when the questions are confusing or when response categories don't allow the respondent enough flexibility of choices. If you are writing an argument that depends on an elaborate questionnaire, consider checking out a book from your library on questionnaire design. Simple questionnaires, however, can be designed without formal training. If you use a questionnaire, type it neatly so that it looks clean, uncluttered, and easy to complete. At the head of the questionnaire you should explain its purpose. Your tone should be courteous and, if possible, you should include some motivational pitch to urge the reader to complete the questionnaire.

INEFFECTIVE EXPLANATION
FOR QUESTIONNAIRE:

The following questionnaire is very important for my research. I need it back by Tuesday, January 19, so please fill it out as soon as you get it. Thanks.
[Doesn't explain purpose; reasons for questionnaire stated in terms of writer's needs, not audience's need]

MORE EFFECTIVE EXPLANATION

This questionnaire is aimed at improving the quality of Dickenson Library for both students and staff. It should take no more than three or four minutes of your time and gives you an opportunity to say what you like and don't like about the present library. Of course, your responses will be kept anonymous. To enable a timely report to the library staff, please return the questionnaire by Tuesday, January 19. Thank you very much.
[Purpose is clear; respondents see how filling out questionnaire may benefit them]

When distributing questionnaires, you should seek a random distribution so that any person in your target population has an equal chance of being selected. Surveys lose their persuasiveness if the respondents are biased or represent just one segment of the total population you intended to survey. For example, if you pass out your library questionnaire only to persons living in dorms, then you won't know how commuting students feel about the library.

USING EVIDENCE FROM
READING: THE ART OF
LIBRARY RESEARCH

Whereas you can sometimes make excellent arguments using only personal experience data, many arguments require data gathered from library research, including books, magazines, journals, newspapers, government documents, computerized data banks, specialized encyclopedias and almanacs, corporate bulletins, and so forth. How to find such data, how to incorporate it into your own writing through summary, paraphrase, and quotation, and how to cite it and document it are treated in detail in Part V of this text (Chapters 17 and 18). Our purpose in this chapter is to examine some of the theoretical and rhetorical issues involved in selecting and using research evidence.

Seeking Clarity: Library Research as an Analysis of a Conversation

As a researcher, do you enter the library solely to support your own position on an issue (Callicles' goal of victory from Chapter 1)? Or are you seeking the fullest possible understanding of the issue (Socrates' goal of clarification)? The most responsible goal is clarification, but the process of reaching this goal often leads you into a confusing morass of conflicting evidence and testimony. Before continuing with a practical discussion of how to use research evidence, let's pause momentarily to examine this knotty problem.

Suppose you are writing an argument claiming that the United States should take immediate measures to combat global warming. Early on in your search for evidence, you come across the following editorial, which appeared in *USA Today* in June 1986.

Imagine a world like this:

Omaha, Neb., sweats through the worst drought in its history. In July 2030, the mercury hits 100 on 20 days. Crops are wiped out; the Midwest is a dust bowl.

New Orleans is under water. The French Quarter has shut down; the Superdome holds a small lake. The governor says property damage will be in the billions.

Washington, D.C., suffers through its hottest summer — 87 days above 90 degrees. Water is rationed; brownouts are routine because utilities can't meet demand for electricity. Federal employees, working half-days in unbearable heat, report an alarming rise in skin cancer across the USA.

Abroad, floods have inundated Bangladesh and Indonesia. The seas are four feet above 1986 levels. The United Nations reports millions will die in famines; shocking climate changes have ruined agriculture.

That sounds far-fetched, but if some scientists' worst fears come true, that could be what our children inherit.

Since the beginning of this century, man has been spewing pollutants into the atmosphere at an ever-increasing rate. Carbon dioxide and chlorofluorocarbons — CFC's — are fouling the air, our life support system. Everything that burns releases carbon dioxide. CFC's are used to make refrigerants, Styrofoam, computer chips, and other products.

In the past century, carbon dioxide in the atmosphere has risen 25 percent. The problem is that carbon dioxide holds in heat, just as the roof of a greenhouse does. That's why the Earth's warming is called the greenhouse effect.

CFC's retain heat, too, and break down the atmosphere's protective layer of ozone. If it is damaged, more of the sun's ultraviolet rays will reach Earth, causing skin cancer and damaging sea life.

Combined with the loss of forests that absorb carbon dioxide, the effects of this pollution could be disastrous. By 2030, Earth's temperature could rise 8 degrees, polar ice caps would melt, weather would change, crops would wilt.

There is growing evidence that these pollutants are reaching ominous levels. At the South Pole, the ozone layer has a "hole" in it—it's been depleted by 40 percent. NASA scientist Robert Watson says: "Global warming is inevitable—it's only a question of magnitude and time."

Some say don't panic, probably nothing will happen. The trouble with that is that we know these pollutants are building, and by the time we are sure of the worst effects, it may be too late. Action is needed, now. The USA must:

—Recognize that global warming may worsen and begin planning responses; more research is needed, too.

—Renew the search for safe, clean alternatives to fossil fuels, nuclear fission, and chlorofluorocarbons.

—Report on the extent of the problem to the world and press for international controls on air pollution.

The possible dimensions of this disaster are too big to just "wait and see." If a runaway train heads for a cliff and the engineer does nothing, the passengers are bound to get hurt. Let's check the brakes before it's too late.

When the students in one of our classes first read this editorial, they found it both persuasive and frightening. The opening scenario of potential disasters—New Orleans under water, unbearable heat, water rationing, floods, ruined agriculture, "alarming rise in skin cancer"—scared the dickens out of many readers. The powerful effect of the opening scenario was increased by the editorial's subsequent use of scientific data: carbon dioxide has increased 25 percent, the ozone layer has been depleted by 40 percent, a NASA scientist says that "[g]lobal warming is inevitable . . ." and so forth. Additionally, a plausible cause-and-effect chain explains the approaching disaster: the spewing of pollutants and the cutting down of forests lead to increased CO_2, which traps heat; use of CFC's breaks down the ozone layer, allowing more ultraviolet radiation to reach earth's surface, thereby causing cancer.

Inexperienced students writing a researched argument might be tempted to quote data from this article, which they would then cite as coming from *USA Today*. Unwittingly, they might even distort the article slightly by writing something like this:

According to *USA Today*, our civilization is on a train ride to disaster unless we put on the brakes. If global warming continues on its present course, by the year 2030, New Orleans will be under water, crops will be wiped out by droughts, . . . [and so forth].

But a second reading of this editorial begins to raise questions and doubts. First of all, the article is couched in "could's" and "might's." If we read carefully, we see that the opening scenario isn't represented as factual, inevitable, or even likely. Rather, it is represented as the "worst fears" of "some scientists." Near the end of the editorial we learn that "[s]ome say don't panic" but we aren't told whether these "some" are respectable scientists, carefree politicians, crackpots, or what. But the most puzzling aspect of this editorial is the gap between the alarming worst-case scenario at the beginning of the editorial and the tepid recommendations at the end. The final "call for action" calls for no real action at all. Recommendations 1 and 3 call for more research and for "international controls on air pollution"—nicely vague terms that create little reader discomfort. The second recommendation—renew the search for safe alternatives—reveals the writer's comfortable American optimism that scientists will find a way out of the dilemma without causing Americans any real distress. (A curious item in Recommendation 2 is the sandwiching of "nuclear fission" between "fossil fuels" and "chlorofluorocarbons." Nuclear fission is *not* a cause of the greenhouse effect and may be a plausible alternative energy source in our effort to combat global warming. But since nuclear power poses other environmental dangers, the writer tosses it in as one of the enemies.) If the "possible dimensions of this disaster" are as great as the opening scenario leads us to believe, then perhaps wrenching changes in our economy are needed to cut down our dependence on fossil fuels.

But what is the actual truth here? How serious is the greenhouse effect and what should the United States do about it? A search for the truth involves us in the sequence of reading strategies suggested in Chapter 2, "The Process of Reading Agruments": (1) reading as a believer; (2) reading as a doubter; (3) seeking out alternative views and asking why the various sides disagree with each other; and (4) evaluating the various positions. When our students applied this strategy to the greenhouse effect, they discovered an unsettling uncertainty among scientists about the facts of the case combined with complex disagreements over values. (You can recreate the same experience for yourselves by reading the anthologized articles on global warming in Part VI of this text.) In your search for clarity, what do you do when the experts disagree?

Coping with Uncertainty: When the Experts Disagree

Coping with disagreement among experts is a skill experienced arguers must develop. If there were no disagreements, of course, there would be no need for argument. It is important to realize that experts can look at the same data, can analyze the same arguments, can listen to the same authorities, and still reach different conclusions. Seldom will one expert's argument triumph over another's in a field of dissenting claims. More often, one expert's argument will modify another's and in turn will be modified by yet another. Your own expertise is not a function of your ability to choose the "right" argument, but of your ability to listen to alternative viewpoints, to understand why people disagree, and to synthesize your own argument from those disagreements.

Here briefly is our analysis of some of the disagreements about the greenhouse effect.

QUESTIONS OF FACT   At the heart of the controversy is the question "How serious is the greenhouse effect?" On the basis of our own research, we discovered that scientists agree on one fact: The amount of carbon dioxide in the earth's atmosphere has increased 7 percent since accurate measurements were first taken during the International Geophysical Year 1957/58. Additionally, scientists seem agreed that the percentage of carbon dioxide has increased steadily since the start of the Industrial Revolution in the 1860s. The statement in the *USA Today* editorial that carbon dioxide has increased by 25 percent is generally accepted by scientists as an accurate estimate of the total increase since 1860.

Where scientists disagree is on the projected effect of this increase. Predictions of global warming are derived from computer models, none of which seems able to encompass all the factors that contribute to global climate, particularly ocean currents and the movements of air masses above the oceans. Because of the enormous complexity of these factors, projections about the future differ considerably from scientist to scientist. *USA Today* took one of the worst-case projections.

QUESTIONS OF VALUE   There is also widespread disagreement on what actions the United States or other countries should take in response to the potential warming of the earth. In general, these disputes stem from disagreements about value. In particular, participants in the conversation give different answers to the following questions:

1. In the face of uncertain threat, do we react as if the threat were definite or do we wait and see? If we wait and see, will we be inviting disaster?

2. How much faith can we place in science and technology? Some people, arguing that necessity is the mother of invention, assume that scientists will get us out of this mess. Others believe that technofixes are no longer possible.

3. How much change in our way of life can we tolerate? What, for example, would be the consequences to our economy and to our

standard of living if we waged an all-out war on global warming by making drastic reductions, say, in our use of carbon fuels? To what extent are we willing to give up the benefits of industrialization?

4. How much economic disruption can we expect other nations to tolerate? What worldwide economic forces, for example, are making it profitable to cut down and burn tropical rain forests? What would happen to the economies of tropical countries if international controls suddenly prevented further destruction of rain forests? What changes in our own economy would have to take place?

Our whole point here is that the problem of global warming is interwoven into a gigantic web of other problems and issues. One of the benefits you gain from researching a complex technical and value-laden issue such as global warming is learning how to cope with ambiguity.

What advice can we give, therefore, when the experts disagree? Here is the strategy we tend to use. First, we try to ferret out the facts that all sides agree on. These facts give us a starting place on which to build an analysis. In the greenhouse controversy, the fact that all sides agree that the amount of CO_2 in the atmosphere has increased by 25 percent and that this amount increases the percentage of infrared radiation absorbed in the atmosphere suggests that there is scientific cause for concern.

Second, we try to determine if there is a majority position among experts. Sometimes dissenting voices stem from a small but prolific group of persons on the fringe. Our instincts are to trust the majority opinions of experts, even though we realize that revolutions in scientific thought almost always start with minority groups. In the case of the greenhouse effect, our own research suggests that the majority of scientists are cautiously concerned but not predicting doomsday. There seems to be a general consensus that increased greenhouse gases will contribute to global warming but how much and how soon, they won't say.

Third, we try as much as possible to focus, not on the testimony of experts, but on the data the experts use in their testimony. In other words, we try to learn as much as possible about the scientific or technical problem and immerse ourselves in the raw data. Doing so in the case of the greenhouse effect helped us appreciate the problems of creating computer models of global climate and especially of gathering data about oceanic impact on climate.

Finally, we try to determine our own position on the values issues at stake because, inescapably, these values influence the position we ultimately take. For example, the authors of this text tend to be pessimistic about technofixes for most environmental problems. We doubt that scientists will solve the problem of greenhouse gases either through finding alternatives to petrocarbon fuels or by discovering ways to eliminate or counteract greenhouse gases. We also tend not to be risk-takers on environmental matters. Thus we prefer to take vigorous action now to slow the increase of greenhouse gases rather than take a wait-and-see attitude. The conclusion of our own research, then, is that the USA Today editorial is irresponsible in two ways: It uses unfair scare tactics in the opening scenario by overstating the fears of most scientists, yet in its conclusion it doesn't call for enough disruption of our present way of life.

What we have attempted to do in the previous section is show you how we try to reach a responsible position in the face of uncertainty. We cannot claim that our position is the right one. We can only claim that it is a reasonable one and a responsible one—responsible to our own understanding of the facts and to our own declaration of values.

WRITING YOUR OWN ARGUMENT: USING EVIDENCE PERSUASIVELY

Once you have arrived at a position on an issue, often after having written a draft that enables you to explore and clarify your own views, you need to select the best evidence possible and to use it persuasively. Whether your evidence comes from research or from personal experience, the following guidelines may be helpful.

When Possible, Select Your Data from Sources Your Reader Will Trust

Other things being equal, choose data from sources you think your reader will trust. After immersing yourself in an issue, you will get a sense of who the participants in a conversation are and what their reputations tend to be. One needs to know the political biases of sources and the extent to which a source has a financial or personal investment in the outcome of a controversy. In the greenhouse controversy, for example, both Carl Sagan (article on pages 261–266) and Dixie Lee Ray (article on pages 596–601) hold Ph.D. degrees in science, and both have national reputations for speaking out in the popular press on technical and scientific issues. Carl Sagan, however, is an environmentalist while Dixie Lee Ray tends to support business and industry. To some audiences, neither of these writers will be as persuasive as more cautious and less visible scientists who publish primarily in scientific journals. Similarly, citing a conservative magazine such as Reader's Digest is apt to be ineffective to liberal audiences just as citing a Sierra Club publication would be ineffective to conservatives.

Increase Persuasiveness of Factual Data by Ensuring Recency, Representativeness, and Sufficiency

Other things being equal, choose data that are recent, representative, and sufficient. The more your data meet these criteria, the more persuasive they are.

Recency: Although some timeless issues don't depend on recent evidence, most issues, especially those related to science and technology or to current political and economic issues, depend on up-to-date information. Make sure your supporting evidence is the most recent you can find.

Representativeness: Supporting examples are more persuasive when the audience believes they are typical examples instead of extreme cases or rare occurrences. Many arguments against pornography, for example, use violent pornography or child pornography as evidence, even though these are extreme cases quite different from the erotica associated, say, with *Playboy Magazine.* These nonrepresentative examples are ineffective if one's purpose is to include such publications as *Playboy Magazine* in the category of pornography. Assuring representativeness is an especially important concern of statisticians, who seek random samples to avoid bias toward one point of view. Seeking representative examples helps you guard against selective use of data—starting with a claim and then choosing only those data that support it, instead of letting the claim grow out of a careful consideration of all the data.

Sufficiency: One of the most common reasoning fallacies, called "hasty generalization" (see Appendix 1), occurs when a person leaps to a sweeping generalization based on only one or two instances. The criterion of sufficiency (which means having enough examples to justify your point) helps you guard against hasty generalization. The key here isn't to cite every possible example, but to convince your audience that the examples you have cited don't exhaust your whole supply. In our experience, lack of sufficiency occurs frequently in personal experience arguments. The student praised earlier for her personal experience data in an argument about rural schools suffers from this problem in the following paragraph:

> My primary reason for supporting the small, rural grade schools over the larger urban schools is the amount of learning that occurs. I am my own proof. I was the only member of my grade from the third to the eighth grade at Fergus Grade School. I relished the privilege of being able to work on two chapters of math, instead of one, especially if I enjoyed the subject. Upon graduation from the eighth grade, I attended a large high school and discovered that I had a better background than students from larger grade schools. I got straight A's.

The problem here is that the writer's one example—herself—isn't sufficient for supporting the claim that rural schools provide quality learning. To support that claim, she would need either more examples or statistical data about the later achievements of students who attended rural grade schools.

In Citing Evidence, Distinguish Fact from Inference or Opinion

In citing research data, you should be careful to distinguish facts from inferences or opinions. A "fact" is a noncontroversial piece of data that is verifiable through observation or through appeal to communally accepted authorities. Although the distinction between a fact and an inference is a fuzzy one philosophically, at a pragmatic level all of the following can loosely be classified as facts.

> The Declaration of Independence was signed in 1776.

> An earthquake took place in San Francisco on the opening day of the World Series in 1989.

> The amount of carbon dioxide in the atmosphere has increased by 7 percent since 1955.

An "inference," on the other hand, is an interpretation or explanation of the facts that may be reasonably doubted. This distinction is important because, when reading as a "doubter," you often call into question a writer's inferences. If you treat these inferences as facts, you are apt to cite them as facts in your own arguments, thereby opening yourself up to easy rebuttal. For the most part, inferences should be handled as testimony rather than as fact.

WEAK: Flohn informs us that the warming of the atmosphere will lead to damaging droughts by the year 2035. [Treats Flohn's inference as a fact about global warming.]

BETTER: Flohn interprets the data pessimistically. He believes that the warming of the atmosphere will lead to damaging droughts by the year 2035. [Makes it clear that Flohn's view is an inference, not a fact.]

To Use Evidence Persuasively, Position it Effectively

Whenever possible, place evidence favorable to your point in rhetorically strong positions in your essay; tuck opposing evidence into rhetorically inconspicuous places. Consider the case of Professor Nutt, who was asked to write a letter of recommendation for Elliot Weasel for a management trainee position at a bank. Professor Nutt remembered Weasel with mixed emotions. On the one hand, Weasel was the most brilliant student Nutt had ever had in class—an excellent mathematical mind, creative imagination, strong writing skills. On the other hand, Weasel was slovenly, rude, irresponsible, and moody. In the first case below, Nutt decides to give Weasel a positive recommendation.

POSITIVE RECOMMENDATION FOR WEASEL

Although Elliot Weasel was somewhat temperamental in my class and occasionally lacked people skills, these problems were the result of brilliance. I am convinced that Weasel is one of the most highly intelligent students I have ever encountered. In fact, in one of my business management classes, he wrote the best term paper I have ever received in five years of teaching management. I gave him an A+ and even learned some new insights from his paper. If he could learn to interact more effectively with others, he would become a superb manager. In sum, I give him a quite high recommendation.

In the next case, Nutt's recommendation is negative.

NEGATIVE RECOMMENDATION FOR WEASEL

Although Elliott Weasel is one of the most intelligent students I have ever encountered, he was somewhat temperamental in my class and occasionally lacked people skills. He would come to class dressed sloppily with unkempt hair and dirty-looking clothes. He also seemed like a loner, was frequently moody, and once refused to participate in a group project. Thus my recommendation of him is mixed. He's highly intelligent and an excellent writer, but I found him rude and hard to like.

Let's analyze the difference between these versions. In the first version, Nutt places the anti-Weasel data in subordinate clauses and phrases and places the pro-Weasel data in main slots, particularly the main clause of the first sentence. The effect is to highlight Weasel's strong points. Because the opening sentence ends with an emphasis on Weasel's brilliance, Nutt brings in additional data to back up the assertion that Weasel is brilliant.

In the second version, Nutt reverses this procedure by putting pro-Weasel data in subordinate positions and highlighting the anti-Weasel data in main clauses. Because the opening sentence ends with an emphasis on Weasel's moodiness and lack of people skills, Nutt brings in additional data to back up these points. Thus through selection of data (deciding which "facts" to put in and which ones to leave out) and through loading of data into main or subordinate slots in the paragraph, Nutt creates a positive impression in the first version and a negative impression in the second. Although neither version could be regarded as untruthful, neither version tells the "whole truth" either, because the necessity to interpret the data means commitment toward some sort of claim, which necessarily shapes the selection and placement of evidence.

FOR CLASS DISCUSSION

Suppose that you developed a questionnaire to ascertain students' satisfaction with your college library as a place to study. Suppose further that you got the following responses to one of your questions (numbers in brackets indicate percentage of total respondents who checked each response):

The library provides a quiet place to study.

Strongly agree   (10%)

Agree   (40%)

Undecided   (5%)

Disagree   (35%)

Strongly disagree   (10%)

Without telling any lies of fact, you can report these data so that they place the current library atmosphere in either favorable or unfavorable light. Working individually or in small groups, use the above data to complete the following sentences:

There seemed to be considerable satisfaction with the library as a quiet place to study. In response to our questionnaire . . . [complete this sentence by selecting data from the above responses].

Students seem dissatisfied with the noise level of the library. In response to our questionnaire . . . [complete this sentence by selecting data from the above responses].

CONCLUSION

Supporting your reasons with evidence or chains of other reasons is essential if you hope to make your arguments persuasive. As we have seen, evidence includes facts, examples, statistics, testimony, and other forms of data, and it can come from personal experience as well as from reading and research. For many issues, your search for evidence leads you into an ambiguous arena of conflicting views. Adapting to a world where experts disagree requires strategies for sorting out the causes of disagreement and establishing reasonable grounds to justify the claims you finally wish to assert. Learning how to evaluate evidence in your sources and how to use evidence responsibly and persuasively is an important skill that develops gradually. We hope this chapter gives you some helpful groundwork on which to build.

In the next chapters we will consider further strategies for making your arguments as persuasive as possible by turning our attention increasingly toward audience.

WRITING ASSIGNMENTS FOR PART II

The first five writing options below are short, skill-building exercises that we call "microthemes." They can be done as overnight out-of-class assignments or as in-class writing or group discussion exercises. These one- or two-paragraph assignments are most successful if approached like games. They are designed to help you learn argumentative "moves" that you can apply later to longer, more formal essays.

The last option is a formal writing assignment that asks you to construct a logical, well-developed argument, putting into practice the principles of structure discussed in Part II.

OPTION 1: A MICROTHEME THAT SUPPORTS A REASON WITH PERSONAL EXPERIENCE DATA   Write a one- or two-paragraph argument in which you support one of the following enthymemes using evidence from personal experience. Most of your microtheme should be devoted to use of personal experience to support the stated reason. However, also include a brief passage supporting the implied warrant for your chosen enthymeme. The opening sentence of your microtheme should be the enthymeme itself, which serves as the thesis statement for your argument.

1. Children should have hobbies because, among other things, hobbies fill up leisure time with enjoyable activity. (Support the stated reason with examples of how hobbies in your life have helped you fill up leisure time with enjoyable activities. Support the warrant by arguing that enjoyable use of leisure time is a good thing for children.)

2. After-school jobs are generally not a good idea for teenagers because they take up too much valuable study time.

3. After-school jobs are beneficial for teenagers because they teach time management.

4. Another reason to oppose a state sales tax is that it is so annoying.

5. X (a teacher/professor of your choosing) is an ineffective teacher because, among other things, he (she) doesn't know how to use homework effectively to promote real learning.

6. X (a teacher/professor of your choosing) is an outstanding teacher because he (she) generously spends so much time outside of class counseling students with personal problems.

7. Any enthymeme (a claim with a because clause) of your choice that can be supported through personal experience. Clear your enthymeme with your instructor before drafting your microtheme.

OPTION 2: A MICROTHEME THAT USES EVIDENCE FROM RESEARCH The purpose of this microtheme is to help you learn how to support reasons with evidence gathered from research. The presentation of data below attempts to simulate the kinds of research evidence one might typically gather on note cards during a research project. (See Chapters 17 and 18 for further advice on incorporating research data into your own writing. For this assignment, assume you are writing for a popular magazine so that you do not need to use academic citations.)

The situation: By means of startling "before and after" photographs of formerly obese people, the commercial diet industry heavily advertises rapid weight loss diets that use liquids and powders or special low-calorie frozen dinners. **Your task:** Drawing on the following data, write a short argument warning people of the hazards of these diets.

Source: Representative Ron Wyden (D–Oregon), chairman of a congressional subcommittee investigating the diet industry:

- Wyden fears that diet programs now include many shoddy companies that use misleading advertisements and provide inadequate medical supervision of their clients.
- "This industry has been built almost overnight on a very shaky foundation."
- "All the evidence says that losing large amounts of weight very fast does more harm than good."
- Wyden believes that the diet industry may need to be federally regulated.

Source: Theodore B. VanItallie, M.D., a founder of the Obesity Research Center at St. Luke's Roosevelt Hospital Center in New York:

- Rapid weight loss systems (such as liquid diets) were originally designed for morbidly obese individuals.
- For people who are only slightly overweight, rapid weight loss can be hazardous.
- When weight loss is too rapid, the body begins using lean muscle mass for fuel instead of excess fat. The result is a serious protein deficiency that can bring on heart irregularities.
- "If more than 25 percent of lost weight is lean body mass, the stage is set not only for early regain of lost weight but for a higher incidence of fatigue, hair loss, skill changes, depression and other undesirable side effects."

Source: Bonnie Blodgett, freelance writer on medical/health issues:

- Rapid weight loss may accelerate formation of gallstones. 179 people are currently suing a major diet company because of gallstone complications while pursuing the company's diet. The company denies responsibility.

- For every five people who start a commercial weight-loss program, only one stays with it long enough to lose a significant amount of weight.

- Up to 90 percent of dieters who lose more than 25 pounds gain it all back within two years.

- Only one in fifty maintains the weight loss for seven years.

- The best way to lose weight is through increased exercise, moderate reduction of calories, and a lifelong change in eating habits.

- Unless one is grossly obese and dieting under a physician's supervision, one should strive to lose no more than 1 or 2 pounds per week.

Source: Philip Kern, M.D., in a study appearing in *The New England Journal of Medicine:*

- Rapid weight loss programs result in the "yo-yo" syndrome—a pattern of compulsive fasting followed by compulsive bingeing.

- This pattern may upset the body's metabolism by producing an enzyme called lipoprotein lipase.

- This protein helps restore fat cells shrunken by dieting.

- It apparently causes formerly fat people to crave fatty foods, thereby promoting regain of lost weight.*

OPTION 3: A MICROTHEME THAT DRAWS ON A NEWSPAPER STORY FOR DATA
Using the following newspaper article "Deaths Spur New Call for Child-Labor Crackdown" as a source, write a microtheme that could be part of an argument calling for increased enforcement of child-labor laws. Begin your microtheme with the following sentence: "Recent evidence suggests that the child-labor problem is more severe than most people realize." Then select data from the story that focus on the extent and severity of the problem.

DEATHS SPUR NEW CALL FOR CHILD-LABOR CRACKDOWN

Two children were killed and 4,000 injured on the job in Washington state 1
last year, Department of Labor and Industries officials said yesterday in proposing legislation to protect youngsters in the workplace.

---

*Source of the above data is Bonnie Blodgett, "The Diet Biz," *Glamour*, January 1991, pp. 136ff.

The department investigated 395 of the 4,000 cases and found nearly 44   2
percent of the employers were violating child-labor laws at the time of a
minor's injury.

"Society places a high value on the well-being of children," said Joe Dear,   3
director of the agency. "That should extend to children in the workplace.
They're more vulnerable. They're more susceptible to intimidation by employers, and they're less knowledgeable about their rights."

It is the third year in a row that the Labor and Industries Department has   4
drafted a bill to strengthen its enforcement capabilities in regulating child-labor laws.

In the past two sessions, the legislation passed the Democrat-controlled   5
House and died in the Republican-dominated Senate.

Attention was focused on child-labor issues in October 1989 when a   6
14-year-old boy died after being struck by two cars while selling candy
door-to-door in the Graham area south of Tacoma.

The state is seeking an injunction to stop the operation of his employer,   7
Teens for Action Against Drugs. The state contends the boy was not supervised properly.

The Pierce County prosecutor's office also has filed criminal misdemeanor   8
charges against owners Christopher and Nikita Spice, accusing them of
failure to register the company with the state, failure to secure work permits
for employees and variances for children under 16, and false advertising.

The other death involved a 12-year-old Oregon boy struck by a car in the   9
Federal Way area. Officials could not provide further information about his
case.

In other incidents, a 16-year-old Spanaway boy cut off three fingers while   10
using a table saw, a 15-year-old girl was burned by a motorized iron in Mount
Vernon, and a 17-year-old boy was burned on the face while pouring molten
aluminum in a Spokane foundry.

Dear said all were performing duties prohibited by child-labor laws. In its   11
year-long study, the department found injured children in every industry, but
particularly in fast-food and retail businesses.

Another study conducted by the University of Washington, Harborview   12
Medical Center and the Labor and Industries Department found 17,000
children under 18 were hurt on the job from 1986 to 1989.

The proposed legislation would allow the department to impose civil   13
penalties on employers who violate the law and to seek felony prosecution for
serious violations. That could mean five years in prison and a fine of $10,000,
Dear said.

For less serious violations, the department could issue citations, and   14
employers could avoid penalty by complying with the regulations.

The maximum charge an employer now faces is a misdemeanor, with a fine   15
of up to $1,000.

OPTION 4: A MICROTHEME THAT DRAWS ON CONFLICTING NEWSPAPER STORIES FOR DATA The following stories appeared on consecutive days in the *Seattle Times*. The first story reports a significant decline in drug use, particularly cocaine, since 1988—a decline contested by Senator Joseph Biden. The second story clarifies Biden's objections to the original report.

Your task: Suppose that you are writing an argument either for or against the thesis that the Bush administration is making significant progress in the war against drugs. Drawing on one or both of these stories, write a paragraph that helps support your thesis. Your paragraph should address the question, "Did drug use in America decline significantly from 1988 to 1990?" In class, be prepared to explain and defend your reasons for the way you summarized and used the data in these conflicting articles.

U.S. COCAINE USE PLUNGES, SURVEY SHOWS

Ronald J. Ostrow

Cocaine use by Americans plunged 45 percent from 1988 levels, according to a government drug survey.   1

The cocaine results, along with other signs of marked improvement reported by the National Institute of Drug Abuse, were sharply disputed by Sen. Joseph Biden, D-Del.   2

The administration's study "actually misses more addicts than it counts," said Biden, chairman of the Senate Judiciary Committee. A study done by the Democratic staff of his committee found the household survey "grossly underestimated the number of hard-core cocaine addicts and weekly heroin users."   3

President Bush, while saying the results suggest "that our hard work is paying off and that our national strategy is having an effect," cautioned that "a declaration of victory would be premature." He pledged no cutback in the stepped-up federal effort against illicit drugs.   4

The survey, conducted from March through June, included these highlights in comparing the latest data with 1988, when the last survey was done: 5

- The number of adolescents using any drug dropped 13 percent, from 1.8 million to 1.6 million. The number of adolescents using cocaine fell 47 percent, from 225,000 to 119,000.

- The number of crack-cocaine smokers stayed stable at 494,000 among the 1.6 million current cocaine users. Individuals are counted as current users if they admit using the substance at least once in the past month.

- Current use of any illicit drug fell from 14.5 million individuals to 12.9 million.

- Daily cocaine users ran counter to the downward trend, increasing from 292,000 to 336,000. Those using cocaine once a week or more dropped from 862,000 to 662,000.

- Despite an overall decline to 6.4 percent of the population engaging in any current illicit drug use, some demographic subgroups were markedly higher. Among 18-to-25-year-olds, 14.9 percent used drugs; among the unemployed, 14 percent; among blacks, 8.6 percent.

- Marijuana remains the most commonly used illegal drug in the country, with 66.5 million Americans, or 33.1 percent of the population, having tried it at least once in their lifetime and 20.5 million having used it at least once over the past year.

- Alcohol and cigarette use continued to decline, as it did from 1985 to 1988. The latest total of 102.9 million current drinkers of alcoholic beverages was down almost 3 million from the 1988 figure. Current cigarette use dropped from 57.1 million to 53.6 million.

The survey was done by conducting interviews in 9,250 randomly chosen 6 homes.

Joining Bush in announcing the results, Secretary of Health and Human 7 Services Louis Sullivan spoke of "marked progress (in) changing attitudes and behaviors as more and more of our neighbors and co-workers have turned away from illegal drugs."

Sullivan also cited favorable results from a survey of cocaine-related cases 8 reaching hospital emergency rooms. Such cases dropped by 9.5 percent, from 8,323 cases in the first quarter of 1990 to 7,532 cases in this year's second quarter.

STUDIES SHOW DRUG PROBLEMS PERSIST

David G. Savage

Researchers working for the Bush administration called thousands of Ameri- 1 cans during the spring and asked: Would you be willing to talk about your use of illegal drugs?

Researchers employed by Senate Democrats tried to answer the similar 2 questions about drug use by zeroing in on persons who were arrested and tested for drugs in jail, and those being admitted to drug treatment centers.

Not surprisingly, the two sets of analysis portray two different pictures of 3 drug abuse in America.

President Bush, reporting on his administration's latest survey, said 4 Wednesday it contained "wonderful and welcome news." Far fewer Americans are using drugs of any kind, concluded the report by the National Institute of Drug Abuse (NIDA).

The Senate Judiciary Committee said its study painted a much bleaker 5 picture, concluding there are about 2.4 million regular cocaine users — four times the estimate in the NIDA survey.

While Bush and his advisers portrayed the drug problem as bad but 6 getting better, Democrats stressed the problem was bad and still bad. Sen. Joe Biden, D-Del., of the Judiciary Committee charged that the administration's estimate of the number of regular cocaine users was "wildly off the mark" because its Household Survey leaves out the homeless and those whose home is prison or a drug treatment center.

Still, both sides in this battle of drug studies agree on an overall conclu- 7 sion: casual drug use is waning in middle America, but cocaine and crack still have a grip on the inner-city.

"You may see declines in drug use in places like Scarsdale, but not in East 8 Harlem," said Mitchell S. Rosenthal, president of the New York-based Phoenix House, a private drug treatment center.

Every other year since 1972, the National Institute on Drug Abuse has 9 asked a statistical sample about their drug use. Those surveyed are interviewed at home and asked to fill out a confidential report. Some 9,259 persons were interviewed this year.

The biennial Household Survey reported a rising tide of marijuana and 10 cocaine use through 1979 and a steady decline since then. When the White House declared a "War on Drugs" in the late 1980s, drug abuse already was on the way down in much of the nation, according to the NIDA surveys.

The 1990 survey gives "the latest and most compelling evidence that drug 11 use in America is declining significantly," Bush said Wednesday.

The Health and Human Services press release highlighted "a dramatic 45 12 percent drop in 'current' cocaine use." This means, according to the data, that an estimated 15 of every 1,000 persons surveyed admitted in 1988 to having used cocaine within the past month, while only 8 of 1,000 said the same this year.

The Senate panel, which came up with higher numbers, drew much of its 13 data from tests of arrested persons in the major cities, as well as tallies of those admitted to drug treatment centers.

The panel and many drug experts say they believe illegal drug use has 14 declined, but not to the extent the NIDA survey suggests.

"As society has become more intolerant of drug use, fewer people are 15 going to talk about their drug use to a researcher who knocks on their door," said Eric Wish, director of the Center for Substance Abuse Research at the University of Maryland. "We just don't know how much of this decline is really a decline in people's willingness to report their drug use."

Ronald Klain, counsel for the Judiciary Committee, said the NIDA survey 16 is "flawed and misleading. About one-fifth of the sample refused to talk, and they didn't talk to the people who are most likely to be addicts," he said.

Charles R. Schuster, NIDA's director, acknowledged that the household 17 survey does not count the homeless or those in prison and other institutions, including college dormitories. "But it does measure 98 percent of the population in the United States 12 years of age and older," he said.

Schuster estimated that half of the 1.5 million persons now in prison may 18 be drug users, and a significant proportion of those crack users. "So the numbers that we are getting for crack cocaine use are obviously an underestimate. . . ."

But Schuster and other HHS officials defended the household survey as an 19 accurate measure of trends, because the survey has been conducted with the same methodology in the 10 times it has been conducted since 1971.

Independent surveys of the prison populations are somewhat inconclusive. 20

OPTION 5: A MICROTHEME THAT USES STATISTICAL DATA TO SUPPORT A POINT
Defend one of the following theses:
Thesis A — "Women (blacks) made only negligible progress toward job equality between 1972 and 1981."
Thesis B — "Women (blacks) made significant progress toward job equality between 1972 and 1981."
Support your thesis with evidence drawn from the table on page 140. You can write your microtheme about the job progress of either women or blacks.

OPTION 6: A FORMAL ARGUMENT USING AT LEAST TWO REASONS IN SUPPORT OF YOUR CLAIM Write a multiparagraph essay in which you develop two or more reasons in support of your thesis or claim. Each of your reasons should be summarizable in a because clause attached to your claim. If you have more than two reasons, develop your most important reason last. Give your essay a self-announcing structure in which you highlight your claim at the end of your introduction and begin your body paragraphs with clearly stated reasons. Open your essay with an attention-grabbing lead that attracts your readers' interest; your introduction should also explain the issue being addressed as well as provide whatever background is needed.

Note that this assignment does not ask you to refute opposing views. Nevertheless, it is a good idea to summarize an opposing view briefly in order to help the reader see the issue more clearly. Because you will not be refuting this view, the best place to summarize it is in your introduction prior to presenting your own claim. (If you place an opposing view in the body of your essay, its prominence obligates you to refute it or concede to it — issues addressed in Part III of this text. If you briefly summarize an

TABLE for Option 5. Employed Persons, by Sex, Race, and Occupation, 1972 and 1981 (selected occupations)

| | 1972 | | | 1981 | | |
| | Total Employed (1,000) | Percentage | | Total Employed (1,000) | Percentage | |
Occupation		Female	Black and Other		Female	Black and Other
Professional, Technical	11,538	39.3	7.2	16,420	44.6	9.9
Accountants	720	21.7	4.3	1,126	38.5	9.9
Dentists	108	1.9	5.6	130	4.6	6.2
Engineers	1,111	0.8	3.4	1,537	4.4	7.3
Lawyers	322	3.8	1.9	581	14.1	4.6
Librarians	158	81.6	7.0	192	82.8	5.7
Physicians	332	10.1	8.2	454	13.7	14.5
Registered nurses	807	97.6	8.2	1,654	96.8	12.3
College teachers	464	28.0	9.2	585	35.2	9.2
Managers, Administrators	8,081	17.6	4.0	11,540	27.5	5.8
Bank officers	430	19.0	2.6	696	37.5	5.5
Office managers	317	41.9	1.0	504	70.6	4.0
Sales managers	574	15.7	1.6	720	26.5	4.6
Clerical Workers	14,329	75.6	8.7	18,564	80.5	11.6
Bank tellers	290	87.5	4.9	569	93.5	7.6
File clerks	274	84.9	18.0	315	83.8	22.9
Secretaries	2,964	99.1	5.2	3,917	99.1	7.2
Skilled Crafts	10,867	3.6	6.9	12,662	6.3	8.5
Carpenters	1,052	0.5	5.9	1,122	1.9	5.8
Construction	2,261	0.6	9.0	2,593	1.9	10.2
Mechanics	1,040	0.5	8.5	1,249	0.6	8.7
Transportation	3,233	4.2	14.8	3,476	8.9	15.5
Bus drivers	253	34.1	17.1	360	47.2	21.1
Truck drivers	1,449	0.6	14.4	1,878	2.7	13.9
Unskilled Labor	4,242	6.0	20.2	4,583	11.5	16.5
Service Workers	9,584	57.0	18.5	12,391	59.2	18.4
Food service	3,286	69.8	13.9	4,682	66.2	14.0
Nurses' aides	1,513	87.0	24.6	1,995	89.2	24.3
Domestic cleaners	715	97.2	64.2	468	95.1	51.5

opposing view in the introduction, however, you use it merely to clarify the issue and hence do not need to treat it at length.)

The following essay illustrates this assignment. It was written by a freshman student whose first language is Vietnamese rather than English. Additional essays written to the same assignment include Sandra Nelson's essay in Chapter 3 (pages 65–68) and the set of essays (some strong, some weak) in the "norming exercise" in Appendix 3 (see pages 755–761). This exercise is aimed at helping you internalize criteria for a strong performance on this assignment.

CHOOSE LIFE!

Dao Do (student)

Should euthanasia be legalized? My classmate Drea and her family think it 1 should be. Drea's grandmother was blind from diabetes. For three years she was constantly in and out of the hospital, but then her kidneys shut down and she became a victim of life supports. After three months of suffering, she finally gave up. Drea believes three-month period was unnecessary, for her grandmother didn't have to go through all of that suffering. If euthanasia were legalized, her family would have put her to sleep the minute her condition worsened. Then, she wouldn't have had to feel pain, and she would have died in peace and with dignity. Despite Drea's strong argument for legalizing euthanasia, I find it is wrong.

First, euthanasia is wrong because no one has the right to take the life of 2 another person. Just as our society discourages suicide, it should discourage euthanasia because in both the person is running away from life and its responsibilities. Some people say that euthanasia or suicide will end suffering and pain. But what proofs do they have for such a claim? Death is still mysterious to us; therefore, we do not know whether death will end suffering and pain or not. What seems to be the real claim is that death to those with illnesses will end *our* pain. Such pain involves worrying over them, paying their medical bills, and giving up so much of our time. Their deaths end our pain rather than theirs. And for that reason, euthanasia is a selfish act, for the outcome of euthanasia benefits us, the nonsufferers, more. Once the sufferers pass away, we can go back to our normal lives.

My second opposition to euthanasia is its unfavorable consequences. 3 Today, euthanasia is performed on those who we think are suffering from incurable diseases or brain death. But what about tomorrow? People might use euthanasia to send old parents to death just to get rid of them faster, so they can get to the money, the possessions, and the real estate. Just think of all the murder cases on TV where children killed their parents so they can get to the fortune. Legalizing euthanasia will increase the number of these murder cases. The right of euthanasia not only encourages corruption, it encourages discrimination. People who suffer pain would be put into categories according to which should live longer and which shouldn't. Perhaps poor people or people of color will be more apt to be euthanized than rich people, or perhaps people with AIDS will be euthanized sooner so that society won't have to spend money on this very expensive disease.

My third objection to euthanasia is that it fails to see the value in suffering.   4
Suffering is a part of life. We only see the value of suffering if we look deeply within our suffering. For example, I never thought my crippled uncle from Vietnam was a blessing to my grandmother until I talked to her. My mother's little brother was born prematurely. As a result of oxygen and nutrition deficiency, he was born crippled. His tiny arms and legs were twisted around his body, preventing him from any normal movements such as walking, picking up things, and lying down. He could only sit. Therefore, his world was very limited, for it consisted of his own room and the garden viewed through his window. Because of his disabilities, my grandmother had to wash him, feed him, and watch him constantly. It was hard but she managed to care for him for forty-three years. He passed away after the death of my grandfather in 1982. Bringing this situation out of Vietnam and into Western society shows the difference between Vietnamese and West's views. In West, my uncle might have been euthanized as a baby. Supporters of euthanasia would have said he wouldn't have any quality of life and that he would have been a great burden. But he was not a burden on my grandmother. She enjoyed taking care of him, and he was always her company after her other children got married and moved away. Neither one of them saw his defect as a form of suffering because it brought them closer together. My uncle was there for us to be thankful to God for not letting us be born with such disabilities. We should appreciate our lives, for they are not so limited.

In conclusion, let us be reminded that we do not have the right to take life,   5
but we do have the right to live. We are free to live life to its fullest. Why anticipate death when it ends everything? Why choose a path we know nothing of? There's always room for hope. In hoping, we'll see that forced death is never a solution. Until we can understand the world after, we should choose to live and not to die.

III

THE RHETORICAL
STRUCTURE OF
ARGUMENTS

8

MOVING YOUR AUDIENCE: FINDING AUDIENCE-BASED REASONS

In Part II, we discussed *logos* — the logical structure of reasons and evidence in an argument. In Part III, we shift from discussing how to structure arguments logically to discussing how to develop persuasive reasons that hook into your audience's values and beliefs. The next chapter continues the focus on persuasion by examining the other two points of the rhetorical triangle, *ethos* and *pathos* (see beginning of Chapter 4).

Though we talk about persuasion in these chapters, we don't intend the Sophists' meaning of *persuasion* that was examined in the debate between Socrates and Callicles. As you will recall, Callicles' interest was not in the "truth," but in simply winning the debate. For Callicles, "truth" became whatever the victor proclaimed. Our meaning of persuasion presupposes an arguer whose position results from a reasoned investigation of evidence, an examination of assumptions, and a commitment to values. Persuasion is the art of making that position as forceful as possible, as likely as possible to gain an audience's adherence.

In the first part of this chapter we discuss the concept of "audience-based" reasons as opposed to "writer-based" reasons. We then explain an invention strategy that may help you find audience-based reasons, especially for arguments that call for action on the part of your audience.

WRITER-BASED REASONS: A COMMON ARGUING MISTAKE

Let's begin by returning to Young Person's argument with Parents over her curfew time. As you may recall from Chapter 1, Young Person's first argument didn't work: "I should be allowed to stay out until 2:00 A.M. because I am sixteen years old." Let's look at the argument using Toulmin's system.

> *Claim:* I should be allowed to stay out until 2:00 A.M.
>
> *Stated Reason:* I am sixteen years old.
>
> *Grounds:* birth certificate, baptismal records, etc. [Parents accept her grounds; they know how old she is!]
>
> *Warrant:* All sixteen-year-olds should be allowed to stay out until 2:00 A.M. [Parents don't buy this warrant.]

As you can see, this argument fails because the warrant, which seems perfectly reasonable to Young Person, isn't acceptable to Parents. Her argument is writer-based, not audience-based.

Her next argument—"I should be able to stay out until 2:00 A.M. because all my friends get to stay out until 2:00 A.M."—is equally futile because, once again, Parents won't accept the warrant.

> *Claim:* I should be allowed to stay out until 2:00 A.M.
>
> *Stated Reason:* My friends get to stay out until 2:00 A.M.
>
> *Grounds:* Jodi's parents let her stay out until 2:00 A.M.; so do Sarah's parents; so do Jim's; so do . . . *ad nauseum.*
>
> *Warrant:* The rules in this family should be based on the rules in other families. [Parents do not accept this warrant.]

We can also think of a number of other writer-based reasons that won't fly with Parents. For example, we recommend that Young Person not try the following argument: "I should be allowed to stay out until 2:00 A.M. because the real fun at Benny's house can't get started until his mom goes to bed." Young Person's rhetorical problem so far is that she has linked her reasons to *her own values* instead of linking them to values that *she and Parents can share.* The reasons Young Person offers here are all writer-based reasons instead of audience-based reasons. In effect, she needs to identify "shared warrants" that won't require extensive backing to gain her parents' acceptance.

AUDIENCE-BASED REASONS: BUILDING A BRIDGE BETWEEN WRITER AND READER

What we are recommending, then, is that Young Person find reasons linked to her parents' values. The search for that link will lead to clarification of the issue and hence will influence the content and shape of the argument itself. Young Person needs to see the world more through her parents' eyes. By attempting to share her parents' views, Young Person might be better prepared to persuade them that her case is reasonable. Indeed, she might even clarify for herself why she desires more freedom.

Perhaps Young Person could try a reason like this:

I should be able to set my own curfew because that will give me the freedom to demonstrate my own maturity to you.

Or, if this reason takes wholesomeness further than she wants to take it, she might put her reason this way:

I should be able to set my own curfew because I need enough freedom to learn through my own mistakes.

These reasons probably link to her parents' values—the desire to see their daughter grow in maturity—and make the case that maturity is best demonstrated when a person is free rather than constrained. We can't say whether this argument will win the night for Young Person, but we can say that it is much more persuasive than giving reasons based only on Young Person's values.

Next let's take a more serious example. Suppose you believed that the government should build a new power generation dam on the near-by Rapid River—a project bitterly opposed by environmentalist groups. Which of the following two arguments would be the most persuasive to this audience (people with strong environmentalist leanings)?

1. The federal government should push ahead with its plan to build a new power generation dam on the Rapid River because the only alternative is a coal-fired plant or a nuclear plant, both of which are much greater environmental hazards than clean, water-generated power.

2. The federal government should push ahead with its plan to build a new power generation dam on the Rapid River because this area needs cheap electricity in order to stimulate the growth of heavy industry.

Although intuitively we know that argument 1 would be more powerful to environmentalists, let's analyze both arguments by using Toulmin's schema in order to see why.

ARGUMENT 1

Claim: The government should build the dam.

Stated Reason: The dam is a lesser environmental hazard than its alternatives (coal or nuclear plants).

Grounds: It doesn't consume petrocarbon fuel, doesn't give off waste gases, doesn't create nuclear waste, etc.

Warrant: Given alternative means of generating power, we should choose those least hazardous to the environment. [This warrant expresses a basic belief or value of environmentalists.]

ARGUMENT 2

Claim: The government should build the dam.

Stated Reason: It will produce cheap electricity, which will stimulate growth of heavy industry.

Grounds: Cheap electricity will keep factory operating costs lower in this area. Low costs will encourage more industries to build factories. Evidence exists of industry interest in locating in places where energy is cheaper.

Warrant: Growth of heavy industry is good. [Environmentalists are not apt to accept this warrant.]

Clearly, the warrant of argument 1 hooks into the values and beliefs of environmentalists, while the warrant of argument 2 is apt to make them wince. To environmentalists, heavy industry is not a good: It means more congestion, more smokestacks, and more pollution. On the other hand, argument 2 might be very persuasive to out-of-work laborers, to whom heavy industry means jobs.

From the perspective of *logos* alone, arguments 1 and 2 are both sound. Both arguments are internally consistent, and both proceed from reasonable premises. But as pieces of persuasion—arguments that work, that move their intended audiences—they have quite different appeals. Argument 1 proceeds from the values of people committed primarily to protecting the environment; argument 2 proceeds from the values of people committed primarily to economic growth and jobs.

Of course, it should be understood that neither argument "proves" that the government should build the dam, for both arguments are open to refutation and counterargument. Facing argument 1, for example, a thoroughgoing environmentalist might counter by arguing that the government shouldn't build any power plant at all. They could argue that energy conservation would obviate the need for a new power plant. Or they might argue that building a dam hurts the environment in ways other than pollution. Our point, then, isn't that argument 1 will persuade environmentalists. Rather, our point is that argument 1 will be more persuasive than 2 because it is rooted in beliefs and values that the intended audience shares.

In many cases, as we shall see shortly, the act of seriously considering the values and beliefs of one's audience can actually change the content of our own ideas. By seeing ourselves through the eyes of others, we begin to change the way we see. The arguments we make will be *different*, depending on to whom we make them.

FOR CLASS DISCUSSION

Working in groups, decide which of the following pairs of reasons is likely to be more persuasive to the specified audience. Be prepared to explain your reasoning to the class as a whole by writing out the implied warrant for each because clause and deciding whether the specific audience would be likely to grant it.

1. Audience: a prospective employer
    a. I would be a good candidate for a summer job at the Happy Trails Dude Ranch because I have always wanted to spend a summer in the mountains and because I like to ride horses.
    b. I would be a good candidate for a summer job at the Happy Trails Dude Ranch because I am a hard worker, because I have had considerable experience serving others in my volunteer work at Mercy Hospital, and because I know how to make guests feel welcome and relaxed.

2. Audience: a prospective buyer of encyclopedias
    a. You should buy these encyclopedias because they are designed especially for students and are written in a more popular, fun-to-read style than its major competitors' encyclopedias.
    b. You should buy these encyclopedias because then I will win my company's sales award and my wife and I will win a free trip to Hawaii.

3. Audience: a group of people who oppose the present grading system on the grounds that it is too competitive
    a. We should keep the present grading system because it prepares people for the competitive world of business.
    b. We should keep the present grading system because it tells students there are certain standards of excellence that must be met if individuals are to reach their full potential.

FINDING AUDIENCE-BASED REASONS: ASKING QUESTIONS ABOUT YOUR AUDIENCE

As the above exercise makes clear, reasons are most persuasive when linked to the audience's values. This principle seems simple enough, yet it is an easy one to forget. Among the most common complaints employers have about job candidates during interviews is candidates' tendency to emphasize what the company can do for the candidate instead of what the candidate can do for the company. Job search experts agree that the best way to prepare for a job interview is to study everything you can about the company in order to relate your skills to the company's problems and needs. The same advice applies to the writers of arguments.

To find out all you can about your audience, we recommend that you ask yourself, early in the writing process, a series of questions that can be grouped into five categories:

1. Who is your audience? Are you writing directly to a decision maker, such as a proposal to a board of directors to start a new research and development project in your company? Or are you writing to a wider, more inclusive audience, such as the general readership of a newspaper or magazine? Most formal arguments in college are written to general audiences, but "case" assignments or arguments written for specific occasions in your life (a letter to the financial aid office arguing for a student loan) can give you practice at writing to specific decision makers.

2. How much does your audience know or care about your issue? Are they currently part of the conversation or do they need quite a bit of background? If you are writing to specific decision makers (for example, the administration at your college about restructuring the intramural program), are they currently aware of the issue and do they care about it? If not, you may need to "shock" them into seeing the problem.

3. What is your audience's current attitude toward your issue? Is your audience opposed to your position on the issue or are they neutral? If neutral, are they open-minded? What other points of view besides your own will your audience be weighing?

4. What weaknesses will your audience find in your own argument? Why might they oppose your view on this issue? What aspects of your position will they find threatening?

5. Finally, what values, beliefs, or assumptions about the world do you and your audience share? Despite differences of view on this issue, where can you find common links with your audience?

Analyzing Your Audience

In answering these questions, you will need to consider your audience closely. If you are writing to specific decision makers, you will have the advantage of knowing precisely who your audience is. If you are writing to a general audience, however, you will have readers with many different points of view. We recommend in this case that you explore closely the views of those who are most likely to oppose your position. If you know as much as possible about your opponents' views, you will be better prepared to direct your argument to neutral audiences, who also will be weighing the views of those who oppose you. In addition, examining opposing views early in the writing process will help you formulate your argument, maybe even modify your claim. An open-minded examination of opposing views is a way of carrying on a heuristic dialogue (see Chapter 1) with the opposition; it is a strategy for discovery.

To analyze opposing views, you should consider both the *logos* of opposing arguments and the unstated forces that have helped shape your opponents' values and beliefs. We like to examine opposing views from the following five perspectives:

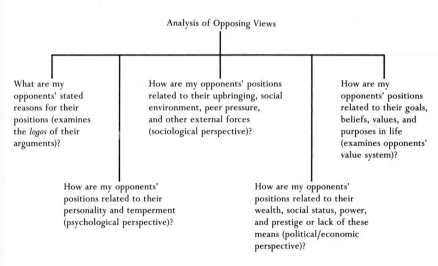

Analysis of Opposing Views

What are my opponents' stated reasons for their positions (examines the *logos* of their arguments)?

How are my opponents' positions related to their upbringing, social environment, peer pressure, and other external forces (sociological perspective)?

How are my opponents' positions related to their goals, beliefs, values, and purposes in life (examines opponents' value system)?

How are my opponents' positions related to their personality and temperment (psychological perspective)?

How are my opponents' positions related to their wealth, social status, power, and prestige or lack of these means (political/economic perspective)?

For example, suppose that you support universal mandatory testing for the AIDS virus. Your audience will be general readers ranging from people who already accept your view to those who deeply oppose it. You intend to aim your argument at those neutral people in the middle, who will also be weighing opposing views. What assumptions could you make about these opponents? Figure 8–1 shows how one student explored this question by making an idea-map adapted from the five perspectives listed above.

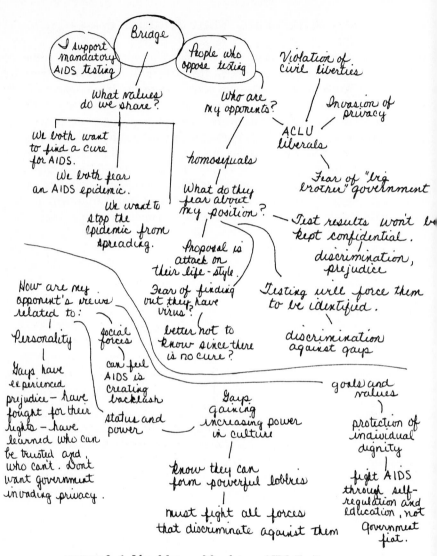

FIGURE 8-1. Idea-Map on Mandatory AIDS Testing

In his map, this writer first explored some of the values he believes he shares with his audience. Under the heading "bridge," he decides that both he and his opponents want to find a cure for AIDS, are afraid of an epidemic, and want to stop the epidemic from spreading. He hopes eventually to construct an argument that ties into these common values. Next he decides that his opponents fall mainly into two groups: homosexuals and "liberals," whom he associates with the ACLU (American Civil Liberties Union). He decides to ask first what each of these groups probably fears about his position. Homosexuals fear finding out whether they have the disease, fear being identified as homosexuals and thus discriminated against, and so forth. Liberals, on the other hand, fear loss of civil liberties. Finally, at the bottom of the map the writer explores how opponents' views might be related to personality, social forces, social status, and goals or values. He comes to the important realization that AIDS is producing a backlash against homosexuals, who recently have made important strides toward gaining acceptance in American society. AIDS testing may be seen as part of that backlash. He is now ready to use this exploration to begin planning out an argumentative strategy.

The next problem this writer must pose, then, is how to develop an argumentative strategy that reduces his audience's fears and uses reasons linked to his audience's values. This writer's thinking might go something like this:

PROBLEM: How can I create an argument rooted in shared values?

POSSIBLE SOLUTIONS: I can try to reduce the audience's fear that mandatory AIDS testing implies a criticism of gay people. I could show my acceptance of gays and my sympathy for victims of AIDS. I could make sure my plan assured confidentiality. I must make it clear that my concern is stopping the spread of the disease and that this concern is shared by the gay community.

PROBLEM: How can I reduce fear that mandatory AIDS testing violates civil liberties?

POSSIBLE SOLUTIONS: I must show that the "enemy" here is the AIDS virus and not victims of the disease. Also, I might cite precedents for how we fight other infectious diseases. For example, many states require marriage license applicants to take a VD test, and on numerous occasions communities have imposed quarantines to halt the spread of epidemics. I could also argue that the rights of the gay community to be free from this disease outweigh individual rights to privacy, especially when confidentiality is assured.

The preceding example shows how a writer's focus on audience can shape the actual invention of the argument.

FOR CLASS DISCUSSION
Working individually or in small groups, make an idea-map similar to Figure 8–1 for one of the following arguments. Then, based on your exploration of audience, plan out an argumentative strategy rooted in audience-based reasons. Follow the thinking process used by the writer of the mandatory AIDS argument: (1) state several problems that the writer must

solve to reach the audience and (2) develop possible solutions to those problems.

1. An argument opposing busing for school integration: Aim the argument at people who believe in the value of integration.
2. An argument limiting the number of terms that can be served by members of Congress: Aim the argument at supporters of an influential incumbent who would no longer be eligible to hold office.
3. An argument supporting a one-dollar-per-gallon increase in gasoline taxes as an energy conservation measure: Aim your argument at business leaders who oppose the tax on the grounds that it will raise the cost of consumer goods.
4. An argument supporting the legalization of cocaine: Aim your argument at readers of *Reader's Digest*, a conservative magazine that supports the current war on drugs.

A GENERAL HEURISTIC FOR DISCOVERING AUDIENCE-BASED REASONS

When you set out to write an argument, you will often have a claim that expresses your position on the issue. But how do you go about thinking of reasons to support it?

The ways we have suggested so far work well for many writers— engaging in discussion with opponents, playing the believing and doubting game, brainstorming for because clauses, and so forth. There is another way, however, to search for ideas—heuristics. Heuristics are structured processes of discovery. They grow out of the assumption that certain patterns of thought recur in many different situations and that learning these patterns gives the writer a powerful strategy for generating ideas and information relevant to a particular case. The heuristic that we will develop here is particularly effective at helping you find audience-based reasons. We introduced you to it briefly in Chapter 3, where we called it the "three approaches" heuristic.

This heuristic is particularly valuable when you are writing proposal or "should" arguments of the kind "We should/should not do X." The heuristic works by focusing your attention sequentially on three different approaches to developing an argument:

1. An "argument from principle" in which you argue that doing X is right (wrong) according to some value, assumption, definition, or belief that you share with your audience. (This strategy is also called by various other names, such as a "definitional strategy" or an "argument from genus or category.")

2. An "argument from consequence" in which you argue that doing X is right (wrong) because doing X will lead to consequences that you and your audience believe are good (bad).

3. An "argument from resemblance" in which you argue that doing X is right (wrong) because doing X is like doing Y, which you and your audience agree is right (wrong).

An Illustration of the Heuristic

In a recent college course, the instructor asked students whether they would report a classmate for plagiarizing a paper. To the instructor's dismay, the majority of students said they would not. The issue question at stake is this: "Should a student report a classmate who plagiarizes an essay?" The teacher wanted to argue "yes," whereas her students argued "no." How could the teacher support her claim?

An argument from principle. One strategy she could use is to argue as follows: "A student should report a classmate for plagiarizing a paper because plagiarism is fraud." We call this an "argument from principle" because it is based on the assumption that the audience opposes fraud as a kind of unchanging rule or law—in short, that it opposes fraud on principle. Such an argument is sometimes also called an "argument from definition or category" because it places the term X (plagiarizing a paper) inside the class or category Y (fraud).

ARGUMENT FROM PRINCIPLE

To think of ideas with this strategy, you conduct the following kind of search:

We should (should not) do X because X is _____ .

Try to fill in the blank with an appropriate adjective or noun (*good, just, ethical, criminal, ugly, violent, peaceful, wrong, inflationary, healing; an act of kindness, terrorism, murder, true art, political suicide,* and so forth). The point is to try to fill in the blank with a noun or adjective that appeals in some way to your audience's values. Your goal is to show that X belongs to the chosen class or category.

In saying that plagiarism is fraud, the teacher assumes that students would report classmates for other kinds of fraud (for example, for counterfeiting a signature on a check, for entering the university's computer system to alter grades, and so forth). In other words, she knows that the term *fraud* has force on the audience because most people will agree that instances of fraud should be reported. Her task is to define *fraud* and show how plagiarism fits that definition. She could show that fraud is an act of deception to obtain a benefit that doesn't rightly belong to a person. She could then argue that plagiarism is such an act in that it uses deception to procure the benefits of a grade that the plagiarizer has not earned. Although the person whose work is plagiarized may not be directly damaged, the reputation and stature of the university is damaged whenever it grants credentials that have been fraudulently earned. The degree earned by a plagiarizer is fraudulent. Although convincing students that plagiarism is fraud won't guarantee that students will report it, it does make such whistle blowing more likely by putting plagiarism inside the class of seriously bad things.

An argument from consequence. Besides arguing from principle, the teacher could argue from consequence: "A student should report a classmate for plagiarizing a paper because the consequences of plagiarism are bad for everyone concerned." This is a consequence argument (X produces these consequences) based on the warrant that these consequences are bad; it shows first that X causes Y and then that Y is bad.

ARGUMENT FROM CONSEQUENCE

To think of reasons using this strategy, conduct the following kind of search:

We should (should not) do X because X leads to these consequences:

—————— , —————— , —————— , —————— .

Then think of consequences that your audience will agree are good or bad, as your argument requires.

Using this strategy, the teacher now focuses on the ill effects that plagiarism can have. She might argue that plagiarism raises the grading curve to the disadvantage of honest students or that it can lead to ill-trained people getting into critical professions. How would you like to undergo brain surgery, she might ask, from someone who cheated her way through medical school? She might argue that acceptance of plagiarism leads to acceptance of moral sloppiness throughout the society — acceptance of tax dodging, of shoddy workmanship, of taking small "loans" from the company till. She might even argue that plagiarism hurts the person who plagiarizes by preventing that person from developing needed skills for later success in life. Finally, she would probably want to argue at some point that reporting plagiarism cases will prevent or limit plagiarism. All these examples would be arguments from consequence.

An argument from resemblance. But there is a third strategy the teacher might employ. She could say, "You should report someone for plagiarizing an essay just as you would report someone for submitting someone else's art project in an art class." Although this argument looks similar to saying that "plagiarism is fraud," it actually represents a different kind of reasoning, what we call reasoning from resemblance or analogy.

In using this strategy, the teacher hopes that her audience will see that if someone else's painting is a piece of property, then someone else's essay is a piece of property also. This recognition in turn will help students see plagiarism as theft, because we typically associate theft with property. The teacher will have to show how an essay represents the same kind of artistic craft as a painting and how cheating works the same way in both art and writing.

ARGUMENT FROM RESEMBLANCE

To think of reasons with this strategy, make the following kind of search:

We should (should not) do X because doing X is like _____.

Then think of analogies or precedents that are similar to doing X but that currently have more force on your audience. Your goal is then to transfer to X the audience's attitude toward the precedent or analogy.

Arguing from analogy in this way is among the most persuasive yet tricky of all argumentative strategies. It is the subject of Chapter 13, which treats resemblance arguments in depth.

These three strategies, then—imagining your argument from the perspectives of principle, consequence, and resemblance—can be useful ways to find reasons for your arguments. The heuristic helps you generate a variety of potential reasons to support your argument; in creating reasons, of course, you will be guided by your knowledge of your audience, trying to create reasons that appeal to their values and beliefs.

When you use the above heuristic for generating ideas, you shouldn't feel you are limited to reasons derived from the heuristic. You can discover all kinds of excellent reasons for your arguments that don't fit neatly into one of the three claim types. Although a reason can often be reworded so that it more clearly fits a strategy, getting the reasons to match the strategies isn't the purpose of the heuristic at all. Rather, its purpose is to stimulate your thinking. It is something to fall back on when your mind gets stuck. With this understanding in mind, you are now ready to try your hand at using the heuristic.

FOR CLASS DISCUSSION

1. Working individually or in small groups, use the strategies of principle, consequence, and resemblance to think of because clauses to support each of the following claims. Try to have at least one because clause from each of the strategies, but generate as many reasons as possible. Don't worry about whether any individual reason exactly fits the strategy. Again, the purpose is to stimulate thinking, not to fill in slots.

   EXAMPLE:

   Claim: Pit bulls make bad pets

   Principle: because they are vicious.

   Consequence: because owning a pit bull leads to conflicts with neighbors.

   Resemblance: because owning a pit bull is a little like having a shell-shocked friend—the friend is wonderful most of the time, but you never know when some event will turn him violent.

   a. The United States should pass a constitutional amendment forbidding abortion
      Principle: because abortion is _____.
      Consequence: because abortion will have the consequences of

      _____, _____, _____.

      Resemblance: because aborting a fetus is like _____.
   b. Marijuana should be legalized.
   c. Libraries should lend movie videocassettes as well as books.
   d. Couples should live together before getting married.
   e. The United States should end its energy dependence on other nations.

   f.-j. Repeat the above exercise, taking a different position on each issue. You might try beginning with the claim "Pit bulls make good pets."

2. Again working individually or in small groups, use the principle/consequence/resemblance heuristic to explore arguments on both sides of the following issues.
   a. Should spanking be made illegal?
   b. Has affirmative action been good or bad for the nation?
   c. Should the United States pass a law mandating universal national

service for all American citizens following graduation from high school or college? (*Universal national service* means being drafted into the military or some alternative means of serving the country.)
 d. Should high schools pass out free contraceptives?
 e. Would it be better to grade college writing classes on the basis of effort rather than performance?

CONCLUSION

This chapter has focused on the need to root one's arguments in the values, beliefs, or assumptions of the audience. Whenever possible, a writer should create reasons with warrants already acceptable to the audience. On many occasions, however, warrants themselves will need extensive backing before an audience will accept them. The category "backing" in Toulmin's schema (if you recall from Chapter 5, backing is the argument needed to support the warrant) shows Toulmin's awareness that any reasonable argument must proceed from agreements shared by the writer and the audience.

The next chapter turns to the concepts of *ethos* and *pathos* as means of persuasion that work together with *logos* to move an audience.

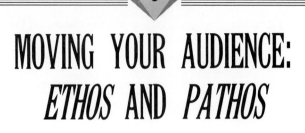

MOVING YOUR AUDIENCE:
ETHOS AND *PATHOS*

The previous chapter focuses on audience-based reasons as a means of moving an audience. In this chapter we turn to the power of *ethos* (the appeal to credibility) and of *pathos* (the appeal to emotions) as further means of enhancing the rhetorical effectiveness of your arguments.

AN OVERVIEW OF
ETHOS AND *PATHOS*

From the outset, you shouldn't think of the three kinds of appeals as, say, separate ingredients in a cake. Thus, you wouldn't say something like "This argument has enough *logos*; now you need to add some *ethos* and *pathos*." It may be helpful, however, to think of these terms as a series of lenses through which you filter and transform your ideas. Thus, if you intensify the *pathos* lens (say, by using more concrete language or vivid examples), the resulting image will appeal more strongly to the audience's emotions. If you change the *ethos* lens (say, by adopting a different tone toward your audience), the projected image of you as a person is subtly altered. If you intensify the *logos* lens (by adding, say, more data for evidence), you draw the reader's attention to the logical appeal of the argument. *Logos*, *ethos*, and *pathos* all work together to create an impact on the reader. The three terms give us a common language to talk about the forces that create that impact.

Consider, for example, the variable effects of the following arguments, all having roughly the same logical appeal:

1. People should adopt a vegetarian diet because only through vegetarianism can we prevent the cruelty to animals that results from factory farming.

2. I hope you enjoyed your fried chicken this evening. You know, of course, how much that chicken suffered just so you could have a tender and juicy meal. Commercial growers cram the chickens so tightly together into cages that they have to have their beaks cut off to keep them from pecking each others' eyes out. The only way to end the torture is to adopt a vegetarian diet.

3. People who eat meat are no better than sadists who torture other sentient creatures in order to enhance their own pleasure. Unless you enjoy sadistic tyranny over others, you have only one choice: Become a vegetarian.

4. People committed to justice might consider the extent to which our love of eating meat requires the agony of animals. A visit to a modern chicken factory — where chickens live their entire lives in tiny darkened coops without room to spread their wings — might raise doubts about our right to inflict such suffering on sentient creatures. Indeed, such a visit might persuade us that vegetarianism is a more just alternative.

Each argument has roughly the same logical core:

Claim:	People should adopt a vegetarian diet.
Stated Reason:	Vegetarianism is the only way to end the suffering of animals caused by factory farming.
Grounds:	the evidence of suffering in commercial chicken farms, where chickens peck each others' eyes out; other evidence of animal suffering in factory farms; evidence that only widespread adoption of vegetarianism will end factory farming
Warrant:	If we have an alternative to inflicting suffering on animals, we should adopt it.

But the impact of each argument on audiences varies. The difference between arguments 1 and 2, most of our students report, is the emotional power of 2. Whereas argument 1 refers only to the abstraction "cruelty to animals," argument 2 paints a vivid picture of chickens with their beaks cut off to prevent their pecking each other blind. Argument 2 makes a stronger appeal to *pathos* (not necessarily a stronger argument) by stirring feelings —hitting the heart, as it were, as well as the head.

The difference between arguments 1 and 3 concerns both *ethos* and *pathos.* Argument 3 appeals to the emotions through such highly charged words as "torture," "sadist," and "tyranny." But argument 3 also draws attention to its writer, and most of our students report not liking that writer very much. His stance is self-righteous and insulting; he prefers shocking his audience by accusing them of sadism rather than by showing empathy for their values. We are not apt to trust such a writer. In contrast, the writer of argument 4 establishes a more positive *ethos.* He establishes rapport with his audience by assuming they are committed to justice and by qualifying his argument with conditional terms such as "might" and "perhaps." He also invites sympathy for his problem — an appeal to *pathos* — by offering a specific description of chickens crammed into tiny coops.

Which of these arguments is best? They all have appropriate uses. Arguments 1 and 4 seem aimed at receptive audiences reasonably open to exploration of the issue, while arguments 2 and 3 seem designed to shock complacent audiences or to rally a group of True Believers. Even argument 3, which borders on being so abusive that it would be ineffective in most instances, might work as a rallying speech at a convention of animal liberation activists.

Our point thus far is that *logos, ethos,* and *pathos* are different aspects of the same whole, different lenses for mixing and coloring the light you project upon the screen. Every choice you make as a writer affects in some way each of the three appeals. The rest of this chapter examines these choices in more detail.

ETHOS: THE APPEAL TO CREDIBILITY

Long ago the classical rhetoricians of Greece and Rome recognized that an argument would be more persuasive if the audience trusted the speaker. Aristotle argued that such trust is created within the speech itself rather than being brought to the speech by the prior reputation of the speaker. In the speaker's manner and delivery, in his tone of voice, in his choice of words, in his arrangement of reasons, in his fairness and sympathy toward opposing views, and in other subtler ways, a speaker could project the image of being a fair-minded, trustworthy person. Aristotle called the impact of the writer's credibility the appeal from *ethos.*

HOW DOES A WRITER
CREATE *ETHOS?*

How does a writer create credibility? We will suggest three ways.

1. Create Credibility by Being Knowledgeable about Your Issue

The first way to gain credibility is to *be* credible; that is, to argue from a strong base of knowledge, to have at hand the examples, personal experiences, statistics, and other empirical data needed to make a sound case. If you have done your homework (people who "do their homework" are highly respected in business, government, and academia) you will command the attention of most audiences.

2. Create Credibility by Demonstrating Fairness

Besides being knowledgeable about your issue, you need to demonstrate fairness and courtesy to opposing views. In Chapter 1, the members of the well-functioning committee differed from the writer of the crank letter by showing respect rather than contempt for opposing views. Because true argument can occur only where persons may reasonably disagree, your *ethos* will be strengthened if you demonstrate that you understand and empathize with other points of view. Of course, there are times when it's effective to scorn an opposing view, but these times are rare, and they occur mainly when you are addressing an audience predisposed toward your position. As a general rule, demonstrating empathy to opposing views is the best strategy.

3. Create Credibility by Building a Bridge to Your Audience

A third means of establishing credibility—building a bridge to your audience—has been treated at length in the previous chapter in our discussion of audience-based reasons. By grounding your argument in shared values and assumptions, you demonstrate your good will and enhance your image as a trustworthy person.

ETHOS AND THE PLACEMENT OF YOUR THESIS: HOW AN ARGUMENT'S ORGANIZATION CAN AFFECT THE WRITER'S IMAGE

To demonstrate the subtlety of *ethos* as a concept, we turn now to a question often asked in our argument classes: "Where should I place my thesis? Should I put it in the introduction so that I tell my readers up front where I stand on an issue, or should I wait until later in the paper to reveal where I stand?" Although this may seem like a small technical matter, the placement of the thesis can profoundly affect an audience's perception of your *ethos*. The standard way of conducting an argument is to state your own position near the beginning of your essay in order to separate your own views from those of the opposition and then to summarize and refute the opposing views.

Rhetorically, however, it is not always advantageous to tell your readers where you stand at the start of your argument or to separate yourself so definitively from your opposition. Sometimes it is to your advantage to keep the issue open, delaying the revelation of your own position until the middle or end of the essay. The effect of an up-front thesis—what we might call the "standard form"—is quite different from that of a delayed thesis. Let's explore this difference in more detail.

Standard Form Arguments

Figure 9–1 shows the format of a typical "standard form" argument—the form that results in what we have called a "self-announcing" structure. Like a tract home or a fast-food restaurant, a standard form argument usually gets the job done, but it does not work well in all environments and for all purposes. Teachers often ask students to write their first arguments in standard form as a way of learning and practicing the basic moves of argumentation. Later, students can experiment with variations on standard form to see the different effects various versions of an argument can have on audiences.

As Figure 9–1 shows, a standard form argument usually begins with an attention grabber, which may be a startling statistic, a dramatic fact, or a real or hypothetical story or example. The attention grabber is usually followed by an explanation of the issue, which in turn is followed by the writer's thesis statement—often the last sentence of the introduction. Sometimes the writer also needs to provide background information (defi-

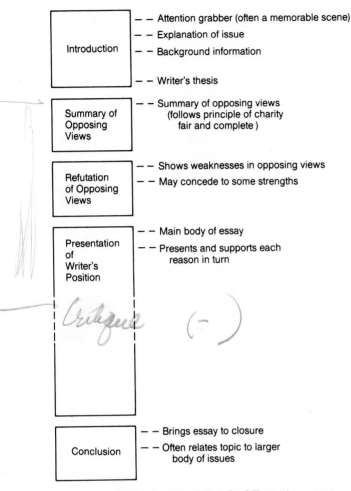

FIGURE 9-1. Diagram of Standard Form Argument

nitions of key terms, historical information about the origins of the issue, explanations of technical matters, and so forth) before presenting the thesis.

The next major part of a typical standard form argument is a summary and refutation of opposing views. If the opposing argument consists of several parts, the writer has two options for organizing this section: The writer can summarize all of the opposing argument before moving to the refutation, or he or she can summarize and refute one part at a time.

After refuting opposing views, the writer proceeds to present his own position and support it. This is usually the longest part of the argument. Frequently the writer will devote a section, often of several paragraphs or more, to the development of each reason.

Finally, the conclusion of a standard form argument serves to bring the whole argument into focus, thus giving the essay a sense of closure.

The standard form, as we have described it here, has several advantages for newcomers to the writing of arguments. For example, the standard form requires you to summarize opposing views and then to refute them, a challenging conceptual skill well worth practicing. Similarly, there are also conceptual advantages to the standard form's requirement that you put your thesis statement into your introduction. By clearly formulating a thesis statement with because clauses, you can see the whole of your argument in miniature. In putting your thesis up front, you have a guide throughout the drafting process. The thesis helps remind you of the purpose, context, and shape of your evolving essay. As your argument becomes increasingly clarified during the drafting process, you can revise your thesis statement to reflect your new intentions.

However, there are many times when the standard form doesn't allow you the subtlety and flexibility necessary to establish an appropriate *ethos*. Let's look now at the differing effect of a delayed thesis argument.

Delayed Thesis Arguments

To illustrate the differences between a standard form and a delayed thesis argument, we have taken a delayed thesis argument by nationally known columnist Ellen Goodman and rewritten it into the standard form. The article appeared shortly after the nation was shocked by a brutal gang rape in New Bedford, Massachusetts, in which a woman was raped on a pool table by patrons of a local bar. We would like you to read both versions and then answer the class discussion exercises that follow.

ELLEN GOODMAN'S ORIGINAL VERSION
(DELAYED THESIS)

Just a couple of months before the pool-table gang rape in New Bedford,   1
Mass., *Hustler* magazine printed a photo feature that reads like a blueprint for the actual crime. There were just two differences between *Hustler* and real life. In *Hustler*, the woman enjoyed it. In real life, the woman charged rape.

There is no evidence that the four men charged with this crime had   2
actually read the magazine. Nor is there evidence that the spectators who yelled encouragement for two hours had held previous ringside seats at pornographic events. But there is a growing sense that the violent pornography being peddled in this country helps to create an atmosphere in which such events occur.

As recently as last month, a study done by two University of Wisconsin 3
researchers suggested that even "normal" men, prescreened college students, were changed by their exposure to violent pornography. After just ten
hours of viewing, reported researcher Edward Donnerstein, "the men were
less likely to convict in a rape trial, less likely to see injury to a victim, more
likely to see the victim as responsible." Pornography may not cause rape
directly, he said, "but it maintains a lot of very callous attitudes. It justifies
aggression. It even says you are doing a favor to the victim."

If we can prove that pornography is harmful, then shouldn't the victims 4
have legal rights? This, in any case, is the theory behind a city ordinance that
recently passed the Minneapolis City Council. Vetoed by the mayor last week,
it is likely to be back before the Council for an overriding vote, likely to
appear in other cities, other towns. What is unique about the Minneapolis
approach is that for the first time it attacks pornography, not because of
nudity or sexual explicitness, but because it degrades and harms women. It
opposes pornography on the basis of sex discrimination.

University of Minnesota Law Professor Catherine MacKinnon, who co- 5
authored the ordinance with feminist writer Andrea Dworkin, says that they
chose this tactic because they believe that pornography is central to "creating
and maintaining the inequality of the sexes. . . . Just being a woman means
you are injured by pornography."

They defined pornography carefully as, "the sexually explicit subordina- 6
tion of women, graphically depicted, whether in pictures or in words." To fit
their legal definition it must also include one of nine conditions that show this
subordination, like presenting women who "experience sexual pleasure in
being raped or . . . mutilated. . . ." Under this law, it would be possible
for a pool-table rape victim to sue *Husler*. It would be possible for a woman to
sue if she were forced to act in a pornographic movie. Indeed, since the law
describes pornography as oppressive to all women, it would be possible for
any woman to sue those who traffic in the stuff for violating her civil rights.

In many ways, the Minneapolis ordinance is an appealing attack on an 7
appalling problem. The authors have tried to resolve a long and bubbling
conflict among those who have both a deep aversion to pornography and a
deep loyalty to the value of free speech. "To date," says Professor MacKinnon, "people have identified the pornographer's freedom with everybody's
freedom. But we're saying that the freedom of the pornographer is the
subordination of women. It means one has to take a side."

But the sides are not quite as clear as Professor MacKinnon describes 8
them. Nor is the ordinance.

Even if we accept the argument that pornography is harmful to women — 9
and I do — then we must also recognize that anti-Semitic literature is harmful
to Jews and racist literature is harmful to blacks. For that matter, Marxist
literature may be harmful to government policy. It isn't just women versus

pornographers. If women win the right to sue publishers and producers, then so could Jews, blacks, and a long list of people who may be able to prove they have been harmed by books, movies, speeches or even records. The Manson murders, you may recall, were reportedly inspired by the Beatles.

We might prefer a library or book store or lecture hall without Mein 10 Kampf or the Grand Whoever of the Ku Klux Klan. But a growing list of harmful expressions would inevitably strangle freedom of speech.

This ordinance was carefully written to avoid problems of banning and 11 prior restraint, but the right of any woman to claim damages from pornography is just too broad. It seems destined to lead to censorship.

What the Minneapolis City Council has before it is a very attractive theory. 12 What MacKinnon and Dworkin have written is a very persuasive and useful definition of pornography. But they haven't yet resolved the conflict between the harm of pornography and the value of free speech. In its present form, this is still a shaky piece of law.

Source: Ellen Goodman, "Minneapolis Pornography Ordinance," *Boston Globe*, 1985.

OUR REWRITE OF THE SAME ARGUMENT INTO STANDARD FORM

Just a couple of months before the pool-table gang rape in New Bedford, 1 Mass., *Hustler* magazine printed a photo feature that reads like a blueprint for the actual crime. There were just two differences between *Hustler* and real life. In *Hustler*, the woman enjoyed it. In real life, the woman charged rape. Of course, there is no evidence that the four men charged with this crime had actually read the magazine. Nor is there evidence that the spectators who yelled encouragement for two hours had held previous ringside seats at pornographic events. But there is a growing sense that the violent pornography being peddled in this country helps to create an atmosphere in which such events occur. One city is taking a unique approach to attack this problem. An ordinance recently passed by the Minneapolis City Council outlaws pornography not because it contains nudity or sexually explicit acts, but because it degrades and harms women. Unfortunately, despite the proponents' good intentions, the Minneapolis ordinance is a bad law because it has potentially dangerous consequences.

Let's begin by looking at the opposing view. The proponents of the 2 Minneapolis City Ordinance argue that pornography should be made illegal because it degrades and humiliates women. To show that it degrades women, they cite a recent study done by two University of Wisconsin researchers that suggests that even "normal" men (prescreened college students) are changed by their exposure to violent pornography. After just ten hours of viewing, reported researcher Edward Donnerstein, "the men were less likely to convict in a rape trial, less likely to see injury to a victim, more likely to see the victim as responsible." Pornography may not cause rape directly, he said, "but it maintains a lot of very callous attitudes. It justifies aggression. It even says you are doing a favor to the victim."

The core of their argument runs as follows: "If something degrades and   3
humiliates women, then it discriminates against women. Pornography degrades and humiliates women. Therefore, pornography discriminates against women." Since empirical evidence is mounting that pornography indeed degrades and humiliates women, pornography, their argument goes, is a form of sex discrimination. University of Minnesota Law Professor Catherine MacKinnon, who co-authored the ordinance with feminist writer Andrea Dworkin, says that they chose to focus on pornography as a form of discrimination because they believe that pornography is central to "creating and maintaining the inequality of the sexes. . . . Just being a woman means you are injured by pornography." They defined pornography carefully as "the sexually explicit subordination of women, graphically depicted, whether in pictures or in words." To fit their legal definition it must also include one of nine conditions that show this subordination, like presenting women who "experience sexual pleasure in being raped or . . . mutilated. . . ." Under this law it would be possible for a woman to sue if she were forced to act in a pornographic movie. Indeed, since the law describes pornography as oppressive to all women, it would be possible for any woman to sue those who traffic in the stuff for violating her civil rights.

In many ways, the Minneapolis ordinance is an appealing solution to an   4
appalling problem. The authors have tried to resolve a long and bubbling conflict among those who have both a deep aversion to pornography and a deep loyalty to the value of free speech. "To date," says Professor MacKinnon, "people have identified the pornographer's freedom with everybody's freedom. But we're saying that the freedom of the pornographer is the subordination of women. It means one has to take a side."

One must concede that the argument is attractive. It seems to give liberal   5
thinkers a way of getting around the problem of free speech. But the reasoning behind the ordinance is flawed because its acceptance could lead to the suppression of a wide range of ideas. Even if we accept the argument that pornography is harmful to women — and I do — then we must also recognize that anti-Semitic literature is harmful to Jews and racist literature is harmful to blacks. For that matter, Marxist literature may be harmful to government policy. It isn't just women versus pornographers. If women win the right to sue publishers and producers, then so could Jews, blacks, and a long list of people who may be able to prove they have been harmed by books, movies, speeches or even records. The Manson murders, you may recall, were reportedly inspired by the Beatles.

We might prefer a library or book store or lecture hall without Mein   6
Kampf or the Grand Whoever of the Ku Klux Klan. But a growing list of
harmful expressions would inevitably strangle freedom of speech. The ordinance was carefully written to avoid problems of banning and prior restraint,
but the right of any woman to claim damages from pornography is just too
broad. It seems destined to lead to censorship. What the Minneapolis City
Council has before it is a very attractive theory. What MacKinnon and
Dworkin have written is a very persuasive and useful definition of pornography. But they haven't yet resolved the conflict between the harm of pornography and the value of free speech. In its present form, this is still a shaky piece
of law.

FOR CLASS DISCUSSION

The following questions are based on Ellen Goodman's pornography essay,
which you have just read. Using whichever version of the essay is most
helpful, prepare answers to the questions. Work either as individuals or in
small groups.

1. In one or two sentences, summarize the argument supporting the
   Minneapolis ordinance.
2. In one or two sentences, summarize Goodman's own argument.
3. Which version of the essay, 1 or 2, did you find most useful in
   answering the preceding two questions?
4. Which version of the essay do you think is most effective? Why?

If you are like our own students, two-thirds of you will prefer Goodman's original version over the standard form version. However, a large
majority of our students reported that the standard form version was more
useful for helping them answer the above questions. By placing the writer's
thesis statement at the end of the introduction ("Unfortunately, despite the
proponents' good intentions, the Minneapolis ordinance is a bad law because it has potentially dangerous consequences"), the standard form version gives you up front a clear summary of the writer's position (question
2). Similarly, by setting off the Minneapolis ordinance as the opposition and
by supplying the syllogistic core of its supporting argument, the standard
form version makes it easier to find and summarize the opposing view.

But even though the argument of the standard form version can be
grasped more quickly, the majority of readers prefer Goodman's original
version. Why is this?

What most people point to is the greater sense of complexity and surprise
in the original version, a sense that comes largely from a delay in presenting

the writer's own position. Whereas in the standard form version the Minneapolis ordinance is the "opposition," in the original version the ordinance isn't so identified until later, creating more reader sympathy for its argument. Because we aren't told from the start that the author will eventually oppose this ordinance, we are led to examine it more open-mindedly, not knowing for sure what judgment will finally emerge. To the extent that she sympathizes with feminist beliefs, Ellen Goodman does not wish to distance herself from those who see pornography as a violation of women's rights. Thus, in her original version the author's sympathy for the Minneapolis ordinance seems real, so real that we are surprised in the last third of the essay when she finally rejects the ordinance. By not laying out her own position at the beginning — as the standard form requires — Goodman lets us enter her own struggle to think through these issues, and her final rejection of the ordinance is made all the more powerful by her obvious sympathy for what the writers of the ordinance are proposing. Thus Goodman's decision about the arrangement of parts turns out to be a decision about how we as audience will feel about both her and her argument, choices that relate to the sense of self that she wishes to project.

It seems clear, then, that a writer's decision about when to reveal an essay's thesis and when to separate the writer's view from the opposition's has considerable importance. If the thesis is revealed early, the writer comes across as more hard-nosed, more sure of her position, more confident about how to divide the ground into friendly and hostile camps, more in control. If the thesis is delayed, the issues are made to seem more complex, the reader's sympathy for the opposition is often increased, and the writer's struggle for clarity is highlighted. Paradoxically, though, such an essay is sometimes more persuasive to opponents because they feel their own position has been generously listened to. It is obvious that the interplay between *pathos* and *ethos* is complex. By delaying her thesis, Goodman projects an image of herself (*ethos*) as sympathetic to feminism and troubled by her own position. This image of herself increases the reader's sympathy (*pathos*) for her dilemma and thus strengthens her argument.

PATHOS: THE APPEAL TO EMOTIONS

At the height of the protest movement against the Vietnam War, a group of protesters "napalmed" a puppy by dousing it with gasoline and setting it on fire. All over the country Americans were outraged by the demonstration. Letters began pouring in to local newspapers protesting the cruel killing of the puppy. The protesters responded as follows: "Why are you outraged by the napalming of a single puppy when you are not outraged by the daily napalming of human babies in Vietnam?"

The protesters' argument depended on *pathos*. *Logos*-centered arguments, the protesters felt, numbed the mind to human suffering. The napalming of the puppy gave presence to the reality of suffering; it reawakened feeling, creating in Americans a gut-level revulsion that, according to protesters, should have been felt all along for the war.

Of course, the napalmed puppy was a real-life event, part of a street theater argument, not a written essay. But the same strategy is often used in written arguments. Anti-abortion arguers use it whenever they present graphic descriptions of the dismembering of a fetus, tiny limb by limb, during the abortion process; proponents of euthanasia use it when they describe the prolonged suffering of a terminally ill patient hooked hopelessly to machines. And students use it when they argue with a professor that their grade should be raised from a C to a B lest the student lose his scholarship and have to return to poverty, shattering the dreams of his dear old grandmother who has vowed not to die until she can witness the first member of her family graduate from college.

Are such appeals to emotion legitimate? Our answer is "yes" if the emotional appeals clarify an issue rather than cloud it. Emotional appeals have an important place in argument because we can know with our hearts as well as with our minds. When used effectively, appeals to emotion help us clarify an issue by revealing its fullest human meaning. That is why arguments are often improved through the use of sensory detail that allows us to "see" the reality of a problem or through stories that make specific cases and instances come alive.

Appeals to emotion become illegitimate, we believe, when they serve to cloud issues rather than to clarify them. The student's argument for a grade of B is, we feel, an illegitimate appeal to emotion. We would argue that a student's grade in a course should be based on his or her performance in the course, not on the student's need. The image of the dear old grandmother postponing death until her grandson's graduation may provide a legitimate motive for the student to study harder, but not for the professor to change a grade. On the other hand, the same image would be both appropriate and effective in a letter from the student's parents urging him to study harder.

HOW DOES A WRITER CREATE *PATHOS*?

How does a writer create emotional appeals in an essay? We will suggest four ways: through concrete language; through examples and illustrations; through word choice, metaphors, and analogies; and through appeals to audience values.

1. Appeal to Emotions by Using Concrete Language

In writing courses, teachers often try to help students develop "voice" or "style." In general, these terms refer to the liveliness, interest level, personality, or beauty of the prose. One of the chief strategies for achieving voice is the effective use of concrete language and specific detail. When used in argument, such language usually heightens *pathos*. We have already seen, at the beginning of this chapter, how specific details about chickens having their beaks removed triggers a stronger emotional response than does the general term "cruelty to animals." For another example, consider the differences between the first and second drafts of the following student argument on the advantages of riding the bus over driving a personal car:

FIRST DRAFT

> People who prefer driving a car to taking a bus think that taking the bus will increase the stress of the daily commute. Just the opposite is true. Not being able to find a parking spot when in a hurry to work or school can cause a person stress. Taking the bus gives a person time to read or sleep, etc. It could be used as a mental break.

Although the argument is logically structured, the lack of details makes it emotionally flat, even dull.

SECOND DRAFT

> Taking the bus can be more relaxing than driving a car. Having someone else behind the wheel gives people time to chat with friends or cram for an exam. They can balance their checkbooks, do homework, doze off, read the daily newspaper, or get lost in a novel rather than foaming at the mouth looking for a parking space. Taking the bus is break time rather than stress time.

In this revision, specific details make the prose livelier by creating images that trigger positive feelings—who wouldn't want some free time to doze off or get lost in a novel?

2. Appeal to Emotions by Using Examples and Illustrations

Stories, examples, and illustrations give your argument a powerful presence. When you move down the ladder of abstraction (going, say, from "living creature" to "animal" to "cow" to "old Bessie out in the barn"), you move from abstractions to specifics. The specifics serve two purposes: As data, they provide evidence that supports your stated reasons; simultaneously, they evoke emotional responses that make your argument more vivid and memorable.

Consider the lack of presence in the following passage written by a student arguing that the core curriculum at his university should include multicultural studies.

EARLY DRAFT

> Another advantage of a multicultural education is that it will help us see our own culture in a broader perspective. If all we know is our own heritage, then we might not be inclined to see anything bad about this heritage because we won't know anything else. But if we study other heritages, then we can see the pros and cons of our own heritage.

The following is a portion of the teacher's end comment in response to this early draft.

TEACHER'S END COMMENT

> Pat, you have the core of an excellent argument here. But you write entirely in abstractions with no concrete examples or detail. For your next draft, think of some snapshot moments to give your argument emotional impact—specific passages from books, specific paintings, specific pieces of music, specific class discussions that illustrate the value of multicultural education.

The next draft was remarkably more persuasive, primarily because of its inclusion of more examples.

REVISED DRAFT

> Another advantage of multicultural education is that it raises questions about traditional Western values. For example, the idea of private property and of ownership is part of the American dream (buying a house with a picket fence in the country, and so forth). It is also one of the basic rights guaranteed in the Constitution of the United States. However, in studying the beliefs of American Indians, students are confronted with an opposing view of property rights. When the U.S. Government wanted to buy land in the Pacific Northwest from Chief Sealth, he replied:
>> The president in Washington sends words that he wishes to buy our land. But how can you buy or sell the sky? The land? The idea is strange to us. If we do not own the freshness of the air and the sparkle of the water, how can you buy them? . . . We are part of the earth and it is part of us. . . . This we know: the earth does not belong to man, man belongs to the earth.
> Our class was shocked when we realized the contrast between Western

values and Chief Sealth's values. One of our best class discussions was initiated by the above quotation from Chief Sealth. Had we not been exposed to a view from another culture, we would have never been led to question the "rightness" of Western values.

The revised draft is much more persuasive. The writer begins by evoking a traditional middle-class American dream—a little house in the country, far from the stress of city life, bordered with a picket fence—which is then immediately undercut by the haunting speech of Chief Sealth. Chief Sealth's vision is not of land domesticated and enclosed, but of land as open, endless, and unobtainable as the sky. In this one brief quotation, the student shows us how a study of Chief Sealth can problematize our belief in private property and thus brings to life his previously abstract point about a benefit of multicultural education.

Another place where writers often use examples to evoke emotions is in their introductions. At the beginning of an argument, a vivid example—real or hypothetical—can shape your audience's emotional response to your issue. In using an opening example, the writer must be careful to fit the example to the claim. To illustrate the potential and the pitfalls of introductory scenes, consider the following vignettes from two different arguments dealing with homeless people in a downtown business area. The first argument, pleading for public support for legislation to help the poor, aims at creating sympathy for homeless people. It opens this way:

> It hurts the most when you come home from the theater on a cold January night. As you pull your scarf tighter around your neck and push your gloved hands deeper into the pockets of your wool overcoat, you notice the man huddled over the sewer grate, his feet wrapped in newspapers. He blows on his hands, then tucks them under his armpits and lies down on the sidewalk with his shoulders over the grate, his bed for the night. There are hundreds like him downtown, and their numbers are growing. Who in our legislature knows or cares about these people?

The second argument, supporting an anti-loitering law to keep homeless people out of a posh shopping area, creates sympathy not for the homeless but for the shoppers.

> Panhandlers used to sit on corners with tin cups. Not any more. I'm not talking here about the legitimate poor—homeless mothers or the blind or crippled. These are ratty, middle-aged woe salesmen drinking fortified wine from a sack or hostile young men with tattoos who appear to be saving their handouts to buy Harley hogs or uzis. They scuttle up behind you, breathing their foul breath down your neck, tap your arm or grab your sleeve, and demand your money. If you try to ignore them, they just keep following you. If you give them change, they ask for folding money. If you don't give them anything, they call you an obscenity. Last week a menacing young man wearing Charlie Manson castoffs assured

me I had money because I was downtown shopping. I'm sure all these poor souls have a tale to explain their present state. But the bottom line is they don't have a *right* to my money, and I do have a right to walk down a public thoroughfare unaccosted.

Each of these scenes makes a case for a particular point of view toward the homeless. They help us see a problem through the eyes of the person making the argument. Although each is effective in its own way, both will face resistance in some quarters. The first scene will strike some as sentimental; the second will strike others as flippant and indifferent. The emotional charge set by an introductory scene can sometimes work against you as well as for you. If you have doubts about an opening scene, test it out on other readers before using it in your final draft.

FOR CLASS DISCUSSION

Suppose that you want to write arguments on the following topics. Working as individuals or in small groups, think of a description, scene, or brief story that could be used in the introduction of your essay to create an emotional appeal favorable to your argument.

1. a. an argument supporting the use of animals for biomedical research
   b. an argument opposing the use of animals for biomedical research
   [Note that the purpose of the first scene is to create sympathy for the use of animals in biomedical research, perhaps by focusing readers' attention on the happy smile of a child cured by a medical breakthrough made possible through animal research. The purpose of the second scene is to create sympathy for the opposing view, perhaps by focusing on the suffering of an animal during an experiment.]

2. a. an argument for a program to restore a national park to its pristine, natural condition
   b. an argument for creating more camping places and overnight sites for recreational vehicles in a national park
   [The purpose of the first scene is to arouse sympathy for restoring a park's beauty; the purpose of the second scene is to arouse sympathy for more camping spaces.]

3. a. an argument favoring mandatory seatbelts laws for auto safety
   b. an argument opposing mandatory seatbelt laws

4. a. an argument favoring TV advertising of condoms
   b. an argument opposing TV advertising of condoms

3. Appeal to Emotions through Appropriate Word Choice, Metaphors, and Analogies

Another way to create emotional appeals is to select words, metaphors, or analogies that have emotional connotations suitable to your purpose. If you oppose a local official, you might call him "a petty bureaucrat," but if you support him, you might call him a "beleaguered administrator." Likewise, the reader's feelings toward the official would be shaped differently depending on whether you called him "assertive" as opposed to "pushy," "decisive" as opposed to "obstinate," or "careful about money" as opposed to "miserly."

Similarly, we can use favorable or unfavorable metaphors, analogies, and other comparisons to shape our audience's emotional response to our arguments. A tax bill might be regarded either as a "poison to the economy" or as "economic medicine"; an insurance salesman might be "like a good neighbor" or "like a voracious shark"; or a new set of audiotapes in the library might be "a valuable new learning tool" or "another cheap educational gadget." In each case, the differing comparisons create differing emotional appeals.

THE PROBLEM OF SLANTED LANGUAGE

The writer's power in choosing one set of words over another raises the problem of how language can be slanted or biased to distort the truth. One of the tricks of the Sophists (see the discussion of Callicles in Chapter 1) is to choose slanted words that bias an argument by evoking emotional responses favorable to the arguer's aims but distortive of the truth. Suppose that you are a real estate developer wishing to attract house buyers to your new subdivision, Paradise Village. Here is what an advertising blurb on Paradise Village might look like.

SLANTED LANGUAGE

> Paradise Village, located on the banks of Clearwater Lake, combines the best of city and country life. Dozens of hiking trails through the Clearwater Woods are only minutes away from your doorstep, while the city itself is virtually at your fingertips. An excellent bus transportation system links Paradise Village with the Metropolis City Center only 15 minutes away.

But consider what a disillusioned homebuyer might say when telling the "truth" about Paradise Village.

THE TRUTH OF THE MATTER

Before buying in Paradise Village, check out carefully the "promises" made in those sales brochures. Clearwater Lake isn't really a lake; it was created by developers by damming up Clearwater Creek, and so far it has been an unattractive pond, full of moss and water bugs but no fish. Certainly it is no place for swimming or boating. Clearwater Woods is simply a couple acres of trees between housing developments. Nowhere within the woods are you free from freeway noise. As for the city being at your fingertips, the bus ride is indeed 15 minutes—at 7:00 A.M. Sunday mornings. But during commuting hours the ride often takes an hour each way. Moreover, buses run infrequently at approximately one-hour intervals during the week and two-hour intervals on weekends.

As the examples show, it is possible to use language deceptively by choosing words that manipulate a reader's response.

But this example raises a more complex philosophical question: To what extent is there really an objective "truth" that can be portrayed fully in language? We tend to think of slanted language as the opposite of objective language or "true" language. But as the next section will suggest, the problem of slanted language is more complex than it at first seems.

A MORE COMPLEX LOOK AT SLANTING

When a witness takes the stand in a trial, he or she swears "to tell the truth, the whole truth, and nothing but the truth." We like to think that "telling the whole truth" is possible in language. We like to believe that objective language tells the whole truth, whereas slanted language distorts it. But can we *ever* tell the whole truth in language? Probably not. When we choose word A rather than word B, when we decide to put this word in the subject slot of our sentence rather than that word, when we select this detail rather than that detail to put into our paragraph, we create bias.

Let's take an illustration, once again focusing on homeless people. When you walk down a city street and see an unshaven man sitting on the sidewalk with his back up against a doorway, wearing old, slovenly clothes, and drinking from a bottle hidden in a sack, what is the "correct" word for this person?

a person on welfare	a disenfranchised person?
a beggar?	a poverty-stricken person?
a wino?	an indigent?
a homeless person?	a bum?
a pauper?	a drunk?
a hobo?	a down and outer?
a panhandler?	a victim of the system?
an unfortunate?	a mendicant?
a transient?	a tramp?
a brother in need?	a scumbag leech on society?

a streetperson?   a loafer?
a destitute?   a person down on his luck?

None of these words is the "correct" term because no such objective or correct term exists. When we choose one of the words, we look at the person through that word's lens. If we call the person a "beggar," for example, we bring up connotations from the historical past, particularly the Bible, where begging provided an opportunity for charity. The word *beggar* is associated with words like *alms*, which one gives to beggars. *Beggar*, then, is a more favorable word than *panhandler*, which conjures up the image of an obnoxious person pestering you for money. Calling the person "homeless," on the other hand, takes our attention off the person's actions and places it on the cause of the problem, in this case a faulty economic system. Likewise, the word *wino* focuses on a cause, but now the cause is alcoholism rather than economics.

Moreover, there is no escape from this phenomenon. We can never find the objective, "true" word. Suppose a social scientist chose a term and stipulated that when he or she used it, the term was perfectly neutral or purely denotative, having no connotations whatsoever. Let's say the social scientist chose the term *streetbound indigents*. But the term immediately takes on connotations simply because it is now the term used by social scientists. Although the scientist can delimit the term painstakingly, it nevertheless becomes social scientific jargon, ripe to be used ironically by all who wish to sneer at homelessness (or at social scientists studying homelessness). Even when used straightforwardly, the term is colored by its scientific origins. The term takes a stance toward its referents just as surely as the terms *Case Study 1* versus *Mary* take different stances toward a psychologist's client.

FOR CLASS DISCUSSION

1. In the Paradise Village example, we suggested that the real estate developer's description of Paradise Village was slanted, whereas the disgruntled homebuyer told the "truth of the matter." But a few moments later we doubted the possibility of a single "truth of the matter" expressible in writing., Working as individuals or as groups, point out ways that the disgruntled homebuyer's description of Paradise Village is also slanted.

2. Divide the class into two groups. The task of the first group is to compose a list of words, analogies, or metaphors that create positive feelings for each of the following classes of people: unemployed people, people who sell used cars, lawyers, college professors, professional wrestlers, hunters, publishers of *Playboy Magazine*, and cheerleaders. The task of the second group is to compose a list that creates negative feelings.

EXAMPLE: Corporate executives

Positive connotations:	industrial leaders, chief executive officers, economic decision-makers, top-level corporation heads
Negative connotations:	fat cats, business tycoons, winners in the corporate rat race, country club elite, business kingpins, business moguls

4. Appeal to Emotions through Sensitivity to Your Audience's Values

We conclude this chapter by returning to the theme introduced in Chapter 8 — finding audience-based reasons. What appeals to a writer's emotions may not necessarily appeal to the emotions of her intended audience.

Suppose that your college or university decided to raise tuition substantially, causing you and many of your classmates to feel truly strapped for funds. Typically, college administrators support tuition increases insofar as they enhance the economic stability of the institution. Students, on the other hand, oppose tuition increases insofar as they impose personal hardships. If you wanted to write a powerful argument against raising tuition, you might choose an emotional appeal based on your own values (sorrowful descriptions of hard-up students). But a better route might be emotional appeals aimed at your audience's values: stories of students who plan to transfer or to drop out of school because of the increased tuition costs. Loss of potential revenues through decreased enrollments probably triggers greater consternation among administrators than your having to borrow another grand from the bank. Likewise, administrators explaining the plan to students should focus on reasons that appeal to students' values; for example, a tuition increase allows hiring and retention of top professors, which leads to a better academic reputation of the college, which leads in turn to higher prestige for students' degrees.

CONCLUSION

In this chapter, we have explored ways that writers can strengthen the persuasiveness of their arguments by creating appeals to *ethos* and to *pathos*. Arguments will be more persuasive if readers trust the credibility of the writer and if the argument appeals to readers' hearts and imaginations as well as to their minds. By being knowledgeable about the issues, by being fair and sympathetic to opposing views, and by establishing common ground with their audiences, writers portray themselves as credible and trustworthy. Through the use of concrete language, vivid examples, effective word choice, and attention to the values of the audience, writers can increase the emotional impact of their arguments. The appeals to credibility and to the emotions, in conjunction with the appeal to logic, work together to create arguments that persuade as well as clarify.

10

ACCOMMODATING YOUR AUDIENCE: TREATING OPPOSING VIEWS IN AN ARGUMENT THAT BOTH CLARIFIES AND PERSUADES

In the previous chapter we discussed ways of moving your audience by appeals to *pathos* and *ethos*. Much of our discussion concerned arguments in process because concern for audience in the early stages of writing is essential for discovering and shaping your argument. In this chapter we are concerned with final products. After you have clarified your argument for yourself and decided on the reasons you will use to support your claim, you still must decide how to treat opposing views — whether to ignore opposing views, to summarize and refute them, to concede to their strengths, or to seek compromise and conciliation. These choices will be determined in part by the stance you wish to take toward your audience and by the image of yourself you wish to project. This chapter addresses these concerns.

AN OPENING EXERCISE: THE CASE OF THE FIRED CHEERLEADERS

As an introduction to our concern for opposing views, consider for a moment "The Case of the Fired Cheerleaders," which we refer to occasionally for illustration throughout this chapter.

To begin this exercise, read the following background information, which describes the context of the case, and then answer the questions on the initial attitude survey that follows.

THE CASE OF THE FIRED CHEERLEADERS

Background Information

In the spring of 1985 a new "sex equity" ruling governing high school sports in the state of _____ required, as part of compliance regulations, that cheerleading squads give equal support to both boys' and girls' teams. When planning for the year, the principal realized that the cheerleading squad was scheduled to cheer at more boys' games than girls' games. His solution, which he arrived at without discussion with the cheerleaders, was to have the cheerleading squad travel to nearby "away" girls' basketball games. (They couldn't go to distant "away" games because of lack of travel funds and overnight chaperone expenses.)

Unfortunately, after school started the principal realized that one girls' "away" game coincided with a home boys' football game. The principal decided to split up the squad, having half of them cheer for the boys' game at home and the other half travel with the girls' basketball team to the "away" game. When told of his decision, however, the cheerleaders refused to accept it, saying that they would go on strike rather than split up their squad for the important boys' football game. After a brief meeting with the principal, in which the cheerleaders reaffirmed their decision to strike, the principal "terminated" the squad and ordered tryouts for new cheerleaders to be chosen before the games.

The next day, after conferring with their parents, the cheerleaders asked to be reinstated saying that they had worked out a compromise way to meet the sex equity guidelines. Their parents would drive them to a distant "away" girls' game and serve as chaperones, thus solving the school's problem of funding the travel and paying a chaperone. The principal said that for insurance reasons the parents' proposal wouldn't work. He refused to reinstate the cheerleaders but told them that if they wanted to be on the new cheerleading squad they could try out like anyone else.

1. Do you think the cheerleaders were justified in refusing to split up the squad?
2. Do you think the principal was justified in "firing" the cheer-leaders?
3. Do you think the principal should have reinstated the cheer-leaders?
4. What are the primary reasons for your choices? Explain briefly.

Now that you know something of the background of this case and have made your initial judgment, please read the following two drafts of a letter to the editor. The writer wants to support the cheerleaders and blame the principal. After you have read the drafts, answer the questions on the survey that follows. It asks you to decide which of the two drafts you think the writer should send to the newspaper.

DRAFT 1

Regarding the dismissal of the cheerleaders at _____, the principal was clearly wrong. He should reinstate the cheerleaders immediately.

First, the principal created the problem, not the cheerleaders. By not discussing the problem with the cheerleaders before he made his decision, the principal created a crisis that could have been avoided. He made up his mind to split up the squad without trying to see the issue from their perspective. He should have realized that cheerleaders are a team, not a collection of individuals. Splitting them up makes it impossible to cheer effectively at an important home football game.

When the matter came to a head, the principal insulted them with a show of force. He called them into his office and ordered them to make up their minds immediately. While such pressure tactics might be common in encyclopedia promotions and used car deals, they hardly seem right in an educational situation. Later, when the cheerleaders worked out a compromise arrangement, the principal dismissed it, quoting some bureaucratic rules about insurance problems.

The only way to set this state of affairs to rest is to reinstate the cheerleaders immediately. Otherwise the cheerleaders should take their case to the school board.

DRAFT 2

Regarding the dismissal of the cheerleaders at _____, both the cheerleaders and the principal seem partly to blame. Both are victims of a communication breakdown. But the principal seems enough at fault that he should reinstate the cheerleaders.

The principal's handling of this difficult case is certainly understand-able. He was caught between a complex set of legal requirements and the demands of the cheerleaders to keep their team together for the home football game. If he had to choose between this rock and a hard place, then his decision to enforce the sex equity guidelines was the right one. I also understand the principal's desire not to back down once he reached a decision. The principal is paid to run the school, and he has the right to see his decisions carried out.

But the principal shouldn't have made that decision in the first place. Long before the situation came to a head, the principal should have discussed the problem with the cheerleaders and their advisor. Certainly another solution could have been reached besides splitting up the team for an important home football game. If he had seen, from the cheerleaders' perspective, the importance of keeping the team together, he never would have gotten himself into the embarrassing position of having to appear like an autocrat.

In the principal's defense, he was working under rigid time constraints and, because of insurance problems, he really couldn't accept the parents' offer to drive the cheerleaders to a later away game. Moreover, his failure to anticipate the cheerleaders' reaction to his decision is merely an act of misjudgment, not malice. True, the cheerleaders bear some of the blame for this whole affair. But the principal is enough at fault that the generous solution is to reinstate the cheerleaders and resolve in the future to involve them in decisions that affect their squad.

SECOND OPINION SURVEY

1. Which draft do you find most persuasive?
2. Which draft do you think the author should submit to the newspaper? Why?

FOR CLASS DISCUSSION

1. Working in small groups, compare notes on which draft you find most persuasive.
2. To aid your discussion, describe the main differences between the two drafts.
3. Take a class poll on the numbers of persons who prefer each of the drafts.
4. What relationship do you find, if any, between a person's initial position on the cheerleader issue (question 1 in the initial opinion survey, page 184) and that person's preference for Draft 1 or Draft 2 as most persuasive?

ONE-SIDED VERSUS TWO-SIDED ARGUMENTS

The previous exercise introduces you to the differences between what rhetoricians call one-sided and two-sided arguments. Draft 1 is a one-sided argument. It presents only the writer's view of the principal's actions without attempting to look at the issue from the principal's perspective. Draft 2, on the other hand, is a two-sided argument. It still attacks the principal, but at various places summarizes the principal's point of view.

Which version is more effective rhetorically? That is, which is apt to be more persuasive to an audience?

According to some research done by communication specialists, if people already agree with the writer's thesis, they usually find one-sided arguments more persuasive. A two-sided argument appears wishy-washy, making the writer look less decisive and the issue somewhat muddier. On the other hand, if people initially disagree with the writer's thesis, a two-sided argument usually seems more persuasive. A one-sided argument often makes opponents defensive and annoyed. A two-sided argument suggests that the writer has listened to the other side and thus tends to defuse anger.

An especially interesting effect has been documented for neutral audiences. In the short range, a one-sided argument generally seems more persuasive to a neutral audience, but such an audience is apt to be easily persuaded in the opposite direction when it subsequently encounters an opposing argument. Although less persuasive in the short run for neutral audiences, a two-sided argument seems more persuasive in the long run. By forewarning an audience of opposing views and then refuting them, the two-sided argument undercuts the surprise of a subsequent counterargument and also exposes its weaknesses.

Now that you've heard from the researchers, go back and examine the results of your own little experiment. Do they bear out the experts' findings? If not, can you think of reasons they might not?

BEGINNING A TWO-SIDED ARGUMENT: SUMMARIZING OPPOSING VIEWS

An effective two-sided argument usually begins with a fair summary of an opposing view. (By "two sides" we mean your position versus one or more positions opposing yours. Often you might need to summarize and refute several different opposing views.) When you summarize opposing views, your own credibility will be enhanced if you follow the "principle of charity." This principle obliges you to make your opponents' best case, stating that case in its best light and avoiding loaded or biased language. You should also avoid a "strawman" summary, which oversimplifies opposing arguments, making them easy to knock over. Consider the differences in the following summaries of an anti-cheerleader argument. The writer of these passages supports the cheerleaders and is angry at a feminist writer who, in opposing the cheerleaders, argued that cheerleaders are an embarrassment to modern women. The feminist's editorial said that cheerleaders are relics from a male chauvinist world that sex equity laws are designed to change. The following passages illustrate fair and unfair ways for this writer to summarize the woman's views.

UNFAIR SUMMARY—LOADED LANGUAGE

Many of these women's libbers who unthinkingly oppose the cheerleaders falsely believe that cheerleaders aren't important to the school. What's the matter with these people? Are they blind? Haven't they been to any football or basketball games lately? These bra-burners think cheerleaders are airheads, but this is an ignorant opinion, as they would find out if they only cared enough to get to know some of these cheerleaders before shooting off their mouths.

Although this summary shows an opposing view, it doesn't effectively enter into that view. By labeling it as "ignorant," the writer reveals a bias that prevents him from really seeing the issue through the opponent's eyes.

UNFAIR SUMMARY—STRAWMAN

Many of the people who oppose the cheerleaders think that cheerleading isn't an important activity and that cheerleaders serve no function other than to stand in front of the crowd and look pretty. They don't realize that cheerleading helps a team win games.

This version oversimplifies the opposing position and is thus a strawman that is easy to knock over. The opponent's point isn't that cheerleaders are unimportant; her point is that cheerleading promotes an inappropriate image for modern, liberated women.

FAIR SUMMARY—FOLLOWS PRINCIPLE
OF CHARITY

A recent guest editorial by Mary _____ opposed the cheerleaders' position. She is unsympathetic to the cheerleaders' request primarily because she sees cheerleading as a sexist activity that trivializes women by presenting them as ornaments or adornments to the real action on the field.

This version role plays the opposing view, trying to state its argument fairly and accurately.

FOR CLASS DISCUSSION

Suppose that a group of parents want to write a joint letter to the editor opposing the cheerleaders and supporting the actions of the principal in the cheerleader case. Working in small groups, role play these parents. Reread Draft 1 (page 184) which is a one-sided argument attacking the principal.

This draft represents the opposing view for your own letter. As a group, prepare three different summaries of the views expressed in Draft 1:

1. an unfair summary using loaded language
2. an unfair strawman summary
3. a fair summary following the principle of charity

After each group has composed its three passages, the recorders should read them aloud to the class as a whole.

Once writers have summarized an opposing view, they have several choices on how to respond to it. They can rebut the view by taking a combative stance, concede to it and then shift the direction of the argument, or seek compromise by listening empathically and reducing threat. Let's examine each strategy in turn.

RESPONSE STRATEGY I: REBUTTING OPPOSING VIEWS

When rebutting or refuting an argument, you attempt to convince readers that the opponent's view is logically flawed, erroneously supported, or in some other way much weaker than the opponent claims.

Using the Toulmin Schema to Find a Strategy for Rebuttal

In planning a rebuttal, the most important principle to keep in mind is that you can attack either your opponent's stated reasons or the often unstated warrants behind those reasons. You have already practiced this kind of thinking when considering Toulmin's "conditions for rebuttal."

Let's illustrate this strategy by continuing with "The Case of the Fired Cheerleaders." For the purposes of this illustration, assume that you want to oppose the feminist argument that cheerleaders are part of an outdated, male chauvinist world. Your opponent's claim with because clause is as follows:

Cheerleading should be abolished because cheerleaders are a sexist symbol of women as ornaments.

Placed into the Toulmin schema, your opponent's enthymemic argument has the following structure:

Claim:	Cheerleading should be abolished.
Stated Reason:	Cheerleaders are a sexist symbol of women as ornaments.
Grounds:	pom poms, short skirts, dance routines, staying on the sidelines, chosen for looks
Warrant:	Sexist symbols showing women as ornaments should be abolished.
Backing:	evidence or argument that stereotypically female behavior causes people not to take women seriously
Conditions of Rebuttal:	unless the cheerleaders haven't acted as mere ornaments; unless under certain conditions, "sexist" symbols are good (and hence shouldn't be called "sexist").
Qualifier:	Original position was not qualified; writer called for abolishment of cheerleading.

Let's suppose that you admire the cheerleaders for having the guts to stand up to the administration and even threaten to go on strike. This action hardly seems to you to be an example of women acting as ornaments. You could therefore use this evidence as a way of attacking your opponent's stated reason. Instead of accepting the opponent's grounds focusing on short skirts and pom poms, you provide new grounds that support a different view of the cheerleaders. Here is how this portion of your rebuttal might go:

REBUTTAL OF STATED REASON

The view that cheerleaders are mere ornaments doesn't hold at all in this case. By having the guts to stand up to the principal, the cheerleaders didn't act like compliant, ornamental females. The cheerleaders demanded to have a voice in determining their role and challenged male authority in the process. Even if one disagrees with their stand, one would have to concede that in confronting the principal, they showed courage and initiative. Given the assertive way they have acted, I find it dismaying to hear Mary _____ condescend to them as if they were mere ornaments. In fact, had he listened to the cheerleaders, the principal could have struck a more substantial blow for sex equity than by giving scrupulous attention to their schedule of performances.

The above argument attacks the opponent's stated reason that cheerleaders are mere ornaments. But it continues to respect the opponent's value system (belief in the modern, independent woman) and thus argues that these cheerleaders showed courage and independence.

But it is also possible to attack the opponent's warrant by attacking the assertion that we ought to abolish all sexist symbols. By attacking the warrant, this rebuttal attacks the feminist value system itself. Here is one way such an argument might proceed:

REBUTTAL OF WARRANT

The "woman as ornament" argument, like many other feminist arguments, is offensive. It tries to eliminate all distinctions between men and women. Mary ———— might as well rail against childbirth, breastfeeding, and the dance of sex itself. Let's not deny it. Cheerleading is indeed an activity where feminine beauty takes center stage. Cheerleaders are sexy. Instead of scorning cheerleaders as "ornaments," I propose celebrating their sexiness as woman's role in a modern fertility rite. The pageantry of a football game, with its archetypal symbols of the male and the female, reflects our natural existence as sexual creatures. Abolishing cheerleaders is like abolishing Eros. Let's leave that kind of repression to the Chinese Communists.

You can see that these are two quite different ways to rebut the original argument. By implying different views of cheerleaders and feminism, they reveal the difference between attacking a stated reason, which keeps the opponent's value system intact, and attacking a warrant, which attacks the value system directly.

FOR CLASS DISCUSSION

Complete each of the following enthymemes by providing the warrant. Then invent plausible grounds and backing for the argument. Finally, consider conditions for rebuttal by suggesting ways to attack the stated reason, the warrant, or both.

1. The Mustangs will win the Pony Football championship because they have the two best running backs in the league.
2. Kids should learn computer programming in school because it teaches reasoning skills.
3. Students should be required to write group essays in college because group or committee writing is very common in the world of work.
4. Majoring in engineering is better than majoring in music because engineers make more money than musicians.
5. It is better to be blind than deaf because blindness cuts you off from things, but deafness cuts you off from people.

Ways to Refute Evidence

Among the most common ways to refute an argument is to find weaknesses in the opponent's use of evidence either in the opponent's grounds or backing. Here are some ways that evidence can be refuted.

DENY THE FACTICITY OF THE DATA

Generally a piece of data can be considered a fact when a variety of observers all agree that the datum corresponds with reality. Often, though, what one writer considers a "fact," another may consider an "interpretation" or simply a case of wrong information. If you have reason to doubt your opponent's facts, then call them into question. Thus, if your opponent reports that the school system's insurance policy doesn't allow parents to drive cheerleaders to an away basketball game, you might examine the policy and report that no such restriction applies.

CITE COUNTEREXAMPLES OR COUNTERTESTIMONY

One of the most effective ways to counter an argument based on examples is to cite a counterexample. If your opponent argues that women are more people-conscious than men, several counterexamples of cold, impersonal women or of kindly, warm-hearted men can cast doubt on the whole claim. The effect of counterexamples is to deny the conclusiveness of the original data. Similarly, citing an authority whose testimony counters other expert testimony is a good way to begin refuting an argument based on testimony.

CAST DOUBT ON THE REPRESENTATIVENESS OR SUFFICIENCY OF EXAMPLES

Examples are powerful only if the audience feels them to be representative and sufficient. If your opponent argues that pool players are true athletes because they excel at many other sports, not just pool, and then cites as an example a local pool player who is also a varsity track star, you could argue that the mentioned player is not typical of all pool players. You could demand that the opponent provide evidence based on a wide sampling of pool players. To conclude your rebuttal, you might cite examples of one or two pool players who were klutzes at other sports.

CAST DOUBT ON THE RELEVANCE OR RECENCY OF THE EXAMPLES, STATISTICS, OR TESTIMONY

The best evidence is up-to-date. In a rapidly changing universe, data that are even a few years out of date are often ineffective. If your opponent uses demographic data to argue that your community doesn't need a new nursing home, you could raise questions about the recency of the data, arguing that the percentage of elderly has increased since the time the data were collected. Another problem with data is their occasional lack of relevance. For example, in arguing that an adequate ozone layer is necessary for preventing skin cancers, it is not relevant to cite statistics on the alarming rise of lung cancers.

CALL INTO QUESTION THE CREDIBILITY OF AN AUTHORITY

One trick of sophistry is to have an authority within one field speak out on issues in a different field. Modern advertising regularly uses this kind of sleight-of-hand whenever movie stars or athletes endorse products about which they have no expertise. The problem of credibility is trickier when an apparent authority has no particular expertise in a specific subfield within the discipline. For example, a psychologist specializing in the appetite mechanisms of monkeys might not be an expert witness on schizophrenic behavior in humans, even though a writer could cite that person as a Ph.D. in psychology. Thus, if you can attack the credibility of the authority, you can sometimes undermine the effectiveness of the testimony. (This procedure is different from the *ad hominem* fallacy discussed in Appendix 1 because it doesn't attack the personal character of the authority but only the authority's expertise on a specific matter.)

QUESTION THE ACCURACY OR CONTEXT OF QUOTATIONS

Frequently evidence based on testimony is distorted by being either misquoted or taken out of context. Often scientists will qualify their findings heavily, but these qualifications will be omitted when their research is reported by the popular media. You can thus attack the use of a quotation by putting it in its original context or by restoring the qualifications accompanying the quotation in its original source.

QUESTION THE WAY STATISTICAL DATA WERE PRODUCED OR INTERPRETED

Appendix 2 provides fuller treatment of how to refute statistics. At this point, however, you should appreciate that you can attack your opponent's statistical evidence by calling into account how the data were gathered, treated mathematically, or interpreted. It can make a big difference, for example, whether you cite raw numbers or percentages or whether you choose large or small increments for the axes of graphs.

Anticipating Your Opposition Throughout Your Essay

Although good writers will often devote a specific section of an essay to refutation, they don't ignore the opposition in the rest of the essay. They will often refer to opposing views even while presenting their own side of the argument. When you draft your essay, try to imagine yourself in a conversation with a reader who has just listened to an opposing view and is weighing its merits against those of your argument. Imagine watching his or her facial expressions as you make your case. At controversial points in your argument, picture your reader recalling an opposing point of view, frowning, giving a shake of the head, and starting to interrupt, "Yes, but. . . . " Your job as a writer is to anticipate those "Yes, but . . . " moments and let your imaginary reader make an opposing case briefly before you go on. The ability to work these opposing views into your arguments gracefully is one hallmark of a skilled writer.

RESPONSE STRATEGY II: CONCESSION TO OPPOSING VIEWS

Sometimes you will encounter portions of an argument that you simply can't refute. If you support the Strategic Defense Initiative (Star Wars), for example, you may not be able to refute your opponent's argument that Star Wars will be extremely expensive or that its chances for success are very slight. Yet you continue to support Star Wars because you believe it is an important bargaining chip in disarmament talks with the Soviets. Your strategy in this case is not to try to refute the opponent's argument. Rather, you concede to it by admitting the expense of Star Wars and its technical difficulties. You then argue, however, that despite the strength of the opposing view, you still support Star Wars and proceed to make your case.

As this example shows, the strategy of a concession argument is to switch from the field of values employed by your opponent to a different field of values more favorable to your position. Whereas your opponent opposed Star Wars because it failed to meet criterion A (acceptable cost) and criterion B (reasonable chance of success), you support it on the basis of criterion C (bargaining chip leading to disarmament), which you introduce into the argument. To put it another way, in a concession argument you don't try to refute your opponent's grounds or warrants. Rather, you find new warrants that you and your audience can share. (For example, an opponent of Star Wars is likely to support nuclear disarmament, so the move to this field of value is a good strategy). Although it may seem that you weaken your own position by conceding to your opponent's argument, you may actually strengthen it by increasing your credibility and gaining your audience's goodwill.

RESPONSE STRATEGY III: A CONCILIATORY APPROACH TO AUDIENCE

A third way to deal with opposing views is to take a conciliatory approach. This strategy is particularly effective if you are writing directly to a decision maker whose views oppose yours. A conciliatory strategy is based in part on the theory that traditional ways of arguing are threatening.* Traditional argument often fails to persuade because people place a high psychological value on preserving their own point of view. Changing one's mind, in a sense, means changing one's identity, taking unsettling risks, loosening a brick in the structure of one's beliefs. Rather than risk change, people tune the arguer out. This assessment of traditional argument has been borne out in psychological studies showing that persons have enormous capacity to resist arguments that somehow threaten their own values, sense of identity, or world view.

A conciliatory strategy tries to reduce those elements in the writer's position that seem to threaten the intended audience. The writer's job is to show that his or her position is not threatening to the opposition *because both writer and opponent share many basic values.* Instead of attacking the opponent for being wrong, the conciliatory writer makes the opponent feel intelligent and valued. The conciliatory writer "listens" carefully to the opponent and refrains from stating his or her own position until demonstrating that the opponent's position is understood. Such "listening" is caring rather than critical in that it tries to understand the speaker's feelings, instead of simply trying to find flaws in the speaker's reasoning. Finally, the writer seldom asks the opponent to accept all of his or her ideas, but just to shift somewhat toward the writer's views. As a precedent, the writer often demonstrates how he or she has already shifted toward the opponent's views, so that the conclusion of a conciliatory argument is often a compro-

---

*See the discussion of Rogerian argument, based on the work of psychologist Carl Rogers, in Richard Young, Alton Becker, and Kenneth Pike, *Rhetoric: Discovery and Change* (New York: Harcourt Brace, 1972).

mise between—or even better, a synthesis of—the opposing positions. (A compromise is a middle ground that neither party particularly likes; a synthesis is a new position that both parties like better than their original positions.)

The key to conciliatory argument, besides the art of good listening, is the ability to point out areas of agreement between the opposing positions. For example, if you support a woman's right to choose abortion and you are arguing with someone completely opposed to abortion, you probably have little chance of changing your opponent's view. You may, however, be able to reduce the threat that your position poses for your audience, a threat that sometimes causes pro-life people to view pro-choice people as baby-killing murderers. After summarizing your audience's position in a sympathetic light, you can then stress how many values you and your audience really share. Depending on what you really believe, you might say, for example, that you too value children, that you too are appalled by people who treat abortion as a form of birth control with no more moral significance than a pulled tooth, that you too agree that an easy acceptance of abortion might lead to a lessening of the value a society places on life, and finally that you too agree that accepting abortion lightly can lead to lack of sexual responsibility.

After building bridges like these between yourself and your opponent, you are then ready to introduce your "however. . . ." Your opponents will be more prepared to consider the areas where you and they disagree if you have already shown the larger, more important areas where you do agree. It is important too that you enter this process with the same openness that you expect of your opponent. That is, you too must risk change.

Here is a brief example of a conciliatory approach in "The Case of the Fired Cheerleaders." The writer of this letter, which is addressed directly to the principal, is a cheerleader's parent. The parent hopes that the principal will accept the compromise proposal of letting the girls cheer at a distant away girls' basketball game later in the season.*

Dear Mr. S———:

As a parent of one of the cheerleaders who have been planning to go on strike, I have an idea for a compromise that may help you end this controversy gracefully. First of all, though, let me assure you that I understand and appreciate your actions in this matter. Since I too believe in sex equity, I am most pleased to see your forceful public endorsement of the guidelines mandated by the state, both in principle and in practice. To tell you the truth, I am a bit disappointed that my daughter would rather cheer for a boys' football game than for a girls' basketball game.

But I can also understand the girls' perspective. They have developed a number of new cheer routines, including several with acrobatic maneu-

---

*Another example of a conciliatory argument is on pages 200–201.

vers, that require the whole team to be present. They feel that if you require them to split up their squad, you are somehow saying that cheerleaders are inconsequential people. Thus their decision to strike is partly, at least, a reaction to their feeling that they have been insulted.

I know of course that you didn't mean to insult them, so is there a way out of this impasse? Other parents and I are hoping that you will accept the girls' compromise proposal to cheer at a later girls' basketball game, but that you let the girls' parents take full responsibility for the whole trip including transportation and insurance. The parents will form a temporary "cheerleading club" like the local soccer club that is not connected in any way to the school. We will provide transportation and chaperones and buy our own temporary insurance for the trip. The girls will show up and cheer for the game, thus meeting the sex equity guidelines, but they will not draw in any way on school funds or require changes in the school's insurance arrangements.

This solution may give you a graceful way of ending the controversy. We certainly hope that you will consider it. Please let me know if we can get together to work out arrangements for this solution.

Sincerely,

Molly ‑‑‑‑‑‑‑

FOR CLASS DISCUSSION

1. In the above letter, what shared values between writer and audience does the writer stress?

2. In what way does the writer's proposal probably represent a compromise on the writer's part?

3. Compare the argumentative strategy of this letter with that of Draft 1 on page 184.
   a. How do the two essays differ in the way they accommodate their audiences?
   b. How do the essays project a different "persona," or image of the writer? How would you describe each persona?
   c. Which strategy do you think is more effective? Why?

Conclusion

This chapter has shown you the difference between one-sided and two-sided arguments and suggested that two-sided arguments are apt to be more persuasive to opposing or neutral audiences. A two-sided argument generally includes a fair summary of the opposing views, followed by either a rebuttal, a concession, or an attempt at synthesis or compromise. How much space your essay devotes to the opposing view depends on the issue you choose and the rhetorical context of your essay.

WRITING ASSIGNMENTS FOR PART III

The writing options for Part III will require you to pay careful attention to the views of your audience. The first option asks you to summarize an opposing view and then to refute it. This assignment calls for a self-announcing structure and asks you to adopt an *ethos* of confident self-assurance about the rightness of your own position.

The second assignment calls for an unfolding, delayed thesis structure in which you arrive at your own position through synthesis with opposing views. In this assignment you adopt an *ethos* of conciliator and listener. If in Option 1 you are something of a boxer giving a knockout punch to your opponent, in Option 2 you are an inviter and synthesis-seeker—someone who knits up wounds rather than going for the kill.

OPTION 1: SUMMARIZING AND REFUTING THE OPPOSITION Whereas the purpose of most arguments is to develop your own position, the purpose of this assignment is to summarize and refute an opposing view. Before drafting this essay, reread Response Strategy I, "Rebutting Opposing Views" (pp. 188–193).

Write a multiparagraph essay in which you summarize a position opposing yours and then show the weaknesses of that position. Each of the reasons in your opponent's argument should be summarizable in because clauses attached to your opponent's claim.

Your essay should have four main sections. The opening section—your introduction—should introduce your issue, give it presence, and briefly indicate your own position on the issue (but not develop that position). Your second section should summarize an opposing view, following the principle of charity. (Make sure that your transition introducing this section makes clear that this is an *opposing view* that you are summarizing; otherwise your readers will assume it is your view and get confused.) Each of the reasons supporting your opponent's position should be clearly highlighted. The third and longest section of your essay should refute the view you have just summarized by attacking in turn each of the reasons summarized earlier. Finally, your last section should provide a conclusion. The following student essay illustrates this assignment.

ABSTRACT VERSUS REPRESENTATIONAL ART

Have you ever come across a painting by Picasso, Mondrian, Pollock, Miro, or any other modern abstract painter of this century and found yourself engulfed in a brightly colored canvas that your senses cannot interpret? Many people, especially out here in the West, would tend to scoff and denounce abstractionism as senseless trash. For instance, these people are disoriented by Miro's bright, fanciful creatures and two-dimensional canvas. They click their tongues and shake their heads at

Mondrian's grid works, declaring the poor guy played too many Scrabble games. They guffaw at Pollock's canvases of splashed paint, and silently shake their heads in sympathy for Picasso, whose gruesome, distorted figures must be a reflection of his mental health. Then, standing in front of a Charlie Russell, the famous Western artist, they'll declare it a work of God. People feel more comfortable with something they can relate to and understand immediately without too much thought. This is the case with the work of Charlie Russell. Being able to recognize the elements in his paintings—such as trees, horses, and cowboys—gives people a safety line to their world of "reality." There are some who would disagree when I say abstract art requires more creativity and artistic talent to produce a good piece than does representational art, but there are many weaknesses in their arguments.

People who look down on abstract art have several major arguments to support their beliefs. First, they feel that artists turn abstract because they are not capable of the technical drafting skills that appear in Remington, Russell, and Rockwell pieces. Therefore they created an art form that anyone was capable of and that was less time consuming and then paraded it as artistic progress. Secondly, they feel that the purpose of art is to create something of beauty in an orderly, logical composition. Russell's compositions are balanced and rational; everything sits calmly on the canvas, leaving the viewer satisfied that he has seen all there is to see. The modern abstractionists, on the other hand, seem to compose their pieces irrationally. For example, upon seeing Picasso's *Guernica*, a girlfriend of mine was confused as to the center of focus and turned to ask me, "What's the point?" Finally, many people feel that art should portray the ideal and real. The exactness of detail in Charlie Russell's work is an example of this. He has been called a great historian because his pieces depict the life style, dress, and events of the times. His subject matter is derived from his own experiences on the trail, and reproduced to the smallest detail.

I agree in part with many of these arguments, and at one time even endorsed them. But now, I believe differently. First I object to the opponent's argument that abstract artists are not capable of drafting—representational drawing—and therefore created a new art form that required little technical skill. Many abstract artists, such as Picasso, are excellent draftsmen. As his work matured, Picasso became more abstract in order to increase the expressive quality of his work. *Guernica* was meant as a protest against the bombing of that city by the Germans. To express the terror and suffering of the victims more vividly, he distorted the figures and presented them in a black and white journalistic manner. If he had used representational image and color, much of the emotional content would've been lost and the piece probably would not have caused the demand for justice that it did. Secondly, I disagree that a piece *must* be logical and aesthetically pleasing to be art. More important, I feel, is the message it conveys to its viewers. It should reflect the ideals and issues of its time and be true to itself, not just a flowery, glossy surface. For example, through his work, Mondrian was trying to present a system of simplicity, logic, and rational order. As a result, his pieces did end up looking like a Scrabble board. Miro created powerful, surrealistic images from his dreams and subconscious. Pollock's huge splatter paint canvases surround the viewer with a fantastic linear environment. All of these artists were trying to evoke a response from society through an expressionistic manner, not just create a pretty picture to be admired and passed by. Finally, abstract artists and representational artists maintain different ideas about "reality." To the representational artist, reality is what he sees with his eyes. This is the reality he *reproduces* on canvas. To the abstract artist, reality is what he feels about what his eyes see. This is the reality he *interprets* on canvas. This can be illustrated by Mondrian's *Trees* series. You can actually see the progression from the early recognizable, though abstracted, *Trees*, to his final solution, the grid system.

A cycle of abstract and representational art began with the first scratching of prehistoric man. From the abstractions of ancient Egypt to representational, classical Rome, returning to abstractionism in early Christian art and so on up to the present day, the cycle has been proved. But this day and age may witness its death through the camera. With film, there is no need to produce finely detailed, historical records manually; the camera does this for us faster and more efficiently. Perhaps we will soon be heading for a time where representational art is nonexistent and artists and their work will be redefined. With abstractionism as the victor of the first battle, maybe another cycle will be touched off and another cyclical interval. Possibly, some time in the distant future—thousands of years from now—art will be physically nonexistent. I heard it said somewhere that some artists even now believe that once they have planned and constructed a piece in their mind, there is no sense doing it with their hands; it has already been done and could never be duplicated. Echoing the birth, life, and death of man, art too would cycle.

OPTION 2: CONCILIATORY STRATEGY   Write a multiparagraph essay that refrains from presenting your position until the conclusion. The opening section introduces the issue and provides needed background. The second section summarizes the views of the opposition in a sympathetic manner. The third section creates a bridge between writer and opponent by pointing out major areas of agreement that writer and opponent have in common. After examining this common ground, the third section then points out areas of disagreement but stresses that these are minor compared with the major areas of agreement already discussed. Finally, the last section presents the writer's position, which, if possible, should be a compromise or synthesis indicating that the writer has shifted his original position (or at least his sympathies) toward the opposition's view and is now asking the opposition to make a similar shift toward the writer's new position. Your goal here, through tone, arrangement, and examination of common values, is to reduce the threat of your argument in the eyes of your opponent. Prior to drafting this essay, reread pages 194–196, where we discuss a conciliatory strategy. The following student essay illustrates this strategy:

Ms. Beth Downey, Owner/Manager
Downey's Music
Grayfish

Dear Ms. Downey:

I would just like to comment on the success of "Downey's Music" in Grayfish and say that, as owner and manager, you have done a wonderful job. I'm sure that you have the most extensive classical music, music teaching books, piano and acoustic guitar inventory of any store in a 100-square-mile area. After working for you for three years, I have encountered music teachers and classical music lovers coming as far as 70 miles to buy their music from Downey's. All have had nothing but compliments for you and for the store. However, I would once again like to bring up the subject of introducing an inventory of electronic music equipment to the store. Since Grayfish is mainly a tourist town, many times a week I have people from touring bands, visiting Canadians, and also locals coming into the store looking for such things as electronic keyboards, electric guitars, and amplifiers. I know that you have qualms about this idea, but I believe that I have a suggestion that we could both agree on.

First, let me restate your reasons for objecting to such a move. You have already stated that if a change will benefit the store, the initial investment is well worth the expense in the long run (e.g., when pianos were added to the inventory). Therefore, I assume that cost is not a factor at this time. However, you feel that the "kind of people" that electronics may draw could possibly offend our present clientele. You feel, as well as others, that the people who are drawn by electronics are often long haired, dirty, and give a bad impression. This would in effect change the store's image. Also, you are afraid that the noise caused by these instruments could turn classical music lovers away from the store. The sounds of electronic instruments are not always pleasing, and since most of our clientele are older, more refined persons, you feel that these sounds will force some to go to other stores. Mainly, however, you are worried about the result that the change in the store's image could have upon a community the size of Grayfish. Many people in this area, I realize, feel that electronic music means heavy rock music, while this in turn means alcohol and drugs.

Basically, I agree with you that Grayfish needs a "classical" music store and that the culture that your store brings to Grayfish greatly enhances the area. I also love classical music and want to see it growing and alive. I also have some of the same fears about adding electronic music to the inventory. I enjoy the atmosphere of Downey's, and I have always enjoyed working there, so I don't want to see anything adverse happen to it either. On the other hand, I feel that if a large electronic music section were added to the store with sound-proof rooms, a "sit and try it" atmosphere, and a catalog inventory large enough to special order anything that a customer might want that is not in the store, it would help immensely in the success of the store. With the way that Downey's is built, on two levels, it would be very easy to accommodate the needs of both departments. Even now we are only using about half the floor space available, while the rest is empty storage area. By building sound-proof rooms on the lower level, we could easily double the in-use floor area, increase our tourist clientele, have the music business in *all* areas cornered for approximately 60 square miles, and also add practice rooms for our present customers to use when they are choosing music.

I know that you are wrestling with this idea of such a drastic change-over, so I would like to propose a solution that I feel we could both agree on. My solution is to start slowly, on a trial basis, and see how it works. I suggest that we start with a few small electronic keyboards, a few electric guitars, and one or two amps. In this way, we could begin to collect the information and literature on other electronic equipment that may be added later on, see how the community responds to such a move, find out how our present clientele reacts, get a feel for the demand in this field, and yet still be a small home-town music store without a great investment in this electronic area. I still feel that a large addition would be more successful, but I also believe that this little test may help prove to you, or disprove to me, that electronic music instruments in this area are in high demand. I honestly feel that electronics could produce fantastic profits for the people who get in the business first. I would love it if these "people" could be the owners and workers at Downey's Music.

Sincerely,

Mary Doe

OPTION 3: A FORMAL ARGUMENT IN THE "STANDARD FORM"   Write a formal argument following the "standard form" as explained on pages 164–166. In essence, this essay combines the two or more reasons assignment on page 139 (Option 6) with the summary and refutation assignment on page 197 (Option 1). A "standard form" argument has a self-announcing structure. Your introduction will present your issue, provide needed background, and announce your thesis. It may also provide a brief forecasting passage to help the reader anticipate the shape of your essay. (See pages 92–94.) In the body of your essay, you summarize and refute opposing views as well as present your own reasons and evidence in support of your position. It is your choice whether you summarize and refute opposing views before or after you have made your own case. Generally, try to end your essay with your strongest arguments.

DRAFTING AND REVISING: SOME ADVICE FOR PEER REVIEWS

We will conclude the assignment options for Part III by providing a general checklist for evaluating drafts. As a writer, you may find such a checklist useful for revising your drafts. But the checklist is most useful, we believe, for readers during an exchange of drafts among peers. When you read a fellow student's draft, your obligation is to provide the most helpful response that you can to enable your colleague to revise his or her argument. The following checklist may help you improve the quality of your responses.

General Checklist for Evaluating Drafts

UNDERSTANDING THE WRITER'S INTENTIONS

- What issue is being addressed in this draft?
- What is the writer's thesis (claim, proposition)?
- Where does the writer choose to reveal the thesis? At the beginning? In the middle? At the end? (See discussion of standard form versus delayed thesis, pages 164–171.)
- Can you summarize the writer's main reasons as because clauses?
- Is the draft a one-sided or two-sided argument?
- What audience seems to be addressed? The opposition? Neutral third party? Fellow believers? Other?
- What stance does the writer take toward opposing views? Tough-minded and combative? Conciliatory? Other?

RECONSTRUCTING THE WRITER'S ARGUMENT

- Can you make a tree diagram, flow chart, or outline of the writer's argument? (See pages 59–65.)
- Summarize the writer's argument in 100–200 words. (If you have trouble summarizing the argument, discuss difficulties with writer. Have him or her talk you through the argument orally and then make recommendations for revision.)

CRITIQUING THE WRITER'S ARGUMENT

- How effective are the writer's supporting reasons? Are there any additional reasons the writer might use?

- Is each reason supported with effective *Grounds* in the form of factual data, evidence, statistics, testimony, or appropriate chains of reasons?
- Do the *Warrants* for any of the reasons need to be explicitly articulated and supported with *Backing*?
- To what extent are the supporting reasons "audience-based" instead of writer-based? (Do each of the supporting enthymemes rest in values shared by the audience? See pages 146–159.)
- Does the writer attend adequately to opposing views? As a reviewer of this draft, how would *you* go about refuting the writer's argument?
- If the writer summarizes opposing views, does he or she follow the "principle of charity"—a fair, accurate, complete summary, making the opponent's "best case" (see pages 186–187)?
- If the writer rebuts the opposition, is the rebuttal clear and effective? How could it be improved?
- Does the writer project an effective *ethos* (see pages 160–171)?
- Does the writer make effective use of *pathos*? How could appeals to *pathos* be strengthened through narratives, specific images and details, metaphor and analogy, or word choice (see pages 171–180)?

CRITIQUING THE ORGANIZATION AND CLARITY OF THE WRITING

- Identify places where the draft is confusing or unclear.
- Do the opening lines engage readers' interest?
- Does the opening introduce the issue and provide enough background?
- If the thesis is presented in the opening, is it clear and is it related effectively to the issue? If the thesis is delayed, is the organization of the draft easy to follow?
- If the essay adopts a "self-announcing" structure (see pages 92–94), does the introduction forecast the organizational structure of the essay? Does the essay follow the structure as forecasted? Are transitions between parts clear?
- If the essay adopts an "unfolding" structure, can you follow the argument? Upon reflection after reading the essay, can you identify the claim and supporting reasons?
- Is the effectiveness of the essay diminished by wordiness, clumsy sentence structure, ineffective passive voice, and other problems of editing, grammar, or style?

SUMMARY OF YOUR RECOMMENDATIONS
AS PEER REVIEWER

- What improvements can be made in quality of the writing?
- What improvements can be made in the main reasons supporting the claim?
- What improvements can be made in the use of data and evidence as *grounds* for the argument?
- What rhetorical changes would you recommend? Adopting a different tone or stance toward audience? Shifting from a one-sided to two-sided argument? Creating more audience-based reasons? Other?

IV

ARGUMENTS IN DEPTH: FIVE CATEGORIES OF CLAIMS

A PREFACE TO PART IV: AN OVERVIEW OF TRUTH CLAIMS AND VALUES CLAIMS

In Parts I, II, and III we discussed the arguing process, the basic structure of arguments, and the relation of arguments to audience. In Part IV, we introduce you to a five-category schema of arguments in order to examine in closer detail the kinds of argumentative "moves" that each category of argument requires. In particular, we suggest ways of using the five-category schema of argument to help you develop different kinds of argument structures. The value of our schema is not that it helps you classify all arguments; in fact, you will come across many arguments that resist and some that defy classification. Rather, the value of the five-category schema is that it helps you generate ideas for an argument by helping you recognize some common patterns that arguments follow. By playing with the categories, by treating a given argument, for example, as if it were a causal or evaluational claim, we open up new avenues of support and refutation.

Chapters 11, 12, and 13 examine arguments about the truth of things, and Chapters 14, 15, and 16 examine arguments about the value of things. (Chapters 14 and 15 discuss general strategies for conducting values arguments; Chapter 16 focuses on specific problems of moral arguments.)

In the previous paragraph we hinted at the difference between arguments about truth and arguments about value. Before turning to the chapters themselves, we should consider for a moment the differences between these kinds of arguments.

WHAT IS A TRUTH ARGUMENT?

Truth arguments involve disputes about the way reality is (or was or will be). Unlike facts, which can be confirmed or disconfirmed by using agreed-on empirical measures, a truth claim involves interpretation of facts, which, like all interpretations, must be supported by reasons.

However, locating the point at which a "fact" turns into a "claim" is a tricky issue. The French mathematician Poincaré said that a fact is something that is "common to several thinking beings and could be common to all." This definition seems simple enough. Water freezes at 32 degrees; Chicago is in Illinois; the state of Illinois did not ratify the Equal Rights Amendment. These are all facts. No problem. But what about the statement "Life is preferable to death." That seems like a statement that could be common to all. But it isn't. The fact that thousands of people voluntarily take their own lives each year establishes that it's not a factual statement. And what makes the number of suicides a fact?—the possibility that we could all go look the information up in a source we all agreed was authoritative and find the same number.

But what about an apparently "factual" statement such as "Joe is literate." Does that mean that Joe can read a newspaper? A traffic sign? A fourth-grade reader? A novel? Or does it mean that he's read a number of books that we've agreed are essential for all educated members of our culture to have read? Anytime an apparent statement of fact requires interpretation (in this case because of a dispute over the definition of *literate*), anytime all who know the thing being referred to don't share a common understanding of that thing, we are in the realm of truth claims, not of facts. Here are some examples of the kinds of truth claims that the next three chapters examine:

Sam is/is not an alcoholic. (X is a Y—definitional argument)

The bombing of Libya will/will not decrease terrorism. (X causes Y—causal argument)

Investing in the stock market is/is not like gambling. (X is like Y— resemblance argument)

WHAT IS A VALUES ARGUMENT?

For many people, the only sort of argument we can legitimately have is over claims of truth. Values, after all, are personal, whereas truth can be looked at objectively. But the notion that values are purely personal is a dangerous one. If for no other reason, it's dangerous because every day we encounter value issues that must be resolved. If you think you deserve a promotion and your boss doesn't, your own sense of self-worth won't let you ignore the resulting values dispute. If you think your community needs a new school and a majority of voters is unpersuaded, you need to articulate your views before election day or else your vote may be wasted.

Values may begin as feelings founded on private experience, but a real value must go beyond these beginnings and be capable of being justified. Otherwise, it remains an opinion, which is a feeling limited to personal experiences, your own private collection of likes and dislikes that couldn't be justified even if it were necessary. But values can be justified; they are transpersonal and shareable. We can articulate criteria that others would agree are significant and coherent and then we can apply those criteria to situations, people, and things and come to some agreement.

Here then are some examples of the kinds of values claims that the following chapters will examine:

Dr. Jones is/is not a good teacher. (X is a good Y—evaluation claim)

Congress should/should not pass a balanced-budget amendment. (We should do X—proposal argument)

Dr. Jones is/is not a good person. (special case of evaluation claim— moral argument)

11

DEFINITION ARGUMENTS: X IS/IS NOT A Y

CASE 1

In 1989 the city of Seattle passed the Family Leave Ordinance, which allowed city employees to use their sick leave to care for a "domestic partner" who is ill. To be eligible for domestic partnership, a couple, whether heterosexual or homosexual, had to file affidavits declaring that they share the same home with their partners, are each other's sole partners, and are responsible for each other's common welfare. For purposes of sick and bereavement leave, domestic partnership was synonymous with marriage. Supporters of this ordinance argued that, in the words of one local columnist, "[i]f sick and bereavement leave is given to married workers, then those in domestic partnerships equivalent to marriage ought to have the same privilege" [Terry Tang, *Seattle Times*, November 2, 1990, p. A10]. Opponents of the ordinance argued that domestic partnerships are not marriages and shouldn't be treated as such.

CASE 2

In August 1985, Charles Manson, who was serving a life sentence for a particularly gruesome murder, came up for parole. A key question facing the parole board was whether Manson was now "mentally competent to reenter society." The criteria for "mental competence" included the following: the ability to tell right from wrong, the ability to feel compunction for his crimes, and the capacity to have normal feelings for other people. The parole board was charged with making a definitional judgment: How might Manson's mental state be classified?

CASE 3

Economist Isabella Sawhill believes that the current distinctions among "poor," "middle income," and "rich" don't help us understand the real problem of poverty in America. She proposes a new term "underclass." According to her definition, the defining characteristic of the underclass is "dysfunctional behavior," which means failure to follow four major norms of middle-class society: (1) Children are supposed to study hard in school; (2) no one is supposed to become a parent until able to afford a child; (3) adults are supposed to hold regular jobs; and (4) everyone is supposed to obey laws. If we use this definition instead of income level, a rich drug dealer may be a member of the underclass while a poor widow might not be. Sawhill believes society can improve the lives of the underclass by changing these dysfunctional characteristics rather than by relieving poverty directly. A new definition thus aims at changing social policy. [Spencer Rich, "Economist: Behavior draws lines between the classes," *Seattle Times*, September 13, 1989, p. A4.]

THE SPECIAL NATURE OF A DEFINITIONAL ISSUE

Many arguments require a definition of key terms. If you are arguing, for example, that after-school jobs are harmful to teenagers because they promote materialism, you will have to define *materialism* somewhere in your argument. Writers regularly define words for their readers either by providing synonyms, by citing a dictionary definition, by stipulating a special definition ("Ordinarily word X means such and so, but in this essay I am using word X to mean this"), or by giving an extended definition in which the writer defines the term and then illustrates the definition with several clarifying examples. This chapter shows you ways to provide such definitions for your readers.

However, this chapter does not focus primarily on writing occasional definitions within arguments. Rather, its purpose is to describe how an entire argument can be devoted to a definitional issue. Definitional arguments, according to our usage, occur whenever people disagree about the actual definition of a term or about the "match" or "fit" between an agreed-on definition and a specific object or concept. For example, an argument about whether or not *Penthouse* magazine is pornographic is a definitional argument; as such it will involve two related issues: (1) What do we mean by "pornographic" (the definition issue)? and (2) Does *Penthouse* fit that definition (the match issue)?

Before proceeding with our explanation of definitional arguments, we will present the writing assignment for Chapter 11. This chapter will be more meaningful to you if you read it in the light of a definitional problem that you will need to solve for one of your own essays.

WRITING ASSIGNMENT FOR CHAPTER 11: EXTENDED DEFINITION/BORDERLINE CASE: IS THIS X A Y?

This assignment asks you to solve a definitional problem. In your essay, you must argue whether or not a given X (a borderline case) belongs to concept Y, which you must define.* You will need to write an extended definition of a concept such as "police brutality," "courageous action," "child abuse," "creative act," "cruelty to animals," "free speech," or another, similar concept that is both familiar yet tricky to define precisely. After you have established your definition, you will need to apply it to a "borderline case," arguing whether the borderline case fits or does not fit the definition. For example:

1. Is a daring bank robbery an "act of courage"?
2. Is accounting a "creative profession"?
3. Are highly skilled videogame players "true athletes"?
4. Is a case like the following an instance of "cruelty to animals"?

> A bunch of starlings build nests in the attic of a family's house, gaining access to the attic through a torn vent screen. Soon the eggs hatch, and every morning at sunrise the family is awakened by the sounds of birds squawking and wings beating against rafters as the starlings fly in and out of the house to feed the hatchlings. After losing considerable early morning sleep, the family repairs the screen. Unable to get in and out, the parent birds are unable to feed their young. The birds die within a day.

One part of your essay should be an extended definition of your Y term (in the above case, cruelty to animals), in which you set forth the criteria for your chosen Y, illustrating each criterion with positive and contrastive examples. Once you have established your definition of Y, you will use it to decide whether your chosen X term (the borderline case—in the preceding case, the repairing of the screen, which leads to the death of the starlings)

*The writing assignment for this chapter, as well as the collaborative exercises for exploration and development of ideas, is based on the work of George Hillocks and his research associates at the University of Chicago. See George Hillocks, Jr., Elizabeth A. Kahn, and Larry R. Johannessen, "Teaching Defining Strategies as a Mode of Inquiry: Some Effects on Student Writing," *Research in the Teaching of English,* 17 (October 1983), pp. 275–284. See also Larry R. Johannessen, Elizabeth A. Kahn, and Carolyn Calhoun Walter, *Designing and Sequencing Prewriting Activities,* Urbana, Ill.: NCTE, 1982.

meets or does not meet the criteria. The rest of this chapter explains this arguing strategy in detail.

THE CRITERIA-MATCH STRUCTURE OF DEFINITIONAL ARGUMENTS

Definitional arguments take the form "X is/is not a Y." This claim can be restated in various ways: "X is/is not a case of Y," "X is/is not an instance of Y," "X does/does not belong to the class of Y," and so forth. The Y term can be either a noun phrase ("Writing graffiti on walls is *vandalism*") or an adjective phrase ("Writing graffiti on walls is *politically useless*" — that is, *"belongs to the class of politically useless things"*).

To appreciate the structure of a definitional argument, consider the shape of a typical definitional claim when its reasons are stated as because clauses: X is a Y because it possesses features A, B, and C. If we expand this enthymeme into a syllogism, it looks like this:

If something possesses features A, B, and C, then it is a Y.

X possesses features A, B, and C.

Therefore, X is a Y.

As this syllogism suggests, a definitional argument usually requires us to develop both the major and the minor premises behind our claim. The major premise requires us to show what conditions need to be met (or what criteria need to be present) before we can call something a Y. ("Everything with features A, B, and C is a Y.") The minor premise requires us to show that X meets these criteria. ("X has features A, B, and C.") The same example placed in Toulmin's schema looks like this:

Enthymeme:	X is a Y because it possesses features A, B, and C.
Claim:	X is a Y.
Stated Reason:	It possesses features A, B, and C.
Grounds:	evidence that it possesses features A, B, and C
Warrant:	Having features A, B, and C is sufficient criteria for calling something a Y.
Backing:	chains of reasons and evidence showing that true Y's have features A, B, and C
Conditions of Rebuttal:	unless X doesn't possess sufficient quantities of features

A, B, and C; unless X possesses, in addition to features A, B, and C, a fourth feature Z, which makes it impossible to be a Y

Qualifier: depends on actual case

As shown above, definitional arguments of the type "X is a Y" tend to have a two-part structure: (1) How do we define Y? and (2) Does X fit that definition? We use the term *criteria-match* to describe this structure, which occurs regularly not only in definitional arguments but also, as we shall see in Chapter 14, in values arguments of the type "X is a good/bad Y." The "criteria" part of the structure defines the Y term by setting forth the criteria that must be met to be considered a Y (these criteria are the warrants for the argument). The "match" part examines whether or not the X term meets these criteria (evidence that X meets the criteria is the grounds for the argument). Let's consider several more examples:

Definitional Claim: Weaving is a craft, not an art.
Criteria part: What are the criteria for a craft?
Match part: Does weaving meet these criteria?

Definitional Claim: Argentina's attempt to take over the Falkland Islands was/was not an act of aggression against Great Britain.
Criteria part: What constitutes an "act of aggression"?
Match part: Did Argentina's attempt to take over the Falklands meet these criteria?

FOR CLASS DISCUSSION
Consider the following definitional claims. Working as individuals or in small groups, identify the criteria issue and the match issue for each of the following claims. (Any of these examples could be potential topics for an "extended definition/borderline case" argument of the kind you are asked to write for this chapter.)

1. Childbirth is/is not a creative art.
2. Writing graffiti on subways is/is not vandalism.
3. The language "spoken" by porpoises is/is not true language.
4. Beauty contests are/are not sexist events.
5. Spiking the football in the end zone is/is not an unsportsmanlike act.
6. Psychology is/is not a true science.
7. Designing advertisements for television is/is not a creative activity.
8. A surrogate mother—one who has had another woman's ferti-

lized egg implanted in her uterus—is/is not the true mother of the child.

9. Cheerleaders are/are not athletes.

10. Poker is/is not a game of luck.

CONCEPTUAL PROBLEMS OF DEFINITION

Before moving on to discuss ways of defining the Y term in a definitional argument, we need to discuss some of the conceptual difficulties of definition. Language, as you quickly discover when you try to analyze it, is a slippery subject. Definitions aren't as easy to make, or as certain, as a handy pocket dictionary might lead you to believe.

Language as a Way of Ordering the World

Language is our primary means of making sense of the world. Through language we convert what psychologist William James called the "buzz and confusion" of the world into a system of classes and relationships that are represented by a network of verbal signs called words. Each naming word in a language depends on our perceiving a set of attributes that any object or concept must have in order to bear that name. Naming words (with the exception of proper names) don't designate particular items but rather attributes of items. Hence, when we want to know what *king* means, we don't need to know every king in history. We simply need to know the characteristics of kings and kingship to understand and use the term. Through naming we are set free from the world of immediate particulars where we can see only this rock or that flower; through naming we are liberated into a shareable world where we possess with other humans the concept "rock" and the concept "flower" along with arbitrary signs—the vocal sounds "rock" and "flower"—that call forth the concepts.

But if naming is the "first act" of language users, it's far from a simple one. Words allow us to share concepts, but they certainly don't assure perfect mutual understanding. Inevitably, as soon as we've named something, someone else will ask "Whaddya mean by that?" Language, for all its wonderful powers, is an arbitrary system that requires agreement among its users before it can work. And it's not always easy to get that agreement. Thus, the second act after naming is defining. And even at the most basic level, defining things can be devilishly complex.

Why Can't We Just Look
in the Dictionary?

"What's so hard about defining?" you might ask. Why not just look in a dictionary? To get a sense of the complexity of defining something, consider the word *red*. What does it mean? Although you might agree with us that *red* is difficult to define in words, you could argue that you can escape the problem simply by pointing to something red. Maybe. But consider the following example cited by I. A. Richards and C. K. Ogden in *The Meaning of Meaning*.

An English explorer, investigating an unknown Congolese language, found himself in a hut with five natives standing around a wooden table. The explorer tapped the table and asked "What's this?" Each of the five Congolese gave him a different answer, causing the explorer to congratulate himself for "working among a people who possessed so rich a language that they had five words for one article" (*Meaning*, p. 78).

Only later did he discover that the natives had understood his apparently straightforward gesture in five different ways. One thought he was asking the word for "wood"; another for "table covering"; the third thought he wanted the word for "hardness"; the fourth for "tapping." Only one guessed his actual intention and gave him the Congolese word for "table." Even when we can point to an object in reality, then, there is possibility for confusion. Think how these difficulties multiply as we move on to words standing for things that can't be pointed toward, words like *love* and *freedom* and *cruelty to animals*.

But let's go back to dictionaries and their limitations in resolving definitional disputes. Say you wanted to resolve the debate over whether or not cheerleaders are athletes by turning to your dictionary. An athlete, according to our dictionary, is "one who is trained to compete in exercises, sports, or games requiring physical strength, agility, or skill." So, are cheerleaders athletes? They do train, and the activity itself of leading cheers would appear to require "strength, agility, and skill." But is it a form of "competition"? Do they "compete" against the rival cheerleaders? And is cheerleading "exercise, sport, or game?" Well, you're going to have to keep looking in your dictionary before you can even begin to address these questions. And take it from us, you won't be able to stop once you've defined all the attributes of your first definition.

Dictionaries usually can't resolve real definitional disputes because their function is to tell us the commonly held meanings of words. That is, their purpose is to tell us what words mean in general usage, without getting into the shades and nuances of meaning that are at the heart of most definitional disputes. People arguing over the definition of *athlete* probably already know the approximate dictionary definition of the word. But words aren't facts and an exact meaning common to all is impossible when words are always changing their meaning over time and between contexts. Moreover, dictionary definitions rarely tell us such things as *to what degree* a given condition must be met before it qualifies for class membership. *How much* do you need to train to qualify as an athlete? *To what extent* must you compete? How strong or agile does an athlete have to be? On all such critical matters, dictionaries are too often silent to settle definitional disputes.

Definitions and the Rule of Justice: At What Point Does X Quit Being a Y?

For some people, all this concern about definition may seem misplaced. How often, after all, have you heard people accuse each other of getting bogged down in "mere semantics"? But how we define a given word can have significant implications for people who must either use the word or have the word used on them. Take, for example, what some philosophers refer to as "the rule of justice." According to this rule, "beings in the same essential category should be treated in the same way." Should an insurance company, for example, treat a woman who needs to miss work following childbirth the same way it treats a woman who needs to miss work following an appendectomy? Should childbirth belong within the category "illness" as far as insurance payments are concerned? Similarly, if a company gives "new baby" leave to a mother, should it also be willing to give "new baby" leave to a father? In other words, is this kind of leave "new mother" leave or is it "new parent" leave? And what if a couple adopts an infant? Should "new mother" or "new parent" leave be available to them also? These questions are all definitional issues involving arguments about what class of beings an individual belongs to and about what actions to take to comply with the "rule of justice," which demands that all members of that class be treated equally.

Let's take a slightly less elevated (and less complex) problem of definitional justice. If your landlord decides to institute a "no pets" rule, then the rule of justice requires that all pets have to go—not just your neighbor's barking dog, but also Mrs. Brown's cat, the kids' hamster downstairs, and your own pet tarantula. In order to keep your friendly spider, though, mightn't you argue that your pet tarantula isn't really a "pet"? Because the rule of justice demands that all pets must be treated equally, the only fair way to save your spider is to get it removed from the class "pets." The rule of justice thus forces the question "How much can any given X vary before it is no longer a Y?"

The rule of justice becomes even harder to apply when we consider X's that grow, evolve, or otherwise change through time. When Young Person back in Chapter 1 argued that she could set her own curfew because she was mature, she raised the question "What are the attributes or criteria of a

'mature' person?" In this case, a categorical distinction between two separate kinds of things ("mature" versus "not mature") evolves into a distinction of degree ("mature enough"). So perhaps we should not ask whether
Young Person is mature, but whether she is "mature enough." At what
point does a child become an adult? (When does a fetus become a human
person? When does a B essay become an A essay? When does a social
drinker become an alcoholic?)

Although we may be able arbitrarily to choose a particular point and
declare, through stipulation, that "mature" means eighteen years old or
that "human person" includes a fetus at conception, or at three months, or
at birth, in the everyday world the distinction between child and adult,
between egg and person, between social drinking and alcoholism seems an
evolution, not a sudden and definitive step. Nevertheless, our language
requires an abrupt shift between classes. In short, applying the rule of
justice often requires us to adopt a digital approach to reality—switches are
either on or off, either a fetus is a human person or it is not—whereas our
sense of life is more analogical—there are numberless gradations between
on and off, there are countless shades of gray between black and white.

As we can see in the above case, the promise of language to fix the buzz
and confusion of the world into an orderly set of categories turns out to be
elusive. In most definitional debates, an argument, not a quick trip to the
dictionary, is required to settle the matter.

CONDUCTING A CRITERIA-
MATCH ARGUMENT

Having raised some philosophical issues about definition, let's now proceed
directly to a discussion of how to conduct a criteria-match argument. When
you prepare to develop and write a definitional argument, you need first to
determine if the criteria or the match or both are primarily at issue.

In some arguments the criteria part—that is, determining the defining
characteristics of Y—is the most difficult. The Minneapolis ordinance
against pornography, referred to in Chapter 9, is an example of this kind of
argument. According to that ordinance, if a magazine or film meets any of
nine criteria, it can be considered pornographic. The major difficulty faced
by drafters of the ordinance was establishing the nine criteria.

In other arguments the match part will take the majority of your time. If
you wanted to argue that your calculus course was badly organized, you
would probably spend most of your time showing examples of disorganization in the course and little time, if any, defining *disorganized.* In still other
arguments—such as the extended definition/borderline case assignment in

this chapter — the criteria and match parts might both demand considerable attention. The point is, however, that all definitional arguments have at their core a criteria-match structure even if one part of the structure can be virtually eliminated in specific cases.

DEFINING THE Y TERM (ESTABLISHING CRITERIA FOR Y)

Unless your Y term is easy to define, you will have to present an extended definition in which you gradually bring your reader step by step toward understanding your criteria. In this section we discuss two methods of definition — Aristotelian and operational.

Aristotelian Definition

In Aristotelian definitions, regularly used in dictionaries, one defines a term by placing it within the next larger class or category and then showing the specific attributes that distinguish the term from other terms within the same category. For example, a *pencil* is a "writing implement" (next larger category) that differs from other writing implements in that it makes marks with lead or graphite rather than ink. You could elaborate this definition by saying "usually the lead or graphite is a long, thin column embedded in a slightly thicker column of wood with an eraser on one end and a sharpened point, exposing the graphite, on the other." You could even distinguish a wooden pencil from a mechanical pencil, thereby indicating again that the crucial identifying attribute is the graphite, not the wooden column.

As you can see, an Aristotelian definition of a Y term creates specific criteria that enable you to distinguish it from the next larger class. But whereas our example of a pencil is relatively easy, most criteria arguments are more complex, requiring you not just to state your criteria but to argue for them. For example, when trying to define *true sports car* for the claim "A Thunderbird is/is not a true sports car," you might have to defend such criteria as these: "A true sports car is an automobile that has seats for only two people" or "A true sports car is an automobile designed specifically for racing on narrow curving roads." Most of the space in the criteria section of your essay would be spent justifying the criteria you have chosen, usually through examples, contrastive examples, and refutation of opposing criteria.

"ACCIDENTAL," "NECESSARY," AND "SUFFICIENT" CRITERIA IN AN ARISTOTELIAN DEFINITION

In constructing Aristotelian definitions it is sometimes helpful to understand and use the concepts of "accidental," "necessary," and "sufficient" criteria. An "accidental" criterion is a usual but not essential feature of a concept. For example, "made out of wood" is an accidental feature of a pencil. Most pencils are made out of wood, but something can still be a pencil even if it isn't made out of wood (a mechanical pencil).

Although the distinction between accidental and essential features is relatively clear when discussing things such as pencils, it gets increasingly cloudy as we move into complex definitional debates (for example, what are the accidental, as opposed to essential, characteristics of sexist acts?).

A "necessary" criterion is an attribute that *must* be present for something to be a Y. For example, "is a writing implement" is a necessary criterion for a pencil; "marks with graphite or lead" is also a necessary criterion. However, neither of these criteria by itself is a sufficient criterion for a pencil. Many writing implements aren't pencils (for example, pens); also, many things that mark with lead or graphite aren't pencils (for example, a lead paperweight will make pencil-like marks on paper). To be a pencil both these criteria together must be present. We say, then, that these two criteria together are *sufficient* criteria for the concept "pencil."

You can appreciate how these concepts can help you carry on a definitional argument with more precision. Felix Ungar might argue that a Thunderbird is not a true sports car because it has rear seats. (To Felix, having seating for only two people is thus a necessary criterion for a true sports car.) Oscar Madison might argue, however, that having two seats is only an accidental feature of sports cars and that a Thunderbird is indeed a true sports car because it has a racy appearance and because it handles superbly on curves. (For Oscar, racy appearance and superb handling are together sufficient criteria for a true sports car.)

FOR CLASS DISCUSSION

Working individually or in small groups, try to determine whether each of the following is a necessary criterion, a sufficient criterion, an accidental criterion, or no criterion for defining the indicated concept. Be prepared to explain your reasoning.

CRITERION	CONCEPT TO BE DEFINED
presence of gills	fish
having yellow hair (applied to person)	blond
born inside the United States	American citizen

CRITERION	CONCEPT TO BE DEFINED
over sixty-five	senior citizen
knows several programming languages for computers	meets foreign language requirement for graduation
line endings form a rhyming pattern	poem
teaches classes at a college	college professor
eats no meat, ever	vegetarian
kills another human being	murderer
good sex life	happy marriage

Placing Aristotelian Definitions in Context

It is important to appreciate how the context of a given argument can affect your definition of a term. The question "Is a tarantula kept in the house a pet?" may actually have opposing answers, depending on the rhetorical situation. You may argue that your tarantula is or is not a pet, depending on whether you are trying to exclude it from your landlord's "no pet" rule or include it in your local talk show's "weird pet contest." Within one context you will want to argue that what your landlord really means by "pet" is an animal (next larger class) capable of disturbing neighbors or harming the landlord's property (criteria that distinguish it from other members of the class). Thus you could argue that your tarantula isn't a pet in your landlord's sense because it is incapable of harming property or disturbing the peace (assuming you don't let it loose!). In the other context you would argue that a pet is "any living thing" (note that in this context the "next larger class" is much larger) with which a human being forms a caring attachment and which shares its owner's domicile. In this case you might say, "Tommy Tarantula here is one of my dearest friends and if you don't think Tommy is weird enough, wait 'til I show you Vanessa, my pet Venus's-flytrap."

To apply the same principle to a different field of debate, consider whether or not obscene language in a student newspaper should be protected by the First Amendment. The purpose of school officials' suspending editors responsible for such language is to maintain order and decency in the school. The school officials thus narrow the category of acts that are protected under the free speech amendment in order to meet their purposes. On the other hand, the American Civil Liberties Union (which has long defended student newspaper editors) is intent on avoiding any precedent that will restrict freedom of speech any more than is absolute necessary. The different definitions of *free speech* that are apt to emerge thus reflect the different purposes of the disputants.

The problem of purpose shows why it is so hard to define a word out of context. Some people try to escape this dilemma by returning to the "original intent" of the authors of precedent-setting documents such as the Constitution. But if we try to determine the original intent of the writers of the Constitution on such matters as "free speech," "cruel and unusual punishment," or the "right to bear arms," we must still ask what their original purposes were in framing the constitutional language. If we can show that those original purposes are no longer relevant to present concerns, we have begun to undermine what would otherwise appear to be a static and universal definition to which we could turn.

Operational Definitions

In some rhetorical situations, particularly those arising in the physical and social sciences, writers need precise definitions that can be measured empirically and are not subject to problems of context and disputed criteria. Consider, for example, an argument involving the concept "aggression." "Do violent television programs increase the incidence of aggression in children?" To do research on this issue a scientist needs a precise, measurable definition of *aggression*. Typically, a scientist might measure "aggression" by counting "the number of blows or kicks a child gives to an inflatable bozo doll over a fifteen-minute period when other play options are available." The scientist might then define "aggressive behavior" as six or more blows to the bozo doll. Such definitions are useful in that they are precisely measurable, but they are also limited in that they omit criteria that may be unmeasurable but important. Is it adequate, for example, to define a "superior student" as someone with a 3.2 GPA or higher? Or is it adequate to define an "aggressive child" as one who pummels bozo dolls instead of playing with trucks?

CONDUCTING THE MATCH
PART OF A
DEFINITIONAL ARGUMENT

As we showed at the beginning of this chapter, a typical enthymeme for a definitional argument is as follows: "X is a Y because it possesses attributes A, B, and C." In the criteria part of the argument you show that A, B, and

C are the necessary and sufficient criteria for something to be called a Y. Then in the match part of your argument you show that X possesses the attributes A, B, and C. Generally you do so by using either examples or analysis.

Suppose you wanted to argue that your history teacher was an "authoritarian." Since he is in some ways rather lax—for example, he doesn't count off for late papers and he doesn't require class attendance—some of your classmates say he isn't authoritarian at all. (They are in effect saying that harsh treatment for late papers and absences is a necessary condition for calling a teacher "authoritarian.") Consequently you establish the following criteria for "authoritarian": repression of alternative points of view and strict adherence to certain arbitrary procedures. You now need to show that your history teacher meets these criteria. You write the following enthymeme to serve as the core of your argument:

> My history professor is an authoritarian because he represses questions and alternate points of view in his class and because he demands strict adherence to arbitrary procedures for doing the assignments.

To support this argument, you would give various examples of his meeting these two criteria: To show his repression of alternative points of view, you might cite, among other examples, the time he embarrassed a student for disagreeing with him on the rightness of Harry Truman's decision to drop the atomic bomb on Hiroshima. And to show his adherence to arbitrary procedures, you could, among other things, mention how he reduces the grade on an essay if the margins aren't precisely one and a half inches.

In other kinds of arguments, you may have to analyze the features of your X rather than just cite examples. For instance, if you argue that one *necessary* criterion for "police brutality" is "intention"—that is, the police officer must intend the harm—then you will need to analyze your borderline case to see if the police officer intentionally (as opposed to accidentally) harmed the victim. If the harm was accidental, then you could relieve the officer of the charge "police brutality." Thus through the power of example or analysis you show that X possesses the attributes of Y.

WRITING YOUR DEFINITIONAL ARGUMENT

With this background, you are now ready to begin writing your "extended definition/borderline case" argument. The following steps should help you in that process.

STARTING POINTS: FINDING A DEFINITIONAL CONTROVERSY

The key to this assignment is finding a good controversy about a definition. A fruitful way to begin is through discussion with others. Perhaps your instructor will use the following discussion exercise in class; if not, start a similar conversation with friends.

FOR CLASS DISCUSSION

1. Suppose you wanted to define the concept "courage." Working in groups, try to decide whether each of the following cases is an example of courage:

   a. A neighbor rushes into a burning house to rescue a child from certain death and emerges, coughing and choking, with the child in his arms. Is the neighbor courageous?

   b. A fireman rushes into a burning house to rescue a child from certain death and emerges with the child in his arms. The fireman is wearing protective clothing and a gas mask. When a newspaper reporter calls him courageous, he says, "Hey, this is my job." Is the fireman courageous?

   c. A teenager rushes into a burning house to recover a memento given to him by his girlfriend, the first love of his life. Is the teenager courageous?

   d. A parent rushes into a burning house to save a trapped child. The fire marshal tells the parent to wait because there is no chance the child can be reached from the first floor. The fire marshal wants to try cutting a hole in the roof to reach the child. The parent rushes into the house anyway and is burned to death. Was the parent courageous?

   e. Are mountain climbers and parachutists courageous in scaling rock precipices or jumping out of airplanes during their leisure hours?

   f. Is a robber courageous in performing a daring bank robbery?

   g. Mutt and Jeff are standing on a cliff high above a lake. Mutt dares Jeff to dive into the water. Jeff refuses, saying it is too dangerous. Mutt double dares Jeff, who still refuses. So Mutt dives into the water and, on surfacing, yells up at Jeff, calling him a coward and taunting him to dive. Jeff starts to dive, but then backs off and takes the trail down to the lake, feeling ashamed and silly. Was Mutt courageous? Was Jeff courageous?

2. As you make your decisions on each of the cases, create and refine the criteria you use.

3. Make up your own series of controversial cases, like those above for "courage," for one or more of the following concepts:
   a. cruelty to animals
   b. child abuse
   c. true athlete
   d. sexual harassment
   e. free speech protected by the First Amendment

Once you complete the preceding exercise, choose one of the most controversial cases within a topic area you enjoy and consider using that as the subject of your essay. Or look back through your idea-log to see if any of your entries focus on definitional issues. Clear your definitional issue with your instructor.

EXPLORATION STAGE I: DEVELOPING CRITERIA FOR YOUR Y TERM

One effective way to discover criteria is to use a definitional heuristic in which you search for cases that are instances of "Y," "not Y," and "maybe Y." You will find that criteria for Y begin to emerge as your group discusses the characteristics of obvious instances of Y, contrastive instances of not Y, and then borderline instances of maybe Y.

Suppose, for example, you wanted to argue the claim that "accounting is/is not a creative profession." Your first goal is to establish criteria for a creative profession. Using this heuristic, you would begin by thinking of examples of obviously creative behaviors, then of contrastive behaviors that seem similar to the previous behaviors but yet are clearly not creative, and then finally of borderline behaviors that may or may not be creative. Your list might look like this:

EXAMPLES OF CREATIVE BEHAVIORS

Beethoven composes a symphony.

An architect designs a house.

Edison invents the light bulb.

An engineer designs a machine that will make widgets in a new way.

A poet writes a poem (later revised to "A poet writes a poem that poetry experts say is beautiful"—see following discussion).

CONTRASTIVE EXAMPLES OF NONCREATIVE BEHAVIORS

A conductor transposes Beethoven's symphony into a different key.

A carpenter builds a house from the architect's plan.

I change a lightbulb in my house.

A factory worker uses the new machine to stamp out widgets.

A graduate student writes stupid "love/dove" poems for birthday cards.

EXAMPLES OF BORDERLINE CASES

A woman gives birth to a child.

An accountant figures out your income tax.

A musician plays Beethoven's symphony with great skill.

A monkey paints an oil painting by smearing paint on canvas: a group of art critics, not knowing a monkey was the artist, call the painting beautiful.

After you have brainstormed for your various cases, develop your criteria by determining what features the "clearly creative" examples have in common and what features the "clearly noncreative" examples lack. Then you refine your criteria by deciding on what grounds you might include or eliminate your borderline cases from the category "creative." For example, you might begin with the following criterion:

DEFINITION: FIRST TRY

For an act to be creative, it must result in an end product that is significantly different from other products.

But then, by looking at some of the examples in your creative and noncreative columns, you decide that just producing a different end product isn't enough. A bad poem might be different from other poems, but you don't want to call a bad poet creative. So you refine your criteria.

DEFINITION: SECOND TRY

For an act to be creative, it must result in an end product that is significantly different from other products and is yet useful or beautiful.

This definition would allow you to include all the acts in your creative column but eliminate the acts in the noncreative column.

Your next step is to refine your criteria by deciding whether to include or reject items in your borderline list. You decide to reject the childbirth case by arguing that creativity must be a mental or intellectual activity, not a natural process. You reject the monkey as painter example on similar grounds, arguing that although the end product may be both original and beautiful, it is not creative because it is not a product of the monkey's intellect. Finally, you reject the example of the musician playing Beethoven's symphony. Like the carpenter who builds the house, the musician possesses great skill but doesn't design a new product; rather, he or she follows the instructions of the designer. (A music major in your group reacts bitterly, arguing that musicians "interpret" music and that such behavior is creative. She notes that the music department is housed in a building called the "Creative Arts Complex." Your group, however, can't figure out a way to reword the definition to include performance rather than production. If you call performing musicians creative, the rest of the group argues, then the rule of justice forces you to call carpenters creative also, because both kinds of craftspeople reproduce the creative intentions of others. Once we call performers creative, they argue, the concept of creativity will get so broad that it will no longer be useful.) Your group's final definition, then, looks like this (with the music major dissenting):

DEFINITION: THIRD TRY

For an act to be creative, it must be produced by intellectual design, and it must result in an end product that is significantly different from other products and is yet useful or beautiful.

Having established these criteria, you are ready for your final borderline case, your original issue of whether or not accounting is a creative profession. Based on your criteria, you might decide that accounting is not generally a creative profession because the final products are not significantly new or different. For the most part, accountants do elaborately complex calculations, but they generally follow established procedures in doing so. However, the profession can sometimes offer creative opportunities when an accountant, for example, develops a new kind of computer program or develops new, improved procedures for handling routine business.

The definitional heuristic thus produces a systematic procedure for developing criteria for a definitional argument. Moreover, it provides an organizational strategy for writing the criteria part of your argument because one good way to conduct a definitional argument is to take your reader step by step through the process of establishing your criteria. In other words, you would use the examples from your list to show your reader first your rough criteria and then your increasingly refined criteria derived from consideration of your borderline cases.

FOR CLASS DISCUSSION

1. Working as a group, try the definitional heuristic on the topic "cruelty to animals" (or some other Y chosen by the instructor or your group). Make three lists.

a. obvious examples of cruelty to animals
b. contrastive examples, that is, behaviors that are not cruel to animals (Try to vary a few features of each entry under "a" above so that the example switches from cruelty to non-cruelty.)
c. borderline cases (Include the starling example from page 211.)

2. Once you have created your list of cases, create a one-sentence definition of "cruelty to animals" following the pattern described earlier for creativity. Your definition should include each of the criteria you have established.

3. In your idea-log, make a similar three-column list for the Y term you have chosen for your own definitional essay. Then create a working definition for your Y term by deciding on your criteria.

EXPLORATION STAGE II: EXPLORING YOUR MATCH ARGUMENT

In doing the earlier class discussion exercises, you have practiced arguing whether borderline cases met your definitions for "courage" or "cruelty to animals." Now try this exercise in your idea-log. List the criteria for your chosen Y term; then freewrite for five or ten minutes exploring whether your borderline case meets each of the criteria. Prior to writing the first draft of your argument, you might also explore your ideas further by doing the eight freewriting tasks in Idea-Log, Set Two (pages 73–75 in Chapter 3).

WRITING THE DISCOVERY DRAFT—A POSSIBLE ORGANIZATIONAL STRUCTURE FOR YOUR ESSAY

You are now ready to write your discovery draft. At this stage it may be helpful to look at a typical organizational structure for an extended definition/borderline case essay. Such an organization is shown in Figure 11–1.

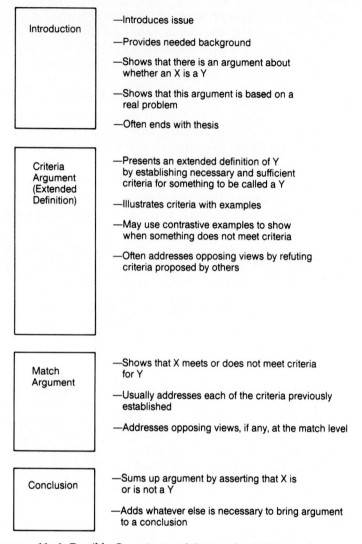

FIGURE 11-1. Possible Organizational Pattern for Definition Argument

The argument typically begins by introducing the reader to the controversy and by showing that the definition of the Y term or the match between the Y definition and the X term is problematic. The body of the essay usually begins with an extended definition of the Y term, followed by an argument showing that the X term does or does not meet the definition. Sometimes a writer will present all the criteria for the Y term before moving to the match argument. At other times, the writer might choose to proceed one criterion at a time by first describing the criterion, arguing that the X term meets it, and then proceeding to the next criterion.

REVISION STAGE

Once you have written a discovery draft, you will better appreciate the complexity of your issue and see it more clearly. As you revise your draft, your goal will be to make your argument clear and persuasive for readers. You might find it helpful at this time to summarize your argument as a claim with because clauses and to test it with Toulmin's schema. Here is how student writer Kathy Sullivan used Toulmin to analyze a draft of her essay examining the possible obscenity of photographs displayed in a gay bar in Seattle. The final version of this essay is printed on pages 234–236.

Enthymeme: The photographs displayed in the Oncore bar are not obscene because they do not violate the community standards of the patrons of the bar, because they do not appeal to prurient interest, because children are not apt to be exposed to them, and because they promote an important social value, safe sex, in order to prevent AIDS.

Claim: The photographs are not obscene.

Stated Reasons: (1) They don't violate community standards; (2) they do not appeal to prurient interests; (3) children are not exposed to them; and (4) they promote an important social purpose of preventing AIDS through safe sex.

Grounds: (1) evidence that most Oncore patrons are homosexual and that these photographs don't offend them (no complaints, etc.); (2) purpose of photographs is not prurient sexuality, they don't depict explicit sexual acts, the only thing complained about by the liquor board is visible body parts; (3) because this is a bar, children aren't allowed; (4) evidence that the purpose of these photographs is to promote safe sex, thus they have a redeeming social value.

Warrant: These criteria come from the definition of obscenity in Black's Law Dictionary, which in turn is based on recent court cases. This is a very credible source.

Backing: arguments showing why the community standards here should be those of the homosexual community rather than the community at large; arguments showing that the social importance of safe sex overrides other considerations

Conditions of
Rebuttal: An opponent might say that the community standards should be those of the Seattle community at large, not those of the gay community. An opponent might say that photographs of male genitalia in a gay bar appeal to prurient interest.

Qualifier: These photographs would be obscene if displayed anywhere but in a gay bar.

As a result of this analysis, Kathy revised her final draft considerably. By imagining where her arguments were weak ("conditions of rebuttal"), she realized that she needed to include more backing by arguing that the community standards to be applied in this case should be those of the homosexual community rather than the community at large. She also added a section arguing that visible genitalia in the photographs didn't make the photos obscene. By imagining how your argument can be rebutted, you will see ways to strengthen your draft. Consequently, we close out this chapter by looking more carefully at the ways a definitional argument can be rebutted.

CONDITIONS FOR REBUTTAL: TESTING A DEFINITIONAL ARGUMENT

In refuting a definitional argument, you need to appreciate its criteria-match structure. Your refutation can attack either the argument's criteria or its match, or both.

Attacking the Criteria

Might an opponent claim that your criteria are not the right ones? This is the most common way to attack a definitional argument. Opponents might say that A, B, and C are only accidental criteria for Y, not necessary and sufficient criteria. Or they might say that A, B, and C are necessary but not sufficient and that you don't have a real Y until you have feature D. For example, you might argue that an action is courageous so long as the doer risks something of value, which you might define as "reputation," "family honor," and so forth. But an opponent might say that an action is truly courageous only if a person risks life and limb. The argument will turn, then, on how much is risked.

Might an opponent find counterexamples—things that possess features A, B, and C but may not be a Y? If you say that cruelty to animals occurs any time a human being intentionally causes an animal to suffer, an opponent might call this criterion into question by bringing up the case of animal research in medicine. Opponents might argue that causing an animal to suffer intentionally is not cruelty to animals so long as the suffering serves a sufficient human good.

Might an opponent cite extraordinary circumstances that weaken your criteria? An opponent may also find that the criteria you've developed are perfectly acceptable in ordinary circumstances but are rendered unacceptable by extraordinary circumstances. If you say that starving the starlings (page 211) is cruelty to animals because the life of the starlings outweighs the inconvenience to the family, an opponent might challenge you by asking, "What if one of the people in the bedroom was ill and needed absolute quiet?" By invoking extraordinary circumstances, an opponent can force us to look at questions of degree—How far are we willing to stretch our criteria?

Might an opponent object to your criteria on the basis of "purpose"? We have seen how definitional arguments occur in context. If your criteria for "sexual harassment" are based on a male view of the world, with the intention of protecting males from being sued for ogling women, might not your criteria be challenged from a woman's perspective?

Attacking the Match

A match argument usually uses examples to show that X indeed possesses characteristics A, B, and C and thus qualifies as a Y.

Might an opponent claim that your examples are too narrow and unrepresentative? The most common way to refute a match argument is to show that the examples are too narrow and unrepresentative. In arguing that Dr. Booley, president of State Technical College, is an imaginative leader, you may have cited as examples Booley's creative handling of a labor dispute with the food service and his institution of a new accounting system. But in so doing, have you ignored other, equally important problem areas on campus where Booley has shown no imagination (for example, the clumsy advising system, low faculty morale, outdated curriculum, poor library, etc.)?

Might an opponent claim that your examples are not accurate? In the previous illustration, an opponent might point out that it was not Dr. Booley's leadership that deserves credit for resolving the labor dispute;

rather, it was Vice President Conehead's steady intervention that won the day.

Will your opponent accuse you of using extreme examples? For example, if you are arguing that pornography is degrading to humans, you may well have turned to extreme instances of child pornography. But might your opponent point out that most pornography is different? Your opponent might simply say: "OK, granted explicit sexual material involving children is degrading to humans. But everything else, so long as it involves consenting adults, is OK."

FOR CLASS DISCUSSION
Read the following two definitional arguments written by students. Both arguments illustrate the "extended definition/borderline case" assignment. In the first argument, the student establishes her own extended definition of *police brutality*. The second writer uses a similar argumentative strategy, except that she works from a definition already established in a law dictionary.

1. Working individually or in small groups, summarize each argument as a definitional claim with because clauses.

2. Identify the criteria used in each article to define its Y term:

   a. Miller's criteria for police brutality

   b. Sullivan's criteria for obscenity

3. Then describe each author's argument showing how her X term (a borderline case) does or does not fit the criteria:

   a. the disorderly drunk case

   b. the photographs in the bar

4. Finally, try to refute both arguments.

POLICE BRUTALITY? THE CASE OF THE DISORDERLY DRUNK

Jean Miller (student)

How can you tell when an act of police brutality occurs? In a recent bull   1
session, some friends and I got into a heated disagreement about the following case: Two policemen confront a drunk who is shouting obscenities on a street corner. The policemen tell the drunk to move on, but he keeps shouting obscenities. When the policemen attempt to put the drunk into the police car, the drunk resists and takes a wild swing at one of the policemen. As his partner later testified, the other cop screamed at the drunk, pinned his arms behind his back, and lifted him so forcefully that the drunk's shoulder was dislocated. Is this police brutality?

My friend Susan says it was. She says a drunk man is usually too uncoordi-   2
nated to be a threat in a fight and that two policemen ought to be able to get a
drunk man into a police car without dislocating a shoulder. They acted out of
anger and meanness. Doug, on the other hand, said that the drunk provoked
the policemen. If the drunk had not resisted arrest, then the use of force
wouldn't have been necessary. But once the drunk took a swing, then the
police were justified in what they did. The dislocated shoulder was simply an
accidental result of justified force. At the time of this discussion I didn't know
where I stood, but now I have concluded that the policemen were guilty of
police brutality.

I base my conclusion on the following definition of "police brutality": I   3
argue that police brutality occurs when a policeman intentionally uses excessive force. The first criterion here is *intentional.* This criterion means that
the officer is using force on purpose with a clear understanding of what he
is doing. For example, if a cop's gun accidentally misfires and shoots a
bystander in the foot, this act is not police brutality since the officer was
not intentionally using force. But if the officer points the gun and pulls
the trigger on purpose, or if the officer purposely uses the gun as a club,
then the action meets the first criterion for police brutality — acting intentionally.

The second criterion in the definition is *excessive.* For example, if a   4
shoplifter took a swing at an officer, the officer would be justified in pinning
the shoplifter's arms and putting handcuffs on him. However, the officer
would not be justified in taking out his nightstick and bashing in the man's
nose. But if the man became violent and suddenly pulled a switchblade, then
the officer is justified in using more force to protect his own life and those of
innocent bystanders. The more clearly the danger presented by the thief, the
more clearly the justification for force on the part of the officer.

If we apply this definition of police brutality — the *intentional* use of   5
excessive force — to the case of the two policemen and the drunk, we can see
that the policemen were indeed brutal. First of all, the policeman's action
appears to be intentional. The officer who pinned the drunk's arm was acting
purposefully in response to the drunk's futile swing. The case thus meets the
first criterion for police brutality — intentional action.

But was the force used by the officer excessive? My own opinion, unlike   6
my friend Doug's, is that the force was excessive. A drunk man taking a wild
swing hardly poses a serious danger to two policemen. Putting handcuffs on
the drunk may have been justified, but lifting the drunk's arm violently
enough to dislocate a shoulder seems like excessive force. The policeman was
angry at the drunk as we can tell from the partner's testimony that he
screamed. The policeman lifted the drunk's arms violently not because he
needed to but because he was angry, and acting out of anger is no justification for that violence. In fact, we can charge policemen with "police brutal-

ity" precisely to protect us from being victims of a policeman's anger. It is the job of the law to punish us, not the policeman's job.

However, it is possible that the drunk's shoulder could have been dislo-   7
cated by his own struggling so that the injury was accidental. In court, I would like to hear a doctor's testimony on how much force is needed to dislocate a shoulder. For now, though, I will say that the officer's anger got out of hand and that the act was thus a case of police brutality. The use of force beyond that necessary to accomplish the policeman's purpose, combined with the policeman's intention to use that force, is a sufficient criterion for a charge of police brutality.

ONCORE, OBSCENITY, AND THE LIQUOR CONTROL BOARD

Kathy Sullivan (student)

In early May, Geoff Menasee, a Seattle artist, exhibited a series of photo-   1
graphs with the theme of "safe sex" on the walls of an inner city, predominantly homosexual restaurant and lounge called the Oncore. Before hanging the photographs, Menasee had to consult with the Washington State Liquor Control Board because, under the current state law, art work containing material that may be considered indecent has to be approved by the board before it can be exhibited. Of the almost thirty photographs, six were rejected by the board because they partially exposed "private parts" of the male anatomy. Menasee went ahead and displayed the entire series of photographs, placing bandaids over the "indecent" areas, but the customers continually removed the bandaids.

The liquor control board's ruling on this issue has caused controversy in   2
the Seattle community. The *Seattle Times* has provided news coverage, and a "Town Meeting" segment was filmed at the restaurant. The central question is this: Should an establishment that caters to a predominantly homosexual clientele be enjoined from displaying pictures promoting "safe sex" on the grounds that the photographs are obscene?

Before I can answer this question, I must first determine whether the art   3
work should truly be classified as obscene. To make that determination, I will use the definition of obscenity in *Black's Law Dictionary*:

> Material is "obscene" if to the average person, applying contemporary community standards, the dominant theme of material taken as a whole appeals to prurient interest, if it is utterly without redeeming social importance, if it goes substantially beyond customary limits of candor in description or representation, if it is characterized by patent offensiveness, and if it is hard core pornography.

An additional criterion is provided by Pember's *Mass Media Laws*: "A work is obscene if it has a tendency to deprave and corrupt those whose minds are open to such immoral influences (children for example) and into whose hands it might happen to fall" (p. 394). The art work in question should not be prohibited from display at predominantly homosexual establishments like the Oncore because it does not meet the above criteria for obscenity.

First of all, to the average person applying contemporary community   4
standards, the predominant theme of Menasee's photographs is not an appeal to prurient interests. The first element in this criterion is "average person." According to Rocky Breckner, manager of the Oncore, 90 percent of the clientele at the Oncore is made up of young white homosexual males. This group therefore constitutes the "average person" viewing the exhibit. "Contemporary community standards" would ordinarily be the standards of the Seattle community. However, this art work is aimed at a particular group of people — the homosexual community. Therefore, the "community standards" involved here are those of the gay community rather than the city at large. Since the Oncore is not an art museum or gallery, which attracts a broad spectrum of people, it is appropriate to restrict the scope of "community standards" to that group who voluntarily patronize the Oncore.

Second, the predominant theme of the photographs is not "prurient   5
interest" nor do the photographs go "substantially beyond public limits of candor." There are no explicit sexual acts found in the photographs; instead, their theme is the prevention of AIDS through the practice of safe sex. Homosexual displays of affection could be viewed as "prurient interest" by the larger community, but same-sex relationships are the norm for the group at whom the exhibit is aimed. If the exhibit were displayed at McDonalds or even the Red Robin it might go "substantially beyond customary limits of candor," but it is unlikely that the clientele of the Oncore would find the art work offensive. The manager stated that he received very few complaints about the exhibit and its contents.

Nor is the material pornographic. The liquor control board prohibited the   6
six photographs based on their visible display of body parts such as pubic hair and naked buttocks, not on the basis of sexual acts or homosexual orientation. The board admitted that the photographs depicted no explicit sexual acts. Hence, it can be concluded that they did not consider the suggestion of same-sex affection to be hard-core pornography. Their sole objection was that body parts were visible. But visible genitalia in art work are not necessarily pornographic. Since other art work, such as Michelangelo's sculptures, explicitly depict both male and female genitalia, it is arguable that pubic hair and buttocks are not patently offensive.

It must be conceded that the art work has the potential of being viewed by   7 children, which would violate Pember's criterion. But once again the incidence of minors frequenting this establishment is very small.

But the most important reason for saying these photographs are not   8
obscene is that they serve an important social purpose. One of Black's criteria is that obscene material is "utterly without redeeming social importance." But these photographs have the explicit purpose of promoting safe sex as a defense against AIDS. Recent statistics reported in the *Seattle Times* show that AIDS is now the leading cause of death of men under forty in the Seattle area. Any methods that can promote the message of safe sex in today's society have strong redeeming social significance.

Those who believe that all art containing "indecent" material should be   9
banned or covered from public view would most likely believe that Menasee's work is obscene. They would disagree that the environment and the clientele should be the major determining factor when using criteria to evaluate art. However, in the case of this exhibit I feel that the audience and the environment of the display are factors of overriding importance. Therefore, the exhibit should have been allowed to be displayed because it is not obscene.

CAUSAL ARGUMENTS: X CAUSES/DOES NOT CAUSE Y

CASE 1

The National Transportation Safety Board concludes in a report that the pilot of Piedmont Flight 467 flew in too fast on his approach and overshot the runway of the Charlotte, N.C., airport, resulting in a crash that injured 34 people. The Air Line Pilots Association, however, disputes the finding and says the accident may have been caused by a "design deficiency" in the Boeing 737 that makes it difficult to obtain reverse thrust and land safely. What caused the crash?

CASE 2

Residents of Vashon Island near Seattle, Washington, gather in a town meeting to debate the value of proposed new ferry service between the island and downtown Seattle. Some islanders oppose the ferry service on the grounds that more convenient ferries will cause more people to move to the island, thereby destroying Vashon's rural character. Supporters say that the proposed ferry service will not attract new residents.

CASE 3

A great national debate in the 1990s is how to fight the drug war. President Bush calls for "zero tolerance for casual use," increased penalties for drug pushers and users, and increased attempts to stop the production of drugs in Third World countries. In contrast many observers say that the only way to solve the drug problem is to legalize drugs, thereby taking the profit out of them. At the heart of this controversy is a series of causal issues. What causes people to take drugs? What will be the consequences of different courses of action? For example, opponents of legalization say that open access to drugs will cause an increase, not a de-

237

crease, in drug usage and that the greatest losers will be minority communities. Proponents of legalization claim that the glamour of drug pushing is itself a cause of drug demand.

CASE 4

During July and August 1986, the death rate for infants rose an unexplained 235 percent in the state of Washington. A medical school professor at the University of Pittsburgh attributes the increase to radioactive fallout from the Chernobyl nuclear accident in Russia. Using weather reports and empirical evidence gathered in Washington state, he documents the increased radiation received on the northwest coast of the United States. He uses this evidence to bolster his argument that low levels of radiation are more dangerous than the scientific community currently believes. Opponents of the professor's hypothesis urge the public to view his argument with caution. They say that other factors may explain the increase in infant mortality.

THE FREQUENCY OF
CAUSAL ARGUMENTS

We encounter causal issues all the time. Was the pilot at error in a recent airline crash? Will better ferry service lead to an influx of new residents on Vashon Island? What is the best way to fight the drug war? What caused a sudden increase in the infant mortality rate in the Pacific Northwest?

Sometimes an argument will be devoted entirely to a causal issue; just as frequently we encounter causal arguments as part of a "should" argument in which the writer argues that we should do X because X *will lead to specified consequences.* Convincing readers how X will lead to these consequences—a causal argument—thus constitutes much of the "should" argument. (Later in this text we call "should arguments" by the more general term "proposal arguments," which we treat at length in Chapter 15.)

An especially common place to find causal arguments is in debates about moral or legal guilt. For example, before we can assign guilt in a crime, we have to show that those being charged were not driven to the act by forces beyond their control. A shrewd attorney might point to her client's life of poverty or to a chemical imbalance such as premenstrual stress syndrome. In one real-life example, a California murderer's sentence was mitigated in part because the defense convinced the jury that the defendant's actions resulted from a diet too heavy in refined sugar. This so-called Twinkie Defense is an extreme case of a causal argument's playing an important role in a judgment about human responsibility.

THE NATURE OF
CAUSAL ARGUING

Typically, causal arguments try to show how one event brings about another. Although causation might at first seem like a fairly straightforward phenomenon, it sometimes raises thorny scientific and philosophic issues. Even if we take the classic illustration of causality—one billiard ball striking another on a pool table—and argue that the movement of the second ball was caused by a transfer of energy from the first ball at the moment of contact, there are some philosophers who argue that the human mind has only inferred causality and that all we can know, for sure, is that first one ball moved and then the other. Imagine how complex this issue becomes when we start talking about humans as well as billiard balls.

When human beings are the focus of a causal argument, the first problem that arises is one of definition. When we say that a given factor X "caused" a person to do Y, we might mean that X "forced her to do Y," thereby negating her free will (for example, my taking a certain drug caused me to fall asleep at the wheel); on the other hand, we might simply mean that factor X "motivated" her to do Y, such that doing Y is still an expression of free will (for example, my desire for more freedom caused me to give up my job and join the circus).

A second problem in dealing with human causality is the complexity of describing the causal mechanism. Because we have free will (or at least appear to), we may choose to respond unpredictably, even perversely, to causal forces. A rock dropped from a roof will always fall to the ground at thirty-two feet per second squared; and a rat zapped for making left turns in a maze will always quit making left turns. But can we predict with certainty any human behavior? Numerous psychological and philosophical schools engage in endless debate over their competing explanations of how causal mechanisms affect human beings.

Fortunately, most causal arguments can avoid the worst of these scientific and philosophic quagmires. As human beings we share a number of assumptions about what causes events in the observable world, and we can depend on the goodwill of our audiences to grant us most of these assumptions. Most of us, for example, would be satisfied with the following explanation for why a car went into a skid: "In a panic the driver locked the brakes of his car, causing the car to go into a skid." This sentence asserts a simple causal chain:

panic → slamming brake pedal → locking brakes → skid

We probably do not need to defend this explanation because the audience will grant the causal connections between events A, B, C, and D. The sequence seems reasonable according to our shared assumptions about psychological causality (panic leads to slamming brake pedal) and physical causality (locked brakes lead to skid).

The writer's task is harder, however, when the causal connections between the events either are not clear or go against common assumptions. Suppose that you are an attorney representing Oilcan Floyd, the driver of the car in the above example. Oilcan is suing the Ramjet Goat Automobile Company, claiming that a faulty brake system, not the driver's panic, caused the car to skid. Here is how you might preview your argument for a jury:

> My Dear Jurors,
> My client's car went into that disastrous skid not because its driver panicked and slammed the brakes. Oh, no. It skidded because of a flaw in the car's brake system. I propose to demonstrate this to you in the following manner: I propose to show first that the driver, Oilcan Floyd, was a professional race car driver with enormous skill handling cars at racetrack speeds in dangerous situations. I will show further that the driver was not in a panic situation when the accident occurred. Oilcan was maneuvering the car in ordinary traffic conditions and would have had no reasons for a panic stop. Finally, I will provide expert witnesses who will testify that the Ramjet Goat automobile that Oilcan was driving has a design flaw in the brake system that could lead to locked braking of all four wheels upon only a gentle touch of the brake pedal.

As Oilcan's attorney, you will be showing a new causal chain:

normal traffic maneuvering → gentle touch → brake locking → skid

This chain has a key link that violates common sense: How can a gentle touch lead to locking of the brakes? Here you must create an argument to show the workings of an unanticipated causal agent—a faulty brake system:

gentle touch → brake locking
caused by
faulty brakes

Your argument must develop in two stages: First, you must refute the causal chain that your audience would ordinarily assume, namely, that the locked brakes occurred during a panic stop. (You will do this by arguing that Oilcan Floyd is a great driver and that traffic conditions were normal.) Second, you must supply an explanation for the causal connection between a gentle touch on the brake pedal and the locked brakes. (You will do this by explaining the mechanical operation of the faulty brake system—for example, explaining how a leaking seal in the brakes' power assist mechanism caused the wheels to lock.) Our point, then, is that you will need to create an argument for causality, rather than just asserting causality or assuming it, whenever a causal connection seems to violate your audience's normal understanding of cause or whenever the audience is unclear about a cause.

DESCRIBING THE LOGICAL STRUCTURE OF A CAUSAL ARGUMENT: BECAUSE CLAUSES AND THE TOULMIN SCHEMA

It is generally easy enough to state a causal argument using because clauses ("Oilcan's gentle touch on the brake pedal caused the car to skid because the brakes had a leaking seal in the power assist mechanism") and then to expand the enthymeme into a syllogism.

Cars with leaking seals in the power assist mechanism will skid with a gentle touch of the brake pedal.

Oilcan's car had such a leak in the power assist mechanism.

Therefore, Oilcan's car skidded with a gentle touch of the brake pedal.

However, for reasons we don't need to explore here in depth, syllogisms in many causal arguments don't work quite the same way as syllogisms in "X is Y" arguments. The reason is that causal arguments are often *how* arguments rather than *why* arguments. The warrant in such an argument is often not a general principle, such as "All men are mortal," but an assertion of one aspect of a specific causal chain. ("Cars with leaking seals in the power assist mechanism will skid with a gentle touch of the brake pedal.") To support the warrant, you therefore need to describe and explain each link in the causal chain. A typical because clause in a causal argument, therefore, summarizes one or two key elements in the causal chain (the leaking seal in the power assist mechanism) rather than describing the entire causal chain.

Despite this problem, however, causal arguments can often be analyzed using the Toulmin schema, which serves to help arguers see the structure of their arguments and to determine the most effective way to support their claims. Here is how Oilcan's attorney might use Toulmin's schema to prepare his or her court case. (It is easiest to apply Toulmin's schema to causal arguments if you think of the grounds as the observable phenomena at any point in the causal chain and the warrants as the shareable assumptions about causality that join links together.) The attorney's first task is to refute the opposition's argument that Oilcan slammed on the brakes in a panic. This argument could be diagrammed as follows:

Enthymeme: Oilcan did not slam brakes in a panic because traffic conditions were normal and because Oilcan is a professional race car driver.

Claim: Oilcan did not slam brakes in a panic.

Stated Reasons: a. Traffic conditions were normal. b. Oilcan is a professional race car driver.

Grounds: a. I will bring in witnesses to testify that traffic conditions were normal. b. I will provide documents and testimony showing that Oilcan Floyd is a professional race car driver.

Warrant: a. since people don't panic in normal traffic conditions. b. since race car drivers rarely panic

Backing: Perhaps I could bring in further testimony from a psychologist on how people drive in normal conditions; further testimony from a race car driver about when a professional would slam brakes?

Conditions of Rebuttal: unless there was a momentary cause for panic even in normal conditions (stung by bee? cat ran across road?); unless Oilcan was not his usual self (sleepy? on drugs? I've got to make sure I establish that he was alert.); unless witnesses are unreliable or disagree with what is meant by "normal"

Qualifier: "very likely"

The attorney's second task is to convince the jury that faulty brakes caused the skid. Here is a Toulmin schema for this argument:

Enthymeme: Faulty brakes caused Oilcan Floyd's car to skid because the brake system had a leaky seal.

Claim: Faulty brakes caused Oilcan Floyd's car to skid.

Stated Reason: The brake system had a leaky seal.

Grounds: expert testimony that brake system had a leaking seal in the power assist mechanism; evidence based on examination of other Ramjet Goat automobiles

Warrant: since a leaking seal in the power assist mechanism can cause wheels to lock with a gentle touch of the brake pedal

Backing: Because leaking seal causes A, which causes B, which causes C, which causes wheels to lock, which causes skid—I will have to make sure my expert witness can describe each of these links to the jury. We'll have to have charts and diagrams of the brake system.

Conditions of Rebuttal: unless Oilcan's car did not have a leaking seal (Can my witness convince jury that *all* Ramjet Goat cars had leaking seals?); unless leaking seals don't always produce skids (Will the opposing attorney argue that wheel locking is rare even with a leaking seal?); unless Oilcan's touch wasn't gentle (Will the jury buy my argument that he didn't panic?)

Qualifier: "in all likelihood" (if I argue effectively!)

FOR CLASS DISCUSSION

1. Working individually or in small groups, create a causal chain to show how the first mentioned item could help lead to the last one.

   a. invention of the automobile   redesign of cities

   b. invention of the automobile   changes in sexual mores

   c. Elvis Presley brings rock and roll to the nation   rise of the drug culture in the 1960's

   d. invention of the telephone   loss of a sense of community in neighborhoods

   e. development of "the pill"   rise in the divorce rate

   f. development of way to prevent rejections in transplant operations   liberalization of euthanasia laws

2. For each of your causal chains, compose a claim with an attached because clause summarizing one or two key links in the causal chain. For example, "The invention of the automobile helped cause the redesign of cities because automobiles made it possible for people to live farther away from their places of work."

WRITING ASSIGNMENT FOR CHAPTER 12: AN ARGUMENT INVOLVING "SURPRISING" OR "DISPUTED" CAUSES

By looking back through your idea-log or by developing new ideas through the exploration tasks at the end of this chapter, choose an issue question about the causes (or consequences) of a trend, event, or other phenomenon.

Write a three- to five-page argument that persuades an audience to accept your explanation of the causes (or consequences) of your chosen phenomenon. Within your essay you should examine alternative hypotheses or opposing views and explain your reasons for rejecting them.

You can imagine your issue either as a puzzle or as a disagreement. If a puzzle, your task will be informational as well as argumentative because your role will be that of an analyst explaining causes or consequences of an event to an audience that doesn't have an answer already in mind. If you see your issue as a disagreement, your task will be more directly argumentative as your goal will be to change an opposing audience's views so that they adhere to your position more than their original one.

The rest of this chapter will help you write your essay by giving you more background about causal arguments and by providing suggestions for each stage of the writing process.

RECOGNIZING DIFFERENT
SORTS OF CAUSAL ISSUES

One of the first things you need to do when preparing a causal argument is to note just what sort of causal relationship you're dealing with. Are you concerned with the causes of a specific event or phenomenon such as the disastrous blowup of the Space Shuttle Challenger, John Lennon's murder, the defeat of the Celtics in the '87 playoffs, or the breakdown in communication between you and your father? Or are you planning to write about the cause of some recurring phenomenon such as cancer, laughter, math anxiety among females, or teen suicide?

With recurring phenomena, you have the luxury of being able to study multiple cases over long periods of time and establishing correlations between suspected causal factors and effects. In some cases you can even intervene in the process and test for yourself whether diminishing a suspected causal factor results in a lessening of the effect or whether increasing the causal factor results in a corresponding increase in the effect. Additionally, you can spend a good deal of time exploring just how the mechanics of causation might work.

But with a one-time occurrence your focus is on the details of the event and specific causal chains that may have contributed to the event. Sometimes evidence has disappeared or changed its nature. You often end up in the position more of a detective than of a scientific researcher and your conclusion will have to be more tentative as a result.

Having briefly stated these words of caution, let's turn now to the various ways you can argue that one event causes another.

THREE WAYS TO ARGUE THAT ONE EVENT CAUSES ANOTHER

First Way: Explain the Causal Mechanism Directly

The most convincing kind of causal argument occurs when you identify every link in the causal chain, showing how X causes A, which causes B, which in turn causes C, which finally causes Y. In some cases, all you have to do is fill in the missing links; in other cases—when your assumptions about causality may seem questionable to your audience—you have to argue for the causal connection with more vigor. Thus, for example, Oilcan Floyd's attorney will have to argue hard to convince the jury that faulty brakes, not a panicked driver, caused the car to skid.

A careful spelling out of each step in the causal chain is the technique used by astronomer Carl Sagan in "The Warming of the World" (pages 261–266), in which he explains the greenhouse effect and predicts its consequences. His causal chain looks like this:

STARTING POINT A	STARTING POINIT B
Cutting down of forests leads to fewer plants on Earth's land surface. Fewer plants lead to more carbon dioxide in the atmosphere. (*Warrant:* because plants convert carbon dioxide to oxygen)	Burning of fossil fuels produces carbon dioxide. (*Warrant:* because carbon dioxide is a product of combustion) Production of carbon dioxide leads to more carbon dioxide in the atmosphere.

LINK 2

More carbon dioxide in atmosphere reduces amount of infrared light radiated into space. (*Warrant:* because carbon dioxide absorbs infrared radiation; Sagan backs this warrant with further explanation.)

LINK 3

Earth heats up. (*Warrant:* because Earth stays cool by reflecting heat back into space through infrared radiation)

LINK 4

Land will become parched; seas will rise. (*Warrant:* because heat causes changes in precipitation patterns causing land to parch; also because heat causes glacial ice to melt)

LINK 5

massive global danger (*Warrant:* because parched farmland and rising seas will cause social and economic upheaval)

Sagan concludes his essay with a proposal based on the above causal argument. Placed into a claim with because clause, Sagan's should argument looks like this:

Nations should initiate worldwide efforts to find alternative energy sources because the continued burning of fossil fuels will lead to global catastrophe.

Thus, in Sagan's essay, a lengthy causal argument in the beginning supports a final should argument.

This causal chain method is also used by student writer Mary Lou Torpey in predicting the consequences of mandatory drug testing (pages 266–268). Figure 12–1 shows Torpey's planning diagram for her argument "What Drugs I Take Is None of Your Business—The Consequences of Mandatory Drug Testing." Her diagram shows the links of the chain beginning with a mandatory drug-testing program and culminating in prejudice against employees with certain treatable disorders such as narcolepsy.

Second Way: Use Various Inductive Methods to Establish a High Probability of a Causal Link

INFORMAL INDUCTION   Although few of us are scientists, all of us practice the scientific method informally through *induction.* Induction is a form of reasoning by which we make generalizations based on a limited number of specific cases. For example, if on several occasions you got a headache after drinking red wine but not after drinking white wine, you would be apt to conclude inductively that red wine causes you to get headaches. However, because there are almost always exceptions to rules arrived at inductively and because we can't be certain that the future will always be like the past, inductive reasoning gives only probable truths, not certain ones.

When your brain thinks inductively, it sorts through data looking for patterns of similarity and difference. Toddlers are thinking inductively when they learn the connection between flipping a wall switch and watching the ceiling light come on. Like scientists, they are holding all variables constant except the position of the switch. But the inductive process does not explain the causal mechanism itself. Thus, through induction you know that red wine gives you a headache, but you don't know how the wine actually works on your nervous system—the causal chain itself.

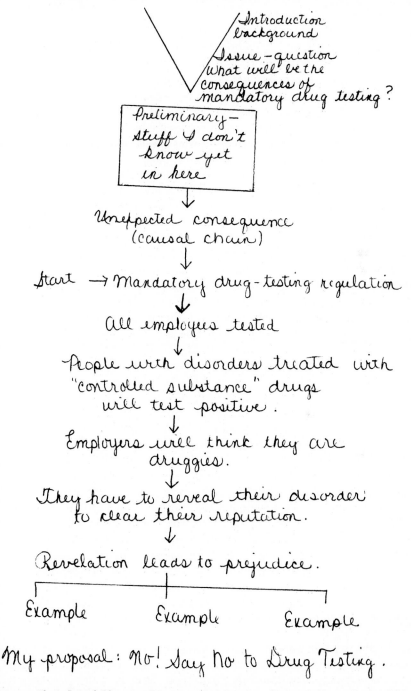

Introduction
background

Issue—question
What will be the
consequences of
mandatory drug testing?

Preliminary—
stuff I don't
know yet
in here

↓

Unexpected consequence
(causal chain)

↓

Start → Mandatory drug-testing regulation

↓

All employees tested

↓

People with disorders treated with
"controlled substance" drugs
will test positive.

↓

Employers will think they are
druggies.

↓

They have to reveal their disorder
to clear their reputation.

↓

Revelation leads to prejudice.

Example   Example   Example

My proposal: No! Say No to Drug Testing.

FIGURE 12–1. Initial Planning Diagram for Mary Lou Torpey's Essay (pages 266–268)

Largely because of its power, the process of induction often can lead you to wrong conclusions. You should be aware of two common fallacies of inductive reasoning that can tempt you into erroneous assumptions about causality. (Both fallacies are treated more fully in Appendix 1.)

The *post hoc, ergo propter hoc* fallacy ("after this, therefore because of this") mistakes precedence for cause. Just because event A regularly precedes event B doesn't mean that event A causes event B. The same reasoning that tells us that flipping a switch causes the light to go on can make us believe that the Chernobyl nuclear disaster caused the rise in infant death rates in the state of Washington (see Case 4, page 238). The nuclear disaster clearly preceded the rise in death rates. But did it clearly *cause* it? Our point is that precedence alone is no proof of causality and that we are guilty of this fallacy whenever we are swayed to believe that X causes Y primarily because X precedes Y.

The *hasty generalization* fallacy occurs when you make a generalization based on too few cases or too little consideration of alternative explanations: You flip the switch, but the light bulb doesn't go on. You conclude—too hastily—that the power has gone off. (Perhaps the light bulb has burned out or the switch is broken.) How many trials does it take before you can make a justified generalization rather than a hasty generalization? It is difficult to say, for sure. Both the *post hoc* fallacy and the *hasty generalization* fallacy remind us that induction requires a leap from individual cases to a general principle and that it is always possible to leap too soon.

SCIENTIFIC EXPERIMENTATION   One way to avoid inductive fallacies is to examine our causal hypotheses as carefully as possible. When we deal with a recurring phenomenon such as cancer, we can create scientific experiments that give us inductive evidence of causality with a fairly high degree of certainty. If, for example, we were concerned that a particular food source such as spinach might contain cancer-causing chemicals, we could test our hypothesis experimentally. We could take two groups of rats and control their environment carefully so that the only difference between them (in theory anyway) was that one group ate large quantities of spinach and the other group ate none. Spinach eating, then, is the one variable between the two groups that we are testing. After a specified period of time, we would check to see what percentage of rats in each group developed cancer. If twice as many spinach-eating rats contracted cancer, we could probably conclude that our hypothesis had held up.

CORRELATION   Still another method of induction is correlation, which expresses a statistical relationship between X and Y. A correlation between X and Y means that when X occurs, Y is likely to occur also, and vice versa. To put it another way, correlation establishes a possibility that an observed link between an X and a Y is a causal one rather than a mere coincidence. The existence of a correlation, however, does not tell us whether X causes Y, whether Y causes X, or whether both are caused by some third phenomenon. For example, there is a fairly strong correlation between nearsightedness and intelligence. (That is, in a given sample of nearsighted people and people with normal eyesight, a higher percentage of the nearsighted people will be highly intelligent. Similarly, in a sample of high-intelligence people and people with normal intelligence, a higher percentage of the high-intelligence group will be nearsighted.) But the direction of causality isn't clear. It could be that high intelligence causes people to read more, thus ruining their eyes (high intelligence causes nearsightedness). Or it could be that nearsightedness causes people to read more, thus raising their intelligence (nearsightedness causes high intelligence). Or it could be that some unknown phenomenon inside the brain causes both nearsightedness and high intelligence.

In recent years, correlation studies have been made stunningly sophisticated through the power of computerized analyses. For example, we could attempt to do the spinach-cancer study without resorting to a scientific experiment. If we identified a given group that ate lots of spinach (for example, vegetarians) and another group that ate little if any spinach (Eskimos) and then checked to see if their rates of cancer correlated to their rates of spinach consumption, we would have the beginnings of a correlation study. But it would have no scientific validity until we factored out all the other variables between vegetarians and Eskimos that might skew the findings — variables such as life-style, climate, genetic inheritance, differences in diet other than spinach, and so forth. Factoring out such variables is one of the complex feats that modern statistical analyses attempt to accomplish. But the fact remains that the most sophisticated correlation studies still cannot tell us the direction of causality or even for certain that there *is* causality.

By way of illustrating the uses of correlation arguments, consider Victor Fuchs' article "Why Married Mothers Work" (pages 268–272). The graph on page 269 shows that the number of married mothers in the workforce has been steadily rising since 1948. Fuchs rejects several common explanations for this phenomenon (growth of feminism, government affirmative action, economic need) on the grounds that the timing is wrong. He proposes another hypothesis: Increased wages and increased job openings in the service sector are for him the best causal candidates because their slow, steady rate of increase correlates with the increase in working married mothers. Moreover, he provides a hypothesis for why women are attracted to service sector jobs (they require less physical strength, offer flexible hours including part-time work, and are located near residential areas).

Note that Fuchs is careful to have two kinds of reasons for his argument. The first is the statistical data that show that the increase of married mothers in the workplace correlates with the increase of wages and the increase of available jobs in the service sector. The second is a hypothesis explaining why increased wages and increased service sector jobs attract married mothers. Whenever you make a causal argument supported by statistical correlations, you should be aware — as is Fuchs — that you must be able to offer some reason for thinking that there is a particular "direction" to the relationship.

CONCLUSION ABOUT INDUCTIVE METHODS   Induction, then, can tell us within varying degrees of certainty whether or not X causes Y. It does not, however, explain the causal mechanism itself. Typically, the because clause structure of an inductive argument would take one of the following three shapes: (1) "Although we cannot explain the causal mechanism directly, we believe that X and Y are very probably causally linked because we have repeatedly observed their conjunction"; (2) ". . . because we have demonstrated the linkage through controlled scientific experiments"; or (3) ". . . because we have shown that they are statistically correlated and have provided a plausible hypothesis concerning the causal direction."

FOR CLASS DISCUSSION
Working individually or in small groups, develop plausible causal chains that might explain the correlations between the following pairs of phenomena:

a. A person registers low stress level on electrochemical stress meter.   Person does daily meditation.

b. Person regularly consumes frozen dinners.   Person is likely to vote for improved rapid transit.

c. High achiever   First-born child

d. Member of the National Rifle Association   Favors tough treatment of criminals

Third Way: Argue by Analogy or Precedent

Another common method of causal arguing is through analogy or precedent. (See also Chapter 13, "Resemblance Arguments," which deals in more depth with the strengths and weaknesses of this kind of arguing.) When you argue through resemblance, you try to find a case that is similar to the one you are arguing about but is better known and less controversial to the reader. If the reader agrees with your view of causality in the similar case, you then try to transfer this understanding to the case at issue. Causal arguments by analogy and precedent are logically weaker than arguments based on causal chains or induction and will typically be used in cases where empirical evidence is weak.

Here are some examples of this method in causal arguing:

1. If you wanted to argue that overcrowding in high-density apartment houses causes dangerous stress in humans, you could compare humans to mice, which develop symptoms of high stress when they are crowded together in cages. (This argument depends on the warrant that humans and mice will respond similarly to the condition of crowding.)

2. If you want to argue that doing regular thinking skills exercises will result in improved thinking ability, you could compare the mind to a muscle and the thinking skills exercises to daily weight training. (Because the audience will probably accept the causal chain of weight training leading to improved physical strength, you hope to transfer that acceptance to the field of mental activity. This argument depends on the warrant that the mind is like a muscle.)

3. If you wanted to argue that a child shouldn't be forced to take piano lessons unless he or she wants to, you could argue that parents can't mold a child like clay; rather, children are like plants—you can't mold them into something that is not in their nature any more than a gardener can mold a tulip into a rose. (This argument depends on the warrant that children are more like plants than like clay.)

All of these arguments have a persuasive power. However, any two things that are alike in some ways (analogous) are different in others (disanalogous), and these differences are apt to be ignored in arguments from analogy. You should realize, then, that the warrant that says X is like Y can almost always be attacked. Psychologists, for example, have pretty much demonstrated that the mind is not like a muscle, and we can all think of ways that children are not like plants. *All* resemblance arguments, therefore, are in some sense "false analogies." But some analogies are so misleading that logicians have labeled them as fallacious—the fallacy of *false analogy*. The *false analogy* fallacy covers those truly blatant cases where the differences between X and Y are too great for the analogy to hold. An example might be the following: "Putting red marks all over students' papers causes great emotional distress just as putting knife marks over their palms would cause great physical distress." It is impossible to draw a precise line, however, between an analogy that has true clarifying and persuasive power and one that is fallacious.

GLOSSARY OF TERMS ENCOUNTERED IN CAUSAL ARGUMENTS

Because causal arguments are often easier to conduct if writer and reader share a few specialized terms, we offer the following glossary for your convenience.

Fallacy of Oversimplified Cause: One of the greatest temptations when establishing causal relationships is to fall into the habit of looking for *the* cause of something. Most phenomena, especially the ones we argue about, will have multiple causes. For example, few presidents have won elections on the basis of one characteristic or event. Usually elections result from a combination of abilities, stances on key issues, personal characteristics, mistakes on the part of the competition, events in the world, and so forth. Similarly, scientists know that a number of different causes must work together to create a disease such as cancer. But though we know all this, we still long to make the world less complex by attributing a single cause to puzzling effects.

Immediate/Remote Causes: Every causal chain links backward indefinitely into the past. An immediate cause is the closest in time to the event being examined. If a normally passive man goes on a killing rampage, the immediate cause may be a brain tumor or a recent argument with his wife that was the "last straw" in a long chain of events. A number of earlier events may have led up to the present—failure to get medical attention for headaches or failure to get counseling when a marriage began to disintegrate. Such causes going further back into the past are considered remote causes. It's sometimes difficult to determine the relative significance of remote causes insofar as immediate causes are so obviously linked to the event whereas remote causes often have to be dug out or inferred. It's difficult to know, for example, just how seriously to take serial murderer Ted Bundy's defense that he was "traumatized" at age twelve by the discovery that he was illegitimate. How big a role are we willing to grant a causal factor so remote in time and so apparently minor in relation to the murder of thirty-five young women?

Precipitating/Contributing Causes: These terms are similar to *immediate* and *remote* causes but don't designate a temporal linking going into the past. Rather, they refer to a main cause emerging out of a background of subsidiary causes. The contributing causes are a set of conditions that give rise to the precipitating cause, which triggers the effect. If, for example, a husband and wife decide to separate, the precipitating cause may be a stormy fight over money, which itself is a symptom of their inability to communicate with each other any longer. All the factors that contribute to that inability to communicate — preoccupation with their respective careers, anxieties about money, in-law problems — may be considered contributing causes. Note that the contributing causes and precipitating cause all coexist simultaneously in time — none is temporally more remote than another. But the marriage might have continued had the contributing causes not finally resulted in frequent angry fighting, which doomed the marriage.

Constraints: Sometimes an effect occurs, not because X happened, but because another factor — a constraint — was removed. At other times a possible effect will not occur because a given constraint prevents it from happening. A constraint is a kind of negative cause that limits choices and possibilities. As soon as the constraint is removed, a given effect may occur. For example, in the marriage we have been discussing, the presence of children in the home might have been a constraint against divorce; as soon as the children graduate from high school and leave home, the marriage may well dissolve.

Necessary/Sufficient Causes: We speak of necessary causes as those that must be present when a given effect takes place. If a necessary cause is absent, the effect cannot take place. Thus the presence of a spark is a necessary cause for the operation of a gasoline engine. A sufficient cause, on the other hand, is one that guarantees a given effect. An electric spark is thus a *necessary cause* for the operation of a gasoline engine but not a *sufficient cause* since other causes must also be present to make the engine work (fuel, etc.). Few causes are ever both necessary and sufficient to bring about a given effect.

FOR CLASS DISCUSSION

The above terms can be used as an effective heuristic for thinking of possible causes of an event. For the following events, try to think of as many causes as possible by making idea-maps with branches labeled *immediate cause, remote cause, precipitating cause, contributing cause,* and *constraint.* (See Figure 12 – 2.)

1. Working individually, make a map identifying causes for one of the following:
   a. your decision to attend your present college
   b. an important event in your life or your family (a divorce, a major move, etc.)
   c. a personal opinion you hold that is not widely shared
2. Working as a group, make a map identifying causes for one of the following:
   a. why many American males began to wear earrings in the mid-1980s
   b. why the majority of teenagers don't listen to classical music

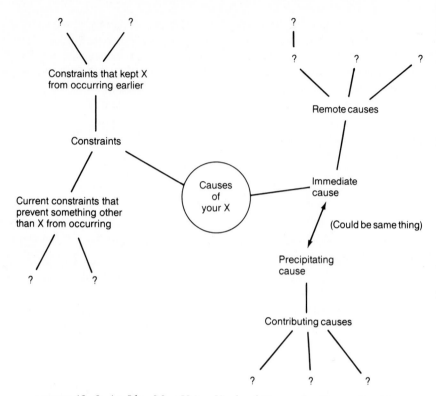

FIGURE 12-2. An Idea-Map Using Kinds of Causes for Generating Ideas

   c. why a sixteen-year-old girl gets pregnant on her third date
   (Invent a hypothetical biography for this girl.)

WRITING YOUR CAUSAL ARGUMENT

The stages of the writing process that we discussed in Chapter 3 can be fruitfully applied to a causal argument. What follows are some suggestions that may help you find a good causal issue and produce an effective argument.

THE STARTING POINT: FINDING A CAUSAL ISSUE

You already may have discovered some good causal issues and recorded them in your idea-log. If not, here are some exploration tasks that might help you get started.

Make a List of People's Unusual Likes and Dislikes

One way to find a causal issue is to make a list of unusual things that anger people, scare them, or inspire their hatred. Alternatively, you can list unusual things that people like, value, or desire. You could then write a causal argument explaining why one of these phenomena produces this emotional response. Try to choose likes or dislikes that are fairly common but are puzzling to explain. Typical titles might be: "Why Are People Afraid of Bats?" "Why Do Certain Students Dislike Writing?" or "Why Do So Many People Like Professional Wrestling?"

Make Lists of Trends and Other Puzzling Phenomena

Besides lists of unusual likes and dislikes, try adding your own X's to the following list.

1. trends
   popularity of expensive basketball shoes for street wear
   growth of punk rock
   decline of nationwide liquor sales
   ?

2. one-time events
   opening of the Berlin Wall
   national voter movement against incumbents in 1990 elections
   Iraq's invasion of Kuwait
   ?

3. repeatable events
   What causes laughter?
   What are the effects of working swing shifts?
   What are the causes of reading difficulties?
   ?

4. other puzzling phenomena
   Why are lotteries popular?
   Why do people watch professional wrestling?
   What was the primary cause of the growth of the budget deficit in the 1980s?

Make Some Idea-Maps to Explore Causes

Another way to find a causal issue is to try out some arguments. Make idea-maps in which you brainstorm possible causes for several of the following phenomena: failure of many sexually active teenagers to use birth control; growth of the home computer industry; decline of interest in home videogames; popularity of rock groups with bisexual identities; increase of popularity of "home birthing" methods; graffiti on. subways; the dominance of blacks in college and professional basketball; popularity of Eddie Murphy movies; success of the Star Wars trilogy; growth in the pornography industry. Then add at least three phenomena of your own to the list.

Make Some Idea-Maps to Explore Consequences

Another fruitful area for idea-maps is to explore possible consequences of real or hypothetical events. What might be the consequences, for example, of some of the following: a cure for cancer; worldwide disarmament; the AIDS epidemic; a heavy tax on families having more than two children; replacement of federal income tax with a federal sales tax; a four-day workweek; several topics of your own choice.

EXPLORATION STAGE

Once you have decided on a causal issue, we recommend that you explore it by going through the eight guided tasks for exploring an argument in "Idea-Log, Set Two" (on pages 73–75). You can also make an idea-map on your causal issue like the ones in the For Class Discussion exercise in the preceding glossary of causal terms.

WRITING THE DISCOVERY DRAFT: TYPICAL WAYS OF ORGANIZING A CAUSAL ARGUMENT

Your goal at the discovery draft stage is to get your developing argument onto paper. At this stage it is useful to know some of the standard ways that a causal argument can be organized. Later, you may decide on a quite different organizational pattern, but these standard ways will help you get started.

PLAN 1   When your purpose is to describe and explain all the links in a causal chain:

- Introduce phenomenon to be explained and show why it is problematical.
- Present your thesis in summary form.
- Describe and explain each link in the causal chain.

Carl Sagan's essay on the greenhouse effect (pages 261–266) follows this format.

PLAN 2   When your purpose is to explore the relative contribution of all causes to a phenomenon or to explore all possible consequences of a phenomenon:

- Introduce the phenomenon to be explained and suggest how or why it is controversial.
- Devote one section to each possible cause/consequence and decide whether it is necessary, sufficient, contributory, remote, and so forth. (Arrange sections so that those causes most familiar to the audience come first and the most surprising ones come last.)

Victor Fuchs's argument "Why Married Mothers Work" (pages 268–272) follows this format.

PLAN 3   When your purpose is to argue for a cause or consequence that is surprising or unexpected to your audience:

- Introduce a phenomenon to be explained and show why it is controversial.
- One by one, examine and reject the causes or consequences your audience would normally assume or expect.
- Introduce your unexpected or surprising cause or consequence and argue for it.

Plans 2 and 3 are similar in that they examine numerous possible causes or consequences. Plan 2, however, tries to establish the relative importance of each cause or consequence, whereas Plan 3 aims at rejecting the causes or consequences normally assumed by the audience and argues for an unexpected surprising cause or consequence. Plan 3 is the strategy used by Mary Lou Torpey (pages 266–268) in arguing for an unexpected consequence of drug testing and by Walter S. Minot in proposing an overlooked cause of the decline in American education (pages 272–274).

PLAN 4   When your purpose is to change your audience's mind about a cause or consequence:

- Introduce issue and show why it is controversial.
- Summarize your opponent's causal argument and then refute it.
- Present your own causal argument.

Plan 4 is a standard structure for all kinds of arguments. This is the structure Oilcan Floyd's attorney would use in court to persuade the jury that faulty brakes caused Oilcan's car to skid.

REVISION: SEEING YOUR ARGUMENT AFRESH

Once you have written a discovery draft, you will have a clearer idea of what you are trying to do in your essay. Through further drafting and discussions with others, your next goal is to clarify your argument for yourself and then finally to make it clear and persuasive for your readers.

If you haven't already done so, now is the time to summarize your argument as a claim with because clauses and to analyze your argument either using the Toulmin schema or making a diagram of your causal chain similar to the one we made for Carl Sagan's essay on the greenhouse effect or that Mary Lou Torpey made for herself (Figure 12–1). In order to strengthen your argument from the perspective of a skeptical audience, pay particular attention to Toulmin's "conditions for rebuttal." Try to see the weaknesses of your argument from an opposing perspective and use that knowledge to bolster your support. The following section shows you some ways to role play an opposing view in order to discover weaknesses in your own argument.

CONDITIONS FOR REBUTTAL: CRITIQUING CAUSAL ARGUMENTS

Because of the strenuous conditions that must be met before causality can be proven, causal arguments are vulnerable at many points. The following strategies will generally be helpful.

If You Described Each Link in a Causal Chain, Would Skeptics Point out Weaknesses in Any of the Links?

As the diagram of Carl Sagan's article suggests, describing a causal chain can be complex business. A skeptic can raise doubts about an entire argument simply by undercutting one of the links. Your best defense is to make a diagram of the linkages and role play a skeptic trying to refute each link in turn. Whenever you find possible arguments against your position, see how you can strengthen your own argument at that point.

If Your Argument Is Based on a Scientific Experiment, Could Skeptics Question the Validity of the Experiment?

The scientific method attempts to demonstrate causality experimentally. If the experiment isn't well designed, however, the demonstration is less likely to be acceptable to skeptical audiences. Here are ways to critique a scientific argument:

Question the findings. Skeptics may have reason to believe that the data collected were not accurate or representative. They might provide alternative data or simply point out flaws in the way the data were collected.

Question the interpretation of the data. Many research studies are divided into a "findings" and a "discussion" section. In the discussion section the researcher analyzes and interprets the data. A skeptic might provide an alternative interpretation of the data or otherwise argue that the data don't support what the original writer claims.

Question the design of the experiment. A detailed explanation of research design is beyond the scope of this text, but we can give a brief example of how a typical experiment did go wrong. A major university recently completed an experiment to test the effect of word processors on students' achievement in Freshman English. They reported that students who used the word processors for revising all their essays did significantly better on a final essay than a control group of students who didn't use word processors.

It turned out, however, that there were at least two major design flaws in the experiment. First, the researchers allowed students to volunteer for the experimental group. Perhaps these students were already better writers than the control group from the start. (Can you think of a causal explanation of why the better students might volunteer to use the computers?) Second, when the teachers graded essays from both the computer group and the control group, the essays were not retyped uniformly. Thus the computer group's essays were typed with "computer perfection" (justified right margins, etc.), whereas the control group's essays were handwritten or typed on ordinary typewriters. Perhaps the readers were affected by the pleasing appearance of the computer-typed essays. More significantly, perhaps the graders were biased in favor of the computer project and unconsciously scored the computer-typed papers higher.

The above example illustrates just a few of the ways a scientific study can be flawed. Our point is that skeptics might not automatically accept your citation of a scientific study as a proof of causality. By considering opposing views in advance, you may be able to strengthen your argument.

If You Have Used Correlation Data, Could Skeptics Argue That the Correlation Is Much Weaker than You Claim or That You Haven't Sufficiently Demonstrated Causality?

As we discussed earlier, correlation data tell us only that two or more phenomena are likely to occur together. They don't tell us that one caused the other. Thus correlation arguments are usually accompanied by hypotheses about causal connections between the phenomena. Correlation arguments can often be refuted as follows:

- Find problems in the statistical methods used to determine the correlation.
- Weaken the correlation by pointing out exceptions.
- Provide an alternative hypothesis about causality.

If You Have Used an Analogy Argument, Could Skeptics Point out Disanalogies?

Although among the most persuasive of argumentative strategies, analogy arguments are also among the easiest to refute. The standard procedure is to counter your argument that X is like Y by pointing out all the ways that X is *not* like Y. Once again, by role playing an opposing view, you may be able to strengthen your own analogy argument.

Could a Skeptic Cast Doubt on Your Argument by Reordering Your Priority of Causes?

Up to this point we've focused on refuting the claim that X causes Y. However, another approach is to concede that X helps cause Y but that X is only one of several contributing causes and not the most significant one at that.

FOR CLASS DISCUSSION

In "Students Who Push Burgers" (pages 272–274), the author, Walter Minot, blames part-time jobs as a primary cause of the decline of educational performance by American students, a decline that leads in turn (so claims Minot) to a decline in our economy. You, however, want to defend the practice of American teenagers holding part-time jobs. Using procedures outlined in this chapter, how might you attempt to weaken Minot's argument and create greater audience adherence to your own?

1. Do a ten-minute freewrite in which you explore ways to undercut Minot's argument and support your own.

2. In groups, discuss your individual responses.

3. Elect one member of your group to give a brief speech before the class, arguing that Minot's essay either fails to see important benefits in part-time work or diverts attention from other, more important causes of the decline of American education.

THE WARMING OF THE WORLD

Carl Sagan

When humans first evolved—in the savannahs of East Africa a few million   1
years ago—our numbers were few and our powers feeble. We knew almost nothing about controlling our environment—even clothing had yet to be invented. We were creatures of the climate, utterly dependent upon it.

A few degrees hotter or colder on average, and our ancestors were in   2
trouble. The toll taken much later by the ice ages, in which average land temperatures dropped some 8°C (centigrade, or Celsius), must have been horrific. And yet, it is exactly such climatic change that pushed our ancestors to develop tools and technology, science and civilization. Certainly, skills in

Source: Carl Sagan, "The Warming of the World," *Parade*, February 3, 1985.

hunting, skinning, tanning, building shelters and refurbishing caves must owe much to the terrors of the deep ice age.

Today, we live in a balmy epoch, 10,000 years after the last major glaciation. In this climatic spring, our species has flourished; we now cover the entire planet and are altering the very appearance of our world. Lately — within the last century or so — humans have acquired, in more ways than one, the ability to make major changes in that climate upon which we are so dependent. The Nuclear Winter findings are one dramatic indication that we can change the climate — in this case, in the spasm of nuclear war. But I wish here to describe a different kind of climatic danger, this one slower, more subtle and arising from intentions that are wholly benign. 3

It is warm down here on Earth because the Sun shines. If the Sun were somehow turned off, the Earth would rapidly cool. The oceans would freeze, eventually the atmosphere itself would condense out and our planet would be covered everywhere by snowbanks of solid oxygen and nitrogen 10 meters (about 30 feet) high. Only the tiny trickle of heat from the Earth's interior and the faint starlight would save our world from a temperature of absolute zero. 4

We know how bright the Sun is; we know how far from it we are; and we know what fraction of the sunlight reaching the Earth is reflected back to space (about 30 percent). So we can calculate — with a simple mathematical equation — what the average temperature of the Earth should be. But when we do the calculation, we find that the Earth's temperature should be about 20°C below the freezing point of water, in stark contradiction to our everyday experience. What have we done wrong? 5

As in many such cases in science, what we've done wrong is to forget something — in this case, the atmosphere. Every object in the universe radiates some kind of light to space; the colder the object, the longer the wavelength of radiation it emits. The Earth — much colder than the Sun — radiates to space mainly in the infrared part of the spectrum, not the visible. Were the Sun turned off, the Earth would soon be indetectable in ordinary visible light, though it would be brilliantly illuminated in infrared light. 6

When sunlight strikes the Earth, part is reflected back into the sky; much of the rest is absorbed by the ground and heats it — the darker the ground, the greater the heating. The ground radiates back upward in the infrared. Thus, for an airless Earth, the temperature would be set solely by a balance between the incoming sunlight absorbed by the surface and the infrared radiation that the surface emits back to space. 7

When you put air on a planet, the situation changes. The Earth's atmosphere is, generally, still transparent to visible light. That's why we can see each other when we talk, glimpse distant mountains and view the stars. 8

But in the infrared, all that is different. While the oxygen and nitrogen in the air are transparent in both the infrared and the visible, minor constituents such as water vapor (H_2O) and carbon dioxide (CO_2) tend to be much more 9 opaque in the infrared. It would be useless for us to have eyes that could see at a wavelength, say, of 15 microns in the infrared, because the air is murky black there.

Accordingly, if you add air to a world, you heat it: The surface now has   10
difficulty when it tries to radiate back to space in the infrared. The atmosphere tends to absorb the infrared radiation, keeping heat near the surface and providing an infrared blanket for the world. There is very little CO_2 in the Earth's atmosphere — only 0.03 percent. But that small amount is enough to make the Earth's atmosphere opaque in important regions of the infrared spectrum. CO_2 and H_2O are the reason the global temperature is not well below freezing. We owe our comfort — indeed, our very existence — to the fact that these gases are present and are much more transparent in the visible than in the infrared. Our lives depend on a delicate balance of invisible gases. Too much blanket, or too little, and we're in trouble.

This property of many gases to absorb strongly in the infrared but not in   11
the visible, and thereby to heat their surroundings, is called the "greenhouse effect." A florist's greenhouse keeps its planty inhabitants warm. The phrase "greenhouse effect" is widely used and has an instructive ring to it, reminding us that we live in a planetary-scale greenhouse and recalling the admonition about living in glass houses and throwing stones. But, in fact, florists' greenhouses do not keep warm by the greenhouse effect; they work mainly by inhibiting the movement of air inside, another matter altogether.

We need look only as far as the nearest planet to see an example of an   12
atmospheric greenhouse effect gone wild. Venus has in its atmosphere an enormous quantity of carbon dioxide (roughly as much as is buried as carbonates in all the rocks of the Earth's crust). There is an atmosphere of CO_2 on Venus 90 times thicker than the atmosphere of the Earth and containing some 200,000 times more CO_2 than in our air. With water vapor and other minor atmospheric constitutents, this is enough to make a greenhouse effect that keeps the surface of Venus around 470°C (900°F) — enough to melt tin or lead.

When humans burn wood or "fossil fuels" (coal, oil, natural gas, etc.),   13
they put carbon dioxide into the air. One carbon atom (C) combines with a molecule of oxygen (O_2) to produce CO_2. The development of agriculture, the conversion of dense forest to comparatively sparsely vegetated farms, has moved carbon atoms from plants on the ground to carbon dioxide in the air. About half of this new CO_2 is removed by plants or by the layering down of carbonates in the oceans. On human time-scales, these changes are irreversible: Once the CO_2 is in the atmosphere, human technology is helpless to remove it. So the overall amount of CO_2 in the air has been growing — at least since the industrial revolution. If no other factors operate, and if enough CO_2 is put into the atmosphere, eventually the average surface temperature will increase perceptibly.

There are other greenhouse gases that are increasingly abundant in the   14

Earth's atmosphere—halocarbons, such as the freon used in refrigerator cooling systems; or nitrous oxide (N_2O), produced by automobile exhausts and nitrogenous fertilizers; or methane (CH_4), produced partly in the intestines of cows and other ruminants.

But let's for the moment concentrate on carbon dioxide: How long, at the   15 present rates of burning wood and fossil fuels, before the global climate becomes significantly warmer? And what would the consequences be?

It is relatively simple to calculate the immediate warming from a given   16 increase in the CO_2 abundance, and all competent calculations seem to be in good agreement. More difficult to estimate are (1) the rate at which carbon dioxide will continue to be put into the atmosphere (it depends on population growth rates, economic styles, alternative energy sources and the like) and (2) feedbacks—ways in which a slight warming might produce other, more drastic, effects.

The recent increase in atmospheric CO_2 is well documented. Over the last   17 century, this CO_2 buildup should have resulted in a few tenths of a degree of global warming, and there is some evidence that such a warming has occurred.

The National Academy of Sciences estimates that the present atmospheric   18 abundance of CO_2 is likely to double by the year 2065, although experts at the academy predict a one-in-20 chance that it will double before 2035— when an infant born today becomes 50 years old. Such a doubling would warm the air near the surface of the Earth by 2°C or 3°C—maybe by as much as 4°C. These are average temperature values; there would naturally be considerable local variation. High latitudes would be warmed much more, although a baked Alaska will be some time coming.

There would be precipitation changes. The annual discharge of rivers   19 would be altered. Some scientists believe that central North America— including much of the area that is now the breadbasket of the world—would be parched in summer if the global temperature increases by a few degrees. There would be some mitigating effects; for example, where plant growth is not otherwise limited, more CO_2 should aid photosynthesis and make more luxuriant growth (of weeds as well as crops). If the present CO_2 injection into the atmosphere continued over a few centuries, the warming would be greater than from all other causes over the last 100,000 years.

As the climate warms, glacial ice melts. Over the last 100 years, the level of   20 the world's oceans has risen by 15 centimeters (6 inches). A global warming of 3°C or 4°C over the next century is likely to bring a further rise in the average sea level of about 70 centimeters (28 inches). An increase of this magnitude could produce major damage to ports all over the world and induce fundamental change in the patterns of land development. A serious speculation is that greenhouse temperature increases of 3°C or 4°C could, in addition, trigger the disintegration of the West Antarctic Ice Sheet, with huge quantities of polar ice falling into the ocean. This would raise sea level by some 6 meters (20 feet) over a period of centuries, with the eventual inundation of all coastal cities on the planet.

There are many other possibilities that are poorly understood, including   21
the release of other greenhouse gases (for example, methane from peat bogs) accelerated by the warming climate. The circulation of the oceans might be an important aspect of the problem. The scientific community is attempting to make an environmental-impact statement for the entire planet on the consequences of continued burning of fossil fuels. Despite the uncertainties, a kind of consensus is in: Over the next century or more, with projected rates of burning of coal, oil and gas, there is trouble ahead.

The problem is difficult for at least three different reasons: 22

(1) We do not yet fully understand how severe the greenhouse conse-   23
quences will be.

(2) Although the effects are not yet strikingly noticeable in everyday life, to   24
deal with the problem, the present generation might have to make sacrifices for the next.

(3) The problem cannot be solved except on an international scale: The   25
atmosphere is ignorant of national boundaries. South African carbon dioxide warms Taiwan, and Soviet coal-burning practices affect productivity in America. The largest coal resources in the world are found in the Soviet Union, the United States and China, in that order. What incentives are there for a nation such as China, with vast coal reserves and a commitment to rapid economic development, to hold back on the burning of fossil fuels because the result might, decades later, be a parched American sunbelt or still more ghastly starvation in sub-Saharan Africa? Would countries that might benefit from a warmer climate be as vigorous in restraining the burning of fossil fuels as nations likely to suffer greatly?

Fortunately, we have a little time. A great deal can be done in decades.   26
Some argue that government subsidies lower the price of fossil fuels, inviting waste; more efficient usage, besides its economic advantage, could greatly ameliorate the CO_2 greenhouse problem. Parts of the solution might involve alternative energy sources, where appropriate: solar power, for example, or safer nuclear fission reactors, which, whatever their other dangers, produce no greenhouse gases of importance. Conceivably, the long-awaited advent of commercial nuclear fusion power might happen before the middle of the next century.

However, any technological solution to the looming greenhouse problem   27
must be worldwide. It would not be sufficient for the United States or the Soviet Union, say, to develop safe and commercially feasible fusion power plants: That technology would have to be diffused worldwide, on terms of cost and reliability that would be more attractive to developing nations than a reliance on fossil fuel reserves or imports. A serious, very high-level look at

patterns of U.S. and world energy development in light of the greenhouse problem seems overdue.

During the last few million years, human technology, spurred in part by   28
climatic change, has made our species a force to be reckoned with on a planetary scale. We now find, to our astonishment, that we pose a danger to ourselves. The present world order is, unfortunately, not designed to deal with global-scale dangers. Nations tend to be concerned about themselves, not about the planet; they tend to have short-term rather than long-term objectives. In problems such as the increasing greenhouse effect, one nation or region might benefit while another suffers. In other global environmental issues, such as nuclear war, all nations lose. The problems are connected: Constructive international efforts to understand and resolve one will benefit the others.

Further study and better public understanding are needed, of course. But   29
what is essential is a global consciousness — a view that transcends our exclusive identification with the generational and political groupings into which, by accident, we have been born. The solution to these problems requires a perspective that embraces the planet and the future. We are all in this greenhouse together.

WHAT DRUGS I TAKE IS NONE OF YOUR BUSINESS — THE CONSEQUENCES OF DRUG TESTING

Mary Lou Torpey (student)

So you have a job interview with a new company tomorrow? Well my   1
advice is to go home, get some rest, and drink plenty of fluids, because chances are you'll have to leave more than just a good impression with your prospective employer. You may have to leave a full specimen bottle to check you out for drug use, too. Imagine having to stand in a line in your business suit with your application in one hand and a steaming cup of urine in the other, waiting to turn each of them in, wondering which one is really more important in the job selection process. Some companies and every branch of the Armed Forces require a witness present during the test so the person being tested doesn't try to switch specimens with someone who is drug or alcohol free. As one can imagine, having to be witnessed during a drug test could give a whole new meaning to the term "stage fright." The embarrassing situation of being drug tested is a real possibility, since mandatory drug testing is becoming more and more prevalent in today's workplaces.

Despite the embarrassment, many employers, including western Washing-   2
ton's largest, Boeing, believe the consequences of mandatory drug testing

would be beneficial. By trying to ensure safe work environments by cutting down on drug abusers who could create potential hazards for other employees, such companies believe that quality in workmanship will improve. They also believe that their employees will operate at peak performance levels to keep productivity up. However, there is a consequence of mandatory drug testing that is not being considered by the employers who have instituted it, a consequence that will be devastating for hundreds of thousands of people.

Perhaps the most potentially damaging result of mandatory drug testing 3 lies with people who have legitimate uses for controlled substance drugs — people like me. I have narcolepsy, a serious lifelong disorder that causes crippling sleepiness without the help of controlled substance drugs, similar to the way a mobility impaired person would be crippled without crutches, a walker, or a wheelchair. In other words, I, as a narcoleptic, must have a controlled substance drug to maintain any sort of normal lifestyle at all. Without amphetamines, I could not drive a car, go to college, read, or even hold a decent conversation without falling asleep.

The damaging consequence of mandatory drug testing here is that if I, or 4 others with a myriad of other chronic disorders requiring the use of controlled substance drugs, such as epilepsy, depression due to chemical imbalance, or a number of other seizure disorders, were seeking employment where a drug test is administered, we would be forced to divulge information about the illness. It should be every person's choice whether or not they will inform their employer, especially if their medications manage their illness adequately.

Having to inform a prospective employer about an illness would open the 5 way for prejudice. In all honesty, why would an employer hire a "sick" person when there are so many "normal" ones on the job market? This prejudice is ironic since people like me with narcolepsy or other "silent disabilities" try so hard to compensate that they make exemplary employees. The way I think of it is like that commercial for "Scrubbing Bubbles." That's the commercial where the little bubbles go down the bathtub drain after making it sparkling clean, shouting "we work hard so you don't have to." When it comes to my job, I work hard so my employer doesn't have to think about making special exceptions for me.

In the case of a random test for employees already with a company, those 6 individuals would be forced to explain why a controlled substance is coming up on their test results. When this happens to an employee who has not previously told his employer about an illness or medication he must take, that employee runs the strong chance of being terminated or prejudiced against in the promotion process. After all, what would make an employer believe an employee's explanation about a necessary drug if the employer already showed so little trust as to administer a test at all?

In addition, the emphasis in drug testing for the abuse of drugs such as 7

Ritalin® and Dexedrine® is making them increasingly difficult to purchase in pharmacies. Quotas are now being put on their production, and some states are working on banning them or making them more and more difficult to get. For example, many times I have taken a prescription to be filled into a pharmacy only to find that they had run out of their allotment and would not have any for a few days. A few days is like a lifetime for most narcoleptics without medication, some of whom can be virtually housebound without it. Imagine, in the hysteria over these drugs caused by being targeted in mandatory drug testing, what would happen if a few days turned into weeks or maybe even a month?

There is no denying the need for programs to address drug and alcohol   8
abuse. The beneficial causes the employers are seeking are reasonable in themselves, but just won't happen through mandatory drug testing. Instead, why can't employers take a positive approach to dealing with substance abuse within the workplace? Employers could set up counseling programs and encourage people with problems to step forward and get help. Employers who show trust and respect for their employees will get trust and respect in return. A positive, caring approach would be better for everyone, considering the far-reaching negative consequences of mandatory drug testing. After all, one should never forget that disorders requiring the use of controlled substance drugs have no prejudice. They can strike anyone at anytime. Believe me, I know.

WHY MARRIED MOTHERS WORK

Victor Fuchs

Among single women ages 25–44 four out of five work for pay, and this   1
proportion has not changed since 1950. Divorced and separated women have also traditionally worked, and their participation rates (about 75 percent) have grown only slightly. The truly astonishing changes have taken place in the behavior of married women with children, as shown in Figure 1. . . .

Why has the participation of married mothers grown so *rapidly* and so   2
steadily? Popular discussions frequently attribute this growth to changes in attitudes that were stimulated by the feminist movement, but the time pattern portrayed in Figure 1 does not lend much support to this view. Betty Friedan's *The Feminine Mystique*, which is often credited with sparking the modern feminist movement, was published in 1963, long after the surge of married mothers into the labor force was under way. Moreover, there is no evidence of any sudden acceleration in response to this movement. Similarly, widespread public expressions of feminism *followed* rather than preceded the rise in the age of marriage and the fall in the birth rate. Divorce is the one variable whose change coincided with the burgeoning feminist movement,

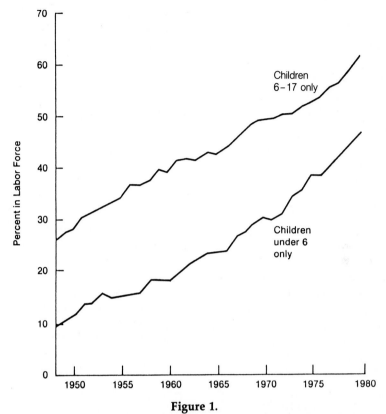

Figure 1.
Labor Force Participation Rates of Married Women with Husband Present, by
Presence and Age of Own Children, 1948–1980
(*Sources:* Employment and Training Administration, *Employment and Training Report of the President, 1980,* table B-4; idem, *Employment and Training Report of the President, 1981,* table B-7.)

rising rapidly between 1965 and 1975. Thus, the feminist writings and discussion, valid as they may be in their own terms, will probably not be viewed by future historians as a basic cause of social change but primarily as a rationale and a rhetoric for changes that were already occurring for other reasons.

Government affirmative action programs are regarded by many as fostering female employment, but the timing again suggests that too much has been claimed for this explanation. These programs, which did not gain force until well into the 1960s, cannot explain the rapid rise in participation of married mothers in the 1950s — a rise that was even more rapid for older women with grown children. The timing of changes in the occupational distribution of employed married women is also contrary to what one would expect if the feminist movement or government affirmative action had a great deal of effect. The proportion who were in professional and technical occupations rose rapidly between 1948 and 1965, from 7.7 percent to 14.7 percent, but thereafter the rate of increase was more modest, only to 17.7 percent by 1979.

One of the most popular explanations for the two-earner family is that the wife's earnings are "needed to help make ends meet." This answer is the one most frequently given by women to survey researchers, and it receives some support from analytical studies that attempt to explain why, at any particular time, some wives work and some don't. There is a strong consensus among economists that, other things held constant, the higher the husband's income, the less likely it is that the wife will work for pay. 4

This explanation, however, does not contribute much to an understanding of changes over time. "Need," in an absolute sense, can hardly be the reason for the rapid rise in labor force participation of married mothers in the 1950s, when the real hourly earnings of their husbands were increasing at an unprecedented pace. Nathan Keyfitz (1980) observed that when women are asked why they work outside the home, they tend to reply that they need the money. "But," he writes, "the answer cannot be correct, since in earlier decades their husbands were earning less, presumably families needed money, and yet wives were content to stay home. Needing money is a universal, a constant, and a first rule of method is that one cannot explain a variable . . . with a constant." 5

One frequently mentioned but inadequately evaluated explanation for the surge of women into paid employment is the spread of time-saving household innovations such as clothes washers and dryers, frozen foods, and dishwashers. There is little doubt that it is easier to combine paid employment with home responsibilities now than it was fifty years ago, but it is not clear whether these time-saving innovations were the *cause* of the rise in female labor force participation or whether they were largely a *response* to meet a demand created by working women. Confusion about this point is most evident in comments that suggest that the rapid growth of supermarkets and fast-food outlets is a cause of women going to work. Similar time-saving organizations were tried at least sixty years ago, but with less success because the value of time was much lower then. The absence of supermarkets and fast-food eating places in low-income countries today also shows that their rapid growth in the United States is primarily a *result* of the rising value of time and the growth of women in the work force, not the reverse. 6

Within the economics profession the explanation that commands the widest consensus is that *higher wages* have attracted more married mothers into the labor force. This explanation is more firmly grounded in economic theory than many of the others and is reasonably consistent with observed behavior, both over time and among families at a given point in time. Ever since the pioneering work of Jacob Mincer (1962), numerous cross-section 7 analyses—studies that examine differences among individual families or groups of families—uniformly report that the probability of a wife's working is *positively* related to her potential wage rate, holding constant spouse's education. This is the opposite of the previously noted *negative* effect of the husband's wage rate on the wife's labor force participation. . . .

In addition to higher wages, the rapid expansion of jobs in the service   8
sector has contributed to the rise in female labor force participation (Fuchs 1968). The service industries (retail trade, financial service, education, health, personal services, public administration) have traditionally offered much greater employment opportunities for women than have mining, manufacturing, construction, and other branches of the industrial sector. For instance, 73 percent of nonfarm female employment was in the service sector in 1960, whereas the comparable figure for males was only 44 percent.

There are many reasons for this large differential. First, most occupations   9
in the service sector do not place a premium on physical strength. Second, hours of work are frequently more flexible in service industries and there are many more opportunities for part-time work. Other things held constant, mothers of small children are more likely to be working in those metropolitan areas where there is large variation in the weekly hours of men (King 1978). This variation is a good indicator of the existence of part-time employment opportunities, and women are much more likely than men to seek part-time employment. Third, service sector jobs are more likely to be located in or near residential areas, thus making them more attractive to women who bear large responsibilities for child care and homemaking.

The propensity of women to seek service sector employment is particularly   10
relevant because it is this sector that has provided nearly all of the additional job opportunities in the U.S. economy since the end of World War II. Between 1947 and 1980 U.S. employment expanded by 39 million; the service sector provided 33 million of these additional jobs. To be sure, some of the growth of service employment is the *result* of the increase in female labor force participation rather than the cause (Fuchs 1981a). Families with working mothers are more likely to eat out, to send their children to nursery school, and to purchase a wide range of personal and professional services. This feedback effect, however, accounts for only a part of the growth of service employment. The major explanation is that rapid increases in output per worker in agriculture and industry cut the demand for labor in those sectors and shifted employment to services. A secondary reason is that consumer demand shifted slightly toward services in response to the growth of real income.

I conclude that the growth of real wages and the expansion of the service   11
sector have been the most important reasons for the growth of female labor force participation. This participation, in turn, has had important effects on marriage, fertility, and divorce, but there is also some feedback from fertility

and divorce to labor force participation. Better control of fertility makes a career in the labor market more promising to women, not only because of a reduction in the *number* of children but also because women now have better control over the *timing* of births. The increase in the *probability* of divorce contributes to the rise in female labor force participation because women recognize that complete commitment to home and husband can leave them in a perilous economic position if the marriage should dissolve. Alimony and child support payments are often inadequate, and are not paid at all in a large proportion of cases. An old song says that "diamonds are a girl's best friend," but today the ability to earn a good wage is likely to prove a more reliable asset.

STUDENTS WHO PUSH BURGERS

Walter S. Minot

A college freshman squirms anxiously on a chair in my office, his eyes   1
avoiding mine, those of his English professor, as he explains that he hasn't finished his paper, which was due two days ago. "I just haven't had the time," he says.

"Are you carrying a heavy course load?"   2
"Fifteen hours," he says — a normal load.   3
"Are you working a lot?"   4
"No, sir, not much. About 30 hours a week."   5
"That's a lot. Do you have to work that much?"   6
"Yeah, I have to pay for my car."   7
"Do you really need a car?"   8
"Yeah, I need it to get to work."   9

This student isn't unusual. Indeed, he probably typifies today's college and   10
high school students. Yet in all the lengthy analyses of what's wrong with American education, I have not heard employment by students being blamed.

I have heard drugs blamed and television — that universal scapegoat. I   11
have heard elaborate theories about the decline of the family, of religion, and of authority, as well as other sociological theories. But nobody blames student employment. The world seems to have accepted the part-time job as a normal feature of adolescence. A parochial school in my town even had a day to honor students who held regular jobs, and parents often endorse this employment by claiming that it teaches kids the value of the dollar.

But such employment is a major cause of educational decline. To argue my   12
case, I will rely on memories of my own high school days and contrast them with what I see today. Though I do have some statistical evidence, my argument depends on what anyone over 40 can test through memory and direct observation.

When I was in high school in the 1950s, students seldom held jobs. Some 13
of us baby-sat, shoveled snow, mowed lawns, and delivered papers, and some
of us got jobs in department stores around Christmas. But most of us had no
regular source of income other than the generosity of our parents.

The only kids who worked regularly were poor. They worked to help their 14
families. If I remember correctly, only about five people in my class of 170
held jobs. That was in a working-class town in New England. As for the rest
of us, our parents believed that going to school and helping around the house
were our work.

In contrast, in 1986 my daughter was one of the few students among 15
juniors and seniors who didn't work. According to Bureau of Labor statistics,
more than 40 percent of high school students were working in 1980, but
sociologists Ellen Greenberger and Laurence Steinberg in "When Teenagers
Work" came up with estimates of more than 70 percent working in 1986,
though I suspect that the figure may be even higher now.

My daughter, however, did not work; her parents wouldn't let her. Inter- 16
estingly, some of the students in her class implied that she had an unfair
advantage over them in the classroom. They were probably right, for while
she was home studying, they were pushing burgers, waiting on tables, or
selling dresses 20 hours a week. Working students have little time for
homework.

I attended a public high school, while she attended a Roman Catholic 17
preparatory school whose students are mainly middle class. By the standards
of my day, her classmates did not "have to" work. Yet many of them were
working 20 to 30 hours a week. Why?

They worked so that they could spend $60 to $100 a week on designer 18
jeans, rock concerts, stereo and video systems, and, of course, cars. They
were living lives of luxury, buying items on which their parents refused to
throw hard-earned money away. Though the parents would not buy such
tripe for their kids, the parents somehow convinced themselves that the kids
were learning the value of money. Yet, according to Ms. Greenberger and Mr.
Steinberg, only about a quarter of these students saved money for college or
other long-term goals.

How students spend their money is their business, not mine. But as a 19
teacher, I have witnessed the effects of their employment. I know that
students who work all evening aren't ready for studying when they get home
from work. Moreover, because they work so hard and have ready cash, they
feel that they deserve to have fun — instead of spending all their free time
studying.

Thus, by the time they get to college, most students look upon studies as a 20
spare-time activity. A survey at Pennsylvania State University showed that
most freshmen believed they could maintain a B average by studying about 20

hours a week. (I can remember when college guidebooks advised two to three hours of studying for every hour in class—30 to 45 hours a week.)

Clearly individual students will pay the price for lack of adequate time 21 studying, but the problem goes beyond the individual. It extends to schools and colleges that are finding it difficult to demand quantity or quality of work from students.

Perhaps the reason American education has declined so markedly is be- 22 cause America has raised a generation of part-time students. And perhaps our economy will continue to decline as full-time students from Japan and Europe continue to out-perform our part-time students.

13

RESEMBLANCE ARGUMENTS: X IS/IS NOT LIKE Y

CASE 1

In May 1987, a controversy arose between Israeli and West German historians over the reinterpretation of the Holocaust, the Nazi attempt to destroy the Jews. According to one West German historian, the Nazi annihilation of the Jews was comparable to Stalin's massacre of the Russian peasants and Pol Pot's murder of his opponents in Cambodia. The effect of this comparison, in the eyes of many Israeli historians, was to diminish the horror of the Holocaust by denying its uniqueness. Israeli historian Shaul Friedlander responded that while the scale and criminality of the murders might be compared, "there is no other example to my knowledge of a government deciding that an entire race of millions of people spread all over a continent is to be brought together by all means at the disposal of the state and eliminated."*

CASE 2

To further her argument against the notion that motherhood is a predestined role for women, a psychiatrist used the following analogy: "Women don't need to be mothers any more than they need spaghetti. But if you're in a world where everyone is eating spaghetti, thinking they need it and want it, you will think so too."†

*From Karen Winkler, "German Scholars Sharply Divided over Place of Holocaust in History," *Chronicle of Higher Education*, May 27, 1987, pp. 4–5.
†From Betty Rollin, "Motherhood: Who Needs It?"

CASE 3

Lawyer Charles Rembar attacked the American Civil Liberties Union (ACLU) for its opposition to the mandatory reporting of AIDS cases. Rembar claimed that the ACLU position didn't take into account the seriousness of the AIDS problem. According to Rembar, the ACLU "clings to once useful concepts that are inappropriate to current problems. Like the French military, which prepared for World War II by building the Maginot Line, which was nicely adapted to the trench warfare of World War I, the ACLU sometimes hauls up legal arguments effective in old libertarian battles but irrelevant to those at hand. . . ."*

CASE 4

When the voting age was reduced from twenty-one to eighteen, many people argued for the lower voting age by saying, "If you are old enough to fight for your country in a war, you are old enough to vote." But author Richard Weaver claimed that this analogy was true "only if you believe that fighting and voting are the same kind of thing which I, for one, do not. Fighting requires strength, muscular coordination and, in a modern army, instant and automatic response to orders. Voting requires knowledge of men, history, reasoning power; it is essentially a deliberative activity. Army mules and police dogs are used to fight; nobody is interested in giving them the right to vote. This argument rests on a false analogy."†

THE DIFFERENCE BETWEEN RESEMBLANCE ARGUMENTS AND DEFINITION ARGUMENTS

In some cases it may seem that a resemblance argument (X is like Y) is not very different from a definitional argument (X is Y). For example, if you were to say that the Sandinista government of Nicaragua was "like" the Somoza regime that it replaced, you might really be making a definitional argument, claiming that both regimes belong to the same class—say, the class "totalitarian governments" or the class "benevolent dictatorships." Their similarities would be restricted to the traits of whatever class they are being put into. In effect, the "like" statement is a definitional claim in which both X and Y are said to belong to class Z.

*From the New York Times, May 15, 1987.
†From Richard M. Weaver, "A Responsible Rhetoric," The Intercollegiate Review, Winter 1976–1977, pp. 86–87.

But if you were to draw an analogy between the Sandinista regime or the Somoza regime and a third thing different in kind from recent Nicaraguan politics — say, to a skin disease or a sporting event — or if you were to argue that some other situation remote in time — say, American Revolutionary politics or nineteenth-century Balkan politics — should serve as a precedent for Nicaragua, the argument moves over into the realm of resemblance. In either case, there are no preexisting definitional criteria to which the event can be matched. There certainly isn't a "Dictionary of Similar Things" we can use to certify the rightness of our comparison. We have to discover and develop the grounds on which the two terms of our comparison are similar.

When we're developing analogies as opposed to establishing definitions, we must be conscious at all times that the two things being compared are essentially different, not members of the same class. In the end we may well be left with several important points of comparison that don't lead to a neat category or concept that somehow "sums" up all the points of comparison and ties them all together. Analogies, in short, reveal different sides of events or things without forcing us to put the things being compared into the same category.

And although the two (or more) things being compared in a relationship of precedence are going to be closer in identity than the terms of an analogy, a precedent doesn't define a term as strictly as does a definition. In a precedent, we are claiming a relationship of resemblance between two actual events. We're saying that this case and that case have sufficient similarities to warrant our drawing similar conclusions from them; we are not saying that the two cases share an identity. The points of comparison between the two may be numerous, but it would be impossible to establish essential conditions that if met would ensure "class membership."

Obviously, an argument of resemblance has to be considerably more tentative than an argument of definition. Suppose, for example, that you wanted to write an argument favoring a balanced federal budget. In one section of your argument you might develop the following claim of resemblance: "Just as a family will go bankrupt if it continually spends more than it makes, so the federal government will go bankrupt if its expenses exceed its revenues." This claim depends on the resemblance between the fiscal problems of the federal government and the fiscal problems of a private family. For many audiences, this comparison might be persuasive: It uses an area of experience familiar to almost everyone (the problem of balancing the family budget) to help make sense of a more complex area of experience (the problem of balancing the federal budget). At its root is the warrant that what works for the family will work for the Fed.

Such an argument can be powerful, but dangerous, if it ignores important differences ("disanalogies") between the terms of comparison. One can think, for instance, of many differences between the economics of a family and that of the federal government. For example, unlike a private family, the federal government prints its own money and does most of its borrowing from its own members. Perhaps these differences negate the claim that family debt and federal debt are similar in their effects. It is thus essential that an argument based on resemblance acknowledge important disanalogies.

THE TENTATIVE NATURE OF RESEMBLANCE ARGUMENTS

One way of illustrating the necessarily tentative nature of a resemblance claim is to look at it via Toulmin's schema. If we take the above example for our illustration, we might get something like this:

Enthymeme:	If the Fed doesn't balance its budget, it will go bankrupt because families that don't balance their budgets go bankrupt.
Claim:	If the Fed doesn't balance its debt, it will go bankrupt.
Stated Reason:	because families that don't balance their budgets go bankrupt
Grounds:	evidence showing that indeed families over-spending their budget do go bankrupt
Warrant:	The economic laws that apply to families apply also to governments.
Backing:	evidence that when governments and families behave in economically similar ways, they suffer similar consequences
Conditions of Rebuttal:	all cases in which governments and families behaved in similar ways and did not suffer similar consequences; all the ways that families and governments differ
Qualifier:	The claim is supported by the analogy only to the extent that family and government economics resemble each other.

As you look at this schema, you can see just how troublesome it would be to support your warrant that economic laws apply equally to families and governments. As noted above, resemblance arguments require you to compare two or more actual cases as opposed to simply applying a concept to an actual case. Whereas the definition of a concept is limited by certain conventions of usage, the comparison between family and government economics is wide open. You have, in sum, undertaken an extraordinary burden of proof since, under the conditions of rebuttal, the possible exceptions to your warrant are in danger of multiplying like exemptions in a tax reform bill (so to speak).

ASSIGNMENT OPTIONS FOR CHAPTER 13

OPTION 1: AN ANALOGY MICROTHEME   Because few arguments are devoted entirely to a resemblance claim and because many arguments from resemblance are used in service of other claims, this assignment asks you simply to write a piece of an argument. Imagine that you are writing a longer argument for or against an X of your choice. As part of your argument you want to influence your reader's emotional or intellectual understanding of X, in either a positive or a negative direction, by comparing it to a more familiar Y. Write the portion of your argument that develops the extended analogy. A good model for this assignment is the argument on pages 281–282. The writer opposes a proficiency exam in writing by comparing it to a proficiency exam in physical fitness. The For Class Discussion exercise on pages 282–283 will give you ideas for topics.

OPTION 2: A PRECEDENCE MICROTHEME   Imagine that you are writing a proposal argument of the kind "We should/should not do X" and that one of your reasons will develop a precedence argument as follows: "We should/should not do X because doing X will lead to the same good/bad consequences that we experienced when we did Y." Write the portion of your argument that develops this precedence claim.

OPTION 3: AN ANALYSIS OF A RESEMBLANCE ARGUMENT   Write an analysis of Jack Greenberg's "Affirmative Action, Quotas and Merit" (pages 687–689), which uses a resemblance argument to support affirmative action programs, or some other resemblance argument provided by your instructor (for example, Peter Singer's argument that human tyranny over animals is analogous to racism or sexism; see his essay on pages 480–492). In your analysis examine the strengths and weaknesses of the analogy or precedence claims being made in the argument and evaluate the argument's overall effectiveness.

An example of an argument analysis is Charles Krauthammer's "Why Lithuania Is Not like South Carolina" (pages 290–292), which is Krauthammer's response to an argument put forth by historian Eric Foner. Foner argued that the Soviet government has the same right to forbid the secession of Lithuania from the Soviet Union as Lincoln had to forbid the secession of South Carolina from the United States. Krauthammer's article analyzes this analogy and rejects it.

THE FIRST TYPE OF RESEMBLANCE ARGUMENT: ARGUMENTS BY ANALOGY

In this section we deal with the first class of resemblance arguments, argument by analogy. Although it's rare to find an entire argument that rests on an analogy, analogies are used extensively in the service of all the other claim types. The ubiquity of analogies in argument is undoubtedly a function of their power to make new relationships clear to reader and writer alike.

The use of analogies can constitute the most imaginative form of argumentation. Consider the case of an outraged prep school student upset about the quality of the high teas at Whitebread-on-Perrier Prep, where he matriculates. Suppose he were to compare his lot to that of a political prisoner in a Russian prison. His resemblance claim would undoubtedly get some attention, particularly from parents paying huge sums of money for their offspring to attend the place.

But getting attention is not enough. In fact, if your argument is particularly weak, getting attention may not be at all desirable. The question now facing our enraged student, the question that faces any author of a resemblance claim, is "How far can I go with this thing?" Analogies can be short and suggestive, used as tools for getting an audience's attention and sympathy, or they can be developed at length and used as tools for guiding their understanding.

Using Undeveloped Analogies

If you put yourself in the shoes of our hypothetical Whitebread-on-Perrier inmate, what would you choose to do? Develop the analogy or let it lie? Our advice would be to get past it as quickly as possible before the disanalogies come back to haunt you. The analogy may serve briefly to suggest certain aspects of the case that you want emphasized—lack of voice in the institution, poor quality of food—but if one goes much past those points of comparison, your suffering is going to pale in comparison to that of the political prisoner. Here, as in many analogies, the differences between the two situations aren't just qualitative but quantitative. And quantitative differences, if extreme, can be fatal to an analogy. In this regard, keep in mind Karl Marx's maxim that "differences in degree, if large enough, become differences in kind."

Using undeveloped analogies to convey feelings and points of view is common in many arguments. The effect is to bring to your argument about topic X (say the importance of discipline to freedom) the full weight, emotion, and understanding your audience already has about Y (the importance of staying on the tracks to the progress of a train). Thus, one writer, arguing against the complexities of recent tax legislation, showed his disgust by drawing an analogy between tax laws and rotting plants or festering wounds.

> It does not take a deep or broadly informed analysis to sense the reek of economic decay and social fester that such irresponsible legislation cultivates.*

Later this writer went on to compare recent tax legislation to an infection by a new virus. Through his use of the analogy, the writer hoped to transfer to the new tax law the audience's already existing revulsion to disease-producing virus.

Using Extended Analogies

Instead of using undeveloped analogies, you may choose to extend your comparison, using your readers' greater understanding of Y to illuminate X. And if your audience is already favorably or unfavorably disposed to Y, then the analogy helps create similar feelings for X. As an example of a claim based on an extended analogy, consider the following excerpt from a professor's argument opposing a proposal to require a writing-proficiency exam for graduation. In the following portion of his argument, the professor compares development of writing skills to the development of physical fitness.

> A writing proficiency exam gives the wrong symbolic messages about writing. It suggests that writing is simply a skill, rather than an active way of thinking and learning. It suggests that once a student demonstrates proficiency then he or she doesn't need to do any more writing.
>
> Imagine two universities concerned with the physical fitness of their students. One university requires a junior-level physical fitness exam in which students must run a mile in less than 10 minutes, a fitness level it considers minimally competent. Students at this university see the physical fitness exam as a one-time hurdle. As many as 70 percent of them can pass the exam with no practice; another 10–20 percent need a few months' training; and a few hopeless couch potatoes must go through exhaustive remediation. After passing the exam, any student can settle

*From C. Thomas Higgins, *Seattle Times*, September 21, 1986.

back into a routine of TV and potato chips having been certified as "physically fit."

The second university, however, believing in true physical fitness for its students, is not interested in minimal competency. Consequently, it creates programs in which its students exercise 30 minutes every day for the entire four years of the undergraduate curriculum. There is little doubt which university will have the most physically fit students. At the second university, fitness becomes a way of life with everyone developing his or her full potential.

If you choose to write an extended analogy such as this, you will focus on the points of comparison that serve your purposes. The writer's purpose in the above case is to support the achievement of mastery rather than minimalist standards as the goal of the university's writing program. Whatever other disanalogous elements are involved (for example, writing requires the use of intellect, which may or may not be strengthened by repetition), the comparison reveals vividly that a commitment to mastery involves more than a minimalist test. The analogy serves primarily to underscore this one crucial point. In reviewing the different groups of students as they "prepare" for the fitness exam, the author makes clear just how irrelevant such an exam is to the whole question of mastery. Typically, then, in developing your analogy you are not developing all possible points of comparison so much as you are bringing out those similarities consistent with the point you are trying to make.

FOR CLASS DISCUSSION

The following is a two-part exercise to help you clarify for yourself how analogies function in the context of arguments. Part 1 is to be done outside of class; part 2 is to be done in class. This exercise is an excellent "Starting Point" task for the *Option 1* writing assignment for this chapter.

PART 1   Think of an analogy that accurately expresses your feeling toward each of the following topics. Then write your analogy in the following one-sentence format:

X is like Y: A, B, C . . . (where X is the main topic being discussed; Y is the analogy; and A, B, and C are the points of comparison).

EXAMPLES

Cramming for an exam to get better grades is like pumping iron for ten hours straight to prepare for a weight-lifting contest; exhausting and counterproductive.

A right-to-lifer bombing an abortion clinic is like a vegetarian bombing a cattle barn: futile and contradictory.

a. Spanking a child to teach obedience is like . . .

b. Building low-cost housing for poor people is like . . .

c. The use of steroids by college athletes is like . . .

d. Mandatory AIDS testing for all U.S. residents is like . . .

e. A legislative proposal to eliminate all federally subsidized student loans is like . . .

f. The effect of American fast food on our health is like . . .

g. The personal gain realized by people who have committed questionable or even illegal acts and then made money by selling book and movie rights is like . . .

In each case, begin by asking yourself how you feel about the subject. If you have negative feelings about a topic, then begin by calling up negative pictures that express those feelings (or if you have positive feelings, call up positive comparisons). As they emerge, test each one to see if it will work as an analogy. An effective analogy will convey both the feeling you have toward your topic and your understanding of the topic. For instance, the writer in the "cramming for an exam" example obviously believes that pumping iron for ten hours before a weight-lifting match is stupid. This feeling of stupidity is then transferred to the original topic—cramming for an exam. But the analogy also clarifies understanding. The writer imagines the mind as a muscle (which gets exhausted after too much exercise and which is better developed through some exercise every day rather than a lot all at once) rather than as a large container (into which lots of stuff can be "crammed").

PART 2   Now, bring your analogies to class and compare them to those of your classmates. Select the best analogies for each of the topics and be ready to say why you think they are good. If you choose, you can then use your analogy as the basis for an extended analogy for this chapter's writing assignment.

THE SECOND TYPE OF RESEMBLANCE ARGUMENT: ARGUMENTS BY PRECEDENT

Precedent arguments are like analogy arguments in that they make comparisons between an X and a Y. In precedent arguments, however, the Y term is always a past event, usually an event where some sort of decision was reached, often a moral, legal, or political decision. An argument by precedent tries to show that a similar decision should or should not be reached for the present issue X because the situation of X is or is not like the situation of Y.

A good example of a precedent argument is the following excerpt from a speech by President Lyndon Johnson in the early years of the Vietnam War:

> Nor would surrender in Vietnam bring peace because we learned from Hitler at Munich that success only feeds the appetite of aggression. The battle would be renewed in one country and then another country, bringing with it perhaps even larger and crueler conflict, as we have learned from the lessons of history.*

Here the audience knows what happened at Munich: France and Britain tried to appease Hitler by yielding to his demand for a large part of Czechoslovakia, but Hitler's armies continued their aggression anyway, using Czechoslovakia as a staging area to invade Poland. By arguing that surrender in Vietnam would lead to the same consequences, Johnson brings to his argument about Vietnam the whole weight of his audience's unhappy knowledge of World War II. Administration white papers developed Johnson's precedent argument by pointing toward the similarity of Hitler's promises with those of the Viet Cong: You give us this and we will ask for no more. But Hitler didn't keep his promise. Why should the Viet Cong?

As with analogies, we often turn to precedents in the early stages of planning an argument. Whereas analogies stimulate our thinking about alternative ways of describing a situation or solving a problem, precedents offer us advice from the past. Let's say, for example, that you are arguing for the mandatory use of seatbelts in cars. Here we might turn to the precedent of a mandatory motorcycle helmet law in our own state or a mandatory seatbelt law in a neighboring state. We would want to review the whole story of how the seatbelt laws were enacted, how opposition arguments were met, what consequences followed their passage, and so forth, to help us plan our own argument. Once we have explored possible arguments using the precedents as guides, we can also cite those precedents in our arguments, using them as evidence as well as structural models.

In a relatively straightforward legal example such as the seatbelt law example, a precedent argument is particularly persuasive. We can see this more clearly if we apply the Toulmin schema to the argument.

> *Enthymeme:* The state should enact a seatbelt law because seatbelt laws have had good consequences in other states.
>
> *Claim:* The state should enact a seatbelt law.
>
> *Stated Reason:* because seatbelt laws have had good consequences in other states

---

*From *Public Papers of the Presidents of the United States,* Vol. 2: *Lyndon B. Johnson,* 1965, p. 794.

> *Grounds:* evidence that seatbelt laws in other states have had good consequences (saved lives, relatively high compliance, few enforcement problems)
>
> *Warrant:* Seatbelt laws will be at least as effective in this state as they have been in the other states that have enacted them.
>
> *Backing:* evidence that there are no significant differences between this state and other states that might diminish the effectiveness of seatbelt laws in this sate
>
> *Conditions of Rebuttal:* acknowledged differences between states that might well impair the effectiveness of a seatbelt law in this state
>
> *Qualifiers:* statements to the effect than even if the seatbelt law is less effective here than it has been in other states it will still improve conditions

As you can see, the key to a precedent argument is showing that the similarities between X and Y outweigh the dissimilarities. In the seatbelt example, it is difficult to imagine how states would differ so that seatbelt laws would be successful in one state but not in another. But if one state is more urban than another (perhaps city drivers are less apt to wear seatbelts because they have to make so many short trips), or if one state regularly elects a Democratic government and the other elects a Republican government (Republicans are generally less tolerant of governmental regulations than Democrats), or if one state has much higher gasoline taxes than another (perhaps people who can afford to drive cars when gasoline is high-priced have a different attitude toward seatbelts than poorer people), then there might be predictable differences in the way citizens would react to a seatbelt law.

FOR CLASS DISCUSSION

1. Consider the following claims of precedent and evaluate just how effective you think each precedent might be in establishing the claim:

   a. Don't vote for Governor Frick for president because governors have not proven to be effective presidents.

   b. I think the Mets will win the pennant next year because they won this year.

   c. American should avoid military involvement in Central America because it will end up in another mess like Vietnam.

2. In 1986, voters in the state of Montana considered an initiative to abolish property taxes. Supporters of the initiative responded to

predictions that it would have disastrous consequences for public services in the state by saying, "Similar dire predictions were made in Massachusetts and California when they passed initiatives to lower property taxes and none of these predictions came to pass, so you can ignore these nay-sayers."

You have been hired by a lobbying group who opposes the initiative. Your task is to do the background research that your group needs in order to refute the above precedent argument. Working in small groups, make a list of research questions you would want to ask.

WRITING YOUR RESEMBLANCE ARGUMENT

The class discussion exercises in this chapter should help you find a starting point for your analogy or precedent and explore its usefulness. The optional microtheme assignments for this chapter will not require as extensive a process as that required for a full-scale argument. After you have written a rough draft of your microtheme, however, we recommend that you examine your argument using Toulmin's scheme. Once again, test your argument by looking carefully at the conditions for rebuttal.

CONDITIONS FOR REBUTTAL: TESTING A RESEMBLANCE ARGUMENT

Once you've written a draft of your resemblance argument, you need to test that argument by attempting to refute it. What follows are some typical questions audiences will raise about arguments of resemblance.

Will My Audience Say I Am Trying to Prove Too Much with My Analogy or Precedent?

The most common mistake people make with resemblance arguments is to ask them to prove more than they're capable of proving. Too often, an analogy is treated as if it were a syllogism or algebraic ratio wherein necessary truths are deduced (*a* is to *b* as *c* is to *d*) rather than as a useful, but basically playful, figure that suggests uncertain but significant insight. The best way to guard against this charge is to qualify your argument and to find other means of persuasion to supplement an analogy or precedent argument.

For a good example of an analogy that tries to do too much, consider President Reagan's attempt to prevent the United States from imposing economic sanctions on South Africa. Reagan wanted to argue that harming South Africa's economy would do as much damage to blacks as to whites. In making this argument, he compared South Africa to a zebra and concluded that one couldn't hurt the white portions of the zebra without also hurting the black.

Now, the zebra analogy works quite well to point up the interrelatedness of whites and blacks in South Africa. But it has no force whatsoever in supporting Reagan's assertion that economic sanctions would hurt blacks as well as whites. To refute this analogy, one need only point out the disanalogies between the zebra stripes and racial groups. (There are, for example, no differences in income, education, and employment between black and white stripes on a zebra.)

Will My Audience Point out Disanalogies in My Resemblance Argument?

Although it is easy to show that a country is not like a zebra, finding disanalogies is sometimes quite tricky. Often displaying the argument in Toulmin terms will help. Here is the Toulmin schema for President Johnson's "Munich analogy" for supporting the war in Vietnam:

> *Enthymeme:* The United States should not withdraw its troops from Vietnam because doing so will have the same disastrous consequences as did giving in to Hitler prior to World War II.
>
> *Claim:* The United States should not withdraw its troops from Vietnam.
>
> *Stated Reason:* because doing so will have the same disastrous consequences as did giving in to Hitler prior to World War II
>
> *Grounds:* evidence that withdrawal of military support backfired in Europe in 1939
>
> *Warrant:* The situation in Europe in 1939 closely parallels the situation in Southeast Asia in 1965.

> *Backing:* evidence of similarities (for example, in political philosophy, goals, and military strength of the enemy; the nature of the conflict between the disputants; and the American commitment to its allies) between the two situations

> *Conditions of Rebuttal:* acknowledged differences between the two situations that might make the outcome of the present situation different from the outcome of the first situation

Laid out like this, some of the problems with the analogy are quickly evident. One has to make a considerable leap to go from undeniably true, historically verifiable grounds to a highly problematic claim. This means that the warrant will have to be particularly strong to license the movement. And although there are undeniable similarities between the two events (as there will be between any two sufficiently complex events), the differences are overwhelming. Thus, during the Vietnam era, critic Howard Zinn attacked the warrant of Johnson's analogy by claiming three crucial differences between Europe in 1938 and Vietnam in 1967.

First, Zinn argued, the Czechs were being attacked from without by an external aggressor (Germany), whereas Vietnam was being attacked from within by rebels as part of a civil war; second, Czechoslovakia was a prosperous, effective democracy, whereas the official Vietnam government was corrupt and unpopular; finally, Hitler wanted Czechoslovakia as a base for attacking Poland, whereas the Viet Cong and North Vietnamese aimed at reunification of their country as an end in itself.*

The Munich example shows again how arguments of resemblance depend on emphasizing the similarities between X and Y and playing down the dissimilarities. One could try to refute the counterargument made by Zinn by arguing first that the Saigon government was more stable than Zinn thinks and second that the Viet Cong and North Vietnamese were driven by goals larger than reunification of Vietnam, namely, communist domination of Asia. Such an argument would once again highlight the similarities between Vietnam and prewar Europe.

Will My Audience Propose a Counteranalogy?

A final way of testing a resemblance claim is to propose an alternative analogy or precedent that counters the original claim. Suppose you wanted to argue for the teaching of creationism along with evolution in the schools

---

*Based on the summary of Zinn's argument in J. Michael Sproule, *Argument: Language and Its Influence* (New York: McGraw-Hill, 1980), pp. 149–150.

and your opponent said that "teaching creationism along with evolution is like teaching the stork theory of where babies come from along with the biological theory." After showing the disanalogies between creationism and the stork theory of reproduction, you could counter with your own analogy: "No, teaching creationism along with evolution is like bilingual education, where you respect the cultural heritage of all peoples." To the extent that your audience values pluralism and the preservation of different beliefs, your analogy may well provide them with a new perspective on the topic, a perspective that allows them to entertain an otherwise alien notion.

FOR CLASS DISCUSSION
Examine the following resemblance claims and then attempt to refute them by pointing out disanalogies between the phenomena being compared.

1. In the following example, the author is arguing that it is not unconstitutional to require drug testing of federal employees. Within the argument the author draws an analogy between testing for drugs and checking for weapons or bombs at an airport. Using the techniques suggested in this chapter, test the soundness of the argument.

> The Constitution does not prohibit all searches and seizures. It makes the people secure in their persons only from "unreasonable" searches and seizures, and there is nothing unreasonable in Reagan's executive order.
> . . . Those who challenge this sensible program [drug testing by urinalysis] ought to get straight on this business of "rights." Like any other employer, the government has a right—within certain well-understood limits—to fix the terms and conditions of employment. The individual's right, if he finds these conditions intolerable, is to seek employment elsewhere. A parallel situation may be observed at every airport in the land. Individuals may have a right to fly, but they have no right to fly without having their persons and baggage inspected for weapons. By the same token, the federal worker who refuses to provide a urine specimen under the president's order can clean out his desk and apply to General Motors or General Electric or Kodak—only to discover that private industry is equally interested in a drug-free work place.*

2. In the following passage, feminist writer Susan Brownmiller argues that pornography expresses prejudice against women just as anti-Semitic propaganda in Hitler's Third Reich expressed prejudice against Jews and "nigger jokes" express prejudice against blacks. She claims that pornography is "anti-female propaganda," which shouldn't be tolerated any more than we tolerate racist propaganda.

> Pornography is the undiluted essence of anti-female propaganda. Yet the very same liberals who were so quick to understand the method and

purpose behind the mighty propaganda machine of Hitler's Third Reich, the consciously spewed-out anti-Semitic caricatures and obscenities that gave an ideological base to the Holocaust and the Final Solution, the very same liberals who, enlightened by blacks, searched their own conscience and came to understand that their tolerance of "nigger" jokes and portrayals of shuffling, rolling-eye servants in movies perpetuated the degrading myths of black inferiority and gave an ideological base to the continuation of black oppression—these very same liberals now fervidly maintain that the hatred and contempt for women that find expression in four-letter words used as expletives and in what are quaintly called "adult" or "erotic" books and movies are a valid extension of freedom of speech that must be preserved as a Constitutional right. [From *Against Our Will* (New York: Simon & Schuster, 1975)]

Analyze Brownmiller's argument. Is she right that pornography is anti-female propaganda? Should we feel the same way about a porno film playing in a downtown "adult" theater that we would feel about an anti-Semitic propaganda film playing in a downtown theater? Working individually or in small groups, create arguments supporting and opposing Brownmiller's analogy.

3. Analyze the strengths and weaknesses of the following argument by Charles Krauthammer, who attempts to refute a resemblance argument made by historian Eric Foner: Lithuania is to Gorbachev as South Carolina was to Lincoln.

WHY LITHUANIA IS NOT LIKE SOUTH CAROLINA

Charles Krauthammer

As Lithuania is slowly strangled, it appeals to the world for help. The 1
world turns away ashamedly. Shame, because we know that the Lithuanian cause is just.

Why? Is it not true, as Columbia University historian Eric Foner asserts, 2
that "there really is a genuine parallel between Lincoln and Gorbachev"? That "Lincoln's position, like Gorbachev's, was that a union, no matter how it was formed, cannot be abandoned." Why do we praise Lincoln for launching a war to save the Union but denounce Gorbachev for much milder actions?

The usual answer—the Lithuanian answer—is an appeal to history. The 3
American South voluntarily joined the American Union. Lithuania was conquered and involuntarily absorbed into the Soviet Union. Its original incorporation being illegitimate, it is not really seceding, it is merely reasserting a

pre-existing independence of which it was robbed 50 years ago when jointly raped by Hitler and Stalin.

But history can be tricky. On the one hand, where exactly does history **4** stop? Lithuania was independent for 20 years between 1920 and 1940, but for more than a hundred years before that it was part of the Russian empire. Which historical period is the norm? The Russian imperium? The brief interregnum of Lithuanian independence? Or the Soviet reality of the past 50 years?

And on the other hand, why was, say, South Carolina's accession to the **5** American Union in 1788 binding on the generation of 1860, which was not even born at the time of incorporation? Why exactly were South Carolinians who had nothing to do with joining the American Union prohibited, by democratic theory no less, from asserting their democratic right to choose their own form of association, or non-association, with the Union?

We need firmer ground on which to base the justice of Lithuania's declara- **6** tion of independence. And it exists. It has nothing to do with history. It has instead to do with democracy, with a new principle of international relations or, rather, an old one that has been revived: the principle of democratic legitimacy. The Lithuanians are right to do what they did because it was an elected government, created by consent of the governed, that decided in the name of the people to secede. It is the democratic origin of that decision, not its history antecedents, that makes it right.

But didn't South Carolina also democratically decide to leave the American **7** Union? By what right did Lincoln make war on it?

The answer is, first, that South Carolina, unlike Lithuania, was not fully **8** democratic. In 1860, 58% of its population was enslaved, denied, among other human rights, the vote. It was a white minority government, we would say today, that voted for secession.

And, second, Lincoln's Union, unlike Gorbachev's, was a democracy. Lin- **9** coln fought to preserve the Union because he believed that secession meant the end of the great American experiment in self-government. If a minority (the South), upon losing an argument (the election of 1860), can just pick up and quit the Union, then the whole idea of republican government becomes a farce. If every disgruntled minority can take up its marbles and secede, then the monarchist and other reactionary critics of the (then) unique American experiment in republican government would be vindicated: man is not fit for self-government. As in classical Rome and Greece, self-government inevitably breaks down into either anarchy or tyranny.

None of this applies to Gorbachev. He is protecting a dictatorial empire, **10** not a democracy. The union he is defending is dedicated to no proposition. Gorbachev has introduced elements of democracy into the U.S.S.R. But ironically, the only part of the U.S.S.R. that can be said to be fully democratic is Lithuania, which has held the U.S.S.R.'s first free multiparty elections. For

Lithuania freely to secede from a nondemocratic union is not to undermine the idea of democratic government but, in fact, to affirm it.

Moreover, today even Lincoln's action would be looked on with far more 11 skepticism. Even if the union is democratic, it hardly seems to us today that it has the right forcibly to suppress the democratically expressed will of a minority for independence. If, for example, Quebec decided tomorrow to secede from Canada, the world would hardly countenance a Lincolnesque invasion of Quebec in the name of the Canadian federal union. Nor would Canada.

So long as a nation, in making its own decisions democratically, does not 12 threaten its neighbors (a condition that a unified Germany, for example, would have to meet), it should be free to choose. Certainly Lithuania meets that test. That is why we are all pulling for Lithuania.

But not fully. When our governments are called upon to support Lith- 13 uania's independence, they are mute. Why? Because while the Lithuanian cause is just, there are other causes in the world — among them the contin- ued success of Gorbachev's attempt to democratize, demilitarize, and deco- lonize the empire that he inherited. This too counts for something.

This tug between the justice of the Lithuanian cause and the need to preserve these other values embodied by Gorbachev is the source of Western paralysis over Lithuania. It is no use trying to justify that paralysis by denying, by appeal to Lincoln, the Lithuanian case. It won't wash. Our paralysis is justified only by admitting that the Lithuanian cause conflicts irreconcilably with other important values.

Some international dilemmas are insoluble. Lithuania presents us with 14 such a dilemma. To try to escape our anguish by denying the just cause of the Lithuanians is to add insult to injury. But we need not condemn ourselves for cowardice. Appeasement is the abandonment of friends simply for one's own safety. Our inaction on Lithuania is grounded in concern not just for our safety but for the reform and eventual liberation of the entire Soviet empire. What Lithuania is experiencing, therefore, is not betrayal, nor is it appease- ment. It is tragedy.

EVALUATION ARGUMENTS: X IS/IS NOT A GOOD Y

CASE 1

A young engineer has advanced to the level of a design group leader. She is now being considered for promotion to a management position. Her present supervisor is asked to write a report evaluating her as a prospective manager. He is asked to pay particular attention to the criteria of "creativity," "leadership," "interpersonal skills," "communication skills," and "technical competence."

CASE 2

A medical research group is asked to prepare guidelines for physicians on the best way to manage insulin-dependent diabetes. Some physicians want strict control of blood sugar levels. These physicians expect patients to take readings of their blood sugars every four hours and to take as many as three or four insulin injections per day. Other physicians allow blood sugars to fluctuate through a wider range of readings. They ask patients to monitor their blood sugars less often and to take only one or two injections per day. Which of these management programs is better? The research group has been asked to deal specifically with the following criteria: risk of long-range complications from diabetes; psychological well-being; and quality of life.

CASE 3

When former tennis star Margaret Court argued that Martina Navratilova's admitted homosexuality kept her from being a proper role model for young tennis players, sports writer Steve Kelley disagreed: "Navratilova is, in fact, an excellent role model. . . . She is self-made. She didn't learn the game playing with the privileged classes. She is honest and well-spoken in interviews. She doesn't kiss off questions with stock cliches. . . . Navratilova is a voracious reader, fluent in four languages. She belongs to the Sierra Club, reads several newspapers a day. She is a political junkie who has the courage of her convictions." Additionally, Kelly admires her courage and integerity in openly acknowledging her relationship with her longtime friend Judy Nelson, an admission that "has cost Navratilova millions in endorsements."*

CASE 4

A regional airline company hires a business consulting firm to evaluate the operations of the company's new hub in a large midwestern city. In the first two years of the hub operation, the company has lost money and is now in trouble. They want the consultants to answer two questions: Is this city a good location for a hub? Is the management team in the hub city doing a good job?

In our roles as citizens and professionals we are continually expected to make difficult evaluations, to defend them, and even to persuade others to accept them. Often we will defend our judgments orally—in committees making hiring and promotion decisions, in management groups deciding which of several marketing plans to adopt, or at parent advisory meetings evaluating the success of school policies. Sometimes, too, we will be expected to put our arguments in writing.

Practice in thinking systematically about the process of evaluation, then, is valuable experience. In this chapter we focus on evaluation arguments of the type "X is/is not a good Y" (or "X is a good/bad Y") and the strategy needed for conducting such arguments.† In Chapter 16, we will return to evaluation arguments to examine in more detail some special problems raised by ethical issues.

WRITING ASSIGNMENT FOR CHAPTER 14: EVALUATE A "CONTROVERSIAL" X

Write an argument in which you evaluate something controversial. Possible examples include the following:

- Is a sales tax a good method of taxation? Which method of income tax is preferable, a flat rate or a progressive rate?

*Steve Kelley, *Seattle Times*, August 26, 1990, C3.

†In addition to the contrasting words *good/bad*, there are a number of other evaluative terms that involve the same kind of thinking: *effective/ineffective, successful/unsuccessful, workable/unworkable,* and so forth. Throughout this chapter, terms such as these can be substituted for *good/bad*.

- Do Top Forty stations play the best music? Is the classic rock music from the late sixties better than the rock music being produced today? What makes some rap music better than other rap music?
- Is *Glory* a great war movie? What is the best horror movie of all time? What is the best James Bond movie? Does the movie *Taxi Driver* deserve the praise it has received from critics? How good was the Mel Gibson *Hamlet*?
- Is [a controversial teacher at your school] a great teacher? During the early Bush administration, was John Sununu a good White House Chief of Staff? Is Arsenio Hall a good talk show host? Was Pete Rose as great a baseball player as is popularly believed? In the early days of the Kuwaiti crisis, was the reputation of Saddam Hussein in the American press a fair one?
- Is *USA Today* a good newspaper? Do network news shows do a good job at giving the news? Are America's prisons effective? How serious a problem is the budget deficit? Have the *Miranda* warnings improved or harmed police enforcement?

The X you choose should be controversial or at least problematic. You would hardly have a surprising essay if you argued that a Mercedes Benz is a good car or that nuclear war is bad. By "controversial" or "problematic," then, we mean that people are apt to disagree with your evaluation of X or that you are somehow opposing the common view of X. By choosing a controversial or problematic X, you will be able to focus on a clear issue. Somewhere in your essay you should summarize opposing views and either refute them or concede to them (see Chapter 10).

Note that this assignment asks you to do something different from a typical movie review, restaurant review, or product review in a consumer magazine. Many reviews are simply informational or analytic, where the writer's purpose is to describe the object or event being reviewed and explain its strengths and weaknesses. In contrast, this assignment calls for an argument, where your purpose is to change someone's mind about the evaluation of X.

The rest of this chapter explains the thinking processes that underlie evaluation arguments and gives you some advice on how to compose an evaluation essay.

THE CRITERIA-MATCH STRUCTURE OF EVALUATION ARGUMENTS

An "X is/is not a good Y" argument follows the same criteria-match structure that we examined in definitional arguments (Chapter 11). A typical claim for such an argument has the following form:

X is/is not a good Y because it meets/fails to meet criteria A, B, and C.

When we expand the preceding enthymeme into a syllogism, it looks like this:

If something meets the criteria A, B, and C, it is a good Y.

X meet the criteria A, B, and C.

Therefore, X is a good Y.

The main difference between an evaluation argument and a definition argument, in terms of structure, involves the Y term. In a definition argument, one argues whether a particular Y term is appropriate, that is, what class to put X into. (Is a tarantula a *pet*?) In an evaluation argument, we know the Y term—that is, what class to put X into (Dr. Choplogic is a *teacher*)—but we don't know whether X is a good or bad instance of that class. (Is Dr. Choplogic a *good* teacher?) As in definition arguments, warrants specify the criteria to be used for the evaluation, whereas the stated reasons and grounds assert that X meets these criteria.

Let's look at some examples that, for the sake of illustration, assert just one criterion for "good" or "bad." (Most arguments will, of course, develop several criteria.) For the first example, we examine only the claim, stated reason, and warrant:

Enthymeme:	Computer-aided instruction (CAI) is an effective teaching method because it encourages self-paced learning.
Claim:	Computer-aided instruction is an effective teaching method.
Stated Reason:	Computer-aided instruction encourages self-paced learning.
Warrant (criterion):	If a teaching method encourages self-paced learning, then it is effective.

To develop this argument, the writer would have to defend both the criterion (warrant) and the match (stated reason). Somewhere in the essay the writer would have to argue that an effective teaching method is one that allows students to work at their own pace; he would also have to argue that

CIA instruction actually meets this criterion. (Of course, if self-paced instruction is the only criterion for effectiveness that the writer is proposing, he will have to justify the great weight he is giving to that criterion, which most readers would not believe is a necessary criterion for effectiveness, much less a sufficient one.)

Let's take a second example, and this time display the complete argument according to the Toulmin schema:

Enthymeme:	Pete Rose is not a Hall of Fame quality ballplayer because he was strong primarily in batting average and career hits but weak in most other categories.
Claim:	Pete Rose does not belong in the Hall of Fame.
Stated Reason:	He wasn't a complete player (he was strong primarily in batting average and career hits but weak in most other categories).
Grounds:	A thorough analysis of Pete Rose's career statistics reveals that in many aspects of fielding, hitting, baserunning, and run production his record is below average.
Warrant:	Well-rounded performance is a necessary criterion for inclusion in the Hall of Fame.
Backing:	evidence that shows that all present members of the Hall of Fame were well-rounded players; testimony from experts arguing that Hall of Fame players should be well rounded
Conditions of Rebuttal:	unless Pete Rose's career records in several areas (e.g., games played, at bats, total career hits, batting average) are so overwhelming that Hall of Fame electors choose to ignore his lack of power, his poor baserunning, his mediocre defense; unless intangibles like competitive zeal are given precedence over the player's record
Qualifier:	Given the surprising nature of this claim—most people who oppose Pete Rose's election to the Hall of Fame do so on the basis of his gambling problems and his income tax evasion, not on the basis of his baseball record—one should acknowledge in the qualifier that one faces an uphill battle. Hence, "Pete Rose *may not* belong in the Hall of Fame" is probably as emphatic a claim as one can expect to get away with.

As is often the case with evaluative arguments, the most challenging task is not to establish the match between X and the criteria, but to gain support for the appropriateness of the criteria. Baseball experts probably will agree that Pete Rose was not a well-rounded ball player. What they will disagree about is whether "well-roundedness" is a necessary criterion for election to the Hall of Fame. Similarly, baseball experts will agree that Pete Rose has damaged his reputation through ethical and legal mistakes. But they will disagree whether those problems should be criteria for excluding Rose from the Hall of Fame.

THE GENERAL STRATEGY FOR EVALUATION ARGUMENTS

The general strategy for evaluation arguments is to establish criteria and then to argue that X meets or does not meet the criteria. In writing your argument, you have to decide whether your audience is apt to accept your criteria or not. If you want to argue, for example, that pit bulls do not make good pets because they are potentially vicious, you can assume that most readers will share your assumption that viciousness is bad. Likewise, if you want to praise the new tax bill because it cuts out tax cheating, you can probably assume readers agree that tax cheating is bad.

Often, however, selecting and defending your criteria are the most difficult parts of a criteria-match argument. For example, people who own pit bulls because they *want* a vicious dog for protection may not agree that viciousness is bad. In this case, you would need to argue that another kind of dog, such as a German shepherd or a doberman, would make a better choice than a pit bull or that the bad consequences of a vicious dog outweigh the benefits. Several kinds of difficulties in establishing criteria are worth discussing in more detail.

The Problem of Standards: What's Normal or What's Ideal?

To get a sense of this problem, consider again Young Person's archetypal argument with The Parents about her curfew (see Chapter 1). She originally argued that staying out until 2:00 A.M. is fair "because all the other kids' parents let their kids stay out late," to which The Parents might respond: "Well, *ideally*, all the other parents should not let their kids stay out that late." Young Person based her criterion for fairness on what is *normal*; her standards arose from common practices of a social group. The Parents, however, argued from what is *ideal*, basing their criteria on some external standard that transcends social groups.

We experience this dilemma in various forms throughout our lives. It is the conflict between absolutes and cultural relativism, between written law and customary practice. There is hardly an area of human experience that escapes the dilemma: Is it fair to get a ticket for going 70 mph on a 65-mph freeway when most of the drivers go 70 mph or higher? Is it better for high schools to pass out free contraceptives to students because the students are having sex anyway (what's *normal*), or is it better not to pass them out in order to support abstinence (what's *ideal*)? When you select criteria for an evaluation argument, you may well have to choose one side or the other of this dilemma, arguing for what is ideal or for what is normal. Neither position should be seen as necessarily better than the other; normal practice may be corrupt just as surely as ideal behavior may be impossible.

The Problem of Mitigating Circumstances

When confronting the dilemma raised by the "normal" versus the "ideal," we sometimes have to take into account circumstances as well as behavior. In particular, we have the notion of "mitigating" circumstances, or circumstances that are extraordinary or unusual enough to cause us to change our standard measure of judgment. Ordinarily it is wrong to be late for work or to miss an exam. But what if your car had a flat tire?

When you argue for mitigating circumstances as a reason for modifying judgment in a particular case, you are arguing against the conditions of both normal behavior and ideal behavior as the proper criterion for judgment. Thus, when you make such an argument, you will likely assume an especially heavy burden of proof. People assume the rightness of usual standards of judgment unless there are compelling arguments for abnormal circumstances.

The Problem of Choosing between Two Goods or Two Bads

Not all arguments of value, of course, clearly deal with bad and good, but with better or worse. Often we are caught between a rock and a hard place. Should we cut pay or cut people? Put our parents in a nursing home or let them stay at home where they have become a danger to themselves? In such cases one has to weigh conflicting criteria, knowing that the choices are too much alike — either both bad or both good.

The Problem of Seductive Empirical Measures

The need to make distinctions among relative goods or relative bads has led many persons to seek quantifiable criteria that can be weighed mathematically. Thus we use grade point averages to select scholarship winners,

MCAT scores to decide who gets into medical school, and student evaluation scores to decide which professor gets the University Teaching Award.

In some cases, such empirical measures can be quite acceptable. But they can be dangerous if they don't adequately measure the value of the people or things they purportedly evaluate. (Some people would argue that they *never* adequately measure anything significant.) To illustrate the problem further, consider the problems of relying on grade point average as a criterion for employment. Many employers rely heavily on grades when hiring college graduates. But according to every major study of the relationship between grades and work achievement, grades are about as reliable as palm reading when it comes to predicting life success. Why do employers continue to rely so heavily on grades? Clearly because it is so easy to classify job applicants according to a single empirical measure that appears to rank order everyone along the same scale.

The problem with empirical measures, then, is that they seduce us into believing that complex judgments can be made mathematically, thus rescuing us from the messiness of alternative points of view and conflicting criteria. Empirical measures seem extremely persuasive next to written arguments that try to qualify and hedge and raise questions. We suggest, however, that a fair evaluation of any X might require such hedging.

The Problem of Cost

A final problem that can crop up in evaluations is cost. In comparing an X to others of its kind, we may find that on all the criteria we can develop, X comes out on top. X is the best of all possible Y's. But if X costs too much, we have to rethink our evaluation.*

If we're looking to hire a new department head at Median State University, and the greatest scholar in the field, a magnificent teacher, a regular dynamo of diplomacy, says she'll come—for a hundred G's a year—we'll probably have to withdraw our offer. Whether the costs are expressed in dollars or personal discomfort or moral repugnance or some other terms, our final evaluation of X must take cost into account, however elusive that cost might be.

---

*We can avoid this problem somewhat by placing items into different classes on the basis of cost. For example, a Mercedes may come out far ahead of a Yugo, but the more relevant evaluative question to ask is, "How does a Mercedes compare to a Cadillac?"

HOW TO DETERMINE CRITERIA FOR YOUR ARGUMENT

Now that we have explored some of the difficulties you may encounter in establishing and defending criteria for your evaluation of X, let's turn to the practical problem of trying to determine criteria themselves. How do you go about finding the criteria you'll need for distinguishing a good teacher from a poor teacher, a good movie from a bad movie, a successful manager from an unsuccessful manager, a healthy diet from an unhealthy diet, and so forth?

Step One: Determine the Category in Which the Object Being Evaluated Belongs

In determining the quality or value of any given X, you must first figure out just what your standard of measure is. You can't begin until you determine what class of things you are putting X into. If, for example, you asked one of your professors to write you a letter of recommendation for a summer job, what "class of things" should the professor put you into? Is he or she supposed to evaluate you as a student? a leader? a worker? a party animal? or what? This is an important question because the criteria for excellence in one class (student) may be very different from criteria for excellence in another class (party animal). To write a useful evaluation, your professor will probably need to put you into the general class "summer job holder" and try to give prospective employers an evaluation based on criteria relevant to a summer job.

As a general rule, fairness requires us to judge X according to the smallest applicable class. For example, your professor would do a better job of evaluating you if he or she placed you not in the general class "summer job holder" but in the smaller class "law office intern" or "highway department flagperson" or "golf course groundsperson" and chose criteria accordingly, since excellence in one kind of summer job might differ considerably from excellence in another job.

We thus recommend placing X into the smallest relevant class because of the apples-and-oranges law. That is, to avoid giving a mistaken rating to a perfectly good apple, you need to make sure you are judging an apple under the class "apple" and not under the next larger class "fruit" or a neighboring class "orange." And to be even more precise, you may wish to evaluate your apple in the class "eating apple" as opposed to "pie apple" because the latter class is supposed to be tarter and the former class juicier and sweeter.

Obviously, there are limits to this law. For example, the smallest possible class of apples would contain only one member—the one being evaluated. At that point, your apple is both the best and the worst member of its class. And hence, evaluation of it is meaningless. Also, we sometimes can't avoid apples-and-oranges comparisons because they are thrust upon us by circumstances, tradition, or some other factor. Thus, the Academy Award judges can't distinguish between tragic movies, comic movies, musicals, and satires when choosing the year's "Best Movie."

Step Two: Determine the Purpose or Function of This Class

Once you have located X in its appropriate class, you should next determine what the purpose or function of this class is. Let's suppose that the summer job you are applying for is tour guide at the city zoo. The function of a tour guide is to make people feel welcome, to give them interesting information about the zoo, to make their visit pleasant, and so forth. Consequently, you wouldn't want your professor's evaluation to praise your term paper on Napoleon Bonaparte or your successful synthesis of some compound in your chemistry lab. Rather, the professor should highlight your dependability, your neat appearance, your good speaking skills, and your ability to work with groups. On the other hand, if you were applying for graduate school, then your term paper on Bonaparte or your chem lab wizardry would be relevant. In other words, the professor has to evaluate you according to the class "tour guide," not "graduate student," and the criteria for each class derive from the purpose or function of the class.

Let's take another example. Suppose that you are the chair of a committee charged with evaluating the job performance of Lillian Jones, director of the admissions office at Clambake College. Ms. Jones has been a controversial manager because several members of her staff have filed complaints about her management style. In making your evaluation, your first step is to place Ms. Jones into an appropriate class, in this case, the general class "manager," and then the more specific class "manager of an admissions office at a small, private college." You then need to identify the purpose or function of these classes. You might say that the function of the general class "managers" is to "oversee actual operations of an organization so that the organization meets its goals as harmoniously and efficiently as possible," whereas the function of the specific class "manager of an admissions office at a small, private college" is "the successful recruitment of the best students possible."

Step Three: Determine Criteria Based on the Purposes or Function of the Class to Which X Belongs

Once you've worked out the purposes of the class, you are ready to work out the criteria by which you judge all members of the class. Criteria for judgment will be based on those features of Y that help it achieve the purposes of its class. For example, once you determine the purpose and function of the position filled by Lillian Jones, you can develop a list of criteria for managerial success:

1. Criteria related to "efficient operation":
   - articulates priorities and goals for the organization
   - is aggressive in achieving goals
   - motivates fellow employees
   - is well organized, efficient, and punctual
   - is articulate and communicates well
2. Criteria related to "harmonious operation":
   - creates job satisfaction for subordinates
   - is well groomed, sets good example of professionalism
   - is honest, diplomatic in dealing with subordinates
   - is flexible in responding to problems and special concerns of staff members
3. Criteria related to meeting specific goals of a college admissions office:
   - creates a comprehensive recruiting program
   - demonstrates that recruiting program works

Step Four: Give Relative Weightings to the Criteria

Even though you have established criteria, you must still decide which of the criteria are most important. In the case of Lillian Jones, is it more important that she bring in lots of students to Clambake College or that she create a harmonious, happy office? These sorts of questions are at the heart of many evaluative controversies. Thus, a justification for your weighting of criteria may well be an important part of your argument.

DETERMINING WHETHER X MEETS THE CRITERIA

Once you've established your criteria, you've got to figure out how well X meets them. You proceed by gathering evidence and examples. The success of the recruiting program at Clambake College can probably be measured empirically, so you gather statistics about applications to the college, SAT scores of applicants, number of acceptances, academic profiles of entering freshmen, and so forth. You might then compare those statistics to those compiled by Ms. Jones' predecessor or to her competitors at other, comparable institutions.

You can also look at what the recruiting program actually does — the number of recruiters, the number of high school visitations, quality of admissions brochures, and other publications. You can also look at Ms. Jones in action, searching for specific incidents or examples that illustrate her management style. For example, you can't measure a trait such as diplomacy empirically, but you can find specific instances where the presence or absence of this trait was demonstrated. You could turn to examples where Ms. Jones may or may not have prevented a potentially divisive situation from occurring or where she offered or failed to offer encouragement at psychologically the right moment to keep someone from getting demoralized. As with criteria-match arguments in definition, one must provide examples of how the X in question meets each of the criteria that have been set up.

Your final evaluation of Ms. Jones, then, might include an overview of her strengths and weaknesses along the various criteria you have established. You might say that Ms. Jones has done an excellent job with recruitment (an assertion you can support with data on student enrollments over the last five years) but was relatively poor at keeping the office staff happy (as evidenced by employee complaints, high turnover, and your own observations of her rather abrasive management style). Nevertheless, your final recommendation might be to retain Ms. Jones for another three-year contract because you believe that an excellent recruiting record is the most important criterion for her position at Clambake. You might justify this heavy weighting of recruiting on the grounds that the institution's survival depends on its ability to attract adequate numbers of good students.

As a way of testing your argument in preparation for your committee's meeting, you lay out your argument according to Toulmin's schema:

Enthymeme: Despite some weaknesses, Ms. Jones has been a good manager of the admissions office at Clambake College because her office's recruitment record is excellent.

Claim: Ms. Jones has been a good manager of the admissions office at Clambake College.

Stated Reason: Her office's recruitment record is excellent.

Grounds: statistical data demonstrating the excellence of the recruitment program

Warrant: Successful recruitment is the most important criterion for rating job performance of the director of admissions.

Backing: Evidence that low recruitment leads to financial problems and even closing of a college; maintaining enrollment through recruitment is the lifeblood of the college. Although her opponents have complained that Ms. Jones has serious problems maintaining harmony among her staff, a happy staff serves no purpose if we don't have enough students to keep the college open.

Conditions of
Rebuttal: unless the recruitment record isn't as good as I have said (NOTE: I'll need to be sure of my standards when I say her record is excellent. Am I arguing about "what's normal" by comparing Clambake's record with other colleges? Or am I arguing about what is ideal? Will one of Jones' critics bring in an argument saying she isn't doing a particularly good job of recruiting? Might they argue that plenty of people in the office could do the same good job of recruitment—after all, Clambake sells itself—without stirring up any of the personnel problems that Ms. Jones has caused?)

Unless the recruitment record isn't the most important criterion. Ms. Jones is obviously weak in maintaining good relationships with staff. How might an opponent argue that staff problems in Ms. Jones' office are severe enough that we ought to search for a new director? I will have to counter that argument some way.

Qualifier: I will need to qualify my general rating of excellent by acknowledging Ms. Jones' weaknesses in some areas. But I want to be definite in saying that recruitment is the most important criterion and that she definitely meets this criterion.

FOR CLASS DISCUSSION

The following small-group exercise can be accomplished in one or two class hours. It gives you a good model of the process you will need to go through in order to write your own evaluation essay. Working in small groups, suppose that you are going to evaluate a controversial member of one of the following classes:

a. a teacher

f. a recent Supreme Court decision

b. a political figure

g. a rock singer or group or MTV video

c. an athlete

h. a dorm or living group

d. a school newspaper

i. a restaurant or college hangout

e. a school policy

j. an X of your choice

1. Choose a controversial member within one of these classes as the specific person, thing, or event you are going to evaluate (Professor Choplogic, the Wild Dog Bar, Madonna, and so forth).
2. Narrow down the general class by determining the smallest relevant class to which your X belongs (from "athlete" to "basketball guard"; from "college hangout" to "college hangout for people who want to hold late-night bull sessions").
3. Make a list of the purposes or functions of that class and then list the criteria that a good member of that class would have to have in order to accomplish the purposes.
4. If necessary, rank order your criteria.
5. Evaluate your X by matching X to each of the criteria.

WRITING YOUR EVALUATION ARGUMENT

STARTING POINT: FINDING AN EVALUATION ISSUE

If you have not already listed some evaluation issues in your idea-log, try creating idea-maps with spokes chosen from among the following categories: *people* (athletes, political leaders, musicians, clergypeople, entertainers, businesspeople); *science and technology* (weapons systems, word-processing programs, spread sheets, automotive advancements, treatments for diseases); *media* (a newspaper, a magazine or journal, a TV program, a radio station, an advertisement); *government and world affairs* (an economic policy, a Supreme Court decision, a law or legal practice, a government custom or practice, a foreign policy); *the arts* (a movie, a book, a building, a painting, a piece of music); *your college or university* (a course, a teacher, a textbook, a curriculum, an administrative policy, the financial aid system); *world of work* (a job, a company operation, a dress policy, a merit pay system, a hiring policy, a supervisor); or any other categories of your choice.

Then brainstorm possibilities for controversial X's that might fit into the categories on your map. As long as you can imagine disagreement about how to evaluate X, you have a potentially good topic for this assignment.

EXPLORATION STAGE

Once you have found an issue and have taken a tentative position on it, explore your ideas by freewriting your responses to the eight guided tasks in Idea-Log Set Two (pages 73–75).

If you have trouble thinking of possible criteria, try using the "three approaches" heuristic (pages 154–159): "X is a good Y because it is _____" (principle); "X is a good Y because it has good consequences" (cause); "X is a good Y because it is like _____" (analogy).

WRITING A DISCOVERY DRAFT: SOME SUGGESTIONS FOR ORGANIZING YOUR EVALUATION ARGUMENT

As you write your discovery draft, you might find useful the following typical structure for an evaluation argument. Of course, many evaluation arguments don't follow this shape, but many do, and you can always alter the shape later if its structure seems too formulaic to you.

- Introduce your issue and show why evaluating X is problematic or controversial.
- Summarize opposing views.
- Refute or concede to opposing views.
- Present your own claim.
    State Criterion 1 and defend it if necessary.
    Show that X meets criterion.
    State Criterion 2 and defend it if necessary.
    Show that X meets criterion.

Continue with additional criteria and match arguments.

- Sum up your evaluation.

REVISION

At this stage you should be able to summarize your argument as a claim with because clauses. In order to test the structure of your argument, you may find it useful to analyze it with the Toulmin scheme. This method will help you see to what extent you need to defend each of your criteria. As the example on evaluating Lillian Jones shows (pages 303–305), the main testing of the argument can occur when you consider the conditions of rebuttal. In the final section of this chapter, we turn to some of the questions you might ask yourself when testing your argument.

CONDITIONS FOR REBUTTAL: TESTING YOUR EVALUATION ARGUMENT

After you've gone through a process like the one sketched out above, you should have a thoughtful rough draft ready for more careful scrutiny. Once again, put yourself in the role of the critic.

Will My Audience Accept My Criteria?

Many evaluative arguments are weak because the writers have simply assumed that readers will accept their criteria. Whenever your audience's acceptance of your criteria is in doubt, you will need to make your warrants clear and provide backing in their support.

Are My Criteria Based on the "Smallest Applicable Class" for X?

For example, the James Bond movie *For Your Eyes Only* will certainly be a failure if you evaluate it in the general class "movies," in which it would have to compete with *Citizen Kane* and other great classics. But if you evaluated it as an "escapist movie" or a "James Bond movie" it would have a greater chance for success and hence of yielding an arguable evaluation.

All of this isn't to say that you couldn't evaluate "escapist movies" as a class of, say, "popular films" and find the whole class deficient. Evaluations of this type are, however, more difficult to argue because of the numbers of items you must take into account.

Will Readers Accept My General Weighting of Criteria?

Another vulnerable spot in an evaluation argument is the relative weight of the criteria. How much anyone weights a given criterion is usually a function of his or her own interests relative to the X in question. You should always ask whether some particular group affected by the quality of X might not have good reasons for weighting the criteria differently.

Will Readers Question My Standard of Reference?

In questioning the criteria for judging X, we can also focus on the standard of reference used — what's normal versus what's ideal. If you have argued that X is bad because it doesn't live up to what's ideal, you can expect some readers to defend X on the basis of what's normal. Similarly, if you argue that X is good because it is better than its competitors, you can expect some readers to point out how short it falls from what is ideal.

Will Readers Criticize My Use of Empirical Measures?

The tendency to mistake empirical measures for criteria is a common one that any critic of an argument should be aware of. As we have discussed earlier, what's most measurable isn't always significant when it comes to assessing the essential traits needed to fulfill whatever function X is supposed to fulfill. A 95-mph fastball is certainly an impressive empirical measure of a pitcher's ability — but if the pitcher doesn't get batters out, that measure is a misleading gauge of performance.

Will Readers Accept My Criteria but Reject My Match Argument?

The other major way of testing an evaluation argument is to anticipate how readers might object to your stated reasons and grounds. Will readers challenge you by finding sampling errors in your data or otherwise find that you used evidence selectively? For example, if you think your opponents will emphasize Lillian Jones' abrasive management style much more heavily than you did, you may be able to undercut their arguments by finding counterexamples that show Ms. Jones acting diplomatically. Be prepared to counter objections to your grounds.

FOR CLASS DISCUSSION

Read the following examples of evaluation arguments. Then, working as individuals or in a group, answer the following questions:

1. What criteria are used to evaluate the X in question?
2. Does the writer create an argument for the appropriateness of these criteria? If so, how effective is it?
3. How effective is the argument that X matches each of the established criteria?
4. How would you go about refuting each of the arguments?

TARNISHED IMAGE OF ACADEMY AWARDS HASN'T DULLED WORLD'S APPETITE FOR THIS FLAWED FARCE

William Arnold

With a worldwide television audience now in excess of a billion people, the   1
annual Academy Awards ceremony officially has entered the record books as
the world's largest spectator event — larger than the World Series, the Super
Bowl and the U.S. presidential election, perhaps all put together.

Moreover, the Oscars are not only the most popular awards in the history   2
of the planet, they are the most written about, most heatedly debated, most
wagered upon, most celebrated in myth and most financially lucrative for the
winners — translating into a hard cash value that has been estimated as high
as $40 million in increased grosses for a Best Picture win.

In short, those little gold statuettes that once again will be handed out   3
tomorrow night are a true phenomenon of 20th-century culture with a
credibility that no other award system comes close to matching — not the
Tonys, the Grammys, the Emmys, the Pulitzers, the People's Choice, the
Medals of Freedom or the Nobel Prizes.

And the extraordinary thing is that this phenomenon defies all reason,   4
analysis and common sense.

Indeed, it is almost universally accepted — and it certainly has dawned on   5
me during my 10 years of covering the event — that the Oscars are just about

Source: William Arnold, "Tarnished Image of Academy Awards," Seattle Post-Intelligencer, March 29, 1987.

the most flawed, tarnished, infuriating and downright perverse awards system ever devised.

In fact, when you sit down and examine the case against the Academy 6
Awards, the evidence seems so overwhelming you begin to wonder why the L.A.P.D. bunco squad doesn't move in and padlock the door of the Dorothy Chandler Pavilion some Oscar night.

Here, in a nutshell, is everything that is wrong with Oscar, the reasons 7
why you should *not* be glued to your television set tomorrow night:

1. The Academy Awards are inherently unfair. The bottom line on the 8
Oscars is that they are not voted upon by any kind of blue-ribbon panel of experts or even a cross section of the movie industry. They are voted upon by the membership of an Academy that is run like a Los Angeles country club. To get in the club one must be nominated by two current members, then voted in by a very picky board of governors.

The current membership totals 4,747, which is, of course, only a fraction 9
of the people who actually work in the film industry.

This group consists of many older, semiretired people. More than 70 10
percent of the director's branch of the Academy, for instance, is over age 60. Many are from the business and promotion side of filmmaking, including studio executives, who are notorious for knowing nothing about films. And they all are subjected to an unbelievable barrage of influence around Oscar time.

Members are regularly wined and dined by publicists, chauffeured to 11
private screenings in limousines and deluged with free gifts and promotional devices.

Even so, it has been estimated that as few as 60 percent of the total 12
membership actually gets out and votes. And it is likely that even fewer actually see the movies that are being voted upon.

Critic Andrew Sarris once reported the average Academy voter saw as few 13
as 12 films a year, and several illustrious members publicly have admitted voting for or against pictures they hadn't seen.

2. The Academy Awards are totally political. Although its publicists 14
don't much like to admit it, the Motion Picture Academy of Arts and Sciences came into existence in 1927 when Louis B. Mayer, the ruler of MGM, decided the industry needed a company union, a means of stalling the formation of the various guilds that later would get a foothold in the business in the '30s.

Though the Academy slowly has gained its independence from the major 15
studios (who angrily pulled out of financing the Oscar show after a British film, "Hamlet," won Best Picture in 1948), the awards themselves have remained so tied to the big studios that more Oscar outcomes have been decided by studio politics and front-office dictate than any other factor. Even

as late as the 1960s, 20th Century-Fox was able to garner Best Picture nominations for big budget flops like "Doctor Doolittle" and "Hello, Dolly" by having its Academy-member employees block vote.

The Oscars also have been influenced by the politics within the member- 16 ship of the Academy itself. Unofficial Academy historians like Mason Wiley and Damien Bona in their book "Inside Oscar" have had a field day tracing how this power has influenced nominations and winners.

For instance, Walter Brennan's record Best Supporting Actor wins in 17 1936, '38 and '39 can be directly attributed to his popularity with the extras (he was once one of them), who were allowed Academy membership in the '30s and held the balance of power with their numbers.

And, of course, the Academy voting record traditionally has bent with the 18 various outside political breezes, as well: scorning the work of blacklisted actors and writers in the redbaiting days, giving Sidney Poitier his Oscar during the height of the civil rights movement in 1964, allowing itself to be swept up in the wave of radical chic of the late 1960s and early '70s to award mavericks like Jane Fonda, George C. Scott and Marlon Brando.

3. The Academy Awards are corrupt. This is a strong statement but 19 how else to describe a measure of artistic achievement so heavily influenced by paid advertising? In one year in the early 1980s in which the ad revenue actually was counted, something like $8 million was spent on Oscar advertising, which is roughly $3,000 spent per Academy voter.

And these ad campaigns have an effect. The older voters who determine 20 the elections have proven to be very swayable by these ads. Skillful Oscar campaigns have amassed Best Picture nominations for such totally forgettable movies as "Anne of a Thousand Days," "Oliver!," "Nicholas and Alexandra," "A Touch of Class," "Cleopatra," and "The Alamo."

The last was an infamous 1960 John Wayne-financed campaign in which a 21 barrage of ads depicted cast members kneeling in prayer under copy warning voters that a loss for "The Alamo" would unleash God's wrath on the movie industry.

These campaigns have become a small industry in Los Angeles not only for 22 the trade papers and cable TV stations that get all the ad revenue, but for the public relations firms that have sprung up to specialize in Oscar races.

A 1983 California Magazine article chronicling John Lithgow's Best Sup- 23 porting Actor run for "The World According to Garp" told an amazing story of how the actor put himself in the hands of media specialists who guided his campaign like a race for the presidency—telling him how to dress, what parties to attend, what kind of car to drive and where to live. (In this case, to no avail. He lost.)

4. The Academy Awards are a lousy measure of movie immortality. 24 To be fair, *all* the movie awards have been poor judges of what ultimately would prove to be lasting. With the benefit of hindsight, the selections of the New York Film Critics, the National Board of Review, the Cannes Film Festival and all the others seem amazingly out of touch with posterity.

But the Oscar choices have been the worst.   25

Looking at its list of past winners, one sees an occasional good Best 26
Picture call ("Casablanca" in '42, "Lawrence of Arabia" in '62) but amazingly few accolades to what we now consider the seminal works of Hollywood art.

No Best Picture honors for "Citizen Kane," "Psycho," "Singin' in the 27
Rain," "2001," "The Searchers," "Dr. Strangelove," "Close Encounters," "Bonnie and Clyde," "Vertigo," "Magnificent Ambersons," "McCabe and Mrs. Miller" or the others that always tend to crop up in the all-time critical 10-best lists.

And a glance at the winning actor lists is even more sobering. The annals 28
of Oscar are clogged with awards for ham performances by the likes of Jose Ferrer, Paul Scofield, George Arliss, Paul Muni and Charles Laughton, but have no place for a Cary Grant.

Oscar voters also have shown themselves to be extraordinarily shallow in 29
other ways, as well.

They're forever rewarding the change-of-pace performance, no matter how 30
dismal (William Hurt as an effeminate homosexual in 1986, Shirley Jones as a hooker in 1960), constantly letting themselves be influenced by cheap sentimentality (Liz Taylor's win in 1960 after nearly dying, Ingrid Bergman's win in 1956 after returning to the Hollywood fold following years of self-imposed exile), consistently second guessing themselves by rewarding the previous year's most worthy loser (Bette Davis' win in 1935 for "Dangerous" when she deserved it for "Of Human Bondage" in 1934).

Because of all this shallowness, snobbishness and stupidity, the Oscars 31
simply have failed to acknowledge the work of what often seems the majority of Hollywood's most important artists.

Alfred Hitchcock, arguably the greatest filmmaker of all time, never took 32
home a Best Director Oscar while the long-forgotten Frank Lloyd took home two and narrowly missed a third. Edward G. Robinson, my personal candidate for the greatest film actor of the sound era, was never nominated in his extraordinary 30-year reign as a top star.

How does one take seriously a movie award that honors Luise Rainer 33
(twice), Ernest Borgnine and Paul Lukas but not Irene Dunne, Carole Lombard, Marilyn Monroe, Jean Harlow, Myrna Loy, Marlene Dietrich, Greta Garbo, Robert Mitchum, James Dean, John Garfield, Tyrone Power, Charles Boyer, Errol Flynn, Charlie Chaplin, Buster Keaton, William Powell, Kirk Douglas and Fred Astaire?

5. The Academy Awards are bad showmanship. I suppose all of the 34
above would be forgivable if the Oscar ceremonies themselves were such a

dandy show that made up for these shortcomings in entertainment value. But the truth is that in all the annals of show business, there probably has been no more tedious, ill-prepared and boring an extravaganza as the annual Oscars consistently have proven themselves to be since their first television broadcast in 1952.

Whole books have been written ridiculing the unbearably cute repartee 35 between the boy and girl presenters, the ponderous acceptance speeches, the unimaginative musical numbers, the tasteless attire of the starlets, the flubbed lines, wrong exits, demonstrations, missed cues and mispronounced names.

Will anyone who experienced them ever forget Greer Garson's 5½-minute 36 acceptance speech in 1942, or Sally Field's embarrassing outburst in 1984 ("You like me — you really like me!"), or Jerry Lewis' excruciating 20-minute ad libbing when the awards inadvertently ended early in 1958, or that tasteless filmed visit in 1976 to the deathbed of a shrunken little thing that once had been Mary Pickford, America's Sweetheart?

Or that prototypical scene of Hollywood vulgarity played year after year in 37 which the stars unload from their limousines before the bleachers of screaming fans? How can one look at what Raymond Chandler called "those awful idiot faces" without feeling, as he did, "a sense of the collapse of human intelligence"?

Indeed, how can anyone in his right mind, in the face of all this well-known 38 evidence of injustice and fraud and epic tackiness, possibly take the Oscars seriously?

Yet they do. By the thousands. By the millions. With China now added to 39 the Oscarcast, by the billions. By almost everyone I know, including the snobbiest critics of the most esoteric film journals. And after a decade of pondering the phenomenon, I think I finally have figured out why.

Like Christmas and Halloween, Oscar night is a phenomenon that has 40 become completely divorced from its origins. It is an annual ritual, part Thanksgiving Day parade, part Kentucky Derby, part Everyone's Senior Prom — a kind of Super Bowl of Celebrity, sanctified by six decades of tradition, united in almost religious communion by the idea that the preservation of human personality on celluloid is a very important thing.

The experience of watching the Academy Awards is a kind of strange 41 cathartic ordeal in which we both voyeuristically witness that great other world of celebrity we will never make and relieve our sense of inadequacy by watching these same people one by one make fools of themselves.

As crazy as it sounds, the ritual has a kind of cleansing effect on the 42 psyche, and I'm convinced it has come to serve a valuable function in our global society. And when it unfolds for the 59th time tomorrow night, I'll be watching. In fact, I wouldn't miss it for the world.

THE MANDATORY MOTORCYCLE-HELMET LAW IS BAD LAW

Bill C. Healy (student)

For most people, Washington's newly re-instated motorcycle-helmet law, 1
which goes into effect today, is no big deal. The reason: Most people do not
ride motorcycles.

For some people, however, especially motorcyclists and politicians, it is a 2
very big deal. During the last 13 years, especially the last legislative session,
the helmet issue has created heated debate with neither side willing to
compromise. The pro-helmet forces want a mandatory law because they say it
will reduce head injuries, deaths, and cost to taxpayers for medical expenses
of unhelmeted riders. Last legislative session, the pro-helmet people won. But
the Legislature made a serious mistake. When we look at the evidence, it's
plain that a mandatory helmet law is a bad law.

Of course, there are some definite benefits to wearing a helmet. A helmet 3
will protect the rider from a head injury in some low-speed accidents. Also a
helmet with a face shield will protect the wearer from being pelted with rain
and hail, thus making it safer for the rider to operate the motorcycle in foul
weather. These benefits mean that responsible motorcyclists will choose to
wear a helmet voluntarily when the conditions are appropriate.

However, a helmet won't protect against head injury when traveling at 4
normal traffic speeds. According to the U.S. Department of Transportation,
"There is no evidence that any helmet thus far, regardless of cost or design, is
capable of rejecting impact stress above 13 mph." The mandatory law is
based on the premise that helmet laws reduce injuries and fatalities. But all
available evidence shows that they do not. A Washington State Patrol Research Report, No. 039, entitled, "An Evaluation of Washington State's
Motorcycle Safety Laws' Effectiveness," reviewed motorcycle fatalities for
five years before and five years after the state's previous experiment with a
mandatory helmet law. It found virtually no change in cause of death rates
with or without a helmet. During 1962–66, when helmet use was voluntary,
47 percent of deaths were due to head injury and 3 percent to neck injury.
During 1967–71, when the state mandated wearing of helmets, 45 percent of
deaths were attributed to head injury and 6 percent to neck injury. Similar
findings were found in other states and by the King County Medical Examiner. It is clear from both state and county records that the mandatory helmet
law provided no relief to fatal accident victims. These figures show a mandatory law did not work in the past, and there is no evidence it will work now.

Another reason why the mandatory helmet law is a bad piece of legislation 5
is that wearing a helmet can actually cause accidents. A helmet restricts the
wearer's hearing and peripheral vision, two senses a motorcyclist desperately
needs for avoiding accidents. Riding a motorcycle while wearing a helmet is

like driving an automobile while wearing earplugs and taping paper over your back and side windows and over the right half of your windshield. The Legislature and the police would not allow a person to operate an automobile under these conditions, yet the Legislature passed, and the police will enforce, these same types of sense restrictions for motorcycle riders. A motorcyclist needs to be able to look over his shoulder quickly and efficiently and to be able to hear side traffic, so as to be a safe, alert and defensive rider. It is having the full use of one's senses that helps a motorcyclist avoid accidents. Isn't that what we really want to do?

Finally, the law infringes on my personal freedom. In the motorcycle   6
helmet case, my right to personal freedom clashes with the state's right to save taxpayers' money on medical expenses. But because the state's side of this argument is so weak, my right to personal freedom outweighs the state's right. What non-motorcyclists don't realize is how much the mandatory helmet law reduces the pleasure of motorcycling. Unlike a seatbelt in a car, which is a very minor inconvenience to wear, a motorcycle helmet is a major inconvenience. Not only does the helmet reduce the pleasure of riding — especially in the summer when a helmet is hot and sticky — but it can't be stored on the motorcycle when you reach your destination. Moreover, you can't use your motorcycle to give a pedestrian a lift. But the biggest inconvenience is the increased risk to my safety. Before today, I was a safe and responsible rider when I rode without a helmet because I believed it increased my chances of survival. I still do, and the fact and figures back me. Today and onward I will be a criminal for doing what I have done since I was 16 — riding the safest way I know how.

Now my life is in jeopardy because a law was passed for motorcyclists by   7
people who do not ride motorcycles. The mandatory helmet law is a bad law. This is something legislators and the governor will never understand unless they ride a motorcycle.

BEAUTY PAGEANT FALLACIES

Debra Goodwin (student)

"You will be beautiful up there on the stage, Jessica," said the beauty   1
pageant director. "You've spent your whole life preparing for this contest. The judges will examine you and all they will see is a perfect ten. You look gorgeous." There are many in our society who believe beauty pageants are a harmless way to celebrate the beauty of women in our culture. These same individuals boast that the beauty pageants provide many opportunities for the winners of such contests. In some contests women are even awarded scholastic scholarships for their beauty. Advocates of beauty pageants claim that

winners of these contests win because of their talent not because of their looks. Despite these claims, I believe that beauty pageants damage our society. First, beauty pageants hurt a woman's self-esteem. Second, beauty contests present women as objects and are thus a kind of pornography. Finally, beauty pageants perpetuate and condone the exploitation of women in our society.

Beauty pageants are harmful because they severely damage a woman's   2
self-esteem by creating an impossible standard of beauty that leads to serious medical and mental problems. My sister Pam pursued her ambition to be a beauty queen. She explained, "I read everything I could find on pageants back to the 1950's to determine if there was a standard of beauty and whether I could seem to fit it. And I could — with the help of heavy makeup to cover my acne scars, enough hair spray to defy gravity for hours, tape for my boobs, and spray adhesive to hold down my swimsuit." Pam felt that being transformed into a beauty queen made absolutely clear how "artificial, dangerous, and self-denying the beauty standard really is." After winning in the local pageants Pam explained, "I was whisked away for a session with two pageant advisors who dissected my body: 'Okay, you really need to work on your legs; we definitely have to find you a better bra.' No mater how I looked, I was inadequate." Pam's obsession with winning in the beauty pageant circle landed her in the hospital diagnosed as anorexic with a severely low self-esteem. After months of counseling, Pam realized that her identity as a woman was replaced by ideas of what others thought she should act and look like.

Unfortunately, Pam's problem is not an isolated case. She said, "There   3
were women who were always making themselves vomit so that they would not gain any weight. Also, there were women in tears during many of our rehearsals because they didn't look exactly like the pageant organizers wanted." According to Ruby Koppes, a retired beauty pageant organizer whom I interviewed, "Diseases such as anorexia and bulimia are very common problems in the beauty pageant ring. Many girls would have to drop out of the contest because they would become ill from erratic dieting methods." The problems that manifest themselves within the beauty pageant circle indicate the extent to which women have been socialized to pursue the elusive ideal of beauty at any cost.

Another reason why beauty pageants are harmful is that they are a subtle   4
form of pornography which portrays women as objects. Although beauty pageants are not usually thought of as pornographic, they have been a major platform for the reduction of women from full human beings into objects. These competitions are such a way of life that we rarely stop to challenge the concept of a woman walking down a platform in a bathing suit, parading in front of a group of male judges who look over her legs, her breasts, and her waist, who compare her bodily measurements with those of other contestants, and who make a choice of the "best" female based primarily on these exterior

solution to the problem of competing needs, he proposes the development of a new industry specializing in thinning and pruning forest lands— making usable products with lumber presently considered scrap and at the same time increasing the quality of forests. [*Seattle Times,* August 27, 1990, A9]

CASE 4

Barry Commoner, director of the Center for the Biology of Natural Systems at Queens College, poses the following dilemma: "To what extent should the choice of production technologies be governed—as it is now —by private, generally short-term, profit-maximizing response to market forces, and to what extent by long-term social concerns like environmental quality?" In examining the problem of atmospheric pollutants, he opts for governmental control based on long-term social concerns. Specifically, he proposes that the government shift from trying to "clean up" pollutants to issuing an outright ban on pollutant-causing technologies. ["Free Markets Can't Control Pollution," *New York Times,* April 15, 1990]

THE NATURE OF
PROPOSAL ARGUMENTS

Although proposal or "should" arguments are the last type we examine, they are among the most common arguments that you will encounter or be called on to write. Their essence is that they call for action. In reading a proposal, the audience is enjoined to make a decision and then to act upon it—to *do* something. Proposal arguments are sometimes called "should" or "ought" arguments because these helping verbs express the obligation to act: "We *should* do X" or "We *ought* to do X."

For instructional purposes, we will distinguish between two kinds of proposal arguments, even though they are closely related and involve the same basic arguing strategies. The first kind we will call "practical proposals," which propose an action to solve some kind of local or immediate problem. A student's proposal to change the billing procedures for scholarship students would be an example of a practical proposal, as would an engineering firm's proposal for the design of a new bridge being planned by a city government. The second kind we will call "policy proposals," in which the writer offers a broad plan of action to solve major social, economic, or political problems affecting the common good. An argument that the United States should adopt a national health insurance plan or that the terms for senators and representatives should be limited to twelve years would be examples of policy proposals.

The primary difference is the narrowness versus breadth of the concern. Practical proposals are narrow, local, and concrete; they focus on the nuts and bolts of getting something done in the here and now. They are often concerned with the exact size of a piece of steel, the precise duties of a new person to be hired, or a close estimate of the cost of paint or computers to be purchased. Policy proposals, on the other hand, are concerned with the broad outline and shape of a course of action, often on a regional, national, or even international issue. What government should do about overcrowding of prisons would be a problem addressed by policy proposals. How to improve the security alarm system for the county jail would be addressed by a practical proposal.

Learning to write both kinds of proposals is valuable. Researching and writing a policy proposal is an excellent way to practice the responsibilities of citizenship. By researching a complex issue, by attempting to weigh the positive and negative consequences of any policy decision, and then by committing yourself to a course of action, you will be doing the kind of thinking necessary for the survival of a democratic society. On the other hand, writing practical proposals may well be among your most important duties on the job. Writing persuasive practical proposals is the lifeblood of engineering companies and construction firms because through such proposals a company wins bids and creates work. In many companies, employees can initiate improvements in company operations through practical proposals, and it is through grant proposals that innovative people gain funding for research or carry on the work of volunteer and nonprofit organizations throughout our society.

THE GENERAL STRUCTURE AND STRATEGY OF PROPOSAL ARGUMENTS

Proposal arguments, whether practical proposals or policy proposals, generally have a three-part structure: (1) description of a problem, (2) proposed solution, and (3) justification for the proposed solution. Luckily, proposal arguments don't require different sorts of argumentative strategies from the ones you have already been using. In the justification section of your proposal argument, you develop because clauses of the kinds you have practiced all along throughout this text.

SPECIAL REQUIREMENTS OF PROPOSAL ARGUMENTS

Although proposal arguments combine elements from other kinds of claims, they differ from other arguments in that they call for action. Calls to action don't entail any strategies that we haven't already considered, but they do entail a unique set of emphases. Let's look briefly at some of the special requirements of proposal arguments.

Adding "Presence" to Your Argument

It's one thing for a person to assent to a value judgment, but it's another thing to act on that judgment. The personal cost of acting may be high for many people in your audience. That means that you have to engage not only your audience's intellect, but their emotions as well. Thus proposal arguments often require more attention to *pathos* than do other kinds of arguments (see pages 171–180).

In most cases, convincing people to act means that an argument must have "presence" as well as intellectual force. An argument is said to have presence when the reader senses the immediacy of the writer's words. Not only does the reader recognize the truth and consistency of the argument, but he experiences its very life. An argument with presence is one in which the reader can share the writer's point of view — the writer's emotions, the force of the writer's personal engagement with the issue — as well as assent to the writer's conclusions.

How does one achieve presence in an argument? There are a number of ways. For one, you can appeal directly to the readers' emotions through the effective use of details, brief scenes, and compelling examples that show the reader the seriousness of the problem you are addressing or the consequences of not acting on your proposal. Consider the following example of presence from a policy argument favoring euthanasia:

> There are hundreds of thousands of persons today living in continuing, sustained, baffled misery, pain, and anguish; thousands literally imprisoned in nursing homes and hospitals; thousands isolated, alone, family gone, just prolonging miserable day after miserable day.
>
> Mist clouds my eyes as I remember the last days of my own father, begging the doctors to let him go home and die peacefully in the room he so loved, overlooking the trees and gardens that he had created over the years.
>
> "No," they said, "you must stay here where we can watch you."
> Maybe brutal is not a strong enough word to describe the situation. And

so my father was refused his sacred right to die with integrity, quality and with some dignity left intact in the life of a proud and good man.*

In addition to scenes such as this, writers can use figurative language such as metaphor and analogy to make the problem being addressed more vivid or real to the audience, or they can shift from abstract language to descriptions, dialogues, statistics, and illustrative narratives. Here is how one student used personal experience in the problem section of her proposal calling for redesign of the mathematics department's introductory calculus curriculum.

My own experience in the Calculus 134 and 135 sequence last year showed me that it was not the learning of calculus that was difficult for me. I was able to catch on to the new concepts. The problem for me was in the fast pace. Just as I was assimilating new concepts and feeling the need to reinforce them, the class was on to a new topic before I had full mastery of the old concept. . . . Part of the reason for the fast pace is that calculus is a feeder course for computer science and engineering. If prospective engineering students can't learn the calculus rapidly, they drop out of the program. The high dropout rate benefits the Engineering School because they use the math course to weed out an overabundance of engineering applicants. Thus the pace of the calculus course is geared to the needs of the engineering curriculum, not to the needs of someone like me who wants to be a high school mathematics teacher and who believes that my own difficulties with math — combined with my love for it — might make me an excellent math teacher.

Here the writer creates presence through an effective *ethos*: She is not a complainer or whiner but a serious student genuinely interested in learning calculus. She has given presence to the problem by calling attention to it in a new way.

OVERCOMING THE NATURAL CONSERVATISM OF PEOPLE

The first difficulty faced by a proposal maker is the innate conservatism of all human beings, whatever their political persuasion. One philosopher refers to this conservatism as the law of inertia, the tendency of all things in the universe, including human beings, to remain at rest if possible. The popular adage "If it ain't broke, don't fix it" is one expression of this

*From William Edelen, *The Idaho Statesman.*

tendency. Hence, proposers of change face an extraordinary burden of proof. Specifically, they have to prove that something needs fixing, that it can be fixed, and that the cost of fixing it will be outweighed by the benefits of fixing it.

The difficulty of proving that something needs fixing is compounded by the fact that frequently the status quo appears to be working. So sometimes when writing a proposal, you can't argue that what we have is bad, but only that what we could have is better. Often, then, a proposal argument will be based not on present evils but on the evils of lost potential. And getting an audience to accept lost potential may be difficult indeed, given the inherently abstract nature of potentiality.

The Difficulty of Predicting Future Consequences

Further, most proposal makers will be forced to predict consequences of a given act. As we've seen in our earlier discussions of causality, it is difficult enough to argue backward from event Y in order to establish that X caused Y. Think how much harder it is to establish that X will, in the future, cause certain things to occur. We all know enough of history to realize that few major decisions have led neatly to their anticipated results. This knowledge indeed accounts for much of our conservatism. All the things that can go wrong in a causal argument can go wrong in a proposal argument as well; the major difference is that in a proposal argument we typically have less evidence for our conjectures.

The Problem of Evaluating Consequences

A final difficulty faced by all proposal arguments concerns the difficulty of evaluating the consequences of the proposal. In government and industry, managers often turn to a tool known as "cost-benefit" analysis to calculate the potential consequences of a given proposal. As much as possible, a cost-benefit analysis tries to reduce all consequences to a single scale for purposes of comparison. Most often, the scale will be money. Although this scale may work well in some circumstances, it can lead to grotesquely inappropriate conclusions in other situations.

Just how does one balance the money saved by cutting Medicare benefits against the suffering of the people denied benefits? How does one translate the beauty of a wilderness area into a dollar amount? On this score, cost-benefit analyses often run into a problem discussed in the previous chapter: the seductiveness of empirical measures. Because something can't be readily measured doesn't mean it can be safely ignored. And finally, what will be a cost for one group will often be a benefit for others. For example, if social security benefits are cut, those on social security will suffer, but current workers who pay for it with taxes will take home a larger paycheck.

These, then, are some of the general difficulties facing someone who sets out to argue in favor of a proposal. Although not insurmountable, they are at least daunting. Given those difficulties, let's now set forth the writing assignment for this chapter and then turn to the question of how one might put together a proposal argument.

WRITING ASSIGNMENT FOR CHAPTER 15: OPTIONS FOR PROPOSAL ARGUMENTS

OPTION 1: A PRACTICAL PROPOSAL ADDRESSING A LOCAL PROBLEM Write a practical proposal offering a solution to a local problem. Your proposal should have three main sections: (1) description of the problem, (2) proposed solution, and (3) justification. You may include additional sections or subsections as needed. Longer proposals often include an "abstract" at the beginning of the proposal to provide a summary overview of the whole argument. (Sometimes called the "executive summary," this abstract may be the only portion of the proposal read by high-level managers.) Sometimes proposals are accompanied by a "letter of transmittal"—a one-page business letter that introduces the proposal to its intended audience and provides some needed background about the writer.

Your proposal can be either an "action" proposal, in which you specify exactly the action that needs to be taken to solve the problem, or a "planning proposal," in which you know what the problem is but don't yet know how to solve it. A planning proposal usually calls for the formation of a committee or task force to address the problem, so that your "solution" doesn't specify an actual solution but rather specifies the mission of the committee you want to establish. To make a planning proposal as effective as possible, you are wise to suggest several ideas for possible solutions, that is, several alternative courses of action that you want the committee to examine in more detail and refine. An example of a practical proposal with a planning focus is included at the end of this chapter ("Restructuring the Washington State High School Dance and Drill Team Association Conference" by student writer Karen Kartes).

Document design is important in practical proposals, which are aimed at busy people who have to make many decisions under time constraints. Because the writer of a practical proposal usually produces the finished document (practical proposals are seldom submitted to newspapers or magazines for publication), he or she must pay particular attention to the attractive design of the document. An effective design helps establish the writer's *ethos* as a quality-oriented professional and helps make the reading of the proposal as easy as possible. Document design includes effective use of headings and subheadings, attractive typeface and layout, flawless editing, and other features enhancing the visual appearance of the document.*

OPTION 2: A POLICY PROPOSAL AS A GUEST EDITORIAL Write a two- to three-page policy proposal suitable for publication as a feature editorial in a college or city newspaper or in some publication associated with a particular group or activity such as a church newsletter or employee bulletin. By "feature editorial" we mean a well-developed argument as opposed to a short "opinion editorial" that simply sets forth an editorial view without development and support. The voice and style of your argument should be aimed at general readers of your chosen publication. Your editorial should have the following features:

1. the identification of a problem (Persuade your audience that this is a genuine problem that needs solving; give it presence.)
2. a proposal for action that will help alleviate the problem
3. a justification of your solution (the reasons that your audience should accept your proposal and act on it)

OPTION 3: A RESEARCHED ARGUMENT PROPOSING PUBLIC POLICY Write a seven- to ten-page proposal argument as a formal research paper, using research data for support. (See Chapters 17 and 18 for advice on writing a researched argument.) Your argument should include all the features of the shorter argument above (Option 2) and also a summary and refutation of opposing views (in the form of alternative proposals and/or differing cost-benefit analyses of your proposal). An example of a researched policy proposal is student writer Brenda Wahler's "Let's Enact Comparable Worth" on pages 348–357.

---

*It is usually a mistake, however, to use all the bells and whistles available on recent hardware and software for desktop publishing. Different styles and sizes of fonts, fancy title pages, and extraneous visuals such as pointing fingers, daggers, stars, and so forth, make you look like a computer doodler rather than a serious writer. Tasteful, conservative use of boldface and underlining is usually the best approach. Even if you have available only a typewriter, you can create several levels of attractive headings by using different combinations of indentation, underlining, and capital letters.

DEVELOPING A PROPOSAL ARGUMENT

Convincing Your Readers That a Problem Exists

There is one argumentative strategy generic to all proposal arguments: awakening in the reader a sense of a problem. Typically, the development of a problem occurs in one of two places in a proposal argument—either in the introduction prior to the presentation of the arguer's proposal claim or in the body of the paper as the first main reason justifying the proposal claim. In the second instance the writer's first because clause has the following structure: "We should do X *because a problem exists (and X will solve it)."*

At this stage of your argument, it's important to give your problem presence. You must get people to see how the problem affects people, perhaps through examples of suffering or other loss or through persuasive statistics and so forth. Your goal is to awaken your readers to the existence of a problem, a problem they may well not have recognized before.

Besides giving presence to the problem, a writer must also gain the readers' intellectual assent to the depth, range, and potential seriousness of the problem. Suppose, for illustration, that you wanted to propose a special tax to increase funding for higher education in your state. In trying to convince taxpayers in your state that a problem exists, what obstacles might you face? First of all, many taxpayers never went to college and feel that they get along just fine without it. They tend to worry more about the quality of roads, social services, elementary and secondary schools, police and fire protection, and so forth. They are not too convinced that they need to worry about professors' salaries or better equipped research labs. Thus, it's not enough to talk about the importance of education in general or to cite figures showing how paltry your state's funding of higher education is.

In order to convince your audience of the need for your proposal, you'll have to describe the consequences of low funding levels in terms they can relate to. You'll have to show them that potential benefits to the state are lost because of inadequate funding. Perhaps you can show the cost in terms of inadequately skilled graduates, disgruntled teachers, high turnover, brain drain to other states, inadequate educational services to farmers and businesspeople, lost productivity, and so forth. Or perhaps you can show your audience examples of benefits realized from better college funding in other states. Such examples give life to the abstract notion of lost potential.

All of this is not to say that you can't or shouldn't argue that higher education is inherently good. But until your reader can see low funding levels as "problematic" rather than "simply the way things are," your proposal stands little chance of being enacted.

Showing the Specifics of Your Proposal

Having decided that there is a problem to be solved, you should lay out your thesis, which is a proposal for solving the problem. Your goal now is to stress the feasibility of your solution, including costs. The art of proposal making is the art of the possible. To be sure, not all proposals require elaborate descriptions of the implementation process. If you are proposing, for example, that a local PTA chapter should buy new tumbling mats for the junior high gym classes, the procedures for buying the mats will probably be irrelevant. But in many arguments the specifics of your proposal— the actual step-by-step methods of implementing it—may be instrumental in winning your audience's support.

You will also need to show how your proposal will solve the problem either partially or wholly. Sometimes you may first need to convince your reader that the problem is solvable, not something intractably rooted in "the way things are," such as earthquakes or jealousy. In other words, expect that some members of your audience will be skeptical about the ability of any proposal to solve the problem you are addressing. You may well need, therefore, to "listen" to this point of view in your refutation section and to argue that your problem is at least partially solvable.

In order to persuade your audience that your proposal can work, you can follow any one of several approaches. A typical approach is to lay out a causal argument showing how one consequence will lead to another until your solution is effected. Another approach is to turn to resemblance arguments, either analogy or precedent. You try to show how similar proposals have been successful elsewhere. Or, if similar things have failed in the past, you try to show how the present situation is different.

The Justification: Convincing Your Reader That Your Proposal Should Be Enacted

This phase of a proposal argument will need extensive development in some arguments and minimal development in others, again depending on your particular problem and the rhetorical context of your proposal. If your audience already acknowledges the seriousness of the problem you are addressing and has simply been waiting for the right solution to come along, then your argument will be successful so long as you can convince your audience that your solution will work and that it won't cost too much. Such arguments depend on the clarity of your proposal and the feasibility of its being implemented.

But what if the costs are high? Or what if your audience doesn't think that the problem you are addressing is particularly serious? In such cases you have to develop your main reasons for believing that X should be done. A good strategy is to use the "three approaches" heuristic described in Chapters 3 and 8. Your purpose is to show how doing X in some way brings "good" to your audience. Here are some examples of how the "three approaches" heuristic can be used for proposal arguments:

Proposal Claim: Our university should abolish fraternities and sororities.

Principle: because they are elitist (or "a thing of the past" or "racist" or "sexist" or whatever)

Consequence: because eliminating the Greek system will improve our school's academics (or "fill our dormitories," "allow us to experiment with new living arrangements," "replace rush with a better freshman orientation," and so forth)

Resemblance: because other universities that have eliminated the Greek system have reported good results

Proposal Claim: We should eliminate mandatory busing of children to achieve racial equality.

Principle: because it is unjust (or "ineffective," "a misuse of judicial authority," "a violation of individual rights," and so forth)

Consequence: because it puts too many psychological burdens on kids (or "costs too much," "destroys neighborhood schools," "makes it difficult to have parental involvement in the schools," "splits up siblings," "causes kids to spend too much time on buses," and so forth)

Resemblance: because busing schoolchildren to solve a social problem such as racism makes about as much sense as sending alcoholics' kids through a detox center to cure their parents

Proposal Claim: Our church should start an active ministry to AIDS patients.

Principle: because doing so would be an act of love (or "justice" or "an example of Christian courage," and so forth)

Consequence: because doing so will help increase community understanding of the disease and also reduce fear

Resemblance: because Jesus ministered to the lepers and in our society AIDS victims have become the outcasts that lepers were in Jesus' society

Each of these arguments attempts to appeal to the value system of the audience. Each tries to show how the proposed action is within the class of things that the audience already values, will lead to consequences desired by the audience, or is similar to something the audience already values (or will alleviate something the audience disvalues).

Touching the Right Pressure Points

Having defined and weighed the problem, having worked out a feasible solution, and having motivated your audience to act on your proposal, you may well wish to take your argument a step further. You may thus have to determine who has the power to act on your proposal and apply arguments directly to that person's or agency's immediate interests. More than any other form of argument, a proposal argument needs finally to be addressed to those with the power to act on the proposal. You need to know to whom or to what your power source is beholden or responsive and what values your power source holds that can be appealed to. You're looking, in short, for pressure points.

While attempting to get a university to improve wheelchair access to the student union building, one student with multiple sclerosis discovered that the university had recently paid $100,000 to put oak trim in a new faculty office building. She knew officials were a bit embarrassed by that figure, and it became an effective pressure point for her essay. "The university can afford to pay $100,000 for oak trim for faculty, but can't spend one quarter of that amount helping its disabled students get full access to the student union building." This hard-to-justify discrepancy put considerable pressure on the administration to find money for more wheelchair ramps. The moral here is that it makes good sense to tie one's proposal as much as possible to the interests of those in power.

SUMMING UP: HOW THE TOULMIN SCHEMA CAN HELP YOU DEVELOP A PROPOSAL ARGUMENT

By way of reviewing what we've discussed about the development of a proposal argument, consider the following proposal argument laid out according to Toulmin's schema and later modified as a result of the Toulmin analysis:

Initial Enthymeme: All college students should be required to take an ethics course because most students are not effective ethical thinkers and because an ethics course would help solve this problem.

Claim: All college students should be required to take an ethics course.

Stated Reasons: a. Students are not effective thinkers about ethical issues; b. An ethics course will help solve this problem.

Grounds: a. evidence that college students lack the ability to think effectively about ethical issues; b. evidence that ethics courses help students think more effectively about ethical issues (e.g., pre- and post-course tests asking students to think coherently about ethical issues; follow-up studies of students who take ethics courses and a control group of students who don't take ethics to see if there are significant differences in ethical behavior)

Warrant for Both A and B: The ability to think effectively about ethical issues is such an important skill that a proposal to develop that skill should be enacted.

Backing: evidence of the benefits of ethical thinking and the costs of ineffective ethical thinking

Conditions of Rebuttal: examples of people who've studied ethics and have been incapable of effective ethical thinking, of effective ethical thinkers who've never had a course in college ethics (perhaps it is the home or the church that teaches ethical thinking, not a college course), or of societies in which effective ethical thinking has not led to the promised benefits

Qualifiers: a statement to the effect that college ethics courses will make it "more likely" that students can think effectively about ethical issues and that more effective ethical thinking will "probably" be beneficial to society

The stated reasons in support of the claim are evaluation and causal claims. The first stated reason—college students are not effective ethical thinkers—is an evaluative claim that requires the writer to create criteria for effective ethical thinking and to show that today's students don't meet the criteria. The second claim—that a course in ethics will help solve this problem—is a causal one and forces the writer to provide evidence that the course will work. The conditions for rebuttal highlight potential weaknesses in the stated reasons and grounds because they point out so many possible exceptions—people who think ethically without taking an ethics course, people who take an ethics course and still don't think ethically, and so forth. The possibility that one really learns ethics in the home or church seems particularly troubling to the argument.

The main warrant for this proposal—that effective ethical thinking is good and that methods for developing it should therefore be enacted—also presents problems. Although your audience might grant that effective ethical thinking is a good thing, plenty of opponents will not grant that an ethics course should be required. Requiring students to take ethics courses means forcing them to forgo other courses, many of which can lay claim to being inherently good as well. Moreover, students uninterested in ethics and professors who don't teach ethics can't be expected to accept the proposal readily because they are the ones who will bear most of the "costs" of implementing it. So the writer has a considerable burden of proof in getting his readers to accept the warrant.

Seeing the argument displayed this way, the writer decided that more support was needed in two places: First, the writer had to find more evidence that ethics courses really work. Second, the writer had to provide a more convincing argument that the benefits of an ethics course were significant enough to justify a required course for all students. The writer decided to do more research into contemporary problems caused by poor ethical thinking in order to bolster his argument that such a course would bring long-range benefits to society. To strengthen his case further, he decided to argue also that ethics courses would in general make for more thoughtful and questioning students. Finally, he turned to a resemblance argument by citing precedents at many liberal arts colleges around the nation where required courses in ethics have been enacted.

FOR CLASS DISCUSSION

The following collaborative task takes approximately two class days to complete. The exercise takes you through the process of creating a proposal argument.

1. In small groups, identify and list several major problems facing students in your college or university.

2. Decide among yourselves which are the most important of these problems and rank them in order of importance.

3. Take your group's number one problem and explore answers to the following questions. Group recorders should be prepared to present your group's answers to the class as a whole:

    a. Why is the problem a problem?

    b. For whom is the problem a problem?

    c. How will these people suffer if the problem is not solved? (Give specific examples.)

    d. Who has the power to solve the problem?

    e. Why hasn't the problem been solved up to this point?

    f. How can the problem be solved? (That is, create a proposal.)

    g. What are the probable benefits of acting on your proposal?

    h. What costs are associated with your proposal?

    i. Who will bear those costs?

    j. Why should this proposal be enacted?

    k. Why is it better than alternative proposals?

4. As a group, draft an outline for a proposal argument in which you:

    a. describe the problem and its significance,

    b. propose your solution to the problem, and

    c. justify your proposal by showing how the benefits of adopting that proposal outweigh the costs.

5. Recorders for each group should write their group's outline on the board and be prepared to explain it to the class.

WRITING THE PROPOSAL ARGUMENT

STARTING POINTS: FINDING A PROPOSAL ISSUE

Since "should" or "ought" issues are among the most common sources of arguments, students who are keeping an idea-log (see Chapter 3) have usually recorded a number of good proposal issues. To think of topics for practical proposals, try making an idea-map of local problems you would like to see solved. For initial spokes, try trigger words such as the following: problems at my university (dorms, parking, registration system, grading system, campus appearance, clubs, curriculum, intramural program, football team); problems in my city or town (dangerous intersections, ugly areas, inadequate lighting, a poorly designed store, a shopping center that needs a specific improvement); problems at my place of work (office design, flow of customer traffic, merchandise display, company policies, customer relations); or problems related to your hobbies, recreational time, life as a consumer, life as a homeowner, and so forth. If you can offer a solution to the problem you identify, consider an action proposal. If you can't solve the problem but believe it is worth serious attention, consider a planning proposal.

To find a topic for policy proposals, stay in touch with the news, which will keep you aware of current debates on regional and national issues. Skimming recent issues of *Time* or *Newsweek*, thumbing through a recent *Wall Street Journal*, or looking at the table of contents in public policy magazines such as *The Atlantic Monthly, The New Republic, National Review,* and others will also give you excellent leads.

You can also try freewriting in response to trigger questions such as these:

- I would really like to solve the problem of . . .

- I believe that X should . . . [substitute for X words such as *my teachers, the president, the school administration, Congress, my boss,* and so forth]

EXPLORATION STAGE

Once you have decided on a proposal issue, we recommend you explore it by trying one or more of the following activities:

Explore ideas by using the "stock issues" heuristic described in Chapter 3. Much of what we say about proposal arguments in this chapter has been influenced by the stock issues questions: (1) Is there really a problem here that has to be solved? (2) Will the proposed solution really solve this problem? (3) Can the problem be solved in a simpler way without disturbing the status quo? (4) Is the proposed solution practical enough that it really stands a chance of being acted upon? (5) What will be the positive and negative consequences of the proposal?

Explore your problem by freewriting answers to the eleven questions (3a. – k.) in the preceding For Class Discussion exercise. These questions cover the same territory as the stock issues heuristic, but the arrangement and number of questions might stimulate additional thought.

Explore ideas for the justification section of your proposal by using the "three approaches" heuristic introduced in Chapter 3 and developed at length in Chapter 8. Briefly, this heuristic invites you to justify your proposal to do X by arguing (1) that doing X is the right thing to do in principle, (2) that doing X will lead to various good consequences, and (3) that doing X (or something similar) has been done with good results elsewhere or that doing X is like doing Y, which we agree is good. This heuristic is particularly powerful for proposal arguments because it focuses on finding audience-based reasons.

Explore ideas for your argument by completing the eight guided journal tasks in Idea-Log Set Two (pages 73–75).

WRITING THE DISCOVERY DRAFT: SOME WAYS TO ORGANIZE A PROPOSAL ARGUMENT

When you write your discovery draft, you may find it helpful to have at hand some plans for typical ways of organizing a proposal argument. What follows are two common methods of organization. Option 1 is the plan most typical for practical proposals. Either Option 1 or Option 2 is an effective plan for a policy proposal.

OPTION 1

- presentation of a problem that needs solving:
  description of problem (give problem presence)
  background, including previous attempts to solve problem
  argument that the problem is solvable (optional)
- presentation of writer's proposal:
  succinct statement of the proposed solution serves as thesis statement
  explain specifics of proposed solution.
- summary and rebuttal of opposing views (In practical proposals, this section is often a summary and rejection of alternative ways of solving the problem.)
- justification persuading reader that proposal should be enacted:
  Reason 1 presented and developed
  Reason 2 presented and developed
  and so forth
- conclusion that exhorts audience to act (Give presence to final sentences.)

OPTION 2

- presentation of issue, including background
- presentation of writer's proposal
- justification
  Reason 1: Show that proposal addresses a serious problem.

Reason 2: Show that proposal will solve problem.
Reason 3: Give additional reasons for enacting proposal.

- summary and refutation of opposing views
- conclusion that exhorts audience to act

REVISION STAGE

Once you have written a discovery draft and have begun to clarify your argument for yourself, you are ready to begin making your argument clear and persuasive for your readers. Once again, exploring your argument using the Toulmin schema should prove useful. Pay particular attention to the ways a skeptical audience might rebut your argument.

CONDITIONS FOR REBUTTAL: TESTING YOUR PROPOSAL ARGUMENT

As we've suggested throughout the foregoing discussion, proposal arguments are vulnerable on many grounds—the innate conservatism of most people, the difficulty of clearly anticipating all the consequences of the proposal, and so forth. What questions, then, can one put specifically to proposal arguments to help us anticipate these vulnerabilities?

Will My Audience Deny That My Problem Is Really a Problem?

The first question to ask of your proposal is "What's so wrong with the status quo that change is necessary?" The second question is "Who loses if the status quo is changed?" Be certain not to overlook this second question. Most proposal makers can demonstrate that some sort of problem exists, but often it is a problem only for certain groups of people. Solving the problem will thus prove a benefit to some people but a cost to others. If your audience examines the problem from the perspective of the potential losers rather than the winners, they can often raise doubts about your proposal.

For example, one state recently held an initiative on a proposed "bottle bill" that would fight litter by permitting the sale of soda and beer only in returnable bottles. Sales outlets would be required to charge a substantial deposit on the bottles in order to encourage people to return them. Proponents of the proposal emphasized citizens as "winners" sharing in the new cleanliness of a landscape no longer littered with cans. In order to refute this argument, opponents showed consumers as "losers" burdened with the high cost of deposits and the hassle of collecting and returning bottles to grocery stores.

Will My Audience Doubt the Effectiveness of My Solution?

Assuming that you've satisfied yourself that a significant problem exists for a significant number of people, a number of questions remain to be asked about the ability of the proposed solution to solve the problem. First, "Does the problem exist for the reasons cited, or might there be alternative explanations?" Here we return to the familiar ground of causal arguments. A proposal supposedly strikes at the cause of a problem. But perhaps striking at that "cause" won't solve the problem. Perhaps you've mistaken a symptom for a cause, or confused two commonly associated but essentially unlinked phenomena for a cause-effect relationship. For example, will paying teachers higher salaries improve the quality of teaching or merely attract greedier rather than brighter people? Maybe more good teachers would be attracted and retained if they were given some other benefit (fewer students? smaller classes? more sabbaticals? more autonomy? more prestige?).

Another way to test your solution is to list all the uncertainties involved. This might be referred to as the "The Devil you know is better than the Devil you don't know" strategy. Remind yourself of all the unanticipated consequences of past changes. Who, for example, would have thought back in the days when aerosol shaving cans were being developed that they might lead to diminished ozone layers, which might lead to more ultraviolet rays getting through the atmosphere from the sun, which would lead to higher incidences of skin cancer? The history of technology is full of such cautionary tales that can be invoked to remind you of the uncertain course that progress can sometimes take.

Will My Audience Think My Proposal Costs Too Much?

The most commonly asked question of any proposal is simply, "Do the benefits of enacting the proposal outweigh the costs?" As we saw above, you can't foresee all the consequences of any proposal. It's easy, before the fact, to exaggerate both the costs and the benefits of a proposal. So, in asking how much your proposal will cost, we urge you to make an honest estimate. Will your audience discover costs you hadn't anticipated—extra financial costs or unexpected psychological or environmental or aesthetic costs? As much as you can, anticipate these objections.

Will My Audience Suggest Counterproposals?

Related to all that's been said so far is the counterproposal. Can you imagine an appealing alternative to both the status quo and the proposal that you're making? The more clearly your proposal shows that a significant problem exists, the more important it is that you be able to identify possible counterproposals. Any potential critic of a proposal to remedy an acknowledged problem will either have to make such a counterproposal or have to argue that the problem is simply in the nature of things. So, given the likelihood that you'll be faced with a counterproposal, it only makes sense to anticipate it and to work out a refutation of it before you have it thrown at you. And who knows, you may end up liking the counterproposal better and changing your mind about what to propose!

FOR CLASS DISCUSSION

The following proposal arguments—both by student writers—illustrate the range of proposal writing. The first argument is a practical proposal, the second a policy proposal. Both arguments are reproduced in typewriter format to illustrate conventional typescript form for formal papers. The first argument, as a practical proposal, uses headings and subheadings. When sent to the intended audience, it is accompanied by a single-spaced letter of transmittal following the conventional format of a business letter. The second argument is a formal research paper using the documentation format of the Modern Language Association. A full explanation of this format occurs in Chapter 18. Working in groups, identify the argumentation strategies used by each writer. Specifically, be able to answer the following questions:

1. Does the writer demonstrate that a problem exists? What strategies does the writer use to demonstrate the problem?

2. Does the writer persuade you that the proposed solution will solve the problem? What strategies does the writer use to try to persuade you that the solution will work?

3. Does the writer attempt to listen to opposing views? How successful is the writer in refuting those views? What strategies does the writer use?

4. Does the writer argue effectively that the solution should be enacted? Does the writer use arguments from principle? from consequence? from resemblance?

5. How would you try to refute each writer's argument?

Karen Kartes
12457 Smith Ave.
Seattle, WA 98146

Joanna Benson
WSDDTA President
Evergreen High School
Seattle, WA 98146

Dear Ms. Benson:

Please find enclosed a proposal for improving the annual Washington state dance and drill team competitions. As an active member of the dance and drill community for the past six years--including experience as a team member, team captain, and now co-advisor--I believe that I have the background to appreciate the complex task that WSDDTA undertakes each year in sponsoring the annual competition. My suggestions for improving the structure of the annual competition might help WSDDTA eliminate some persistent problems felt by participants, spectators, and judges.

Basically, I believe that the competition would be more enjoyable if the program were shortened and focused. The enclosed proposal suggests two ways of doing so: through qualifying regional competitions or through separate competitions for the two genres of dance and drill.

The ultimate goal of the WSDDTA's annual competition is to create a rewarding experience for participants and a high level of entertainment for spectators by bringing out the best possible performance from the competing teams. I have found great joy in performing and choreographing, and I hope that through this proposal I can perhaps contribute to enhancing the public image of dance and drill throughout the state. Thank you very much for considering my ideas.

Sincerely,

Karen Kartes
Kennedy Drill Co-Advisor

A PROPOSAL TO RESTRUCTURE THE WASHINGTON STATE HIGH SCHOOL

DANCE AND DRILL TEAM ASSOCIATION COMPETITION

Submitted to the Washington State
Dance and Drill Team Association

Karen Kartes
Drill Co-Advisor
Kennedy High School

SUMMARY

The present structure of the annual dance and drill team competition sponsored by the Washington State Dance and Drill Team Association (WSDDTA) creates animosity among teams, confusion for viewers, and stress for judges. Additionally, the number of participants makes the competition too lengthy and too taxing for all involved.

The WSDDTA should create a task force to solve the problem of an unwieldy state competition. This proposal suggests two possible solutions to be considered by the task force: (1) regional qualifying competitions preceding the state competition or (2) separate competitions for the two genres of dance and drill.

BACKGROUND ON THE WSDDTA COMPETITION

The WSDDTA is a group of elected representatives selected from the advisors of statewide high school dance and drill teams. As a coordinating group, the WSDDTA's primary function is to work with a host high school in Washington state to prepare for the annual state competition, a Friday to Sunday weekend event open to any high school dance or drill team wishing to attend. Each participating team performs for a huge audience of spectators and is critiqued and rated by judges with many years' experience in dance and drill.

1

PROBLEMS WITH THE CURRENT CONFERENCE STRUCTURE

Several factors in the current structure cause the
event to be unfocused, lengthy, tiresome, and demoralizing
for weaker teams.

1. The talent level among the 60+ participating teams
is too disparate. Some teams have much more skill and
experience than others. It does not seem fair for more
technically sophisticated teams to perform beside simpler
teams at an event which is supposed to be the presentation
of the brightest and best work being done in the dance and
drill world. A thirty-six member team from a large suburban
high school with two faculty advisors and a professional
choreographer will put to shame an eight-member team from a
tiny rural school that might not even have a full-time
advisor. Competing with these ''incredible'' teams often
creates feelings of hopelessness and embarrassment among
the weaker teams. Rather than improve from year to year as a
result of being intermingled with superior teams (the hope
of the WSDDTA), these weaker teams lose motivation.

2. The present competition doesn't distinguish
adequately between the genres of dance and drill. Strict
military-style drill teams are judged on the same basis as
jazzy, dance-oriented novelty squads. Normally, drill
teams use sharp movements and employ marching technique,
whereas dance squads incorporate complex footwork and
flowing, interpretive movements. Although the WSDDTA is
proud of this variety, it is as unfair as pitting figure

2

skaters against speed skaters. The WSDDTA judging scale is far too broad if it can be applied to both of these vastly different types of teams. As the judging now stands, teams upset with their final rating blame their scores on judges who ''love dance and hate drill'' or vice versa. Each year teams don't know whether to focus on drill or on dance in order to improve their ratings at the annual competition. The result is a lessening of overall quality, since teams embark on a neverending crusade to find the perfect style ''to please the judges'' rather than honing to perfection a style appropriate for their team.

   3. The competition is too big an event for one high school to host. Approximately five thousand people pouring into one school is taxing on the organizers and creates an enormous strain on the physical facilities of the school. Organizers report exhaustion from trying to handle the logistics of such a large competition. The spectators, jammed into the seating area of a standard high school gymnasium, complain of heat, of inadequate drinking fountains and restrooms, of the impossibility of locating a performer for congratulations or a message, and even of claustrophobia.

   4. The conference is too long and too emotionally and physically taxing on participants, spectators, and judges. As a spectator, team member, and team advisor, I have witnessed first-hand the stress and fatigue of the conference. Every year complaints flow from spectators and

participants about the excessive length of the conference, the hours of sitting, and the tedious waiting--problems compounded by uncomfortable physical conditions in an overcrowded gymnasium. The length is hardest on the performers, who are emotionally and physically drained from months of practicing before the competition begins and who are nervous and anxious throughout the whole weekend.

PROPOSAL

The WSDDTA should select a task force which would decide how to best limit the current scope and length of the competition. What follows are two possible ways in which the competition could be improved. If the scope of the conference is narrowed in either of the following ways, the length of the conference would naturally diminish.

One possible solution: Establishing regional qualifying competitions. Having regional competitions in order to qualify for the state conference would ensure a shorter program involving only top teams. About fifteen teams would attend each regional competition. All teams would perform and be judged, but only three or four would continue on to compete at the state level.

A second possible solution: Hold separate competitions for dance and drill. This alternative would call for two separate state conferences, one for dance squads and one for drill teams. This alternative would require the WSDDTA to separate into two distinct

4

associations. One group would organize a competition for dance squads, the other for drill teams.

Other than separation by genre, the organization of state competitions would be similar to the present structure, except that the size of the competition would be cut in half and the judging system would focus on each particular genre.

JUSTIFICATION

For a number of reasons, limiting the scope of the current state conference would promote quality performances and would increase interest in the sport of dance and drill.

First, with either proposed solution implemented, state judges would be forced to tighten and clarify their criteria for excellence. Their comments would be more respected by teams because criticisms would not be so vague, general, and ambiguous--a problem caused currently by the mixing of genres and by the wide difference in talent levels.

Second, either solution would improve the quality of performances. With regional competitions, teams would strive for higher standards; they would know they had to achieve a certain status to make it to state, just as other sports teams do. At the state level, the head-to-head competition of the best teams would stimulate stronger performances without dilution from weaker teams. With competitions divided by genres, performances would improve because there would no longer be confusion about criteria for excellence.

Third, when teams work harder to achieve a higher standard of excellence, more people will want to stay on the team and more will want to join. Teams' performances at their home schools will boost school spirit and team morale and attract talented new members. Old members will be rewarded with fond memories of success at state and will want to improve further, and new members will yearn to achieve that satisfaction.

Finally, as teams improve and state conferences become more comfortable and enjoyable, more people will take interest in the sport of dance and drill. The great quality and entertainment value of an organized, fair, focused competition will bring about the respect, recognition, and interest that dance and drill activities deserve. Providing the best possible entertainment for audiences is a guaranteed lifeline for the continuation of these activities.

CONCLUSION

By limiting the scope of the statewide competition, the WSDDTA can simultaneously increase the enjoyment of participants and spectators at competitions while also improving the quality of teams throughout the state and enhancing the public image of dance and drill.

Brenda Wahler

Professor Smith

English 380

May 13, 1988

LET'S ENACT COMPARABLE WORTH

''Sandra'' works as a Secretary III at a large
university. To get her job, she needed a high school diploma
and two years prior experience. She must manage a small
office, supervise other clerical employees, order supplies
and keep books in addition to regular clerical duties such
as typing and taking shorthand. There are two male and 328
female Secretary III's at the University (Remick 11).

''Jack'' is a Traffic Guide at the same university. He
needed a valid driver's license to get his job. He collects
parking fees and directs visitors to parking areas and
offices. Seventy-five percent of the Traffic Guides at the
university are male (Remick 11).

Jack earns a higher salary than Sandra. They work for
the same employer and are represented by the same union. Why
is it that Sandra, with a job requiring more education, more
experience, and more responsibility than Jack's job, earns
less than Jack? Why is it that, on a nationwide average,
women earn only 63 cents to every dollar earned by men (Beck
22)?

Wahler   2

One reason for the disparity in earnings is that many jobs are, for all practical purposes, segregated by sex. While there is no <u>legal</u> barrier to women or men who wish to enter non-traditional occupations, the fact remains that whether from intentional discrimination, conscious and unconscious social pressure, or any other cause, many individuals work in jobs dominated by one sex or the other. When this tendency is combined with the historical pattern of paying women less than men, the result is the current situation where jobs held mostly by women tend to pay less than jobs held predominantly by men.

Comparable worth is a solution to the problem. In spite of U.S. Commission on Civil Rights chairman Clarence Pendleton, Jr.'s remark that comparable worth is the ''looniest idea since 'Loony Tunes''' (382), comparable worth is in fact a well thought out, workable idea. In essence, it attempts to compare unlike jobs in an impartial manner in order to free wage guidelines of discriminatory features. Different jobs are broken down into common factors such as education level needed for the job, responsibility required, physical effort needed, dangers and hazards, and other conditions or requirements. Points are assigned to each factor, and by comparing the results from various jobs, the relative value of each job is indicated.

The reader may think the above method of comparing unlike jobs is an untested and extremely complicated idea.

Wahler   3

This is not the case. Corporate America, the government, and other institutions have used systems such as this--called point factor job evaluation systems--for nearly fifty years (Remick 2, Bergmann). Businesses and government have long needed to compare jobs in terms of their relative values, whether comparing janitors to chauffeurs or comparing the governor of a state to the chairman of the board of a major corporation. The question is not if unlike jobs can be compared. They can and they are. The real question is this: Given evidence that jobs held predominantly by women tend to pay less than they are worth, shall the situation be changed, and if so, how?

Those who feel that there is no reason to change the situation, and thus oppose comparable worth, make several criticisms. First, they deny that there is a problem. They try to explain away differences in pay by saying that women are more likely to leave work to care for children or to follow a spouse in a job transfer, thus hurting their seniority. Critics also suggest that women tend to be less skilled and less educated, and so are employed in more low-paying jobs than are many men. But studies disprove this assertion. In a study done at a large university with a non-academic support staff of over 6000 people, jobs where more than 70 percent of the personnel were one sex or the other were singled out and compared. When these ''sex segregated'' jobs were compared (with factors such as seniority and education level compensated for), there was a 20 percent gap between the wages paid in ''men's''

occupations and those paid in ''women's'' occupations
(Remick 10). In other words, there is a substantial
disparity in wages that cannot be explained except by the
common denominator of women holding many of the lower paying
jobs.

The next criticism is that jobs held most by women are
simply not worth as much. This is a very common reason given
for the low wages of these jobs. But a very effective
rebuttal to this was given by Miller, who pointed out that
secretarial work was once a field dominated by men,
particularly before the turn of the century, and had been
considered work with upward mobility, good status, and good
pay. All of these benefits have declined in real terms, and
this decline parallels the shift from male to female
dominance in this area of work. The same thing has happened
in the garment trade, in teaching, and in other areas where
women have come to dominate jobs that were once considered
''men's work'' (Miller).

Another argument is heard. Not only can differences in
pay be explained away, opponents declare, but in fact women
themselves are of questionable value in the workforce. The
reasoning was once given that women were only going to work
until they married, or were working merely for a little
extra ''mad money.'' But for most women, this is not the
case. Even the still heard argument that the workforce is
dominated by upper middle class women who primarily need
''psychic gratification'' (Picus) does not hold up. Women
work for need as well as for a sense of self worth. The

reality is that in 1950, 70 percent of American households
were headed by men who were the sole supporters of their
family; by 1984, the figure had plummeted to less than 15
percent (Rosenberg 337).

Women are in the workforce today because they must be.
Some are sole supporters of a family: divorced women,
single parents, widows. Others have a spouse who is disabled
or unemployed. And even in a more traditional two-adult
household, two incomes are increasingly necessary in order
to simply make ends meet.

Therefore, it is clear that women are a vital part of
the workforce and are here to stay. It is also clear that it
makes no sense to downgrade the value of a job simply
because it is normally held by women. It must furthermore be
noted that it would be impossible to solve the problem by
expecting all working women to enter high-paying ''non-
traditional'' occupations. First, there are simply not
enough openings to accommodate such a large influx of
workers, and second, the jobs held by many women are
valuable. The world would be a much less satisfactory place
if there were no secretaries, nurses, lab technicians,
elementary school teachers, or housekeepers.

Now it is time to deal with the criticism that
comparable worth is unworkable due to its potential high
cost and negative effect on the economy. Opponents cite
predictions of 9.7 percent inflation and tremendous
unemployment (Pendleton 384). But in nations such as
Australia, where 30 percent raises were given in

traditional women's occupations to bring about pay equity,

no such dire circumstances arose (Bergmann). Not only does

it appear that the economy can handle comparable worth pay

adjustments, but also the cost is not as great as critics

like to claim. In the state of Minnesota, where comparable

worth in the public sector was implemented by legislation,

it cost the state about 11 million dollars a year for four

years. This affected 8000 workers and amounted to about

four percent of the state's salary budget (''Pay Equity'').

The facts are in stark contrast to Mr. Pendleton's

assertion that comparable worth could cost 6.4 <u>billion</u>

dollars per state per year on into the indefinite future

(Pendleton 382)! In the city of Los Angeles, comparable

worth for municipal workers was achieved through collective

bargaining and will cost the city a total of twelve million

dollars (''Pay Equity''). Similar relatively reasonable

costs have been true for many of the states which have

implemented comparable worth as well as for municipalities

such as Colorado Springs, San Francisco, San Jose, and

Spokane (Miller).

Another misconception based on the potential for very

high costs is that comparable worth must be implemented due

to litigation settlements involving back pay. The lawsuit

of the American Federation of State, County and Municipal

Employees against the state of Washington was anticipated

by some to cost as much as a billion dollars if back pay was

awarded for the twelve years it took to settle the dispute.

But the case was settled out of court without back pay, and

will cost 103 million dollars. Considering the settlement will affect some 35,000 workers, the amount is not as large as it may seem (''Montana's comp''). If past history is a reliable indicator, the great majority of comparable worth disputes will be settled by legislation, collective bargaining, or policy decisions--not lawsuits.

Another source of misinformation comes from the fact that billions of dollars are spent each year on regular pay increases for workers. Some of the misleading statistics on the cost of comparable worth come from studies that include scheduled pay increases along with the figures for pay equity increases.

Finally, there is the question of the impact on the so-called free market. The argument is that wages should be set by supply and demand, prevailing market conditions, and so on (Hackett 336). The problem is that there is no market that is not already influenced by government policy, taxation policy, union agreements, traditional biases (including sexism), and a host of other factors. In fact, even the ''law'' of supply and demand has limits. One can see that in the field of nursing, for example, where wages have not in fact risen to the degree necessary to respond to a shortage of qualified nurses. Likewise, in spite of a glut of lawyers that is observable in some areas, lawyers' fees have not shown signs of being lowered in substantial amounts. It seems that there are already many factors influencing wages above and beyond the ''free market.''

With comparable worth, different jobs can be compared

on a more objective basis, eliminating sex, race, and other
unfair criteria so that a more truly accurate evaluation is
applied to the value of a job. Not all ''women's'' jobs may
see an increase in pay, and some ''men's'' jobs that have
also been traditionally undervalued may see raises. As
mentioned earlier, the procedures for bringing about equity
in wages by comparing unlike jobs have long been in use and
are workable.

Comparable worth can be implemented in several ways.
In government, it can be achieved through legislation,
through union negotiations, or through executive policy
decision making. In the private sector, unions again can
effectively act to bring about pay equity. Management in the
private sector can also choose to implement comparable
worth for a number of reasons, among them the potential for
higher productivity by workers who have increased morale
based on full recognition of the value of the work they do.
Large corporations such as AT&T have already implemented
the policy of comparable worth and are pleased with the
results.

Barbara Bergmann, professor of economics at the
University of Maryland, points out, ''Nobody's pay need go
down. Nor will budgets or profits be wiped out'' (112).
Existing law prohibits lowering wages for the purpose of
achieving pay equity (BNA 116-19). When budgets allow it,
comparable worth is implemented along with and in addition
to regular salary increases. In areas of budget
constraints, comparable worth can still be brought about by

making adjustments in pay increases that have already been budgeted for. Although some individuals may be unhappy to see smaller than usual pay increases for a few years, it is not a permanent condition. Furthermore, it is moral and just to correct past inequities, especially when workers in all jobs ultimately benefit from the improved working conditions that can come about from higher morale, lower turnover, and better productivity.

A case in point is the city of Colorado Springs, Colorado. Comparable worth has been implemented for municipal workers in that city, and the mayor, a conservative male Republican, has answered criticism in just this fashion: ''We did something fair and just, and in return we got ourselves great employee morale, lower turnover, and higher productivity. Isn't that what the private sector is always looking for?'' (Picus).

It can be said that comparable worth is a promising and logical answer to the problem of the traditional undervaluing of jobs held predominantly by women. It is becoming policy across the country in both liberal and conservative enclaves. It is a valuable system worthy of bipartisan support. The time has come to take this step toward ending once and for all discrimination against women in the workplace.

Works Cited

Beck, Melinda, Gloria Borger, and Diane Weathers. ''Women's Work--And Wages.'' Newsweek 9 July 1984: 22-23.

Bergmann, Barbara R. ''Pay Equity--How to Argue Back.'' Ms. Nov 1985: 112.

The Bureau of National Affairs, Inc. The Comparable Worth Issue: A BNA Special Report. Washington: BNA Books, 1981.

Hackett, Clifford. ''Better from a Distance.'' Commonweal 31 May 1985: 336+.

Miller, Joyce D. Letter. New York Times 3 June 1982: A18.

''Montana's Comparable Worth Different Than Washington's.'' Bozeman Daily Chronicle 19 Aug 1986: 4.

''Pay Equity for Jobs Held by Women: How States and Cities Put It into Practice.'' Christian Science Monitor 19 June 1985: 4.

Pendleton, Clarence M., Jr. ''Comparable Worth Is Not Pay Equity: Loony Tunes and the Tooth Fairy.'' Vital Speeches of the Day 1 Apr 1985: 382-84.

Picus, Joy. ''Comparable Worth Concept Will Prevail.'' Editorial. Los Angeles Times 18 Sept 1985: sec. II:5.

Remick, Helen. Beyond Equal Pay for Equal Work: Comparable Worth in the State of Washington. Wellesley College, Center for Research on Women, Wellesley: May 1978.

Rosenberg, Jan. ''Judging on the Merits.'' Commonweal 31 May 1985: 337-40.

16

SPECIAL PROBLEMS WITH ETHICAL ARGUMENTS

The line between ethical arguments ("Is X morally good?") and other kinds of values disputes is often pretty thin. Many apparently straightforward practical values issues can turn out to have an ethical dimension to them. For example, in deciding what kind of car to buy, most people would base their judgments on criteria such as cost, reliability, safety, comfort, stylishness, and so forth. But some people might feel morally obligated to buy the most fuel-efficient car, or not to buy a car from a manufacturer whose investment or labor policies they found morally repugnant. Depending on how large a role ethical considerations played in the evaluation, we might choose to call this an ethical argument as opposed to a simpler kind of values argument. In any case, we here devote a separate chapter to ethical arguments because we believe they represent special difficulties to the student of argumentation. Let's take a look now at some of those special difficulties.

SPECIAL DIFFICULTIES OF ETHICAL ARGUMENTS
Uncertainty about the Role of "Purpose"

One crucial difficulty with ethical arguments concerns the role of "purpose" in defining criteria for judgment. In Chapter 14, we assumed that every class of beings has a purpose, that the purpose should be defined as narrowly as possible, and that the criteria for judgment derive directly from that purpose. For example, the purpose of a computer repairperson is to analyze the problem with my computer, to fix it, and to do so in a timely and cost-efficient manner. Once I formulate this purpose, it is easy for me to define criteria for a good computer repairperson.

In ethics, however, the place of purpose is much fuzzier. Just what is the purpose of human beings? Before I can begin to determine what ethical duties I have to myself and to others, I'm going to have to address this question; and because the chance of reaching agreement on that question remains remote, many ethical arguments are probably unresolvable. In ethical discussions we don't ask what a "manager" or a "judge" or a "point guard" is supposed to do in situations relevant to the respective classes; we're asking what John Doe is supposed to be or what Jane Doe is supposed to do with her life. Who they are or what their social function is makes no difference to our ethical assessment of their actions or traits of character. A morally bad person may be a good judge and a morally good person may be a bad manager.

The Problem of Warrants in Ethical Arguments

As the discussion so far has suggested, disagreements about ethical issues often stem from different systems of belief. We might call this problem the problem of warrants. That is, people disagree because they do not share common assumptions on which to ground their arguments.

If, for example, you say that good manners are necessary for keeping us from reverting to a state of raw nature, your implied warrant is that raw nature is bad. But if you say that good manners are a political tool by which a ruling class tries to suppress the natural vitality of the working class, then your warrant is that liberation of the working classes from the corrupt habits of the ruling class is good. It would be difficult, therefore, for people representing these opposing belief systems to carry on a reasonable discussion of etiquette — their whole assumptions about value, about the role of the natural self, and about political progress are different. This is why ethical arguments are often so acrimonious — they frequently lack shared warrants to serve as starting places for argument.

It is precisely because of the problem of warrants, however, that you should try to confront issues of ethics with rational deliberation. The arguments you produce may not persuade others to your view, but they should lay out more clearly the grounds and warrants of your own beliefs. Such arguments serve the purpose of clarification. By drafting essays on ethical issues, you begin to see more clearly what you believe and why you believe it. Although the arguments demanded by ethical issues require rigorous thought, they force us to articulate our most deeply held beliefs and our richest feelings.

AN OVERVIEW OF MAJOR ETHICAL SYSTEMS

When faced with an ethical issue, such as the issue of whether terrorism can be justified, we must move from arguments of good or bad to arguments of right or wrong. The terms *right* and *wrong* are clearly different from the terms *good* and *bad* when the latter terms mean simply "effective" (meets purposes of class, as in "This is a good stereo system") or "ineffective" (fails to meet purposes of class, as in "This is a bad cookbook"). But "right" and "wrong" often also differ from what seems to be a moral use of the terms *good* and *bad*. We might say, for example, that warm sunshine is good in that it brings pleasure and that cancer is bad in that it brings pain and death, but that is not quite the same thing as saying that sunshine is "right" and cancer is "wrong." It is the problem of "right" and "wrong" that ethical arguments confront.

Thus it is not enough to say that terrorism is "bad"; obviously everyone, including most terrorists, would agree that terrorism is "bad" in that it causes suffering and anguish. If we want to condemn terrorism on ethical grounds, we have to say that it's also "wrong" as well as "bad." In saying that something's wrong, we're saying that all people ought to refrain from doing it. We're also saying that acts that are morally "wrong" are in some way blameworthy and deserve censure, a conclusion that doesn't necessarily follow a negative nonethical judgment, which might lead simply to our not buying something or not hiring someone. From a nonethical standpoint, you may even say that someone like Abu Nidal is a "good" terrorist in that he fully realizes the purposes of the class "terrorist": He causes great damage with a minimum of resources, brings a good deal of attention to his cause, and doesn't (as of this writing) get caught. The ethical question here, however, is not whether or not Nidal is a good member of the class, but whether it is wrong for such a class to exist.

In asking the question "Ought the class 'terrorist' exist?" or, to put it more colloquially, "Are there ever cases where terrorism is justified?" we need to seek some consistent approach or principle. In the phrase used by some philosophers, ethical judgments are typically "universalizable" statements. That is, when we oppose a terrorist act, our ethical argument (assuming it's a coherent one) should be capable of being generalized into an ethical principle that will hold for all similar cases. Ethical disputes usually involve clashes between such principles. For example, a pro-terrorist might say, "My ends justify my means," whereas an antiterrorist might say, "The sanctity of human life is not to be violated for any reason." The differences in principles such as these account for different schools of ethical thought.

There are many different schools of ethical thought—too many to present in this chapter. But to help you think your way through ethical issues, we'll look at some of the most prevalent methods of resolving ethical questions. The first of these methods, "naive egoism," is really less a method than a retreat from method. It doesn't represent a coherent ethical view, but it is a position that many people lapse into on given issues. It represents, in short, the most seductive alternative to rigorous ethical thought.

Naive Egoism

Back in Chapter 1, we touched on the morality of the Sophists and suggested that their underlying maxim was something like "might makes right." That is, in ethical terms, they were essentially egoists who used other people with impunity to realize their own ends. The appeal of this position, however repugnant it may sound when laid out like this, is enormous. It is a rationalization for self-promotion and pleasure seeking. We are all prone to sink into it occasionally. In recent years, people have gotten rich by rationalizing this position into an "enlightened egoism" and by arguing, in numerous best-selling books with words like *Number One* or *Self* in the titles, that if we all follow the bidding of our egos, we'll be happy.

On closer examination, this philosophy proves to be incoherent, incapable of consistent application. Not many philosophers take it seriously, however persistently it returns with new sets of disciples. It should be noted, however, that philosophers don't reject naive egoism simply because they believe "selfishness is bad." Rather, philosophers tend to assess ethical systems according to such factors as their scope (how often will principles derived from a system provide a guide for our moral action?) and their precision (how clearly can we analyze a given situation using the tools of the system?) rather than their intuition about whether the system is right or wrong.

Although naive egoism has great scope (you can always ask "What's in it for me?"), it is far from precise, as we'll try to show. Take the case of young Ollie Unger, who has decided that he wants to quit living irrationally and to join some official school of ethical thought. The most appealing school at the moment—recommended to him by a philosophy major over at the Phi Upsilon Nu house—is the "I'm Number One!" school of scruples. He heads downtown to their opulent headquarters and meets with the school's guru, one Dr. Pheelgood.

"What's involved in becoming a member of your school?" Ollie inquires.

"Ahhh, my apple-cheeked chum, that's the beauty of it. It's so simple.

You just give me all your worldly possessions and do whatever I tell you to do."

Ollie's puzzled. He had in mind something a bit more, well, gratifying. He was hoping for something closer to the Playboy philosophy of eat, drink, and make merry—all justified through rational thought.

"You seem disappointed," Pheelgood observes. "What's the matter?"

"Well, gee, it just doesn't sound like I'm going to be number one here. I thought that was the idea. To look out for numero uno."

"Of course not, silly boy. This is after all the 'I'm Number One School of Scruples.' And I, *moi*, am the I who's Number One. There can be only one Number One, of course, and since I founded the school, I'm it."

"But I thought the idea of your school was for everyone to have the maximum amount of enjoyment in life."

Peevishness clouds Pheelgood's face. "Look here, Unger, if I arrange things for you to have a good time, my day has to dim. The demand that I curb my own pleasure for the sake of your own, well that's simply subversive, undermines the very foundation of this philosophy. Next you'll be asking me to open soup kitchens and retread the downtrodden. If I'm to look out for Number One, then you've got to act entirely differently from me. I take, you give. Capiche? If you want to be Number One, then you go somewhere else. After paying me to teach you how to do it, of course."

With that, we'll stop the dialogue. As should be obvious by now, it's very difficult to systematize egoism. You have two sets of demands in constant conflict—the demands of your own personal ego and those of everyone else's. It's impossible, hence, to universalize a statement that all members of the school could hold equally without contradicting all other members of the school. Thus, for example, if I write a book saying that it's okay to rip people off to satisfy their own desires, I am authorizing others to steal my book and prevent me from realizing my own desires for profit. In the end, the philosophy is not only contradictory, but also not very efficient at delivering the desired end product—personal gratification.

That's not to say, of course, that people can't or don't act on the principle of me-firstism. It's just to say that it's impossible to systematize it without returning us to what philosopher Thomas Hobbes called the condition of nature, wherein life is "nasty, brutish, and short." The immediate practical problem of any survival-of-the-fittest school of morals is that it benefits a few (the fittest of the fit) at the expense of the many. Some egoists try to get around this problem by conceding that we must limit our self-gratification either by entering into contracts or institutional arrangements with others or by sacrificing short-term interests for long-term ones. We might, for example, give to the poor now in order to avoid a revolution of the masses later. But once they've let the camel's nose of concern for others into the tent, it's tough to hang onto egoistic philosophy. Having considered naive egoism, let's turn to a pair of more workable alternatives.

Consequences or Principles as the Grounds of Ethics

In shifting to the two most common forms of ethical thought, we shift point of view from "I" to "us." Both groups, those who make ethical judgments according to the consequences of any act and those who make ethical judgments according to the conformity of any act with a principle, are guided by their concern for the whole of humanity rather than simply the self.

AN APPROACH THROUGH CONSEQUENCES

Perhaps the best-known example of evaluating acts according to their ethical consequences is John Stuart Mill's Utilitarianism. The goal of Utilitarianism, according to Mill, is "the greatest good for the greatest number." It is a very down-to-earth philosophy that grew out of nineteenth-century British philosophers' concern to demystify ethics and to make it work in the practical world.

As Mill makes clear, a focus on ethical consequences allows you readily to assess a wide range of acts. You can apply the principle of utility—which says that an action is morally right if it produces a greater net value (benefits minus costs) than any available alternative action—to virtually any situation and it will help you reach a decision. Obviously, however, it's not always easy to make the calculations called for by the principle, since, like any prediction of the future, an estimate of consequences is conjectural. In particular, it's often very hard to assess the long-term consequences of any action. Too often, Utilitarianism seduces us into a short-term analysis of a moral problem simply because long-term consequences are very difficult to predict.

AN APPROACH THROUGH PRINCIPLES

Any ethical system based on principles will ultimately rest on one or two moral tenets that we are duty-bound to uphold, no matter what the consequences. Sometimes the moral tenets come from religious faith—for example, the Ten Commandments. At other times, however, the principles are derived from philosophical reasoning, as in the case of German philosopher Immanual Kant. Kant held that no one should ever use another person as a means to his own ends and that everyone should always act as if his acts were the basis of universal law. In other words, Kant held that we were duty-bound to respect other people's sanctity and to act in the same way that we would want all other people to act. The great advantage of such a system is its clarity and precision. We are never overwhelmed by a multiplicity of contradictory and difficult-to-quantify consequences; we simply make sure we are not violating a principle of our ethical system and proceed accordingly.

THE TWO SYSTEMS COMPARED

In the eyes of many people, a major advantage of a system such as Utilitarianism is that it impels us to seek out the best solution, whereas systems based on principle merely enjoin us not to violate a principle by our action. In turn, applying an ethical principle will not always help us resolve necessarily relativistic moral dilemmas. For instance, what if none of our available choices violates our moral principles? How do we choose among a host of permissible acts? Or what about situations where none of the alternatives is permitted by our principles. How might we choose the least bad alternative?

To further our comparison of the two systems, let's ask what a Mill or a Kant might say about the previously mentioned issue of terrorism. Here the Kantian position is clear: To kill another person to realize your own ends is palpably evil and forbidden.

But a follower of Mill will face a less clear choice. A Utilitarian could not automatically rule out terrorism or any other means so long as it led ultimately to the greatest good for the greatest number. If a nation is being slowly starved by those around it, if its people are dying, its institutions crumbling and its future disappearing, who's to say that the aggrieved nation is not justified in taking a few hundred lives to improve the lot of hundreds of thousands? The Utilitarian's first concern is to determine if terrorism will most effectively bring about that end. So long as the desired end represents the best possible net value and the means are effective at bringing about that end, the Utilitarian can, in theory anyway, justify almost any action.

Given the shared cultural background and values of most of us, not to mention our own vulnerability to terrorism, the Kantian argument is probably very appealing here. Indeed, Kantian ethical arguments have overwhelming appeal for us when the principle being invoked is already widely held within our culture, and when the violation of that principle will have clear and immediate negative consequences for us. But in a culture that doesn't share that principle and for whom the consequences of violation are positive rather than negative, the argument will undoubtedly appear weaker, a piece of fuzzy-headed idealism.

FOR CLASS DISCUSSION

Working as individuals or in small groups:

1. Try to formulate a Utilitarian argument to persuade terrorist leaders in a country such as Libya to stop terrorist action.
2. Try to formulate an ethical principle or rule that would permit terrorism.

Some Compromise Positions Between Consequences and Principles

In the end, most of us would not be entirely happy with an ethic that forced us to ignore either principles or consequences. We all have certain principles that we simply can't violate no matter what the consequences. Thus, for example, some of us would not have dropped the bomb on Hiroshima even if it did mean saving many lives ultimately. And certainly, too, most of us will compromise our principles in certain situations if we think the consequences justify it. For instance, how many of us would not deceive, harm, or even torture a kidnapper to save the life of a stolen child? Indeed, over the years, compromise positions have developed on both sides to accommodate precisely these concerns.

Some "consequentialists" have acknowledged the usefulness of general rules for creating more human happiness over the long run. To go back to our terrorism example, a consequentialist might oppose terrorist action on the grounds that "Thou shalt not kill another person in the name of greater material happiness for the group." This acknowledgment of an inviolable principle will still be based on a concern for consequences — for instance, a fear that terrorist acts may lead to World War III — but having such a principle allows the consequentialist to get away from a case-by-case analysis of acts and to keep more clearly before himself the long-range consequences of acts.

Among latter-day ethics of principle, meanwhile, the distinction between absolute obligation and what philosophers call *prima facie* obligation has been developed to take account of the force of circumstances. An absolute obligation would be an obligation to follow a principle at all times, no matter what. A *prima facie* obligation, on the other hand, is an obligation to do something "other things being equal," that is, in a normal situation. Hence, to use a classic moral example, you would not, other things being equal, cannibalize an acquaintance. But if there are three of you in a lifeboat, one is dying and the other two will surely die if they don't get food, your *prima facie* obligation not to eat another might be waived. (However, the Royal Commission, which heard the original case, took a more Kantian position and condemned the action of the seamen who cannibalized their mate.)

These, then, in greatly condensed form, are the major alternative ways of thinking about ethical arguments. Let's now briefly summarize the ways you can use your knowledge of ethical thought to develop your arguments and refute those of others.

DEVELOPING AN ETHICAL ARGUMENT

To help you see how familiarity with these systems of ethical thought can help you develop an ethical argument, let's take an example case. How, for example, might we go about developing an argument in favor of abolishing the death penalty?

Our first task is to examine the issue from the two points of view just discussed. How might a Utilitarian or a Kantian argue that the death penalty should be abolished? The argument on principle, as is usually the case, would appear to be the simpler of the two. Taking another life is difficult to justify under most ethical principles. For Kant, the sanctity of human life is a central tenet of ethics. Under Judeo-Christian ethics, meanwhile, one is told that "Vengeance is Mine, saith the Lord" and "Thou shalt not kill."

But, unfortunately for our hopes of simplicity, Kant argued in favor of capital punishment:

> There is no sameness of kind between death and remaining alive even under the most miserable conditions, and consequently there is no equality between the crime and the retribution unless the criminal is judicially condemned and put to death.*

Kant is here invoking an important principle of justice—that punishments should be proportionate to the crime. Kant appears to be saying that this principle must take precedence over his notion of the supreme worth of the individual. Some philosophers think he was being inconsistent in taking this position. Certainly, in establishing your own position, you could support a case against capital punishment based on Kant's principles, even if Kant himself did not reach the same conclusion. But you'd have to establish for your reader why you are at odds with Kant in this case. Kant's apparent inconsistency here illustrates how powerfully our intuitive judgments can affect our ethical judgment.

Likewise, with the Judeo-Christian position, passages can be found in the Bible that would support capital punishment, notably, the Old Testament injunction to take "an eye for an eye and a tooth for a tooth." The latter principle is simply a more poetic version of "let the punishment fit the crime." Retribution should be of the same kind as the crime. And the commandment "Thou shalt not kill" is often interpreted as "Thou shalt not commit murder," an interpretation that not only permits just wars or killing in self-defense but is also consistent with other places in the Bible that

---

*From Immanuel Kant, *The Metaphysical Elements of Justice.*

suggest that people have not only the right but the obligation to punish wrongdoers and not leave their fate to God.

So, there appears to be no clearcut argument in support of abolishing capital punishment on the basis of principle. What about an argument based on consequences? How might abolishing capital punishment result in a net good that is at least as great as allowing it?

A number of possibilities suggest themselves. First, in abolishing capital punishment, we rid ourselves of the possibility that someone may be wrongly executed. To buttress this argument, we might want to search for evidence of how many people have been wrongly convicted of or executed for a capital crime. In making arguments based on consequence we must, whenever possible, offer empirical evidence that the consequences we assert exist—and exist to the degree we've suggested.

There are also other possible consequences that a Utilitarian might mention in defending the abolition of capital punishment. These include leaving open the possibility that the person being punished will be reformed, keeping those charged with executing the murderer free from guilt, putting an end to the costly legal and political process of appealing the conviction, and so forth.

But in addition to calculating benefits, you will need also to calculate the costs of abolishing the death penalty and to show that the net result favors abolition. Failure to mention such costs is a serious weakness in many arguments of consequence. Moreover, in the issue at hand, the consequences that favor capital punishment—deterrence of further capital crimes, cost of imprisoning murderers, and so forth—are well known to most members of your audience.

In our discussion of capital punishment, then, we employed two alternative ways of thinking about ethical issues. In pursuing an argument from principle, we looked for an appropriate rule that permitted or at least did not prohibit our position. In pursuing an argument from consequence, we moved from what's permissible to what brings about the most desirable consequences. Most ethical issues, argued thoroughly, should be approached from both perspectives, so long as irreconcilable differences don't present themselves.

Should you choose to adopt one of these perspectives to the exclusion of the other, you will find yourself facing many of the problems mentioned above. This is not to say that you can't ever go to the wall for a principle or focus solely on consequences to the exclusion of principles; it's simply that you will be hard-pressed to convince those of your audience who happen to be of the other persuasion and demand different sorts of proof. For the purpose of developing arguments, we encourage you to consider both the relevant principles and the possible consequences when you evaluate ethical actions.

TESTING ETHICAL ARGUMENTS

Perhaps the first question you should ask in setting out to analyze your draft of an ethical argument is, "To what extent is the argument based on consequences or on ethical principles?" If it's based exclusively on one of these two forms of ethical thought, then it's vulnerable to the sorts of criticism discussed above. A strictly principled argument that takes no account of the consequences of its position is vulnerable to a simple cost analysis. What are the costs in the case of adhering to this principle? There will undoubtedly be some, or else there would be no real argument. If the argument is based strictly on consequentialist grounds, we should ask if the position violates any rules or principles, particularly such commandments as the Golden Rule—"Do unto others as you would have others do unto you"—which most members of our audience adhere to. By failing to mention these alternative ways of thinking about ethical issues, we undercut not only our argument but our credibility as well.

Let's now consider a more developed examination of the two positions, starting with some of the more subtle weaknesses in a position based on principle. In practice people will sometimes take rigidly "principled" positions because they live in fear of "slippery slopes"; that is, they fear setting precedents that might lead to ever more dire consequences. Consider, for example, the slippery slope leading from birth control to euthanasia if you have an absolutist commitment to the sanctity of human life. Once we allow birth control in the form of condoms or pills, the principled absolutist would say, then we will be forced to accept birth control "abortions" in the first hours after conception (IUDs, "morning after" pills), then abortions in the first trimester, then in the second or even the third trimester. And once we have violated the sanctity of human life by allowing abortions, it is only a short step to euthanasia and finally to killing off all undesirables.

One way to refute a slippery-slope argument of this sort is to try to dig a foothold into the side of the hill to show that you don't necessarily have to slide all the way to the bottom. You would thus have to argue that allowing birth control does not mean allowing abortions (by arguing for differences between a fetus after conception and sperm and egg before conception), or that allowing abortions does not mean allowing euthanasia (by arguing for differences between a fetus and a person already living in the world).

Consequentialist arguments have different kinds of difficulties. As discussed before, the crucial difficulty facing anyone making a consequentialist argument is to calculate the consequences in a clear and reliable way. Have you considered all significant consequences? If you project your scenario of consequences further into the future (remember, consequentialist arguments are frequently stronger over the short term than over the long term, where many unforeseen consequences can occur), can you identify possibilities that work against the argument?

As also noted above, consequentialist arguments carry a heavy burden of empirical proof. What evidence can you offer that the predicted consequences will in fact come to pass? Do you offer any evidence that alternative consequences won't occur? And just how do you prove that the consequences of any given action are a net good or evil?

In addition to the problems unique to each of the two positions, ethical arguments are vulnerable to the more general sorts of criticism, including consistency, recency, and relevance of evidence. Obviously, however, consequentialist arguments will be more vulnerable to weaknesses in evidence, whereas arguments based on principle are more open to questions about consistency of application.

FOR CLASS DISCUSSION

1. Prior to beginning this exercise, read the following short story by Ursula Le Guin. Then, working individually or in small groups, prepare answers to the following questions:
   a. How would someone such as Mill evaluate the actions of those who walk away?
   b. How would someone such as Kant evaluate the same action?
   c. If you are working in groups, try to reach a group consensus on how the action should be evaluated. Recorders for the group should explain how your group's evaluation differs from a Utilitarian or a Kantian approach.
2. Read "The Case for Torture" (pages 404–406) by philosopher Michael Levin. Levin creates an argument that torture not only can be justified but is positively mandated under certain circumstances. Analyze Levin's argument in terms of our distinction between arguments from principle and arguments from consequence.
3. In "The Case for Torture," Levin mentions the possibility of some "murkier" cases in which it is difficult to draw a line demarcating the legitimate use of torture. Try to come up with several examples of these "murkier" cases and explain what makes them murky.

THE ONES WHO WALK AWAY FROM OMELAS (VARIATIONS ON A THEME BY WILLIAM JAMES)

Ursula Le Guin

With a clamor of bells that set the swallows soaring, the Festival of Summer   1
came to the city Omelas, bright-towered by the sea. The rigging of the boats

Source: Ursula Le Guin, "The Ones Who Walk Away from Omelas," *The Wind's 12 Quarters* (New York: Harper & Row, 1975).

in harbor sparkled with flags. In the streets between houses with red roofs and painted walls, between old moss-grown gardens and under avenues of trees, past great parks and public buildings, processions moved. Some were decorous: old people in long stiff robes of mauve and grey, grave master workmen, quiet, merry women carrying their babies, and chatting as they walked. In other streets the music beat faster, a shimmering of gong and tambourine, and the people went dancing, the procession was a dance. Children dodged in and out, their high calls rising like the swallows' crossing flights over the music and the singing. All the processions wound towards the north side of the city, where on the great water-meadow called the Green Fields boys and girls, naked in the bright air, with mud-stained feet and ankles and long, lithe arms, exercised their restive horses before the race. The horses wore no gear at all but a halter without bit. Their manes were braided with streamers of silver, gold, and green. They flared their nostrils and pranced and boasted to one another; they were vastly excited, the horse being the only animal who has adopted our ceremonies as his own. Far off to the north and west the mountains stood up half encircling Omelas on her bay. The air of morning was so clear that the snow still crowning the Eighteen Peaks burned with white-gold fire across the miles of sunlit air, under the dark blue of the sky. There was just enough wind to make the banners that marked the racecourse snap and flutter now and then. In the silence of the broad green meadows one could hear the music winding through the city streets, farther and nearer and ever approaching, a cheerful faint sweetness of the air that from time to time trembled and gathered together and broke out into the great joyous clanging of the bells.

Joyous! How is one to tell about joy? How describe the citizens of Omelas? 2

They were not simple folk, you see, though they were happy. But we do 3 not say the words of cheer much any more. All smiles have become archaic. Given a description such as this one tends to make certain assumptions. Given a description such as this one tends to look next for the King, mounted on a splendid stallion and surrounded by his noble knights, or perhaps in a golden litter borne by great-muscled slaves. But there was no king. They did not use swords, or keep slaves. They were not barbarians. I do not know the rules and laws of their society, but I suspect that they were singularly few. As they did without monarchy and slavery, so they also get on without the stock exchange, the advertisement, the secret police, and the bomb. Yet I repeat that these were not simple folk, not dulcet shepherds, noble savages, bland utopians. They were not less complex than us. The trouble is that we have a bad habit, encouraged by pedants and sophisticates, of considering happiness as something rather stupid. Only pain is intellectual, only evil interesting. This is the treason of the artist: a refusal to admit the banality of evil and the terrible boredom of pain. If you can't lick 'em, join 'em. If it hurts, repeat it. But to praise despair is to condemn delight, to embrace violence is to lose hold of everything else. We have almost lost hold; we can no longer describe a happy man, nor make any celebration of joy. How can I tell you about the people of Omelas? They were not naïve and happy children — though their children were, in fact, happy. They were mature, intelligent, passionate adults whose lives were not wretched. O miracle! but I wish I could describe it better. I wish I could convince you. Omelas sounds in my words like a city in a fairy tale, long ago and far away, once upon a time. Perhaps it would be best if you imagined it as your own fancy bids, assuming it will rise to the occasion, for certainly I cannot suit you all. For instance, how about technology? I think that there would be no cars or helicopters in and above the streets; this follows from the fact that the people of Omelas are happy people. Happiness is based on a just discrimination of what is necessary, what is neither necessary nor destructive, and what is destructive. In the middle category, however — that of the unnecessary but undestructive, that of comfort, luxury, exuberance, etc. — they could perfectly well have central heating, subway trains, washing machines, and all kinds of marvelous devices not yet invented here, floating light-sources, fuelless power, a cure for the common cold. Or they could have none of that: it doesn't matter. As you like it. I incline to think that people from towns up and down the coast have been coming in to Omelas during the last days before the Festival on very fast little trains and double-decked trams, and that the train station of Omelas is actually the handsomest building in town, though plainer than the magnificent Farmers' Market. But even granted trains, I fear that Omelas so far strikes some of you as goody-goody. Smiles, bells, parades, horses, bleh. If so, please add an orgy. If an orgy would help, don't hesitate. Let us not, however, have temples from which issue beautiful nude priests and priestesses already half in ecstasy and ready to copulate with any man or woman, lover or stranger, who desires union with the deep godhead of the blood, although that was my first idea. But really it would be better not to have any temples in Omelas — at least, not manned temples. Religion yes, clergy no. Surely the beautiful nudes can just wander about, offering themselves like divine soufflés to the hunger of the needy and the rapture of the flesh. Let them join the processions. Let tambourines be struck above the copulations, and the glory of desire be proclaimed upon the gongs, and (a not unimportant point) let the offspring of these delightful rituals be beloved and looked after by all. One thing I know there is none of in Omelas is guilt. But what else should there be? I thought at first there were no drugs, but that is puritanical. For those who like it, the faint insistent sweetness of *drooz* may perfume the ways of the city, *drooz* which first brings a great lightness and brilliance to the mind and limbs, and then after some hours a dreamy languor, and wonderful visions at last of the very arcana and inmost secrets of the Universe, as well as exciting the pleasure of sex beyond all belief; and it is not habit-forming. For more modest tastes I think there ought to be beer. What else, what else belongs in the joyous city? The sense of victory, surely, the celebration of courage. But as we did without clergy, let us do without soldiers. The joy built upon successful slaughter is not the right kind of joy; it will not do; it is fearful and it is trivial. A boundless and generous contentment, a magnanimous triumph felt not against some outer enemy but in communion with the finest and fairest in the souls of all men everywhere and the splendor of the world's summer: this is what swells the hearts of the people of Omelas, and the victory they celebrate is that of life. I really don't think many of them need to take *drooz.*

Most of the processions have reached the Green Fields by now. A marvel- **4**
ous smell of cooking goes forth from the red and blue tents of the provi-
sioners. The faces of small children are amiably sticky; in the benign grey
beard of a man a couple of crumbs of rich pastry are entangled. The youths
and girls have mounted their horses and are beginning to group around the
starting line of the course. An old woman, small, fat, and laughing, is passing
out flowers from a basket, and tall young men wear her flowers in their
shining hair. A child of nine or ten sits at the edge of the crowd alone, playing
on a wooden flute. People pause to listen, and they smile, but they do not
speak to him, for he never ceases playing and never sees them, his dark eyes
wholly rapt in the sweet, thin magic of the tune.

He finishes, and slowly lowers his hands holding the wooden flute. **5**

As if that little private silence were the signal, all at once a trumpet sounds **6**
from the pavilion near the starting line: imperious, melancholy, piercing. The
horses rear on their slender legs, and some of them neigh in answer. Sober-
faced, the young riders stroke the horses' necks and soothe them, whisper-
ing, "Quiet, quiet, there my beauty, my hope. . . . " They begin to form in
rank along the starting line. The crowds along the racecourse are like a field
of grass and flowers in the wind. The Festival of Summer has begun.

Do you believe? Do you accept the festival, the city, the joy? No? Then let **7**
me describe one more thing.

In a basement under one of the beautiful public buildings of Omelas, or **8**
perhaps in the cellar of one of its spacious private homes, there is a room. It
has one locked door, and no window. A little light seeps in dustily between
cracks in the boards, secondhand from a cobwebbed window somewhere
across the cellar. In one corner of the little room a couple of mops, with stiff,
clotted, foul-smelling heads, stand near a rusty bucket. The floor is dirt, a
little damp to the touch, as cellar dirt usually is. The room is about three
paces long and two wide: a mere broom closet or disused tool room. In the
room a child is sitting. It could be a boy or a girl. It looks about six, but
actually is nearly ten. It is feeble-minded. Perhaps it was born defective, or
perhaps it has become imbecile through fear, malnutrition, and neglect. It
picks its nose and occasionally fumbles vaguely with its toes or genitals, as it
sits hunched in the corner farthest from the bucket and the two mops. It is

afraid of the mops. It finds them horrible. It shuts its eyes, but it knows the mops are still standing there; and the door is locked; and nobody will come. The door is always locked; and nobody ever comes, except that sometimes — the child has no understanding of time or interval — sometimes the door rattles terribly and opens, and a person, or several people, are there. One of them may come in and kick the child to make it stand up. The others never come close, but peer in at it with frightened, disgusted eyes. The food bowl and the water jug are hastily filled, the door is locked, the eyes disappear. The people at the door never say anything, but the child, who has not always lived in the tool room, and can remember sunlight and its mother's voice, some-times speaks. "I will be good," it says. "Please let me out. I will be good!" They never answer. The child used to scream for help at night, and cry a good deal, but now it only makes a kind of whining, "eh-haa, eh-haa," and it speaks less and less often. It is so thin there are no calves to its legs; its belly protrudes; it lives on a half-bowl of corn meal and grease a day. It is naked. Its buttocks and thighs are a mass of festered sores, as it sits in its own excrement continually.

They all know it is there, all the people of Omelas. Some of them have **9** come to see it, others are content merely to know it is there. They all know that it has to be there. Some of them understand why, and some do not, but they all understand that their happiness, the beauty of their city, the tender-ness of their friendships, the health of their children, the wisdom of their scholars, the skill of their makers, even the abundance of their harvest and the kindly weathers of their skies, depends wholly on this child's abominable misery.

This is usually explained to children when they are between eight and **10** twelve, whenever they seem capable of understanding; and most of those who come to see the child are young people, though often enough an adult comes, or comes back, to see the child. No matter how well the matter has been explained to them, these young spectators are always shocked and sickened at the sight. They feel disgust, which they had thought themselves superior to. They feel anger, outrage, impotence, despite all the explanations. They would like to do something for the child. But there is nothing they can do. If the child were brought up into the sunlight out of that vile place, if it were cleaned and fed and comforted, that would be a good thing, indeed; but if it were done, in that day and hour all the prosperity and beauty and delight of Omelas would wither and be destroyed. Those are the terms. To exchange all the goodness and grace of every life in Omelas for that single, small improve-ment: to throw away the happiness of thousands for the chance of the happiness of one: that would be to let guilt within the walls indeed.

The terms are strict and absolute; there may not even be a kind word **11** spoken to the child.

Often the young people go home in tears, or in a tearless rage, when they **12** have seen the child and faced this terrible paradox. They may brood over it for weeks or years. But as time goes on they begin to realize that even if the child could be released, it would not get much good of its freedom: a little vague pleasure of warmth and food, no doubt, but little more. It is too degraded and imbecile to know any real joy. It has been afraid too long even to be free of fear. Its habits are too uncouth for it to respond to humane treatment. Indeed, after so long it would probably be wretched without walls about it to protect it, and darkness for its eyes, and its own excrement to sit in. Their tears at the bitter injustice dry when they begin to perceive the terrible justice of reality, and to accept it. Yet it is their tears and anger, the trying of their generosity and the acceptance of their helplessness, which are perhaps the true source of the splendor of their lives. Theirs is no vapid, irresponsible happiness. They know that they, like the child, are not free. They know compassion. It is the existence of the child, and their knowledge of its existence, that makes possible the nobility of their architecture, and poignancy of their music, the profundity of their science. It is because of the child that they are so gentle with children. They know that if the wretched one were not there snivelling in the dark, the other one, the flute-player, could make no joyful music as the young riders line up in their beauty for the race in the sunlight of the first morning of summer.

Now do you believe in them? Are they not more credible? But there is one more thing to tell, and this is quite incredible. 13

At times one of the adolescent girls or boys who go to see the child does not go home to weep or rage, does not, in fact, go home at all. Sometimes also a man or woman much older falls silent for a day or two, and then leaves home. These people go out into the street, and walk down the street alone. They keep walking, and walk straight out of the city of Omelas, through the beautiful gates. They keep walking across the farmlands of Omelas. Each one goes alone, youth or girl, man or woman. Night falls; the traveler must pass down village streets, between the houses with yellow-lit windows, and on out into the darkness of the fields. Each alone, they go west or north, towards the mountains. They go on. They leave Omelas, they walk ahead into the darkness, and they do not come back. The place they go towards is a place even less imaginable to most of us than the city of happiness. I cannot describe it at all. It is possible that it does not exist. But they seem to know where they are going, the ones who walk away from Omelas. 14

V

WRITING FROM SOURCES: THE ARGUMENT AS A FORMAL RESEARCH PAPER

17

UNLOCKING THE LIBRARY: STRATEGIES FOR FINDING AND SELECTING SOURCES

Although the "research paper" is a common writing assignment in college, students are often baffled by their professor's expectations when they are given a research paper assignment. The problem is that students often think of research writing as presenting information rather than as creating an argument. One of our business school colleagues calls these sorts of research papers "data dumps." "You ask students to write a research paper on the American banking system," he will tell you, "and they fill you up a truck load of information on banking and unload it on your desk. 'There's your fresh load of info, Prof; you make sense out of it.'"

But a research paper shouldn't be a data dump. Like any other essay, it should use its data to support a thesis. Consider the following excerpt from an article in *Family Circle*, a typical supermarket magazine for the home consumer:

> Despite the enormous expansion of the female labor force in recent years (the number of working women has doubled since 1960), there has been little improvement in women's economic position. In 1939 American women earned 63 cents to a man's dollar. Today, they earn 64 cents to a man's dollar. In 1984 the median income of women who worked full time, year-round was $14,479, while similarly employed men earned $23,218. A woman with four years of college still earns less than a male high school dropout.*

*From Sylvia Ann Hewlett, "How Our Laws Hurt Working Mothers and Their Families," *Family Circle*, October 21, 1986, p. 54.

This essay has many features of a good research paper. Note that it has a clear thesis (". . . there has been little improvement in women's economic position"). Note also that the author's supporting data come from research, that is, from external sources rather than personal experience—data she has found by reading books, journals, newspapers, statistics, and so forth.

However, there is one major difference between this essay and a formal academic research paper. In this essay, we can't check her data. Because the essay has no citations and no list of works cited, we can't tell where she got her information; we have no way of verifying her figures, of deciding about the reliability of her sources. The purpose of citations and a bibliography in an academic research paper is to enable readers to follow the trail of the author's research. Perhaps the writer has misquoted somebody, has taken information out of context or from a biased source, has fallen victim to some of the statistical traps we discuss in Appendix 2, and so forth. If a research essay is properly "documented" (accurate use of citations placed in correct form), it is possible to locate all the sources and verify the author's data. The proper formats for citations and bibliography entries are simply conventions within an academic discipline to facilitate the reader's retrieval of the original sources. These conventions, like other jargon shared by people with special interests, permit rapid communication among those familiar with the discipline.

Thus, you will find that writing an argument as a formal research paper draws on the same argumentation skills you have been using all along. What distinguishes a formal research argument from less formal arguments is more extensive use of research data to support the writer's argument and special care in documenting sources properly. In this chapter and the next, we look at the special skills you will need to use sources effectively.

FORMULATING A RESEARCH QUESTION

The best way to avoid writing a data dump essay is to begin with a good research question—the formulation of a problem or issue that your essay will address. The research question, usually in the form of an issue question, will give you a guiding purpose in doing your library research. If you begin only with a general topic—say, the American banking system—all you can do is look at books and articles on banks, dozens and dozens of them perhaps. But to what purpose? What are you looking for?

If, on the other hand, you come to the library with a clearly formulated issue question, then you know what you are looking for in your research. For example, you might formulate specific issue questions on the American banking system such as these: "Will the elimination of tax deductions for consumer loans substantially reduce demand for car loans from banks?" Or "Will the elimination of tax deductions for consumer loans benefit banks?"

Searching for a Research Question: Exploring Your Interests

The sooner you can settle on a research question, the easier it will be for you to find the source materials you need in a time-saving, efficient manner. The exploration methods we suggested in Chapter 3, particularly in Idea-Log 1, can help you find a research topic that interests you.

A good way to begin an exploration is to freewrite for ten minutes or so, reflecting on recent readings that have stimulated your interest, on recent events that have sparked arguments, or on personal experiences that might open up onto public issues. If you have no idea for a topic, try starting with the trigger question "What possible topics am I interested in?" If you already have an idea for a topic area, explore why you are interested in it. Search for the personal connections or the particular angles that most intrigue you. Here is how Lynnea, a student writer, began exploring a topic related to police work. She chose this topic because she had a friend who was a patrol officer.

LYNNEA'S FIRST FREEWRITE

Why am I attracted to this issue? What personal connections do I have?

My friend is a police officer and has been telling me about some of the experiences he has had while walking "the beat" downtown. The people he has to deal with are mostly street-people: bums, gang members, drug dealers, etc. He tells me how he just harasses them to get them to move on and to leave the area, or he looks for a reason to give them a ticket so that eventually they will accumulate a few unpaid tickets, and they will have to go to jail. My friend told me about an experience where an alcoholic tramp started banging his bags against the patrol car after he and his partner had walked about a block away to begin their night shift. The bum started yelling at them to come back and kept hitting and throwing himself against the car. "OK, what are you doing that for?" they asked. The bum stammered that he wanted to go to "detox." They told the tramp that they would not take him to detox, and so he kept on banging the car. What can be done about these people? Not only the alcoholics and bums, but what about the gang members, prostitutes, drug dealers, etc.? The police forces out on the streets at night seem to be doing little more than just ruffling a few feathers, but what else can they do under the circumstances?

Upon finishing this freewrite, Lynnea was certain she wanted to write her research argument on something related to police work. The topic interested her, and having a patrol officer as a friend gave her an opportunity for interview data. She decided she was most interested in gangs and called her friend to get some more insights. Several days later, she met her friend at a local restaurant during his lunch break. After that meeting, she again did a freewrite.

LYNNEA'S SECOND FREEWRITE

Today I went with my friend for a cup of coffee to discuss some possible topics for my paper. He took me to a coffee shop where several of the officers in the area meet for lunch. I had wanted to ask Bob specific questions about gangs in the area, but when we joined the rest of the officers, I didn't have the chance. However, something they brought into the discussion *did* interest me. They were talking about a woman who had recently graduated from the academy and was now trying to pass the student officer's phase. This woman, I was informed, was 4'9" and weighed about 90 pounds. Apparently, at the academy she couldn't perform many of the physical exercises that her fellow trainees could. Where most of the men could pull a trigger between 80 and 90 times during the allotted time, she could pull the trigger of her police issue .38 revolver only once. And she was so tiny that they had to make a booster seat for the patrol car. One of the instructors said that her being in the academy was a joke. Well, it does seem that way to me. I can imagine this woman trying to handle a situation. How could she handcuff someone who resisted arrest? It seems dangerous that someone who is so weak should be allowed to be on patrol duty. I wouldn't want her as my back-up.

Lynnea now knew she had a topic that interested her. She wanted to research women patrol officers, specifically the success rate of small women. She formulated her initial research question this way: "Can a small, physically weak woman, such as this 4'9" police candidate, make a good patrol officer?" Her initial thesis was that small, physically weak women could not make good patrol officers, but she wanted to keep an open mind, using argument as a means of clarification. As this chapter progresses, we will return occasionally to Lynnea's research project. (Her final argument essay is reproduced in full at the end of Chapter 18).

Another Means of Searching for a Research Question: Browsing the Library

Another effective means of searching for a research question is to browse through the indexes to periodicals in your library. Locate a recent periodical index (such as the *Readers' Guide to Periodical Literature* or the *Social Science*

Index—see next section), turn to topic areas of interest to you, and look at the titles of articles published in the past two or three years. Often these titles will suggest controversies that you would like to explore further. Then, by skimming several of these articles and examining the sources that these authors cite, you can get a feel for the different voices in the conversation. An alternative method is to locate the general shelf section in the library where recent books on your topic are housed. Then you can browse through the books, looking particularly at the introductions, titles of chapters, and bibliographies of articles at the back. Frequently these materials will give you a hint of the controversies going on in the field.

LOCATING LIBRARY MATERIALS

To be a good researcher, you need to know how to unlock the resources of your college's or university's library. Because most students think of "books" when they enter a library, they tend to focus on the bookshelves and neglect the wealth of other resources a library contains, particularly articles in magazines and journals, statistical reports from government agencies, articles and editorials in newspapers (often on microfilm or microfiche), congressional records, and so forth. Books, of course, are important, but they tend to be less current than periodical sources. The key is to become skilled at using *all* of a library's resources.

USING THE CARD CATALOG

The library's card catalog is your first source of information about the library's holdings. Indexed by subject, title, and author, cards in the card catalog identify most of the library's holdings: books, magazines and journals (but not the titles of articles in them), newspapers, theses and dissertations, major government documents (but not minor ones), and most multimedia items including records, cassettes, and filmstrips.

Each book in the library has at least three cards—a title card, an author card, and a subject card. Figure 17–1 shows a subject card for one of the books Lynnea used in her research. Filed under the subject heading "POLICEWOMEN," this card shows the book's title (*Women Police; A Study of the Development and Status of the Women Police Movement*), its author (Chloe Owings), and other information. This book would have two additional cards—one filed under "Owings" in the author file and one under *"Women*

Dewey Decimal System
call number

Subject heading

POLICEWOMEN.

Author's name

Book title

363.22   **Owings, Chloe.**
0w3W   Women police; a study of the development and status of
              the women police movement. With a pref. by Mina C.
              Van Winkle . . . written for the International Associa-
Number of pages   tion of Policewomen. Montclair, N.J., Patterson Smith,
in book   1969.

Place,
publisher,
date of
publication

Number of pages —— xxii, 337 p. 22 cm. (Patterson Smith reprint series in criminology, law
in preface   enforcement, and social problems, no. 28)

Size of   Reprint of the 1925 ed. ——   Shows that 1969
book   Bibliography: p. 299-306.   book is a reprint of
                                                      an earlier 1925 book

Book has a
bibliography   1. Policewomen. I. Title.

                    HV8023.08   1969   363.2'2   69-14941
Additional headings ISBN 0-87585-028-6   MARC
where entry cards are
indexed
                    Library of Congress

                    International Standard Book Number

FIGURE 17–1. Book Entry in Card Catalog

Police; A Study of . . ." under the title file. The call number at the left (a Dewey Decimal System number—see below) indicates where the book can be found in the stacks.

To help you find cards in the files, you should know something about the rules of alphabetizing:

- Subjects and titles are alphabetized word by word (*On Becoming a Person* comes before *On Matrimony*) and then letter by letter (*Neutral Zone* comes before *Neutrons in Electromicroscopy*).

- In alphabetizing, follow the rule "nothing comes before something." In other words, a blank space comes before the letter *a*. *Sea Through a Sailor's Eyes* comes before *Seatbelts and Other Controversies* (the blank space after "Sea" comes before the *t* in "Seatbelts").

- Abbreviations are arranged as though spelled out (for example, "St. Augustine" is filed in the S section under "Saint Augustine").

- Titles containing numbers are filed as though the numbers were spelled out (*2000 Leagues under the Sea*) is filed under *Two Thousand Leagues . . .*).

- Articles (*a, an,* and *the*) and their foreign language equivalents are disregarded for purposes of alphabetizing (*A Midsummer Night's Dream* is filed under the *M*'s).

- Names beginning with "Mc" or "Mac" are filed under "Mac" ("McKinnon" comes before "MacRae").

To find the book in the stacks, you will need to know the two major systems for shelving books—the Dewey Decimal System, which uses a series of numbers and decimals, and the Library of Congress System, which uses letters followed by numbers. The Library of Congress system is used by most college and university libraries, although they may have an older book collection still classified in the Dewey Decimal System.

DEWEY DECIMAL SYSTEM

000	General Works
100	Philosophy and Related Disciplines
200	Religion
300	Social Sciences
400	Language
500	Pure Science
600	Technology and Applied Science
700	The Arts
800	Literature and Rhetoric
900	General Geography and History

LIBRARY OF CONGRESS SYSTEM

A	General Works, Polygraphy
B	Philosophy, Psychology, and Religion
C	Auxiliary Sciences of History
D	General and Old World History (except America)
E–F	American History
G	Geography, Anthroplogy, Manners and Customs, Folklore, Recreation
H	Social Science, Statistics, Economics, Sociology
J	Political Science
K	Law
L	Education
M	Music
N	Fine Arts
P	Language and Literature
Q	Science
R	Medicine
S	Agriculture, Plant and Animal Industry, Fish Culture, Fisheries, Hunting, Game Protection
T	Technology
U	Military Science
V	Naval Science
Z	Bibliography and Library Science

Each of these headings is further subdivided according to an elaborate system of subclassifications. For example, in the Library of Congress System the book by William C. Grimm called *Familiar Trees of America* is filed under QK481 (Q = Science; K = Botany; 481 = North American trees). Knowing something of the system's logic helps you browse.

USING PERIODICAL AND NEWSPAPER INDEXES

Often the best sources of information come from periodicals (magazines and scholarly journals) and from newspapers. The library's card catalog doesn't help you find titles of articles appearing in these periodical sources.

For that task, you need to use indexes. Most libraries locate their indexes in a central area in the reference section of the library, so it is usually a simple matter to find out where they are housed. In this section we will list the major indexes that you should know about; then we'll give you some instructions on how to use them.

The Most Important Indexes

What follows is a list of what we consider the most important and useful indexes. We begin with "current affairs" indexes, useful for finding information on current controversies and issues related to public affairs. Then we turn to a variety of more specialized indexes.

CURRENT AFFAIRS

1. *Readers' Guide to Periodical Literature.* The best-known index to periodical literature. Includes popular, general interest topics such as current events, famous people, movie reviews, and hobbies. Focuses primarily on "general audience" magazines such as *Time, Newsweek, Popular Mechanics, National Geographic, Scientific American,* and so forth.

2. *Social Sciences Index.* Covers all subjects and disciplines within the social sciences, including anthropology, area studies, psychology, political science, and sociology. (Before 1974 this was called *Social Sciences and Humanities Index.*) Although this index lists some articles from popular magazines, it concentrates on articles published in scholarly journals carried in academic libraries. Articles listed in this index will often be more technical and academic, aimed at professional scholars rather than the general audience.

3. *Biography Index.* Quarterly and annual index to biographical material in current books and periodicals. Here is where you should turn if you want to find out biographical information about a person.

4. *Business Periodical Index.* This index covers articles on all business-related topics such as advertising, public relations, marketing, management, and topics relating to economics.

5. *General Science Index.* A subject index to articles in general science periodicals. Covers areas such as biology, botany, chemistry, environment and conservation, medicine and health, physics, zoology.

6. *New York Times Index.* Subject index to the *New York Times,* giving exact references to date, page, and column and including brief synopses of articles.

7. *Wall Street Journal Index.* Monthly and annual index to the *Wall Street Journal.* Organized in two parts: (1) corporate news indexed by name of company, and (2) general news indexed by subject.

8. *Public Affairs Information Service (P.A.I.S.) Bulletin.* Lists articles, pamphlets, and books dealing with economic and social conditions, public administration, politics, and international relations. This index is especially useful for topics related to current public policy, domestic or international.

SPECIALIZED INDEXES: EDUCATION

1. *Education Index.* Indexes by author and subject about 300+ periodicals, proceedings, and yearbooks covering all phases of education. Especially good coverage of topics related to children and child development.

2. *Current Index to Journals in Education.* Detailed author and subject index for articles from more than seven hundred education and education-related journals.

SPECIALIZED INDEXES: HISTORY AND 'LITERATURE

1. *America: History and Life.* Includes abstracts of scholarly articles on the history of the United States and Canada.

2. *Annual Bibliography of English Language and Literature.* Subject index of scholarly articles in English language and literature. Literature section is arranged chronologically and includes articles on the major writers of each century.

3. *Historical Abstracts.* Includes abstracts of scholarly articles on world history (excluding United States and Canada) from 1775 to 1945.

4. *Humanities Index.* Subject index to various topics in the humanities, including archaeology, classics, folklore, history, language and literature, politics, performing arts, philosophy, and religion. (Before 1974 this was called *Social Sciences and Humanities Index.*)

5. *MLA (Modern Language Association) International Bibliography of Books and Articles in Modern Language and Literature.* Comprehensive index of scholarly articles on the languages and literature of various countries. Arranged by national literatures with subdivisions by literary periods.

SPECIALIZED INDEXES: NURSING AND MEDICAL SCIENCES

1. *Cumulative Index to Nursing and Allied Health Literature.* Major index for topics related to nursing and public health.

2. *Index Medicus.* Monthly index, by subject, of periodical literature on medicine and medical-related topics. Covers publication in all principal languages.

SPECIALIZED INDEXES: PHILOSOPHY
AND RELIGION

1. *Philosopher's Index.* Author and subject index to scholarly articles in books and periodicals. Subject section includes abstracts of articles.

2. *Religion Index One: Periodicals.* Subject and author index to scholarly articles on topics in religion. Protestant in viewpoint, but also indexes a number of Catholic and Jewish periodicals.

SPECIALIZED INDEXES: PSYCHOLOGY
AND SOCIOLOGY

1. *Psychological Abstracts.* Subject and author index covering books, journals, technical reports, and scientific documents. Each item includes an abstract.

2. *Social Sciences Index.* See under Current Affairs on page 385.

3. *Applied Science and Technology Index.* Subject index to periodical articles in fields of aeronautics and space sciences, automation, earth sciences, engineering, physics, telecommunications, transportation, and related topics.

4. *Biological and Agricultural Index.* Subject index to English-language periodicals in the agricultural and biological sciences.

5. *General Science Index.* See above under Current Affairs.

How to Use Periodical Indexes

Once you locate these indexes in the library, you will quickly get the hang of using them. Most of the indexes listed above (with the exception of the *New York Times Index*) are used in approximately the same way. In general, each volume in an index lists articles that appeared in journals and magazines for a one-year period. The year is stated on the outside cover of the index volume and sometimes at the top of each page. To use the index, you have to be flexible in selecting subject headings. Lynnea, for example, found most of her articles indexed under "policewomen," but one index used the heading "women" and the subheading "and police." It is often difficult to know what headings an index will use, but because most indexes cross-reference listings under a variety of headings, with patience and perseverance you can usually track down what you want.

Because indexes are generally bound by year, you need to look in a different volume for each year you wish to search. Thus, if you wanted to find all the articles written on women in police forces between 1980 and 1990, you would need to look under the subject heading "policewomen" in ten separate volumes. Each entry uses a series of abbreviations (you may have to look in the explanatory codes at the front of the index to decipher some of them) that give you all the information you need to locate the article. Figures 17-2, 17-3, and 17-4 show entries on policewomen from the *Readers' Guide,* the *Social Sciences Index,* and the *Public Affairs Information Service (P.A.I.S.) Bulletin.*

When you find entries that seem relevant to your topic, jot down the title of the article; the name of the magazine or journal; and the volume, year, and page numbers (remember that the year often doesn't appear in the entry; the year is on the cover of the volume).

Once you have a preliminary list of articles, you will need to find out how your library shelves its periodical collection so that you can retrieve the journals or magazines you need. (Small libraries can afford only small collections of journals, so you may have to cross some of your titles off your list or depend on interlibrary loan.)

Special case: Using the New York Times Index. When you want to find newspaper stories in the *New York Times,* you have to use a slightly

---

Police questioning
The case of common sense vs. Miranda. E. H. Methvin.
il *Read Dig* 131:96–100 Ag '87
Crime and the Constitution [Miranda Rule] D. O. Relin
and C. Lawrence. il *Sch Update* 120:10–11 D 4 '87
The Meese lie [effort to overturn Miranda decision]
S. Gillers. *Nation* 244:205 F 21 '87
Viva Miranda [Justice Dept. offensive against Miranda
decision] J. Toobin. *New Repub* 196:11–12 F 16 '87
Police radar *See* Radar in traffic control
Police shootings
Best intentions: Edmund Perry's path from Harlem to
Exeter to death on a street in Morningside Heights
[excerpt] R. S. Anson. il. pors map *N Y* 20:30–45
My 11 '87
Charges of racism [black youth A. Griffin killed by
Montreal police] L. Van Dusen. il. *Macleans* 100:14+
N 30 '87
Shot by a cop [J. Yates of Cleveland] D. O. Relin.
il por *Sch Update* 120:7 D 4 '87
Police television shows *See* Television broadcasting—Crime
programs ——————————————————— Heading
Policewomen ————————————————
Barbara Schein finally ⌐gets a shot at walking the beat. —— Title of article
A. Abrahams. il⌐pors *People Wkly* 27:139–40 My 4 ——
'87
Jury awards $900,000 to black female officer in Detroit —— Author of article
police case [case of C. Preston] *Jet* 72:33 Ap 27 '87
Policies, Insurance *See* Insurance
Policy analysis *See* Policy sciences
Policy Analysis for California Education
Bridging the gap between policy and research [interview
with M. W. Kirst] D. B. Strother, il por *Phi Delta
Kappan* 69:161–4 O '87
Data: a by-product of reform. C. Pipho. il *Phi Delta
Kappan* 69:102–3 O '87
Policy loans *See* Insurance, Life—Policy loans
Policy Management Systems Corp.
One insider bet his boat on this stock. G. G. Marcial.
Bus Week p100 S 7 '87

Shows that
article
contains
a portrait and
illustration

Shows that article appeared
in *People Weekly,* volume
27, pages 139–40,
May 4, 1987.

FIGURE 17-2. Entry from *Readers' Guide,* 1987

Poles in France
Immigration and emigration
History
Comparative immigrant history: Polish workers in the Ruhr area and the north of France. C. Klessmann. *J Soc Hist* 20:335–53 Wint '86
Police
See also
Communication in police work
Conflict of interests (Police)
Criminal investigation
Decision making in police work
Detectives
Off-duty police
Police patrol
Sardino, Thomas J.
Secret service
Tamm, Quinn, 1910–1986
Administration
See Police administration
Alcoholism
Alcoholism and the police officer: impact on police administrators. H. W. Stege. *Police Chief* 53:82–4 Mr '86
Amount of education, experience, etc.
Education and training requirements in law enforcement: a national comparison. A. D. Sapp. *Police Chief* 53:48+ N '86
Learning the skills of policing. D. H. Bayley and E. Bittner. *Law Contemp Probl* 47:35–59 Aut '84
Subject heading ——————— **Attitudes**
Attitudes of police toward violence. S. L. Brodsky and G. D. Williamson. *Psychol Rep* 57:1179–80 D '85 pt2
Title ——— A comparison of male and female peace officers'
Author ——— stereotypic perceptions of women and women peace officers. L. K. Lord. bibl *J Police Sci Adm* 14:83–97 Je '86
Contains bibliography ——— Police solidarity and tolerance for police misbehavior.
Article appears ——— D. Lester and W. T. Brink. *Psychol Rep* 57:326 Ag in *Journal of Police* ——— '85
Science Administration, **Budget**
June 1986, volume 14, *See* Police—Finance
pages 83–97 **Diseases and hygiene**
Cardiovascular intervention among police officers: a two-year report. R. A. Mostardi and others. il *Police Chief* 53:32–4 Je '86
Disease risk and mortality among police officers: new evidence and contributing factors. J. M. Violanti and others. bibl *J Police Sci Adm* 14:17–23 Mr '86
Management of training-related injury. P. A. Callicutt. il *FBI Law Enforc Bull* 55:16–24 My '86
NYC's physical performance testing program. D. B. Jordan and S. Schwartz. *Police Chief* 53:29–30 Je '86

FIGURE 17–3. Entry from *Social Sciences Index,* 1986

different procedure. Each volume of the *New York Times Index* contains a year's worth of condensed news stories arranged chronologically by subject. At the back of the volume, a supplementary index lists all headings with an extensive system of cross-references. By looking under the appropriate headings in this supplementary index, you will find listed, by date, all the year's articles indexed under that heading. For example, the 1988 volume of the *New York Times Index* (Figure 17–5) shows that stories about women in police appeared on March 29 and on December 29. Figure 17–6 shows the mini-summary of the December 29 story from the front of

POLICE, MOUNTED

Doeren, Stephen E. Mounted patrol programs in law enforcement, tables *Police Studies 12:10-17 Spring '89*
Based on a survey of 25 US police departments.

POLICE, PRIVATE

United States, Nat. Inst. of Justice. Office of Communication and Research Utilization. Public policing—privately provided. Chaiken, Marcia and Jan Chaiken. Je '87 iii+44p tables (Issues and practices) (SD cat. no. J 28.23:P 96)—*Washington, DC 20531*
Issues related to contracts between municipal governments and private companies for delivery of services.

POLICE QUESTIONING

Praet, Bruce D. Defending the practice of photographing field detainees. il *Police Chief 55:52-5 N '88*
Experience of the Orange, California, police department; analysis of recent decisions. ———— Subject heading

POLICEWOMEN ———————————— Title

Authors ———— Garrison, Carole G. and others. Utilization of police women. il tables chart *Police Chief 55:32-5+S '88* ———— Shows that article appeared in *Police Chief,*

Brief contents { Based on survey responses from International Association of Police Women members in the U.S., Guam, and Canada.

POLICY SCIENCES
See also
Public policy

Bartlett, Robert V., ed. Symposium: Policy and impact assessment. bibls tables charts *Policy Studies R 8:73-178 Autumn '88*
Jointly sponsored by the International Association for Impact Assessment and the Policy Studies Organization.
Policy-making and administration based on a priori analysis of predictable impacts; 11 articles.

Bulmer, Martin and others, ed. The goals of social policy. '89 xvi+330p bibls table charts index (LC 88-35552) (ISBN 0-04-445131-8) $49.95; (ISBN 0-04-445132-6) pa—*Unwin Hyman*
Based on papers presented at a conference held at the Department of Social Science, London School of Economics, Dec. 17-18, 1987.
Academic study and practice.

September 1988, Volume 55, pages 32-35, plus additional pages

FIGURE 17-4. Entry from *Public Affairs Information Service (P.A.I.S.) Bulletin,* 1989

the volume in the section headed "POLICE." A citation to the original story shows that it appeared on December 29, section II, page 1, column 2. To read the full story, you would turn to your library's collection of the *New York Times.*

USING COMPUTER SEARCHES

Now that library indexing systems are becoming increasingly computerized, the old-fashioned, one-volume-at-a-time, hands-on searching method described above is becoming obsolete. However, methods of using on-line

WOLZIEN, VALERIE. See also
Book Reviews—Murder at the PTA Luncheon (Book), My 22
WOMACK, CECIL. See also
Music, Je 25
WOMACK, JAMES. See also
Sheldahl Inc, F 19, Mr 16
WOMACK, LINDA. See also
Music, Je 25
WOMAN (MAGAZINE)
Magazine will be acquired by Conde Nast Publications Inc (S). N 16.IV,19:4
WOMAN'S WORKSHOP (NEWSLETTER). See also
Women, O 5
WOMC-FM (RADIO STATION). See also
Radio, Mr 1
WOMEN. See also —— **Main Heading**
Abortion, Ja 29, F 6,10,29, Mr 6, Jl 29, S 26,27,29
Accounting and Accountants, Jl 12
Acquired Immune Deficiency Syndrome (AIDS), F 20, Mr 6, My 24, Jl 15, Ag 11,14
Advertising, Ja 14, Je 1
Afghanistan, Mr 27, Ap 2, Je 12, D 12
Age, Chronological, S 1
Aged, My 15
Agriculture, Ja 3, F 28
Airlines and Airplanes, F 29, Mr 10, S 13
Airports, My 30
Alcoholism, F 21, Je 19, O 13
Anglican Churches, Jl 20, Ag 2,7,8,14, N 8
Anorexia Nervosa, F 11
Apparel, F 21, Mr 9,11,21,31, Ap 10,12,16,17,19,22, My 1, 21,29,30, Je 12, Jl 29, S 25,29, O 11, N 4,8,22, D 13,18,23
Art, Ja 3,15,22, N 20, D 1
Athletics and Sports, Ja 26,31, My 26, Je 8,9,14, Jl 22, S 23, O 2
Banks and Banking, Mr 9
Baseball, Mr 8,20,21,25, Je 2, Ag 12
Basketball, F 15, Mr 5,18,20,25,27,28, Ap 1,3,4,8,27, N 2, 11,12,15, D 20,29
Bathrooms, My 10
Beer, Ap 10
Birth Control and Family Planning, Ja 29, F 6, Jl 28, Ag 4, S 15
Birth Defects, Ap 27, Je 6, S 28
Blood Pressure, My 15
Boats and Boating, Je 13
Bohemian Club, S 4
Bones, Mr 29
Books and Literature, Mr 20, Ap 21, My 5
Boy Scouts of America, F 14,17, Jl 17, Ag 28
Brooklyn College, My 19
Bulimia, Ag 25
Bush, George (Mrs), D 11
California, University of, Mr 24
Cancer, Ja 7,21, F 2,16, Mr 11,22, My 31, Je 30, S 7,11,21, 29, O 27, N 10,13,16,17,20,28
Cartoons and Cartoonists, N 27
Century Association, N 27
Chemicals, D 15
Child Care, Jl 25
Chilton Club (Boston, Mass), O 30
China, People's Republic of, D 15
Cuba, Ja 5
Curling, F 2
Dartmouth College, S 21, O 19
Data Processing (Computers), Jl 5,10
Dating (Social), Je 21
Deerfield Academy (Mass), Ja 31
Defense, Department of, My 24
Diamonds, D 18
Drug Addiction and Abuse, Je 23, O 30
Drug Traffic, N 29, D 4
Education and Schools, F 22, O 30, N 30
Electronics, D 15
Emotions, Ag 23
Endometriosis, Mr 8
Engineering and Engineers, Mr 9,30
Ethiopia, My 19, Ag 25
Etiquette, My 11
Executives and Management, Ja 25, My 11, Ag 14, S 25
Exercise, S 5
Families and Family Life, My 22, N 6
Federal Aviation Administration (FAA), Ap 29
Fencing (Sport), Je 25
Fires and Firemen, My 22
Food, Ag 31
Forest Service, US, My 10
Fort Orange Club (Albany, NY), O 8
Friars Club, Jl 19, Ag 27, N 9
Fur, Ap 2
Furniture, Ap 14
Gambling, N 29
Games, Jl 17
Government Employees, Mr 29
Great Britain, Je 3
Guinea-Bissau, Ja 3
Handicapped, Je 18
Harvard University, F 21, My 11,24,26, D 2
Hats and Caps, Mr 25, Ap 24, Je 14
Heart, Ag 3
History, Ja 9
Homeless Persons, Ja 24, D 22
Honda of America Manufacturing Inc, Mr 24
Horse Racing, Mr 6,7,20
Housework, D 8
Housing, Mr 27
Humor and Wit, N 20
Indians, American, O 30
Industrial and Occupational Hazards, Ag 2, O 4,5
Insurance, F 28
International Trade and World Market, Jl 4
Ireland, Northern, My 2
Israel, State of, N 29, D 22
Japan, D 4
Jews, Mr 14,30, My 20, Ag 29, D 2
Jonathan Club (Los Angeles), My 6
Jump Rope, Jl 20
Kissing, D 11
Labor, Ja 18, F 2,12,14, My 30, Je 16,19,30, Jl 31, Ag 14, O 12,16, N 27
Lacrosse, My 22
Latin America, Jl 27
Lear's (Magazine), F7
Legal Profession, F 12, Mr 6, Ap 22, Jl 22, Ag 8,11, S 2,30, N 11
Life Insurance, S 5
Lupus Erythematosus, Ap 3
Magazines, My 30
Malaysia, Je 5
Marriages, S 1
Mathematics, Jl 20, N 1
Medicine and Health, Ja 14, Ap 10, Jl 10, O 16, D 9,11,15
Mental Health and Disorders, O 12
Methodist Church, My 4
Murders and Attempted Murders, My 23,24, Je 1
Music, Je 5, O 22, D 25
Names, Personal, Ja 10, F 27, Ap 20
Nashville (Tenn), F 14
Nebraska, O 21
New Hampshire, S 12
New Jersey, Ja 24
New York, City University of (CUNY), My 16, S 30
New York State—Economic Conditions and Trends, Ap 9,19
New York State—Politics and Government, My 20
New York University, Ag 30
Newcomb College, Mr 30
News and News Media, F 4, Ap 14, Jl 14, Ag 3
Plastic Surgery, Ag 28, S 6 —— **Subheading**
Police, Mr 29, D 29 —— **Articles in March 29 and December 29 issues of *New York Times***
Population, Je 5
Pregnancy and Obstetrics
Presbyterian Church, F 14
Presidential Election of 1984, Jl 18
Presidential Election of 1988, My 10,17,19,30, Je 2,17,19, 21,27, Jl 6,18,24,25,28, Ag 14,17,19 29, S 6,11, O 5,27
Presidential Elections (US), Jl 28, Ag 5

FIGURE 17-5. Index in back of *New York Times Index*, 1988

POLICE (cont.)

Louisa O Dixon, first woman to be Mississippi's Commissioner of Public Safety, wins over most of the doubters in her department, which includes highway patrol, narcotics bureau, crime laboratory, medical examiner's office and law-enforcement training academy; appointment is part of Gov Ray Mabus's continuing effort to bring new ideas to Mississippi government; photo (M), D 22,1,18:5

New Jersey State Trooper Jerome W Johnson is arrested on charges he planned to sell cocaine he confiscated from drug courier who turned out to be an undercover detective (S), D 24,1,30:6

Hemphill, Texas, where black man, Loyal Garner Jr, died in police custody last December, is divided between whites who view incident as tragedy with no villains and blacks embittered by acquittal of three white law-enforcement officers; photos; map (S), D 25,1,18:4

New York City Police Department, in hopes of attracting more women to careers in police work while helping to ease domestic burdens of employees with pre-school children, begins building on-site day care centers in its Manhattan headquarters building; Judith Dynia, civilian official who is in charge of project, comments; photo (S), D 29,11,1:2

Correction of Dec 29 article on plans for day-care center at Police Headquarters in New York City, D 31,1,3:2

POLICE, FRATERNAL ORDER OF. See also
Presidential Election of 1988, O 9

POLICE ATHLETIC LEAGUE (PAL). See also
Children and Youth, Jl 10
Photo of Police Athletic League carnival in Central Park. New York City, Ag 11,11,2:3

POLICE CHIEFS, INTERNATIONAL ASSN OF (LOS ANGELES, CA). See also
Police, My 6

POLICE FOUNDATION. See also
Child Abuse, Mr 15
Koch, Edward I (Mayor), My 24
Police, Ja 31, My 24, N 21
Annual winter benefit dance of New York City Police Foundation at Police Headquarters is held on Feb 11; photo (S), F 12,11,2:3

POLICELLA, ANTHONY. See also
Kinney System Inc, My 4

POLICY AND MANAGEMENT, OFFICE OF (CONN). See also
Prisons and Prisoners, Je 26

POLICY COMMUNICATIONS INC
William Lilley 3d announces that he is forming his own firm, Policy Communications Inc, to provide policy analysis, lobbying and communications services; photo (S), Mr 2,IV,4:5

POLICY STUDIES, INSTITUTE FOR. See also
United States Politics and Government, Jl 13

Summary of story [annotation]

Story appears in December 29, Section II, page 1, column 2. [annotation]

(S)=short article
(M)=medium article
(L)=long [annotation]

FIGURE 17-6. Story Summary from *New York Times Index*

computer searches vary so much from institution to institution that it is impossible to describe a single, generalized method of conducting a computer search.

Many libraries now have simple, easy-access computer terminals for searching specific databases. One typical system, called INFOTRAC, provides rapid access to a multiyear database of popular journals and magazines. However, the number of entries in the data bank is much smaller than the number in the *Readers' Guide to Periodical Literature* or the *Social Sciences Index* so that INFOTRAC is a good starting place but not an adequate source for an extensive search for periodicals. INFOTRAC is easy to use because of its simple menu options and clear prompts. In general, you type in the subject heading you wish to search and then select from a menu of subheadings. When you have identified the heading and sub-heading of your choice, you can ask the computer to list its entries in that category. You can either read the entries from the screen or ask for a hard copy printout.

In addition to small, primarily undergraduate systems such as INFO-TRAC, many libraries offer in-house computerized searching of specialized databases such as ERIC (Educational Research Information Center) or NEXIS (for news and public affairs). Most libraries also provide exhaustive, professional on-line searches from a variety of national and international databases. These searches usually require the assistance of a reference librarian and are often quite expensive. The key to these searches is providing the right array of subject headings, called "descriptors," so that you adequately narrow your topic (otherwise you end up paying for hundreds of titles) without getting it so narrow that you miss key titles. Ask your librarian for help.

USING OTHER LIBRARY SOURCES

Besides being a storehouse for books and periodicals, your library has a wealth of material in the reference section that may be useful to you in finding background information, statistics, and other kinds of evidence. Here are some sources that we have found particularly useful in our own research.

1. *Encyclopedias.* For getting quick background information on a topic, you will often find that a good encyclopedia is your best bet. Besides the well-known general-purpose encyclopedias such as the *Encyclopedia Britannica*, there are excellent specialized encyclopedias devoted to in-depth coverage of specific fields. Among the ones you might find most useful are these:

> The International Encyclopedia of the Social Sciences
> Dictionary of American History
> Encyclopedia of World Art
> McGraw-Hill Encyclopedia of Science and Technology

2. *Facts on File.* These interesting volumes give you a year-by-year summary of important news stories. If you wish to assemble a chronological summary of a news event such as the fall of Pete Rose, the opening of the Berlin Wall, or the controversy over the Mapplethorpe photographs, *Facts on File* gives you a summary of the events along with information about

exact dates so that you can find the full stories in newspapers. A special feature is a series of excellent maps in the back of each volume, allowing you to find all geographical place names that occur in the year's news stories. The front cover of each volume explains how to use the series.

3. *Statistical Abstracts of the United States.* Don't even consider picking up one of these volumes if you don't have some spare time. You will get hooked on the fascinating graphs, charts, and tables compiled by the Bureau of Statistics. For statistical data about birth rates and abortions, marriages and divorces, trends in health care, trends in employment and unemployment, nutritional habits, and a host of other topics, these yearly volumes are a primary source of quantitative information about life in the United States.

4. *Congressional Abstracts.* For people working on current or historical events related to politics or any controversy related to the public sector, this index can guide you to all debates about the topic in the Senate or the House of Representatives.

5. *Book Review Digest.* For writers of argument, this series can be a godsend because it provides not only a brief summary of a book but also excerpts from a variety of reviews of the book, allowing the writer to size up quickly the conversation surrounding the book's ideas. To use *Book Review Digest*, you need to know the publishing date of the book for which you want to find reviews. Generally, reviews first appear in the same year the book was published and for several years thereafter. If you want to read reviews, for example, of a book appearing in 1985, you would probably find them in the 1985, 1986, and (if the book were very popular or provocative) 1987 volumes of *Book Review Digest*.

FOR CLASS DISCUSSION
Working in groups, visit your college's library and learn to use the indexes and other sources listed in the preceding pages. Choose an issue of interest to the members of your group (preferably one about current public affairs so that you can find sources from *The New York Times Index* and *Congressional Abstracts*); then locate titles of two or three articles addressing your issue from as many of the indexes and sources as possible. Group members can divide up the work, each person taking several indexes as a special project and then teaching the others how to use them. Your goal is to feel confident that you can use these indexes to unlock most of the resources contained in your library.

BEYOND THE LIBRARY

As you pursue your research project, consider ways you might gather information or ideas through field research as well as library research—

interviews, questionnaires, polls, field observations, and so forth. Review Chapter 7 for suggestions on using field research in argumentation.

USING YOUR SOURCES: SITTING DOWN TO READ

Once you have developed a working bibliography of books and articles and have gathered a collection of materials, how do you go about reading and notetaking? There is no easy answer here. At times you need to read articles carefully, fully, and empathically — reading as a believer and as a doubter, as discussed in Chapter 2, trying to understand various points of view on your issue, seeing where the disagreements are located, and so forth. Your goal at this time is to clarify your own understanding of the issue in order to join responsibly the on-going conversation.

At other times you need to read quickly, skimming an article in search of a needed piece of information, an alternative view, or a timely quotation. All these considerations and others — how to get your ideas focused, how to take notes, how to incorporate source material into your own writing, and how to cite and document your sources — are the subjects of the next chapter.

18

USING AND DOCUMENTING SOURCES

The previous chapter helped you pose a good research question and begin unlocking some of the resources of your library. This chapter helps you see what to do with your sources once you have found them — how to use them to clarify your own thinking and how to incorporate them into your writing through effective use of quotations, paraphrases, and summaries along with appropriate conventional formats for citations and documentation.

CLARIFYING YOUR OWN THINKING: THE CASE OF LYNNEA

In the previous chapter, we followed Lynnea's progress as she posed her research question on the effectiveness of policewomen and began her search for sources. Once Lynnea located several articles on policewomen, she found a quiet spot in the library and began to read. She was guided by two related questions: What physical requirements must someone meet in order to be an effective patrol officer? How successful have policewomen been when assigned to patrol duty? After reading some recent articles, Lynnea noticed that writers often referred to significant earlier studies, particularly a 1984 study called *Policewomen on Patrol, Final Report* by P.B. Bloch and D. Anderson. Lynnea tracked down this study as well as several others referred to in the first articles she read.

Both Lynnea's experience and her research strategy are typical. As a researcher becomes familiar with the ongoing conversation on an issue, she will notice that recent writers frequently refer to the same earlier studies or to the same earlier voices in the conversation. In scientific writing, this background reading is so important that the introductions to scientific studies usually include a "review of the literature" section, wherein writers summarize important research done to date on the question under investigation and identify areas of consensus and disagreement.

Therefore, during the first hours of her research project, Lynnea conducted her own "review of the literature" concerning women on patrol. During an early visit to her university's writing center, she reported that she had found three kinds of studies:

1. Studies attempting to identify the attitude of the police establishment (overwhelmingly male) toward women entering the police profession and the attitude of the general public toward women patrol officers. Although the findings weren't entirely consistent, Lynnea reported that male police officers generally distrusted women on patrol and felt that women didn't have the required physical strength or stamina to be patrol officers. The public, however, was more accepting of women patrol officers.

2. Studies attempting to evaluate the success of women on patrol by examining a variety of data such as arrests made, use of force, firing of weapons, interviews with persons involved in incidents, evaluation reports by superiors, and so forth. Lynnea reported that these studies were generally supportive of women police officers and showed that women cops were as successful as men cops.

3. Studies examining the legal and political battles fought by women to gain access to successful careers in police work. Lynnea reported being amazed at how much prejudice against women was evident in the police establishment.

At a writing center conference Lynnea confessed that, as a result of her readings, she was beginning to change her mind: She was now convinced that women could be effective patrol officers. But she wasn't convinced that *all* women could be effective officers any more than *all* men could be. She still felt that minimum size and strength requirements should be necessary. The problem was, she reported, that she couldn't find any information related to size and strength issues. Moreover, the research on women police officers did not mention anything about the size or strength of the women being studied. Were these successful patrol officers "big, husky" women Lynnea asked, or "petite" women? She left the writing center in pursuit of more data.

Lynnea's dilemma is again typical. As we discussed in Chapter 7, the search for clarification often leads to uncertainty. As you immerse yourself in the conversation surrounding an issue, you find that the experts often disagree and that no easy answers emerge. Your goal under these circumstances is to find the best reasons available and to support them with the best evidence you can muster. But the kind of uncertainty Lynnea felt is both healthy and humbling. If your own research leads to similar feelings, we invite you to reread those sections of Chapter 7 where, in our discussion of the greenhouse effect, we suggest our own strategy for coping with ambiguity.

We'll leave Lynnea at this point to take up the technical side of writing research arguments. Besides using research to clarify your own thinking, you also need to have strategies for note taking and for incorporating the results of your reading into your own writing through proper citations and documentation.

DEVELOPING A GOOD SYSTEM OF NOTE TAKING

There is no one right way to take notes. For short research papers, many students keep all their notes in a spiral notebook; others use a system of 3×5 cards (for bibliographic information) and 5×8 cards (for actual notes). A few technological types are even using database software on their personal computers. Whatever system you use, the key is to take notes that are complete enough so that you don't have to keep going back to the library to reread your sources. Some students get around this problem by photocopying all articles they might use in their essays, but this is an expensive habit that may in the long run be less efficient than careful note taking in the first place.

It is much easier to take good notes for a research project if you have your issue question clearly formulated. When you know your issue question, you can anticipate how information from books and articles is apt to get incorporated into your essay. Sometimes you will need to write an accurate summary of a whole article as part of your research notes; at other times you may want to jot down only some facts or figures from an article; at still other times you may want to copy a passage word for word as a potential quotation. There is no way to know what kind of notes you will need to take on each book or article unless you can predict what kind of thesis you will be supporting. We therefore continue our comments on the art of note taking as we discuss ways information can be used in a research essay.

INCORPORATING SOURCES INTO YOUR ARGUMENT: SOME GENERAL PRINCIPLES

To illustrate different ways that you can use a source, we will use the following brief article from the magazine *Science '86*.

READING, WRITING, AND (UGH!) YOU KNOW WHAT

Ann Arbor, Mich. — Not only are American high school students worse at mathematics than their Japanese and Chinese peers, they start falling behind in kindergarten.   1

That's one conclusion of a five-year study done by psychologist Harold Stevenson and graduate student Shin-ying Lee, both of the University of Michigan, and psychologist James Stigler of the University of Chicago. The study also shows for the first time that parents must share the blame.   2

More than 2,000 children in kindergarten and the first and fifth grades were tested and interviewed in Minneapolis, in Sendai, Japan, and in Taipei, China. The researchers composed the test for each grade from math problems found in textbooks in all three cities.   3

All the children in each grade performed equally well on reading and general intelligence tests, but math scores differed from the start. While average scores for U.S. and Chinese kindergarten students were the same, Japanese kindergartners scored about 10 percent higher. First graders in the U.S. were surpassed by their peers in both China and Japan by an average of 10 percent. Then the gap widened. The top U.S. fifth-grade class scored below the lowest Japanese class and the second lowest Chinese class. Of the 100 highest scoring fifth graders, one was American.   4

A crucial difference is time: Chinese and Japanese students spend more hours in math class and attend school some 240 days a year, Americans about 180. But another difference, the researchers found, is parental influence. Chinese and Japanese parents give their children more help with math homework than U.S. parents, who tended to believe that "ability" was the premier reason for academic success, according to the researchers' interviews. Chinese and Japanese parents, in contrast, most often said "effort" was most important. And more than 90 percent of U.S. parents believed the schools did   5

Source: "Reading, Writing, and (Ugh!) You Know What," *Science '86* (May 1986), pp. 7–8.

an "excellent" job teaching math and other subjects; most Japanese and Chinese parents said the schools did a "fair" job.

"American parents are very involved in teaching reading," says Stigler. **6** "But they seem to think that teaching math is the school's job. It's as if it gets them off the hook."

Citing Information

Sometimes the complete argument of an article may not be relevant to your essay. Often you will use a piece of information from the article. For example, let's suppose you are writing an argument claiming that American society, as a whole, values individual creativity more than does Japanese society. You plan to contrast an open classroom in an American grade school with a more regimented Japanese classroom. At the end of the passage, you might write something like this:

> Not only is education in Japan more regimented than it is in the United States, it continues through a much longer school year. A typical Japanese grade school student attends classes 240 days a year compared with 180 days a year in the United States (*Science '86* 7). Although such a system might produce more academic achievement, it provides little time for children to be children, to play and daydream—essential ingredients for nurturing creativity.

Here the total argument of the *Science '86* article isn't relevant to the writer's essay. He has borrowed only the small detail about the length of the school year (which, of course, the writer documents by means of a citation in parentheses). In his original notecards, the writer would not have had to summarize the whole *Science '86* article. By knowing his research question, he would have known that only this piece of information was relevant.

Summarizing an Argument: Different Contexts Demand Different Summaries

On other occasions, however, you may need to summarize the entire argument of an essay, or at least a major portion of the argument. How you summarize it depends once again on the context of your own essay because your summary must focus on your own thesis. To illustrate how context influences a summary, we will examine passages by two different writers, Cheryl and Jeff, each of whom uses the *Science '86* article, but in the context of different arguments. Cheryl is writing on the issue of heredity versus environment in the determination of scholastic achievement. She is making the causal claim that environment plays a key role in scholastic high achievement. Jeff, on the other hand, is writing on American mathematics education. He is making the evaluation claim that American mathematics education is in a dangerous shambles. Both writers include a summary of the *Science '86* article,* but their summaries are written in different ways in order to emphasize different aspects of the article.

PASSAGE FROM CHERYL'S ESSAY ON HEREDITY VERSUS ENVIRONMENT

Another argument showing the importance of environment on scholastic achievement comes from a research study done by psychologists at the University of Chicago and the University of Michigan (*Science '86*). These researchers compared the mathematics achievement of 2000 kindergartners, first graders, and fifth graders from the United States, Japan, and China. At the beginning of the study the researchers determined that the comparison groups were equal in terms of reading ability and general intelligence. But the American students were far behind in mathematics achievement. At the first grade level, the researchers reported, American students were 10 percent behind Japanese and Chinese students and considerably further behind by the end of the fifth grade. In fact, only one American student scored in the top 100 of all students.

What is significant about this study is that heredity seems to play no factor in accounting for the differences between American students and their Japanese and Chinese counterparts since the comparison groups were shown to be of equal intelligence at the beginning of the study. The researchers attribute the differences between the groups to the time they spent on math (Japanese students go to class 240 days per year while Americans are in class only 180 days per year) and to parental influence. According to the study, American parents believe that native "ability" is the key factor in math achievement and don't seem to push their children as much. Japanese and Chinese parents, however, believe that "effort" is the key factor and spend considerably more time than American parents helping their children with their math homework (8). Thus, it is the particular environment created by Chinese and Japanese societies, not inherited intelligence, that accounts for the greater math achievement of children in those cultures.

PASSAGE FROM JEFF'S ESSAY ON THE FAILURE OF MATHEMATICS EDUCATION IN THE UNITED STATES

Further evidence of the disgraceful nature of mathematics education in the United States is the dismal performance of American grade school students in mathematics achievement tests as compared to children from other cultures. One study, reported in the magazine *Science '86*, revealed that American kindergarten students scored 10 percent lower on mathe-

---

*The citations follow the MLA format described later in this chapter.

matics knowledge than did kindergarteners from Japan. This statistic suggests that American parents don't teach arithmetical skills in the home to preschoolers the way Japanese parents do.

But the most frightening part of the study showed what happens by the fifth grade. The best American class in the study scored below the worst Chinese or Japanese class, and of the top 100 students only one was an American (8). The differences between the American students and their Chinese and Japanese counterparts cannot be attributed to intelligence because the article reports that comparison groups were matched for intelligence at the beginning of the study. The difference can be accounted for only by the quality of education and the effort of students. The researchers who did this study attributed the difference first of all to time. According to the study, Chinese and Japanese students spend 240 days per year in school while Americans spend only 180. The second reason for the difference is parental influence, since Japanese and Chinese parents spend much more time than American parents helping their children with mathematics. The study suggests that if we are to do anything about mathematics education in the United States we need a revolution not only in the schools but in the home.

FOR CLASS DISCUSSION
Although both passages above summarize the *Science '86* article, they use the article to support somewhat different claims. Working as individuals or in groups, prepare short answers to the following questions. Be ready to elaborate on your answers in class if called on to defend them.

1. What makes each passage different from a data dump?
2. In what ways are the summaries different? (Compare the summaries to each other and to the original article.)
3. How does the difference between the summaries reflect a different purpose in each passage?

Article Summaries as a Note-Taking Tool

Both Cheryl's passage and Jeff's summarize the *Science '86* article accurately. To be able to write summaries such as these when you compose your rough drafts, you need to have the articles at hand (by photocopying them from the library) or you need to have written summaries of the articles in your notecards. We strongly recommend the second practice—writing summaries of articles in your notecards when their arguments seem relevant to your research project. Taking notes this way is time-consuming in the short run but time-efficient in the long run. The act of summarizing forces you to read the article carefully and to perceive its whole argument. It also steers you away from the bad habit of noting facts or information from an article without perceiving how the information supports a meaning. Because summary writing is a way of reading as a believer (see Chapter 2), it helps you listen to the various voices in the conversation about your issue.

Paraphrasing Portions of an Argument

Whereas a summary places a whole argument in a nutshell by leaving out supporting details but keeping the main argument, a paraphrase is about the same length as the original but places the ideas of the original in the writer's own words. Paraphrase often includes pieces of quotation worked neatly into the writer's passage. When you are summarizing a short article, such as the *Science '86* article used in the previous section, parts of your summary can blend into paraphrase. The distinction isn't important. What is important is that you avoid plagiarism by making sure you are restating the original argument in your own words. Generally you should avoid paraphrasing a lengthy passage because then you will simply be turning someone else's argument into your own words. A good research argument weaves together supporting material from a variety of sources; it doesn't paraphrase someone else's argument.

Quoting

Inexperienced writers tend to quote too much material and at too great a length. To see a skillful use of quotations, look again at the *Science '86* article we have been using as an illustration. That article is actually a summary of a much longer and more technical research study written by the researchers Stevenson, Shin-ying Lee, and Stigler. Note that the summary includes only two kinds of quotation: quotation of the single words *ability, effort, excellent,* and *fair;* and a brief quotation from Stigler to conclude the article.

The first kind of quotation — quoting individual words or short phrases — is a matter of accuracy. The writer summarizing the original research study wanted to indicate the exact terms the researchers used at key points in their argument. The second kind of quotation — quoting a brief passage from an article — has a different purpose. Sometimes writers want to give readers a sense of the flavor of their original source, particularly if the source speaks in a lively, interesting style. At other times a writer wishes to quote a source exactly on an especially important point, both to highlight the point and to increase readers' confidence that the writer has elsewhere been summarizing or paraphrasing accurately. The ending quotation in the *Science '86* article serves both purposes.

As a general rule, avoid too much quotation, especially long quotations. Remember that a research essay, like any other essay, should present *your* argument in *your* voice. When you use summary and to a lesser extent paraphrase, you are in command because you are fitting the arguments of your sources to your own purposes. When you quote, on the other hand, you are lifting material from a different context with a different purpose and plunking it into an alien home, inevitably mixing voices and styles. Too much quotation is the hallmark of a data dump essay; the writer strings together other people's words instead of creating his own argument.

INCORPORATING SOURCES INTO YOUR ARGUMENT: TECHNICAL ADVICE ON SUMMARIZING, PARAPHRASING, AND QUOTING

As a research writer, you need to be able to move back and forth gracefully between conducting your own argument and using material from your research in the form of summary, paraphrase, or quotation. For purposes of illustration, we ask you to read the following essay entitled "The Case for Torture" by Michael Levin. We will assume you want to use Levin's ideas in an argument that you are writing. You will need to be familiar with Levin's essay in order to understand our explanations of summary, paraphrase, and quotation.

THE CASE FOR TORTURE

Michael Levin

It is generally assumed that torture is impermissible, a throwback to a   1
more brutal age. Enlightened societies reject it outright, and regimes suspected of using it risk the wrath of the United States.

I believe this attitude is unwise. There are situations in which torture is not   2
merely permissible but morally mandatory. Moreover, these situations are moving from the realm of imagination to fact.

Death: Suppose a terrorist has hidden an atomic bomb on Manhattan   3
Island which will detonate at noon on July 4 unless . . . (here follow the usual demands for money and release of his friends from jail). Suppose, further, that he is caught at 10 A.M. of the fateful day, but — preferring death

Source: Michael Levin, "The Case for Torture," *Newsweek,* June 7, 1982.

to failure — won't disclose where the bomb is. What do we do? If we follow due process — wait for his lawyer, arraign him — millions of people will die. If the only way to save those lives is to subject the terrorist to the most excruciating possible pain, what grounds can there be for not doing so? I suggest there are none. In any case, I ask you to face the question with an open mind.

Torturing the terrorist is unconstitutional? Probably. But millions of lives 4 surely outweigh constitutionality. Torture is barbaric? Mass murder is far more barbaric. Indeed, letting millions of innocents die in deference to one who flaunts his guilt is moral cowardice, an unwillingness to dirty one's hands. If *you* caught the terrorist, could you sleep nights knowing that millions died because you couldn't bring yourself to apply the electrodes?

Once you concede that torture is justified in extreme cases, you have 5 admitted that the decision to use torture is a matter of balancing innocent lives against the means needed to save them. You must now face more realistic cases involving more modest numbers. Someone plants a bomb on a jumbo jet. He alone can disarm it, and his demands cannot be met (or if they can, we refuse to set a precedent by yielding to his threats). Surely we can, we must, do anything to the extortionist to save the passengers. How can we tell 300, or 100, or 10 people who never asked to be put in danger, "I'm sorry, you'll have to die in agony, we just couldn't bring ourselves to . . . "

Here are the results of an informal poll about a third, hypothetical, case. 6 Suppose a terrorist group kidnapped a newborn baby from a hospital. I asked four mothers if they would approve of torturing kidnappers if that were necessary to get their own newborns back. All said yes, the most "liberal" adding that she would like to administer it herself.

I am not advocating torture as punishment. Punishment is addressed to 7 deeds irrevocably past. Rather, I am advocating torture as an acceptable measure for preventing future evils. So understood, it is far less objectionable than many extant punishments. Opponents of the death penalty, for example, are forever insisting that executing a murderer will not bring back his victim (as if the purpose of capital punishment were supposed to be resurrection, not deterrence or retribution). But torture, in the cases described, is intended not to bring anyone back but to keep innocents from being dispatched. The most powerful argument against using torture as a punishment or to secure confessions is that such practices disregard the rights of the individual. Well, if the individual is all that important — and he is — it is correspondingly important to protect the rights of individuals threatened by terrorists. If life is so valuable that it must never be taken, the lives of the innocents must be saved even at the price of hurting the one who endangers them.

Better precedents for torture are assassination and pre-emptive attack. No 8 Allied leader would have flinched at assassinating Hitler, had that been possible. (The Allies did assassinate Heydrich.) Americans would be angered to learn that Roosevelt could have had Hitler killed in 1943 — thereby shortening the war and saving millions of lives — but refused on moral grounds. Similarly, if nation A learns that nation B is about to launch an unprovoked attack, A has a right to save itself by destroying B's military capability first. In the same way, if the police can by torture save those who would otherwise die at the hands of kidnappers or terrorists, they must.

Idealism: There is an important difference between terrorists and their victims that should mute talk of the terrorists' "rights." The terrorist's victims are at risk unintentionally, not having asked to be endangered. But the terrorist knowingly initiated his actions. Unlike his victims, he volunteered for the risks of his deed. By threatening to kill for profit or idealism, he renounces civilized standards, and he can have no complaint if civilization tries to thwart him by whatever means necessary.

Just as torture is justified only to save lives (not extort confessions or recantations), it is justifiably administered only to those *known* to hold innocent lives in their hands. Ah, but how can the authorities ever be sure they have the right malefactor? Isn't there a danger of error and abuse? Won't We turn into Them?

Questions like these are disingenuous in a world in which terrorists proclaim themselves and perform for television. The name of their game is public recognition. After all, you can't very well intimidate a government into releasing your freedom fighters unless you announce that it is your group that has seized its embassy. "Clear guilt" is difficult to define, but when 40 million people see a group of masked gunmen seize an airplane on the evening news, there is not much question about who the perpetrators are. There will be hard cases where the situation is murkier. Nonetheless, a line demarcating the legitimate use of torture can be drawn. Torture only the obviously guilty, and only for the sake of saving innocents, and the line between Us and Them will remain clear.

There is little danger that the Western democracies will lose their way if they choose to inflict pain as one way of preserving order. Paralysis in the face of evil is the greater danger. Some day soon a terrorist will threaten tens of thousands of lives, and torture will be the only way to save them. We had better start thinking about this.

For incorporating Levin's ideas into your own writing, you have a number of options.

Summary

When you wish to include a writer's complete argument (or a large sustained portion of it) in your own essay, you will need to summarize it. For a detailed explanation of how to summarize, see Chapter 2. Summaries can be quite long or very short. The following condensation of Levin's essay illustrates a short summary.

> Levin believes that torture can be justifiable if its purpose is to save innocent lives and if it is certain that the person being tortured has the power to save those lives. Torture is not justifiable as punishment. Levin likens the justified use of torture to the justified use of assassination or preemptive strikes in order to preclude or shorten a war.

This short passage summarizes the main points of the Levin argument in a few sentences. As a summary, it condenses the whole down to a small nutshell. For an example of a somewhat longer summary, see Chapter 2, pages 25–27.

Paraphrase

Unlike summary, which is a condensation of an essay, a paraphrase is a "translation" of an essay into the writer's own words. It is approximately the same length as the original, but converts the original into the writer's own voice. Be careful when you paraphrase to avoid both the original writer's words and the original writer's grammatical structure and syntax. If you follow the original sentence structure while replacing occasional words with synonyms, you are cheating: That practice is plagiarism, not paraphrase. Here is a paraphrase of paragraph 4 in Levin's essay:

> Levin asks whether it is unconstitutional to torture a terrorist. He believes that it probably is, but he argues that saving the lives of millions of innocent people is a greater good than obeying the Constitution. Although torture is brutal, so is letting innocent people die. In fact, Levin believes that we are moral cowards if we don't torture a guilty individual in order to save millions of lives.

This paraphrase of paragraph 4 is approximately the same length as the original paragraph. The purpose of a paraphrase is not to condense the original, but to turn the original into one's own language. Even though you are not borrowing any language, you will still need to cite the source to indicate that you are borrowing ideas.

Block Quotation

Occasionally, you will wish to quote an author's words directly. You must be meticulous in copying down the words *exactly* so that you make no changes. You must also be fair to your source by not quoting out of context. When the quoted material takes up more than three lines in your original source, use the following block quotation method:

In his argument supporting torture under certain circumstances, Levin is careful to insist that he doesn't see torture as punishment but solely as a way of preventing loss of innocent lives:

> I am not advocating torture as punishment. Punishment is addressed to deeds irrevocably past. Rather, I am advocating torture as an acceptable measure for preventing future evils. So understood, it is far less objectionable than many extant punishments.

Here the writer wants to quote Levin's words as found in paragraph 7. Because the passage to be quoted is longer than three lines, the writer uses the block quotation method. Note that the quotation is introduced with a colon and that no quotation marks are used. The block format with indentations takes the place of quotation marks.

Inserted Quotation

If the passage you wish to quote is less than three lines, you can insert it directly into your own sentences by using quotation marks instead of the block method:

> In his argument favoring torture, Levin is careful to distinguish between torture and punishment. "I am not advocating torture as punishment," Levin asserts. "Punishment is addressed to deeds irrevocably past. Rather, I am advocating torture as an acceptable measure for preventing future evils."

Here the writer breaks the same quotation into parts so that no part is longer than three lines. Thus the writer uses quotation marks rather than the block quotation method.

If the inserted quotation is a complete sentence in your own essay, then it should begin with a capital letter. The quotation is usually separated from preceding explanatory matter by a colon or comma. However, if the quotation is not a complete sentence in your own essay, then you insert it using quotation marks only and begin the quotation with a small letter.

QUOTATION AS INDEPENDENT SENTENCE

According to Levin, "Punishment is addressed to deeds irrevocably past."

QUOTATION AS CLAUSE OR PHRASE THAT IS NOT AN INDEPENDENT SENTENCE

Levin claims that punishment is concerned with "deeds irrevocably past," while torture is aimed at "preventing future evils."

In the first example, the quotation begins with a capital *P* because the quotation comprises an independent sentence. Note that it is separated from the preceding phrase by a comma. In the second example the quotations do not comprise independent sentences. They are inserted directly into the writer's sentence, using quotation marks only.

Shortening or Modifying Quotations

Sometimes you wish to quote the exact words from a source, but in order to make the quotation fit gracefully into your own sentence you need to alter it in some way, either by shortening it, by changing it slightly, or by adding explanatory material to it. There are several ways of doing so: through judicious selection of phrases to be quoted or through use of ellipses and brackets.

SHORTEN A PASSAGE BY SELECTING ONLY KEY PHRASES FOR QUOTING

> In his argument favoring torture, Levin is careful to distinguish between torture and punishment. "I am not advocating torture as punishment," Levin asserts, but only "as an acceptable measure for preventing future evils."

Here the writer quotes only selected pieces of the longer passage and weaves them into her own sentences.

USE ELLIPSIS TO OMIT MATERIAL FROM A QUOTATION

> Levin continues by distinguishing torture from capital punishment:
> Opponents of the death penalty . . . are forever insisting that executing a murderer will not bring back his victim. . . . But torture . . . is intended not to bring anyone back but to keep innocents from being dispatched.

In this block quotation from paragraph 7, the writer uses ellipses in three places. Made with three spaced periods, an ellipsis indicates that words have been omitted. Note that the second ellipsis in the above passage seems to contain four periods. The first period ends the sentence; the last three periods are the ellipsis.

USE BRACKETS TO MAKE SLIGHT CHANGES IN A QUOTATION OR TO ADD EXPLANATORY MATERIAL

> According to Levin, "By threatening to kill for profit or idealism, he [the torturer] renounces civilized standards."

The writer puts "the torturer" in brackets to indicate the antecedent of the quoted pronoun "he." This passage is from paragraph 9.

> According to Levin, "[T]orture [is] an acceptable measure for preventing future evils."

This passage, from paragraph 7, changes the original slightly: a small *t* has been raised to a capital *T,* and the word *as* has been changed to *is.* These changes are indicated by brackets. You don't usually have to indicate when you change a small letter to a capital or vice versa. But it is important to do so here because the writer is actually changing the grammar of the original by converting a phrase into a sentence.

Using Quotations within Quotations

Sometimes you may wish to quote a passage that already has quotation marks within it. If you use the block quotation method, keep the quotation marks exactly as they are in the original. If you use the inserted quotation method, then use single quotation marks (') instead of double marks (") to indicate the quotation within the quotation.

> Levin is quick to dismiss the notion that a terrorist has rights:
>> There is an important difference between terrorists and their victims that should mute talk of the terrorists' "rights." The terrorist's victims are at risk unintentionally, not having asked to be endangered. But the terrorist knowingly initiated his actions.

Because the writer uses the block quotation method, the original quotation marks around *rights* remain. See the original passage in paragraph 9.

> Levin claims that "an important difference between terrorists and their victims . . . should mute talk of the terrorists' 'rights.'"

Here the writer uses the inserted quotation method. Therefore the original double quotation marks (") around *rights* have been changed to single quotation marks ('), which on a typewriter are made with an apostrophe.

An Extended Illustration: Martha's Argument

To help you get a feel for how a writer integrates brief quotations into paraphrases or summaries, consider the following passage written by Martha, a student who was disturbed by a class discussion of Levin's essay. Several classmates argued that Levin's justification of torture could also be used to justify terrorism. Martha did not believe that Levin's argument could be applied to terrorism. Here is the passage from Martha's argument that summarizes Levin. (Page references in Martha's passage refer to the original *Newsweek* source that she used—part of the MLA citation system to be described shortly.)

> Now it may seem that if terrorism is always wrong then torture should always be wrong also since torture, even more so than terrorism, is a

barbaric practice from a pre-civilized age. But philosopher Michael Levin shows a flaw in this reasoning. Torture is justifiable, says Levin, but only in some cases. First of all, he says that torture should be applied only to those *"known* to hold innocent lives in their hands" and only if the person being tortured is clearly guilty and clearly can prevent a horrible act from occurring (13). Levin uses the example of using torture on a captured terrorist to find the location of an atomic bomb set to go off on Manhattan Island. The principle here is that you are saving the lives of millions of innocent bystanders by applying systematic pain to one person who "renounc[ed] civilized standards" (13) when becoming a terrorist. For Levin, saving the lives of innocent bystanders is a higher moral imperative than refusing to torture the person who can prevent the deaths. In fact, Levin claims, refusal to torture the terrorist is "moral cowardice, an unwillingness to dirty one's hands" (13). "If life is . . . valuable," Levin argues, then "the lives of the innocents must be saved even at the price of hurting the one who endangers them" (13).

We can now return to the problem I posed earlier. If Levin is able to justify torture under some conditions, why can't we also justify terrorism under some conditions? The answer is that . . . [Martha's argument continues].

FOR CLASS DISCUSSION
Working as individuals or as small groups, prepare brief answers for the following questions:

1. How is Martha's passage different from a data dump?
2. Without being able to read her whole essay, can you determine Martha's purpose for summarizing Levin within her own argument on terrorism? If so, what is her purpose?
3. Why did the writer use brackets [ ] within one quotation and ellipses (. . .) within another?
4. What effects did Martha achieve by using only short quotations instead of longer block quotations from Levin's argument?

Signaling Directions: The Use of Attributive Tags

In all of our examples of citing, summarizing, paraphrasing, and quoting, the writers have used attributive tags to signal to readers which ideas are the writer's own and which ideas are being taken from another source. Attributive tags are phrases such as the following: "according to the researchers . . . ," "Levin claims that . . . ," "the author continues . . . ," and so forth. Such phrases signal to the reader that the material immediately following is from the cited source. Parenthetical citations are used only to give readers follow-up information on where the source can be found, not to indicate that the writer is using a source. The source being cited should always be mentioned in the text. Note how confusing a passage becomes if these attributive tags are omitted.

CONFUSING ATTRIBUTION

Now it may seem that if terrorism is always wrong then torture should always be wrong also since torture, even more so than terrorism, is a barbaric practice from a pre-civilized age. But there is a flaw in this reasoning. Torture should be applied only to those *"known* to hold innocent lives in their hands (Levin 13)" and only if the person being tortured is clearly guilty and clearly can prevent a terrorist act from occurring. A good example is using torture on a captured terrorist to find the location of an atomic bomb set to go off on Manhattan Island.

Although this writer cites Levin as the source of the quotation, it is not clear just when the borrowing from Levin begins or ends. For instance, is the example of the captured terrorist on Manhattan Island the writer's own or does it come from Levin? As the following revision shows, the use of attributive tags within the text makes it clear exactly where the writer's ideas leave off and a borrowed source begins or ends.

CLEAR ATTRIBUTION

Now it may seem that if terrorism is always wrong then torture should always be wrong also since torture, even more so than terrorism, is a barbaric practice from a pre-civilized age. But **philosopher Michael Levin shows** a flaw in this reasoning. Torture is justifiable, **says Levin,** but only in some cases. First of all, **he says that** torture should be applied only to those *"known* to hold innocent lives in their hands" and only if the person being tortured is clearly guilty and clearly can prevent a horrible act from occurring (13). **Levin uses** the example of using torture on a captured terrorist to find the location of an atomic bomb set to go off on Manhattan Island.

AVOIDING PLAGIARISM

Plagiarism, a form of academic cheating, is always a serious academic offense. You can plagiarize in one of two ways: (1) by borrowing another person's ideas without indicating the borrowing with attributive tags in the text and a proper citation, or (2) by borrowing another person's language without putting the borrowed language in quotation marks or block indentations. The first kind of plagiarism is usually outright cheating; the writer usually knows he is stealing material and tries to disguise it.

The second kind of plagiarism, however, often begins in a hazy never-never land between paraphrasing and copying. We refer to it in our classes as "lazy cheating" and still consider it a serious offense, like stealing from your neighbor's vegetable garden because you are too lazy to do your own planting, weeding, and harvesting. Anyone who appreciates how hard it is to write and revise even a short passage will appreciate why it is wrong to take someone else's language ready-made. Thus, in our classes, we would fail a paper that included the following passage. (Let's call the writer Lucy.)

> Another argument showing the importance of environment on scholastic achievement comes from a research study done by psychologists at the University of Chicago and the University of Michigan (*Science* '86 7, 8). The study shows that parents must share the blame for the poor math performance of American students. In this study more than 2,000 children in kindergarten and the fifth grade were tested and interviewed in Minneapolis, in Sendai, Japan, and in Taipei, China. The researchers made up a test based on math problems found in textbooks used in all three cities. All the children in each grade performed equally well on reading and general intelligence tests, but their math scores differed from the start. The kindergarteners from Japan scored about 10 percent higher than American kindergarteners. The gap widened by the fifth grade. The top U.S. fifth-grade class scored below the lowest Japanese class and the second lowest Chinese class. Of the 100 highest scoring fifth graders, one was American (*Science* '86 8).

FOR CLASS DISCUSSION

Do you think it was fair to flunk Lucy's essay? She claimed she wasn't cheating since she gave two different parenthetical citations accurately citing the *Science* '86 article as her source. Before answering this question, compare the above passage with the original article on pages 399–400; also compare the above passage with the opening paragraph from Cheryl's summary (page 401) of the *Science* '86 article. What justification could a professor use for giving an A to Cheryl's essay while flunking Lucy's essay?

Note Taking to Avoid Plagiarism

When you takes notes on books or articles, be extremely careful to put all borrowed language in quotation marks. If you write summaries of arguments, as we strongly recommend you do, take time at the note-taking stage to put the summaries in your own words. If you wish to paraphrase an important passage, make sure you either copy the original into your notes word for word and indicate that you have done so (so that you can paraphrase it later) or paraphrase it entirely in your language when you take the notes. Inadvertent plagiarism can occur if you copy something in your notes word for word and then later assume that what you copied was actually a paraphrase.

DOCUMENTING YOUR SOURCES

To many students, the dreariest aspect of research writing is documenting their sources — that is, getting citations in the proper places and in the correct forms. As we noted at the beginning of this chapter, however, documentation of sources is a service to readers who may want to follow up on your research. Documentation in the proper form allows them to find your sources quickly.

There are two questions that you must answer to ensure proper documentation: "When do I cite a source?" and "What format do I use?"

When to Cite Sources

As a general rule, cite everything you borrow. Some students take this rule to unnecessary extremes, arguing that everything they "know" comes from somewhere. They end up citing lectures, conversations with a friend, notes from an old high school class, and so forth. Use common sense. If you successfully avoid writing a data dump essay, then your research will be used to support a thesis, which will reflect your own individual thinking and synthesis of material. You will know when you are using evidence from your own personal experience as source material and when you are using evidence you got from doing library research. Document all the material you got from the library or from another external source.

What Format to Use

Formats for citations and bibliographies vary somewhat from discipline to discipline. At the present time, footnotes have almost entirely disappeared from academic writing as a means of citing sources. Rather, citations for quotations or paraphrased material are now usually made in the text itself by putting brief identifying symbols inside parentheses.

OVERVIEW OF THE MLA AND APA SYSTEMS OF DOCUMENTATION*

The two main systems used today for academic essays aimed at general college audiences are the MLA (Modern Language Association) system, generally favored in the humanities, and the APA (American Psychological Association) system, generally favored in the social sciences. Other general systems are sometimes encountered—for example, the *University of Chicago Manual of Style*—and many specialized disciplines such as biology or chemistry have their own style manuals. But familiarity with the MLA and APA systems should serve you well throughout college. The sample research argument written by Brenda Wahler (pages 348–357) follows the MLA style. The sample research argument written by Lynnea Clark (pages 428–439) follows the APA style.

Citations in Parentheses in the Text

Neither the MLA nor the APA system uses footnotes to document sources. In both systems a source is cited by means of a brief parenthetical reference following the quotation or the passage in which the source is used. The formats for these parenthetical references vary slightly in the two systems and will be explained shortly.

Bibliographies at the End of the Paper

In both the MLA and the APA styles, a list of all the sources you have cited is included at the end of the research paper. In the MLA system, this bibliographic list is called "Works Cited." In the APA system this list is called "References." In both systems, entries are listed alphabetically by author (if no author is given for a particular source, then that source is alphabetized by title).

Let's look at how the two style systems would have you cite the Levin article on torture. The article appears in the June 7, 1982, issue of *Newsweek* on page 13. In the MLA style the complete bibliographic reference would be placed at the end of the paper under "Works Cited," where it would appear as follows:

---

*Our description of the MLA style is taken from Joseph Gibaldi and Walter S. Achtert, *MLA Handbook for Writers of Research Papers*, 3rd ed. New York: MLA, 1988. Our description of the APA style is taken from *Publication Manual of the American Psychological Association*, 3rd ed. Washington, D.C.: APA, 1983.

MLA: Levin, Michael. ''The Case for Torture.'' Newsweek

7 June 1982: 13.

In the APA system, the complete bibliographic reference would be placed at the end of the paper under "References," where it would appear as follows:

APA: Levin, M. (1982, June 7). The case for torture.

Newsweek, p. 13.

When you refer to this article in the text—using either system—you place a brief citation in parentheses.

IN-TEXT CITATION: MLA SYSTEM   In the MLA system, you place the author's name and the page number of the cited source in parentheses. (If the author's name is mentioned in a preceding attributive tag, then only the page number needs to be placed in parentheses.)

Torture, claims one philosopher, should only be

applied to those ''known to hold innocent lives in their

hands'' and only if the person being tortured is clearly

guilty and clearly can prevent a terrorist act from

occurring (Levin 13).

or

Torture, claims Michael Levin, should only be applied

to those ''known to hold innocent lives in their hands'' and

only if the person being tortured is clearly guilty and

clearly can prevent a terrorist act from occurring (13).

If readers wish to follow up on the source, they will look up the Levin article in the "Works Cited" at the end. If more than one work by Levin has been used as sources in the essay, then you would include in the in-text citation an abbreviated title of the article following Levin's name.

(Levin, ''Torture'' 13)

Once Levin has been cited the first time and it is clear that you are still quoting from Levin, then you need put in parentheses only the page number and eliminate the author's name.

IN-TEXT CITATION: APA SYSTEM   In the APA system, you place the author's name and the date of the cited source in parentheses. If you are quoting a particular passage or citing a particular table, include the page number where the information is found. Use a comma to separate each element of the citation and use the abbreviation *p.* or *pp.* before the page number. (If the author's name is mentioned in a preceding attributive tag, then only the date needs to be placed in parentheses.)

Torture, claims one philosopher, should only be applied to those ''<u>known</u> to hold innocent lives in their hands'' and only if the person being tortured is clearly guilty and clearly can prevent a terrorist act from occurring (Levin, 1982, p. 13).

or

Torture, claims Michael Levin, should only be applied to those ''<u>known</u> to hold innocent lives in their hands'' and only if the person being tortured is clearly guilty and clearly can prevent a terrorist act from occurring (1982, p. 13).

If readers wish to follow up on the source, they will look for the 1982 Levin article in the "References" at the end. If Levin had published more than one article in 1982, the articles would be distinguished by small letters placed alphabetically after the date:

(Levin, 1982a)

or

(Levin, 1982b)

In the APA style, if an article or book has more than one author, the word *and* is used to join them in the text but the ampersand (&) is used to join them in the reference:

Smith and Peterson (1983) found that . . .

More recent data (Smith & Peterson, 1983) have

shown . . .

What follows is a description of the format for the end-of-text bibliographic entries under "Works Cited" in the MLA system and under "References" in the APA system.

FORM FOR ENTRIES IN "WORKS CITED" (MLA) AND "REFERENCES" (APA)

General Format for Books

MLA: Author. Title. Edition. City of Publication:

       Publisher, year.

APA: Author. (Year of Publication). Title. City of

       Publication: Publisher.

ONE AUTHOR

MLA: Hamilton, Edith. The Greek Way to Western

       Civilization. New York: Norton, 1930.

APA: Hamilton, E. (1930). The Greek way to western

       civilization. New York: W. W. Norton.

In the MLA style, author entries include first names and middle initials. In the APA style only the initials of the first and middle names are given, unless full names are needed to distinguish persons with the same initials. In the APA style only the first word and proper names in a title are capitalized. Note also that the year of publication follows immediately after the author's name. In the MLA system, names of publishers have standard abbreviations, listed on pages 214–216 in the *MLA Handbook for Writers of Research Papers*, cited earlier. In the APA system, names of publishers are not usually abbreviated, except for the elimination of unnecessary words such as *Inc., Co.,* and *Publishers.*

TWO LISTINGS FOR ONE AUTHOR

MLA: Doig, Ivan. Dancing at the Rascal Fair. New York:

       Atheneum, 1987.

       - - - . English Creek. New York: Atheneum, 1984.

In the MLA style, when two or more works by one author are cited, the works are listed in alphabetical order by title. For the second and all additional entries, type three hyphens and a period in place of the author's name. Then skip two spaces and type the title.

APA: Doig, I. (1984). English Creek. New York: Atheneum.

Doig, I. (1987). <u>Dancing at the rascal fair</u>. New
York: Atheneum.

Selfe, C. L. (1984a). The predrafting processes
of four high- and four low-apprehensive
writers. <u>Research in the teaching of English</u>,
<u>18</u>, 45-64.

Selfe, C. L. (1984b). <u>Reading as writing and
revising strategy</u>. ERIC Document Reproduction
Service No. ED 244 295.

In APA style, when an author has more than one entry in "References," the author's name is repeated and the entries are listed chronologically (oldest to newest) rather than alphabetically. When two entries by the same author have the same date, they are then listed in alphabetical order. Lower-case letters are added after the year of publication to distinguish them from each other when cited by date in the text.

TWO OR MORE AUTHORS

MLA: Rieke, Richard D., and Malcolm O. Sillars.

<u>Argumentation</u>. 2nd ed. Glenview: Scott, 1984.

APA: Rieke, R. D., & Sillars, M. O. (1984).

<u>Argumentation</u> (2nd ed.). Glenview, IL: Scott,
Foresman.

Note that the APA style uses the ampersand (&) to join the names of multiple authors.

USING ET AL. *FOR WORKS WITH SEVERAL AUTHORS*

MLA: Maimon, Elaine P. et al. <u>Writing in the Arts and
Sciences</u>. Cambridge: Winthrop, 1981.

In the MLA system, if there are four or more authors, you have the option of using *et al.* (meaning "and others") after the name of the first author listed on the title page.

APA: Maimon, E. P., Belcher, G. L., Hearn, G. W.,
Nodine, B. F., & O'Connor, F. W. (1981).

<u>Writing in the arts and sciences</u>. Cambridge:
Winthrop.

APA style allows the use of *et al.* only when there are six or more authors for one work.

ANTHOLOGY WITH AN EDITOR

MLA: Rabkin, Norman, Ed. Approaches to Shakespeare.

New York: McGraw-Hill, 1964.

APA: Rabkin, N. (Ed.). (1964). Approaches to

Shakespeare. New York: McGraw-Hill.

ESSAY IN AN ANTHOLOGY OR OTHER COLLECTION

MLA: Stein, Robert B., Lon Polk, and Barbara Bovee

Polk. ''Urban Communes.'' Old Family/New

Family. Ed. Nona Glazer-Malbin. New York:

Nostrand, 1975. 171-88.

APA: Stein, R. B., Polk, L., & Polk, B. B. (1975). Urban

communes. In N. Glazer-Malbin (Ed.), Old

family/new family (pp. 171-188). New York: D.

Van Nostrand.

BOOK IN A LATER EDITION

MLA: Valette, Rebecca M. Modern Language Testing. 2nd

ed. New York: Harcourt, 1977.

Williams, Oscar, ed. A Little Treasury of Modern

Poetry. Rev. ed. New York: Scribner's, 1952.

APA: Valette, R. M. (1977). Modern language testing

(2nd ed.). New York: Harcourt, Brace,

Jovanovich.

Williams, O. (Ed.). (1952). A little treasury of

modern poetry (rev. ed.). New York: Scribner's.

MULTIVOLUME WORK

Cite the whole work when you have used more than one volume of the work.

MLA: Churchill, Winston S. A History of the English-

Speaking Peoples. 4 vols. New York: Dodd,

1956-58.

APA: Churchill, W. S. (1956-1958). History of the

English-speaking peoples (Vols. 1-4). New

York: Dodd, Mead.

Include the volume number when you have used only one volume of a multivolume work.

MLA: Churchill, Winston S. The Great Democracies. New

York: Dodd, 1957. Vol. 4 of A History of the

English-Speaking Peoples. 4 vols. 1956-58.

APA: Churchill, W. S. (1957). A history of the English-

speaking peoples: Vol. 4. The great

democracies. New York: Dodd, Mead.

REFERENCE WORK WITH FREQUENT EDITIONS

MLA: Pei, Mario. ''Language.'' World Book

Encyclopedia. 1976 ed.

In citing familiar reference works under the MLA system, you don't need to include all the normal publication information.

APA: Pei, M. (1976). Language. In World book

encyclopedia (Vol. 12, pp. 62-67). Chicago:

Field Enterprises.

APA does not give a specific example for use of a reference book. The APA manual directs the writer to follow an example similar to the source and to include more information rather than less.

LESS FAMILIAR REFERENCE WORK WITHOUT FREQUENT EDITIONS

MLA: Ling, Trevor O. ''Buddhism in Burma.'' Dictionary

of Comparative Religion. Ed. S. G. F. Brandon.

New York: Scribner's, 1970.

APA: Ling, T. O. (1970). Buddhism in Burma. In S. G. F.

Brandon (Ed.). Dictionary of comparative

religion. New York: Scribner's.

EDITION IN WHICH ORIGINAL AUTHOR'S WORK IS PREPARED BY AN EDITOR

MLA: Brontë, Emily. Wuthering Heights. Ed. V. S.

Pritchett. Boston: Houghton, 1956.

APA: Brontë, E. (1956). Wuthering Heights (V. S.

Pritchett, ed.). Boston: Houghton, Mifflin.

(Original work published 1847)

TRANSLATION

MLA: Camus, Albert. The Plague. Trans. Stuart Gilbert.

New York: Modern Library, 1948.

APA: Camus, A. (1948). The plague (S. Gilbert, Trans.).

New York: Modern Library. (Original work

published 1947)

In APA style, the date of the translation is placed after the author's name; the date of original publication of the work is placed in parentheses at the end of the reference. In text, this book would be cited

(Camus, 1947/1948)

CORPORATE AUTHOR (A COMMISSION, COMMITTEE, OR OTHER GROUP)

MLA: American Medical Association. The American

Medical Association's Handbook of First Aid

and Emergency Care. New York: Random, 1980.

APA: American Medical Association. (1980). The

American Medical Association's handbook of

first aid and emergency care. New York: Random

House.

ANONYMOUS WORK

MLA: WordStar Training Guide. 2nd ed. San Rafael:

MicroPro International, 1983.

APA: WordStar training guide. (1983). (2nd ed.). San

Rafael, CA: MicroPro International.

REPUBLISHED WORK (FOR EXAMPLE, A NEWER PAPERBACK PUBLISHED AFTER THE ORIGINAL HARDBOUND)

MLA: Sagan, Carl. The Dragons of Eden: Speculations on

the Evolution of Human Intelligence. 1977. New

York: Ballantine, 1978.

APA: Sagan, C. (1978). The dragons of Eden: Speculations

on the evolution of human intelligence. New

York: Ballantine. (Originally published

in 1977)

General Format for Articles

MLA: Author. ''Article Title.'' Magazine or Journal

Title volume number (Date): inclusive pages.

APA: Author. (Date). Article title. Magazine or

Journal Title, volume number, inclusive pages.

SCHOLARLY JOURNAL WITH CONTINUOUS ANNUAL PAGINATION

MLA: Brée, Germaine. ''Women's Voices in Cross-

Cultural Exchange.'' Contemporary French

Civilization 5 (1981): 403-10.

APA: Brée, G. (1981). Women's voices in cross-cultural

exchange. Contemporary French Civilization,

5, 403-410.

SCHOLARLY JOURNAL WITH EACH ISSUE PAGED SEPARATELY

MLA: Tetlock, Philip E. ''Testing Deterrence Theory:

Some Conceptual and Methodological Issues.''

Journal of Social Issues 43.4 (1987): 85-91.

APA: Tetlock, P. E. (1987). Testing deterrence theory:

Some conceptual and methodological issues.

Journal of Social Issues 43(4), 85-91.

Note that in both systems when each issue is paged separately, both the volume (in this case, 43) and the issue number (in this case, 4) are given.

MAGAZINE ARTICLE

> MLA: Angier, Natalie. ''A 'Stupid' Cell with All the
>
> Answers.'' <u>Discover</u> Nov. 1986: 70-83.
>
> APA: Angier, N. (1986, November). A ''stupid'' cell
>
> with all the answers. <u>Discover</u>, pp. 70-83.

Note that the above form is for a magazine published each month. The next entry shows the form for a magazine published each week.

ANONYMOUS ARTICLE

> MLA: ''The Rebellious Archbishop.'' <u>Newsweek</u> 11 July
>
> 1988: 38.
>
> APA: The rebellious archbishop. (1988, July 11).
>
> <u>Newsweek</u>, p. 38.

REVIEW

> MLA: Bliven, Naomi. ''Long, Hot Summer.'' Rev. of <u>We</u>
>
> <u>Are</u> <u>Not</u> <u>Afraid</u>: <u>The</u> <u>Story</u> <u>of</u> <u>Goodman,</u>
>
> <u>Schwerner,</u> <u>and</u> <u>Cheney</u> <u>and</u> <u>the</u> <u>Civil</u> <u>Rights</u>
>
> <u>Campaign</u> <u>of</u> <u>Mississippi</u>, by Seth Cagin and
>
> Philip Dray. <u>New</u> <u>Yorker</u> 11 July 1988: 81+.

This is a review of a book. The *81+* indicates that the review continues later in the magazine. For both movie and book reviews, if the reviewer's name is not given, begin with the title of the reviewed work, preceded by "Rev. of" in the MLA system or "[Review of title]" in the APA system. Begin with the title of the review if the review is titled but not signed.

> APA: Bliven, N. (1988, July 11). Long, hot summer
>
> [Review of <u>We</u> <u>are</u> <u>not</u> <u>afraid</u>: <u>The</u> <u>story</u> <u>of</u>
>
> <u>Goodman,</u> <u>Schwerner,</u> <u>and</u> <u>Cheney</u> <u>and</u> <u>the</u> <u>civil</u>
>
> <u>rights</u> <u>campaign</u> <u>of</u> <u>Mississippi</u>]. <u>New</u> <u>Yorker</u>,
>
> p. 81+

NEWSPAPER ARTICLE

MLA: Healy, Tim. ''The Politics of Real Estate.''

Seattle Times 14 June 1988: 1E.

APA: Healy, T. (1988, June 14). The politics of real

estate. The Seattle Times, p. 1E.

Note that the section is indicated if each section is paged separately.

NEWSPAPER EDITORIAL

MLA: Smith, Charles Z. ''Supreme Court Door Opens for a

Minority.'' Editorial. Seattle Times 14 July

1988: 18A.

APA: Smith, C. Z. (1988, July 14). Supreme court door

opens for a minority [Editorial]. The Seattle

Times, p. 18A.

LETTER TO THE EDITOR OF A MAGAZINE OR NEWSPAPER

MLA: Fleming, Deb. Letter. Ms. July 1988: 14.

APA: Fleming, D. (1988, July). [Letter to the editor].

Ms., p. 14.

Include a title if one is given to the letter in the publication.

INFORMATION SERVICE SUCH AS ERIC (EDUCATIONAL RESOURCES INFORMATION CENTER) OR NTIS (NATIONAL TECHNICAL INFORMATION SERVICE)

MLA: Eddy, P. A. The Effects of Foreign Language Study

in High School on Verbal Ability as Measured by

the Scholastic Aptitude Test-Verbal.

Washington: Center for Applied Linguistics,

1981. ERIC ED 196 312.

APA: Eddy, P. A. (1981). The effects of foreign

language study in high school on verbal ability

as measured by the Scholastic Aptitude Test-

<u>Verbal</u>. Washington, D.C.: Center for Applied
Linguistics. (ERIC Document Reproduction
Service No. ERIC ED 196 312)

Miscellaneous Materials

FILMS, FILMSTRIPS, SLIDE PROGRAMS, AND VIDEOTAPES

MLA: <u>Chagall</u>. Videocassette. Dir. by Kim Evans. Ed.
Melvyn Bragg. London Weekend Television, 1985.

APA: Evans, K. (Director), & Bragg, M. (Editor).
(1985). <u>Chagall</u> [Videocassette]. London,
England: London Weekend Television.

TELEVISION AND RADIO PROGRAMS

MLA: <u>Korea: The Forgotten War</u>. Narr. by Robert Stack.
KCPQ, Seattle. 27 June 1988.

APA: Stack, R. (Narrator). (1988, June 27). <u>The
forgotten war</u>. KCPQ Seattle.

INTERVIEW

MLA: Rockwood, Hisako. Personal interview. 27 Feb.
1988.

APA: Rockwood, H. (1988, February 27). [Personal
interview].

The APA publication manual says to omit nonrecoverable materials—such
as personal correspondence, personal interviews, lectures, and so forth—
from "References" at the end. However, in college research papers, professors usually like to have such information included.

LECTURE, ADDRESS, OR SPEECH

MLA: North, Oliver. Speech. Washington Policy Council.
Seattle, 20 July 1988.

APA: North, O. (1988, July 20). Speech presented to
Washington Policy Council, Seattle.

In the MLA system, if the title of the speech is known, give the title in quotation marks in place of the word "Speech." The *Publication Manual of the American Psychological Association* has no provisions for citing lectures, addresses, or speeches because these are nonrecoverable items. However, the manual gives authors leeway to design citations for instances not covered explicitly in the manual. This format is suitable for college research papers.

For more complicated entries, consult the *MLA Handbook for Writers of Research Papers*, third edition, or the *Publication Manual of the American Psychological Association*, third edition. Both books should be available in your library or bookstore.

CONCLUSION

If you see research writing as a variation on the thesis-governed writing you do for all your argument essays, you shouldn't have any particular difficulty writing an argument as a research paper. Keep in mind the issue question, thesis, and purpose of your own essay as a guide to taking notes and incorporating sources into your own work. Avoid data dumping by using borrowed material as a way of supporting your own argument instead of as an end in itself. Take particular care to indicate the beginning and end of borrowed material by putting attributive tags in your text and indicate any borrowed language with quotation marks or block indentations. Simply add the conventions of documentation appropriate to your topic and field, and you will have produced a satisfying research paper.

FOR CLASS DISCUSSION

1. Read Brenda's essay, pages 348–357, which is an example of a fully documented argument using the MLA style. Go to your library and locate several of the sources she has cited in her essay. Read one or two of the articles she cites and then prepare a brief report on whether or not she uses those sources accurately and fairly.

2. Read Lynnea's essay (following this section), which is an example of a fully documented argument using the APA style. Give this essay the same scrutiny requested for Brenda's essay. Go to your library and locate several of the sources she has cited in her essay. Then prepare a brief report on whether or not she uses those sources accurately and fairly.

Women Police Officers:

Should Size and Strength Be Criteria for Patrol Duty?

Lynnea Clark

English 301

15 November 1990

Running Head: WOMEN POLICE

This research paper follows the APA style for format and documentation.

Women Police Officers:

Should Size and Strength Be Criteria for Patrol Duty?

A marked patrol car turns the corner at 71st and Franklin Avenue and cautiously proceeds into the parking lot of an old shopping center. About a dozen gang members, dressed in their gang colors, stand alert, looking down the alley that runs behind the store. As the car moves toward the gathering, they suddenly scatter in all directions. Within seconds, several shots are fired from the alley. Switching on the overhead emergency lights, the officer bolts from the car when he sees two figures running past him. ''Freeze! Police!'' the officer yells. The men dart off in opposite directions. Chasing one, the policeman catches up to him, and, observing no gun, tackles him. After a violent struggle, the officer manages to handcuff the man, just as the backup unit comes screeching up.

This policeman is my friend. The next day I am with him as he sits at a cafe with three of his fellow officers, discussing the incident. One of the officers comments, ''Well, at least you were stronger than he was. Can you imagine if Connie Jones was on patrol duty last night?'' ''What a joke,'' scoffs another officer, ''How tall is she anyway?'' ''About 4'10" and 90 pounds,'' says the third officer. ''She could fit in my backpack.'' Connie Jones (not her real name) has just completed police academy training and has been assigned to patrol duty in _____ . Because she is so small, she has to have a booster seat in her patrol car and has been given a special gun, since she can barely manage to pull the trigger of a standard police-issue .38 revolver. Although she passed the physical requirements at the academy, which involved speed and endurance running, situps, and monkey bar tests, most of the officers in her department doubt her ability to perform competently as a patrol officer. But nevertheless she is on patrol because men and women receive equal assignments in most of today's police forces. But is this a good policy? Can a person who is significantly small and weak make an effective patrol officer?

Because the ''small and weak'' people in question are almost always women, the issue becomes a woman's issue. Considerable research has been done on women in the police force, and much of it suggests that women, who are on the average smaller and weaker than men, can perform competently in law enforcement, regardless of their size or strength. More specifically, most research concludes that female police workers in general perform just as well as their fellow officers in patrolling situations. A major study by Bloch and Anderson (1984), commissioned by the

Urban Institute, revealed that in the handling of violent
situations, women performed well. In fact, women and men
received equally satisfactory evaluation ratings on their
overall performances.

In another more recent study (Grennan, 1987) examining
the relationship between outcomes of police - citizen
confrontations and the gender of the involved officers,
female officers were determined to be just as productive as
male officers in the handling of violent situations. In his
article on female criminal justice employment, Potts (1982)
reviews numerous studies on evaluation ratings of
policewomen and acknowledges that ''the predominant weight
of evidence is that women are equally capable of performing
police work as are men'' (p. 11). Additionally, female
officers score higher on necessary traits for leadership
(p. 10), and it has been often found that women are better
at dealing with rape and abuse victims. Again, a study
performed by Grennan (1987), concentrating on male and
female police officers' confrontations with citizens,
revealed that the inborn or socialized nurturing ability
possessed by female police workers makes them ''just as
productive as male officers in the handling of a violent
confrontation'' (p. 84).

This view has been strengthened further by the recent
achievement of Katherine P. Heller, who was honored by

receiving the nation's top award in law enforcement for
1990 (Proctor, 1990). Heller, a United States park
policewoman, risked her life by stepping in the open to
shoot dead an assailant while he levelled his gun to shoot
at her fellow police officer. Five feet three inches and 107
pounds, Heller is not only the first woman to be awarded
with Police Officer of the Year, but she is also the smallest
recipient ever. Maybe Heller's decisiveness will help lay
to rest doubts about many women's abilities as police
workers.

However, despite the evidence provided by the above
cited research, I am not convinced. Although these studies
show that women make effective police officers, I believe
the studies must be viewed with skepticism. My concern is
public safety. In light of that concern, the evidence
suggests that police departments should set stringent size
and strength requirements for patrol officers, even if
these criteria exclude many women.

First of all, the research studies documenting the
success of women as patrol officers are marred by two major
flaws: the amount of evidence gathered is scanty and the way
that the data have been gathered doesn't allow us to study
factors of size and strength. Because of minimal female
participation in patrol work prior to the past decade,
limited amounts of research and reports exist on the issue.

And of the research performed, many studies have not been
based on representative samples. Garrison, Grant, and
McCormick (1988) found that

> [l]iterature on women in patrol or nontraditional
> police roles tends to be idiosyncratic. . . .
> Many of the observations written about a
> relatively small number of women performing
> successfully in a wider range of police tasks
> support the assumption that they are exceptions
> rather than the norm. (p. 32)

Similarly, Bloch and Anderson (1984) note that in the
course of their study

> it was not possible to observe enough incidents
> to be sure that men and women are equally capable
> in all such situations. It is clear from the
> incidents which were described that women
> performed well in the few violent situations
> which did arise. (p. 61)

Another problem with the available research is that
little differentiation has been made within the large group
of women being considered; all women officers seem to be
grouped and evaluated based on only two criteria: that they
are on the police force and that they are female. But like
men, women come in all shapes and sizes. To say that women as
a class make effective or ineffective police workers is to

make too general a claim. The example of women officers such as Katherine Heller proves that <u>some</u> women make excellent patrol cops. But, presumably, <u>some</u> women probably would not make good patrol cops just as some men would not. The available data do not allow us to determine whether size and strength are factors. Because no size differentiation has been made within the groups of women officers under observation in the research studies, it is impossible to conclude whether or not smaller, weaker women performed patrol duties as well as larger, stronger women did. In fact, for Bloch and Anderson's study (which indicates that, from a performance viewpoint, it is appropriate to hire women for patrol assignments on the same basis as men) both men and women had to meet a minimum height requirement of 5'7". Therefore, the performance of smaller, weaker women in handling violent situations remained unevaluated. Thus the data show that many women are great cops; the data do <u>not</u> show that many small women with minimal strength make great cops.

The case of Katherine Heller might seem to demonstrate that smaller women can perform patrol duties successfully. Heller acknowledged in an interview in <u>Parade</u> magazine that ninety percent of her adversaries will be bigger than herself (Proctor, 1990, p. 5). But she is no fluttering fluffball; rather, she has earned the reputation for being an extremely aggressive cop and has compensated for her size by her bearing. But how many women (or men) of Heller's size or smaller could maintain such ''officer presence''? How can we be certain that Heller is in fact representative of small women rather than being an exception?

This question leads to my second reason for supporting stringent size and strength requirements: Many police officers, both male and female, have real doubts about the abilities of small and physically weak patrol workers, most of whom are women. In a study done by Vega and Silverman (1982), almost 75% of male police officers felt that women were not strong enough to handle the demands of patrol duties, and 42% felt women lacked the needed assertiveness to enforce the law vigorously (p. 32). Unfortunately, however, because of frequent media reports of discrimination and sexism among police personnel and because of pressure from the Equal Employment Opportunity Commission (EEOC) on police agencies and other employers (Vega & Silverman, 1982; Lord, 1986), these reservations and attitudes have not been seriously taken into account. The valid concerns and opinions of police workers who feel that some women officers are not strong enough to deal effectively with violent situations have been asphyxiated

by the smoldering accusations of civil rights activists and
feminists, who see only layers of chauvinism, conservatism,
cynicism, and authoritarianism permeating our law
enforcement agencies. These activists view the problem as
being only a ''women'' issue rather than a ''size'' issue.
But the fact remains that both male and female officers
think that many patrol workers are incapable of handling
violent situations because of small stature and lack of
physical strength. Another policewoman belonging to the
same department as Connie Jones explained, ''She [Jones]
doesn't have the authoritarian stance needed to compensate
for her size. She's not imposing and is too soft spoken.
Once she responded to a call and was literally picked up and
thrown out the door'' (anonymous personal communication,
October 6, 1990).

Finally, patrol duties, unlike other areas of police
work, constitute one of the few jobs in our society that may
legitimately require above average strength. Because the
job involves great personal risk and danger, the concern
for public safety overrides the concern for equal rights in
this instance. Patrolling is a high visibility position in
police departments as opposed to jobs such as radio
dispatching, academy training, or clerical duties. Patrol
workers directly face the challenges presented by the
public, and violence is always a threat for officers on

patrol (Vega & Silverman, 1982; Grennan, 1987). Due to the
nature of patrol work, officers many times must cope with
violent situations by using physical force, such as that
needed for subduing individuals who resist arrest. However,
pressure from liberal groups has prevented special
consideration being given to these factors of patrol duty.
As long as student officers pass the standard academy
Physical Ability Test (in addition to the other academy
requirements), then they are eligible for patrol
assignments; in fact, everyone out of the academy must go on
patrol. But the minimum physical requirements are not
challenging. According to Lord (1986), police agencies
''struggle to find a nondiscriminatory, empirically valid
entry level physical agility test which does not
discriminate against women by overemphasizing upper body
strength'' (Lord, 1986, p. 91). In short, the liberal agenda
leading to women on patrol has forced the lowering of
strength requirements.

Without establishing minimum size and strength
requirements for patrol workers, police departments are not
discharging their duties with maximum competency or
effectiveness. Police training programs stress that police
officers should be able to maintain an authoritarian
presence in the face of challenges and possess the ability
to diffuse a situation just by making an appearance. But

some individuals who are able to pass basic training
programs still lack the size needed to maintain an imposing
physical stance. And as many citizens obviously do not
respect the uniform, police workers must possess the
strength to efficiently handle violent encounters. Even if
size and strength requirements have a disproportionate
impact on women, these physical standards are <u>lawful</u>, so
long as they relate to the demands of the job and
''constitute valid predictors of an employee's performance
on the job'' (Steel & Lovrich, 1987, p. 53). Patrol duties
demand highly capable and effective workers, and in order to
professionalize law-enforcement practices and to maintain
the degree of order necessary for a free society, police
agencies must maintain a high level of competency in their
street-patrol forces.

References

Bloch, P., & Anderson, D. (1974). Police women on patrol: Final report. Washington, D.C.: Police Foundation.

Garrison, C., Grant, N., & McCormick, K. (1988). Utilization of police women. The Police Chief, 55(9), 32-73.

Golden, K. (1981). Women as patrol officers: A study of attitudes. Police Studies, 4(3), 29-33.

Grennan, S. (1987). Findings on the role of officer gender in violent encounters with citizens. Journal of Police Science and Administration, 15(1), 78-84.

Igbinovia, P. (1987). African women in contemporary law enforcement. Police Studies, 10(1), 31-34.

Lord, L. (1986). A comparison of male and female peace officers' stereotypic perceptions of women and women peace officers. Journal of Police Science and Administration, 14(2), 83-91.

Potts, L. (1981). Equal employment opportunity and female criminal justice employment. Police Studies, 4(3), 9-19

Proctor, P. (1990, September 30). ''I didn't have time to taste the fear.'' Parade Magazine, pp. 4-5.

Steel, B., & Lovrich, N., Jr. (1987). Equality and efficiency tradeoffs in affirmative action--real or imagined? The case of women in policing. The Social Science Journal, 24(1), 53-67.

Vega, M., & Silverman, I. (1982). Female police officers as viewed by their male counterparts. Police Studies, 5(1), 31-39.

VI

AN ANTHOLOGY OF ARGUMENTS

A PREFACE TO THE ANTHOLOGY, INCLUDING GUIDE QUESTIONS FOR ANALYZING ARGUMENTS

OVERVIEW OF THE ANTHOLOGY

Up to this point, we've concentrated mostly on how to write arguments. In Part VI of this text we present a number of finished arguments for you to study. These aren't intended to be "model" arguments in the sense that simply by imitating them you can be guaranteed a great argument. By now, it should be clear that writing is more complex than that. What typically makes these arguments worthy of our attention is the writers' commitment to and knowledge of their subjects and their ability to find a form appropriate to what they have to say. Often, the least "imitable" aspects of an essay are the keys to the essay's success. But this doesn't mean we can't learn something about how to write better arguments from reading a variety of good arguments. And, provided that we don't treat the essays with too much reverence, provided that we're willing to play with them as well as imitate them, we can certainly adapt specific features of various essays to our own ends.

Here we would underscore the need to make the essays work for you.

Every argument has a specific occasion, a set of circumstances that gave rise to the writer's choice of voice, structure, and evidence. In order to "translate" another writer's argument to your own occasion, you'll need to make adjustments. An essay you like very much may deal with its topic in an irreverent and funny way; but when you turn to your own topic, you may find humor inappropriate and distracting. Data that are extremely persuasive in one writer's argument may be almost wholly unpersuasive or even irrelevant in the context of your own argument. But by the same token, you may well find that the same author's adroit use of narrative illustrations will serve your essay well. Our advice is to use the following essays as models only in the sense that they are analogues of, not patterns for, arguments you might want to write. The essays represent a range of choices that other writers have made, and in that sense are intended to expand your own sense of available options.

One good method for dealing with the essays in this section is to approach them in the manner of the bricoleur mentioned by French anthropologist Claude Levi-Strauss. A bricoleur is a sort of jack-of-all-trades who keeps a large supply of diverse materials on hand in order to "make do" with them: "A particular cube of oak could be a wedge to make up for the inadequate length of a plank of pine or it could be a pedestal—which would allow the grain and polish of the old wood to show to advantage. In one case it will serve as an extension, in the other as material." If you examine the essays with the bricoleur's irreverent eye for new possibilities and adapt them for your own use, you do them more honor than if you passively "appreciate" them or mechanically ape them.

In order to help you see these essays in the proper spirit, we've attempted to place some of them in the context of the ongoing conversation that they come from. Instead of standing as the last word on some problematical subject, they are presented as positions on an issue. However eloquent and persuasive they may be, each should be recognized as one voice in a conversation. Indeed, we may well decide that one of the essays is right and another wrong. But even then, the essay of choice will almost always be understood differently by virtue of the fact that we've considered another point of view. After reading divergent points of view on a given subject, the reader is left with the responsibility to synthesize what's given and to create yet another point of view. This process of synthesis and dissent is the very lifeblood of argument.

The anthology addresses twelve important social issues. The first four issues are arranged as pro/con pairs so that you can analyze opposing arguments head to head. In the remaining eight issues, we have added additional voices to each of the conversations, blurring somewhat the neatness of sharply contrasted pro/con perspectives but imitating more closely the complexity of actual conversations. Seldom are there just two positions on an issue. Almost always, disputants express a wide range of views with many overlapping areas of agreement and disagreement. The later sections of this anthology reflect this complexity.

As you read through the arguments in Part VI, you might want to keep in mind the question of where each of them fits into a larger context of issues—those recurrent questions and dilemmas that we struggle with in different guises all the time. No matter what the specific issue is, certain recurring patterns of concern keep cropping up such as the conflict between principles and consequences in ethical arguments, or between spiritual and material values, individual rights and public duties, duties to self and duties to others, short-range consequences and long-range consequences, and commitment to tradition and commitment to progress. For example, whether you are considering a proposal for mandatory drug testing or for a new zoning regulation to prevent homeowners from building too high a fence, you are dealing with the conflict between "rights of the individual" and "rights of the society." One advantage of an anthology of arguments is that in reading through them, you can see for yourself how frequently these large issues recur in different guises.

GUIDE QUESTIONS FOR THE ANALYSIS AND EVALUATION OF ARGUMENTS

As you read various arguments from this anthology, we hope that you will internalize habits of analysis and evaluation that we believe are essential for arguers. These habits derive from the principles of argument analysis covered throughout this text so that what follows is simply a summary and review of concepts you have already studied.

Questions for Analyzing and Evaluating a Conversation

Whenever you read a pro/con pair or a wide range of arguments addressing the same issue, we recommend that you follow the principles of reading described in Chapter 2.

1. *What does each argument say?* (Reading as a believer, be able to summarize each argument, stating its main claim and supporting reasons in a single sentence, if possible.)

2. *How can each argument be doubted?* (Reading as a doubter, search for weaknesses in the argument and for important questions that you would like to raise if you could talk to the author.)

3. *Why do the disputants disagree?* (Do they disagree about the "facts of the case"? About key definitions? About appropriate comparisons and analogies? About values, assumptions, and beliefs?)

4. *Which arguments appear to be stronger?* (Which arguments seem most persuasive to you? Before you could take a stand on the issue yourself, what further questions would you need to have answered? Which of your own assumptions, values, and beliefs would you have to examine further and clarify?)

Questions for Analyzing and Evaluating an Individual Argument

The previous questions ask you to examine arguments in the context of the conversations to which they belong. This next set of questions asks you to look closely at a single argument, examining in detail its structure, its argumentative strategies, and its rhetorical force. The questions apply the principles described in Parts II and III of this text.

1. *How effective is the writer at creating logical appeals?*
   - What is the claim?
   - What reasons support the claim?
   - What are the grounds and warrants for each of the reasons?
   - How effective is the argument, particularly its use of evidence (grounds) and its support of its basic assumptions (warrants)?
   - Does the argument exhibit any of the *logos* fallacies explained in Appendix 1?

2. *How effective is the writer at creating ethical appeals?*
   - What *ethos* does the writer project? What is the writer's stance toward the audience?
   - Is the writer's *ethos* effective?
   - Does the writer commit any of the *ethos* fallacies explained in Appendix 1?

3. *How effective is the writer at creating emotional appeals?*
   - How effective is the writer at using audience-based reasons?
   - How effective is the writer's use of concrete language, word choice, powerful examples, and analogies for enhancing the emotional appeal of the argument?

4. *How could the writer's argument be refuted?*
   - Can the writer's grounds be attacked or called into question?
   - Can the writer's warrants be attacked or called into question?

THE EXCLUSIONARY RULE: DO LAWS PROTECTING SUSPECTS' RIGHTS BENEFIT SOCIETY?

LET OUR POLICE TAKE ON THE DRUG DEALERS

Charles Brandt

Charles Brandt, past president of the Delaware Trial Lawyers Association, opposes the "exclusionary rule" — a Supreme Court decision that limits the ways police can collect evidence. Police departments "now find their hands cuffed, their eyes blinded and their ears plugged by the very laws they have sworn to uphold."

One evening last March, Sgt. Byron Simms and two other undercover Washington, D.C., police officers spotted a flashy new Lincoln illegally parked in one of the city's drug-ravaged neighborhoods. A passenger stepped out, removed a large plastic bag from the trunk, and got back in the car. 1

Suspecting a drug transaction, the narcotics officers followed the Lincoln to a shopping center. There the suspect, later identified as Gary K. Most, Jr., took the bag into a small grocery. 2

Within a half-hour, Most returned without the bag. Simms, posing as a shopper, went into the store, where he spotted the bag behind the checkout counter. He questioned the manager and two clerks, who said Most had asked them to keep an eye on it. 3

When Simms lifted the bag, he felt hard, pebble-like objects inside—"rocks" of crack, experience told him. Sure enough, he pulled out 272 small plastic bags of crack, with a street value of $23,000.

Although Most was sentenced to ten years in prison, last June the U.S. Court of Appeals overturned the verdict on the ground that his rights had been violated. If one of the clerks had opened the bag and showed the evidence to Simms, that would have been acceptable. But according to the rules of evidence, Simms, trained to recognize criminal behavior and to identify drugs, didn't have the right to pick up the bag in the first place. And so Gary Most went free.

- On February 8, 1989, a federal judge dismissed crack charges against a Jamaican drug dealer because a Denver SWAT team—carrying a valid search warrant—had failed to knock on the door before battering it down.

- In April 1989 an appellate court in Alaska dropped a charge against a bartender who had sold drugs to undercover state troopers from his jacket hanging some 15 feet from the bar. The court ruled that because the jacket was not within the bartender's reach, the troopers should have gotten a search warrant for the jacket.

- Alabama police were recently tipped off that a vehicle was transporting guns and drugs. With their own guns drawn, they surrounded the car and noticed a partially smoked marijuana joint on the dashboard. They ordered the occupants to get out. On July 21, 1989, the Alabama Court of Criminal Appeals decided that the police could not have been sure of their informant's reliability, declared the seizure of an automatic pistol and drugs illegal and remanded the case to the lower court—without the key evidence. Of course, minus this evidence, the case probably will never be retried.

Every day in America, drug dealers walk away from their crimes because of legal hair-splitting. Police departments, trying to follow court guidelines on proper procedure by studying cases like those above, now find their hands cuffed, their eyes blinded and their ears plugged by the very laws they have sworn to uphold. The sad result is that today, all over the country, drug markets operate flagrantly, protected by rules that exclude authorities better than any steel door.

"Exclusionary Rule." Why do we force our cops to stand by impotently, watching criminals ply their trade as if they had diplomatic immunity? The major cause of such rulings that defy common sense is the 1961 Supreme Court case of *Mapp v. Ohio.* Police had accidentally found pornographic pamphlets and photos in the Mapp house while searching for a bombing suspect. The Supreme Court ruled that since the search was warrantless, evidence of other illegalities discovered had to be excluded in court.

This "exclusionary rule" had its most devastating impact on one area of 11
law enforcement: drug arrests. Before the Mapp decision, a police officer
could stop and search a drug dealer or user on suspicion. An anonymous tip
from a neighbor was enough to justify a house search warrant. Today,
because of the exclusionary rule, there is a barrage of court rulings on proper
ways to gather evidence. Police practically *need* a search warrant to gather
enough facts to *get* one.

On November 1, 1987, for example, a resident of an Atlantic Beach, Fla., 12
apartment complex found a three-year-old boy wandering the parking lot.
She called the police. When they questioned the boy, he ran to an apartment,
saying, "Mama's in there." The door was ajar and swung open as police
knocked. The officers announced their presence. Getting no response, they
drew their weapons and entered. They could see marijuana and drug paraphernalia in the bedroom, where the boy's mother and one David Emory
Eason were asleep.

Police then obtained a search warrant for the rest of the apartment, which 13
held even more drugs. Eason was charged with drug possession. But not for
long. On June 28, 1989, the District Court of Appeal of Florida dismissed the
case because the police had not obtained a search warrant *before* their initial
visit to the apartment.

A Columbia University study compared the number of narcotics-possession 14
arrests during a six-month period just prior to the Mapp decision and the
same period the following year. The study found that arrests were cut in half.
Furthermore, it noted that "convictions have been harder to obtain since
Mapp."

Steven Schlesinger, former director of the Bureau of Justice Statistics, 15
estimated in *Crime and Public Policy* that the exclusionary rule derailed
45,000 to 55,000 *serious* criminal cases in 1977–78 alone. And this didn't
include arrests that never happened because, while the cop felt sure drugs
were being dealt right under his nose, he knew he didn't have enough
evidence to obtain a search warrant.

Balancing Act. The exclusionary rule has become the police officer's 16
nightmare. The courts cranked out so many restrictions on police that the
1960s have been called the "criminal-law revolution." It wasn't enough to
require a search warrant: the search also had to be limited to a narrowly
specified crime, and the warrant had to list facts amounting to "probable
cause" for arrest. If the police presented facts suggesting stolen television
sets, for example, the warrant would not allow a search for drugs in a desk
drawer. Then the courts began to pass judgment on the "reliability" of
information that went into the "probable cause" argument.

To do his job, a police officer now has to balance a 3342-page law book on 17
his head. Prof. Wayne R. LaFave's standard treatise, *Search and Seizure*,
cited by judges in many of the decisions described in this article, is based

entirely on interpretations of the one sentence in the Fourth Amendment. Each year the book grows larger.

Defenders of the exclusionary rule say that "police training" on these 18 issues has promoted greater professionalism in police departments. But the price of this noble goal is far fewer drug arrests — and brisk open-air drug markets in every fair-sized city.

Citizens' Rights. I was a prosecutor and Chief Deputy Attorney General 19 for Delaware when many of the present rules were created. I know firsthand how they affected drug enforcement. They constrained the police to operate in slow motion, while drug traffickers picked up frightening speed.

I rode with experienced cops who could tell just by looking at a known 20 dealer whether or not he was carrying drugs. Yet they couldn't search and arrest him. Instead, they could only hope that someday they would be able to get a paid addict to help an undercover cop make a "controlled buy." Even then, in order to protect the informant, weeks would have to pass before an arrest could be made — during which time the dealer would continue to pollute the community with drugs.

Capt. Ronald M. Huston of the Wilmington, Del., police force says that 21 countless criminals walk the streets with impunity, carrying both drugs and guns. One is a major dealer with lavish homes in Delaware and New Jersey. He is known by the federal Drug Enforcement Administration, but is basically untouchable. "Dealers tell us about him, but that's not enough to get a warrant," says Huston. "Unless someone comes forward to wear a body mike, we can't get enough admissible evidence to search him."

In addition to being a prosecutor, I've served as a defense attorney and 22 have seen from the inside how criminals use the rules to protect their activities. Thus an arrest that once took a couple of police officers a few hours now often takes a whole squad many months. Cops can't confront a problem directly. They have to go undercover at great cost to the public — and at the risk of their lives.

In the 1960s, police conduct in some areas of the country against civil- 23 rights demonstrators and minorities enraged the public and justly brought police procedures under scrutiny. But today our drug-plagued society needs to ask: is it the police who pose a threat in our neighborhoods — or the drug dealers carrying attack rifles?

"I don't believe criminal rights are a civil-rights issue," says one black 24 police chief, Reuben Greenberg of Charleston, S.C. "Drug crime mostly affects the poor. They are trapped in their neighborhoods because they can't afford to move. It is their rights I am concerned about, for criminals now have an overwhelming advantage."

End the Nitpicking. Americans did not live in a police state before the 25 Mapp decision. We have other laws to protect citizens from overzealous police. Australia, Canada, England, France, Japan and West Germany have no exclusionary rules, and they aren't police states. No other democracy protects the rights of criminals over society's right to peace and security—and no other democracy has anywhere near America's drug problem. It is no coincidence that our drug problem greatly worsened after *Mapp v. Ohio.*

There is a ray of hope, however. In 1984 the Supreme Court created the 26 "good faith" exception to the exclusionary rule. A search warrant that is "largely error-free," but technically imperfect, can provide evidence in court if the police acted in "objectively reasonable reliance" on it. Previously, if an "i" were undotted or a "t" uncrossed, the evidence was thrown out.

Unfortunately, the good-faith rule doesn't apply to searches *without* a 27 warrant. It cannot be used to justify seizing a hidden machine gun under a raincoat, for example, or cocaine suspected to be in a car—or any of the evidence described in this article.

Clearly, the good-faith exception doesn't go far enough. As Cornelius J. 28 Behan, Baltimore County, Maryland, police chief, asserts, "It is time to revisit the entire area of admissible evidence to see if it is blocking the way to the truth."

Congress should hold hearings on the subject. And the public ought to 29 join in the debate—this is not a matter just for lawyers arguing behind closed doors. People need to make *their* voices heard by their Congressmen.

Am I suggesting that our cherished Constitutional rights be abrogated? 30 Absolutely not! But the exclusionary rule is a judge-made rule of courtroom evidence, *not* a Constitutional right. We need to protest the way the Constitution has been nitpicked by judges and the truth banished from courthouses.

American law is dynamic and has always changed with the times. We are in 31 the middle of a drug epidemic. We don't need protection from the cop on the beat—we need protection from criminals. And our police can't fight drugs if they are hamstrung by laws that defy common sense.

LIBERALS AND CRIME

George Kannar

Law professor George Kannar defends the exclusionary rule on the grounds that its benefits outweigh its disadvantages. "Despite 20 years of debate and study, no one has come up with any better devices for protecting individual rights in the criminal justice process."

By a quarter of an inch, I missed growing up as the son of an Irish cop in   1
New York City. Because my father flunked the height exam, I ended up as the son of an international automobile executive instead. Only in America. I consequently came of age in a faraway country with stylish people and broad boulevards, a Spanish-speaking Paris; with gauchos, and pampas, and steak every day. A beautiful country where the judiciary was weak, where habeas corpus was usually ignored, and where official investigations were unhampered by cumbersome procedures. A society as cosmopolitan and sophisticated as our own, in which a few years later thousands of innocent men, women, and children were kidnapped, tortured, and made to "disappear." And all as part of a good-faith effort, performed by sincere officers, to re-establish "law and order."

In 1968 Richard Nixon was elected president by talking about crime and   2
the liberals' supposed "softness" on it, as exemplified by the Warren Court. This year George Bush was elected by talking about crime again. But in 1988 there is an important difference. Having controlled the White House for 16 of the last 20 years, and having appointed every Supreme Court justice for the last 21, the Republicans ought rightfully to be explaining why their lengthy reign has apparently done so little to assuage Americans' fear of crime. Yet the Warren Court's legacy endures. Those rules that let criminals off on "technicalities" — *Miranda*, the exclusionary rule, and miscellaneous procedural contortions that delay final resolution of so many cases — have not been stricken from the law, even in the Burger/Rehnquist era. The reason is simple: despite 20 years of debate and study, no one has come up with any better devices for protecting individual rights in the criminal justice process.

In other respects, America has become much tougher on its criminals since   3
Earl Warren left the Court. Because of stricter sentencing laws (particularly new "habitual offender" statutes), as well as changes in judicial sensibilities, according to David C. Anderson's *Crimes of Justice,* since 1968 the inmate population in this country has more than tripled. The United States now incarcerates a greater percentage of its population than any industrialized country except the Soviet Union and South Africa. As Elliot Curie pointed out in *Confronting Crime,* such massive "incapacitation" has indeed kept crime

rates lower than they would otherwise have been — not because of any deterrent effect, but simply by keeping would-be criminals off the streets.

Still, this vast increase in punishment has not satisfied anyone, and has not **4** come without substantial costs, both human and financial. At latest count, according to Anderson, 36 states were under expensive court orders to relieve prison overcrowding, whose truly hellish human consequences no reader of *Presumed Innocent* or *The Bonfire of the Vanities* can doubt. We require new prison beds at the rate of a thousand every week. This cannot go on forever, and communities throughout the country balk at the idea of paying for more prisons, or letting them be built nearby. Budget pressures and community resistance are far more responsible for the nation's many furlough programs and work-release alternatives than are woolly-headed liberals or weak-kneed judges.

But, aside from distorting our discussion of crime control for the last two **5** decades, have there been any socially significant costs to those Warren Court "technicalities"? The evidence is overwhelming that the Warren Court — clumsily, and no doubt in part by accident — in fact managed to enhance protection of individual liberties (greater insurance than ever that "it can't happen here") without any real dilution of legitimate law enforcement efforts. If anything, the reality is just the opposite of what the public thinks. Sentimental liberalism has not been a major problem. The problem comes from the other side. Conservative sentimentalism, particularly on our highest court, has in complex ways probably impaired both constitutional rights *and* effective law enforcement.

Consider the exclusionary rule, the remedy the Warren Court imposed on **6** the states to enforce the Fourth Amendment's protections against unreasonable search and seizure. The premise of the rule is simple: if evidence is obtained unconstitutionally, it may not be introduced at trial. The reasons for it, originally, were two. First, it was thought to corrupt the system of justice for courts to use the products of illegal searches — a "judicial integrity" rationale. Second, it was hoped that police would conduct fewer illegal searches if they knew the result would not help gain convictions — a "deterrence" rationale.

Because the Burger Court discarded the "judicial integrity" idea, recent **7** criticism of the exclusionary rule has focused on its deterrent purpose. Does it make sense, as Benjamin Cardozo once put it, to "let the criminal go free because the constable has blundered"? Taking the analysis at this level, the answer is easy: in the case of a well-intentioned officer, doing his or her level best to observe constitutional proprieties, it certainly does not make sense. If the officer was *already* trying to do what was right, what deterrent purpose could possibly be served by suppressing the evidence obtained?

But if we don't intend for the Constitution to become a dead letter, then **8** *some* kind of enforcement mechanism is essential. And constructing a work-able constitutional remedy means taking a *systemic* view of the criminal justice process, not one that focuses sentimentally on the "innocent," well-meaning cop. The Burger/Rehnquist Court consistently gave in to just such sentimentalism. A prime culprit is the so-called "good faith" exception to the exclusionary rule. This sensible-sounding change allows the use of illegally gathered evidence when the officer who obtained it did not know that what he did was wrong. The Burger Court created this exception to "protect" the officer who relied upon what later turned out to be a defective search warrant, issued by a magistrate based on insufficient evidence. Many conservatives have urged the Court to create a "good faith" exception for mistakes com-mitted by the officer himself, an exception deleted from the latest drug bill only at the very last minute.

But if such an exception becomes available, what smart officer, at a pretrial suppression hearing, will *not* say that he "meant well" — and believe it? Of course he "means well"; fighting crime is hard, boring, and highly dangerous work. People don't do it so that they can become millionaires. Moreover, even if the question is narrower — whether the police officer sincerely thought his actions were permitted by the Constitution — does society want the officer's opinion to be the only one that matters? Although individual cases of suppressing "good faith" evidence may seem stupid, the only real alternative is to delegate the entire matter to the individual cop. With all the considerable respect that's due our law enforcement officers, trusting solely in the individual officer's "good faith" would create a com-pletely lawless system. The effective result of a broad "good faith" exception of the sort now widely proposed would be to eliminate entirely the opportu-nity for meaningful judicial review.

In its obsession with the predicament of the forgivably mistaken officer — its uncontrollable frustration at seeing undeniably guilty individuals go free — the Burger Court abdicated its prime institutional responsibility within the criminal justice system: to establish comprehensible and enforceable ground rules.

The Fourth Amendment's "warrant clause" could easily be read to estab-lish an ironclad rule that searches and arrests may be conducted only with a formal written warrant, issued by a magistrate on the basis of sworn testi-mony establishing "probable cause." Even the Warren Court recognized that such an absolute rule was inadequate for the myriad unanticipated situations of modern life. Consequently, that Court, and the ones before it, allowed a few "jealously and carefully drawn" exceptions, for example allowing police to search suspects for weapons while making an arrest, and to inspect automobiles without detaining the driver while a warrant is obtained or allowing him to drive away.

The Burger Court consistently failed to recognize that exceptions of this

sort can only be kept from swallowing the rule if they are *kept* narrowly —
and clearly — limited. Out of a misplaced zeal to punish individual malefac-
tors, it began behaving like a neighborhood police court; cluttering its docket
with insignificant cases simply because it could not bear the sight of particular individuals going free. In the process, the Republican-dominated Court
converted Fourth Amendment jurisprudence into the impossibly confused
quagmire it is today — piling exception upon exception, creating exceptions
to exceptions, until not even the legal treatise writers can figure out exactly
what the law is, or conscientious officers figure out how to act. In short, it
was the conservative Burger Court, not the liberal Warren Court, that made
search and seizure law a labyrinth of muddled "technicalities." And then
opponents of the exclusionary rule seized upon the mess conservatives had
themselves created as an excuse for abolishing the rule completely.

Because releasing clearly guilty suspects to vindicate the Constitution is   **13**
indeed unattractive, it is frequently proposed to replace the exclusionary rule
with some kind of civil damage suit by the person whose rights are violated.
In fact, such tort remedies *already* exist, and everyone knows from long
experience that juries will hardly ever award any substantial damages against
a cop, even to an innocent citizen. "Everyone" includes the police themselves, which means lawsuits will never have any serious deterrent value. Civil
lawsuits also put the burden of enforcing the Constitution on the shoulders
of private citizens who may not, individually, have the time, resources, or
inclination to pursue every violation. For all its faults, the exclusionary rule is
at least self-executing. Although there are various ideas floating around to
address these questions, no one has really shown how to get around the basic
problem that a civil action simply has no credible bite.

Criminal prosecution of errant police — another oft-suggested alternative   **14**
to the exclusionary rule — wouldn't work either. According to Professor
Stephen A. Saltzburg of the University of Virginia (now deputy head of the
Justice Department's Criminal Division), both the federal government and his
home state have long had perfectly fine criminal statutes on their books
prohibiting illegal searches. No officer, however, has ever been convicted
under the federal statue, and the Virginia one, in all its history, has never
once been used. And vigorously prosecuting cops would just make it impossible for the district attorneys and the officers to work together anyway.

What about the supposed costs of enforcing the exclusionary rule with   **15**
rigor? Of course there are individual horror cases: the man who raped your
wife — or you — but goes free because a well-intentioned officer accidentally
goofed. Still, despite the terrible human pain such incidents inflict, any
policy-maker or justice who worries obsessively about criminals going free
because of "soft" criminal procedures faces a statistical uphill battle in a
society where half the crimes go unreported, two-thirds of those reported go

unsolved, and four out of every five crimes committed therefore never get to court at all.

Even among cases that get to court, the "cost" of the exclusionary rule is   16 very small. Critics often cite a 1982 report by the National Institute of Justice reviewing the experience of California, which allegedly concluded that 4.8 percent of state court prosecutions fail because evidence has been thrown out on exclusionary rule grounds. In fact, 4.8 percent is the proportion of *rejected* cases in which the prosecution fails for search and seizure reasons. In other words, only one out of every 20 that are *dismissed* can be blamed on the exclusionary rule. The percentage of *all* criminal cases that founder on search and seizure issues is 0.8 percent, hardly a major public policy concern.

A comprehensive 1979 General Accounting Office study of the exclusion-   17 ary rule's effect on federal prosecutions found similar results. According to the GAO, in only 1.3 percent of the federal cases was any evidence excluded on Fourth Amendment grounds. And in more than half of those cases — a factor that is usually overlooked — the defendant was convicted *anyway*. In other words, the effective cost of the exclusionary rule to federal prosecutors, *before* the Burger Court created the "good faith" standard, was — at worst — a negligible 0.65 percent. And since the vast majority of these cases involve drug possession, rather than violent offenses against person or property, the threat to public order represented by the rule diminishes to the vanishing point. A 1979 study of Washington, Salt Lake City, Los Angeles, and New Orleans found in all those cities exactly one homicide case that was aborted because of the exclusionary rule, and no rape arrests at all.

Although politicians still clamor for exclusionary rule reform, in light of   18 these realities it is no surprise that growing numbers of law enforcement experts agree with Reagan-appointed FBI Director William Sessions, who told the Senate Judiciary Committee during his confirmation hearings in 1987, "As a former judge, . . . I know that the protections that are afforded by the exclusionary rule are extremely important to . . . fair play, and the proper carrying out of the law enforcement responsibility. . . . [B]y and large, I am happy with it the way it is."

FOR CLASS DISCUSSION

1. Analyze and evaluate the debate on the exclusionary rule by applying the first set of guide questions from pages 443–444. How do you account for the disagreement between Brandt and Kannar?

2. Choose one of the arguments for closer analysis, applying the second set of guide questions on page 444.

AN OPTIONAL WRITING ASSIGNMENT Interview a police officer, trial lawyer, or judge about his or her views on the exclusionary rule or on the *Miranda* rule, which requires disclosure of a suspect's right to remain silent. Write a report to your class on the results of your interview.

BIRTH CONTROL AND THE SCHOOLS: SHOULD HIGH SCHOOLS DISPENSE CONTRACEPTIVES?

CLEAR MESSAGE TO TEENS: "IT'S OK TO HAVE SEX"

Joan Beck

Dismayed by the decision of New York City school officials to dispense free contraceptives to high school students, Chicago Tribune columnist Joan Beck argues that the decision is a mistake. It won't be effective at stopping pregnancy or disease, and it will further undermine the efforts of parents to teach moral values.

Whatever his intentions, the message that New York City Schools Chancellor Joseph Fernandez is proposing to give students in the city's 120 high schools is clear: It's OK to have sex. 1

Fernandez has asked the city Board of Education to agree to make free condoms available to all 261,000 high-school students, regardless of their age. Not in a school-based health clinic. Not in connection with sex education. Not just if they have a parent's permission. 2

Simply, free condoms for the asking from male and female staff volunteers during the school day. 3

The Board of Education is expected to give its approval next month. 4

What has persuaded Fernandez to take such a controversial step is   5
concern about AIDS. New York City has the nation's highest rate of AIDS
cases among adolescents, and 20 percent of all teens in this country who have
the deadly disease live there.

But it's hard to jump from those facts, however worrisome, to giving out   6
condoms free in all the New York City high schools.

The number of cases of AIDS diagnosed among teens is still small com-   7
pared with the national toll. Of the 154,917 cumulative cases of AIDS
reported to the Centers for Disease Control by the end of October, only 604
were diagnosed among 13- to 19-year-olds.

Not all these teens acquired the AIDS virus through sexual activity. Drug   8
users who share needles now account for a substantial and growing percentage of AIDS cases.

Does that mean Fernandez will next propose handing out clean, free   9
needles in the schools?

What Fernandez should remember is that the lessons adults think they are   10
teaching children aren't necessarily the messages young people pick up.

The chancellor may think he's warning students to be responsible about   11
sex. But what the teens are most likely to hear is that the school says it's all
right for high-schoolers to have sex and that sex has school backing, right up
there with reading, writing and arithmetic.

How can parents teach teen-agers moral values and counsel them against   12
premature sexual activity, for which they are probably not psychologically
ready, and which may have consequences they are unprepared for? The
school will be telling these adolescents it expects them to be having sex.

By giving out condoms — and at least tacit permission to be sexually   13
active — the schools also will be making it harder than ever for girls to say
no. Teen-agers who don't want to be rushed into sex for very good reasons
already have lost most of the backing they used to get from society.

Little in popular culture now supports premarital abstinence. And boys   14
who customarily pressure girls with everyone-does-it, what's-the-matter-
with-you? arguments will now be able to point out that even the school makes
that assumption.

Fernandez tries to counter criticism about handing out condoms —   15
without counseling or sex education — by saying, "People at any age have
ready access to condoms at supermarkets and drugstores without the benefit
of an educational or counseling component." But since access to condoms is
so easy at supermarkets and drugstores, why is it necessary for the schools
also to hand them out? Any teen who is reluctant to make a public purchase
would probably be even less likely to ask for them at school.

There are other problems. Condoms are not a totally sure protection   16 against the AIDS virus any more than they are 100 percent effective in preventing pregnancy. At best, they offer only safer sex, not safe sex—a distinction that is easily lost on adolescents. They also require responsible, unfailing use, a self-discipline that many teen-agers seem unable to muster for a variety of reasons.

Little clear evidence exists that efforts to reduce teen-age pregnancies by 17
encouraging the use of contraceptives have been successful on a large scale, even when they have involved much more sex education and counseling than New York City high-schoolers get.

Yet, almost no efforts are being made—except by parents and churches 18
—to persuade teens that the only sure protection against pregnancy and sexually transmitted AIDS is abstinence.

Fernandez may be correct in assuming that sexual activity among teens of 19
high-school age is so pervasive that it justifies his condom plan. But it is also possible that expecting students to be sexually active will increase the number of them who are—and could even raise the incidence of adolescent pregnancy and AIDS.

Before the city's Board of Education approves Fernandez's plan, it might 20
pause to consider how poorly the New York schools—and most other big, urban systems—succeed in their traditional task. When the schools can't even do a good job of teaching academics, it's grasping at straws to expect they can be effective in reducing AIDS and teen pregnancies.

The real problem is that we are reduced to grasping at straws. 21

SCHOOL BIRTH-CONTROL CLINICS: NECESSARY EVIL

Charles Krauthammer

The social good of preventing pregnancy, says syndicated columnist Charles Krauthammer, outweighs the social harm of implying that sex is OK. "The sex battle is lost. The front-line issue is pregnancy."

The latest outrage of American life: The pill goes to school. There are now 1
72 "comprehensive health clinics" in or near the nation's public high schools.

Very comprehensive. More than a quarter dispense and more than half 2
prescribe birth-control devices. When the New York City Board of Education found out that two of its clinics were in the dispensing business, it ordered them to cease and desist.

Secretary of Education William Bennett has waxed eloquent on the sub- 3
ject. He is surely right that birth control in the schools makes sexual activity

legitimate and represents an "abdication of moral authority." Clinics are not only an admission by adults that they cannot control teen-age sexuality, but also tacit consent, despite the "just say no" rhetoric.

Unfortunately, there are two problems: not just sex, but pregnancy. As in 4
all social policy, there is a choice to be made. Is it worth risking the implicit message that sex is OK in order to decrease pregnancies?

(Clinic opponents sometimes argue that birth-control dispensaries do not 5
decrease the number of pregnancies, a contention that defies both intuition and the evidence.)

Bennett is right about the nature of the message. But he vastly overesti- 6
mates its practical effect. Kids do not learn their morals at school. (Which is why the vogue for in-school drug education will prove an expensive failure.) They learn at home. Or they used to.

Now they learn from the culture, most notably from the mass media. Your 7
four-eyed biology teacher and your pigeon-toed principal say don't. The Pointer Sisters say do. To whom are you going to listen?

My authority for the image of the grotesque teacher and moronic principal 8
is "Porky's," the wildly popular teen sex flick that has spawned imitators and sequels. My authority for the fact that teen-age sex control is an anachronism is Madonna. "Papa don't preach," she sings. "I'm gonna keep my baby."

The innocent in the song is months—nine months, to be precise— 9
beyond the question of sex. Her mind is already on motherhood.

Kids are immersed in a mass culture that relentlessly says yes. A squeak 10
from the schools saying no, or a tacit signal saying maybe, is not going to make any difference. To pretend otherwise is grossly to misread what shapes popular attitudes.

What a school can credibly tell kids depends a lot on whether they grew up 11
on the Pillsbury dough boy or on a grappling group of half-nudes frenzied with Obsession.

Time to face facts. Yes, birth-control clinics are a kind of surrender. But at 12
Little Big Horn, surrender is the only sound strategy. Sex oozes from every pore of the culture, and there's not a kid in the world who can avoid it. To shut down school birth-control clinics in order to imply the contrary is a high-minded but very costly exercise in message sending. Costly because the message from the general culture will prevail anyway, and sex without contraception means babies.

The sex battle is lost. The front-line issue is pregnancy. Some situations 13
are too far gone to be reversed. They can only be contained. Containment here means trying at least to prevent some of the personal agony and social pathology that invariably issue from teen-age pregnancy.

Not that the sexual revolution can never be reversed. It can, in principle. In 1
our time, the vehicle might be AIDS. The association of sex and sin elicits
giggles. The association of sex and death elicits terror. Nevertheless, the
coming counter-revolution, like all cultural revolutions, will not be made in
the schools. It will happen outside—in movies and the newsmagazines, on
the soaps and MTV—and then trickle down to the schools. As usual, they
will be the last to find out.

I am no more pleased than the next parent to think that in 10 years' time 1⁵
my child's path to math class will be adorned with a tasteful display of
condoms in the school's clinic window. But by then it will be old hat.

The very word "condom" has broken through into the national conscious- 1⁶
ness, i.e., network TV. It was uttered for the first time ever on a prime-time
entertainment show, "Cagney and Lacey." Condoms will now find their place
beside bulimia, suicide, incest, and spouse murder in every child's mental
world.

If the schools ignore that world, it will not change a thing. Neglect will 1⁷
make things worse. In a sex-soaked culture, school is no shelter from the
storm. Only a monastery is, if it doesn't have cable.

FOR CLASS DISCUSSION

1. Analyze and evaluate the debate over the dispensing of birth
   control in the schools by applying the first set of guide questions
   from pages 443–444. How do you account for the disagreement
   between Beck and Krauthammer?

2. Choose one of the arguments for closer analysis, applying the
   second set of guide questions on page 444.

OPTIONAL WRITING ASSIGNMENTS

1. Both Beck and Krauthammer dislike the idea of birth control clinics in
the schools. Explain to someone who hasn't read this textbook or hasn't
taken your writing class how the disagreement between Krauthammer and
Beck turns on the difference between "what's ideal" and "what's normal"
as explained on pages 298–299.

2. Despite widespread knowledge about birth control and despite easy
access to condoms in drug stores, many teenagers still become pregnant.
Write a causal argument explaining why sexually active teenagers often
don't practice safe sex even when they know better.

THE BOMBING OF HIROSHIMA: SHOULD THE UNITED STATES HAVE DROPPED THE BOMB?

REFLECTIONS ON THE BOMB: OF ACCIDENTAL JUDGMENTS AND CASUAL SLAUGHTERS

Kai Erikson

Kai Erikson, professor of sociology at Yale, argues that the "decision" to drop the bomb wasn't the result of a rational judgment arising from considered debate. Had there been debate, Erikson argues, there were options available far preferable to the mass destruction of civilians.

The bombings of Hiroshima and Nagasaki, which took place forty years   1
ago this month, are among the most thoroughly studied moments on human record. Together they constitute the only occasion in history when atomic weapons were dropped on living populations, and together they constitute the only occasion in history when a decision was made to employ them in that way.

I want to reflect here on the second of those points. The "decision to   2
drop" — I will explain in a minute why quotation marks are useful here — is a fascinating historical episode. But it is also an exhibit of the most profound importance as we consider our prospects for the future. It is a case history well worth attending to. A compelling parable.

If one were to tell the story of that decision as historians normally do, the   3
details arranged in an ordered narrative, one might begin in 1938 with the
discovery of nuclear fission, or perhaps a year later with the delivery of
Einstein's famous letter to President Roosevelt. No matter what its opening
scene, though, the tale would then proceed along a string of events — a
sequence of appointees named, committees formed, reports issued, orders
signed, arguments won and lost, minds made up and changed — all of it
coming to an end with a pair of tremendous blasts in the soft morning air over
Japan.

The difficulty with that way of relating the story, as historians of the   4
period all testify, is that the more closely one examines the record, the harder
it is to make out where in the flow of events something that could reasonably
be called a decision was reached at all. To be sure, a kind of consensus
emerged from the sprawl of ideas and happenings that made up the climate
of wartime Washington, but looking back, it is hard to distinguish those pivotal moments in the story when the crucial issues were identified, debated,
reasoned through, resolved. The decision, to the extent that one can even
speak of such a thing, was shaped and seasoned by a force very like
inertia.

Let's say, then, that a wind began to blow, ever so gently at first, down the   5
corridors along which power flows. And as it gradually gathered momentum
during the course of the war, the people caught up in it began to assume,
without ever checking up on it, that it had a logic and a motive, that it had
been set in motion by sure hands acting on the basis of wise counsel.

Harry Truman, in particular, remembered it as a time of tough and lonely   6
choices, and titled his memoir of that period *Year of Decisions*. But the bulk
of those choices can in all fairness be said to have involved confirmation of
projects already under way or implementation of decisions made at other
levels of command. Brig. Gen. Leslie R. Groves, military head of the Manhattan Project, was close to the mark when he described Truman's decision as
"one of noninterference — basically, a decision not to upset the existing
plans." And J. Robert Oppenheimer spoke equally to the point when he
observed some twenty years later: "The decision was implicit in the project. I
don't know whether it could have been stopped."

In September of 1944, when it became more and more evident that a bomb   7
would be produced in time for combat use, Franklin Roosevelt and Winston
Churchill met at Hyde Park and initialed a brief *aide-mémoire*, noting, among
other things, that the new weapon "might, perhaps, after mature consideration, be used against the Japanese." This document does not appear to have
had any effect on the conduct of the war, and Truman knew nothing at all
about it. But it would not have made a real difference in any case, for neither
chief of state did much to initiate the "mature consideration" they spoke of
so glancingly, and Truman, in turn, could only suppose that such matters

had been considered already. "Truman did not inherit the question," writes Martin J. Sherwin, "he inherited the answer."

What would "mature consideration" have meant in such a setting as that anyway?   8

First of all, presumably, it would have meant seriously asking whether the   9 weapon should be employed at all. But we have it on the authority of virtually all the principal players that no one in a position to do anything about it ever really considered alternatives to combat use. Henry L. Stimson, Secretary of War:

> At no time, from 1941 to 1945, did I ever hear it suggested by the President, or by any other responsible member of the government, that atomic energy should not be used in the war.

Harry Truman:

> I regarded the bomb as a military weapon and never had any doubt that it should be used.

General Groves:

> Certainly, there was no question in my mind, or, as far as I was ever aware, in the mind of either President Roosevelt or President Truman or any other responsible person, but that we were developing a weapon to be employed against the enemies of the United States.

Winston Churchill:

> There never was a moment's discussion as to whether the atomic bomb should be used or not.

And why should anyone be surprised? We were at war, after all, and with the most resolute of enemies, so the unanimity of that feeling is wholly understandable. But it was not, by any stretch of the imagination, a product of mature consideration.

"Combat use" meant a number of different things, however, and a second   10 question began to be raised with some frequency in the final months of the war, all the more insistently after the defeat of Germany. Might a way be devised to demonstrate the awesome power of the bomb in a convincing enough fashion to induce the surrender of the Japanese without having to destroy huge numbers of civilians? Roosevelt may have been pondering something of the sort. In September of 1944, for example, three days after initialing the Hyde Park *aide-mémoire,* he asked Vannevar Bush, a trusted science adviser, whether the bomb "should actually be used against the Japanese or whether it should be used only as a threat." While that may have been little more than idle musing, a number of different schemes were explored within both the government and the scientific community in the months following.

One option involved a kind of *benign strike*: the dropping of a bomb on 11
some built-up area, but only after advance notice had been issued so that
residents could evacuate the area and leave an empty slate on which the
bomb could write its terrifying signature. This plan was full of difficulties. A
dud under those dramatic circumstances might do enormous damage to
American credibility, and, moreover, to broadcast any warning was to risk the
endeavor in other ways. Weak as the Japanese were by this time in the war, it
was easy to imagine their finding a way to intercept an incoming airplane if
they knew where and when it was expected, and officials in Washington were
afraid that it would occur to the Japanese, as it had to them, that the venture
would come to an abrupt end if American prisoners of war were brought into
the target area.

The second option was a *tactical strike* against a purely military target — 12
an arsenal, railroad yard, depot, factory, harbor — without advance notice.
Early in the game, for example, someone had nominated the Japanese fleet
concentration at Truk. The problem with this notion, however — and there is
more than a passing irony here — was that no known military target had a
wide enough compass to contain the whole of the destructive capacity of the
weapon and so display its full range and power. The committee inquiring into
likely targets wanted one "more than three miles in diameter," because
anything smaller would be too inadequate a canvas for the picture it was
supposed to hold.

The third option was to stage a kind of *dress rehearsal* by detonating a 13
bomb in some remote corner of the world — a desert or empty island, say — to
exhibit to international observers brought in for the purpose what the device
could do. The idea had been proposed by a group of scientists in what has
since been called the Franck Report, but it commanded no more than a
moment's attention. It had the same problems as the benign strike: the risk of
being embarrassed by a dud was more than most officials in a position to
decide were willing to take, and there was a widespread feeling that any
demonstration involving advance notice would give the enemy too much
useful information.

The fourth option involved a kind of *warning shot*. The thought here was 14
to drop a bomb without notice over a relatively uninhabited stretch of enemy
land so that the Japanese high command might see at first hand what was in
store for them if they failed to surrender soon. Edward Teller thought that an
explosion at night high over Tokyo Bay would serve as a brilliant visual
argument, and Adm. Lewis Strauss, soon to become a member (and later
chair) of the Atomic Energy Commission, recommended a strike on a local
forest, reasoning that the blast would "lay the trees out in windrows from the
center of the explosion in all directions as though they were matchsticks,"
meanwhile igniting a fearsome firestorm at the epicenter. "It seemed to me,"
he added, "that a demonstration of this sort would prove to the Japanese that

we could destroy any of their cities at will." The physicist Ernest O. Lawrence may have been speaking half in jest when he suggested that a bomb might be used to "blow the top off" Mount Fujiyama, but he was quite serious when he assured a friend early in the war."The bomb will never be dropped on people. As soon as we get it, we'll use it only to dictate peace."

Now, hindsight is too easy a talent. But it seems evident on the face of it   15 that the fourth of those options, the warning shot, was much to be preferred over the other three, and even more to be preferred over use on living targets. I do not want to argue the case here. I do want to ask, however, why that possibility was so easily dismissed.

The fact of the matter seems to have been that the notion of a demonstra-   16 tion was discussed on only a few occasions once the Manhattan Project neared completion, and most of those discussions were off the record. So a historian trying to reconstruct the drift of those conversations can only flatten an ear against the wall, as it were, and see if any sense can be made of the muffled voices next door. It seems very clear, for example, that the options involving advance notice were brought up so often and so early in official conversations that they came to *mean* demonstration in the minds of several important players. If a James Byrnes, say, soon to be named Secretary of State, were asked why one could not detonate a device in unoccupied territory, he might raise the problem posed by prisoners of war, and if the same question were asked of a James Bryant Conant, another science adviser, he might speak of the embarrassment that would follow a dud—thus, in both cases, joining ideas that had no logical relation to each other. Neither prisoners of war nor fear of failure, of course, posed any argument against a surprise demonstration.

There were two occasions, however, on which persons in a position to   17 affect policy discussed the idea of a nonlethal demonstration. Those two conversations together consumed no more than a matter of minutes, so far as one can tell at this remove, and they, too, were off the record. But they seem to represent virtually the entire investment of the government of the United States in "mature consideration" of the subject.

The first discussion took place at a meeting of what was then called the   18 Interim Committee, a striking gathering of military, scientific and government brass under the chairmanship of Secretary Stimson. This group, which included James Byrnes and Chief of Staff Gen. George C. Marshall, met on a number of occasions in May of 1945 to discuss policy issues raised by the new bomb, and Stimson recalled later that at one of their final meetings the members "carefully considered such alternatives as a detailed advance warning or a demonstration in some uninhabited area." But the minutes of the meeting, as well as the accounts of those present, suggest otherwise. The only exchange on the subject, in fact, took place during a luncheon break, and while we have no way of knowing what was actually said in that conversation, we do know what conclusion emerged from it. One participant, Arthur H. Compton, recalled later:

> Though the possibility of a demonstration that would not destroy human lives was attractive, no one could suggest a way in which it could be made so convincing that it would be likely to stop the war.

And the recording secretary of the meeting later recalled:

> Dr. Oppenheimer . . . said he doubted whether there could be devised any sufficiently startling demonstration that would convince the Japanese they ought to throw in the sponge.

Two weeks later, four physicists who served as advisers to the Interim **19** Committee met in Los Alamos to consider once again the question of demonstration. They were Arthur Compton, Enrico Fermi, Ernest Lawrence and Robert Oppenheimer — as distinguished an assembly of scientific talent as could be imagined — and they concluded, after a discussion of which we have no record: "We can propose no technical demonstration likely to bring an end to the war; we see no acceptable alternative to direct military use." That, so far as anyone can tell, was the end of it.

We cannot be sure that a milder report would have made a difference, for **20** the Manhattan Project was gathering momentum as it moved toward the more steeply pitched inclines of May and June, but we can be sure that the idea of a demonstration was at that point spent. The Los Alamos report ended with something of a disclaimer ("We have, however, no claim to special competence. . . . "), but its message was clear enough. When asked about that report nine yeai s later in his security hearings, Oppenheimer said, with what might have been a somewhat defensive edge in his voice, "We did not think exploding one of those things as a firecracker over the desert was likely to be very impressive."

Perhaps not. But those fragments are telling for another reason. If you **21** listen to them carefully for a moment or two, you realize that these are the voices of nuclear physicists trying to imagine how a strange and distant people will react to an atomic blast. These are the voices of nuclear physicists dealing with psychological and anthropological questions about Japanese culture, Japanese temperament, Japanese will to resist — topics, we must assume, about which they knew almost nothing. They did not know yet what the bomb could actually do, since its first test was not to take place for another month. But in principle, at least, Oppenheimer and Fermi reflecting on matters relating to the Japanese national character should have had about the same force as Ruth Benedict and Margaret Mead reflecting on matters relating to high-energy physics, the first difference being that Benedict and Mead would not have presumed to do so, and the second being that no one in authority would have listened to them if they had.

The first of the two morals I want to draw from the foregoing — this being   22
a parable, after all — is that in moments of critical contemplation, it is often
hard to know where the competencies of soldiers and scientists and all the
rest of us begin and end. Many an accidental judgment can emerge from such
confusions.

But what if the conclusions of the scientists had been correct? What if   23
some kind of demonstration had been staged in a lightly occupied part of
Japan and it *had* been greeted as a firecracker in the desert? What then?

Let me shift gears for a moment and discuss the subject in another way. It   24
is standard wisdom for everyone in the United States old enough to remember
the war, and for most of those to whom it is ancient history, that the
bombings of Hiroshima and Nagasaki were the only alternative to an all-out
invasion of the Japanese mainland involving hundreds of thousands and
perhaps millions of casualties on both sides. Unless the Japanese came to
understand the need to surrender quickly, we would have been drawn by an
almost magnetic force toward those dreaded beaches. This has become an
almost automatic pairing of ideas, an article of common lore. If you lament
that so many civilians were incinerated or blown to bits in Hiroshima and
Nagasaki, then somebody will remind you of the American lives thus saved.
Truman was the person most frequently asked to account for the bombings,
and his views were emphatic on the subject:

> It was a question of saving hundreds of thousands of American lives. I don't mind
> telling you that you don't feel normal when you have to plan hundreds of thou-
> sands of complete, final deaths of American boys who are alive and joking and
> having fun while you are doing your planning. You break your heart and your
> head trying to figure out a way to save one life. The name given to our invasion
> plan was "Olympic," but I saw nothing godly about the killing of all the people
> that would be necessary to make that invasion. I could not worry about what
> history would say about my personal morality. I made the only decision I ever knew
> how to make. I did what I thought was right.*

Veterans of the war, and particularly those who had reason to suppose   25
that they would have been involved in an invasion, have drawn that same

---

*Merle Miller notes, in *Plain Speaking: An Oral Biography of Harry S. Truman,* that Truman may have had
moments of misgiving: "My only insight into Mr. Truman's feeling about the Bomb and its dropping, and it isn't
much, came one day in his private library at the Truman Memorial Library. In one corner was every book ever
published on the Bomb, and at the end of one was Horatio's speech in the last scene of *Hamlet.*" Truman had
underlined these words:

And let me speak to the yet unknowing world
How these things came about. So shall you hear
Of carnal, bloody, and unnatural acts,
Of accidental judgments, casual slaughters,
Of deaths put on by cunning and forced cause,
And, in this upshot, purposes mistook
Fall'n on the inventors' heads.

connection repeatedly, most recently Paul Fussell in the pages of *The New Republic.* Thank God for the bomb, the argument goes, it saved the lives of countless numbers of us. And so, in a sense, it may have.

But the destruction of Hiroshima and Nagasaki had nothing to do with it. 26 It only makes sense to assume, even if few people were well enough positioned in early August to see the situation whole, that there simply was not going to be an invasion. Not ever.

For what sane power, with the atomic weapon securely in its arsenal, 27 would hurl a million or more of its sturdiest young men on a heavily fortified mainland? To imagine anyone ordering an invasion when the means were at hand to blast Japan into a sea of gravel at virtually no cost in American lives is to imagine a madness beyond anything even the worst of war can induce. The invasion had not yet been called off, granted. But it surely would have been, and long before the November 1 deadline set for it.

The United States did not become a nuclear power on August 6, with the 28 destruction of Hiroshima. It became a nuclear power on July 16, when the first test device was exploded in Alamogordo, New Mexico. Uncertainties remained, of course, many of them. But from that moment on, the United States knew how to produce a bomb, knew how to deliver it and knew it would work. Stimson said shortly after the war that the bombings of Hiroshima and Nagasaki "ended the ghastly specter of a clash of great land armies," but he could have said, with greater justice, that the ghastly specter ended at Alamogordo. Churchill came close to making exactly that point when he first learned of the New Mexico test:

> To quell the Japanese resistance man by man and conquer the country yard by yard might well require the loss of a million American lives and half that number of British. . . . Now all that nightmare picture had vanished.

It *had* vanished. The age of inch-by-inch crawling over enemy territory, 29 the age of Guadalcanal and Iwo Jima and Okinawa, was just plain over.

The point is that once we had the bomb and were committed to its use, the 30 terrible weight of invasion no longer hung over our heads. The Japanese were incapable of mounting any kind of offensive, as every observer has agreed, and it was our option when to close with the enemy and thus risk casualties. So we could have easily afforded to hold for a moment, to think it over, to introduce what Dwight Eisenhower called "that awful thing" to the world on the basis of something closer to mature consideration. We could have afforded to detonate a bomb over some less lethal target and then pause to see what happened. And do it a second time, maybe a third. And if none of those demonstrations had made a difference, presumably we would have had to strike harder: Hiroshima and Nagasaki would still have been there a few weeks later for that purpose, silent and untouched—"unspoiled" was the term Gen. H.H. Arnold used—for whatever came next. Common lore also has it that there were not bombs enough for such niceties, but that seems not to have been the case. The United States was ready to deliver a third bomb toward the end of August, and Groves had already informed Marshall and Stimson that three or four more bombs would be available in September, a like number in October, at least five in November, and seven in December, with substantial increases to follow in early 1946. Even if we assume that Groves was being too hopeful about the productive machinery he had set in motion, as one expert close to the matter has suggested, a formidable number of bombs would have been available by the date originally set for invasion.

Which brings us back to the matter of momentum. The best way to tell the   31 story of those days is to say that the "decision to drop" had become a force like gravity. It had taken life. The fact that it existed supplied its meaning, its reason for being. Elting E. Morison, Stimson's biographer, put it well.

> Any process started by men toward a special end tends, for reasons logical, biological, aesthetic or whatever they may be, to carry forward, if other things remain equal, to its climax. [This is] the inertia developed in a human system. . . . In a process where such a general tendency has been set to work it is difficult to separate the moment when men were still free to choose from the moment, if such there was, when they were no longer free to choose.

I have said very little about Nagasaki so far because it was not the subject   32 of any thought at all. The orders of the bomber command were to attack Japan as soon as the bombs were ready. One was ready on August 9. Boom. When Groves was later asked why the attack on Nagasaki had come so soon after the attack on Hiroshima, leaving so little time for the Japanese to consider what had happened to them, he simply said: "Once you get your opponent reeling, you keep him reeling and never let him recover." And that is the point, really. There is no law of nature that compels a winning side to press its superiority, but it is hard to slow down, hard to relinquish an advantage, hard to rein the fury. The impulse to charge ahead, to strike at the throat, is so strong a habit of war that it almost ranks as a reflex, and if that thought does not frighten us when we consider our present nuclear predicament, nothing will. Many a casual slaughter can emerge from such moods.

If it is true, as I have suggested, that there were few military or logistic   33 reasons for striking as sharply as we did and that the decision to drop moved in on the crest of an almost irreversible current, then it might be sensible to ask, on the fortieth anniversary of the event, what some of the drifts were that became a part of that larger current. An adequate accounting would have to consider a number of military, political and other matters far beyond the reach of this brief essay, the most important of them by far being the degree to which the huge shadow of the Soviet Union loomed over both official meetings and private thoughts. It is nearly impossible to read the remaining record without assuming that the wish to make a loud announcement to the Russians was a persuasive factor in the minds of many of the principal participants. There were other drifts as well, of course, and I would like to note a few of the sort that sometimes occur to social scientists.

For one thing, an extraordinary amount of money and material had been invested in the Manhattan Project—both of them in short supply in a wartime economy—and many observers thought that so large a public expense would be all the more willingly borne if it were followed by a striking display of what the money had been spent for.

And, too, extraordinary investments had been made in men and talent, both of them in short supply in a wartime economy. The oldest of the people involved in the Manhattan Project—soldiers, engineers and scientists—made sacrifices in the form of separated families, interrupted careers and a variety of other discomforts, and it makes a certain psychological sense that a decisive strike would serve as a kind of vindication for all the trouble. The youngest of them, though, had been held out of combat, thus avoiding the fate of so many men of their generation, by accidents of professional training, personal skill and sheer timing. The project was their theater of war, and it makes even more psychological sense that some of them would want the only shot they fired to be a truly resonant one.

The dropping of such a bomb, moreover, could serve as an ending, something sharp and distinct in a world that had become ever more blurred. The Grand Alliance was breaking up, and with it all hope for a secure postwar world. Roosevelt was dead. The future was full of ambiguity. And, most important, everybody was profoundly tired. In circumstances like that, a resounding strike would serve to clarify things, to give them form, to tidy them up a bit.

There are other matters one might point to, some of them minor, some of them major, all of them strands in the larger weave. There was a feeling, expressed by scientists and government officials alike, that the world needed a rude and decisive shock to awaken it to the realities of the atomic age. There was a feeling, hard to convey in words but easy to sense once one has become immersed in some of the available material, that the bomb had so much power and majesty, was so compelling a force, that one was almost required to give it birth and a chance to mature. There was a feeling, born of war, that for all its ferocity the atomic bomb was nevertheless no more than a minor increment on a scale of horror that already included the firebombings of Tokyo and other Japanese cities. And there was a feeling, also born of war, that living creatures on the other side, even the children, had somehow lost title to the mercies that normally accompany the fact of being human.

The kinds of points I have been making need to be stated either very precisely or in some detail. I have not yet learned to do the former; I do not have space enough here for the latter. So let me just end with the observation that human decisions do not always emerge from reflective counsels where facts are arrayed in order and logic is the prevailing currency of thought. They emerge from complex fields of force, in which the vanities of leaders and the moods of constituencies and the inertias of bureaucracies play a critical part. That is as important a lesson as one can learn from the events of 1945 — and as unnerving a one.

The bombings of Hiroshima and Nagasaki supply a rich case study for **39** people who must live in times like ours. It is not important for us to apportion shares of responsibility to persons who played their parts so long ago, and I have not meant to do so here: these were unusually decent and compassionate people for the most part, operating with reflexes that had been tempered by war. We need to attend to such histories as this, however, because they provide the clearest illustrations we have of what human beings can do — this being the final moral to be drawn from our parable — when they find themselves in moments of crisis and literally have more destructive power at their disposal than they know what to do with. That is as good an argument for disarming as any that can be imagined.

HIROSHIMA: A SOLDIER'S VIEW

Paul Fussell

Paul Fussell — who had been wounded in action in the European theater — gives us a shocking, soldier's view of a war that aroused visceral hatred on both sides. "Experience whispers that the pity is not that we used the bomb to end the Japanese war but that it wasn't ready earlier to end the German one."

Many years ago in New York I saw on the side of a bus a whiskey ad which **1** I've remembered all this time, for it's been for me a model of the brief poem. Indeed, I've come upon few short poems subsequently that evinced more genuine poetic talent. The ad consisted of two lines of "free verse," thus:

In life, experience is the great teacher.
In Scotch, Teacher's is the great experience.

For present purposes we can jettison the second line (licking our lips ruefully as it disappears), leaving the first to encapsulate a principle whose banality suggests that it enshrines a most useful truth. I bring up the matter this August, the thirty-sixth anniversary of the A-bombing of Hiroshima and Nagasaki, to focus on something suggested by the long debate about the ethics, if any, of that affair: namely, the importance of experience, sheer vulgar experience, in influencing, if not determining, one's views about the first use of the bomb. And the experience I'm talking about is that of having come to grips, face to face, with an enemy who designs your death. The experience is common to those in the infantry and the Marines and even the line Navy, to those, in short, who fought the Second World War mindful always that their mission was, as they were repeatedly told, "to close with the enemy and destroy him." I think there's something to be learned about that war, as well as about the tendency of historical memory unwittingly to resolve ambiguity, by considering some of the ways testimonies emanating from experience complicate attitudes about the cruel ending of that cruel war.

"What did you do in the Great War, Daddy?" The recruiting poster 2 deserves ridicule and contempt, of course, but its question is embarrassingly relevant here. The problem is one that touches on the matter of social class in America. Most of those with firsthand experience of the war at its worst were relatively inarticulate and have remained silent. Few of those destined to be destroyed if the main islands had had to be invaded went on to become our most eloquent men of letters or our most impressive ethical theorists or professors of history or international jurists. The testimony of experience has come largely from rough diamonds like James Jones and William Manchester, who experienced the war in the infantry and the Marine Corps. Both would agree with the point, if not perhaps the tone, of a remark about Hiroshima made by a naval officer menaced by the kamikazes off Okinawa: "Those were the best burned women and children I ever saw." Anticipating objection from the inexperienced, Jones, in his book *WWII*, is careful to precede his chapter on Hiroshima with one detailing the plans already in motion for the infantry assaults on the home islands of Kyushu, scheduled for November 1945, and ultimately Honshu. The forthcoming invasion of Kyushu, he notes, "was well into its collecting and stockpiling stages before the war ended." (The island of Saipan was designated a main ammunition and supply base for the invasion, and if you visit it today you can see some of the assembled stuff still sitting there.) "The assault troops were chosen and already in training," Jones reminds us, and he illuminates the situation by the light of experience:

> What it must have been like to some old-timer buck sergeant or staff sergeant who had been through Guadalcanal or Bougainville or the Philippines, to stand on some beach and watch this huge war machine beginning to stir and move all around him and know that he very likely had survived this far only to fall dead on the dirt of Japan's home islands, hardly bears thinking about.

On the other hand, John Kenneth Galbraith is persuaded that the Japanese would have surrendered by November without an invasion. He thinks the atom bombs were not decisive in bringing about the surrender and he implies that their use was unjustified. What did he do in the war? He was in the Office of Price Administration in Washington, and then he was director of the United States Strategic Bombing Survey. He was thirty-seven in 1945, and I don't demand that he experience having his ass shot off. I just note that he didn't. In saying this I'm aware of its offensive implications ad hominem. But here I think that approach justified. What's at stake in an infantry assault is so entirely unthinkable to those without experience of one, even if they possess very wide-ranging imaginations and sympathies, that experience is crucial in this case.

A similar remoteness from experience, as well as a similar rationalistic   3
abstraction, seems to lie behind the reaction of an anonymous reviewer of William Manchester's *Goodbye Darkness: A Memoir of the Pacific War* for the *New York Review of Books.* First of all the reviewer dislikes Manchester's calling the enemy Nips and Japs, but what really shakes him (her?) is this passage:

> After Biak the enemy withdrew to deep caverns. Rooting them out became a bloody business which reached its ultimate horrors in the last months of the war. You think of the lives which would have been lost in an invasion of Japan's home islands — a staggering number of Americans but millions more of Japanese — and you thank God for the atomic bomb.

Thank God for the atomic bomb. From this, "one recoils," says the reviewer. One does, doesn't one?

In an interesting exchange last year in the *New York Review of Books,*   4
Joseph Alsop and David Joravsky set forth the by now familiar arguments on both sides of the debate. You'll be able to guess which sides they chose once you know that Alsop experienced capture by the Japanese at Hong Kong in 1942 and that Joravsky made no mortal contact with the Japanese: a young soldier, he was on his way to the Pacific when the war ended. The editors of the *New York Review* have given their debate the tendentious title "Was the Hiroshima Bomb Necessary?" — surely an unanswerable question (unlike "Was It Effective?") and one suggesting the intellectual difficulties involved in imposing ex post facto a rational ethics on this event. Alsop focuses on the power and fanaticism of War Minister Anami, who insisted that Japan fight to the bitter end, defending the main islands with the same means and tenacity with which it had defended Iwo and Okinawa. He concludes: "Japanese surrender could never have been obtained, at any rate without the honor-satisfying bloodbath envisioned by . . . Anami, if the hideous destruction of Hiroshima and Nagasaki had not finally galvanized the peace advocates into tearing up the entire Japanese book of rules." The Japanese planned to deploy the undefeated bulk of their ground forces, over two million men, plus 10,000 kamikaze planes, in a suicidal defense. That fact, says Alsop, makes it absurd to "hold the common view, by now hardly challenged by anyone, that the decision to drop the two bombs on Japan was wicked in itself, and that

President Truman and all others who joined in making or who [like Oppen-heimer] assented to this decision shared in the wickedness." And in explana-tion of "the two bombs" Alsop adds: "The true, climactic, and successful effort of the Japanese peace advocates . . . did not begin in deadly earnest until *after* the second bomb had destroyed Nagasaki. The Nagasaki bomb was thus the trigger to all the developments that led to peace."

Joravsky, now a professor of history at Northwestern, argues on the other 5 hand that those who decided to use the bomb on cities betray defects of "reason and self-restraint." It all needn't have happened, he asserts, "if the U.S. government had been willing to take a few more days and to be a bit more thoughtful in opening the age of nuclear warfare." But of course in its view it wasn't doing that: that's a historian's tidy hindsight. The government was ending the war conclusively, as well as irrationally remembering Pearl Harbor with a vengeance. It didn't know then what everyone knows now about leukemia and carcinoma and birth defects. History, as Eliot's "Geron-tion" notes,

> has many cunning passages, contrived corridors
> And issues, deceives with whispering ambitions,
> Guides us by vanities. . . .
>   Think
> Neither fear nor courage saves us. Unnatural vices
> Are fathered by our heroism. Virtues
> Are forced upon us by our impudent crimes.

Understanding the past means feeling its pressure on your pulses and that's harder than Joravsky thinks.

The Alsop–Joravsky debate, which can be seen as reducing finally to a 6 collision between experience and theory, was conducted with a certain civi-lized respect for evidence. Not so the way the new scurrilous agitprop *New Statesman* conceives those favoring the bomb and those opposing. They are, on the one hand, says Bruce Page, "the imperialist class-forces acting through Harry Truman," and, on the other, those representing "the humane, democratic virtues" — in short, "fascists" opposed to "populists." But ironi-cally the bomb saved the lives not of any imperialists but only of the low and humble, the quintessentially democratic huddled masses — the conscripted enlisted men manning the fated invasion divisions. Bruce Page was nine years old when the war ended. For a man of that experience, phrases like "imperial-ist class-forces" come easily, and the issues look perfectly clear.

He's not the only one to have forgotten, if he ever knew, the savagery of 7 the Pacific war. The dramatic postwar Japanese success at hustling and merchandising and tourism has (happily, in many ways) effaced for most people important elements of the assault context in which Hiroshima should be viewed. It is easy to forget what Japan was like before it was first destroyed and then humiliated, tamed, and constitutionalized by the West. "Implacable, treacherous, barbaric" — those were Admiral Halsey's characterizations of the enemy, and at the time few facing the Japanese would deny that they fit to a T. One remembers the captured American airmen locked for years in packing crates, the prisoners decapitated, the gleeful use of bayonets on civilians. The degree to which Americans register shock and extraordinary shame about the Hiroshima bomb correlates closely with lack of information about the war.

And the savagery was not just on one side. There was much sadism and   8
brutality — undeniably racist — on ours. No Marine was fully persuaded of his manly adequacy who didn't have a well-washed Japanese skull to caress and who didn't have a go at treating surrendering Japs as rifle targets. Herman Wouk remembers it correctly while analyzing Ensign Keith in *The Caine Mutiny:* "Like most of the naval executioners of Kwajalein, he seemed to regard the enemy as a species of animal pest." And the enemy felt the same way about us: "From the grim and desperate taciturnity with which the Japanese died, they seemed on their side to believe they were contending with an invasion of large armed ants." Hiroshima seems to follow in natural sequence: "This obliviousness on both sides to the fact that the opponents were human beings may perhaps be cited as the key to the many massacres of the Pacific war." Since the Japanese resisted so madly, let's pour gasoline into their emplacements and light it and shoot the people afire who try to get out. Why not? Why not blow them all up? Why not, indeed, drop a new kind of big bomb on them? Why allow one more American high school kid to see his intestines blown out of his body and spread before him in the dirt while he screams when we can end the whole thing just like that?

On Okinawa, only weeks before Hiroshima, 123,000 Japanese and Ameri-   9
cans *killed* each other. "Just awful" was the comment not of some pacifist but of MacArthur. One million American casualties was his estimate of the cost of the forthcoming invasion. And that invasion was not just a hypothetical threat, as some theorists have argued. It was genuinely in train, as I know because I was to be in it. When the bomb ended the war I was in the 45th Infantry Division, which had been through the European war to the degree that it had needed to be reconstituted two or three times. We were in a staging area near Reims, ready to be shipped across the United States for final preparation in the Philippines. My division was to take part in the invasion of Honshu in March 1946. (The earlier invasion of Kyushu was to be carried out by 700,000 infantry already in the Pacific.) I was a twenty-one-year-old second lieutenant leading a rifle platoon. Although still officially in one piece, in the German war I had already been wounded in the leg and back severely enough to be adjudged, after the war, 40 percent disabled. But even if my legs buckled whenever I jumped out of the back of the truck, my condition was held to be satisfactory for whatever lay ahead. When the bombs dropped and

news began to circulate that "Operation Olympic" would not, after all, take place, that we would not be obliged to run up the beaches near Tokyo assault-firing while being mortared and shelled, for all the fake manliness of our façades we cried with relief and joy. We were going to live. We were going to grow up to adulthood after all. When the *Enola Gay* dropped its package, "There were cheers," says John Toland, "over the intercom; it meant the end of the war."

Those who cried and cheered are very different from high-minded, guilt-   10
ridden GIs we're told about by the late J. Glenn Gray in *The Warriors* (1959). During the war in Europe Gray was an interrogator in the Counter Intelligence Corps, and in that capacity he underwent the war at division level. After the war he became a professor of philosophy at Colorado College (never, I've thought, the venue of very much reality) and a distinguished editor of Heidegger. There's no doubt that Gray's outlook on everything was noble and elevated. But *The Warriors,* his meditation on modern soldiering, gives every sign of remoteness from experience. Division headquarters is miles behind the places where the soldiers experience terror and madness and relieve these pressures by sadism. "When the news of the atomic bombing of Hiroshima and Nagasaki came," Gray asks us to believe, "many an American soldier felt shocked and ashamed." But why, we ask? Because we'd bombed civilians? We'd been doing that for years and, besides the two bombs, wiped out 10,000 Japanese troops, not now often mentioned, John Hersey's kindly physicians and Jesuit priests being more touching. Were Gray's soldiers shocked and ashamed because we'd obliterated whole towns? We'd done that plenty of times. If at division headquarters some felt shocked and ashamed, down in the rifle companies none did, although Gray says they did:

> The combat soldier knew better than did Americans at home what those bombs meant in suffering and injustice. The man of conscience realized intuitively that the vast majority of Japanese in both cities were no more, if no less, guilty of the war than were his own parents, sisters, or brothers.

I find this canting nonsense: the purpose of dropping the bombs was not to "punish" people but to stop the war. To intensify the shame he insists we feel, Gray seems willing to fiddle the facts. The Hiroshima bomb, he says, was dropped "without any warning." But actually, two days before, 720,000 leaflets were dropped on the city urging everyone to get out and indicating that the place was going to be obliterated. Of course few left.

Experience whispers that the pity is not that we used the bomb to end the   11
Japanese war but that it wasn't ready earlier to end the German one. If only it could have been rushed into production faster and dropped at the right moment on the Reich chancellery or Berchtesgaden or Hitler's military head-quarters in East Prussia or — Wagnerian *coup de théâtre* — at Rommel's phony state funeral, most of the Nazi hierarchy could have been pulverized

immediately, saving not just the embarrassment of the Nuremburg trials but the lives of about four million Jews, Poles, Slavs, gypsies, and other "sub-humans," not to mention the lives and limbs of millions of Allied and Axis soldiers. If the bomb could have been ready even as late as July 1944, it could have reinforced the Von Stauffenberg plot and ended the war then and there. If the bomb had only been ready in time, the men of my infantry platoon would not have been killed and maimed.

All this is not to deny that like the Russian revolution, the atomic bombing 12 of Japan was a vast historical tragedy, and every passing year magnifies the dilemma into which it has thrown the contemporary world. As with the Russian revolution there are two sides — that's why it's a tragedy rather than a disaster — and unless we are simple-mindedly cruel, like Bruce Page, we need to be painfully aware of both at once. To observe that from the viewpoint of the war's victims-to-be the bomb was precisely the right thing to drop is to purchase no immunity from horror. See, for example, the new book *Unforgettable Fire: Pictures Drawn by Atomic Bomb Survivors,* issued by the Japan Broadcasting Corporation and distributed here by Pantheon Books. It presents a number of amateur colored-pencil, pastel, and water-color depictions of the scene of the Hiroshima bombing made by the middle-aged and elderly survivors for a peace exhibition in 1975. In addition to the heartrending pictures the book offers brief moments of memoir, not for the weak-stomached:

> While taking my severely wounded wife out to the riverbank . . . , I was horrified indeed at the sight of a stark naked man standing in the rain with his eyeball in his palm. He looked to be in great pain but there was nothing I could do for him. I wonder what became of him. Even today, I vividly remember the sight. It was simply miserable.

The drawings and paintings, whose often childish style makes them doubly touching, are of skin hanging down, breasts torn off, people bleeding and burning, dying mothers nursing dead babies. A bloody woman holds a bloody child in the ruins of a house, and the artist remembers her calling, "Please help this child! Someone, please help this child! Please help! Someone, please." As Samuel Johnson said of the smothering of the innocent Desdemona in another tragedy, "It is not to be endured." Nor, we should notice, is an infantryman's account of having his arm blown off in the Arno Valley in Italy in 1944:

> I wanted to die and die fast. I wanted to forget this miserable world. I cursed the war, I cursed the people who were responsible for it, I cursed God for putting me here . . . to suffer for something I never did or knew anything about. For this was hell, and I never imagined anything or anyone could suffer so bitterly. I screamed and cursed. Why? Why? What had I done to deserve this? But no answer came. I yelled for medics, because subconsciously I wanted to live. I tried to apply

my right hand over my bleeding stump, but I didn't have the strength to hold it. I looked to the left of me and saw the bloody mess that was once my left arm; its fingers and palm were turned upward, like a flower looking to the sun for its strength.

The future scholar-critic of rhetoric who writes *The History of Canting in* 13 *the Twentieth Century* will find much to study in the utterances of those who dilate on the wickedness of the bomb-droppers. He will realize that such utterance can perform for the speaker a valuable double function. First, it can display the fineness of his moral weave. And second, by implication it can also inform the audience that during the war he was not socially so unfortunate as to find himself at the cutting edge of the ground forces, where he might have had to compromise the pure clarity of his moral vision by the experience of weighing his own life against other people's. Down there, which is where the other people were in the war, is the place where coarse self-interest is the rule. When the young soldier with the wild eyes comes at you firing, do you shoot him in the foot, hoping he'll be hurt badly enough to drop or mis-aim the gun with which he is going to kill you, or do you shoot him in the chest and make certain he stops being your mortal enemy? It would be stupid to expect soldiers to be very sensitive humanitarians ("Moderation in war is imbecility" — Admiral of the Fleet Lord Fisher); actually, only the barest decencies can be expected of them. They didn't start the war, except in the terrible sense hinted in Frederic Manning's observation based on his experience in the Great War: "War is waged by men; not by beasts, or by gods. It is a peculiarly human activity. To call it a crime against mankind is to miss at least half its significance; it is also the punishment of a crime." Knowing that fact by experience, soldiers have every motive for wanting a war stopped, by any means.

The predictable stupidity, parochialism, and greed in the postwar interna- 14 tional mismanagement of the whole nuclear problem should not tempt us to misimagine the circumstances of the bomb's first "use." Nor should our well-justified fears and suspicions occasioned by the capture of the nuclear business by the mendacious classes (cf. Three Mile Island) tempt us to infer retrospectively extraordinary corruption, cruelty, and swinishness in those who decided to drop the bomb. Times change. Harry Truman was not a fascist, but a democrat. He was as close to a real egalitarian as we've seen in high office for a very long time. He is the only president in my lifetime who ever had the experience of commanding a small unit of ground troops obliged to kill people. He knew better than his subsequent critics what he was doing. The past, which as always did not know the future, acted in ways that ask to be imagined before they are condemned. Or even before they are simplified.

FOR CLASS DISCUSSION

1. Analyze and evaluate the disagreement over the bombing of Hiroshima by applying the first set of guide questions from pages 443–444.
2. Choose one of the arguments for closer analysis, applying the second set of guide questions on page 444.
3. Fussell's argument doesn't seem to fit the standard kinds of argumentative patterns discussed elsewhere in this text. Explore some of the differences between Fussell's argument and a standard argument with a self-announcing structure.

OPTIONAL WRITING ASSIGNMENT You are a junior senator recently appointed to the Senate Armed Forces Committee. The president has asked Congress to develop guidelines for the Pentagon to use in determining when the use of nuclear weapons is justified.

Drawing on personal experience, your reading of the preceding essays, and any other research you may have done on the subject, prepare a brief report responding to the president's charge. Begin by believing/doubting the following statement: "The use of nuclear weapons is *never* justified." If you decided that the United States ought never to use nuclear weapons, your report should say why. If you decide that nuclear weapon use is justified under certain conditions, indicate what criteria ought to be invoked. Think of examples for each of the following: situations in which nuclear weapons would clearly be called for; situations in which nuclear weapons would clearly not be called for; situations in which one may or may not decide to use nuclear weapons.

HUMAN USE OF ANIMALS: DO ANIMALS HAVE RIGHTS?

REVIEW OF *ANIMALS, MEN AND MORALS*

Peter Singer

Philosopher Peter Singer, in this review of a book of essays on the exploitation of animals, argues that humans are guilty of "speciesism" in their belief that animals exist for human use. Animals have rights, argues Singer, because animals can suffer.

We are familiar with Black Liberation, Gay Liberation, and a variety of other movements. With Women's Liberation some thought we had come to the end of the road. Discrimination on the basis of sex, it has been said, is the last form of discrimination that is universally accepted and practiced without pretense, even in those liberal circles which have long prided themselves on their freedom from racial discrimination. But one should always be wary of talking of "the last remaining form of discrimination." If we have learned anything from the liberation movements, we should have learned how difficult it is to be aware of the ways in which we discriminate until they are forcefully pointed out to us. A liberation movement demands an expansion of our moral horizons, so that practices that were previously regarded as natural and inevitable are now seen as intolerable.

Animals, Men and Morals is a manifesto for an Animal Liberation movement. The contributors to the book may not all see the issue this way. They

1

2

are a varied group. Philosophers, ranging from professors to graduate students, make up the largest contingent. There are five of them, including the three editors, and there is also an extract from the unjustly neglected German philosopher with an English name, Leonard Nelson, who died in 1927. There are essays by two novelist/critics, Brigid Brophy and Maureen Duffy, and another by Muriel the Lady Dowding, widow of Dowding of Battle of Britain fame and the founder of "Beauty Without Cruelty," a movement that campaigns against the use of animals for furs and cosmetics. The other pieces are by a psychologist, a botanist, a sociologist, and Ruth Harrison, who is probably best described as a professional campaigner for animal welfare.

Whether or not these people, as individuals, would all agree that they are   3
launching a liberation movement for animals, the book as a whole amounts to
no less. It is a demand for a complete change in our attitudes to nonhumans.
It is a demand that we cease to regard the exploitation of other species as
natural and inevitable, and that, instead, we see it as a continuing moral
outrage. Patrick Corbett, Professor of Philosophy at Sussex University,
captures the spirit of the book in his closing words:

> . . . We require now to extend the great principles of liberty, equality and frater-
> nity over the lives of animals. Let animal slavery join human slavery in the
> graveyard of the past.

The reader is likely to be skeptical. "Animal Liberation" sounds more like   4
a parody of liberation movements than a serious objective. The reader may
think: We support the claims of blacks and women for equality because
blacks and women really are equal to whites and males — equal in intelligence
and in abilities, capacity for leadership, rationality, and so on. Humans and
nonhumans obviously are not equal in these respects. Since justice demands
only that we treat equals equally, unequal treatment of humans and nonhumans cannot be an injustice.

This is a tempting reply, but a dangerous one. It commits the non-racist   5
and non-sexist to a dogmatic belief that blacks and women really are just as
intelligent, able, etc., as whites and males — and no more. Quite possibly this
happens to be the case. Certainly attempts to prove that racial or sexual
differences in these respects have a genetic origin have not been conclusive.
But do we really want to stake our demand for equality on the assumption
that there are no genetic differences of this kind between the different races
or sexes? Surely the appropriate response to those who claim to have found
evidence for such genetic differences is not to stick to the belief that there are
no differences, whatever the evidence to the contrary; rather one should be
clear that the claim to equality does not depend on IQ. Moral equality is
distinct from factual equality. Otherwise it would be nonsense to talk of the
equality of human beings, since humans, as individuals, obviously differ in
intelligence and almost any ability one cares to name. If possessing greater

intelligence does not entitle one human to exploit another, why should it entitle humans to exploit nonhumans?

Jeremy Bentham expressed the essential basis of equality in his famous 6 formula: "Each to count for one and none for more than one." In other words, the interest of every being that has interests are to be taken into account and treated equally with the like interests of any other being. Other moral philosophers, before and after Bentham, have made the same point in different ways. Our concern for others must not depend on whether they possess certain characteristics, though just what concern involves may, of course, vary according to such characteristics.

Bentham, incidentally, was well aware that the logic of the demand for 7 racial equality did not stop at the equality of humans. He wrote:

> The day *may* come when the rest of the animal creation may acquire those rights which never could have been withholden from them but by the hand of tyranny. The French have already discovered that the blackness of the skin is no reason why a human being should be abandoned without redress to the caprice of a tormentor. It may one day come to be recognized that the number of the legs, the villosity of the skin, or the termination of the *os sacrum*, are reasons equally insufficient for abandoning a sensitive being to the same fate. What else is it that should trace the insuperable line? Is it the faculty of reason, or perhaps the faculty of discourse? But a full-grown horse or dog is beyond comparison a more rational, as well as a more conversable animal, than an infant of a day, or a week, or even a month, old. But suppose they were otherwise, what would it avail? The question is not, Can they *reason*? nor Can they *talk*? but, Can they *suffer*?

Surely Bentham was right. If a being suffers, there can be no moral justification for refusing to take that suffering into consideration, and, indeed, to count it equally with the like suffering (if rough comparisons can be made) of any other being.

So the only question is: Do animals other than man suffer? Most people 8 agree unhesitatingly that animals like cats and dogs can and do suffer, and this seems also to be assumed by those laws that prohibit wanton cruelty to such animals. Personally, I have no doubt at all about this and find it hard to take seriously the doubts that a few people apparently do have. The editors and contributors of *Animals, Men and Morals* seem to feel the same way, for although the question is raised more than once, doubts are quickly dismissed each time. Nevertheless, because this is such a fundamental point, it is worth asking what grounds we have for attributing suffering to other animals.

It is best to begin by asking what grounds any individual human has for 9 supposing that other humans feel pain. Since pain is a state of consciousness, a "mental event," it can never be directly observed. No observations, whether behavioral signs such as writhing or screaming or physiological or neurological recordings, are observations of pain itself. Pain is something one feels, and one can only infer that others are feeling it from various external indications. The fact that only philosophers are ever skeptical about whether other humans feel pain shows that we regard such inference as justifiable in the case of humans.

Is there any reason why the same inference should be unjustifiable for other animals? Nearly all the external signs which lead us to infer pain in other humans can be seen in other species, especially "higher" animals such as mammals and birds. Behavioral signs — writhing, yelping, or other forms of calling, attempts to avoid the source of pain, and many others — are present. We know, too, that these animals are biologically similar in the relevant respects, having nervous systems like ours which can be observed to function as ours do. **10**

So the grounds for inferring that these animals can feel pain are nearly as good as the grounds for inferring other humans do. Only nearly, for there is one behavioral sign that humans have but nonhumans, with the exception of one or two specially raised chimpanzees, do not have. This, of course, is a developed language. As the quotation from Bentham indicates, this has long been regarded as an important distinction between man and other animals. Other animals may communicate with each other, but not in the way we do. Following Chomsky, many people now mark this distinction by saying that only humans communicate in a form that is governed by rules of syntax. (For the purposes of this argument, linguists allow those chimpanzees who have learned a syntactic sign language to rank as honorary humans.) Nevertheless, as Bentham pointed out, this distinction is not relevant to the question of how animals ought to be treated, unless it can be linked to the issue of whether animals suffer. **11**

This link may be attempted in two ways. First, there is a hazy line of philosophical thought, stemming perhaps from some doctrines associated with Wittgenstein, which maintains that we cannot meaningfully attribute states of consciousness to beings without language. I have not seen this argument made explicit in print, though I have come across it in conversation. The position seems to me very implausible, and I doubt that it would be held at all if it were not thought to be a consequence of a broader view of the significance of language. It may be that the use of public, rule-governed language is a precondition of conceptual thought. It may even be, although personally I doubt it, that we cannot meaningfully speak of a creature having an intention unless that creature can use a language. But states like pain, surely, are more primitive than either of these, and seem to have nothing to do with language. **12**

Indeed, as Jane Goodall points out in her study of chimpanzees, when it comes to the expression of feelings and emotions, humans tend to fall back on non-linguistic modes of communication which are often found among apes, such as a cheering pat on the back, an exuberant embrace, a clasp of hands, and so on. Michael Peters makes a similar point in his contribution to **13**

Animals, Men and Morals when he notes that the basic signals we use to convey pain, fear, sexual arousal, and so on are not specific to our species. So there seems to be no reason at all to believe that a creature without language cannot suffer.

The second, and more easily appreciated way of linking language and the existence of pain is to say that the best evidence that we can have that another creature is in pain is when he tells us that he is. This is a distinct line of argument, for it is not being denied that a non-language-user conceivably could suffer, but only that we could know that he is suffering. Still, this line of argument seems to me to fail, and for reasons similar to those just given. "I am in pain" is not the best possible evidence that the speaker is in pain (he might be lying) and it is certainly not the only possible evidence. Behavioral signs and knowledge of the animal's biological similarity to ourselves together provide adequate evidence that animals do suffer. After all, we would not accept linguistic evidence if it contradicted the rest of the evidence. If a man was severely burned, and behaved as if he were in pain, writhing, groaning, being very careful not to let his burned skin touch anything, and so on, but later said he had not been in pain at all, we would be more likely to conclude that he was lying or suffering from amnesia than that he had not been in pain.

Even if there were stronger grounds for refusing to attribute pain to those who do not have a language, the consequences of this refusal might lead us to examine these grounds unusually critically. Human infants, as well as some adults, are unable to use language. Are we to deny that a year-old infant can suffer? If not, how can language be crucial? Of course, most parents can understand the responses of even very young infants better than they understand the responses of other animals, and sometimes infant responses can be understood in the light of later development.

This, however, is just a fact about the relative knowledge we have of our own species and other species, and most of this knowledge is simply derived from closer contact. Those who have studied the behavior of other animals soon learn to understand their responses at least as well as we understand those of an infant. (I am not referring to Jane Goodall's and other well-known studies of apes. Consider, for example, the degree of understanding achieved by Tinbergen from watching herring gulls.) Just as we can understand infant human behavior in the light of adult human behavior, so we can understand the behavior of other species in the light of our own behavior (and sometimes we can understand our own behavior better in the light of the behavior of other species).

The grounds we have for believing that other mammals and birds suffer are, then, closely analogous to the grounds we have for believing that other humans suffer. It remains to consider how far down the evolutionary scale this analogy holds. Obviously it becomes poorer when we get further away from man. To be more precise would require a detailed examination of all that we know about other forms of life. With fish, reptiles, and other vertebrates the analogy still seems strong, with molluscs like oysters it is much weaker. Insects are more difficult, and it may be that in our present state of knowledge we must be agnostic about whether they are capable of suffering.

If there is no moral justification for ignoring suffering when it occurs, and **18** it does occur in other species, what are we to say of our attitudes toward these other species? Richard Ryder, one of the contributors to *Animals, Men and Morals*, uses the term "speciesism" to describe the belief that we are entitled to treat members of other species in a way in which it would be wrong to treat members of our own species. The term is not euphonious, but it neatly makes the analogy with racism. The non-racist would do well to bear the analogy in mind when he is inclined to defend human behavior toward nonhumans. "Shouldn't we worry about improving the lot of our own species before we concern ourselves with other species?" he may ask. If we substitute "race" for "species" we shall see that the question is better not asked. "Is a vegetarian diet nutritionally adequate?" resembles the slave-owner's claim that he and the whole economy of the South would be ruined without slave labor. There is even a parallel with skeptical doubts about whether animals suffer, for some defenders of slavery professed to doubt whether blacks really suffer in the way whites do.

I do not want to give the impression, however, that the case for Animal **19** Liberation is based on the analogy with racism and no more. On the contrary, *Animals, Men and Morals* describes the various ways in which humans exploit nonhumans, and several contributors consider the defenses that have been offered, including the defense of meat-eating mentioned in the last paragraph. Sometimes the rebuttals are scornfully dismissive, rather than carefully designed to convince the detached critic. This may be a fault, but it is a fault that is inevitable, given the kind of book this is. The issue is not one on which one can remain detached. As the editors state in their Introduction:

> Once the full force of moral assessment has been made explicit there can be no rational excuse left for killing animals, be they killed for food, science, or sheer personal indulgence. We have not assembled this book to provide the reader with yet another manual on how to make brutalities less brutal. Compromise, in the traditional sense of the term, is simple unthinking weakness when one considers the actual reasons for our crude relationships with the other animals.

The point is that on this issue there are few critics who are genuinely **20** detached. People who eat pieces of slaughtered nonhumans every day find it hard to believe that they are doing wrong; and they also find it hard to imagine what else they could eat. So for those who do not place nonhumans beyond the pale of morality, there comes a stage when further argument seems pointless, a stage at which one can only accuse one's opponent of hypocrisy and reach for the sort of sociological account of our practices and the way we defend them that is attempted by David Wood in his contribution to this book. On the other hand, to those unconvinced by the arguments, and unable to accept that they are merely rationalizing their dietary preferences and their fear of being thought peculiar, such sociological explanations can only seem insultingly arrogant.

The logic of speciesism is most apparent in the practice of experimenting 2 on nonhumans in order to benefit humans. This is because the issue is rarely obscured by allegations that nonhumans are so different from humans that we cannot know anything about whether they suffer. The defender of vivisection cannot use this argument because he needs to stress the similarities between man and other animals in order to justify the usefulness to the former of experiments on the latter. The researcher who makes rats choose between starvation and electric shocks to see if they develop ulcers (they do) does so because he knows that the rat has a nervous system very similar to man's, and presumably feels an electric shock in a similar way.

Richard Ryder's restrained account of experiments on animals made me 2 angrier with my fellow men than anything else in this book. Ryder, a clinical psychologist by profession, himself experimented on animals before he came to hold the view he puts forward in his essay. Experimenting on animals is now a large industry, both academic and commercial. In 1969, more than 5 million experiments were performed in Britain, the vast majority without anesthetic (though how many of these involved pain is not known). There are no accurate U.S. figures, since there is no federal law on the subject, and in many cases no state law either. Estimates vary from 20 million to 200 million. Ryder suggests that 80 million might be the best guess. We tend to think that this is all for vital medical research, but of course it is not. Huge numbers of animals are used in university departments from Forestry to Psychology, and even more are used for commercial purposes, to test whether cosmetics can cause skin damage, or shampoos eye damage, or to test food additives or laxatives or sleeping pills or anything else.

A standard test for foodstuffs is the "LD50." The object of this test is to 23 find the dosage level at which 50 percent of the test animals will die. This means that nearly all of them will become very sick before finally succumbing or surviving. When the substance is a harmless one, it may be necessary to force huge doses down the animals, until in some cases sheer volume or concentration causes death.

Ryder gives a selection of experiments, taken from recent scientific jour- 24 nals. I will quote two, not for the sake of indulging in gory details, but in order to give an idea of what normal researchers think they may legitimately do to other species. The point is not that the individual researchers are cruel men, but that they are behaving in a way that is allowed by our speciesist attitudes. As Ryder points out, even if only 1 percent of the experiments involve severe pain, that is 50,000 experiments in Britain each year, or nearly 150 every day (and about fifteen times as many in the United States, if Ryder's guess is right). Here then are two experiments:

O. S. Ray and R. J. Barrett of Pittsburgh gave electric shocks to the feet of 1,042 mice. They then caused convulsions by giving more intense shocks through cup-shaped electrodes applied to the animals' eyes or through pressure spring clips attached to their ears. Unfortunately some of the mice who "successfully completed Day One training were found sick or dead prior to testing on Day Two." [*Journal of Comparative and Physiological Psychology*, vol. 67, 1969, pp. 110–116]

At the National Institute for Medical Research, Mill Hill, London, W. Feldberg and S. L. Sherwood injected chemicals into the brains of cats — "with a number of widely different substances, recurrent patterns of reaction were obtained. Retching, vomiting, defaecation, increased salivation and greatly accelerated respiration leading to panting were common features." . . .

The injection into the brain of a large dose of Tubocuraine caused the cat to jump "from the table to the floor and then straight into its cage, where it started calling more and more noisily whilst moving about restlessly and jerkily . . . finally the cat fell with legs and neck flexed, jerking in rapid clonic movement, the condition being that of a major [epileptic] convulsion . . . within a few seconds the cat got up, ran for a few yards at high speed and fell in another fit. The whole process was repeated several times within the next ten minutes, during which the cat lost faeces and foamed at the mouth."

The animal finally died thirty-five minutes after the brain injection. [*Journal of Physiology*, vol. 123, 1954, pp. 148–167]

There is nothing secret about these experiments. One has only to open any **25** recent volume of a learned journal, such as the *Journal of Comparative and Physiological Psychology*, to find full descriptions of experiments of this sort, together with the results obtained — results that are frequently trivial and obvious. The experiments are often supported by public funds.

It is a significant indication of the level of acceptability of these practices **26** that, although these experiments are taking place at this moment on university campuses throughout the country, there has so far as I know, not been the slightest protest from the student movement. Students have been rightly concerned that their universities should not discriminate on grounds of race or sex, and that they should not serve the purposes of the military or big business. Speciesism continues undisturbed, and many students participate in it. There may be a few qualms at first, but since everyone regards it as normal, and it may even be a required part of a course, the student soon becomes hardened and, dismissing his earlier feelings as "mere sentiment," comes to regard animals as statistics rather than sentient beings with interests that warrant consideration.

Argument about vivisection has often missed the point because it has been 27
put in absolutist terms: Would the abolitionist be prepared to let thousands
die if they could be saved by experimenting on a single animal? The way to
reply to this purely hypothetical question is to pose another: Would the
experimenter be prepared to experiment on a human orphan under six
months old, if it were the only way to save many lives? (I say "orphan" to
avoid the complication of parental feelings, although in doing so I am being
overfair to the experimenter, since the nonhuman subjects of experiments are
not orphans.) A negative answer to this question indicates that the experimenter's readiness to use nonhumans is simple discrimination, for adult apes,
cats, mice, and other mammals are more conscious of what is happening to
them, more self-directing, and, so far as we can tell, just as sensitive to pain as
a human infant. There is no characteristic that human infants possess that
adult mammals do not have to the same or a higher degree.

(It might be possible to hold that what makes it wrong to experiment on a 28
human infant is that the infant will in time develop into more than the
nonhuman, but one would then, to be consistent, have to oppose abortion,
and perhaps contraception, too, for the fetus and the egg and sperm have the
same potential as the infant. Moreover, one would still have no reason for
experimenting on a nonhuman rather than a human with brain damage severe
enough to make it impossible for him to rise above infant level.)

The experimenter, then, shows a bias for his own species whenever he 29
carries out an experiment on a nonhuman for a purpose that he would not
think justified him in using a human being at an equal or lower level of
sentience, awareness, ability to be self-directing, etc. No one familiar with the
kind of results yielded by these experiments can have the slightest doubt that
if this bias were eliminated the number of experiments performed would be
zero or very close to it.

If it is vivisection that shows the logic of speciesism most clearly, it is the 30
use of other species for food that is at the heart of our attitudes toward them.
Most of *Animals, Men and Morals* is an attack on meat-eating — an attack
which is based solely on concern for nonhumans, without reference to arguments derived from considerations of ecology, macrobiotics, health, or religion.

The idea that nonhumans are utilities, means to our ends, pervades our 31
thought. Even conservationists who are concerned about the slaughter of
wild fowl but not about the vastly greater slaughter of chickens for our tables
are thinking in this way — they are worried about what we would lose if there
were less wildlife. Stanley Godlovitch, pursuing the Marxist idea that our
thinking is formed by the activities we undertake in satisfying our needs,
suggests that man's first classification of his environment was into Edibles

and Inedibles. Most animals came into the first category, and there they have remained.

Man may always have killed other species for food, but he has never **32** exploited them so ruthlessly as he does today. Farming has succumbed to business methods, the objective being to get the highest possible ratio of output (meat, eggs, milk) to input (fodder, labor costs, etc.). Ruth Harrison's essay "On Factory Farming" gives an account of some aspects of modern methods, and of the unsuccessful British campaign for effective controls, a campaign which was sparked off by her *Animal Machines* (London: Stuart, 1964).

Her article is in no way a substitute for her earlier book. This is a pity **33** since, as she says, "Farm produce is still associated with mental pictures of animals browsing in the fields . . . of hens having a last forage before going to roost. . . . " Yet neither in her article nor elsewhere in *Animals, Men and Morals* is this false image replaced by a clear idea of the nature and extent of factory farming. We learn of this only indirectly, when we hear of the code of reform proposed by an advisory committee set up by the British government.

Among the proposals, which the government refused to implement on the **34** grounds that they were too idealistic, were *"Any animal should at least have room to turn around freely."*

Factory farm animals need liberation in the most literal sense. Veal calves **35** are kept in stalls five feet by two feet. They are usually slaughtered when about four months old, and have been too big to turn in their stalls for at least a month. Intensive beef herds, kept in stalls only proportionately larger for much longer periods, account for a growing percentage of beef production. Sows are often similarly confined when pregnant, which, because of artificial methods of increasing fertility, can be most of the time. Animals confined in this way do not waste food by exercising, nor do they develop unpalatable muscle.

"A dry bedded area should be provided for all stock." Intensively kept **36** animals usually have to stand and sleep on slatted floors without straw, because this makes cleaning easier.

"Palatable roughage must be readily available to all calves after one **37** *week of age."* In order to produce the pale veal housewives are said to prefer, calves are fed on an all-liquid diet until slaughter, even though they are long past the age at which they would normally eat grass. They develop a craving for roughage, evidenced by attempts to gnaw wood from their stalls. (For the same reason, their diet is deficient in iron.)

"Battery cages for poultry should be large enough for a bird to be able to **38** *stretch one wing at a time."* Under current British practice, a cage for four or five laying hens has a floor area of twenty inches by eighteen inches, scarcely larger than a double page of the *New York Review of Books*. In this

space, on a sloping wire floor (sloping so the eggs roll down, wire so the dung drops through) the birds live for a year or eighteen months while artificial lighting and temperature conditions combine with drugs in their food to squeeze the maximum number of eggs out of them. Table birds are also sometimes kept in cages. More often they are reared in sheds, no less crowded. Under these conditions all the birds' natural activities are frustrated, and they develop "vices" such as pecking each other to death. To prevent this, beaks are often cut off, and the sheds kept dark.

How many of those who support factory farming by buying its produce **39** know anything about the way it is produced? How many have heard something about it, but are reluctant to check up for fear that it will make them uncomfortable? To non-speciesists, the typical consumer's mixture of ignorance, reluctance to find out the truth, and vague belief that nothing really bad could be allowed seems analogous to the attitudes of "decent Germans" to the death camps.

There are, of course, some defenders of factory farming. Their arguments **40** are considered, though again rather sketchily, by John Harris. Among the most common: "Since they have never known anything else, they don't suffer." This argument will not be put by anyone who knows anything about animal behavior, since he will know that not all behavior has to be learned. Chickens attempt to stretch wings, walk around, scratch, and even dustbathe or build a nest, even though they have never lived under conditions that allowed these activities. Calves can suffer from maternal deprivation no matter at what age they were taken from their mothers. "We need these intensive methods to provide protein for a growing population." As ecologists and famine relief organizations know, we can produce far more protein per acre if we grow the right vegetable crop, soy beans for instance, than if we use the land to grow crops to be converted into protein by animals who use nearly 90 percent of the protein themselves, even when unable to exercise.

There will be many readers of this book who will agree that factory **41** farming involves an unjustifiable degree of exploitation of sentient creatures, and yet will want to say that there is nothing wrong with rearing animals for food, provided it is done "humanely." These people are saying, in effect, that although we should not cause animals to suffer, there is nothing wrong with killing them.

There are two possible replies to this view. One is to attempt to show that **42** this combination of attitudes is absurd. Roslind Godlovitch takes this course in her essay, which is an examination of some common attitudes to animals. She argues that from the combination of "animal suffering is to be avoided" and "there is nothing wrong with killing animals" it follows that all animal life ought to be exterminated (since all sentient creatures will suffer to some degree at some point in their lives). Euthanasia is a contentious issue only because we place some value on living. If we did not, the least amount of suffering would justify it. Accordingly, if we deny that we have a duty to exterminate all animal life, we must concede that we are placing some value on animal life.

This argument seems to be valid, although one could still reply that the **43** value of animal life is to be derived from the pleasures that life can have for them, so that, provided their lives have a balance of pleasure over pain, we are justified in rearing them. But this would imply that we ought to produce animals and let them live as pleasantly as possible, without suffering.

At this point, one can make the second of the two possible replies to the **44** view that rearing and killing animals for food is all right so long as it is done humanely. This second reply is that so long as we think that a nonhuman may be killed simply so that a human can satisfy his taste for meat, we are still thinking of nonhumans as means rather than as ends in themselves. The factory farm is nothing more than the application of technology to this concept. Even traditional methods involve castration, the separation of mothers and their young, the breaking up of herds, branding or ear-punching, and of course transportation to the abattoirs and the final moments of terror when the animal smells blood and senses danger. If we were to try rearing animals so that they lived and died without suffering, we should find that to do so on anything like the scale of today's meat industry would be a sheer impossibility. Meat would become the prerogative of the rich.

I have been able to discuss only some of the contributions to this book, **45** saying nothing about, for instance, the essays on killing for furs and for sport. Nor have I considered all the detailed questions that need to be asked once we start thinking about other species in the radically different way presented by this book. What, for instance, are we to do about genuine conflicts of interest like rats biting slum children? I am not sure of the answer, but the essential point is just that we *do* see this as a conflict of interest, that we recognize that rats have interests too. Then we may begin to think about other ways of resolving the conflict — perhaps by leaving out rat baits that sterilize the rats instead of killing them.

I have not discussed such problems because they are side issues compared **46** with the exploitation of other species for food and for experimental purposes. On these central matters, I hope that I have said enough to show that this book, despite its flaws, is a challenge to every human to recognize his attitudes to nonhumans as a form of prejudice no less objectionable than racism or sexism. It is a challenge that demands not just a change of attitudes, but a change in our way of life, for it requires us to become vegetarians.

Can a purely moral demand of this kind succeed? The odds are certainly **47** against it. The book holds out no inducements. It does not tell us that we will become healthier, or enjoy life more, if we cease exploiting animals. Animal Liberation will require greater altruism on the part of mankind than any other liberation movement, since animals are incapable of demanding it for themselves, or of protesting against their exploitation by votes, demonstrations, or bombs. Is man capable of such genuine altruism? Who knows? If this book does have a significant effect, however, it will be a vindication of all those who have believed that man has within himself the potential for more than cruelty and selfishness.

THE CASE FOR THE USE OF ANIMALS IN BIOMEDICAL RESEARCH

Carl Cohen

Medical school professor Carl Cohen argues that animals cannot have rights because animals have no moral consciousness. Although we are obligated to treat animals humanely, we cannot act as though the life of an animal were equal to the life of a human. The animal liberation movement, if followed to its logical conclusion, will have dire consequences for humanity.

Using animals as research subjects in medical investigations is widely 1 condemned on two grounds: first, because it wrongly violates the *rights* of animals, and second, because it wrongly imposes on sentient creatures much avoidable *suffering*. Neither of these arguments is sound. The first relies on a mistaken understanding of rights; the second relies on a mistaken calculation of consequences. Both deserve definitive dismissal.

Why Animals Have No Rights

A right, properly understood, is a claim, or potential claim, that one party 2 may exercise against another. The target against whom such a claim may be registered can be a single person, a group, a community, or (perhaps) all humankind. The content of rights claims also varies greatly: repayment of loans, nondiscrimination by employers, noninterference by the state, and so on. To comprehend any genuine right fully, therefore, we must know *who* holds the right, *against whom* it is held, and *to what* it is a right.

Alternative sources of rights add complexity. Some rights are grounded in 3 constitution and law (e.g., the right of an accused to trial by jury); some rights are moral but give no legal claims (e.g., my right to your keeping the promise you gave me); and some rights (e.g., against theft or assault) are rooted both in morals and in law.

The differing targets, contents, and sources of rights, and their inevitable 4 conflict, together weave a tangled web. Notwithstanding all such complications, this much is clear about rights in general: they are in every case claims, or potential claims, within a community of moral agents. Rights arise, and can be intelligibly defended, only among beings who actually do, or can, make moral claims against one another. Whatever else rights may be, therefore, they are necessarily human; their possessors are persons, human beings.

The attributes of human beings from which this moral capability arises 5 have been described variously by philosophers, both ancient and modern: the inner consciousness of a free will (Saint Augustine); the grasp, by human reason, of the binding character of moral law (Saint Thomas Aquinas); the self-conscious participation of human beings in an objective ethical order (G.W.F. Hegel); human membership in an organic moral community (F.H. Bradley); the development of the human self through the consciousness of other moral selves (G.H. Mead); and the underivative, intuitive cognition of the rightness of an action (L.A. Prichard). Most influential has been Immanuel Kant's emphasis on the universal human possession of a uniquely moral will and the autonomy its use entails. Humans confront choices that are purely moral; humans — but certainly not dogs or mice — lay down moral laws, for others and for themselves. Human beings are self-legislative, morally *auto-nomous.*

Animals (that is, nonhuman animals, the ordinary sense of that word) lack   **6** this capacity for free moral judgment. They are not beings of a kind capable of exercising or responding to moral claims. Animals therefore have no rights, and they can have none. This is the core of the argument about the alleged rights of animals. The holders of rights must have the capacity to comprehend rules of duty, governing all including themselves. In applying such rules, the holders of rights must recognize possible conflicts between what is in their own interest and what is just. Only in a community of beings capable of self-restricting moral judgments can the concept of a right be correctly invoked.

Humans have such moral capacities. They are in this sense self-legislative,   **7** are members of communities governed by moral rules, and do possess rights. Animals do not have such moral capacities. They are not morally self-legislative, cannot possibly be members of a truly moral community, and therefore cannot possess rights. In conducting research on animal subjects, therefore, we do not violate their rights, because they have none to violate. . . .

Genuinely moral acts have an internal as well as an external dimension.   **8** Thus, in law, an act can be criminal only when the guilty deed, the actus reus, is done with a guilty mind, mens rea. No animal can ever commit a crime; bringing animals to criminal trial is the mark of primitive ignorance. The claims of moral rights are similarly inapplicable to them. Does a lion have a right to eat a baby zebra? Does a baby zebra have a right not to be eaten? Such questions, mistakenly invoking the concept of right where it does not belong, do not make good sense. Those who condemn biomedical research because it violates "animal rights" commit the same blunder.

In Defense of Speciesism

Abandoning reliance on animal rights, some critics resort instead to animal   **9** sentience — their feelings of pain and distress. We ought to desist from the imposition of pain insofar as we can. Since all or nearly all experimentation on animals does impose pain and could be readily forgone, say these critics, it should be stopped. The ends sought may be worthy, but those ends do not justify imposing agonies on humans, and by animals the agonies are felt no less. The laboratory use of animals (these critics conclude) must therefore be ended — or at least very sharply curtailed.

Argument of this variety is essentially utilitarian, often expressly so; it is 10 based on the calculation of the net product, in pains and pleasures, resulting from experiments on animals. Jeremy Bentham, comparing horses and dogs with other sentient creatures, is thus commonly quoted: "The question is not, Can they reason? nor Can they talk? but, Can they suffer?"

Biomedical Research Must Still Proceed

Animals certainly can suffer and surely ought not to be made to suffer 11 needlessly. But in inferring, from these uncontroversial premises, that biomedical research causing animal distress is largely (or wholly) wrong, the critic commits two serious errors.

The first error is the assumption, often explicitly defended, that all sentient 12 animals have equal moral standing. Between a dog and a human being, according to this view, there is no moral difference; hence the pains suffered by dogs must be weighed no differently from the pains suffered by humans. To deny such equality, according to this critic, is to give unjust preference to one species over another; it is "speciesism." The most influential statement of this moral equality of species was made by Peter Singer:

> The racist violates the principles of equality by giving greater weight to the interests of members of his own race when there is a clash between their interests and the interests of those of another race. The sexist violates the principle of equality by favoring the interests of his own sex. Similarly the speciesist allows the interests of his own species to override the greater interests of members of other species. The pattern is identical in each case.

This argument is worse than unsound; it is atrocious. It draws an offensive 13 moral conclusion from a deliberately devised verbal parallelism that is utterly specious. Racism has no rational ground whatever. Differing degrees of respect or concern for humans for no other reason than that they are members of different races is an injustice totally without foundation in the nature of the races themselves. Racists, even if acting on the basis of mistaken factual beliefs, do grave moral wrong precisely because there is no morally relevant distinction among the races. The supposition of such differences had led to outright horror. The same is true of the sexes, neither sex being entitled by right to greater respect or concern than the other. No dispute here.

Between species of animate life, however — between (for example) humans   14
on the one hand and cats or rats on the other — the morally relevant differences are enormous, and almost universally appreciated. Humans engage in
moral reflection; humans are morally autonomous; humans are members of
moral communities, recognizing just claims against their own interest.
Human beings do have rights; theirs is a moral status very different from that
of cats or rats.

Speciesism Is Necessary

I am a speciesist. Speciesism is not merely plausible; it is essential for right   15
conduct, because those who will not make the morally relevant distinctions
among species are almost certain, in consequence, to misapprehend their true
obligations. The analogy between speciesism and racism is insidious. Every
sensitive moral judgment requires that the differing natures of the beings to
whom obligations are owed be considered. If all forms of animate life — or
vertebrate animal life — must be treated equally, and if therefore in evaluating
a research program the pains of a rodent count equally with the pains of a
human, we are forced to conclude (1) that neither humans nor rodents
possess rights, or (2) that rodents possess all the rights that humans possess.
Both alternatives are absurd. Yet one or the other must be swallowed if the
moral equality of all species is to be defended. . . .

Those who claim to base their objection to the use of animals in biomedical   16
research on their reckoning of the net pleasures and pains produced make a
second error, equally grave. Even if it were true — as it is surely not — that
the pains of all animate beings must be counted equally, a cogent utilitarian
calculation requires that we weigh all the consequences of the use, and of the
nonuse, of animals in laboratory research. Critics relying (however mistakenly) on animal rights may claim to ignore the beneficial results of such
research, rights being trump cards to which interest and advantage must give
way. But an argument that is explicitly framed in terms of interest and benefit
for all over the long run must attend also to the disadvantageous consequences of not using animals in research, and to all the achievements attained
and attainable only through their use. The sum of the benefits of their use is
utterly beyond quantification. The elimination of horrible disease, the increase of longevity, the avoidance of great pain, the saving of lives, and the
improvement of the quality of lives (for humans and for animals) achieved
through research using animals is so incalculably great that the argument of
these critics, systematically pursued, establishes not their conclusion but its
reverse: to refrain from using animals in biomedical research is, on utilitarian
ground, morally wrong.

When balancing the pleasures and pains resulting from the use of animals   17
in research, we must not fail to place on the scales the terrible pains that

would have resulted, would be suffered now, and would long continue had animals not been used. Every disease eliminated, every vaccine developed, every method of pain relief devised, every surgical procedure invented, every prosthetic device implanted — indeed, virtually every modern medical therapy is due, in part or in whole, to experimentation using animals. Nor may we ignore, in the balancing process, the predictable gains in human (and animal) well-being that are probably achievable in the future but that will not be achieved if the decision is made now to desist from such research or to curtail it. . . .

The Absurd Consequences of Animal Rights

Finally, inconsistency between the profession and the practice of many 18 who oppose research using animals deserves comment. This frankly ad hominem observation aims chiefly to show that a coherent position rejecting the use of animals in medical research imposes costs so high as to be intolerable even to the critics themselves.

One cannot coherently object to the killing of animals in biomedical 19 investigations while continuing to eat them. Anesthetics and thoughtful animal husbandry render the level of actual animal distress in the laboratory generally lower than that in the abattoir. So long as death and discomfort do not substantially differ in the two contexts, the consistent objector must not only refrain from all eating of animals but also protest as vehemently against others eating them as against others experimenting on them. No less vigorously must the critic object to the wearing of animal hides in coats and shoes, to employment in any industrial enterprise that uses animal parts, and to any commercial development that will cause death or distress to animals. . . .

Scrupulous vegetarianism, in matters of food, clothing, shelter, commerce, 20 and recreation, and in all other spheres, is the only fully coherent position the critic may adopt. At great human cost, the lives of fish and crustaceans must also be protected, with equal vigor, if speciesism has been forsworn. A very few consistent critics adopt this position. It is the reductio ad absurdum of the rejection of moral distinctions between animals and human beings.

FOR CLASS DISCUSSION

1. Analyze and evaluate the debate on the use of animals for medical research by applying the first set of guide questions from pages 443–444. How do you account for the disagreement between Singer and Cohen?

2. Choose one of the arguments for closer analysis, applying the second set of guide questions on page 444.

OPTIONAL WRITING ASSIGNMENTS

1. Suppose you have a friend who hasn't taken this class or read this textbook but who is interested in argument. Suppose further that one evening you explained to your friend a bit about Toulmin's schema using grounds, warrants, backing, and so forth. Your friend picked up the notion of grounds quite quickly, but seemed confused about warrants. Write a letter to your friend explaining the concept of warrants and illustrating it with the disagreement between Singer and Cohen over animals rights.

2. A group of animal rights activists has taken over your university's biomedical research lab to protest its inhumane treatment of experimental animals. A national TV network features the protest on the six o'clock news. Your oldest friend sees the feature and calls you to find out what's going on. She hasn't thought much about the issue and is curious to find out how you stand.

After hanging up, you decide you've given a pretty lame response. You gather some information, including the following: (1) The lab conducts primarily AIDS and cancer research; (2) the lab was cited in a recent accreditation report for several "minor" violations, including unsanitary pens and overcrowding, but received provisional accreditation; (3) the lab receives $2.5 million in federal aid annually. You read the preceding essays and get ready to write a letter to your friend explaining more precisely how you feel about the use of experimental animals in medical research and why you feel that way.

CIVIL DISOBEDIENCE: IS REFUSAL TO OBEY LAWS EVER JUSTIFIED?

LETTER FROM BIRMINGHAM JAIL IN RESPONSE TO PUBLIC STATEMENT BY EIGHT ALABAMA CLERGYMEN

Martin Luther King, Jr.

On April 12, 1963, eight Alabama clergymen signed the following public statement urging "outsiders" to halt the racial demonstrations they had instigated. Writing from the Birmingham jail, Martin Luther King, Jr., gave a compelling justification for his actions: "I am in Birmingham because injustice is here."

We the undersigned clergymen are among those who, in January, issued "An Appeal for Law and Order and Common Sense," in dealing with racial problems in Alabama. We expressed understanding that honest convictions in racial matters could properly be pursued in the courts, but urged that decisions of those courts should in the meantime be peacefully obeyed.

Since that time there had been some evidence of increased forbearance and a willingness to face facts. Responsible citizens have undertaken to work on various problems which cause racial friction and unrest. In Birmingham, recent public events have given indication that we all have opportunity for a new constructive and realistic approach to racial problems.

Source: Martin Luther King, Jr., "Letter from Birmingham Jail," *Why We Can't Wait* (New York: Harper & Row, 1964).

However, we are now confronted by a series of demonstrations by some of our Negro citizens, directed and led in part by outsiders. We recognize the natural impatience of people who feel that their hopes are slow in being realized. But we are convinced that these demonstrations are unwise and untimely.

We agree rather with certain local Negro leadership which has called for honest and open negotiation of racial issues in our area. And we believe this kind of facing of issues can best be accomplished by citizens of our own metropolitan area, white and Negro, meeting with their knowledge and experience of the local situation. All of us need to face that responsibility and find proper channels for its accomplishment.

Just as we formerly pointed out that "hatred and violence have no sanction in our religious and political traditions," we also point out that such actions as incite to hatred and violence, however technically peaceful those actions may be, have not contributed to the resolution of our local problems. We do not believe that these days of new hope are days when extreme measures are justified in Birmingham.

We commend the community as a whole, and the local news media and law enforcement officials in particular, on the calm manner in which these demonstrations have been handled. We urge the public to continue to show restraint should the demonstrations continue, and the law enforcement officials to remain calm and continue to protect our city from violence.

We further strongly urge our own Negro community to withdraw support from these demonstrations, and to unite locally in working peacefully for a better Birmingham. When rights are consistently denied, a cause should be pressed in the courts and in negotiations among local leaders, and not in the streets. We appeal to both our white and Negro citizenry to observe the principles of law and order and common sense.

Signed by:

C. C. J. Carpenter, D.D., LL.D., *Bishop of Alabama*
Joseph A. Durick, D.D., *Auxiliary Bishop, Diocese of Mobile, Birmingham*
Rabbi Milton L. Grafman, *Temple Emanu-El, Birmingham, Alabama*
Bishop Paul Hardin, *Bishop of the Alabama-West Florida Conference of the Methodist Church*
Bishop Nolan B. Harmon, *Bishop of the North Alabama Conference of the Methodist Church*
George M. Murray, D.D., LL.D., *Bishop Coadjutor, Episcopal Diocese of Alabama*
Edward V. Ramage, *Moderator, Synod of the Alabama Presbyterian Church in the United States*
Earl Stallings, *Pastor, First Baptist Church, Birmingham, Alabama*

Following is the letter Martin Luther King, Jr., wrote in response to the clergymen's public statement.

April 16, 1963

My Dear Fellow Clergymen:

While confined here in the Birmingham city jail, I came across your recent **1** statement calling my present activities "unwise and untimely." Seldom do I pause to answer criticism of my work and ideas. If I sought to answer all the criticisms that cross my desk, my secretaries would have little time for anything other than such correspondence in the course of the day, and I would have no time for constructive work. But since I feel that you are men of genuine good will and that your criticisms are sincerely set forth, I want to try to answer your statement in what I hope will be patient and reasonable terms.

I think I should indicate why I am here in Birmingham, since you have **2** been influenced by the view which argues against "outsiders coming in." I have the honor of serving as president of the Southern Christian Leadership Conference, an organization operating in every southern state, with head-quarters in Atlanta, Georgia. We have some eighty-five affiliated organizations across the South, and one of them is the Alabama Christian Movement for Human Rights. Frequently we share staff, educational and financial resources with our affiliates. Several months ago the affiliate here in Birmingham asked us to be on call to engage in a nonviolent direct-action program if such were deemed necessary. We readily consented, and when the hour came we lived up to our promise. So I, along with several members of my staff, am here because I was invited here. I am here because I have organizational ties here.

But more basically, I am in Birmingham because injustice is here. Just as **3** the prophets of the eighth century B.C. left their villages and carried their "thus saith the Lord" far beyond the boundaries of their home towns, and just as the Apostle Paul left his village of Tarsus and carried the gospel of Jesus Christ to the far corners of the Greco-Roman world, so am I compelled to carry the gospel of freedom beyond my own home town. Like Paul, I must constantly respond to the Macedonian call for aid.

Moreover, I am cognizant of the interrelatedness of all communities and **4** states. I cannot sit idly by in Atlanta and not be concerned about what happens in Birmingham. Injustice anywhere is a threat to justice everywhere. We are caught in an inescapable network of mutuality, tied in a single garment of destiny. Whatever affects one directly, affects all indirectly. Never again can we afford to live with the narrow, provincial "outside agitator" idea. Anyone who lives inside the United States can never be considered an outsider anywhere within its bounds.

You deplore the demonstrations taking place in Birmingham. But your **5** statement, I am sorry to say, fails to express a similar concern for the conditions that brought about the demonstrations. I am sure that none of you would want to rest content with the superficial kind of social analysis that deals merely with effects and does not grapple with underlying causes. It is unfortunate that demonstrations are taking place in Birmingham, but it is even more unfortunate that the city's white power structure left the Negro community with no alternative.

In any nonviolent campaign there are four basic steps: collection of the   6 facts to determine whether injustices exist; negotiation; self-purification; and direct action. We have gone through all these steps in Birmingham. There can be no gainsaying the fact that racial injustice engulfs this community. Birmingham is probably the most thoroughly segregated city in the United States. Its ugly record of brutality is widely known. Negroes have experienced grossly unjust treatment in the courts. There have been more unsolved bombings of Negro homes and churches in Birmingham than in any other city in the nation. These are the hard, brutal facts of the case. On the basis of these conditions, Negro leaders sought to negotiate with the city fathers. But the latter consistently refused to engage in good-faith negotiation.

Then, last September, came the opportunity to talk with leaders of Bir-   7 mingham's economic community. In the course of the negotiations, certain promises were made by the merchants — for example, to remove the stores' humiliating racial signs. On the basis of these promises, the Reverend Fred Shuttlesworth and the leaders of the Alabama Christian Movement for Human Rights agreed to a moratorium on all demonstrations. As the weeks and months went by, we realized that we were the victims of a broken promise. A few signs, briefly removed, returned; the others remained.

As in so many past experiences, our hopes had been blasted, and the   8 shadow of deep disappointment settled upon us. We had no alternative except to prepare for direct action, whereby we would present our very bodies as a means of laying our case before the conscience of the local and the national community. Mindful of the difficulties involved, we decided to undertake a process of self-purification. We began a series of workshops on nonviolence, and we repeatedly asked ourselves: "Are you able to accept blows without retaliating?" "Are you able to endure the ordeal of jail?" We decided to schedule our direct-action program for the Easter season, realizing that except for Christmas, this is the main shopping period of the year. Knowing that a strong economic-withdrawal program would be the by-product of direct action, we felt that this would be the best time to bring pressure to bear on the merchants for the needed change.

Then it occurred to us that Birmingham's mayoral election was coming up   9 in March, and we speedily decided to postpone action until after election day. When we discovered that the Commissioner of Public Safety, Eugene "Bull" Connor, had piled up enough votes to be in the run-off, we decided again to postpone action until the day after the run-off so that the demonstrations could not be used to cloud the issues. Like many others, we waited to see Mr. Connor defeated, and to this end we endured postponement after postponement. Having aided in this community need, we felt that our direct-action program could be delayed no longer.

You may well ask: "Why direct action? Why sit-ins, marches and so forth? 10 Isn't negotiation a better path?" You are quite right in calling for negotiation. Indeed, this is the very purpose of direct action. Nonviolent direct action seeks to create such a crisis and foster such a tension that a community which has constantly refused to negotiate is forced to confront the issue. It seeks so to dramatize the issue that it can no longer be ignored. My citing the creation of tension as part of the work of the nonviolent-resister may sound rather shocking. But I must confess that I am not afraid of the word "tension." I have earnestly opposed violent tension, but there is a type of constructive, nonviolent tension which is necessary for growth. Just as Socrates felt that it was necessary to create a tension in the mind so that individuals could rise from the bondage of myths and half-truths to the unfettered realm of creative analysis and objective appraisal, so must we see the need for nonviolent gadflies to create the kind of tension in society that will help men rise from the dark depths of prejudice and racism to the majestic heights of understanding and brotherhood.

The purpose of our direct-action program is to create a situation so 11 crisis-packed that it will inevitably open the door to negotiation. I therefore concur with you in your call for negotiation. Too long has our beloved Southland been bogged down in a tragic effort to live in monologue rather than dialogue.

One of the basic points in your statement is that the action that I and my 12 associates have taken in Birmingham is untimely. Some have asked: "Why didn't you give the new city administration time to act?" The only answer that I can give to this query is that the new Birmingham administration must be prodded about as much as the outgoing one, before it will act. We are sadly mistaken if we feel that the election of Albert Boutwell as mayor will bring the millennium to Birmingham. While Mr. Boutwell is a much more gentle person than Mr. Connor, they are both segregationists, dedicated to maintenance of the status quo. I have hope that Mr. Boutwell will be reasonable enough to see the futility of massive resistance to desegregation. But he will not see this without pressure from devotees of civil rights. My friends, I must say to you that we have not made a single gain in civil rights without determined legal and nonviolent pressure. Lamentably, it is an historical fact that privileged groups seldom give up their privileges voluntarily. Individuals may see the moral light and voluntarily give up their unjust posture; but, as Reinhold Niebuhr has reminded us, groups tend to be more immoral than individuals.

We know through painful experience that freedom is never voluntarily 13 given by the oppressor; it must be demanded by the oppressed. Frankly, I have yet to engage in a direct-action campaign that was "well timed" in the view of those who have not suffered unduly from the disease of segregation. For years now I have heard the word "Wait!" It rings in the ear of every Negro with piercing familiarity. This "Wait" has almost always meant "Never." We must come to see, with one of our distinguished jurists, that "justice too long delayed is justice denied."

We have waited for more than 340 years for our constitutional God-given 14 rights. The nations of Asia and Africa are moving with jetlike speed toward gaining political independence, but we still creep at horse-and-buggy pace toward gaining a cup of coffee at a lunch counter. Perhaps it is easy for those who have never felt the stinging darts of segregation to say, "Wait." But when you have seen vicious mobs lynch your mothers and fathers at will and drown your sisters and brothers at whim; when you have seen hate-filled policemen curse, kick, and even kill your black brothers and sisters; when you see the vast majority of your twenty million Negro brothers smothering in an airtight cage of poverty in the midst of an affluent society; when you suddenly find your tongue twisted and your speech stammering as you seek to explain to your six-year-old daughter why she can't go to the public amusement park that has just been advertised on television, and see tears welling up in her eyes when she is told that Funtown is closed to colored children, and see ominous clouds of inferiority beginning to form in her little mental sky, and see her beginning to distort her personality by developing an unconscious bitterness toward white people; when you have to concoct an answer for a five-year-old son who is asking: "Daddy, why do white people treat colored people so mean?"; when you take a cross-country drive and find it necessary to sleep night after night in the uncomfortable corners of your automobile because no motel will accept you; when you are humiliated day in and day out by nagging signs reading "white" and "colored"; when your first name becomes "nigger," your middle name becomes "boy" (however old you are) and your last name becomes "John," and your wife and mother are never given the respected title "Mrs."; when you are harried by day and haunted by night by the fact that you are a Negro, living constantly at tiptoe stance, never quite knowing what to expect next, and are plagued with inner fears and outer resentments; when you are forever fighting a degenerating sense of "nobodiness" — then you will understand why we find it difficult to wait. There comes a time when the cup of endurance runs over, and men are no longer willing to be plunged into the abyss of despair. I hope, sirs, you can understand our legitimate and unavoidable impatience.

You express a great deal of anxiety over our willingness to break laws. 15 This is certainly a legitimate concern. Since we so diligently urge people to obey the Supreme Court's decision of 1954 outlawing segregation in the public schools, at first glance it may seem rather paradoxical for us consciously to break laws. One may well ask: "How can you advocate breaking some laws and obeying others?" The answer lies in the fact that there are two types of laws: just and unjust. I would be the first to advocate obeying just laws. One has not only a legal but a moral responsibility to obey just laws. Conversely, one has a moral responsibility to disobey unjust laws. I would agree with St. Augustine that "an unjust law is no law at all."

Now, what is the difference between the two? How does one determine **16** whether a law is just or unjust? A just law is a man-made code that squares with the moral law or the law of God. An unjust law is a code that is out of harmony with the moral law. To put it in the terms of St. Thomas Aquinas: An unjust law is a human law that is not rooted in eternal law and natural law. Any law that uplifts human personality is just. Any law that degrades human personality in unjust. All segregation statutes are unjust because segregation distorts the soul and damages the personality. It gives the segregator a false sense of superiority and the segregated a false sense of inferiority. Segregation, to use the terminology of the Jewish philosopher Martin Buber, substitutes an "I–it" relationship for an "I–thou" relationship and ends up relegating persons to the status of things. Hence, segregation is not only politically, economically and sociologically unsound, it is morally wrong and sinful. Paul Tillich has said that sin is separation. Is not segregation an existential expression of man's tragic separation, his awful estrangement, his terrible sinfulness? Thus it is that I can urge men to obey the 1954 decision of the Supreme Court, for it is morally right; and I can urge them to disobey segregation ordinances, for they are morally wrong.

Let us consider a more concrete example of just and unjust laws. An **17** unjust law is a code that a numerical or power majority group compels a minority group to obey but does not make binding on itself. This is *difference* made legal. By the same token, a just law is a code that a majority compels a minority to follow and that it is willing to follow itself. This is *sameness* made legal.

Let me give another explanation. A law is unjust if it is inflicted on a **18** minority that, as a result of being denied the right to vote, had no part in enacting or devising the law. Who can say that the legislature of Alabama which set up that state's segregation laws was democratically elected? Throughout Alabama all sorts of devious methods are used to prevent Negroes from becoming registered voters, and there are some counties in which, even though Negroes constitute a majority of the population, not a single Negro is registered. Can any law enacted under such circumstances be considered democratically structured?

Sometimes a law is just on its face and unjust in its application. For **19** instance, I have been arrested on a charge of parading without a permit. Now, there is nothing wrong in having an ordinance which requires a permit for a parade. But such an ordinance becomes unjust when it is used to maintain segregation and to deny citizens the First-Amendment privilege of peaceful assembly and protest.

I hope you are able to see the distinction I am trying to point out. In no 20
sense do I advocate evading or defying the law, as would the rabid segregationist. That would lead to anarchy. One who breaks an unjust law must do
so openly, lovingly, and with a willingness to accept the penalty. I submit that
an individual who breaks a law that conscience tells him is unjust, and who
willingly accepts the penalty of imprisonment in order to arouse the conscience of the community over its injustice, is in reality expressing the
highest respect for law.

Of course, there is nothing new about this kind of civil disobedience. It was 21
evidenced sublimely in the refusal of Shadrach, Meshach and Abednego to
obey the laws of Nebuchadnezzar, on the ground that a higher moral law was
at stake. It was practiced superbly by the early Christians, who were willing to
face hungry lions and the excruciating pain of chopping blocks rather than
submit to certain unjust laws of the Roman Empire. To a degree, academic
freedom is a reality today because Socrates practiced civil disobedience. In
our own nation, the Boston Tea Party represented a massive act of civil
disobedience.

We should never forget that everything Adolf Hitler did in Germany was 22
"legal" and everything the Hungarian freedom fighters did in Hungary was
"illegal." It was "illegal" to aid and comfort a Jew in Hitler's Germany. Even
so, I am sure that, had I lived in Germany at the time, I would have aided and
comforted my Jewish brothers. If today I lived in a Communist country where
certain principles dear to the Christian faith are suppressed I would openly
advocate disobeying that country's antireligious laws.

I must make two honest confessions to you, my Christian and Jewish 23
brothers. First, I must confess that over the past few years I have been
gravely disappointed with the white moderate. I have almost reached the
regrettable conclusion that the Negro's great stumbling block in his stride
toward freedom is not the White Citizen's Counciler or the Ku Klux Klanner,
but the white moderate, who is more devoted to "order" than to justice; who
prefers a negative peace which is the presence of tension to a positive peace
which is the presence of justice; who constantly says: "I agree with you in the
goal you seek, but I cannot agree with your methods of direct action"; who
paternalistically believes he can set the timetable for another man's freedom;
who lives by a mythical concept of time and who constantly advises the Negro
to wait for a "more convenient season." Shallow understanding from people
of good will is more frustrating than absolute misunderstanding from people
of ill will. Lukewarm acceptance is much more bewildering that outright
rejection.

I had hoped that the white moderate would understand that law and order 24
exist for the purpose of establishing justice and that when they fail in this
purpose they become the dangerously structured dams that block the flow of

social progress. I had hoped that the white moderate would understand that the present tension in the South is a necessary phase of the transition from an obnoxious negative peace, in which the Negro passively accepted his unjust plight, to a substantive and positive peace, in which all men will respect the dignity and worth of human personality. Actually, we who engage in nonviolent direct action are not the creators of tension. We merely bring to the surface the hidden tension that is already alive. We bring it out in the open, where it can be seen and dealt with. Like a boil that can never be cured so long as it is covered up but must be opened with all its ugliness to the natural medicines of air and light, injustice must be exposed, with all the tension its exposure creates, to the light of human conscience and the air of national opinion before it can be cured.

In your statement you assert that our actions, even though peaceful, must 25 be condemned because they precipitate violence. But is this a logical assertion? Isn't this like condemning a robbed man because his possession of money precipitated the evil act of robbery? Isn't this like condemning Socrates because his unswerving commitment to truth and his philosophical inquiries precipitated the act by the misguided populace in which they made him drink hemlock? Isn't this like condemning Jesus because his unique God-consciousness and never-ceasing devotion to God's will precipitated the evil act of crucifixion? We must come to see that, as the federal courts have consistently affirmed, it is wrong to urge an individual to cease his efforts to gain his basic constitutional rights because the quest may precipitate violence. Society must protect the robbed and punish the robber.

I had also hoped that the white moderate would reject the myth concern- 26 ing time in relation to the struggle for freedom. I have just received a letter from a white brother in Texas. He writes: "All Christians know that the colored people will receive equal rights eventually, but it is possible that you are in too great a religious hurry. It has taken Christianity almost two thousand years to accomplish what it has. The teachings of Christ take time to come to earth." Such an attitude stems from a tragic misconception of time, from the strangely irrational notion that there is something in the very flow of time that will inevitably cure all ills. Actually, time itself is neutral; it can be used either destructively or constructively. More and more I feel that the people of ill will have used time much more effectively than have the people of good will. We will have to repent in this generation not merely for the hateful words and actions of the bad people but for the appalling silence of the good people. Human progress never rolls in on wheels of inevitability; it comes through the tireless efforts of men willing to be co-workers with God, and without this hard work, time itself becomes an ally of the forces of social stagnation. We must use time creatively, in the knowledge that the time is always ripe to do right. Now is the time to make real the promise of democracy and transform our pending national elegy into a creative psalm of brotherhood. Now is the time to lift our national policy from the quicksand of racial injustice to the solid rock of human dignity.

You speak of our activity in Birmingham as extreme. At first I was rather 27 disappointed that fellow clergymen would see my nonviolent efforts as those of an extremist. I began thinking about the fact that I stand in the middle of two opposing forces in the Negro community. One is a force of complacency, made up in part of Negroes who, as a result of long years of oppression, are so drained of self-respect and a sense of "somebodiness" that they have adjusted to segregation; and in part of a few middle-class Negroes who, because of a degree of academic and economic security and because in some ways they profit by segregation, have become insensitive to the problems of the masses. The other force is one of bitterness and hatred, and it comes perilously close to advocating violence. It is expressed in the various black nationalists groups that are springing up across the nation, the largest and best-known being Elijah Muhammad's Muslim movement. Nourished by the Negro's frustration over the continued existence of racial discrimination, this movement is made up of people who have lost faith in America, who have absolutely repudiated Christianity, and who have concluded that the white man is an incorrigible "devil."

I have tried to stand between these two forces, saying that we need 28 emulate neither the "do-nothingism" of the complacent nor the hatred and despair of the black nationalist. For there is the more excellent way of love and nonviolent protest. I am grateful to God that, through the influence of the Negro church, the way of nonviolence became an integral part of our struggle.

If this philosophy had not emerged, by now many streets of the South 29 would, I am convinced, be flowing with blood. And I am further convinced that if our white brothers dismiss as "rabble-rousers" and "outside agitators" those of us who employ nonviolent direct action, and if they refuse to support our nonviolent efforts, millions of the Negroes will, out of frustration and despair, seek solace and security in black-nationalist ideologies — a development that would inevitably lead to a frightening racial nightmare.

Oppressed people cannot remain oppressed forever. The yearning for 30 freedom eventually manifests itself, and that is what has happened to the American Negro. Something within has reminded him of his birthright of freedom, and something without has reminded him that it can be gained. Consciously or unconsciously, he has been caught up by the *Zeitgeist,* and with his black brothers of Africa and his brown and yellow brothers of Asia, South America and the Caribbean, the United States Negro is moving with a sense of great urgency toward the promised land of racial justice. If one recognizes this vital urge that has engulfed the Negro community, one should readily understand why public demonstrations are taking place. The

Negro has many pent-up resentments and latent frustrations, and he must release them. So let him march; let him make prayer pilgrimages to the city hall; let him go on freedom rides — and try to understand why he must do so. If his repressed emotions are not released in nonviolent ways, they will seek expression through violence; this is not a threat but a fact of history. So I have not said to my people: "Get rid of your discontent." Rather, I have tried to say that this normal and healthy discontent can be channeled into the creative outlet of nonviolent direct action. And now this approach is being termed extremist.

But though I was initially disappointed at being categorized as an extrem- **31** ist, as I continued to think about the matter I gradually gained a measure of satisfaction from the label. Was not Jesus an extremist for love: "Love your enemies, bless them that curse you, do good to them that hate you, and pray for them which despitefully use you, and persecute you." Was not Amos an extremist for justice: "Let justice roll down like waters and righteousness like an ever-flowing stream." Was not Paul an extremist for the Christian gospel: "I bear in my body the marks of the Lord Jesus." Was not Martin Luther an extremist: "Here I stand; I cannot do otherwise, so help me God." And John Bunyan: "I will stay in jail to the end of my days before I make a butchery of my conscience." And Abraham Lincoln: "This nation cannot survive half slave and half free." And Thomas Jefferson: "We hold these truths to be self-evident, that all men are created equal. . . . " So the question is not whether we will be extremists, but what kind of extremists we will be. Will we be extremists for hate or for love? Will we be extremists for the preservation of injustice or for the extension of justice? In that dramatic scene on Calvary's hill three men were crucified. We must never forget that all three were crucified for the same crime — the crime of extremism. Two were extremists for immorality, and thus fell below their environment. The other, Jesus Christ, as was an extremist for love, truth and goodness, and thereby rose above his environment. Perhaps the South, the nation and the world are in dire need of creative extremists.

I had hoped that the white moderate would see this need. Perhaps I was **32** too optimistic; perhaps I expected too much. I suppose I should have realized that few members of the oppressor race can understand the deep groans and passionate yearnings of the oppressed race, and still fewer have the vision to see that injustice must be rooted out by strong, persistent and determined action. I am thankful, however, that some of our white brothers in the South have grasped the meaning of this social revolution and committed themselves to it. They are still all too few in quantity, but they are big in quality. Some — such as Ralph McGill, Lillian Smith, Harry Golden, James McBride Dabbs, Ann Braden and Sarah Patton Boyle — have written about our struggle in eloquent and prophetic terms. Others have marched with us down nameless streets of the South. They have languished in filthy, roach-infested jails, suffering the abuse and brutality of policemen who view them as "dirty nigger-lovers." Unlike so many of their moderate brothers and sisters, they have recognized the urgency of the moment and sensed the need for powerful "action" antidotes to combat the disease of segregation.

Let me take note of my other major disappointment. I have been so greatly 33 disappointed with the white church and its leadership. Of course, there are some notable exceptions. I am not unmindful of the fact that each of you has taken some significant stands on this issue. I commend you, Reverend Stallings, for your Christian stand on this past Sunday, in welcoming Negroes to your worship service on a nonsegregated basis. I commend the Catholic leaders of this state for integrating Spring Hill College several years ago.

But despite these notable exceptions, I must honestly reiterate that I have 34 been disappointed with the church. I do not say this as one of those negative critics who can always find something wrong with the church. I say this as a minister of the gospel, who loves the church; who was nurtured in its bosom; who has been sustained by its spiritual blessings and who will remain true to it as long as the cord of life shall lengthen.

When I was suddenly catapulted into the leadership of the bus protest in 35 Montgomery, Alabama, a few years ago, I felt we would be supported by the white church. I felt that the white ministers, priests and rabbis of the South would be among our strongest allies. Instead, some have been outright opponents, refusing to understand the freedom movement and misrepresenting its leaders; all too many others have been more cautious than courageous and have remained silent behind the anesthetizing security of stained-glass windows.

In spite of my shattered dreams, I came to Birmingham with the hope that 36 the white religious leadership of this community would see the justice of our cause and, with deep moral concern, would serve as the channel through which our just grievances could reach the power structure. I had hoped that each of you would understand. But again I have been disappointed.

I have heard numerous southern religious leaders admonish their wor- 37 shipers to comply with a desegregation decision because it is the law, but I have longed to hear white ministers declare: "Follow this decree because integration is morally right and because the Negro is your brother." In the midst of blatant injustices inflicted upon the Negro, I have watched white churchmen stand on the sideline and mouth pious irrelevancies and sanctimonious trivialities. In the midst of a mighty struggle to rid our nation of racial and economic injustice, I have heard many ministers say: "Those are social issues, with which the gospel has no real concern." And I have watched many churches commit themselves to a completely otherworldly religion which makes a strange, un-Biblical distinction between body and soul, between the sacred and the secular.

I have traveled the length and breadth of Alabama, Mississippi and all the 38 other southern states. On sweltering summer days and crisp autumn mornings I have looked at the South's beautiful churches with their lofty spires pointing heavenward. I have beheld the impressive outlines of her massive religious-education buildings. Over and over I have found myself asking: "What kind of people worship here? Who is their God? Where were their voices when the lips of Governor Barnett dripped with words of interposition and nullification? Where were they when Governor Wallace gave a clarion call for defiance and hatred? Where were their voices of support when bruised and weary Negro men and women decided to rise from the dark dungeons of complacency to the bright hills of creative protest?"

Yes, these questions are still in my mind. In deep disappointment I have 39 wept over the laxity of the church. But be assured that my tears have been tears of love. There can be no deep disappointment where there is not deep love. Yes, I love the church. How could I do otherwise? I am in the rather unique position of being the son, the grandson, and the great-grandson of preachers. Yes, I see the church as the body of Christ. But, oh! How we have blemished and scarred that body through social neglect and through fear of being nonconformists.

There was a time when the church was very powerful — in the time when 40 the early Christians rejoiced at being deemed worthy to suffer for what they believed. In those days the church was not merely a thermometer that recorded the ideas and principles of popular opinion; it was a thermostat that transformed the mores of society. Whenever the early Christians entered a town, the people in power became disturbed and immediately sought to convict the Christians for being "disturbers of the peace" and "outside agitators." But the Christians pressed on, in the conviction that they were "a colony of heaven," called to obey God rather than man. Small in number, they were big in commitment. They were too God-intoxicated to be "astronomically intimidated." By their effort and example they brought an end to such ancient evils as infanticide and gladiatorial contests.

Things are different now. So often the contemporary church is a weak, 41 ineffectual voice with an uncertain sound. So often it is an archdefender of the status quo. Far from being disturbed by the presence of the church, the power structure of the average community is consoled by the church's silent — and often even vocal — sanction of things as they are.

But the judgment of God is upon the church as never before. If today's 42 church does not recapture the sacrificial spirit of the early church, it will lose its authenticity, forfeit the loyalty of millions, and be dismissed as an irrelevant social club with no meaning for the twentieth century. Every day I meet young people whose disappointment with the church has turned into outright disgust.

Perhaps I have once again been too optimistic. Is organized religion too 43 inextricably bound to the status quo to save our nation and the world?

Perhaps I must turn my faith to the inner spiritual church, the church within the church, as the true *ekklesia* and the hope of the world. But again I am thankful to God that some noble souls from the ranks of organized religion have broken loose from the paralyzing chains of conformity and joined us as active partners in the struggle for freedom. They have left their secure congregations and walked the streets of Albany, Georgia, with us. They have gone down the highways of the South on tortuous rides for freedom. Yes, they have gone to jail with us. Some have been dismissed from their churches, have lost the support of their bishops and fellow ministers. But they have acted in the faith that right defeated is stronger than evil triumphant. Their witness has been the spiritual salt that has preserved the true meaning of the gospel in these troubled times. They have carved a tunnel of hope through the dark mountain of disappointment.

I hope the church as a whole will meet the challenge of this decisive hour. 44 But even if the church does not come to the aid of justice, I have no despair about the future. I have no fear about the outcome of our struggle in Birmingham, even if our motives are at present misunderstood. We will reach the goal of freedom in Birmingham and all over the nation, because the goal of America is freedom. Abused and scorned though we may be, our destiny is tied up with America's destiny. Before the pilgrims landed at Plymouth, we were here. Before the pen of Jefferson etched the majestic words of the Declaration of Independence across the pages of history, we were here. For more than two centuries our forebears labored in this country without wages; they made cotton king; they built the homes of their masters while suffering gross injustice and shameful humiliation — and yet out of a bottomless vitality they continued to thrive and develop. If the inexpressible cruelties of slavery could not stop us, the opposition we now face will surely fail. We will win our freedom because the sacred heritage of our nation and the eternal will of God are embodied in our echoing demands.

Before closing I feel impelled to mention one other point in your statement 45 that has troubled me profoundly. You warmly commended the Birmingham police force for keeping "order" and "preventing violence." I doubt that you would have so warmly commended the police force if you had seen its dogs sinking their teeth into unarmed, nonviolent Negroes. I doubt that you would so quickly commend the policemen if you were to observe their ugly and inhuman treatment of Negroes here in the city jail; if you were to watch them push and curse old Negro women and young Negro girls; if you were to see them slap and kick old Negro men and young boys; if you were to observe them, as they did on two occasions, refuse to give us food because we wanted to sing our grace together. I cannot join you in your praise of the Birmingham police department.

It is true that police have exercised a degree of discipline in handling the 46 demonstrators. In this sense they have conducted themselves rather "nonviolently" in public. But for what purpose? To preserve the evil system of segregation. Over the past few years I have consistently preached that nonviolence demands that the means we use must be as pure as the ends we seek. I have tried to make clear that it is wrong to use immoral means to attain moral ends. But now I must affirm that it is just as wrong, or perhaps even more so, to use moral means to preserve immoral ends. Perhaps Mr. Connor and his policemen have been rather nonviolent in public, as was Chief Pritchett in Albany, Georgia, but they have used the moral means of nonviolence to maintain the immoral end of racial injustice. As T. S. Eliot has said: "The last temptation is the greatest treason: To do the right deed for the wrong reason."

I wish you had commended the Negro sit-inners and demonstrators of **47** Birmingham for their sublime courage, their willingness to suffer and their amazing discipline in the midst of great provocation. One day the South will recognize its real heroes. They will be the James Merediths, with the noble sense of purpose that enables them to face jeering and hostile mobs, and with the agonizing loneliness that characterizes the life of the pioneer. They will be old, oppressed, battered Negro women, symbolized in a seventy-two-year-old woman in Montgomery, Alabama, who rose up with a sense of dignity and with her people decided not to ride segregated buses, and who responded with ungrammatical profundity to one who inquired about her weariness: "My feets is tired, but my soul is at rest." They will be the young high school and college students, the young ministers of the gospel and a host of their elders, courageously and nonviolently sitting in at lunch counters and willingly going to jail for conscience' sake. One day the South will know that when these disinherited children of God sat down at lunch counters, they were in reality standing up for what is best in the American dream and for the most sacred values in our Judaeo-Christian heritage, thereby bringing our nation back to those great wells of democracy which were dug deep by the founding fathers in their formulation of the Constitution and the Declaration of Independence.

Never before have I written so long a letter. I'm afraid it is much too long **48** to take your precious time. I can assure you that it would have been much shorter if I had been writing from a comfortable desk, but what else can one do when he is alone in a narrow jail cell, other than write long letters, think long thoughts and pray long prayers?

If I have said anything in this letter that overstates the truth and indicates **49** an unreasonable impatience, I beg you to forgive me. If I have said anything that understates the truth and indicates my having a patience that allows me to settle for anything less than brotherhood, I beg God to forgive me.

I hope this letter finds you strong in faith. I also hope that circumstances **50** will soon make it possible for me to meet each of you, not as an integrationist or a civil-rights leader but as a fellow clergyman and a Christian brother. Let us all hope that the dark clouds of racial prejudice will soon pass away and the deep fog of misunderstanding will be lifted from our fear-drenched communities, and in some not too distant tomorrow the radiant stars of love and brotherhood will shine over our great nation with all their scintillating beauty.

Yours for the cause of Peace and Brotherhood
MARTIN LUTHER KING, JR.

CIVIL DISOBEDIENCE: DESTROYER OF DEMOCRACY

Lewis H. Van Dusen, Jr.

Attorney Lewis H. Van Dusen, Jr., a Rhodes scholar and graduate of Harvard Law School, distinguishes between "conscientious disobedience" — in which one willingly accepts punishment in order to make a moral protest — and active group disobedience aimed at changing laws. "[C]ivil disobedience [e.g., the kind practiced by Martin Luther King, Jr.], whatever the ethical rationalization, is still an assault on our democratic society, an affront to our legal order and an attack on our constitutional government."

As Charles E. Wyzanski, Chief Judge of the United States District Court in   1
Boston, wrote in the February, 1968, *Atlantic:* "Disobedience is a long step
from dissent. Civil disobedience involves a deliberate and punishable breach
of legal duty." Protesters might prefer a different definition. They would
rather say that civil disobedience is the peaceable resistance of conscience.

The philosophy of civil disobedience was not developed in our American   2
democracy, but in the very first democracy of Athens. It was expressed by the
poet Sophocles and the philosopher Socrates. In Sophocles's tragedy, Antigone chose to obey her conscience and violate the state edict against
providing burial for her brother, who had been decreed a traitor. When the
dictator Creon found out that Antigone had buried her fallen brother, he
confronted her and reminded her that there was a mandatory death penalty
for this deliberate disobedience of the state law. Antigone nobly replied, "Nor
did I think your orders were so strong that you, a mortal man, could overrun
the gods' unwritten and unfailing laws."

Conscience motivated Antigone. She was not testing the validity of the law   3
in the hope that eventually she would be sustained. Appealing to the judgment of the community, she explained her action to the chorus. She was not
secret and surreptitious — the interment of her brother was open and public.
She was not violent; she did not trespass on another citizen's rights. And
finally, she accepted without resistance the death sentence — the penalty for
violation. By voluntarily accepting the law's sanctions, she was not a revolutionary denying the authority of the state. Antigone's behavior exemplifies
the classic case of civil disobedience.

Socrates believed that reason could dictate a conscientious disobedience of   4
state law, but he also believed that he had to accept the legal sanctions of the
state. In Plato's *Crito*, Socrates from his hanging basket accepted the death
penalty for his teaching of religion to youths contrary to state laws.

The sage of Walden, Henry David Thoreau, took this philosophy of   5
nonviolence and developed it into a strategy for solving society's injustices.

Source: Reprinted with permission from the February 1969 issue of the *ABA* Journal, the Lawyer's Magazine, published by the American Bar Association.

First enunciating it in protest against the Mexican War, he then turned it to use against slavery. For refusing to pay taxes that would help pay the enforcers of the fugitive slave law, he went to prison. In Thoreau's words, "If the alternative is to keep all just men in prison or to give up slavery, the state will not hesitate which to choose."

Sixty years later, Gandhi took Thoreau's civil disobedience as his strategy to wrest Indian independence from England. The famous salt march against a British imperial tax is his best-known example of protest. 6

But the conscientious law breaking of Socrates, Gandhi and Thoreau is to be distinguished from the conscientious law testing of Martin Luther King, Jr., who was not a civil disobedient. The civil disobedient withholds taxes or violates state laws knowing he is legally wrong, but believing he is morally right. While he wrapped himself in the mantle of Gandhi and Thoreau, Dr. King led his followers in violation of state laws he believed were contrary to the Federal Constitution. But since Supreme Court decisions in the end generally upheld his many actions, he should not be considered a true civil disobedient. 7

The civil disobedience of Antigone is like that of the pacifist who withholds paying the percentage of his taxes that goes to the Defense Department, or the Quaker who travels against State Department regulations to Hanoi to distribute medical supplies, or the Vietnam war protester who tears up his draft card. This civil disobedient has been nonviolent in his defiance of the law; he has been unfurtive in his violation; he has been submissive to the penalties of the law. He has neither evaded the law nor interfered with another's rights. He has been neither a rioter nor a revolutionary. The thrust of his cause has not been the might of coercion but the martyrdom of conscience. 8

Was the Boston Tea Party Civil Disobedience?

Those who justify violence and radical action as being in the tradition of our Revolution show a misunderstanding of the philosophy of democracy. 9

James Farmer, former head of the Congress of Racial Equality, in defense of the mass action confrontation method, has told of a famous organized demonstration that took place in opposition to political and economic discrimination. The protesters beat back and scattered the law enforcers and then proceeded to loot and destroy private property. Mr. Farmer then said he was talking about the Boston Tea Party and implied that violence as a method for redress of grievances was an American tradition and a legacy of our revolutionary heritage. While it is true that there is no more sacred document than our Declaration of Independence, Jefferson's "inherent right of rebellion" was predicated on the tyrannical denial of democratic means. If there is no popular assembly to provide an adjustment of ills, and if there is no court system to dispose of injustices, then there is, indeed, a right to rebel. 10

The seventeenth century's John Locke, the philosophical father of the 11
Declaration of Independence, wrote in his *Second Treatise on Civil Government:* "Wherever law ends, tyranny begins . . . and the people are absolved
from any further obedience. Governments are dissolved from within when the
legislative [chamber] is altered. When the government [becomes] . . . arbitrary disposers of lives, liberties and fortunes of the people, such revolutions
happen. . . ."

But there are some sophisticated proponents of the revolutionary redress 12
of grievances who say that the test of the need for radical action is not the
unavailability of democratic institutions but the ineffectuality of those institutions to remove blatant social inequalities. If social injustice exists, they
say, concerted disobedience is required against the constituted government,
whether it be totalitarian or democratic in structure.

Of course, only the most bigoted chauvinist would claim that America is 13
without some glaring faults. But there has never been a utopian society on
earth and there never will be unless human nature is remade. Since inequities
will mar even the best-framed democracies, the injustice rationale would allow
a free right of civil resistance to be available always as a shortcut alternative
to the democratic way of petition, debate and assembly. The lesson of history
is that civil insurgency spawns far more injustices than it removes. The
Jeffersons, Washingtons and Adamses resisted tyranny with the aim of promoting the procedures of democracy. They would never have resisted a
democratic government with the risk of promoting the techniques of tyranny.

Legitimate Pressures and Illegitimate Results

There are many civil rights leaders who show impatience with the process of 14
democracy. They rely on the sit-in, boycott or mass picketing to gain speedier
solutions to the problems that face every citizen. But we must realize that the
legitimate pressures that won concessions in the past can easily escalate into
the illegitimate power plays that might extort demands in the future. The
victories of these civil rights leaders must not shake our confidence in the
democratic procedures, as the pressures of demonstration are desirable only if
they take place within the limits allowed by law. Civil rights gains should
continue to be won by the persuasion of Congress and other legislative bodies
and by the decision of courts. Any illegal entreaty for the rights of some can
be an injury to the rights of others, for mass demonstrations often trigger
violence.

Those who advocate taking the law into their own hands should reflect 15
that when they are disobeying what they consider to be an immoral law, they
are deciding on a possibly immoral course. Their answer is that the process
for democratic relief is too slow, that only mass confrontation can bring
immediate action, and that any injuries are the inevitable cost of the pursuit

of justice. Their answer is, simply put, that the end justifies the means. It is this justification of any form of demonstration as a form of dissent that threatens to destroy a society built on the rule of law.

Our Bill of Rights guarantees wide opportunities to use mass meetings, **16** public parades and organized demonstrations to stimulate sentiment, to dramatize issues and to cause change. The Washington freedom march of 1963 was such a call for action. But the rights of free expression cannot be mere force cloaked in the garb of free speech. As the courts have decreed in labor cases, free assembly does not mean mass picketing or sit-down strikes. These rights are subject to limitations of time and place so as to secure the rights of others. When militant students storm a college president's office to achieve demands, when certain groups plan rush-hour car stalling to protest discrimination in employment, these are not dissent, but a denial of rights to others. Neither is it the lawful use of mass protest, but rather the unlawful use of mob power.

Justice Black, one of the foremost advocates and defenders of the right of **17** protest and dissent, has said:

> . . . Experience demonstrates that it is not a far step from what to many seems to be the earnest, honest, patriotic, kind-spirited multitude of today, to the fanatical, threatening, lawless mob of tomorrow. And the crowds that press in the streets for noble goals today can be supplanted tomorrow by street mobs pressuring the courts for precisely opposite ends.

Society must censure those demonstrators who would trespass on the **18** public peace, as it must condemn those rioters whose pillage would destroy the public peace. But more ambivalent is society's posture toward the civil disobedient. Unlike the rioter, the true civil disobedient commits no violence. Unlike the mob demonstrator, he commits no trespass on others' rights. The civil disobedient, while deliberately violating a law, shows an oblique respect for the law by voluntarily submitting to its sanctions. He neither resists arrest nor evades punishment. Thus, he breaches the law but not the peace.

But civil disobedience, whatever the ethical rationalization, is still an **19** assault on our democratic society, an affront to our legal order and an attack on our constitutional government. To indulge civil disobedience is to invite anarchy, and the permissive arbitrariness of anarchy is hardly less tolerable than the repressive arbitrariness of tyranny. Too often the license of liberty is followed by the loss of liberty, because into the desert of anarchy comes the man on horseback, a Mussolini or a Hitler.

Violations of Law Subvert Democracy. Law violations, even for ends **20** recognized as laudable, are not only assaults on the rule of law, but subversions of the democratic process. The disobedient act of conscience does not ennoble democracy; it erodes it.

First, it courts violence, and even the most careful and limited use of **21** nonviolent acts of disobedience may help sow the dragon-teeth of civil riot. Civil disobedience is the progenitor of disorder, and disorder is the sire of violence.

Second, the concept of civil disobedience does not invite principles of 22 general applicability. If the children of light are morally privileged to resist particular laws on grounds of conscience, so are the children of darkness. Former Deputy Attorney General Burke Marshall said: "If the decision to break the law really turned on individual conscience, it is hard to see in law how [the civil rights leader] is better off than former Governor Ross Barnett of Mississippi who also believed deeply in his cause and was willing to go to jail."

Third, even the most noble act of civil disobedience assaults the rule of 23 law. Although limited as to method, motive and objective, it has the effect of inducing others to engage in different forms of law breaking characterized by methods unsanctioned and condemned by classic theories of law violation. Unfortunately, the most patent lesson of civil disobedience is not so much nonviolence of action as defiance of authority.

Finally, the greatest danger in condoning civil disobedience as a permissi- 24 ble strategy for hastening change is that it undermines our democratic processes. To adopt the techniques of civil disobedience is to assume that representative government does not work. To resist the decisions of courts and the laws of elected assemblies is to say that democracy has failed.

There is no man who is above the law, and there is no man who has a right 25 to break the law. Civil disobedience is not above the law, but against the law. When the civil disobedient disobeys one law, he invariably subverts all law. When the civil disobedient says that he is above the law, he is saying that democracy is beneath him. His disobedience shows a distrust for the democratic system. He is merely saying that since democracy does not work, why should he help make it work. Thoreau expressed well the civil disobedient's disdain for democracy:

> As for adopting the ways which the state has provided for remedying the evil, I know not of such ways. They take too much time and a man's life will be gone. I have other affairs to attend to. I came into this world not chiefly to make this a good place to live in, but to live in it, be it good or bad.

Thoreau's position is not only morally irresponsible but politically repre- 26 hensible. When citizens in a democracy are called on to make a profession of faith, the civil disobedients offer only a confession of failure. Tragically, when civil disobedients for lack of faith abstain from democratic involvement, they help attain their own gloomy prediction. They help create the social and political basis for their own despair. By foreseeing failure, they help forge it. If citizens rely on antidemocratic means of protest, they will help bring about the undemocratic result of an authoritarian or anarchic state.

How far demonstrations properly can be employed to produce political and   27
social change is a pressing question, particularly in view of the provocations
accompanying the National Democratic Convention in Chicago last August
and the reaction of the police to them. A line must be drawn by the judiciary
between the demands of those who seek absolute order, which can lead only
to a dictatorship, and those who seek absolute freedom, which can lead only
to anarchy. The line, wherever it is drawn by our courts, should be respected
on the college campus, on the streets and elsewhere.

Undue provocation will inevitably result in overreaction, human emotions   28
being what they are. Violence will follow. This cycle undermines the very
democracy it is designed to preserve. The lesson of the past is that democracies will fall if violence, including the intentional provocations that will lead
to violence, replaces democratic procedures, as in Athens, Rome and the
Weimar Republic. This lesson must be constantly explained by the legal
profession.

We should heed the words of William James: 29

> Democracy is still upon its trial. The civic genius of our people is its only bulwark
> and . . . neither battleships nor public libraries nor great newspapers nor boom-
> ing stocks: neither mechanical invention nor political adroitness, nor churches nor
> universities nor civil service examinations can save us from degeneration if the
> inner mystery be lost.

> That mystery, at once the secret and the glory of our English-speaking race,
> consists of nothing but two habits. . . . One of them is habit of trained and
> disciplined good temper towards the opposite party when it fairly wins its innings.
> The other is that of fierce and merciless resentment toward every man or set of men
> who break the public peace. (James, *Pragmatism*, 127 – 28).

FROM *THE CRITO*

Plato

Socrates, who was himself ill-served by the state, here argues in favor of a citizen's absolute obligation to obey the rules of the state. He has been unjustly sentenced to die, and his friend Crito urges him to escape from prison. Socrates declines on ethical grounds.

SOCRATES: . . . Ought a man to do what he admits to be right, or ought he to betray the right?   1

CRITO: He ought to do what he thinks right.   2

SOCRATES: But if this is true, what is the application? In leaving the prison against the will of the Athenians, do I wrong any? Or rather do I not wrong those whom I ought least to wrong? Do I not desert the principles which are acknowledged by us to be just — what do you say?   3

CRITO: I cannot tell, Socrates; for I do not know.   4

SOCRATES: Then consider the matter in this way: — Imagine that I am about to play truant (you may call the proceeding by any name which you like), and the laws of the government come and interrogate me: "Tell us, Socrates," they say: "what are you about? Are you not going by an act of yours to overturn us — the laws, and the whole state, as far as in you lies? Do you imagine that a state can subsist and not be overthrown, in which the decisions of law have no power, but are set aside and trampled upon by individuals?" What will be our answer, Crito, to these and the like words? Any one, and especially a rhetorician, will have a good deal to say on behalf of the law which requires a sentence to be carried out. He will argue that this law should not be set aside; and shall we reply, "Yes, but the state has injured us and given an unjust sentence." Suppose I say that?   5

CRITO: Very good, Socrates.   6

SOCRATES: "And was that our agreement with you?" the law would answer; "or were you to abide by the sentence of the state?" And if I were to express my astonishment at their words, the law would probably add: "Answer, Socrates, instead of opening your eyes — you are in the habit of asking and answering questions. Tell us, — What complaint have you to make against us which justifies you in attempting to destroy us and the state? In the first place did we not bring you into existence? Your father married your mother by our aid and begat you. Say whether you have any objection to urge against those of us who regulate marriage?" None, I should reply. "Or against those of us who after birth regulate the nurture and education of children, in which you also were trained? Were not the laws, which have the charge of education,   7 right in commanding your father to train you in music and gymnastics?" Right, I should reply. "Well then, since you were brought into the world and nurtured and educated by us, can you deny in the first place that you are our child and slave, as your fathers were before you? And if this is true you are not on equal terms with us; nor can you think that you have a right to do to us what we are doing to you. Would you have any right to strike or revile or do any other evil to your father or your master, if you had one, because you have been struck or reviled by him, or received some other evil at his hands? — you would not say this? And because we think right to destroy you, do you think that you have any right to destroy us in return, and your country as far as in you lies? Will you, O professor of true virtue, pretend that you are justified in this? Has a philosopher like you failed to discover that our country is more to be valued and higher and holier far than mother or father or any ancestor, and more to be regarded in the eyes of the gods and of men of understanding? Also to be soothed, and gently and reverently entreated when angry, even more than a father, and either to be persuaded, or if not persuaded, to be obeyed? And when we are punished by her, whether with imprisonment or stripes, the punishment is to be endured in silence, and if she leads us to wounds or death in battle, thither we follow as is right; neither may any one yield or retreat or leave his rank, but whether in battle or in a court of law, or in any other place, he must do what his city and his country order him; or he must change their view of what is just: and if he may do no violence to his father or mother, much less may he do violence to his country." What answer shall we make to this, Crito? Do the laws speak truly, or do they not?

CRITO: I think that they do　　　　　　　　　　　　　　　　　　8

SOCRATES: Then the laws will say, "Consider, Socrates, if we are speaking　9 truly that in your present attempt you are going to do us an injury. For, having brought you into the world, and nurtured and educated you, and given you and every other citizen a share in every good which we had to give, we further proclaim to any Athenian by the liberty which we allow him, that if he does not like us when he has become of age and has seen the ways of the city, and made our acquaintance, he may go where he pleases and take his goods with him. None of us laws will forbid him or interfere with him. Any one who does not like us and the city, and who wants to emigrate to a colony or to any other city, may go where he likes, retaining his property. But he who has experience of the manner in which we order justice and administer the state, and still remains, has entered into an implied contract that he will do as we command him. And he who disobeys us is, as we maintain, thrice wrong; first, because in disobeying us he is disobeying his parents; secondly, because we are the authors of his education; thirdly, because he has made an agreement with us that he will duly obey our commands; and he neither obeys them nor convinces us that our commands are unjust; and we do not rudely impose them, but give him the alternative of obeying or convincing us; — that is what we offer, and he does neither.

"These are the sort of accusations to which, as we were saying, you, **10** Socrates, will be exposed if you accomplish your intentions; you, above all other Athenians." Suppose now I ask, why I rather than anybody else? They will justly retort upon me that I above all other men have acknowledged the agreement. "There is clear proof," they will say, "Socrates, that we and the city were not displeasing to you. Of all Athenians you have been the most constant resident in the city, which, as you never leave, you may be supposed to love. For you never went out of the city either to see the games, except once when you went to the Isthmus, or to any other place unless when you were on military service; nor did you travel as other men do. Nor had you any curiosity to know other states or their laws: your affections did not go beyond us and our state; we were your special favourites, and you acquiesced in our government of you; and here in this city you begat your children, which is a proof of your satisfaction. Moreover, you might in the course of the trial, if you had liked, have fixed the penalty at banishment; the state which refuses to let you go now would have let you go then. But you pretended that you preferred death to exile, and that you were not unwilling to die. And now you have forgotten these fine sentiments, and pay no respect to us the laws, of whom you are the destroyer; and are doing what only a miserable slave would do, running away and turning your back upon the compacts and agreements which you made as a citizen. And first of all answer this very question: Are we right in saying that you agreed to be governed according to us in deed, and not in word only? Is that true or not?" How shall we answer, Crito? Must we not assent?

CRITO: We cannot help it, Socrates. **11**

SOCRATES: Then will they not say: "You, Socrates, are breaking the cove- **12** nants and agreements which you made with us at your leisure, not in any haste or under any compulsion or deception, but after you have had seventy years to think of them, during which time you were at liberty to leave the city, if we were not to your mind, or if our covenants appeared to you to be unfair. You had your choice, and might have gone either to Lacedaemon or Crete, both which states are often praised by you for their good government, or to some other Hellenic or foreign state. Whereas you, above all other Athenians, seemed to be so fond of the state, or, in other words, of us her laws (and who would care about a state which has no laws?), that you never stirred out of her; the halt, the blind, the maimed were not more stationary in her than you were. And now you run away and forsake your agreements. Not so, Socrates, if you will take our advice; do not make yourself ridiculous by escaping out of the city.

"For just consider, if you transgress and err in this sort of way, what good **13** will you do either to yourself or to your friends? That your friends will be driven into exile and deprived of citizenship, or will lose their property, is tolerably certain; and you yourself, if you fly to one of the neighboring cities, as, for example, Thebes or Megara, both of which are well governed, will come to them as an enemy, Socrates, and their government will be against you, and all patriotic citizens will cast an evil eye upon you as a subverter of the laws, and you will confirm in the minds of the judges the justice of their own condemnation of you. For he who is a corrupter of the laws is more than likely to be a corrupter of the young and foolish portion of mankind. Will you then flee from well-ordered citizens and virtuous men? and is existence worth having on these terms? Or will you go to them without shame, and talk to them, Socrates? And what will you say to them? What you say here about virtue and justice and institutions and laws being the best things among men? Would that be decent of you? Surely not. But if you go away from well-governed states to Crito's friends in Thessaly, where there is a great disorder and licence, they will be charmed to hear the tale of your escape from prison, set off with ludicrous particulars of the manner in which you were wrapped in a goatskin or some other disguise, and metamorphosed as the manner is of runaways; but will there be no one to remind you that in your old age you were not ashamed to violate the most sacred laws from a miserable desire of a little more life? Perhaps not, if you keep them in a good temper; but if they are out of temper you will hear many degrading things; you will live, but how? — as the flatterer of all men, and the servant of all men; and doing what? — eating and drinking in Thessaly, having gone abroad in order that you may get a dinner. And where will be your fine sentiments about justice and virtue? Say that you wish to live for the sake of your children — you want to bring them up and educate them — will you take them into Thessaly and deprive them of Athenian citizenship? Is this the benefit which you will confer upon them? Or are you under the impression that they will be better cared for and educated here if you are still alive, although absent from them: for your friends will take care of them? Do you fancy that if you are an inhabitant of Thessaly they will take care of them, and if you are an inhabitant of the other world that they will not take of them? Nay: but if they who call themselves friends are good for anything, they will — to be sure they will.

"Listen, then, Socrates, to us who have brought you up. Think not of life **14** and children first, and of justice afterwards, but of justice first, that you may be justified before the princes of the world below. For neither will you nor any that belong to you be happier or holier or juster in this life, or happier in another, if you do as Crito bids. Now you depart in innocence, a sufferer and not a doer of evil; a victim, not of the laws of men. But if you go forth, returning evil for evil, and injury for injury, breaking the covenants and agreements which you have made with us, and wronging those whom you ought least of all to wrong, that is to say, yourself, your friends, your country, and us, we shall be angry with you while you live, and our brethren, the laws in the world below, will receive you as an enemy; for they will know that you have done your best to destroy us. Listen, then, to us and not to Crito."

This, dear Crito, is the voice which I seem to hear murmuring in my ears, 15 like the sound of the flute in the ears of the mystic; that voice, I say, is humming in my ears, and prevents me from hearing any other. And I know that anything more which you may say will be vain. Yet speak, if you have anything to say.

CRITO: I have nothing to say, Socrates. 16

SOCRATES: Leave me then, Crito, to fulfill the will of God, and to follow 17 whither he leads.

_____

FOR CLASS DISCUSSION

1. Analyze and evaluate the disagreement between Martin Luther King, Jr., and Lewis Van Dusen, Jr., over the ethics of civil disobedience by applying the first set of guide questions from pages 443–444. How do you account for their disagreement?

2. To what extent do you think that Van Dusen, Jr., and Socrates agree on their reasons for disapproving civil disobedience?

3. Choose one of the arguments for closer analysis, applying the second set of guide questions on page 444.

OPTIONAL WRITING ASSIGNMENTS

1. You are a successful civil rights attorney. The principal of your child's junior high school has approached you with a concern. It seems that none of the social studies textbooks discusses the concept of civil disobedience. He wants to provide the social studies teachers with a statement on civil disobedience.

Drawing on the preceding essays, personal experience and any other research you may have done, write a brief explanation of the role of civil disobedience in a democracy. Before you start writing, believe/doubt the following statement: "There is no place for civil disobedience in a modern democracy." Whatever you decide about that statement, construct a brief explanation of your view that would be appropriate for use in an eighth grade textbook.

2. Two days before the manuscript for this text was sent off to the publisher, the United States began its aerial bombardment of Iraq, setting off waves of war protest on college campuses. One of the authors of this text had scheduled a midterm examination on the day of a protest march; several students went on the march and missed the exam. The next day they asked if it was all right to take the exam a day late. Write a letter to the instructor arguing what his policy should be regarding students who miss exams because of war protests.

CENSORSHIP AND PORNOGRAPHY: SHOULD A DEMOCRATIC SOCIETY SUPPRESS PORNOGRAPHIC OR OBSCENE WORKS?

PORNOGRAPHY, OBSCENITY, AND THE CASE FOR CENSORSHIP

Irving Kristol

New York University Professor Irving Kristol argues that a liberal today "ought to favor a liberal form of censorship." Basing his arguments on the moral relevance of art, Kristol says bluntly: "If you care for the quality of life in our American democracy, then you have to be for censorship."

Being frustrated is disagreeable, but the real disasters in life begin when 1 you get what you want. For almost a century now, a great many intelligent, well-meaning and articulate people have argued eloquently against any kind of censorship of art and entertainment. Within the past ten years, courts and legislatures have found these arguments so persuasive that censorship is now a relative rarity in most states.

Is there triumphant exhilaration in the land? Hardly. Somehow, things 2 have not worked out as they were supposed to, and many civil-libertarians have said this was not what they meant. They wanted a world in which

Eugene O'Neill's *Desire under the Elms* could be produced, or James Joyce's *Ulysses* published, without interference. They got that, of course; but they also got a world in which homosexual rape is simulated on the stage, in which the public flocks to witness professional fornication, in which New York's Times Square has become a hideous marketplace for printed filth.

But does this really matter? Might not our disquiet be merely a cultural 3
hangover? Was anyone ever corrupted by a book?

This last question, oddly enough, is asked by the same people who seem 4
convinced that advertisements in magazines or displays of violence on television *do* have the power to corrupt. It is also asked, incredibly enough and in all sincerity, by university professors and teachers whose very lives provide the answer. After all, if you believe that no one was ever corrupted by a book, you have also to believe that no one was ever improved by a book. You have to believe, in other words, that art is morally trivial and that education is morally irrelevant.

To be sure, it is extremely difficult to trace the effects of any single book 5
(or play or movie) on any reader. But we all know that the ways in which we use our minds and imaginations do shape our characters and help define us as persons. That those who certainly know this are moved to deny it merely indicates how a dogmatic resistance to the idea of censorship can result in a mindless insistence on the absurd.

For the plain fact is that we all believe that there is a point at which the 6
public authorities ought to step in to limit the "self-expression" of an individual or a group. A theatrical director might find someone willing to commit suicide on the stage. We would not allow that. And I know of no one who argues that we ought to permit public gladiatorial contests, even between consenting adults.

No society can be utterly indifferent to the ways its citizens publicly 7
entertain themselves. Bearbaiting and cockfighting are prohibited only in part out of compassion for the animals; the main reason is that such spectacles were felt to debase and brutalize the citizenry who flocked to witness them. The question with regard to pornography and obscenity is whether they will brutalize and debase our citizenry. We are, after all, not dealing with one book or one movie. We are dealing with a general tendency that is suffusing our entire culture.

Pornography's whole purpose, it seems to me, is to treat human beings 8
obscenely, to deprive them of their specifically human dimension. Imagine a well-known man in a hospital ward, dying an agonizing death. His bladder and bowels empty themselves of their own accord. His consciousness is overwhelmed by pain, so that he cannot communicate with us, nor we with him. Now, it would be technically easy to put a television camera in his room and let the whole world witness this spectacle. We don't do it—at least not yet—because we regard this as an obscene invasion of privacy. And what

would make the spectacle obscene is that we would be witnessing the extinguishing of humanity in a human animal.

Sex — like death — is an activity that is both animal and human. There are 9 human sentiments and human ideals involved in this animal activity. But when sex is public, I do not believe the viewer can see the sentiments and the ideals, but sees only the animal coupling. And that is why when most men and women make love, they prefer to be alone — because it is only when you are alone that you can make love, as distinct from merely copulating. When sex is a public spectacle, a human relationship has been debased into a mere animal connection.

But even if all this is granted, it doubtless will be said that we ought not to 10 be unduly concerned. Free competition in the cultural marketplace, it is argued by those who have never otherwise had a kind word to say for laissez-faire, will dispose of the problem; in the course of time, people will get bored with pornography and obscenity.

I would like to be able to go along with this reasoning, but I think it is 11 false, and for two reasons. The first reason is psychological, the second, political.

In my opinion, pornography and obscenity appeal to and provoke a kind of 12 sexual regression. The pleasure one gets from pornography and obscenity is infantile and autoerotic; put bluntly, it is a masturbatory exercise of the imagination. Now, people who masturbate do not get bored with masturbation, just as sadists don't get bored with sadism, and voyeurs don't get bored with voyeurism. In other words, like all infantile sexuality, it can quite easily become a permanent self-reinforcing neurosis. And such a neurosis, on a mass scale, is a threat to our civilization and humanity, nothing less.

I am already touching upon a political aspect of pornography when I 13 suggest that it is inherently subversive of civilization. But there is another political aspect, which has to do with the relationship of pornography and obscenity to democracy, and especially to the quality of public life on which democratic government ultimately rests.

Today a "managerial" conception of democracy prevails — wherein de- 14 mocracy is seen as a set of rules and procedures, and *nothing but* a set of rules and procedures, by which majority rule and minority rights are reconciled into a state of equilibrium. Thus, the political system can be fully reduced to its mechanical arrangements.

There is, however, an older idea of democracy — fairly common until about 15 the beginning of this century — for which the conception of the quality of public life is absolutely crucial. This idea starts from the proposition that democracy is a form of self-government, and that you are entitled to it only if that "self" is worthy of governing. Because the desirability of self-government depends on the character of the people who govern, the older idea of democracy was very solicitous of the condition of this character. This older democracy had no problem in principle with pornography and obscenity; it censored them; it was not about to permit people to corrupt themselves.

But can a liberal — today — be for censorship? Yes, but he ought to favor **16** a liberal form of censorship.

I don't think this is a contradiction in terms. We have no problem con- **17** trasting *repressive* laws governing alcohol, drugs and tobacco with laws *regulating* (that is, discouraging the sale of) alcohol, drugs and tobacco. We have not made smoking a criminal offense. We have, however, and with good liberal conscience, prohibited cigarette advertising on television. The idea of restricting individual freedom, in a liberal way, is not at all unfamiliar to us.

I therefore see no reason why we should not be able to distinguish **18** repressive censorship from liberal censorship of the written and spoken word. In Britain, until a few years ago, you could perform almost any play you wished — but certain plays, judged to be obscene, had to be performed in private theatrical clubs. In the United States, all of us who grew up using public libraries are familiar with the circumstances under which certain books could be circulated only to adults, while still other books had to be read in the library. In both cases, a small minority that was willing to make a serious effort to see an obscene play or book could do so. But the impact of obscenity was circumscribed, and the quality of public life was only marginally affected.

It is a distressing fact that any system of censorship is bound, upon **19** occasion, to treat unjustly a particular work of art — to find pornography where there is only gentle eroticism, to find obscenity where none really exists, or to find both where the work's existence ought to be tolerated because it serves a larger moral purpose. That is the price one has to be prepared to pay for censorship — even liberal censorship.

But if you look at the history of American or English literature, there is **20** precious little damage you can point to as a consequence of the censorship that prevailed throughout most of that history. I doubt that many works of real literary merit ever were suppressed. Nor did I notice that hitherto suppressed masterpieces flooded the market when censorship was eased.

I should say, to the contrary, that literature has lost quite a bit now that so **21** much is permitted. It seems to me that the cultural market in the United States today is awash in dirty books, dirty movies, dirty theater. Our cultural condition has not improved as a result of the new freedom.

I'll put it bluntly: if you care for the quality of life in our American **22** democracy, then you have to be for censorship.

DEFENDING INTELLECTUAL FREEDOM

Eli M. Oboler

Responding directly to Kristol's argument, Obolor claims that Kristol "has clearly failed to consider the most basic of all issues in the censorship/ noncensorship dispute."

The Henry Luce Professor of Urban Values at New York University, Irvin   1
Kristol, was rather less than urbane in his strictures against pornography and obscenity—or what he defines as such—in his March 23, 1971 article, "Pornography, Obscenity, and the Case for Censorship," which first appeared in the *New York Times* magazine and was recently reprinted in two issues of this *Newsletter* (September and November, 1971). He has exhumed a great many of the tired old pro-censorship arguments, but added a new dimension; he has coined a new phrase, "liberal censorship," which, despite all protestations to the contrary, is clearly a contradiction in terms.

Indeed, his whole essay is on the hyperbolic, exaggerated level illustrated   2
by his undocumented statement that ". . . pornography . . . is inherently and purposefully subversive of civilization and its institutions." He is even more specific and direct in this: ". . . if you care for the quality of life in our American democracy, then you have to be for censorship." Blithely, he sells creative art down the river: "There are . . . some few works of art that are in the special category of the comic-ironic 'bawdy' (Boccaccio, Rabelais). It is such works of art tł at are likely to suffer at the hands of the censor. *That is the price* [my italics] one has to be prepared to pay for censorship—even liberal censorship." Snick-snack! Off with Boccaccio's head! Snip-snip! Eliminate Rabelais! And Joyce and Swift and Henry Miller and—but Kristol, contrary to all factual evidence, says, "If you look at the history of American or English literature, there is precious little damage you can point to as a consequence of the censorship that prevailed throughout most of that history."

Let alone the gross inexactitude of this dogmatic opinion, Kristol really   3
ought to do a little study of the hundreds of years and thousands of literary creations between the writing of *Beowulf* and the first English legal censorship, that of Edmund Curll's *Venus in the Cloister,* in 1727. During those centuries after centuries, "most" of the history of English literature occurred. The quoted statement is only one of many examples of Kristollian *obiter dicta* which have a nice, ringing sound—but are actually quite hollow of solid fact, when closely examined.

It is really almost incredible that he would seriously make such a state-   4
ment as "very few works of literature—of real literary merit, I mean—ever

were suppressed; and those that were, were not suppressed for long." The long, long list of Anne Haight's well-known *Banned Books* is a simple answer to the first claim; and it is certainly a specious, unsound argument to say that "those that were, were not suppressed for long." *Any* length of time is contrary to the fundamental tenets of freedom of speech and expression in which, presumably, "liberal" Kristol believes.

Incidentally, near the end of his article, he admits that "We had censorship 5 of pornography and obscenity for 150 years," which in simple mathematical process would indicate that censorship began in 1821. This is a most interesting date, just about 93 years after it historically began! Kristol, as I said, needs at least a capsule course in the facts of the story of censorship.

If Kristol's facts were right, one might be willing to consider the logic of 6 his argumentation, which, on the whole, is rather persuasive. But if "liberal" censorship has to be based on misinformation and exaggeration, then it is no more worth the consideration of reasonable men and women than *il*liberal censorship.

Admittedly, this brief reply to Kristol is itself a polemic, rather than in a 7 reasonable vein. The reader is referred to my forthcoming book for a lengthy, historically based, positive set of facts and arguments concerning the merits and demerits of censorship of writings about sex. Suffice it here, in a necessarily limited space, to say that Kristol has clearly failed to consider the most basic of all issues in the censorship/noncensorship dispute.

In a long perspective, the fear of the word is really the fear of the human. 8 Like reverse Terences, those who censor and favor censorship are really saying, "I am human, but everything human is alien to me." Men and women are men and women *because* of their sexual drives, and denial of this fact by even a never-ending line of censors—liberal *or* illiberal!—will not eliminate maleness and femaleness and the male-female relationship. The censor will never outlast biology.

PORNOGRAPHY HURTS WOMEN
FROM *AGAINST OUR WILL: MEN, WOMEN AND RAPE*

Susan Brownmiller

Feminist author Susan Brownmiller argues against pornography insofar as its primary effect is to raise male self-esteem by degrading women and reducing them to "adult toys . . . to be used, abused, broken and discarded."

Pornography has been so thickly glossed over with the patina of chic these   1
days in the name of verbal freedom and sophistication that important distinctions between freedom of political expression (a democratic necessity), honest sex education for children (a societal good) and ugly smut (the deliberate devaluation of the role of women through obscene, distorted depictions) have been hopelessly confused. Part of the problem is that those who traditionally have been the most vigorous opponents of porn are often those same people who shudder at the explicit mention of any sexual subject. Under their watchful, vigilante eyes, frank and free dissemination of educational materials relating to abortion, contraception, the act of birth, and female biology in general is also dangerous, subversive and dirty. (I am not unmindful that frank and free discussion of rape, "the unspeakable crime," might well give these righteous vigilantes further cause to shudder.) Because the battle lines were falsely drawn a long time ago, before there was a vocal women's movement, the antipornography forces appear to be, for the most part, religious, Southern, conservative and right-wing, while the pro-porn forces are identified as Eastern, atheistic and liberal.

But a woman's perspective demands a totally new alignment, or at least a   2
fresh appraisal. The majority report of the President's Commission on Obscenity and Pornography (1970), a report that argued strongly for the removal of all legal restrictions on pornography, soft and hard, made plain that 90 percent of all pornographic material is geared to the male heterosexual market (the other 10 percent is geared to the male homosexual taste), that buyers of porn are "predominantly white, middle-class, middle-aged married males" and that the graphic depictions, the meat and potatoes of porn, are of the naked female body and of the multiplicity of acts done to that body.

Discussing the content of stag films, "a familiar and firmly established part   3
of the American scene," the commission report dutifully, if foggily, explained, "Because pornography historically has been thought to be primarily a masculine interest, the emphasis in stag films seems to represent the preferences of the middle-class American male. Thus male homosexuality and bestiality are relatively rare, while lesbianism is rather common."

The commissioners in this instance had merely verified what purveyors of **4**
porn have always known: hard-core pornography is not a celebration of
sexual freedom; it is a cynical exploitation of female sexual activity through
the device of making all such activity, and consequently all females, "dirty."
Heterosexual male consumers of pornography are frankly turned on by
watching lesbians in action (although never in the final scenes, but always as
a curtain raiser); they are turned off with the sudden swiftness of a water
faucet by watching naked men act upon each other. One study quoted in the
commission report came to the unastounding conclusion that "seeing a stag
film in the presence of male peers bolsters masculine esteem." Indeed. The
men in groups who watch the films, it is important to note, are *not* naked.

When male response to pornography is compared to female response, a **5**
pronounced difference in attitude emerges. According to the commission,
"Males report being more highly aroused by depictions of nude females, and
show more interest in depictions of nude females than [do] females." Quoting
the figures of Alfred Kinsey, the commission noted that a majority of males
(77 percent) were "aroused" by visual depictions of explicit sex while a
majority of females (68 percent) were not aroused. Further, "females more
often than males reported 'disgust' and 'offense.'"

From whence comes this female disgust and offense? Are females sexually **6**
backward or more conservative by nature? The gut distaste that a majority of
women feel when we look at pornography, a distaste that, incredibly, it is no
longer fashionable to admit, comes, I think, from the gut knowledge that we
and our bodies are being stripped, exposed and contorted for the purpose of
ridicule to bolster that "masculine esteem" which gets its kick and sense of
power from viewing females as anonymous, panting playthings, adult toys,
dehumanized objects to be used, abused, broken and discarded.

This, of course, is also the philosophy of rape. It is no accident (for what **7**
else could be its purpose?) that females in the pornographic genre are
depicted in two cleanly delineated roles: as virgins who are caught and
"banged" or as nymphomaniacs who are never sated. The most popular and
prevalent pornographic fantasy combines the two: an innocent, untutored
female is raped and "subjected to unnatural practices" that turn her into a
raving, slobbering nymphomaniac, a dependent sexual slave who can never
get enough of the big, male cock.

There can be no "equality" in porn, no female equivalent, no turning of **8**
the tables in the name of bawdy fun. Pornography, like rape, is a male
invention, designed to dehumanize women, to reduce the female to an object
of sexual access, not to free sensuality from moralistic or parental inhibition.
The staple of porn will always be the naked female body, breasts and genitals
exposed, because as man devised it, her naked body is the female's "shame,"
her private parts the private property of man, while his are the ancient, holy,
universal, patriarchal instrument of his power, his rule by force over *her.*

Pornography is the undiluted essence of anti-female propaganda. Yet the   **9**
very same liberals who were so quick to understand the method and purpose
behind the mighty propaganda machine of Hitler's Third Reich, the consciously spewed-out anti-Semitic caricatures and obscenities that gave an
ideological base to the Holocaust and the Final Solution, the very same
liberals who, enlightened by blacks, searched their own conscience and came
to understand that their tolerance of "nigger" jokes and portrayals of shuffling, rolling-eyed servants in movies perpetuated the degrading myths of
black inferiority and gave an ideological base to the continuation of black oppression — these very same liberals now fervidly maintain that the hatred and
contempt for women that find expression in four-letter words used as expletives and in what are quaintly called "adult" or "erotic" books and movies are
a valid extension of freedom of speech that must be preserved as a Constitutional right.

To defend the right of a lone, crazed American Nazi to grind out propa-   **10**
ganda calling for the extermination of all Jews, as the ACLU has done in the
name of free speech, is, after all, a self-righteous and not particularly courageous stand, for American Jewry is not currently threatened by storm
troopers, concentration camps and imminent extermination, but I wonder if
the ACLU's position might change if, come tomorrow morning, the book-
stores and movie theaters lining Forty-second Street in New York City were
devoted not to the humiliation of women by rape and torture, as they
currently are, but to a systematized commercially successful propaganda
machine depicting the sadistic pleasures of gassing Jews or lynching blacks?

Is this analogy extreme? Not if you are a woman who is conscious of the   **11**
ever-present threat of rape and the proliferation of a cultural ideology that
makes it sound like "liberated" fun. The majority report of the President's
Commission on Obscenity and Pornography tried to pooh-pooh the opinion of
law enforcement agencies around the country that claimed their own concrete
experience with offenders who were caught with the stuff led them to
conclude that pornographic material is a causative factor in crimes of sexual
violence. The commission maintained that it was not possible at this time to
scientifically prove or disprove such a connection.

But does one need scientific methodology in order to conclude that the   **12**
antifemale propaganda that permeates our nation's cultural output promotes
a climate in which acts of sexual hostility directed against women are not only
tolerated but ideologically encouraged? A similar debate has raged for many
years over whether or not the extensive glorification of violence (the gangster
as hero; the loving treatment accorded bloody shoot-'em-ups in movies,
books and on TV) has a causal effect, a direct relationship to the rising rate
of crime, particularly among youth. Interestingly enough, in this area —
nonsexual and not specifically related to abuses against women — public
opinion seems to be swinging to the position that explicit violence in the

entertainment media does have a deleterious effect; it makes violence commonplace, numbingly routine and no longer morally shocking.

More to the point, those who call for a curtailment of scenes of violence in 13 movies and on television in the name of sensitivity, good taste and what's best for our children are not accused of being pro-censorship or against freedom of speech. Similarly, minority group organizations, black, Hispanic, Japanese, Italian, Jewish, or American Indian, that campaign against ethnic slurs and demeaning portrayals in movies, on television shows and in commercials are perceived as waging a just political fight, for if a minority group claims to be offended by a specific portrayal, be it Little Black Sambo or the Frito Bandido, and relates it to a history of ridicule and oppression, few liberals would dare to trot out a Constitutional argument in theoretical opposition, not if they wish to maintain their liberal credentials. Yet when it comes to the treatment of women, the liberal consciousness remains fiercely obdurate, refusing to be budged, for the sin of appearing square or prissy in the age of the so-called sexual revolution has become the worst offense of all.

A PHILOSOPHER LOOKS AT THE PORN DEBATE

F. M. Christensen

In this interview from Playboy Magazine, *Canadian philosopher F. M. Christensen argues that "nothing is more human than sexual fantasies and feelings. . . . Emotional reactions against pornography tell more about the complainant's own sexual inhibitions than about pornography."*

How many times have you sat through an antiporn diatribe or listened to a   1
fundamentalist rail against erotica and wondered, Who will stand up for pornography? We asked Canadian philosopher Dr. F. M. Christensen to respond to some of the clichéd antiporn arguments.

PLAYBOY: Is pornography a recent phenomenon?

CHRISTENSEN: Humans have produced pornography for thousands of years. The artists of ancient Greece, India and Japan produced quite a bit of sexually explicit art. In ancient Tahiti, family entertainment included the portrayal of a variety of sex acts, and ancient Polynesians held nude beauty contests. In most early societies, evidently pornography was not considered disgusting or degrading.

PLAYBOY: Why do we have pornography?

CHRISTENSEN: Pornography is something like theater or spectator sports.   5
Humans can get enjoyment by watching others because we have the ability to fantasize. In particular, we fantasize about sex; in fact, it's so natural that we even fantasize in our sleep. Pornography is a simple extension of sexual fantasy. It is an alternative way of satisfying, albeit imperfectly, some very strong needs and desires.

Fantasies Are Natural

PLAYBOY: But some people say that that makes pornography dehumanizing.

CHRISTENSEN: On the contrary, nothing is more human than sexual fantasies and feelings. If anyone is trying to dehumanize us, it is those who would denigrate our sexuality.

PLAYBOY: Does pornography turn people into sex objects?

CHRISTENSEN: Our long tradition of devaluing the body, and sex in particular, underlies this charge. An exercise video tape has just as much focus on the physical body — or the body as object — as does a pornographic movie. Why is sex object a common charge while exercise object is not?

PLAYBOY: Does pornography reduce people to body parts?   **10**

CHRISTENSEN: Look through almost any *non*erotic magazine and you will find advertisements and articles featuring hair, hands, hips, feet, etc. They may be selling foot powder or explaining how to keep hips in trim or how to reduce back pain. They are never condemned for reducing people to body parts. The real reason for the attack on pornography is that some people consider sex organs shameful.

A Limited View

PLAYBOY: Is pornography very narrow-minded? Does it present people as being nothing but sexual beings; does it carry the message that sex is all we're good for?

CHRISTENSEN: Most pornography has a limited scope; it contains little else besides sex. This is partly because sexual activity has been excluded from socially respectable portrayals of human experience; it has been driven out into a realm by itself. But almost all events, from sports to concerts, are specialized in their content. They all portray a limited view of human life. There are magazines that specialize in sports, food, music, hobbies, fashion, etc. Do these publications portray people as whole human beings? Do movies or novels that do *not* have sex scenes deny our completeness? No. Human wholeness in no way precludes focusing on one aspect of ourselves at a time.

You presume that pornography makes all women angry. This is not true. In fact, many of them enjoy sexually explicit presentation. Video dealers report that women and couples rent most X-rated movies. There are many women who *are* angered by pornography. However, the main reason for their anger stems from the bodily shame we've all been conditioned to feel. Those feelings are not healthy, and the best way to solve this problem is to educate people to be comfortable with their bodies. Another reason for women's anger is that they feel their careers have been restricted. In the past, they were largely limited to being sex partners and mothers and were not valued by society for their intelligence or creativity. Consequently, emphasis on a woman's desirability to men is seen as something bad in itself. The solution to this problem is not to eliminate attraction between the sexes but to continue to expand women's opportunities.

PLAYBOY: Do men's-magazines' images of women create an unreal standard   **15** of beauty?

CHRISTENSEN: The women pictured in, say, *Playboy* have faces and figures that the average woman can't match. Hence, comparison with them can only make a woman feel inferior and insecure. This is obviously not a legitimate objection to nudity itself. Should *Playboy* publish pictures of less attractive women? That wouldn't really satisfy those who object to pornography, for they don't make this same charge about idealization elsewhere in the media and the culture. For instance, children on television and in the movies are almost always cute and charming. The models in women's fashion magazines are certainly above average in attractiveness. How does an average man feel when he compares himself with most male movie stars? He certainly can't match their looks or status. But the real point here is that neither the media nor pornography creates the ideal of beauty. Every culture has its standard of physical attractiveness, and those who fall short feel inadequate. This problem will exist with or without pornography.

PLAYBOY: Is pornography male propaganda? It portrays women as being sexually assertive and uninhibited, and that is just not necessarily so.

CHRISTENSEN: In this respect, pornography is no different from any other fiction. It is *not* real life; its characters are idealized; they fulfill someone's fantasy. Does good always triumph over evil? Does true love always last forever? These are fantasies, too — not portrayals of real life. In fact, avoiding depicting sexuality in a work is more unrealistic, for it suggests that women and men are *non*sexual.

A Desire to Share Pleasure

PLAYBOY: Does pornography promote rape?

CHRISTENSEN: Some radical feminists make charges like that, but they are   20
absurd when applied to nonviolent pornography. It's important to realize that these people make similar libelous claims about men and male sexuality in general. They say that all men are by nature violent. These extremists see antifemale messages everywhere. To them, sexual comments are never appreciative, only hostile. Similarly, then, they view pornography as another expression of men's desire to dominate women, not of their desire to have and share sexual pleasure.

Emotional reactions against pornography tell more about the complainant's own sexual inhibitions than about pornography. The fact is that these arguments are false and, indeed, potentially very harmful. Anyone who hears them should counter with the truth.

CENSORSHIP IS A MATTER OF CLASSIFICATION

Charles Krauthammer

We are all censors, argues columnist Charles Krauthammer, if we believe that material permissible on late-night cable TV is not permissible on network TV during the children's hour. The issue is not censorship but classification.

When Dan Rather reports on the banned-in-Cincinnati exhibit of Robert   1
Mapplethorpe's photographs, he does not show the homoerotic, pedophilic or sadomasochistic pictures, the ones that brought the police and the courts, the American Civil Liberties Union and Jesse Helms, the censors and libertarians into the game.

Television will show you the exquisite flower pictures and the tamer   2
portraits. It *tells* you about the nasty ones.

Similarly, this newspaper does not publish, say, Mapplethorpe's self-por-   3
trait in leather with bull whip inserted in his rectum. Why not? This is quite obviously censorship. Why is the ACLU not protesting?

Because everyone, ACLU included, favors censorship in principle. No one   4
protests the banning of Mapplethorpe's nastier pictures from television and newspapers, because there is a consensus that some things are not to be shown on the mass media.

But as the media becomes less mass — as you go, for example, from   5
network to cable to videocassette — more and more is permitted, until we reach the point where just about anything is permitted for viewing in the privacy of one's own bedroom.

This arrangement, which might be called censorship by classification,   6
enjoys wide support because it is a reasonable way for a pluralistic society to deal with the question of obscenity and public standards. The question with Mapplethorpe is how to classify his art.

Should it be classified as so outrageous and degrading as to be reserved for   7
the most private sanctum (the home)? Or is it serious enough to deserve placement in a public institution such as an art gallery?

Note that even the museum curators who exhibit Mapplethorpe are careful   8
to place the most offensive pictures in special rooms under special cover. Even they accept the principle of segregation.

Why? For two reasons.   9

First, not to segregate is to risk assaulting the unwitting. To show, say on   10
"The CBS Evening News," a picture of one man urinating into the mouth of another (also in the Mapplethorpe exhibit) would be to assault the sensibili-

ties of millions who did not seek it out. That violates the classic liberal dictum that you can do what you want to yourself so long as you do not harm others.

The other reason is that, even if people aren't harming others, society has 11 an interest in what people do to themselves. Libertarians don't like this kind of paternalism, but most people in this democracy believe that society has the right to prevent consenting adults from, say, drug-taking or self-mutilation (selling a kidney for money, for example).

In short, society has the right—the duty, even—to protect people 12 against themselves.

We know that drugs can injure. But can art? 13

"What reason is there to think that anyone was ever corrupted by a 14 book?" Irving Kristol asks. "This last question, oddly enough, is asked by the very same people who seem convinced that advertisements in magazines or displays of violence on television do indeed have the power to corrupt."

Of course art can corrupt. "If you believe that no one was ever corrupted 15 by a book," Kristol points out, "you have also to believe that no one was ever improved by a book (or a play or a movie). You have to believe, in other words, that all art is morally trivial . . . No one, not even a university professor, believes that."

It is precisely because words and images have the power to degrade that 16 society tries to restrict certain kinds of material to the smallest possible audience. That is why strip joints and porno houses are segregated into combat zones. Some things may not be displayed on billboards. Some may not be shown on TV. Some may not be shown in public galleries.

What goes where? That is the issue. It is one not of principle but of 17 classification. It is thus far less cosmic than Pat Buchanan and the ACLU would like us to think. Take away all the posturing, and the issue with Mapplethorpe is not, as the civil libertarians pretend, "Are you for or against censorship?" The issue is "Where on the spectrum do you place Mapplethorpe?"

For what it's worth, where do I? Having seen the catalog, though not the 18 exhibit, I find his work too melancholy to be offensive, too decadent to be pornographic. Given current cultural norms—the slasher/skin flicks one can see nightly on cable, for example—even his rougher stuff is, in my view, correctly placed in a public art gallery.

The people of Cincinnati may, however, have a different standard. If they 19 believe that Mapplethorpe's rougher stuff ranks a rung lower, why should they not be permitted to decide that it is too degrading to warrant public exhibit?

Let these pictures be accessible to Cincinnatians by mail-order catalog for 20 study behind closed doors. That is no more attack on the First Amendment than keeping these pictures off television.

The sophisticates howl at this judgment. They sneer at the yahoos of Ohio   21
for their small, censoring minds. Well, if the sophisticates and the civil
libertarians are so outraged by censorship, are they prepared to defend my
project to have the bullwhip-in-rectum study blown up and featured on a
Times Square billboard?

FOR CLASS DISCUSSION

1. Analyze and evaluate the dispute on the censorship of pornography by applying the first set of guide questions from pages 443–
   444. How do you account for the disagreement between Kristol
   and Oboler and between Brownmiller and Christensen? Pay particular attention to disagreements about the facts of the case as
   well as to disagreements in assumptions, beliefs, and values.
2. Choose one of the arguments for closer analysis, applying the
   second set of guide questions on page 444.

OPTIONAL WRITING ASSIGNMENT   You are the editor of your campus newspaper. While you were on vacation, your assistant editor reviewed an
exhibition of works of art deemed obscene by a recent presidential commission. Inspired by the openness of the exhibit, your second-in-command has
written an impassioned defense of the exhibit, replete with four-letter
words and nearly a half page of explicit photos of stunningly naked inter-
twined bodies. The student senate, in response to numerous complaints,
has decided to review your newspaper's funding and scheduled a hearing.
You will be asked to read testimony at the hearing. You must tell the senate
members what you propose to do about your assistant editor and why.
Drawing on the preceding essays, personal experience, and any other research you may have done, write a two-page presentation suitable for your
student senate.

THE LEGALIZATION OF DRUGS: WOULD AMERICA BE BETTER OFF OR WORSE OFF IF DRUGS WERE LEGALIZED?

THE FEDERAL DRUGSTORE

An Interview with Michael S. Gazzaniga

In this interview, Michael S. Gazzaniga, Professor of Neuroscience at Dartmouth Medical School, provides a scientific perspective on drug use and abuse. Gazzaniga's own stance is a scientifically cautious belief that the benefits of legalizing drugs outweigh the costs.

Q: Professor Gazzaniga, as you know, there are those who have recom-   1
mended the decriminalization of drugs. Before we take up a concrete proposal coming in from that quarter, we want to ask you a question or two, the answers to which will shed light on any such proposal. The first question is this:

It is said that the drug crack is substantively different from its parent drug,   2
cocaine, in that it is, to use the term of Professor van den Haag, "crimogenic." In other words a certain (unspecified) percentage of those who take crack are prompted to — well, to go out and commit mayhem of some kind. Is that correct?

A: No, not in the way you put it, What you are asking is, Is there something   3
about how crack acts on the brain that makes people who take it likelier to
commit crime?

Let's begin by making it clear what crack is. It is simply cocaine that has   4
been mixed with baking soda, water, and then boiled. What this procedure
does is to permit cocaine to be smoked. Now any drug ingested in that
way — i.e., absorbed by the lungs — goes more efficiently to the brain, and
the result is a quicker, more intense experience. That is what crack gives the
consumer. But its impact on the brain is the same as with plain cocaine and,
as a matter of fact, amphetamines. No one has ever maintained that these
drugs are "crimogenic."

The only study I know about that inquires into the question of crack   5
breeding crime reports that most homicides involving crack were the result
not of the use of crack, but of dealer disputes. Crack did not induce users to
commit crimes. Do some crack users commit crimes? Of course. After all,
involvement in proscribed drug traffic is dangerous. Moreover, people who
commit crimes tend to use drugs at a high rate, though which drug they
prefer varies from one year to the next.

Q: You are telling us that an increase in the use of crack would not mean an   6
increase in crime?

A: I am saying that what increase there would be in crime would not be simply   7
the result of the pharmacology of that drug. Look, let's say there are
200,000 users/abusers of crack in New York City — a number that reflects
one of the current estimates. If so, and if the drug produced violent tendencies in all crack users, the health-care system would have come to a
screeching halt. It hasn't. In fact, in 1988 the hospitals in New York City (the
crack capital of the world) averaged only seven crack-related admissions,
citywide, a day. The perception of crack-based misbehavior is exaggerated
because it is the cases that show up in the emergency rooms that receive
public notice, and the whole picture begins to look very bleak. All of this is to
say: when considering any aspect of the drug problem, keep in mind the
matter of selection of the evidence.

It is prudent to recall that, in the past, dangerous and criminal behavior   8
has been said to have been generated by other drugs, for instance marijuana
(you remember *Reefer Madness?*). And bear it in mind that since cocaine is
available everywhere, so is crack available everywhere, since the means of
converting the one into the other are easy, and easily learned. It is important
to note that only a small percentage of cocaine users actually convert their
stuff to crack. Roughly one in six.

Q: Then would it follow that even if there were an increase in the use of crack,   9
the legalization of it would actually result in a decrease in crime?

A: That is correct.   10

Q: Isn't crack a drug whose addictive power exceeds that of many other   11 drugs? If that is the case, one assumes that people who opt to take crack do so because it yields the faster and more exhilarating satisfactions to which you make reference.

A: That is certainly the current understanding, but there are no solid data on   12
the question. Current observations are confounded by certain economic variables. Crack is cheap —

Q: Why? If cocaine is expensive, how can crack be cheap?   13

A: Cocaine costs $1,000 per ounce if bought in quantity. One ounce can   14
produce one thousand vials of crack, each of which sells for $5. The drug abuser is able to experience more drug episodes. Crack being cheap, the next high can come a lot more quickly and since there is a down to every up, or high, the cycle can become intense.

So yes, crack is addictive. So is cocaine. So are amphetamines. The special   15
punch of crack, as the result of going quickly via the lungs to the brain, may prompt some abusers to want more. By the way, it is the public knowledge that crack acts in this way that, as several studies document, causes most regular cocaine users to be cautious about crack. The casual-to-moderate user very clearly wants to stay in that category. So, all you can say is that there is a *perception,* widely shared, that crack is more addictive. Whether it is, isn't really known. One thing we do know is that crack does not begin to approach tobacco as a nationwide health hazard. For every crack-related death, there are three hundred tobacco-related deaths.

Q: You are confusing us. You say that because of the especially quick effects   16
that come from taking crack, there is a disposition on the part of the user to want more. Isn't that a way of saying that it is more addictive? If someone, after smoking, say, ten cigarettes, begins to want cigarettes every day, isn't tobacco "addictive," as you say it is? Or are you saying that crack finds most users indifferent to the highs it brings on, and for *that* reason it can't be said to be more addictive than cocaine?

A: The current, official definition of an addict is someone who compulsively   17
seeks psychoactive drugs. The definition, you will note, focuses on human behavior, not on pharmacologic action on the brain. In respect of crack, there are factors that might lead to a higher rate of addiction. Some of these factors are certainly social in nature and some may be pharmacologic. The purported higher rate of addiction among crack users could be due to social values, for instance the low cost of crack. We simply don't know as yet.

Keep in mind our experience with LSD. When it was fashionable to take it,   18
droves did so. But LSD has unpleasant side-effects, and eventually the use of it greatly diminished. In drugs, as in much else, there is a strong tendency to follow the herd. Sorting out the real threat from the hyperbole takes time.

Another example of hyperbole is the recent claim that there were 375,000   19
"crack babies" born last year; how could that possibly be, when the govern-

ment (the National Institutes on Drug Abuse) informs us that there were only 500,000 crack *users* last year? Exaggeration and misinformation run rampant on this subject.

Q: Well, if crack were legally available alongside cocaine and, say, marijuana, 20 what could be the reason for a consumer to take crack?

A: You need to keep your drug classifications straight. If your goal were, 21 pure and simple, to get high, you might try crack or cocaine, or some amphetamine. You wouldn't go for marijuana, which is a mild hallucinogen and tranquilizer. So, if you wanted to be up and you didn't have much time, you might go to crack. But then if it were absolutely established that there was a higher addiction rate with crack, legalization could, paradoxically, diminish its use. This is so because if cocaine were reduced to the same price as crack, the abuser, acknowledging the higher rate of addiction, might forgo the more intensive high of crack, opting for the slower high of cocaine. Crack was introduced years ago as offering an alluring new psychoactive experience. But its special hold on the ghetto is the result of its price. Remember that — on another front — we know that 120-proof alcohol doesn't sell as readily as the 86 proof, not by a long shot, even though the higher the proof, the faster the psychological effect that alcohol users are seeking.

Q: The basic question, we take it, has got to be this: It is everywhere assumed 22 that if drugs were legal, their consumption would increase. That guess is based on empirical observations of a past phenomenon. Mr. Bennett, for instance, has said that when Prohibition ended, the consumption of alcohol increased by 400 per cent. What are your comments on that?

A: Books and even careers have been built around studies of the Eighteenth 23 Amendment. Arguments about its meaning continue to rage in the scientific journals. Arguments always continue when available data are inconclusive.

Most experts insist that the rate of alcohol use before Prohibition was the 24 same as after. Some qualify that assertion by pointing out that the pre-Prohibition rate of consumption was not realized again until years after Prohibition was over. From this we are invited to conclude that, in that sense, Prohibition was really successful — i.e., it interrupted many potential drinkers on their way to the saloon. And then some point out that although alcohol was freely available during Prohibition, it was harder to get in some parts of America. Even so overall consumption was rising (some say to pre-Prohibition levels) toward the middle and end of Prohibition.

Frankly, here is what's important: *There is a base rate of drug abuse, and* 25 *it is achieved one way or another.* This is so even though there are researchers who point to different rates of abuse in different cultures. The trouble with that generality is that it is usually made without taking into account correlative factors, such as national traditions, the extent of educa-

tion programs available, and so on. In which connection, I think the Federal
Government should establish a study group to collect drug information from
different cultures in an effort to get useful leads.

Q: Is there evidence that the current consumption of drugs is restrained by   26
their illegality? We have read that ninety million Americans have experimented, at one time or another, with illegal drugs. Would more than ninety
million have experimented with them if drugs had been legal?

A: I think illegality has little if anything to do with drug consumption — and,   27
incidentally, I am certain that far more than ninety million Americans have at
some point or other experimented with an illegal drug.

This gets to the issue of actual availability. Drugs are everywhere, simply   28
everywhere. In terms of availability, drugs might just as well be legal as
illegal. Now it has been argued that legalization will create a different social
climate, a more permissive, more indulgent climate. It is certainly conceivable,
primarily for that reason, that there would be greater initial use — the result
of curiosity. But the central point is that human beings in all cultures tend to
seek out means of altering their mental state, and that although some will
shop around and lose the powers of self-discipline, most will settle down to a
base rate of use, and a much smaller rate of abuse, and those rates are pretty
much what we have in the United States right now.

Q: Then the factor of illegality, in your opinion, does not weigh heavily? But,   29
we come to the critical question, if ninety million (or more) Americans have
experimented with the use of drugs, why is drug abuse at such a (relatively)
low level?

A: If you exclude tobacco, in the whole nation less than 10 per cent of the   30
adult population abuses drugs. That is, 9 to 12 million adult Americans abuse
drugs. That figure includes alcohol, by the way, and the figure remains fairly
constant.

Consider alcohol. In our culture alone, 70 to 80 per cent of us use alcohol,   31
and the abuse rate is now estimated at 5 to 6 per cent. We see at work here a
major feature of the human response to drug availability, namely, the inclination to moderation. Most people are adjusted and are intent on living productive lives. While most of us, pursuing that goal, enjoy the sensations of
euphoria, or anxiety reduction, or (at times) social dis-inhibition or even
anaesthesia, we don't let the desire for these sensations dominate our behavior. Alcohol fills these needs for many people and its use is managed intelligently.

It is worth noting that the largest proportion of this drug is sold to the   32
social drinker, not the drunk, just as most cocaine is sold to the casual user,
not the addict. Now, early exposure to alcohol is common and inevitable, and
youthful drinking can be extreme. Yet studies have shown that it is difficult
to determine which drunk at the college party will evolve into a serious
alcoholic. What is known is that the vast majority of early drinkers stop

excessive drinking all by themselves. In fact, drug use of all types drops off radically with age.

Q: Wait a minute. Are you telling us that there is only a 10 per cent chance 33 that any user will become addicted to a drug, having experimented with it?
A: The 10 per cent figure includes all drugs except tobacco. The actual risk 34 for abuse of some drugs is much lower. Consider last year's National Household Survey (NHS), which was carried out by the National Institutes on Drug Abuse. It is estimated that some 21 million people tried cocaine in 1988. But according to the NHS only three million defined themselves as having used the drug at least once during the month preceding their interview. Most of the three million were casual users. Now think about it. *All* the cocaine users make up 2 per cent of the adult population, and the addicts make up less than one-quarter of 1 per cent of the total population. These are the government's own figures. Does that sound like an epidemic to you?
Q: But surely an epidemic has to do with the rate at which an undesirable 35 occurrence is increasing. How many more cocaine users were there than the year before? Or the year before that?
A: The real question is whether or not more and more Americans are becom- 36 ing addicted to something. Is the rate of addiction to psychoactive substances going up? The answer to that is a flat no. Are there fads during which one drug becomes more popular than another as the drug of abuse? Sure. But, when one drug goes up in consumption, others go down. Heroin use is down, and so is marijuana use. That is why the opiate and marijuana pushers are trying to improve their purity — so they can grab back some of their market share, which apparently they have done for heroin in New York City.

But, having said that, you should know that the actual use of cocaine and 37 all other illicit drugs is on the decline, according to the NHS. The just-published National High School Survey carried out by the University of Michigan reports that the same is true among high-school students. Crack is used at such a low rate throughout the country that its use can hardly be measured in most areas.
Q: Well, if a low addiction rate is the rule, how do we come to terms with the 38 assertion, which has been made in reputable circles, that over 40 per cent of Americans fighting in Vietnam were using heroin and 80 per cent marijuana?
A: Stressful situations provoke a greater use of drugs. Vietnam was one of 39 them. But what happens when the soldiers come home?
That point was examined in a large study by Dr. Lee Robbins at Washing- 40 ton University. During the Vietnam War, President Nixon ordered a study on the returning vets who seemed to have a drug problem. (Nixon didn't know what he was looking for, but he was getting a lot of flak on the point that the war was producing a generation of addicts.) Dr. Robbins chose to study those

soldiers returning to the United States in 1971. Of the 13,760 Army enlisted me who returned and were included in her sample, 1,400 had a positive urine test for drugs (narcotics, amphetamines, or barbiturates). She was able to re-test 495 men from this sample a few months later. The results were crystal clear: Only 8 per cent of the men who had been drug positive in their first urine tests remained so. In short, over 90 per cent of them, now that they were back home, walked away from drug use. And all of them knew how to get hold of drugs, if they had wanted them. Incidentally, Dr. Robbins did a follow-up study a couple of years later on the same soldiers. She reported there had not been an increase in drug use.

Q: Aha! You are saying that under special circumstances, the use of drugs 41 increases. Well, granted there was stress in Vietnam. Isn't there stress also in American ghettos?

A: Floyd Bloom of the Scripps Medical Institute — one of the foremost brain 42 scientists in the country — has posited that most psychoactive drugs work on the brain's reward systems. There is good neurobiologic research to support this idea. It is an idea that can easily be understood and applied to everyday life.

What it tells you is that some people want artificial ways of getting their 43 kicks out of life, but also that some people need those artificial crutches. If you live in poverty and frustration, and see few rewards available to you, you are likelier than your better-satisfied counterpart to seek the escape of drugs, although the higher rate of consumption does not result in a higher rate of addiction. Virtually every study finds this to be the case with one possibly interesting twist. A recent Department of Defense study showed that drug use in the military was lower for blacks than for whites, the reverse of civilian life. (It is generally agreed that the military is the only institution in our country that is successfully integrated.) In short, environmental factors play an important role in the incidence of drug use.

Q: So you are saying that there are social circumstances that will raise the 44 rate of consumption, but that raising the rate of consumption doesn't in fact raise the rate of addiction. In other words, if 50 per cent of the troops in Vietnam had been using crack, this would not have affected the rate at which, on returning to the United States, they became addicted. They would have kicked the habit on reaching home?

A: That's the idea. Drug consumption can go up in a particular population, 45 fueled by stress, but the rate of addiction doesn't go up no matter what the degree of stress. Most people can walk away from high drug use if their lives become more normal. Of course, the stress of the ghetto isn't the only situation that fuels high drug consumption. Plenty of affluent people who for some reason or another do not find their lives rewarding also escape into drugs.

Q: If it is true, then, that only a small percentage of those who take crack will   **46**
end up addicted, and that that is no different from the small percentage who,
taking one beer every Saturday night, will become alcoholics, what is the
correct way in which to describe the relative intensity of the addictive element
in a particular drug?

A: That is an interesting question and one that can't satisfactorily be an-   **47**
swered until much more research is done. There are conundrums. Again, it is
estimated that 21 million people tried cocaine in 1988. Yet, of those, only 3
million currently use it, and only a small percentage are addicted. As for
crack, it is estimated that 2.5 million have used it, while only a half million
say they still do, and *that* figure includes the addicted and the casual user.
Some reports claim that as many as one half of crack users are addicted. As I
have said, crack is cheap, and for that reason may be especially attractive to
the poor. That is a non-pharmacological, non-biological factor, the weight of
which we have not come to any conclusions about. We don't even have
reliable data to tell us that crack creates a greater rate of addiction than, say,
cocaine. My own guess is it doesn't. Remember that the drug acts on the same
brain systems that cocaine and amphetamines do.

What is needed, in order to answer your question, is a science of compara-   **48**
tive pharmacology where the various psychoactive drugs could be compared
against some kind of common physiological/psychological measure. Doing
that would be difficult, which is one of the reasons why those data don't exist.
How do you capture fluctuating moods and motivations? There are times
when the smallest dose of a drug can have a sublime effect on someone, while
at another time it takes ten times the dose to have any noticeable effect. These
are tough problems to quantify and study, even in the laboratory.

Q: To what extent is the addictive factor affected by education? Here is what I   **49**
mean by this: Taking a drug, say heroin or cocaine or crack—or, for that
matter, alcohol—is a form of Russian roulette, using a ten-cartridge revolver. Now, presumably, an educated person, concerned for his livelihood,
wouldn't take a revolver with nine empty cartridges and one full cartridge,
aim it at his head, and pull the trigger. But granted, decisions of that kind are
based on ratiocinative skills. And we have to assume these skills don't exist
even among college students. If they did, there would be no drinking in
college, let alone drug taking. Comments?

A: Most people perceive themselves as in control of their destiny. They do not   **50**
think the initial exposure will ruin their lives, because of their perceived
self-control, and they are right. Take the most difficult case, tobacco—the
most highly addictive substance around. In a now classic study, Stanley
Schächter of Columbia University formally surveyed his highly educated
colleagues at Columbia. At the same time, he polled the working residents of

Amagansett, a community on Long Island where he summered. He first determined who were ongoing smokers, and who had been smokers. He took into account how long they had smoked, what they had smoked, and all other variables he could think of.

It wasn't long before the picture began to crystallize. Inform a normally 51 intelligent group of people about the tangible hazards of using a particular substance and the vast majority of them simply stop. It wasn't easy for some, but in general they stopped, and they didn't need treatment programs, support programs, and all the rest. Dr. Schachter concluded, after this study, that it is only the thorny cases that show up at the treatment centers, people who have developed a true addiction. For those people, psychological prophylactics, including education, are of little or no value. Yet it is these people that are held up as examples of what happens when one uses drugs. This is misleading. It creates an unworkable framework for thinking about the problem. Most people can voluntarily stop using a psychoactive substance, and those people who do continue to use it can moderate their intake to reduce the possibility of health hazards. This is true, as I say, for most substances, but I repeat, less true for tobacco because of its distinctively addictive nature. The people who unwisely continue to use tobacco tend to smoke themselves into major illness even though they are amply warned that this is likely to happen.

Q: So no matter how widely you spread the message, it is in fact going to be 52 ignored, both by PhDs and by illiterates?

A: If they are real abusers, yes. That is the reason for the high recidivism rate 53 among graduates of drug treatment centers. Here we are talking about the true addicts. Education appears not to help the recalcitrant abusers, who are the ones that keep showing up at health centers.

Yet, manifestly, education contributes to keeping the abuse rate as low as 54 it is. I think the message gets to the ghetto, but where there are other problems — the need for an artificial reward — drugs are going to be taken by many people because the excruciating pain of a current condition overrides long-term reason. In short, the ghetto citizen or the psychologically isolated person might well decide that the probability of living a better life is low, so grab some rewards while you can.

Q: At what level of intelligence is a potential drug user influenced to take a 55 less dangerous, rather than a more dangerous, drug? I mean, if it were known to all PhDs that crack was more dangerous than marijuana, that the small percentage who became addicted to crack would suffer greater biological change from it, up to and including death, in contrast to comparatively lenient sentences from addiction to marijuana, what percentage of PhDs would be influenced to stay away from the hard stuff, compared to illiterate 17-year-old ghetto dwellers?

A: Again, this is difficult to answer because the educational message interacts 56 with innumerable social problems. For example, drug abuse is three times greater among the unemployed. Someone who is unemployed on Monday might be re-employed on Friday, and this may stop, or reduce, his use of drugs. Gainful employment has a bigger effect in a case like this than education does. But in general, education plays a big role, and this is established. Remember, we are a health-oriented society, and we do care about our bodies and minds, by and large. Marijuana is a mild drug, compared to crack, for a variety of biological and psychological reasons. There are studies showing that casual-to-moderate cocaine users will not go the crack route because of fear of a greater chance of addiction or of an immediate physiological crisis. A recent issue of the *New England Journal of Medicine* reports that cocaine use contributes to heart disease in a rather muted way. However, crack may have a far greater impact and be responsible for a much more serious increase in drug-related heart failures. Does that kind of thing influence a kid in the ghetto? I think the message does get there. It certainly gets to Park Avenue first, however.

Q: In that case, education, even in the popular media, is likely to influence 57 primarily the educated classes. That has to mean that the uneducated class will suffer more addiction than the educated class.

A: Well, again, people in the lowest socio-economic status will continue to 58 consume more drugs, but that doesn't change the addiction rate. Still, legalization shouldn't change the current figures, since drugs are literally available everywhere in the ghetto. They are also available on every college campus. They are available in prisons! I suppose if one wants to conjure up fresh problems brought on by legalization, they will center on the folks living on Park Avenue, where drugs are less easily secured, not the ghetto. Legalization of drugs would reduce crime in the ghetto, and much that is positive would follow.

Q: If the number of addicts would be increased by decriminalization, is the 59 trade-off worth it? Is it wise to decriminalize, even if by doing so: we a) abort the $150-billion per-year drug-crime business; b) release $10 billion in federal money now going to the pursuit of drug merchants; c) end the corruption of government subsidized by drug dealers; and d) come upon a huge sum of money available to give treatment to addicts? Is this, in your judgment, a moral recommendation to make, given our knowledge of the psychological problems we are talking about?

A: Are you asking me to commit myself at this point to the question of 60 whether that trade-off is wise?

Q: Well, no, not quite yet. Let me describe a situation, the concrete situation I 61 spoke of a while ago, and ask you to comment on it in the light of the questions put to you above.

Suppose that drugs were made available. All of them, legally, in a Federal 62 Drugstore. But above each of the common drugs — crack, cocaine, heroin, hash, marijuana, amphetamines, LSD, etc.—there was a graphic description of what addiction to that drug would do to you. Suppose a situation in which, for instance, over the punch bowl at the far left of the counter that contained crack were written: "This drug will create an appetite to take another dose. That appetite is very strong. If you become an addict, you will want to take as many as twenty of these every day, and the results of doing so will be serious for your health. With overuse, you may suffer a heart attack and die."

By contrast, let's say that the placard directly above the punch bowl that   63
houses marijuana were to say: "Not addictive, but chronic use may lead to cancer, chromosome damage, birth deformities in future children, memory loss, paranoia, and depression." Is there any reason to suppose that this kind of merchandising will have the effect of propelling the majority of consumers either to taking no drugs at all, or to taking the less dangerous drugs? For example, marijuana over, say, cocaine?

A: For those not intent on self-abuse, yes. After all, as I said, we are a   64
health-oriented society. Hard-liquor sales are down, and, for that matter, so are wine sales. You can now buy low-cholesterol popcorn and so on. We want our kicks, but within a knowledgeable health-safety framework. On the other hand, for those intent on self-abuse, drug consumption will continue. Self-abuse occurs at all levels of our society, not only in the ghetto. Remember, most people in America are not living in ghettos, and a certain percentage of them are addicted to something. I think we as a society ought to focus attention on addiction groups and see if some factors can be isolated that might help out. Currently, drug treatment programs, which should more accurately be called drug management programs, need a lot of help. Treatment is not a reality for most of these centers. As I have already indicated, the recidivism rate is high at drug centers and this in part reflects the fact the drug centers get only the tough cases, the hard-core abusers that can not stop abuse themselves. Much more research is key.

Q: All right then, presumably the price of the drugs available for sale at the   65
Federal Drugstore will be low enough to discourage black-market activity. Would such Federal Drugstores eliminate black-market activity altogether?

A: No, of course not. The criminal mind is ever inventive. Special services will   66
be supplied, like home-delivery services, and the inevitable (and positively illegal) pushing to children. There will be new drugs dreamed up, and they will have their own market until they are isolated, and then will be sold legally. But, the vast majority of the crime network ought to crumble. The importance of that cannot be underestimated.

Q: So, the Federal Drugstores would obviously charge the cost of providing   67
the drugs and the overhead of retailing them. Let's suppose that they could then double the acquisition cost without activating black-market competition; if double proved too much, they would simply lower the price. Whatever; profits would go to the treatment centers and toward more advertising of the

dangers of drug abuse, and indeed of drug consumption. Do you have any difficulty with that?

A: No, but I would caution against setting up a plan that found the govern- **68** ment playing the role of pusher. If the drug-treatment centers were dependent on income from the Drugstore, the bureaucrats running the store might be tempted to increase profits. Once Congress comes around to thoughtfully considering legalization, the actual mechanisms will have to be carefully thought out.

Q: What would be your prediction, as a scientist, of what the advent of the **69** Federal Drugstore, combined with a program of intensified education, would accomplish in the next ten years?

A: Drug-consumption rates will bounce around, related as they are to envi- **70** ronmental factors, fads, and a host of other factors. Drug-abuse rates will not change much, if at all. Yet many of the negative social consequences of keeping drugs illegal will be neutralized. The health costs of drug abuse will always be with us. We should try to focus on those problems with more serious neurobiologic and neurobehavioral research and help where we can to reduce the percentage that fall victim. I am an experimental scientist, and like most people can see that the present system doesn't work. We need to try another approach. If for whatever reason, legalization doesn't improve the situation, it would take five minutes to reverse it.

DRUGS AN ESSENTIAL PART OF MODERN LIFE

Bruce Sterling

The drug problem is not going to go away "because it is part of us, and inherent in the way we live and think." Arguing that Americans are not simply seeking intoxicants but "performance enhancers," writer Bruce Sterling concludes that the "war against drugs is a lost cause; the only question is how many will die in the service of empty rhetoric."

Every society gets the drug problem it deserves. Drug hunger is essential 1
to our modern way of life; it's a constant, like electricity or air pollution.

We lie to ourselves about drugs and their attraction for us. Because of 2
that, we risk being blindsided in the 21st century—when the hidden cultural
logic of drug use will reach a bizarre crescendo.

Not long ago, President Bush told an audience of astonished Amish people 3
that Wall Street yuppies use cocaine. That uncomfortable truth discredits the
silly myth that drugs are the exclusive province of derelicts, teen-agers,
bohemians and the *lumpen.*

Those well-heeled professionals do cocaine not because it's fun (although 4
it is), but because it gives them a vital short-term edge that helps them
prosper in the crazed environment of a futures pit.

The coming thing in drugs is not intoxicants but performance enhancers. 5
In the future, we won't use drugs to "escape reality," but to lash ourselves to
superhuman effort.

You can see this trend coming. The cozy, dreamy days of marijuana and 6
LSD are history; what people want now is crack, amphetamine, and anabolic
steroids—headlong speed and muscle by order.

Steroids provide no pleasurable "high"—in fact, they ruin your sleep, 7
your temper, and your complexion—but it's estimated that 1 million Americans abuse them. The market is vast and growing, and the steroids scandal of
the latest Olympics perversely gave this market a tremendous popular boost.

The reasons are obvious. Ben Johnson is, in fact, the fastest man in the 8
world. He may have been deprived of his gold medal, but of his frankly
superhuman abilities there is no doubt. Athletes are caught in a bind that will
eventually spread into many other corners of society.

Put yourself in Johnson's place. (It will happen soon enough, so you might 9
as well get used to it.) Steroids enhance strength, but soon we are going to
discover substances that will enhance memory, intelligence, mood, sexuality.

The drugs we have today already do this, in halting ways—amphetamine, 10
for instance, has been found to raise the intelligence quotient by about 10
points, though for short periods and at great cost to health.

As we come to understand our own neurochemistry, we are going to 11
discover a galaxy of extremely potent substances with greater specificity and
fewer side effects. The drugs we use today are mostly vegetable extracts that
crudely mimic human biochemistry.

But beta-endorphin, for instance, is a natural human-brain chemical, an 12
analgesic 10,000 times more potent than morphine. The high-technology
development of drugs will lead us eventually to abuse our own body chemistry.

With the advent of monoclonal antibodies and genetic engineering, we are 13
learning to produce pure biochemicals cheaply, artificially, by the ton. Imagine the vast coca fields of South America reduced to a few stainless-steel vats
neatly hidden in a basement in Medellin or San Francisco.

Cheaper drugs, better quality, less risk, more profit — the logic of indus- 14
trial commerce is powerful. We have found no way to defeat the black-market
drug industry, and the social, financial and technological factors are all
strongly on its side.

Now imagine yourself as a 21st century student, taking entrance exams 15
for the law, or for medicine, while your fellow students enjoy the secret
luxury of an unusually vivid and detailed memory, enhanced IQ, and perfect
concentration. Could you resist that temptation when "everyone else is doing
it" — and the cost of failure means the sacrifice of your ambitions?

Or imagine yourself as a failing television journalist, when the reporters on 16
the other networks can instantly remember every campaign promise the
president ever made. Imagine yourself being a 21st century president, and
facing some cunning Panamanian drug monarch who never sleeps.

The irresistible logic of drugs confounds all attempts at repression, creat- 17
ing a maelstrom of money, guns and violence that has turned our inner cities
into war zones. The problem isn't stopping there, and it's not going to stop
anywhere else in our society, either, because it is part of us, and inherent in
the way we live and think.

Drugs are a technology like others. Like nuclear power, for instance, the 18
tremendous potency of high-tech pharmacology has fearsome side effects.
We are not masters of the destiny of our technology; the changes it brings to
our society may force us into dilemmas we never would have chosen.

That is the milieu in which we were born and raised; it is part of the culture 19
all around us — the culture that invented cosmetic surgery, genetic engineering, antibiotics, telephones, jet travel, and a thousand other glittering short-
cuts to the Artificial Paradise. Our unstoppable cultural hunger for drugs is
overwhelming evidence for this simple fact.

Already, we are investing billions in the basic medical research that will 20
open a Pandora's box. The alternative is Luddism — to virtuously ignore this

medical knowledge and plod on with the burdens of schizophrenia, cancer, AIDS, Alzheimer's disease, and the simple God-given limits of what we used to call "the human condition."

Ladies and gentlemen, we are not going to accept those limits, under any 21 circumstances. We may give them pious lip service, but when it comes to the crunch, we will vote otherwise with our bloodstreams.

Sooner or later, we will stop trying to bail back the sea with a fork, and 22 come to terms with this horrifically powerful transformation in our lives. The war against drugs is a lost cause; the only question is how many will die in the service of empty rhetoric.

AMERICAN DEMAND IS AT THE HEART OF THE CURRENT COCAINE PLAGUE

Joan Beck

The heart of the drug problem is America's insatiable craving for drugs. Until we establish zero tolerance for casual drug use, says syndicated columnist Joan Beck, the problem will only get worse — at enormous human costs.

In careful English, Colombia's weary President Virgilio Barco looked into 1
the television cameras last week and said, "Those of you who depend on cocaine have created the largest, most vicious criminal enterprise the world has ever known."

It was as blunt as he could afford to be, dependent as he now is on what 2
help the U.S. decides to give him against the drug czars who are terrorizing his country virtually at will.

But Barco's real message needs to be driven home: Americans are largely 3
responsible for Colombia's cocaine terrorism.

Unless Americans pay attention to what Barco is saying, all of President 4
Bush's carefully balanced new drug offensive will fall woefully short.

It's Americans who are pouring billions of dollars into South America — 5
reward for Colombians who grow and process and deliver cocaine. It's basically American money that is destabilizing the Colombian government, destroying its legal system, killing innocent people and enriching and empowering evil people who may be so entrenched that legal government is now endangered.

The drug problem isn't caused only by Colombian growers or drug czars 6
or crooked officials or smugglers. They are all responding to an avid, insatiable market. It is largely American demand that is responsible for the supply-side horrors.

Bush did say as much in his talk on Tuesday, putting responsibility for the 7
drug problem on "everyone who uses drugs. Everyone who sells drugs. And every one who looks the other way."

But his words were much too mild to drive home the crucial message. 8

This is an ugly chapter in American history. The richest, most powerful 9
nation in the world is letting its greedy appetite for drugs destroy a poor Third World country and endanger other Andean nations as well. Now we may have to send armed forces resources to Colombia to battle evils largely created by U.S. money and illicit American indulgences.

Those who use drugs, those who sell drugs and those who look the other 10
way are also doing incalculable damage to the U.S. itself.

The billions of dollars that have gone to South America to pay for drugs 11 have exacerbated our dismal balance of trade and damaged our economy.

Far worse, the flood of money that pours into areas of urban poverty in the 12 United States is destroying what chance existed to help many people into stable, self-supporting, mainstream lives.

The suburbanite who drives into a drug-dealing neighborhood to buy 13 crack from a kid on the corner is handing him a powerful and obvious message: The way to get money isn't to stay in school or try to get an entry-level job. The way out of poverty is drugs.

Nothing drug czar William Bennett or Bush or anyone else can devise by 14 way of education will ever be as powerful as the message that comes with the money handed out through the car window in exchange for drugs.

Drug abuse used to be brushed off as a "victimless crime." Tell that to the 15 hundreds of thousands of babies born addicted to the cocaine their mothers took during pregnancy. Try explaining it to the kids as they grow up with damaged brains and other problems.

Cocaine users whose money pays for the flashy lifestyles of drug dealers 16 and indirectly for the drugs that ruin so many inner-city families are doing essentially the same kind of harm as the dealers and pushers. They are just as responsible for the new "no-parent families" where children of an absent father and a crack-using mother are essentially left to fend for themselves.

And the drug users also are responsible for the enormous drain on the 17 American economy their self-indulgence is costing the rest of us. Bush wants $7.9 billion to fight drugs in the coming fiscal year, an increase of about $2.2 billion over current spending. But that's just the tip of an iceberg of social, economic and human costs that push up the bills for welfare, health care, unemployment, low productivity and law enforcement.

The president did call for us to demonstrate "zero tolerance for casual 18 use." He wasn't specific enough about the tougher penalties he said he wanted. And the capacities of law-enforcement agencies, courts and prisons are limited.

But "zero tolerance for casual use" would do more to win the war against 19 drugs than all the expensive measures intended to reduce the supply of narcotics. That includes zero tolerance for drug use by entertainers, athletes, workers, health-care personnel, business executives, parents, government employees, "nice" people from the suburbs and especially everyone who is a role model for young people.

The war against drugs isn't going to be won for us in Colombia or by drug 20 agents seizing record shipments of cocaine in secluded Florida landing strips or by William Bennett or George Bush, but by the most powerful weapon of all; changing social attitudes. It's up to all of us to stop the demand.

It hurts to be ashamed of the United States. 21

DRUG WAR IS LOST; HERE'S WHAT TO DO NOW

Mike Royko

Mike Royko, the street-smart columnist from Chicago, gives five reasons why the drug war is lost. His solution is to legalize drugs. "If people want to sniff away their nose or addle their brain, so be it."

Poor William Bennett, the nation's chief drug warrior. He's outgunned, 1 outnumbered, underfinanced and overwhelmed. In other words, he can't win.

The other side—those who use drugs, make drugs, sell drugs, and profit 2 from drugs—has become too big and powerful.

As we've just seen in Colombia, one of the world's biggest drug suppliers, 3 if a presidential candidate displeases the drug kings, they just kill him.

Sure, the Colombian authorities are putting on a big show, rounding up 4 the usual suspects and all that. But for what? The judges there are afraid that if they send any of the biggies to jail, they'll be murdered, too. Which they will.

And as we've just seen in this country, if the price is right, almost anyone 5 can be corrupted. One of the top federal agents in the famous "French Connection" case has been nailed for being part of a big drug deal. Once he was a hero chasing the bad guys. Now he's one of the bad guys.

There really isn't any "drug war," because the war has long been lost for a 6 number of reasons.

- **Reason one:** Popular demand. Many Americans choose to use drugs. Some are back-alley crackheads who will eventually die. Others are outwardly respectable coke sniffers who will slowly screw up their lives. And still others are pot smokers who won't hurt themselves any more than a person who has two or three martinis after work. Drugs are used at every level of society, from the ghetto to the penthouse.

- **Reason two:** The profits are staggering. The street pusher makes big money. His supplier makes bigger bucks. The smugglers make even more. The foreign suppliers make billions. Entire governments are corrupted or intimidated. Law-enforcement people, from the patrolman up to and beyond judges, are bought off. And when bribe money doesn't talk, automatic weapons do.

- **Reason three:** There just aren't enough cops to make a tiny dent in the drug industry. Chicago has about 3 million people, give or take a few hundred thousand illegal aliens.

  That gives us one cop for every 265 people. But not really. At any given moment, some are on vacation, some on sick leave, some shuffling papers. And they're working three shifts and on weekends. So realistically, we probably don't have one working cop for every 1,500 people.

And they're busy with other chores — chasing speeders and drunken drivers; breaking up family fights or tavern brawls; looking for muggers, porch climbers, rapists, flashers, killers, and people who don't buy their auto stickers.

There are 135 cops assigned to full-time narcotics duty. That's one for every 22,222 Chicagoans. So if every dealer *and* cokehead did his or her selling and sniffing on a street in broad daylight, the local narcs couldn't keep up with them. And if they did — well, that leads us to the next problem.

- **Reason four:** Where would we put them? The local jails, the state prisons, the federal prisons — just about every slammer in the country — are overcrowded. Build more, you say? We are, and the taxpayers are already screaming that they pay too much.

  Hire more cops? That costs money. Build rehabilitation centers? Drug-detention camps? More money. We want it both ways — solve the problem, but don't send the bill to me.

- **Reason five:** The local authorities say they can't cope with the drug industry, that the flow has to be stopped at the borders or at the sources. The problem is that there are thousands of ways and thousands of places to bring drugs in. And there aren't enough border patrols, Coast Guard boats and planes, federal narcs or anything else to stop the flow.

  And we're not going to send troops into Colombia, Peru, Mexico, or any of the other big exporting nations to shoot it out with the armies of the drug cartels.

  Those governments don't want us there. Even if they did, we'd have to become a permanent occupying military force, which is impossible. And once we left, the drug tycoons would be back in business. Meanwhile, our importers would find other sources. So what is the solution?

Well, Bill Bennett can keep making speeches and pleading for more federal bucks, while knowing he won't get them. And we can keep telling our children to "just say no," while a certain percentage of them will be saying yes. 7

Or we can say: Let's call off the war and make the best of the peace. We can view drugs the way we view liquor. 8

If you want it, and are of legal age and have the price, you can have booze. If you want to become a lush, that's a problem for you, your liver, and your family. 9

Liquor can be a terrible curse for some people, but for most it isn't. And at 10 least we don't have gangs blasting one another and innocent bystanders for territorial rights. Plus, we collect a tax on every sip.

Yes, I'm saying that we might as well legalize the junk. Put taxes on it, 11 license the distributors, establish age limits, and treat it like hooch. If people want to sniff away their nose or addle their brain, so be it.

They're doing it now, anyway, and at least we'd be rid of the gun battles, 12 the corruption, and the wasted money and effort trying to save the brains and noses of those who don't want them saved.

It is this society's position that if you choose to be a falling-down drunken 13 bum and wind up in the gutter, that is your right. So if you want to sniff or snort or puff your way into the gutter, that should be your right, too.

AGAINST THE LEGALIZATION OF DRUGS

James Q. Wilson

Noted professor and former member of the National Council for Drug Abuse Prevention James Q. Wilson compares contemporary arguments for cocaine legalization to earlier arguments for heroin legalization. Focusing on the disquieting consequences, he rejects drug legalization as costly and dehumanizing, leading to huge increases in crime, addiction, and violence.

In 1972, the President appointed me chairman of the National Advisory   1
Council for Drug Abuse Prevention. Created by Congress, the Council was charged with providing guidance on how best to coordinate the national war on drugs. (Yes, we called it a war then, too.) In those days, the drug we were chiefly concerned with was heroin. When I took office, heroin use had been increasing dramatically. Everybody was worried that this increase would continue. Such phrases as "heroin epidemic" were commonplace.

That same year, the eminent economist Milton Friedman published an   2
essay in *Newsweek* in which he called for legalizing heroin. His argument was on two grounds: as a matter of ethics, the government has no right to tell people not to use heroin (or to drink or to commit suicide); as a matter of economics, the prohibition of drug use imposes costs on society that far exceed the benefits. Others, such as the psychoanalyst Thomas Szasz, made the same argument.

We did not take Friedman's advice. (Government commissions rarely do.) I   3
do not recall that we even discussed legalizing heroin, though we did discuss (but did not take action on) legalizing a drug, cocaine, that many people then argued was benign. Our marching orders were to figure out how to win the war on heroin, not to run up the white flag of surrender.

That was 1972. Today, we have the same number of heroin addicts that we   4
had then—half a million, give or take a few thousand. Having that many heroin addicts is no trivial matter; these people deserve our attention. But not having had an increase in that number for over fifteen years is also something that deserves our attention. What happened to the "heroin epidemic" that many people once thought would overwhelm us?

The facts are clear: a more or less stable pool of heroin addicts has been   5
getting older, with relatively few new recruits. In 1976 the average age of heroin users who appeared in hospital emergency rooms was about twenty-seven; ten years later it was thirty-two. More than two-thirds of all heroin users appearing in emergency rooms are now over the age of thirty. Back in the early 1970's, when heroin got onto the national political agenda, the

typical heroin addict was much younger, often a teenager. Household surveys show the same thing—the rate of opiate use (which includes heroin) has been flat for the better part of two decades. More fine-grained studies of inner-city neighborhoods confirm this. John Boyle and Ann Brunswick found that the percentage of young blacks in Harlem who used heroin fell from 8 percent in 1970–71 to about 3 percent in 1975–76.

Why did heroin lose its appeal for young people? When the young blacks   6 in Harlem were asked why they stopped, more than half mentioned "trouble with the law" or "high cost" (and high cost is, of course, directly the result of law enforcement). Two-thirds said that heroin hurt their health; nearly all said they had had a bad experience with it. We need not rely, however, simply on what they said. In New York City in 1973–75, the street price of heroin rose dramatically and its purity sharply declined, probably as a result of the heroin shortage caused by the success of the Turkish government in reducing the supply of opium base and of the French government in closing down heroin-processing laboratories located in and around Marseilles. These were short-lived gains for, just as Friedman predicted, alternative sources of supply—mostly in Mexico—quickly emerged. But the three-year heroin shortage interrupted the easy recruitment of new users.

Health and related problems were no doubt part of the reason for the   7 reduced flow of recruits. Over the preceding years, Harlem youth had watched as more and more heroin users died of overdoses, were poisoned by adulterated doses, or acquired hepatitis from dirty needles. The word got around: heroin can kill you. By 1974 new hepatitis cases and drug-overdose deaths had dropped to a fraction of what they had been in 1970.

Alas, treatment did not seem to explain much of the cessation in drug use.   8 Treatment programs can and do help heroin addicts, but treatment did not explain the drop in the number of *new* users (who by definition had never been in treatment) nor even much of the reduction in the number of experienced users.

No one knows how much of the decline to attribute to personal observa-   9 tion as opposed to high prices or reduced supply. But other evidence suggests strongly that price and supply played a large role. In 1972 the National Advisory Council was especially worried by the prospect that U.S. servicemen returning to this country from Vietnam would bring their heroin habits with them. Fortunately, a brilliant study by Lee Robins of Washington University in St. Louis put that fear to rest. She measured drug use of Vietnam veterans shortly after they had returned home. Though many had used heroin regularly while in Southeast Asia, most gave up the habit when back in the United States. The reason: here, heroin was less available and sanctions on its use were more pronounced. Of course, if a veteran had been willing to pay enough—which might have meant traveling to another city and would certainly have meant making an illegal contact with a disreputable dealer in a threatening neighborhood in order to acquire a (possibly) dangerous dose — he could have sustained his drug habit. Most veterans were unwilling to pay this price, and so their drug use declined or disappeared.

Reliving the Past

Suppose we had taken Friedman's advice in 1972. What would have hap- 10 pened? We cannot be entirely certain, but at a minimum we would have placed the young heroin addicts (and, above all, the prospective addicts) in a very different position from the one in which they actually found themselves. Heroin would have been legal. Its price would have been reduced by 95 percent (minus whatever we chose to recover in taxes). Now that it could be sold by the same people who make aspirin, its quality would have been assured — no poisons, no adulterants. Sterile hypodermic needles would have been readily available at the neighborhood drugstore, probably at the same counter where the heroin was sold. No need to travel to big cities or unfamiliar neighborhoods — heroin could have been purchased anywhere, perhaps by mail order.

There would no longer have been any financial or medical reason to avoid 11 heroin use. Anybody could have afforded it. We might have tried to prevent children from buying it, but as we have learned from our efforts to prevent minors from buying alcohol and tobacco, young people have a way of penetrating markets theoretically reserved for adults. Returning Vietnam veterans would have discovered that Omaha and Raleigh had been converted into the pharmaceutical equivalent of Saigon.

Under these circumstances, can we doubt for a moment that heroin use 12 would have grown exponentially? Or that a vastly larger supply of new users would have been recruited? Professor Friedman is a Nobel Prize–winning economist whose understanding of market forces is profound. What did he think would happen to consumption under his legalized regime? Here are his words: "Legalizing drugs might increase the number of addicts, but it is not clear that it would. Forbidden fruit is attractive, particularly to the young."

Really? I suppose that we should expect no increase in Porsche sales if we 13 cut the price by 95 percent, no increase in whiskey sales if we cut the price by a comparable amount — because young people only want fast cars and strong liquor when they are "forbidden." Perhaps Friedman's uncharacteristic lapse from the obvious implications of price theory can be explained by a misunderstanding of how drug users are recruited. In his 1972 essay he said that "drug addicts are deliberately made by pushers, who give likely prospects their first few doses free." If drugs were legal it would not pay anybody to produce addicts, because everybody would buy from the cheapest source. But as every drug expert knows, pushers do not produce addicts. Friends or acquaintances do. In fact, pushers are usually reluctant to deal with non-users because a non-user could be an undercover cop. Drug use spreads in the same way any fad or fashion spreads: somebody who is already a user urges his friend to try, or simply shows already-eager friends how to do it.

But we need not rely on speculation, however plausible, that lowered **14** prices and more abundant supplies would have increased heroin usage. Great Britain once followed such a policy and with almost exactly those results. Until the mid-1960's, British physicians were allowed to prescribe heroin to certain classes of addicts. (Possessing these drugs without a doctor's prescription remained a criminal offense.) For many years this policy worked well enough because the addict patients were typically middle-class people who had become dependent on opiate painkillers while undergoing hospital treatment. There was no drug culture. The British system worked for many years, not because it prevented drug abuse, but because there was no problem of drug abuse that would test the system.

All that changed in the 1960's. A few unscrupulous doctors began passing **15** out heroin in wholesale amounts. One doctor prescribed almost 600,000 heroin tablets — that is, over thirteen pounds — in just one year. A youthful drug culture emerged with a demand for drugs far different from that of the older addicts. As a result, the British government required doctors to refer users to government-run clinics to receive their heroin.

But the shift to clinics did not curtail the growth in heroin use. Through- **16** out the 1960's the number of addicts increased — the late John Kaplan of Stanford estimated by fivefold — in part as a result of the diversion of heroin from clinic patients to new users on the streets. An addict would bargain with the clinic doctor over how big a dose he would receive. The patient wanted as much as he could get, the doctor wanted to give as little as needed. The patient had an advantage in this conflict because the doctor could not be certain how much was really needed. Many patients would use some of their "maintenance" dose and sell the remaining part to friends, thereby recruiting new addicts. As the clinics learned of this, they began to shift their treatment away from heroin and toward methadone, an addictive drug that, when taken orally, does not produce a "high" but will block the withdrawal pains associated with heroin abstinence.

Whether what happened in England in the 1960's was a mini-epidemic or **17** an epidemic depends on whether one looks at numbers or at rates of change. Compared to the United States, the numbers were small. In 1960 there were 68 heroin addicts known to the British government; by 1968 there were 2,000 in treatment and many more who refused treatment. (They would refuse in part because they did not want to get methadone at a clinic if they could get heroin on the street.) Richard Hartnoll estimates that the actual number of addicts in England is five times the number officially registered. At a minimum, the number of British addicts increased by thirtyfold in ten years; the actual increase may have been much larger.

In the early 1980's the numbers began to rise again, and this time nobody 18 doubted that a real epidemic was at hand. The increase was estimated to be 40 percent a year. By 1982 there were thought to be 20,000 heroin users in London alone. Geoffrey Pearson reports that many cities—Glasgow, Liverpool, Manchester, and Sheffield among them—are now experiencing a drug problem that once had been largely confined to London. The problem, again, was supply. The country was being flooded with cheap, high-quality heroin, first from Iran and then from Southeast Asia.

The United States began the 1960's with a much larger number of heroin 19 addicts and probably a bigger at-risk population than was the case in Great Britain. Even though it would be foolhardy to suppose that the British system, if installed here, would have worked the same way or with the same results, it would be equally foolhardy to suppose that a combination of heroin available from leaky clinics and from street dealers who faced only minimal law-enforcement risks would not have produced a much greater increase in heroin use than we actually experienced. My guess is that if we had allowed either doctors or clinics to prescribe heroin, we would have had far worse results than were produced in Britain, if for no other reason than the vastly larger number of addicts with which we began. We would have had to find some way to police thousands (not scores) of physicians and hundreds (not dozens) of clinics. If the British civil service found it difficult to keep heroin in the hands of addicts and out of the hands of recruits when it was dealing with a few hundred people, how well would the American civil service have accomplished the same tasks when dealing with tens of thousands of people?

Back to the Future

Now cocaine, especially in its potent form, crack, is the focus of attention. 20 Now as in 1972 the government is trying to reduce its use. Now as then some people are advocating legalization. Is there any more reason to yield to those arguments today than there was almost two decades ago?*

I think not. If we had yielded in 1972 we almost certainly would have had 21 today a permanent population of several million, not several hundred thousand, heroin addicts. If we yield now we will have a far more serious problem with cocaine.

---

*I do not here take up the question of marijuana. For a variety of reasons—its widespread use and its lesser tendency to addict—it presents a different problem from cocaine or heroin. For a penetrating analysis, see Mark Kleiman, *Marijuana: Costs of Abuse, Costs of Control* (Greenwood Press, 217 pp., $37.95).

Crack is worse than heroin by almost any measure. Heroin produces a 22
pleasant drowsiness and, if hygienically administered, has only the physical
side effects of constipation and sexual impotence. Regular heroin use inca-
pacitates many users, especially poor ones, for any productive work or social
responsibility. They will sit nodding on a street corner, helpless but at least
harmless. By contrast, regular cocaine use leaves the user neither helpless
nor harmless. When smoked (as with crack) or injected, cocaine produces
instant, intense, and short-lived euphoria. The experience generates a powerful desire to repeat it. If the drug is readily available, repeat use will occur.
Those people who progress to "bingeing" on cocaine become devoted to the
drug and its effects to the exclusion of almost all other considerations — job,
family, children, sleep, food, even sex. Dr. Frank Gawin at Yale and Dr.
Everett Ellinwood at Duke report that a substantial percentage of all high-
dose, binge users become uninhibited, impulsive, hypersexual, compulsive,
irritable, and hyperactive. Their moods vacillate dramatically, leading at times
to violence and homicide.

Women are much more likely to use crack than heroin, and if they are 23
pregnant, the effects on their babies are tragic. Douglas Besharov, who has
been following the effects of drugs on infants for twenty years, writes that
nothing he learned about heroin prepared him for the devastation of cocaine.
Cocaine harms the fetus and can lead to physical deformities or neurological
damage. Some crack babies have for all practical purposes suffered a dis-
abling stroke while still in the womb. The long-term consequences of this
brain damage are lowered cognitive ability and the onset of mood disorders.
Besharov estimates that about 30,000 to 50,000 such babies are born every
year, about 7,000 in New York City alone. There may be ways to treat such
infants, but from everything we now know the treatment will be long,
difficult, and expensive. Worse, the mothers who are most likely to produce
crack babies are precisely the ones who, because of poverty or temperament,
are least able and willing to obtain such treatment. In fact, anecdotal evidence
suggests that crack mothers are likely to abuse their infants.

The notion that abusing drugs such as cocaine is a "victimless crime" is 24
not only absurd but dangerous. Even ignoring the fetal drug syndrome,
crack-dependent people are, like heroin addicts, individuals who regularly
victimize their children by neglect, their spouses by improvidence, their
employers by lethargy, and their coworkers by carelessness. Society is not
and could never be a collection of autonomous individuals. We all have a
stake in ensuring that each of us displays a minimal level of dignity, responsibility, and empathy. We cannot, of course, coerce people into goodness, but
we can and should insist that some standards must be met if society itself —
on which the very existence of the human personality depends — is to persist.
Drawing the line that defines those standards is difficult and contentious, but
if crack and heroin use do not fall below it, what does?

The advocates of legalization will respond by suggesting that my picture is   25
overdrawn. Ethan Nadelmann of Princeton argues that the risk of legalization is less than most people suppose. Over 20 million Americans between the
ages of eighteen and twenty-five have tried cocaine (according to a government survey), but only a quarter million use it daily. From this Nadelmann
concludes that at most 3 percent of all young people who try cocaine develop
a problem with it. The implication is clear: make the drug legal and we only
have to worry about 3 percent of our youth.

The implication rests on a logical fallacy and a factual error. The fallacy is   26
this: the percentage of occasional cocaine users who become binge users
when the drug is illegal (and thus expensive and hard to find) tells us
nothing about the percentage who will become dependent when the drug is
legal (and thus cheap and abundant). Drs. Gawin and Ellinwood report, in
common with several other researchers, that controlled or occasional use of
cocaine changes to compulsive and frequent use "when access to the drug
increases" or when the user switches from snorting to smoking. More cocaine
more potently administered alters, perhaps sharply, the proportion of "controlled" users who become heavy users.

The factual error is this: the federal survey Nadelmann quotes was done in   27
1985, *before* crack had become common. Thus the probability of becoming
dependent on cocaine was derived from the responses of users who snorted
the drug. The speed and potency of cocaine's action increases dramatically
when it is smoked. We do not yet know how greatly the advent of crack
increases the risk of dependency, but all the clinical evidence suggests that
the increase is likely to be large.

It is possible that some people will not become heavy users even when the   28
drug is readily available in its most potent form. So far there are no scientific
grounds for predicting who will and who will not become dependent. Neither
socio-economic background nor personality traits differentiate between casual and intensive users. Thus, the only way to settle the question of who is
correct about the effect of easy availability on drug use, Nadelmann or Gawin
and Ellinwood, is to try it and see. But that social experiment is so risky as to
be no experiment at all, for if cocaine is legalized and if the rate of its abusive
use increases dramatically, there is no way to put the genie back in the bottle,
and it is not a kindly genie.

Have We Lost?

Many people who agree that there are risks in legalizing cocaine or heroin   29
still favor it because, they think, we have lost the war on drugs. "Nothing we
have done has worked" and the current federal policy is just "more of the
same." Whatever the costs of greater drug use, surely they would be less
than the costs of our present, failed efforts.

That is exactly what I was told in 1972 — and heroin is not quite as bad a **30** drug as cocaine. We did not surrender and we did not lose. We did not win, either. What the nation accomplished then was what most efforts to save people from themselves accomplish: the problem was contained and the number of victims minimized, all at a considerable cost in law enforcement and increased crime. Was the cost worth it? I think so, but others may disagree. What are the lives of would-be addicts worth? I recall some people saying to me then, "Let them kill themselves." I was appalled. Happily, such views did not prevail.

Have we lost today? Not at all. High-rate cocaine use is not commonplace. **31** The National Institute of Drug Abuse (NIDA) reports that less than 5 percent of high-school seniors used cocaine within the last thirty days. Of course this survey misses young people who have dropped out of school and miscounts those who lie on the questionnaire, but even if we inflate the NIDA estimate by some plausible percentage, it is still not much above 5 percent. Medical examiners reported in 1987 that about 1,500 died from cocaine use: hospital emergency rooms reported about 30,000 admissions related to cocaine abuse.

These are not small numbers, but neither are they evidence of a nationwide **32** plague that threatens to engulf us all. Moreover, cities vary greatly in the proportion of people who are involved with cocaine. To get city-level data we need to turn to drug tests carried out on arrested persons, who obviously are more likely to be drug users than the average citizen. The National Institute of Justice, through its Drug Use Forecasting (DUF) project, collects urinalysis data on arrestees in 22 cities. As we have already seen, opiate (chiefly heroin) use has been flat or declining in most of these cities over the last decade. Cocaine use has gone up sharply, but with great variation among cities. New York, Philadelphia, and Washington, D.C., all report that two-thirds or more of their arrestees tested positive for cocaine, but in Portland, San Antonio, and Indianapolis the percentage was one-third or less.

In some neighborhoods, of course, matters have reached crisis propor- **33** tions. Gangs control the streets, shootings terrorize residents, and drug-dealing occurs in plain view. The police seem barely able to contain matters. But in these neighborhoods — unlike at Palo Alto cocktail parties — the people are not calling for legalization, they are calling for help. And often not much help has come. Many cities are willing to do almost anything about the drug problem except spend more money on it. The federal government cannot change that; only local voters and politicians can. It is not clear that they will.

It took about ten years to contain heroin. We have had experience with **34** crack for only about three or four years. Each year we spend perhaps $11 billion on law enforcement (and some of that goes to deal with marijuana) and perhaps $2 billion on treatment. Large sums, but not sums that should lead anyone to say, "We just can't afford this any more."

The illegality of drugs increases crime, partly because some users turn to **35** crime to pay for their habits, partly because some users are stimulated by certain drugs (such as crack or PCP) to act more violently or ruthlessly than they otherwise would, and partly because criminal organizations seeking to control drug supplies use force to manage their markets. These also are serious costs, but no one knows how much they would be reduced if drugs were legalized. Addicts would no longer steal to pay black-market prices for drugs, a real gain. But some, perhaps a great deal, of that gain would be offset by the great increase in the number of addicts. These people, nodding on heroin or living in the delusion-ridden high of cocaine, would hardly be ideal employees. Many would steal simply to support themselves, since snatch-and-grab, opportunistic crime can be managed even by people unable to hold a regular job or plan an elaborate crime. Those British addicts who get their supplies from government clinics are not models of law-abiding decency. Most are in crime, and though their per-capita rate of criminality may be lower thanks to the cheapness of their drugs, the total volume of crime they produce may be quite large. Of course, society could decide to support all unemployable addicts on welfare, but that would mean that gains from lowered rates of crime would have to be offset by large increases in welfare budgets.

Proponents of legalization claim that the costs of having more addicts **36** around would be largely if not entirely offset by having more money available with which to treat and care for them. The money would come from taxes levied on the sale of heroin and cocaine.

To obtain this fiscal dividend, however, legalization's supporters must first **37** solve an economic dilemma. If they want to raise a lot of money to pay for welfare and treatment, the tax rate on the drugs will have to be quite high. Even if they themselves do not want a high rate, the politicians' love of "sin taxes" would probably guarantee that it would be high anyway. But the higher the tax, the higher the price of the drug, and the higher the price the greater the likelihood that addicts will turn to crime to find the money for it and that criminal organizations will be formed to sell tax-free drugs at below-market rates. If we managed to keep taxes (and thus prices) low, we would get that much less money to pay for welfare and treatment and more people could afford to become addicts. There may be an optimal tax rate for drugs that maximizes revenue while minimizing crime, bootlegging, and the recruitment of new addicts, but our experience with alcohol does not suggest that we know how to find it.

The Benefits of Illegality

The advocates of legalization find nothing to be said in favor of the current **38** system except, possibly, that it keeps the number of addicts smaller than it would otherwise be. In fact, the benefits are more substantial than that.

First, treatment. All the talk about providing "treatment on demand" **39**
implies that there is a demand for treatment. That is not quite right. There are
some drug-dependent people who genuinely want treatment and will remain
in it if offered; they should receive it. But there are far more who want only
short-term help after a bad crash: once stabilized and bathed, they are back
on the street again, hustling. And even many of the addicts who enroll in a
program honestly wanting help drop out after a short while when they
discover that help takes time and commitment. Drug-dependent people have
very short time horizons and a weak capacity for commitment. These two
groups — those looking for a quick fix and those unable to stick with a
long-term fix — are not easily helped. Even if we increase the number of
treatment slots — as we should — we would have to do something to make
treatment more effective.

One thing that can often make it more effective is compulsion. Douglas **40**
Anglin of UCLA, in common with many other researchers, has found that the
longer one stays in a treatment program, the better the chances of a reduction
in drug dependency. But he, again like most other researchers, has found
that drop-out rates are high. He has also found, however, that patients who
enter treatment under legal compulsion stay in the program longer than
those not subject to such pressure. His research on the California civil-com-
mitment program, for example, found that heroin users involved with its
required drug-testing program had over the long term a lower rate of heroin
use than similar addicts who were free of such constraints. If for many addicts
compulsion is a useful component of treatment, it is not clear how compulsion could be achieved in a society in which purchasing, possessing, and
using the drug were legal. It could be managed, I suppose, but I would not
want to have to answer the challenge from the American Civil Liberties Union
that it is wrong to compel a person to undergo treatment for consuming a
legal commodity.

Next, education. We are now investing substantially in drug-education **41**
programs in the schools. Though we do not yet know for certain what will
work, there are some promising leads. But I wonder how credible such
programs would be if they were aimed at dissuading children from doing
something perfectly legal. We could, of course, treat drug education like
smoking education: inhaling crack and inhaling tobacco are both legal, but
you should not do it because it is bad for you. That tobacco is bad for you is
easily shown; the Surgeon General has seen to that. But what do we say
about crack? It is pleasurable, but devoting yourself to so much pleasure is
not a good idea (though perfectly legal)? Unlike tobacco, cocaine will not give
you cancer or emphysema, but it will lead you to neglect your duties to
family, job, and neighborhood? Everybody is doing cocaine, but you should
not?

Again, it might be possible under a legalized regime to have effective **42**
drug-prevention programs, but their effectiveness would depend heavily, I

think, on first having decided that cocaine use, like tobacco use, is purely a matter of practical consequences; no fundamental moral significance attaches to either. But if we believe—as I do—that dependency on certain mind-altering drugs *is* a moral issue and that their illegality rests in part on their immorality, then legalizing them undercuts, if it does not eliminate altogether, the moral message.

That message is at the root of the distinction we now make between   **43** nicotine and cocaine. Both are highly addictive; both have harmful physical effects. But we treat the two drugs differently, not simply because nicotine is so widely used as to be beyond the reach of effective prohibition, but because its use does not destroy the user's essential humanity. Tobacco shortens one's life, cocaine debases it. Nicotine alters one's habits, cocaine alters one's soul. The heavy use of crack, unlike the heavy use of tobacco, corrodes those natural sentiments of sympathy and duty that constitute our human nature and make possible our social life. To say, as does Nadelmann, that distinguishing morally between tobacco and cocaine is "little more than a transient prejudice" is close to saying that morality itself is but a prejudice.

The Alcohol Problem

Now we have arrived where many arguments about legalizing drugs begin: is   **44** there any reason to treat heroin and cocaine differently from the way we treat alcohol?

There is no easy answer to that question because, as with so many human   **45** problems, one cannot decide simply on the basis either of moral principle or of individual consequences; one has to temper any policy by a common-sense judgment of what is possible. Alcohol, like heroin, cocaine, PCP, and marijuana, is a drug—that is, a mood-altering substance—and consumed to excess it certainly has harmful consequences: auto accidents, barroom fights, bedroom shootings. It is also, for some people, addictive. We cannot confidently compare the addictive powers of these drugs, but the best evidence suggests that crack and heroin are much more addictive than alcohol.

Many people, Nadelmann included, argue that since the health and finan-   **46** cial costs of alcohol abuse are so much higher than those of cocaine or heroin abuse, it is hypocritical folly to devote our efforts to preventing cocaine or drug use. But as Mark Kleiman of Harvard has pointed out, this comparison is quite misleading. What Nadelmann is doing is showing that a *legalized* drug (alcohol) produces greater social harm than *illegal* ones (cocaine and heroin). But of course. Suppose that in the 1920's we had made heroin and cocaine legal and alcohol illegal. Can anyone doubt that Nadelmann would now be writing that it is folly to continue our ban on alcohol because cocaine and heroin are so much more harmful?

And let there be no doubt about it—widespread heroin and cocaine use **47** are associated with all manner of ills. Thomas Bewley found that the mortality rate of British heroin addicts in 1968 was 28 times as high as the death rate of the same age group of non-addicts, even though in England at the time an addict could obtain free or low-cost heroin and clean needles from British clinics. Perform the following mental experiment: suppose we legalized heroin and cocaine in this country. In what proportion of auto fatalities would the state police report that the driver was nodding off on heroin or recklessly driving on a coke high? In what proportion of spouse-assault and child-abuse cases would the local police report that crack was involved? In what proportion of industrial accidents would safety investigators report that the forklift or drill-press operator was in a drug-induced stupor or frenzy? We do not know exactly what the proportion would be, but anyone who asserts that it would not be much higher than it is now would have to believe that these drugs have little appeal except when they are illegal. And that is nonsense.

An advocate of legalization might concede that social harm—perhaps **48** harm equivalent to that already produced by alcohol—would follow from making cocaine and heroin generally available. But at least, he might add, we would have the problem "out in the open" where it could be treated as a matter of "public health." That is well and good, *if* we knew how to treat—that is, cure—heroin and cocaine abuse. But we do not know how to do it for all the people who would need such help. We are having only limited success in coping with chronic alcoholics. Addictive behavior is immensely difficult to change, and the best methods for changing it—living in drug-free therapeutic communities, becoming faithful members of Alcoholics Anonymous or Narcotics Anonymous—require great personal commitment, a quality that is, alas, in short supply among the very persons—young people, disadvantaged people—who are often most at risk for addiction.

Suppose that today we had, not 15 million alcohol abusers, but half a **49** million. Suppose that we already knew what we have learned from our long experience with the widespread use of alcohol. Would we make whiskey legal? I do not know, but I suspect there would be a lively debate. The Surgeon General would remind us of the risks alcohol poses to pregnant women. The National Highway Traffic Safety Administration would point to the likelihood of more highway fatalities caused by drunk drivers. The Food and Drug Administration might find that there is a non-trivial increase in cancer associated with alcohol consumption. At the same time the police would report great difficulty in keeping illegal whiskey out of our cities, officers being corrupted by bootleggers, and alcohol addicts often resorting to crime to feed their habit. Libertarians, for their part, would argue that every citizen has a right to drink anything he wishes and that drinking is, in any event, a "victimless crime."

However the debate might turn out, the central fact would be that the 50 problem was still, at that point, a small one. The government cannot legislate away the addictive tendencies in all of us, nor can it remove completely even the most dangerous addictive substances. But it can cope with harms when the harms are still manageable.

Science and Addiction

One advantage of containing a problem while it is still containable is that it 51 buys time for science to learn more about it and perhaps to discover a cure. Almost unnoticed in the current debate over legalizing drugs is that basic science has made rapid strides in identifying the underlying neurological processes involved in some forms of addiction. Stimulants such as cocaine and amphetamines alter the way certain brain cells communicate with one another. That alteration is complex and not entirely understood, but in simplified form it involves modifying the way in which a neurotransmitter called dopamine sends signals from one cell to another.

When dopamine crosses the synapse between two cells, it is in effect 52 carrying a message from the first cell to activate the second one. In certain parts of the brain that message is experienced as pleasure. After the message is delivered, the dopamine returns to the first cell. Cocaine apparently blocks this return, or "reuptake," so that the excited cell and others nearby continued to send pleasure messages. When the exaggerated high produced by cocaine-influenced dopamine finally ends, the brain cells may (in ways that are still a matter of dispute) suffer from an extreme lack of dopamine, thereby making the individual unable to experience any pleasure at all. This would explain why cocaine users often feel so depressed after enjoying the drug. Stimulants may also affect the way in with other neurotransmitters, such as serotonin and noradrenaline, operate.

Whatever the exact mechanism may be, once it is identified it becomes 53 possible to use drugs to block either the effect of cocaine or its tendency to produce dependency. There have already been experiments using desipramine, imipramine, bromocriptine, carbamazepine, and other chemicals. There are some promising results.

Tragically, we spend very little on such research, and the agencies funding 54 it have not in the past occupied very influential or visible posts in the federal bureaucracy. If there is one aspect of the "war on drugs" metaphor that I dislike, it is its tendency to focus attention almost exclusively on the troops in the trenches, whether engaged in enforcement or treatment, and away from the research-and-development efforts back on the home front where the war may ultimately be decided.

I believe that the prospects of scientists in controlling addiction will be 55
strongly influenced by the size and character of the problem they face. If the
problem is a few hundred thousand chronic, high-dose users of an illegal
product, the chances of making a difference at a reasonable cost will be much
greater than if the problem is a few million chronic users of legal substances.
Once a drug is legal, not only will its use increase but many of those who then
use it will prefer the drug to the treatment: they will want the pleasure,
whatever the cost to themselves or their families, and they will resist —
probably successfully — any effort to wean them away from experiencing the
high that comes from inhaling a legal substance.

If I Am Wrong . . .

No one can know what our society would be like if we changed the law to 56
make access to cocaine, heroin, and PCP easier. I believe, for reasons given,
that the result would be a sharp increase in use, a more widespread degrada-
tion of the human personality, and a greater rate of accidents and violence.

I may be wrong. If I am, then we will needlessly have incurred heavy costs 57
in law enforcement and some forms of criminality. But if I am right, and the
legalizers prevail anyway, then we will have consigned millions of people,
hundreds of thousands of infants, and hundreds of neighborhoods to a life of
oblivion and disease. To the lives and families destroyed by alcohol we will
have added countless more destroyed by cocaine, heroin, PCP, and whatever
else a basement scientist can invent.

Human character is formed by society; indeed, human character is incon- 58
ceivable without society, and good character is less likely in a bad society.
Will we, in the name of an abstract doctrine of radical individualism, and with
the false comfort of suspect predictions, decide to take the chance that
somehow individual decency can survive amid a more general level of degra-
dation?

I think not. The American people are too wise for that, whatever the 59
academic essayists and cocktail-party pundits may say. But if Americans
today are less wise than I suppose, then Americans at some future time will
look back on us now and wonder, what kind of people were they that they
could have done such a thing?

FOR CLASS DISCUSSION

1. Analyze and evaluate the dispute on the legalization of drugs by applying the first set of guide questions from pages 443–444. How do you account for the enormous disagreements between Wilson and those arguing that drugs should be legalized?

2. Choose one of the arguments for closer analysis, applying the second set of guide questions on page 444.

OPTIONAL WRITING ASSIGNMENT   Your state has an initiative on the ballot to legalize all drugs. Because you are a well-known writer of book blurbs, celebrated for your ability to summarize seven-hundred-page tomes in a few paragraphs, you have been asked by both sides to write up their side of the case for the voters' pamphlet. You can't help yourself. You're broke. You take on both clients. Now the day of truth has arrived. Your deadline is tomorrow. Drawing on the preceding essays, personal experience, and any other research you may have done, write two-hundred-fifty-word arguments for and against drug legalization suitable for use in a voting pamphlet.

GLOBAL WARMING: HOW SERIOUS IS THE GREENHOUSE EFFECT? WHAT SHOULD AMERICA DO ABOUT IT?

ENDLESS SUMMER: LIVING WITH THE GREENHOUSE EFFECT

Andrew C. Revkin

Claiming that global warming is coming and may in fact already be here, Andrew C. Revkin predicts alarming consequences ranging from loss of coastal lands to devastating droughts. "The only way to eliminate the greenhouse problem completely would be to return the world to its preindustrial state."

On June 23 (1988) the United States sizzled as thermometers topped 100   1
degrees in 45 cities from coast to coast: 102 in Sacramento; 103 in Lincoln, Nebraska; 101 in Richmond, Virginia. In the nation's heartland the searing heat was accompanied by a ruinous drought that ravaged crops and prompted talk of a dust bowl to rival that of the 1930s. Heat waves and droughts are nothing new, of course. But on that stifling June day a top atmospheric scientist testifying on Capitol Hill had a disturbing message for his senatorial audience: Get used to it.

This wasn't just a bad year, James Hansen of the NASA Goddard Institute   2 for Space Shuttles told the Senate committee, or even the start of a bad decade. Rather, he could state with "99 percent confidence" that a recent, persistent rise in global temperature was a climatic signal he and his colleagues had long been expecting. Others were still hedging their bets, arguing there was room for doubt. But Hansen was willing to say what no one had dared to say before. "The greenhouse effect," he claimed, "has been detected and is changing our climate now."

Until this year, despite dire warnings from climatologists, the greenhouse   3
effect has seemed somehow academic and far off. The idea behind it is simple: gases accumulating in the atmosphere as by-products of human industry and agriculture — carbon dioxide, mostly, but also methane, nitrous oxide, ozone, and chlorofluorocarbons — let in the sun's warming rays but don't let excess heat escape. As a result, mean global temperature has probably been rising for decades. But the rise has been so gradual that it has been masked by the much greater, and ordinary, year-to-year swings in world temperature.

Not anymore, said Hansen. The 1980s have already seen the four hottest   4
years on record, and 1988 is almost certain to be hotter still. Moreover, the seasonal, regional, and atmospheric patterns of rising temperature — greater warming in winters than summers, greater warming at high latitudes than near the equator, and a cooling in the stratosphere while the lower atmosphere is warmer — jibe with what computer models predict should happen with greenhouse heating. And the warming comes at a time when, by rights, Earth should actually be cooler than normal. The sun's radiance has dropped slightly since the 1970s, and dust thrown up by recent volcanic eruptions, especially that of Mexico's El Chichon in 1982, should be keeping some sunlight from reaching the planet.

Even though most climatologists think Hansen's claims are premature,   5
they agree that warming is on the way. Carbon dioxide levels are 25 percent higher now than they were in 1860, and the atmosphere's burden of greenhouse gases is expected to keep growing. By the middle of the next century the resulting warming could boost global mean temperatures from three to nine degrees Fahrenheit. That doesn't sound like much, but it equals the temperature rise since the end of the last ice age, and the consequences could be devastating. Weather patterns could shift, bringing drought to once fertile areas and heavy rains to fragile deserts that cannot handle them. As run-off from melting glaciers increases and warming seawater expands, sea level could rise as much as six feet, inundating low-lying coastal areas and islands. There would be dramatic disruptions of agriculture, water resources, fisheries, coastal activity, and energy use.

"Average climate will certainly get warmer," says Roger Revelle, an ocean-   6
ographer and climatologist at the University of California at San Diego. "But what's more serious is how many more hurricanes we'll have, how many more droughts we'll have, how many days above one hundred degrees." By Han-

sen's reckoning, where Washington now averages one day a year over 100 degrees, it will average 12 such scorchers annually by the middle of the next century.

Comparable climate shifts have happened before, but over tens of cen-   7 turies, not tens of years. The unprecedented rapid change could accelerate the already high rate of species extinction as plants and animals fail to adapt quickly enough. For the first time in history humans are affecting the ecological balance of not just a region but the entire world, all at once. "We're altering the environment far faster than we can possibly predict the consequences," says Stephen Schneider, a climate modeler at the National Center for Atmospheric Research in Boulder, Colorado. "This is bound to lead to some surprises."

Schneider has been trying to generate interest in the greenhouse effect   8 since the early 1970s, although largely unsuccessfully. Frightening as the greenhouse effect is, the task of curbing it is so daunting that no one has been willing to take the necessary steps as long as there was even a tiny chance that the effect might not be real. Since greenhouse gases are chiefly the result of human industry and agriculture, it is not an exaggeration to say that civilization itself is the ultimate cause of global warming. That doesn't mean nothing can be done; only that delaying the effects of global warming by cutting down on greenhouse-gas emissions will be tremendously difficult, both technically and politically. Part of the problem is that predicting exactly what will happen to the local climate, region by region, is a task that's still beyond the power of even the most sophisticated computer model.

Some parts of the world could actually benefit from climate change, while   9 others could suffer tremendously. But for the foreseeable future the effects will be uncertain. No nation can plan on benefiting, and so, says Schneider, we must all "hedge our global bets," by reducing emissions of greenhouse gases. "The longer we wait to take action," he says, "and the weaker the action, the larger the effect and the more likely that it will be negative." Says meteorologist Howard Ferguson, assistant deputy minister of the Canadian Atmospheric Environment Service, "All the greenhouse scenarios are consistent. These numbers are real. We have to start behaving as if this is going to happen. Those who advocate a program consisting only of additional research are missing the boat."

While the greenhouse effect threatens to make life on Earth miserable, it is   10 also part of the reason life is livable in the first place. For at least the last 100,000 years atmospheric carbon dioxide, naturally generated and consumed by animals and plants, was in rough equilibrium, at a couple of hundred parts per million. Without this minute but critical trace to hold in heat, the globe's mean temperature would be in the forties instead of a comfortable 59 degrees. The amount of carbon dioxide has risen and fallen a bit, coinciding with the spread and retreat of glaciers as ice ages have come and gone. But until the Industrial Revolution, atmospheric carbon dioxide levels never rose above a manageable 280 parts per million.

Then, beginning early in the nineteenth century, the burning of fossil 11 fuels, especially coal, took off. By 1900, carbon dioxide levels in the atmosphere had begun to rise steadily, reaching 340 parts per million last year.

Levels of the other greenhouse gases have also risen. Methane, for exam- 12 ple, is generated primarily by bacterial decomposition of organic matter — particularly in such places as landfills, flooded rice paddies, and the guts of cattle and termites — and by the burning of wood. Methane concentration in the atmosphere has grown steadily as Earth's human population has grown, rising one percent a year over the last decade. Levels of chlorofluorocarbons, which are used as refrigerants, as cleaning solvents, and as raw materials for making plastic foam, have climbed 5 percent annually.

The amount of nitrous oxide in the atmosphere has quickly increased as 13 well, with about a third of the total added by human activity — much of that emitted by nitrogen-based fertilizers, and half of that from just three nations: China, the Soviet Union, and the United States. This gas is also released by the burning of coal and other fossil fuels, including gasoline. And ozone, which forms a beneficial shield against ultraviolet radiation when high in the stratosphere, is an efficient greenhouse gas when it appears at airliner altitudes — as it increasingly does, since it too is a by-product of fossil fuel burning.

All these gases are far more efficient at absorbing infrared energy (the 14 invisible radiation that ordinarily carries Earth's excess heat into space) than is carbon dioxide. Indeed, atmospheric chemists have estimated that the combined warming effect of these trace gases will soon equal or exceed the effect from carbon dioxide. And even as growth has slowed in the industrialized nations, the Third World is rushing full tilt into development. All told, billions of tons of greenhouse gases enter the atmosphere each year.

The big question is, given the inexorable buildup of these gases — a 15 growth that even the most spirited optimists concede can only be slowed, not stopped — what will the specific effects be? It's hard to say, because the relationship between worldwide climate and local weather is such a complex phenomenon to begin with. The chaotic patterns of jet streams and vortices and ocean currents swirling around the globe and governing the weather still confound meteorologists; in fact, weather more than two weeks in the future is thought by some to be inherently unpredictable.

So far, the best answers have come from computer models that simulate 16 the workings of the atmosphere. Most divide the atmosphere into hundreds of boxes, each of which is represented by mathematical equations for wind, temperature, moisture, incoming radiation, outgoing radiation, and the like. Each mathematical box is linked to its neighbors, so it can respond to changing conditions with appropriate changes of its own. Thus, the model behaves the way the world does—albeit at a very rough scale. A typical model divides the atmosphere vertically into boxes that are several hundred miles on a side.

Climate modelers can play with "what if" scenarios to see how the world 17 would respond to an arbitrary set of conditions. Several years ago, for example, computer models were used to bolster the theory of nuclear winter, which concluded that smoke and dust lofted into the atmosphere in a nuclear war would block sunlight and dangerously chill the planet. To study the greenhouse effect, climatologists first used models to simulate current conditions, then instantly doubled the amount of carbon dioxide in the atmosphere. The computer was allowed to run until conditions stabilized at a new equilibrium, and a map could be drawn showing changes in temperature, precipitation, and other factors.

But Hansen's latest simulations—the ones he used in his startling con- 18 gressional testimony—are more sophisticated. In them he added carbon dioxide to the atmosphere stepwise, just as is happening in the real world. The simulations, begun in 1983, took so much computer time that they were not completed and published until this summer.

Even the best climate model, however, has to oversimplify the enormous 19 complexity of the real atmosphere. One problem is the size of the boxes. The model used at the National Center for Atmospheric Research, for example, typically uses boxes 4.5 degrees of latitude by 7 degrees of longitude—about the size of the center's home state of Colorado—and treats them as uniform masses of air. While that's inherently inaccurate—the real Colorado contains such fundamentally different features as the Rocky Mountains and the Great Plains—using smaller boxes would take too much computing power.

Another problem is that modelers must estimate the influence of vegeta- 20 tion, ice and snow, soil moisture, terrain, and especially clouds, which reflect lots of sunlight back into space and also hold in surface heat. "Clouds are an important factor about which little is known," says Schneider. "When I first started looking at this in 1972, we didn't know much about the feedback from clouds. We don't know any more now than we did then."

So it is not surprising that while the more than a dozen major global 21 climate models in use around the world tend to agree on the broadest phenomena, they differ wildly when it comes to regional effects. And, says Robert Cess, a climate modeler at the State University of New York at Stony Brook, "The smaller the scale, the bigger the disagreement."

That makes it extremely hard to get national and local governments to 22 take action. Says Stephen Leatherman, director of the Laboratory for Coastal Research at the University of Maryland, "Unless you can put something down on paper and show the effects on actual locations—even actual buildings—then it's just pie in the sky."

There are, however, some consequences of a warming Earth that will be 23 universal.Perhaps the most obvious is a rise in sea level. "If we went all out to slow the warming trend, we might stall sea level rise at three to six feet," says Robert Buddemeier of Lawrence Livermore National Laboratory, who is studying the impact of sea-level rise on coral reefs. "But that's the very best you could hope for." And a six-foot rise, Buddemeier predicts, would be devastating.

It would, for one thing, render almost all low coral islands uninhabitable. 24 "Eventually," Buddemeier says, "a lot of real estate is going to go underwater." For places like the Marshall Islands in the Pacific, the Maldives off the west coast of India, and some Caribbean nations, this could mean nothing less than national extinction. "You're really looking at a potential refugee problem of unprecedented dimensions," says Buddemeier. "In the past, people have run away from famine or oppression. But they've never been physically displaced from a country because a large part of it has disappeared."

Coastal regions of continents or larger islands will also be in harm's way, 25 particularly towns or cities built on barrier islands and the fertile flat plains that typically surround river deltas. Bangladesh, dominated by the Ganges-Brahmaputra-Meghna Delta, is the classic case, says Buddemeier. "It's massively populated, achingly poor, and something like a sixth of the country is going to go away."

Egypt will be in similar trouble, according to a study by economist James 26 Broadus and several colleagues at Woods Hole Oceanographic Institution. Like the Ganges-Brahmaputra-Meghna, the soft sediments of the Nile Delta are subsiding. Given even an intermediate scenario for sea-level rise by the year 2050, Egypt could lose 15 percent of its arable land, land that currently houses 14 percent of its population and produces 14 percent of its gross domestic product.

One mitigating factor for some coastal nations that are still developing, 27 such as Belize and Indonesia, is that they generally have committed fewer resources to the coastline than their developed counterparts — Australia, for example, or the United States, with such vulnerable cities as Galveston and Miami. "Developed countries have billions invested in a very precarious, no-win situation," Buddemeier says. "The less developed countries will have an easier time adapting."

Indeed, the impact on coastal cities in developed countries may be enor- 28 mous. The Urban Institute, a non-partisan think tank, is completing a study for the Environmental Protection Agency on what a three-foot sea level rise would do to Miami. Miami is particularly vulnerable. Not only is it a coastal city, but it is nearly surrounded by water, with the Atlantic to the east, the Everglades to the west, and porous limestone beneath — "one of the most permeable aquifers in the world," says William Hyman, a senior research associate at the institute. "The aquifer in Miami is so porous that you'd actually have to build a dike down one hundred fifty feet beneath the surface to keep water from welling up." In an unusually severe storm nearby Miami Beach would be swept by a wall of water up to 16 feet above the current sea level.

Storms are an even greater danger to Galveston, which Leatherman has 29 studied extensively. Given just a couple of feet in sea-level rise, a moderately bad hurricane, of the type that occurs about once every ten years, would have the destructive impact of the type of storm that occurs once in a century. And Galveston is typical of a whole range of resort areas on the eastern and Gulf coasts, such as Atlantic City, New Jersey ("almost the whole New Jersey coast, really," says Leatherman); Ocean City, Maryland; and Myrtle Beach, South Carolina. "The point is, all these cities have been built on low-lying sandy barrier islands, mostly with elevations no higher than ten feet above sea level," Leatherman says. "Just a small rise in sea level will result in a lot of complications."

Even as cities become more vulnerable to moderate storms, the intensity of 30 hurricanes may increase dramatically, says Kerry Emanuel, a meteorologist at MIT. Hurricane intensity is linked to the temperature of the sea surface, Emanual explains. According to his models, if the sea warms to predicted levels, the most intense hurricanes will be 40 to 50 percent more severe than the most intense hurricanes of the past 50 years.

James Titus, director of the Environmental Protection Agency's Sea Level 31 Rise Project, says communities will have two choices: build walls or get out of the way. For cities such as New York or Boston the answer may well be to build walls. But for most other coastal regions, picking up and moving may work out better. One of the first examples of a regional government making a regulation based on the greenhouse effect took place in Maine last year. The state approved regulations allowing coastal development with the understanding that if sea level rises enough to inundate a property, the property will revert to nature, with the owner footing the bill for dismantling or moving structures.

Another worldwide consequence of global warming is increased precipita- 32 tion: warmer air will mean more evaporation of ocean water, more clouds, and an overall rise in rain and snow of between 5 and 7 percent. But it won't be evenly distributed. One climate model at Princeton University's Geophysical Fluid Dynamics Laboratory predicts that central India will have doubled precipitation, while the centers of continents at middle latitudes — the midwestern United States, for example — will actually have much drier summers than they have now (this summer's drought could, in other words, be a foretaste). Some arid areas, including southern California and Morocco, will have drier winters; and winters are when such areas get most of their precipitation. Moreover, the effect may be self-perpetuating: drier soil, says Syukuro Manabe, the climatologist who developed the model, leads to even hotter air.

The changes could be political dynamite for nations that already argue 33 over water resources. A prime example is Egypt and Sudan, both of which draw their lifeblood from the north-flowing Nile. Sudan has been trying to divert a bigger share of the river's water; but downstream, Egypt is experiencing one of Africa's fastest population explosions and will need every drop of water it can get. A string of droughts in the Sudan could make the conflict far worse. The same situation occurs in many other parts of the world.

Not all the tensions will be international. Within nations, local effects of 34 global warming will cause internecine fights for increasingly scarce water. In the United States, for example, western states have long argued over who owns what fraction of the water in such rivers as the Colorado. In California 42 percent of the water comes from the Sacramento and San Joaquin river basins, which are fed by runoff from the Sierra Nevada and other mountain ranges. Most of the water falls as snow in the winter, which melts in the spring to feed the rivers, reservoirs, and subterranean aquifers. The state's normal strategy for water management calls for keeping the reservoirs low in winter, to provide protection against floods, and keeping them as high as possible in summer, to ensure an adequate supply for the giant farming operations in the Central Valley (one of the most productive agricultural regions in the world) and for arid southern California.

Peter Gleick of the Pacific Institute for Studies in Development, Environ- 35 ment and Security, in Berkeley, California, has devised a widely praised model that predicts a dramatic disruption of the state's water supply in the event of global warming, even if total precipitation remains unchanged. It focuses on the Sacramento River basin, which alone provides 30 percent of the state's water for agriculture in the Central Valley.

According to the model, higher temperatures will mean that what falls in 36 winter will increasingly be rain, not snow, and that more of it will run off right away. California may get the same amount of total annual run-off, but the water-distribution system won't be able to deal with it. "California will get the worst of all possible worlds — more flooding in the winter, less available water in the summer," Gleick says. "This will reverberate throughout the state." San Francisco Bay will feel a secondary effect. As freshwater supplies shrink in the summer, seawater, which has already infiltrated freshwater aquifers beneath the low-lying Sacramento Delta, will continue its push inland. Rising sea level will just compound the effect.

Food is another crucial resource that will be affected by the global green- 37 house. Taken by itself, a rise in atmospheric carbon dioxide might not be so bad. For many crops more carbon dioxide might not be so bad. For many crops more carbon dioxide means a rise in the rate of photosynthesis and, therefore, in growth; and with increased carbon dioxide some plants' use of water is more efficient, according to studies done in conventional glass greenhouses. Also, as the planet gets warmer, crops might be cultivated farther north. But as usual, things are not so simple. A temperature rise of only 3.5 degrees in the tropics could reduce rice production by more than 10 percent.

In temperate regions also, the picture is mixed. Cynthia Rosenzweig, a **38** researcher based at Goddard, has been using crop-growth computer models to predict effects of carbon dioxide buildup and climate change on wheat, the most widely cultivated crop in the world. Plugging in temperature changes derived from the Goddard climate model, Rosenzweig tested a world with doubled carbon dioxide levels. Because the Goddard model is bad at predicting precipitation, she did separate runs for normal and dry conditions. She found that in normal years the wheat grew better, thanks to the extra carbon dioxide. But in dry years there was a marked increase in crop failures, because of excessive heat. Given the likelihood that heat waves and droughts are increasing, she says, no one should count on better yields in years to come.

The nations most likely to reap the benefits of warmer climate are Canada **39** and the Soviet Union, much of whose vast land area is too cold for large-scale crop cultivation. There has even been speculation that these countries might go slowly on controlling the greenhouse effect, or even oppose such control; anyone who has spent the winter in Moscow or Saskatoon would be sorely tempted by the prospect of better weather.

But again, atmospheric scientists stress that no nation can count on **40** benefits. "The models suggest that ecological zones will shift northward," says planetary scientist Michael McElroy of Harvard. "The southwestern desert to the Grain Belt; the Grain Belt to Canada. There might be winners and losers if this shift occurs slowly. But suppose it shifts so fast that ecosystems are unable to keep up?" For example, he says, there is a limit to the distance that a forest can propagate in a year. "If it is unable to propagate fast enough, then either we have to come in and plant trees, or else we'll see total devastation and the collapse of the ecosystem."

According to Irving Mintzer, a senior associate with the Energy and **41** Climate Project of the World Resources Institute in Washington, there is another reason to be leery of projections for regional agricultural benefits. Just because climatic conditions conducive to grain cultivation move north, that doesn't mean that other conditions necessary for agricultural super-powerdom will be present. Much of Canada, for example, does not have the optimum type of soil for growing wheat and corn.

Wildlife will suffer, too. In much of the world, wilderness areas are **42** increasingly hemmed in by development, and when climate shifts, these fragile ecosystems won't be able to shift with it. Plants will suddenly be unable to propagate their seeds, and animals will have no place to go. Species in the Arctic, such as caribou, may lose vital migratory routes as ice bridges between islands melt.

In the United States the greatest impact will likely be on coastal wetlands: **43** the salt marshes, swamps, and bayous that are among the world's most diverse and productive natural habitats. James Titus of the Environmental Protection Agency estimates that a five-foot rise in sea level—not even the worst-case scenario—would destroy between 50 and 90 percent of America's wetlands. Under natural conditions marshes would slowly shift inland. But with levees, condominiums, and other man-made structures in the way, they can't. The situation is worst in Louisiana, says Titus, which has 40 percent of U.S. wetlands (excluding those in Alaska); much of the verdant Mississippi River delta may well vanish.

In many parts of the tropics, low forests of mangrove trees thrive in the 44 shallow waters along coastlines. Their dense networks of roots and runners are natural island-building systems, trapping sediment and cushioning the damaging effects of tropical storms. But rising sea levels will flood the mangroves; the natural response would be for them to shift with the tide, spreading their roots farther inland. But in places where development has encroached on the shore, the mangrove forests will feel the same squeeze that will threaten marshes.

The only way to eliminate the greenhouse problem completely would be to 45 return the world to its preindustrial state. No one proposes that. But researchers agree that there is plenty that can be done to at least slow down the warming. Energy conservation comes first: using less coal, finding more efficient ways to use cleaner-burning fossil fuels, and taking a new look at nonfossil alternatives, everything from solar and geothermal energy to—yes, even some environmentalists are admitting it—nuclear power.

Getting the world's fractious nations to agree to a program of remedial 46 measures sounds extremely difficult, but Stephen Schneider sees signs that it may not be impossible. Schneider was one of more than 300 delegates from 48 countries who attended the International Conference on the Changing Atmosphere, which took place in Toronto, coincidentally, just a week after Hansen's congressional testimony. It was, says Schneider, the "Woodstock of CO2" (an obvious reference to the "Woodstock of Physics" meeting held last year, during which news of the high-temperature superconductors exploded into the public consciousness).

The meeting was the first large-scale attempt to bridge the gap between 47 scientists and policymakers on a wide range of atmospheric problems, including not just the greenhouse effect but also acid rain and the depletion of the protective layer of ozone in the stratosphere. Four days of floor debates, panel discussions, and closed-door sessions produced an ambitious manifesto calling for, among other things, the following:

- A 20 percent reduction in carbon dioxide emissions by industrialized nations by the year 2005, using a combination of conservation efforts and reduced consumption of fossil fuels. A 50 percent cut would eventually be needed to stabilize atmospheric carbon dioxide.

- A switch from coal or oil to other fuels. Burning natural gas, for example, produces half as much carbon dioxide per unit of energy as burning coal.

- Much more funding for development of solar power, wind power, geothermal power, and the like, and efforts to develop safe nuclear power.

- Drastic reductions in deforestation, and encouragement of forest replanting and restoration.

- The labeling of products whose manufacture does not harm the environment.

- Nearly complete elimination of the use of chlorofluorocarbons, or CFCs, by the year 2000.

Of all the anti-greenhouse measures, the last should prove easiest to 48 achieve. Although CFCs are extremely persistent, remaining in the upper atmosphere for decades, and although they are 10,000 times more efficient than carbon dioxide at trapping heat, the process of controlling them has been underway for years, for reasons having nothing to do with the greenhouse effect. Since the early 1970s atmospheric scientists have known that CFCs could have destructive effects on ozone. CFCs were banned from spray cans in the United States and Canada in the late 1970s, and the appearance of a "hole" in the ozone layer over Antarctica in the early 1980s created an international consensus that CFCs must go. Last year 53 nations crafted an agreement that will cut CFC production by 50 percent over the next decade; the chemicals may well be banned altogether by the turn of the century.

CFCs are a special case, however. Since they are entirely man-made, and 49 since substitutes are available or under development, control is straightforward. "There are only thirty-eight companies worldwide that produce CFCs," says Pieter Winsemius, former minister of the environment of the Netherlands. "You can put them all in one room; you can talk to them. But you can't do that with the producers of carbon dioxide — all the world's utilities and industries."

Also, there is a lack of basic information on the flow of carbon dioxide and 50 the other greenhouse gases into and out of the atmosphere and biosphere. Just as one example, there is no good estimate of how much carbon dioxide, methane, and nitrous oxide are produced by fires, both man-made and naturally occurring. "We need to better assess global biomass burning as a source of greenhouse gases," says Joel Levine of the NASA Langley Research Center in Hampton, Virginia. "We have to understand what we're actually doing when we burn tropical forests and when we burn agricultural stubble after harvest. We don't know on a global basis what the contribution is."

Remarkably, the conference spurred some specific promises from political 51 leaders rather than just vague platitudes. Standing before a 40-foot-wide photorealist painting of a cloud-studded skyscape, prime ministers Brian Mulroney of Canada and Gro Harlem Brundtland of Norway pledged that their countries will slow fossil fuel use and forgive some Third World debt, allowing developing countries to grow in a sustainable way. Says Schneider, "In the fifteen years that I've been trying to convince people of the seriousness of the greenhouse effect, this is the first time I've seen a broad consensus: First, there is a consensus that action is not premature. Second, that solutions have to occur on a global as well as a national scale."

In the end, the greatest obstacle facing those who are trying to slow the   52 output of greenhouse gases is the fundamental and pervasive nature of the human activities that are causing the problem: deforestation, industrialization, energy production. As populations boom, productivity must keep up. And even as the developed nations of the world cut back on fossil fuel use, there will be no justifiable way to prevent the Third World from expanding its use of coal and oil. How can the developed countries expect that China, for example, which has plans to double its coal production in the next 15 years in order to spur development, will be willing or even able to change course?

And then there is poverty, which contributes to the greenhouse effect by   53 encouraging destruction of forests. "Approximately seventy-five percent of the deforestation occurring in the world today is accounted for by landless people in a desperate search for food," says Jose Lutzenberger, director of the Gaia Foundation, an influential Brazilian environmental group. Commercial logging accounts for just 15 percent of tropical forest loss worldwide. Unfortunately for the atmosphere and the forests themselves, working out an agreement with the tropical timber industry will be far easier than eliminating rural poverty.

Industrialized nations, which created most of the greenhouse problem,   54 should lead the way to finding solutions, says State Department official Richard Benedick, who represented the United States during negotiations for cuts in CFCs and who was a conference attendee. The first priority, he says, should be strong conservation efforts — an area in which the United States lags far behind such countries as Japan. The effect of such measures, Benedick feels, can only be positive and the cost is not great. "Certain things make sense on their own merits," he says. Technology can be transferred to developing countries. In some Third World nations a partial solution can be as simple as modernizing energy production and distribution. Upgrading India's electric power system, Benedick says, could double the effective energy output of existing coal-fired power plants.

Addressing the conference, Canadian minister of energy Marcel Masse   55 noted that there is cause for optimism. One need look no further than the energy crisis of a decade ago. From 1979 to 1985, thanks primarily to conservation, substantial cuts were made in the use of fossil fuels by industrialized nations. Only since 1986 and the current oil glut, said Masse, has there been a resurgence in oil use and coal burning.

Michael McElroy concluded, "If we choose to take on this challenge, it appears that we can slow the rate of change substantially, giving us time to develop mechanisms so that the cost to society and the damage to ecosystems can be minimized. We could alternatively close our eyes, hope for the best, and pay the cost when the bill comes due." **56**

GLOBAL WARMING: DIPLOMACY'S NEXT GREAT CHALLENGE

James R. Udall

Udall assumes that global warming will be disastrous unless nations worldwide cooperate to develop an environmental policy to combat the greenhouse effect. In this essay, Udall outlines some preliminary ideas for such a policy.

As Cold War tensions ease, there is a growing recognition among interna-   1
tional leaders and policymakers that developing a timely, equitable, and effective strategy for abating global warming will be their next great diplomatic challenge.

Over the last two years, concern about global warming has grown expo-   2
nentially. Last January, the National Academy of Sciences warned President Bush that "global environmental change may well be the most pressing international issue of the next century," adding, "the future welfare of human society is . . . at risk." On Capitol Hill, where six bills to abate global warming have been introduced, Tennessee Senator Al Gore has said, "The question is whether the world's political system can find a new equilibrium before the world's climate system loses its current one . . . The winds of change are approaching hurricane force."

According to climatologist Stephen Schneider of the National Center for   3
Atmospheric Research, computer models of the world's climate suggest that, absent a worldwide effort to reduce greenhouse gas emissions, a temperature rise of three to nine degrees Fahrenheit is likely by 2050. Such a radical shift in temperature is guaranteed to trigger economic and social upheaval on an unimaginable scale. Its ecological impacts—ice caps melting, farm crops wilting, entire forests dying—will be catastrophic. One fact not yet grasped by many is that the Earth's thermostat has no upper limit; the warming will continue, theoretically for centuries, unless and until humankind acts to stop it.

As the world warms, oceans will march inland. A one- or two-meter sea   4
level rise, possible by 2100, would devastate many cities, including New Orleans, New York, Venice, and Bangkok; submerge much of the Netherlands, Bangladesh, and Egypt; and even erase entire nations like the low-lying Maldive Islands off India. A recent illustration in *Scientific American* showed what Florida might look like by the year 2200: the southern two hundred miles of the state, from Key West past Miami to West Palm Beach, would be submerged under the Atlantic Ocean. Like many of global warming's potential impacts, this one is difficult to credit and nearly impossible to fathom.

Computerized climate models are far from infallible, but global warming   5
seems destined to become a planetary emergency, a global crisis born of one

ineluctable reality: Modern societies have been forged from, and are sustained by, fossil fuels—oil, coal, and natural gas. Burning these fuels releases immense quantities of greenhouse gases, the most important of which is carbon dioxide (CO_2). CO_2 is not a "pollutant" that can be "scrubbed," trapped, or otherwise eliminated—it is a fundamental *by-product* of the combustion process. This means that global warming has been simmering for a long time. Until recently, though, it has been one of the hidden costs of progress.

It is nearly impossible to overstate how difficult it will be for the world's   6
leaders, policymakers, and diplomats to forge a coordinated response to the threat of global warming. This is true even though devising a strategy to combat global warming is not like finding a cure for cancer. The ailment's causes—fossil fuel usage and rampant deforestation—are known. Its symptoms—acid rain, urban air pollution, and ozone depletion—are ubiquitous. Prescribing a cure is child's play; filling it though, will be a Herculean task. Any effort to halt climate change must be global in scope; it will last for decades, even centuries; and, in one fashion or another, it will affect the lives of nearly everyone on the planet.

During recent months there has been a flurry of scientific and diplomatic   7
discussions aimed at reaching some informal agreement on how best to proceed. Under the auspices of the United Nations, multilateral working groups are attempting to resolve some of the uncertainties about the greenhouse effect and lay the groundwork for further initiatives. Meanwhile, diplomats have begun to brainstorm ways of crafting an abatement agreement that will enable the overarching interest of a stable climate to surmount each nation's tendency to act in its own selfish interest.

At a meeting at The Hague in March, the leaders of seventeen countries,   8
including France, Norway, Hungary, Japan, Kenya, West Germany, and the Netherlands, proposed to broaden the mandate of the United Nations Environmental Program (UNEP). Transforming UNEP into something approaching an "Environmental Security Council" was a radical idea, said Norwegian Prime Minister Gro Harlem Brundtland, "but any approach . . . less ambitious would not serve us."

Only in the last year have many heads of state begun to understand that   9
the threat of global warming has dramatically altered the political and economic landscape. For decades the prevailing assumption has been that the world's fossil-fuel-based economy would eventually be constrained by oil, gas, and coal depletion. But global warming has turned that paradigm on its head: It now appears that the atmosphere's ability to assimilate fossil-fuel wastes will be the limiting factor. The question is no longer how much oil, gas, and coal we have, but how much we can afford to burn.

According to the best estimates now available, stabilizing the climate will   10
require slashing fossil fuel combustion by at least half from current levels.

Since fossil fuel usage is predicted to *double* over the next four decades as population grows, this clearly represents an immense challenge.

In principle, there are three ways to reduce CO_2 emissions. The first is 11 through voluntary or mandatory conservation. The second is by wringing more work out of fossil fuels, burning them more efficiently. The third is by replacing fossil fuels with other energy sources such as hydroelectricity, solar power, biofuels, and nuclear power.

Since the Earth's atmosphere is a commons, logic suggests that no coun- 12 try has an incentive to control its CO_2 emissions — unless it has ironclad assurances that other countries will also control theirs. In recent months, many scientists and international leaders have called for a CO_2 treaty, enforced with trade sanctions and a fossil fuel levy, or "climate protection tax." It has been widely suggested that such a treaty might be modeled after the 1987 Montreal Protocol, signed by more than forty nations, to phase out the production of ozone-depleting chlorofluorocarbons.

But many aspects of the global warming phenomenon promise to make the 13 drafting of a "Law of the Atmosphere" a torturous and perhaps ultimately futile exercise. Among the potential stumbling blocks:

- There is no scientific consensus that global warming has yet begun. It may be another decade before scientists can detect a clear "signal" that the predicted warming is occurring.

- The impacts of global warming will vary from place to place. For example, low-lying countries like the Netherlands and Bangladesh have more to fear from a sea-level rise than landlocked countries like Bolivia or Czechoslovakia. The U.S. Corn Belt may suffer recurring droughts, but Canada and the U.S.S.R. may experience a net gain in arable land.

- Many governments currently subsidize energy to make it cheap. (Energy prices in the U.S.S.R., for example, remain pegged at 1928 levels; and in real terms, gasoline prices in the U.S. are now at a historic low.) Abating global warming will require discouraging the usage of fossil fuels by making them more expensive. This will be unpopular.

- With the exception of a few large countries like the U.S., China, and U.S.S.R., which together produce about fifty-two percent of global CO_2, most nations are responsible for only a minuscule portion of total CO_2 releases.

- Global warming's worst impacts are remote in space and time. Most politicians and diplomats will not live to see the dramatic rise in temperatures now predicted.

- Monitoring and enforcing a CO_2 treaty would be very difficult, if not impossible.

- Reductions in CO_2 emissions by rich countries could be negated by increased CO_2 emissions in fast-growing developing countries.

Perhaps the largest hurdle that such a treaty must surmount is the **14** tremendous existing disparities in energy use between rich and poor nations. For example, two hundred fifty million Americans produce about nine times more CO_2 than the nearly one billion inhabitants of India. Prime Minister Gandhi has made it clear that India will not scale back its ambitious development plans to accommodate what he sees as an excessive life-style here.

"Seventy-five percent of CO_2 emissions come from industrialized nations; **15** they have caused the problem," says United Nations Environmental Program's Noel Brown. "Why should poor countries, which haven't shared the benefits of fossil fuel use, now be asked to share the burdens?" In all likelihood, such disputes may torpedo attempts to negotiate a CO_2 reduction treaty — unless that treaty links national security, economic, social, energy, and environmental concerns to create a win/win situation for all countries. The outlines of such a grand compromise are faintly visible: developed countries would slash their CO_2 emissions, forgive much of the Third World's $1.3 trillion debt burden, and increase foreign aid to speed the transmission of energy efficiency technologies to poorer nations. In exchange, those nations would agree to stabilize their populations and cease tropical deforestation, which is responsible for about twenty percent of the CO_2 problem.

Since the world cannot be weaned from fossil fuels overnight, the best **16** short-term tactic for reducing CO_2 emissions is to wring more work out of fossil fuels, to burn them more efficiently. A recent study by the World Resources Institute concluded that developed countries could halve fossil fuel usage by embracing new conservation and efficiency initiatives. The United States has a special responsibility in this regard: Americans are five percent of the world's population, but produce twenty-three percent of the world's CO_2; on a per capita basis, this works out to a staggering eighteen tons of CO_2 annually. "If the United States doesn't take the lead to cut emissions, no other nation has the slightest incentive to reduce theirs," says Brooks Yeager, former Sierra Club Washington, D.C., representative.

Increased energy efficiency would have many salutary benefits for the **17** United States in addition to its climatic impact: It would reduce our trade deficits, enhance our industrial competitiveness, improve our national security, and assuage vexing environmental problems like urban smog and acid rain. Moreover, new efficiency initiatives could simply build on the progress we have already made. According to energy expert Amory Lovins, since 1973 the United States has gotten *seven* times as much new energy from efficiency savings as from *all* net increases in energy supply. But in the last two years United States energy consumption has begun to grow, reaching an all-time high in 1989.

We are backsliding. And if developing countries continue to blindly emu- 18
late our thriftless practices, there will be no hope of preventing worldwide
CO_2 emissions from spiraling upward. One bellwether is China. To power
their industrialization program, the Chinese plan to nearly double coal consumption in the next decade. By 2025 China may be the world's largest
emitter of CO_2, largely because of its reliance on outmoded technologies, a
point Lovins illustrates with an example:

> A few years ago China decided it was time people had refrigerators, and built more
> than 100 refrigerator factories. Unfortunately, an inefficient design was chosen —
> thereby committing China to billions of dollars' worth of electric capacity to serve
> those refrigerators — and millions of tons of unnecessary CO_2 emissions. The story
> is much the same throughout the Third World and the Soviet bloc. The Soviet
> economy is almost twice as energy intensive as ours, coal burning threatens to
> make much of Eastern Europe uninhabitable, and East Germans are the only
> people to produce more CO_2 per capita than Americans. These political, cultural,
> and economic realities underscore how difficult it will be to implement an interna-
> tional treaty to reduce global warming.

For his part, Lovins argues that a coercive treaty isn't needed, because energy
efficiency breakthroughs and advances in renewable energy will enable us to
replace fossil fuels — and make money doing it. Says he: "The fallacy that
abatement will be costly and inconvenient is warping the debate. Reducing
CO_2 (by using energy efficiency to displace fossil fuels) won't be a sacrifice,
nor will it cost extra: in general, it will work *better* and cost *less* than what
we're doing now."

If Lovins is right, diplomats and leaders do not need to waste years 19
grappling with thorny questions (How should CO_2 reductions be appor-
tioned? Which countries should bear the largest burdens? How can reluctant
countries be strong-armed into going along?) while negotiating an unimagin-
ably complex treaty that may be impossible to enforce. Instead, they should
focus their efforts on developing energy policies and shaping market forces to
help people, companies, and nations behave in their self-interest.

A landmark April 1989 study by the Swedish State Power Board illustrates 20
this point. The study documented how, over the next twenty years, Sweden
could expand its economy by half, phase out the nuclear power that makes
two-fifths of its electricity, reduce the CO_2 output of its heat-and-power
sector by a third, and make electrical services cheaper — all at the same time!
How? By combining efficiency improvements, some switching to natural gas
and biofuels, and environmental dispatch (using the cleanest fuels first).

Energy efficiency may also prove to be the biggest key to advancing 21
progress in the Third World. If developing countries continue to squander
much, even most, of their capital on supplying more energy to be inefficiently
used, they will not have the money left to buy the things that were supposed

to use the energy in the first place. Conversely, energy efficiency can free up enormous amounts of money to finance development's essential tasks.

If poor countries "did it right the first time"—if they leapfrogged our 22 mistakes, straight to the most resource-efficient infrastructure—they could theoretically expand their economies roughly tenfold with no increase in their greenhouse gas emissions. Meanwhile, if rich nations followed a path similar to that outlined for Sweden they could improve their standard of living while using several-fold *less* energy than now. A few decades from now, we would all meet in the middle.

But to make this scenario a reality, Japan, the United States and the 23 European Community will have to forge an "Ecological Alliance" with hand-to-mouth countries like India, China, Brazil, Mexico, Kenya, Poland, and yes, even the Soviet Union to help them create a sustainable energy future. This is a mind-boggling task on the order of a new Marshall Plan, and it will take money—lots of it.

Where to get it? The world currently spends $900 billion each year on 24 military and defense. The Worldwatch Institute suggests that we redefine security in ecological rather than military terms—and divert one-sixth, or $150 billion, to environmental defense. But why stop there? If, as it sometimes seems, nations require an adversary to maintain their cohesiveness, well, let global warming be the foil. It is the common enemy. Of course ancient antagonisms will not vanish overnight, but from an ecological perspective, armies are vestigial.

A century from now historians may conclude that the threat of global 25 warming was the best thing that ever happened to the environment. Humanity has an enormous investment in a stable climate, and global warming gives us a compelling, selfish, economic incentive to change patterns of energy use that have proved so harmful to the environment. But whether global warming will help unite the world's nations or simply aggravate preexisting differences is an open question.

This is a decisive moment in history. Can mankind, in Noel Brown's words, 26 "make a quantum conceptual leap, look beyond our paralyzing manias, and mobilize human energy and creativity in defense of the Earth"? Will global warming galvanize us into overcoming our weaknesses as a species? Can we muster the will to resolve the growing disconsonance between natural laws and human laws? Can we radically reorder our priorities and break our addiction to fossil fuels?

Every crisis has a silver lining, a flip side. Because global warming sub- 27 sumes everything from acid rain to urban smog to rainforest destruction, a successful effort to control it will simultaneously resolve many other heretofore intractable environmental problems. If, however, humanity, led by the international diplomatic community, fails to rise to the challenge, these problems can only mount until they overwhelm the biosphere.

THE GREENHOUSE BLUES:
KEEP COOL ABOUT GLOBAL WARMING

Dixy Lee Ray

Arguing that computer modeling hasn't adequately accounted for ocean surfaces, for different absorption bands of greenhouse gases, and for sun-spot activity, this former chair of the Atomic Energy Commission casts doubt on the inevitability of global warming. "What the greenhouse debate needs most is a dose of healthy skepticism."

The year 1988 ended on a high note of hysteria, one that was to continue 1 well into 1989. The issue fueled by an unusually hot, dry summer, was global warming. NASA's James Hansen testified at a Senate hearing that the high temperatures presaged the onset of the long-debated "greenhouse effect" and global warming due to buildup of carbon dioxide in the atmosphere. Forgotten were the harsh winters of 1978 (when barges carrying coal and heating oil froze in river ice and more than 200 people lost their lives in the cold weather) and 1982.

Memory is a capricious thing, Perhaps the early winter months of 1989 2 will remind prophets of global warming that nature can be fickle. Only days after *Time* magazine featured as its "Man" of the Year for 1988 a doomed Planet Earth, perishing from human mismanagement and greenhouse overheat, Alaska experienced the worst cold in its history. Twenty locations in our most northerly state recorded their lowest-ever temperatures, mainly in the range of −50 to −65 degrees Fahrenheit. The cold did not begin to move south until the first week in February, when it seeped down from Alaska on both sides of the Rocky Mountains, bringing near-record lows to the Pacific Northwest and throughout the Midwest, south to Texas, and eventually to the mid-Atlantic and New England states. Proponents of the "greenhouse-effect-is-here-global-warming-has-begun" theory were very quiet during these weeks.

Seeing Infrared

To be fair, even if there is a potential for increased temperatures due to 3 enhancement of the greenhouse effect, no one would expect it to occur all at once or without intervening cold spells. So let us examine the situation more closely.

Earth, with its blanket of atmosphere, constitutes a "greenhouse." This **4**
fact has never been at issue. Indeed, were it not for the greenhouse function
of air, the Earth's surface would be like the moon's, bitterly cold (-270
degrees Fahrenheit) at night and unbearably hot ($+212$ degrees) during the
day. Although the amount of solar energy reaching the moon is similar to
that reaching the Earth, the Earth's atmosphere permits incoming solar
radiation to penetrate. When that warms the surface, infrared heat is radiated
back. The "greenhouse gases" — carbon dioxide, water vapor, methane,
hydrocarbons — all absorb longwave (infrared) radiation. This process moder-
ates the surface temperature. Let us therefore rejoice and be glad that the
Earth does indeed function as a greenhouse!

In addition, the greenhouse gases are all produced by nature as well as by **5**
human activity. For example, carbon dioxide comes from the respiration of all
living things, and from forest fires, decaying vegetation, and volcanoes, as
well as from humans burning fossil fuel. The total amount divides about
$50/50$ between what nature produces and what people can be blamed for.
Hydrocarbons come from growing plants, especially evergreens such as the
pines and firs that cause the "blue haze" of the Great Smoky Mountains and
other areas where coniferous forests abound. Hydrocarbons also come from
various industrial activities and incomplete combustion in automobiles. Both
hydrocarbons and methane enter the atmosphere from the "burping" of cows
and other ruminants. The contribution of hydrocarbons to our air is also
about evenly divided between nature and human activities. Methane comes
from swamps, termites, coal mines, and rice paddies. Approximately 90
percent of methane comes from nature and only about 10 percent from
human activity.

Contrary Computer Models

These gases have always been present in the atmosphere, but in total they **6**
have been increasing during the last century. Carbon dioxide, the most
carefully measured, has increased 25 percent since the Industrial Revolution.
The current rate of increase in carbon dioxide plus the other greenhouse
gases is about 1 percent a year. Assuming this rate continues, the amount of
greenhouses gases will double in this century.

According to the leading computer models of climate scientists, the rise in **7**
carbon dioxide concentration since the middle of the 19th century should
have caused measurable warming of 1 to 5 degrees centigrade (2 to 9 degrees
Fahrenheit). But it hasn't! The temperature has oscillated and the overall rise
is in the range of 0.3 to 0.7 degrees centigrade. (Nobody knows what has
happened in the Southern Hemisphere, which is 90 percent ocean, because
oceanic temperature measurements are so scarce.)

Recall that the public furor started June 1988, when NASA scientist James   8
Hansen testified in the U.S. Senate that the greenhouse effect was here and
changing the climate. He said he was 99 percent sure of it and that "1988
would be the warmest year on record . . . unless there is some remarkable,
improbable cooling in the remainder of the year." Well, there was. (Ask them
in Alaska!) While Hansen was testifying, the eastern tropical Pacific Ocean
cooled drastically. The temperature dropped 7 degrees quite suddenly and is
now at near-record lows. No one knows why. The phenomenon is called La
Niña, to contrast it with the warmer El Niño current. Such cooling has
occurred 19 times in the last 102 years. But Hansen didn't consider La Niña
because his computer model didn't take sea temperatures into account even
though sea water covers 73 percent of Earth's surface. When a NASA
scientist talks "global" it's hard to imagine that he would ignore 73 percent
of the globe's surface — but he did.

Another possible explanation for the absence of the warming predicted by   9
the computer models: both carbon dioxide and water vapor have several
absorption bands besides the infrared. While longwave (infrared) radiation
may be kept *in*, some shorter waves of the incoming solar radiation may be
kept *out* (by the combined effect of carbon dioxide and water) so that less heat
becomes available to be trapped in the first place. Nature has many feedback
and self-regulating mechanisms of which this is only one.

Eddy's Sun Spots

There also may be cosmic forces at work that influence Earth temperatures   10
more than does the greenhouse effect. John Eddy of the National Center for
Atmospheric Research has found an interesting correlation between decades
of low sunspot activity and cold periods such as the "Little Ice Age" of the
17th century, when there was a virtual absence of sunspot activity between
1645 and 1715. (During the winter of 1683–84, recorded in the novel *Lorna
Doone*, the trees of Somerset could be heard bursting in the cold.) Conversely, Eddy found that decades of high sunspot activity coincided with
warm temperatures on Earth. If Eddy's theory holds up, the high solar
activity of the mid-20th century accounts for the period's unusual warmth,
and Earth may soon enter a slow return to colder temperatures. (Ice ages
recur about every 10,000 to 12,000 years, and it is now 11,000 years since
the last one.)

While most environmentalists blame deforestation and the burning of   11
fossil fuel for the carbon dioxide increase, they generally fail to take into
account the role of volcanoes in affecting the composition of the atmosphere.
We are currently near the peak of a 500-to-600-year cycle of volcanic activity,

which may have something to do with the carbon dioxide increase. The quantity of air-polluting materials produced by man during his entire existence on Earth does not begin to equal the quantities of toxic gases and particulates spewed forth into the atmosphere from just three volcanic eruptions: Krakatau in Indonesia in 1883, Mount Katmai in Alaska in 1912, and Hekla in Iceland in 1947. Mount St. Helens pumped out 910,000 metric tons of carbon dioxide during six months in 1982, not including the eruption.

Switch To Nuclear

Despite the uncertainty about whether we are now experiencing global warm- 12 ing, it is prudent to reduce the production of greenhouse gases through human activity. Because no one really knows what the ultimate consequences of the increases in carbon dioxide and other greenhouse gases might be, we should reduce man's contribution wherever possible. While there is no need to take draconian measures that would damage our standard of living, there are several things we can do.

For starters, we can phase out the use of fossil fuel for generating 13 electricity and turn to technology with no known adverse impact on the atmosphere — nuclear power. We can shift to an essentially all-electric economy. We can turn, once again, to electric buses and trains and eventually to electric automobiles. For air travel we could replace fossil fuels with hydrogen. New ceramics materials and ceramics-metal compounds can overcome the former problem of embrittlement resulting from the absorption of hydrogen into metal. Recent advances in storage technology promise to ease the necessity for large, heavy, high-pressure, low-temperature hydrogen storage tanks.

Sapling Hopes

We can also take advantage of photosynthesis to absorb carbon dioxide and 14 produce oxygen. Those who urge preservation of old growth, or "climax," forests on the basis of their contribution to the oxygen-carbon dioxide balance in the atmosphere overlook the fact that old trees metabolize far less rapidly than young ones (like humans and most living things). Indeed, old trees contribute little to removing carbon dioxide or producing oxygen, whereas a forest of young trees will remove carbon dioxide from the air at a rate of five or six tons per acre. Reforestation, therefore, is far more effective in carbon dioxide reduction than is preservation of existing forests. We should also vastly increase the use of plants in urban areas, where air pollution is usually worse than in rural regions.

In considering possible carbon dioxide mitigating actions, it is important to 15
keep in mind that these steps are feasible for an advanced, highly technical
industrialized society with plenty of electricity. Around the world, however,
fossil fuel burning will inevitably continue for many years. In China, for
example, 936 million metric tons of coal were burned in 1987–88. Who is
going to tell them to stop or to change? What alternatives do they have? No
matter what we do in the United States, or even throughout the Western
world, the carbon dioxide from man-made sources is bound to rise. Should
global warming occur, it is estimated that no nation, acting alone, could
affect it by more than 10 percent. We should nevertheless do what we can to
reduce our own carbon dioxide contribution—proper stewardship of the
Earth demands nothing less.

To do so, we need not be panicked into precipitous and costly "corrective" 16
actions that only reduce our standard of living. We can phase out fossil
fuels—replacing them with nuclear power and other fuels such as hydrogen
—in a deliberate, responsible way. We can also plant lots of trees.

Apocalypse No

A final note on the supposedly dire consequences of a global temperature rise 17
of 1.5 to 4.5 degrees centigrade over the next 50 years: Such a climate
change, should it occur, is not nearly so drastic a change for humans as a
move by an Alaskan to Palm Springs. Elevated temperatures would have
greater impact on agriculture and vegetation in general. But with plants,
temperature is hardly the only determinant of growth. Perhaps as important
are the duration and quality of light (latitude is significant here), soil moisture, and the amounts, timing, and duration of rainfall, and the possibilities
for irrigation. A warmer Earth—and the changes in rainfall that might
accompany it—would make some areas of farmland more fertile or less fertile
than today. But that hardly constitutes global environment doom.

Nor do the predictions of melting ice caps and possible inundation of 18
low-lying areas. Most weather specialists predict that a global temperature
rise of 1.5 to 4.5 degrees centigrade—enough to dislodge Antarctica ice
submerged under the surface—would cause the sea level to rise by one and a
half to four and a half feet. Should this happen, a number of cities would be
vulnerable to flooding of the sort that Venice and Holland have coped with for
centuries. Some beachfronts would be gradually moved back a few miles, and
some people would have to move. The inconvenience of all this should not be
minimized, but it is hardly apocalypse.

Is a global warming on the way? Maybe sometime, but it is not here now. 19
Why do so many people believe in the dire forecasts? Perhaps the historian
Hans Morgenthau was right when he wrote in 1946, "The intellectual and

moral history of mankind is the story of insecurity, of the anticipation of impending doom, of metaphysical anxieties." John Maddox, editor of the British journal *Nature*, says, "But these days there also seems to be an underlying cataclysmic sense among people. Scientists don't seem to be immune to this."

Well, they ought to be. What the greenhouse debate needs most is a dose 20 of healthy skepticism.

GLOBAL CLIMATIC TRENDS

H. E. Landsberg

This atmospheric scientist argues that the great complexity of Earth's climate system and the impossibility of creating reliable computer models make it impossible to predict what the effect of increased CO_2 concentrations might be.

There is little doubt that urbanization and industrialization have affected the climate of fairly substantial areas occupied by man. . . . By far the most troublesome atmospheric alteration has been the steady increase in *carbon dioxide* (CO_2). This and a few other minor gases have been lumped together under the term "greenhouse" gases. Their action is supposed to increase surface temperature, somewhat analogous to the glass panes of a greenhouse (actually an incomplete interpretation of greenhouse action). Undeniably CO_2 has steadily increased on a global basis, probably since the 1860s, and at an accelerated rate since the end of World War II. Systematic global measurements started during the International Geophysical Year 1957/8. Since then it has risen about 7 percent. The total increase since 1860 has been from 280 ppmV (parts per million by volume) to 335 ppmV. These are the established facts. They have prompted a staggering amount of literature pertaining to the climatic consequences of a continuing increase in atmospheric CO_2. The potential of a rising CO_2 level in the atmosphere to raise global temperatures at the surface has been discussed on and off ever since Svante Arrhenius advanced the idea in 1896. There is general agreement that the infrared-absorbing qualities of this gas will reduce the outgoing radiation from earth to space and thus raise the surface temperature. At the same time the radiation from the gas itself would cool the stratosphere.

No Agreement

The question about this temperature rise is how much, how soon, and with what regional distribution. There is no agreement on that. Some of it is a result of the initial uncertainties. These include principally the projections for future CO_2 increases. There had been the contention that this is primarily due to the increases in the use of fossil fuels. The calculations had shown that the past increase of CO_2 corresponded to about one-half of the CO_2 produced by combustion of the reasonably well-known consumption of fossil fuels. This was extrapolated to the future with scenarios of exponential increases in the use of fossil fuels. It must be said here that not all the CO_2 increase is caused by fossil fuel use. There have also been some decreases in uptake of CO_2 by vegetation, caused by deforestation especially in tropical areas. According to some estimates the depletion is presently at the rate of nearly 8 million hectares annually. However, the potential increase of other biomass as a result of additional CO_2 remains to be fully quantified.

The whole carbon cycle and the transfers from the various reservoirs' soil,   3 sea, and plant cover have not been adequately represented in past considerations, as pointed out in an excellent . . . review by [B.] Bolin. He points out that the regional biogeochemical processes are important for climatic models and have so far been inadequately considered: "Important feedback mechanisms may therefore have been overlooked, some of which may possibly cause natural climatic oscillations. Important also are the man-made changes in the surface of the land and the fact that on longer time scales ecosystems are hardly static."

A Cascade Of Uncertainty

The whole CO_2 climate problem is, in the words of Kellogg and Schware, a   4 "cascade of uncertainty." There is recognition that the prime problem lies with the scenarios. Kellogg and Schware proceed with the assumption that by the year 2000 atmospheric CO_2 will have risen to 360 ppmV and that it will have doubled from the pre-industrial level by 2035. While they admit the need for research to improve knowledge they proceed to discuss dire consequences. They are quite conservative compared with more alarming views by [H.] Flohn. He writes "the possibility of a drastic rapid climatic modification on a large scale must be envisaged," setting a critical limit at 450 ppmV with "catastrophic" possibilities at higher levels. Without much reference to the uncertainties this is elaborated in a report of the International Institute for Applied Systems Analysis. It is partly based on a paleoclimatic scenario, the hypsithermal of the Holocene, when global temperatures were estimated to have been 1.5° C above the present. CO_2 and the infrared-absorbing trace gases methane, nitrous oxide, and the chlorofluoromethanes are expected to constitute 70 percent and 30 percent, respectively, of the absorbing mixture. By the year 2050 the pre-industrial CO_2 has doubled and a 4°C global temperature rise is projected. Rain belts will be shifted, some areas will have more droughts, the polar ice will melt rapidly, coastal areas will become submerged. Doom will be there.

Such views prompted some scientists to propose policy changes that   5 would postpone the evil day. Many of the scenarios had envisaged an annual use increment for fossil fuel of 4 percent. It was thus natural to urge a "low-risk" energy policy. Actually there had already been a slow-down to an annual increase of 2¾ percent, presumably due to economic factors. Yet the predictions of temperature increases of several degrees in 50 – 70 years continued with adverse effects on the United States, the Soviet Union, and China:

"It now appears that the possible global climate change may be very disruptive to some societies. It may trigger shifts in agricultural patterns, balances of trade, and habitual ways of life for many people — and eventually, a few centuries from now, may even force abandonment of low-lying land due to a rise in sea level."

With such prospects being bandied about it is not surprising that legislative concern is being aroused. Thus subcommittees of the U.S. House of Representatives held hearings on carbon dioxide research and the greenhouse effect. Fortunately there was very cautious scientific testimony. It brought out that there are widely different results from various models used to simulate the CO_2 effect. It also indicated that it would probably take centuries to melt the Western Antarctic ice sheet. Even though there is a fair amount of consensus that the greenhouse effect is real, there remains a wide range of opinion as to the magnitude and the rate at which climatic change will occur and, in particular, about the changes that will take place on the all-important regional scale. **6**

Deceptive Models

Because so many conclusions are based on the mathematical–numerical modeling of climate, it is imperative to take a critical look at the various models. The fact that they appear in the exact framework of mathematics is deceiving because they can only simulate nature successfully if they represent all variables and their interactions. With the present state of knowledge that is virtually impossible. Hence it is also not surprising that various modelers have used different approaches and parameterizations to achieve approximations. The tests of validity have usually been that they present a fair representation of the current mean value of a climatic element and its annual variation. Yet when they are employed to project, say, the global mean temperature for the case of doubled atmospheric CO_2 the answers vary widely. . . . **7**

Where lie the problems? There are many. The question of the biospheric reservoir has already been pointed out (Bolin, 1982). The study also clearly stated the inadequate consideration of storage and circulation of CO_2 in the ocean. It is quite clear, as others have also pointed out, that the circulation of the deep sea is not well known and the available data are insufficient to verify current theories about that circulation. We know very little about the CO_2 transfer to greater depths in the ocean and the depth of the thermocline and its role in this transfer remains to be explored. In a . . . study of the turn-over of the deep waters of the world oceans it was concluded that their replacement-time is between 200 and 500 years. No such time lag appears in any of the climate models. The question of evaporation from the ocean and its **8** thermal effect, the role of increased water vapor in the atmosphere, the proper cloud cover for a higher-temperature earth and its albedo effect, other surface albedo changes with numerous interelement feedbacks, both positive and negative, call for intensified efforts for modeling, observations for the verification of models, and a highly conservative attitude with respect to conclusions.

There have been a number of statements that a CO_2-induced warming has 9 already occurred and that there is observational evidence for it. These refer particularly to shrinkage of the Antarctic ice sheets and sea level changes. However, there is no detectable decrease of Antarctic sea ice in 9 years of satellite observations. There are, as in all such elements, notable fluctuations. In satellite observations between 1967 and 1981 there are ice increases of considerable magnitude. These obscure any CO_2-induced trend and the postulate of such a trend is purely speculative. Also calculated temperature rises of $0.14°C$ because of CO_2 and $0.1°C$ because of other trace gas increases for the 1970–80 decade simply disappear in the noisy climatic temperature pattern. There has been an estimate of sea-level rises. These amount to about 10 cm in a century and are probably due to some general melting of the earth's ice and snow cover. Natural warming since the last decades of the nineteenth century is probably a major cause. It is unlikely that clear evidence of a CO_2 induced temperature rise, if it occurs, will be discovered before 2000. . . .

The current stand of the CO_2-climate question has been . . . comprehen- 10 sively discussed. . . . It is worth noting here that the eminent atmospheric scientist, F.K. Hare, states the only thing agreed upon is the atmosphere CO_2 increase. He then states:

The volume is a long litany of uncertainties — of the internal transport processes in the ocean, of ocean atmosphere interaction, of the magnitude of forest and soil carbon wastage, of the future course of fossil-fuel consumption.

He also notes the many "ifs" that lead to the uncertainties. Were the models right, were CO_2 increase to continue, were the present assumptions of the role of the oceans correct, then an unprecedented post-glacial climatic change in global climate could occur next century.

At the end of this brief review of the CO_2 problem it is perhaps worthwhile 11 to quote the laconic opinion of the members of the Executive Committee of the World Meteorological Organization. . . . This committee noted

[the] increasing amount of CO_2 released into the atmosphere as a result of human activity may have far-reaching consequences on the global climate, but the present state of knowledge does not permit any reliable prediction to be made of future CO_2 concentrations or their impact on climate.

APOCALYPSE AGAIN

Peter Shaw

"Predictions of the end of the world" are "as old as human history itself,"
claims Peter Shaw, who argues that the greenhouse effect is just one of a
series of doomsday predictions that terrify the human imagination in times
of prosperity. Like previous doomsday scenarios, Shaw argues, this one is
based on the flimsiest of scientific evidence and blindness to counterevi-
dence.

> *Some say the world will end in*
> *fire,*
> *Some say in ice.*
> ROBERT FROST

Predictions of the end of the world, as old as human history itself and   1
lately a subject of scholarly inquiry, have by no means abated in our own
time. Nor are those who believe in such predictions confined to isolated
religious sects, as was the case as recently as the 19th century. While such
sects do continue regularly to spring up and disappear, predictions of catastrophe have become the virtual orthodoxy of society as a whole. Journalists,
educators, churchmen, and philosophers daily endorse one or another script
foretelling the end of individual life, of human civilization, or of the entire
earth. Some say the world will end in fire—through the conflagration of a
nuclear holocaust; some say in ice—through the same event, this time
precipitating a "nuclear winter."

Fire and ice. We need only add earth and air to include within the   2
apocalyptic genre all four of the elements understood as basic by the Greeks,
and water to include the biblical account of the flood. Contemporary prophe-
cies of flood are stated in apparently scientific terms: as a result of global
warming, the polar ice caps will melt and inundate the world's major cities. As
for earth and air, we anticipate the disappearance of the one thanks to the
erosion of farmland and shorelines, while the other is to be depleted of its
ozone, if not first saturated with carbon dioxide or poisoned by man-made
pollutants.

Pagan man projected his fears outward; contemporary man internalizes.   3
Like biblical man (at least to that very limited extent) he holds himself, or
more accurately his own society, responsible for the coming end of the world.
Not only the disaster allegedly threatened by pollutants but every prospective
modern apocalypse stipulates man rather than the gods or nature as the

primal cause. And the charge is always the same: whether it is to be by fire or by ice, mankind faces extinction as a punishment for its impiety.

The continuities and discontinuities between ancient and modern imagina- 4 tions of disaster would amount to no more than curiosities if it were the case that superstitious fears had been replaced by rational ones. But it is not the case. On the contrary, given the best scientific understanding of reality available to early man, it made sense for him to ascribe natural disasters, present and future, to the gods. Later, it made sense for the Greeks to ascribe such disasters to some wayward or even malign characteristic of matter itself. Nor was Empedocles a simpleton for regarding the personification of the elements by gods as a persuasive account of reality. Would that our own conceptions of apocalypse were similarly founded on the best available scientific understanding. Instead, most if not all of the disasters currently being predicted have gained widespread credence *despite* a lack of scientific basis, or even in the face of definitive counterevidence.

Without question the most spectacular example of such a wholly supposi- 5 tious theory has to do with the so-called greenhouse effect. The greenhouse effect itself, as every school child knows, is simply the process by which the earth's atmosphere traps enough heat from the sun to create a habitable planet. As for the disaster scenario that bears the same name, it posits, in the words of a New York *Times* editorial, an increased "warming of the atmosphere by waste gases from a century of industrial activity." The *Times* goes on:

> The greenhouse theory holds that certain waste gases let in sunlight but trap heat, which otherwise would escape into space. Carbon dioxide has been steadily building up through the burning of coal and oil — and because forests, which absorb the gas, are fast being destroyed.

Now, aside from the mistaken assumption that forests worldwide are decreasing in size (they are not), the theory of a runaway greenhouse effect, otherwise known as global warming, presents even its advocates with a variety of internal contradictions. In the first place, the earth has a number of mechanisms for ameliorating fluctuations in global temperature: a significant rise in temperature, for example, leads to increased evaporation from the oceans; this is followed by the formation of clouds that shield the sun and then by a compensating drop in temperature. Too, if the greenhouse theory were valid, a global warming trend should be observable in records of temperatures soon after the jump in man-made carbon dioxide that is the result of modern industrial activity. Yet if there has been such a rise over the past one hundred years, it does not follow but precedes the onset of modern industrialism, and anyway it amounts to a barely detectable change of no more than one degree Fahrenheit over the entire period.

Here is a particularly significant problem for any hypothesis—the lack of   6
evidence. Purveyors of the global-warming theory counter it by pointing to
computer projections which show a catastrophic upward trend in the *next*
century. Once again, however, a knotty problem presents itself: computer
models, writes Andrew R. Solow, a statistician at Woods Hole Oceanographic
Institution, "have a hard time reproducing current climate from current data.
They cannot be expected to predict future climate with any precision."

Does any of this detract from the persuasive power of the global-warming   7
theory? Apparently not. As in certain forms of religion, the less evidence, the
more faith. And in the resultant climate of belief (as it deserves to be called),
not only the lack of evidence but even outright counterevidence can work
to a theory's benefit. According to the late Leon Festinger, Henry W.
Riecken, and Stanley Schachter, the authors of the classic study, *When
Prophecy Fails* (1956), "Although there is a limit beyond which belief will
not stand disconfirmation, it is clear that the introduction of contrary evidence can serve to increase the conviction and enthusiasm of a believer." So it
has been during the most recent phase of prediction, which itself represents a
revival of the great irruption of ecological warnings that dominated the early
1970's.

The central document in that earlier wave was *Limits to Growth*, a report   8
issued by the Club of Rome in 1972 foretelling a worldwide doom brought on
by the combined forces of "resource depletion," overpopulation, pollution,
and starvation. The future conjured up by computer simulation in *Limits to
Growth* bore a certain resemblance to the still more spectacularly stated
predictions of Paul Ehrlich in his 1968 book, *Population Bomb*. Ehrlich had
offered specific dates for specific catastrophes: 1983, for example, would see
a precipitous decline in American harvests and the institution of food rationing, by which time a billion people worldwide would have already starved to
death. The Club of Rome, more cautiously, assigned likely years for the
exhaustion of specific resources: petroleum (1992), silver (1985), natural gas
(1994), mercury (1985), tin (1987).

In 1982 one of the authors of the Club of Rome report had to admit that   9
his predictions were not coming true. Yet he was not repentant. There may
have been a postponement, a temporary reprieve, but man and the earth still
remained poised on the brink of cataclysm. Presumably Paul Ehrlich, who
never recanted, felt the same way. Just so have members of religious sects
always responded when their confidently predicted apocalypses pass without
incident.

True, the general public and even some members of the sect begin to fall   10
away after such disappointments; in our time, both Paul Ehrlich and the Club
of Rome did fade out of the spotlight. But instructively, and in contrast to the
sects studied in *When Prophecy Fails,* they did so without having been

exposed to the full glare of adverse publicity and ridicule that used to attend the collapse of prophecy. Perhaps that is why so little time elapsed before the public could be brought to credit similar predictions.

For even as the "population bomb" failed to explode on schedule, or **11**
ecological disaster to strike, new predictions of not only global but galactic proportions were being prepared. By the late 1980's these were receiving the same respectful, credulous hearing as their forerunners, and were being promoted just as avidly by the press. In the case of nuclear winter, the most publicized apocalypse, the cycle from prediction to publicity to disconfirmation took only a few years, from approximately 1985 to 1988; yet once again the end came without bringing ridicule or discredit to the theoreticians.

Nuclear winter was at once a prediction of what would happen after a **12**
nuclear war and the claim that an identical disaster, never detected in the geological record, had already taken place once before, in the age of the dinosaurs. A giant explosion, the theory went, had been caused on earth by a "nemesis" or "death star" wheeling in from far out in the universe and returning so quickly whence it had come as to be invisible to the most far-seeing of modern telescopes. The clouds of dust kicked up by that explosion had shielded the sun and thus caused the earth's vegetation to wither, bringing about the extinction of the dinosaurs by cold and starvation. The lesson for the mid-1980's was clear: intermediate-range nuclear missiles should not be emplaced in Western Europe and disarmament should commence forthwith.

As chance would have it, not long after the nuclear-winter theory gained **13**
currency there was a giant volcanic eruption at Mount St. Helens in the state of Washington. It was followed by the spreading of just such dark clouds as had been described — but without any hint of the predicted effect on vegetation or climate. At about the same time, too, paleontologists demonstrated that the dinosaurs could not possibly have been the casualties of a single, catastrophic event, since they had disappeared over a period of some thousands of years. Finally, a check of some of the nuclear-winter projections exposed gaping errors of math and physics.

As a result of these and other refutations of the theory. nuclear winter died **14**
its own death-by-theoretical-starvation. But so quickly was its place taken by similar predictions, similarly linked to geopolitical issues, that the event seems to have almost entirely escaped notice. Nuclear winter remains today in the public mind as a proven hypothesis, vying for popularity with its mirror opposite, the greenhouse effect.

Actually, not so long ago (as the journalist John Chamberlain has pointed **15**
out) we were being assured that we were living not in a warming but in a "cooling world." In the 1970's, as *Science* magazine reported in 1975, meteorologists were "almost unanimous" that such a trend was taking place,

and that its consequences, especially for agriculture, were potentially disastrous. Climatologists, according to *Fortune* magazine, warned that the cooling trend "could bring massive tragedies for mankind." A decade later, all of this quite forgotten, the opposite theory of global warming has drifted past the rocks of evidentiary lac'·, tumbled safely through the falls of skepticism, and sailed triumphantly onto the smooth lake of public respect.

The status of global warming as an unassailable, self-evident truth was 16 recently confirmed by the reaction to a scientific report that challenges its assumptions. This report, compiled at the National Oceanic and Atmospheric Administration and duly described on the front page of the New York *Times* and other newspapers, traces U.S. temperatures since 1895. It shows that the putative one-degree rise in temperature worldwide over the past hundred years, a figure widely accepted even by many of those skeptical of the global-warming scenario, is wrong for the United States. As the *Times* headline put it: "U.S. Data Since 1895 Fail to Show Warming Trend."

The reaction was immediate. All of the experts consulted by the *Times* 17 were in agreement that the report does not set back the global-warming theory by so much as an iota. Prominent among these experts was Dr. James E. Hansen, director of the National Aeronautic and Space Administration's Institute for Space Studies in Manhattan, a leading proponent of global warming and the man who produced the data showing a one-degree rise in global temperature. "We have to be careful about interpreting things like this," he warned, and went on to explain that the United States covers only a small portion of the earth's surface. Besides, the steadiness of the temperature readings could be a "statistical fluke." Note the implicit distinction here: we must be "careful" in interpreting data that appear reassuring, but it is virtually our duty to indulge any strongly felt premonitions of disaster even if they are based on the flimsiest evidence, or none.

The concept of the "statistical fluke" could easily be applied to many 18 current predictions, but is not. Thus, the acidification of a number of freshwater lakes in the eastern United States is considered not a fluke but a definite trend, even though it might be taken to fall well within the range of natural fluctuations. Similarly, the disturbing deaths of numerous dolphins during the summer of 1988 were traced to the same pattern of human depredation of the environment supposed to be causing acid rain and other ecological catastrophes. Later, it developed that the dolphins were killed by a so-called "red tide" of algae — itself first seen as a man-created scourge but then conceded to be a natural phenomenon. Here, in other words, was a genuine statistical fluke; but it was never labeled as such since it exonerated industrial man.

It does not give pause either to the catastrophists or to their credulous 19 promoters in the media that some predictions cancel out others. Dr. Hansen, for example, suggests that the absence of a warming trend, as shown by the new study, might be "the result of atmospheric pollutants reflecting heat away from earth." Yet these are the same pollutant particles supposedly responsible for global warming in the first place. Now it develops that the particles they carry with them counter the greenhouse effect. In fact, Dr. Hansen is worried that "anti-pollution efforts are reducing the amount of these particles and thus reducing the reflection of heat" away from the earth. It is surely a measure of the power of catastrophic thinking that what may have been the first public revelation of an actual decrease in man-made atmospheric pollutants should prompt the fear that such a decrease itself portends the direst consequences.

What all this suggests is that we have come to depend at any given **20** moment on a constant degree of threat. When times are bad — because of war, depression, or real natural disasters — proximate fears tend to dominate the imagination. When times are good — through the conquest of disease and famine, the achievement of high employment, prosperity, and an upward curve of longevity — apprehension has to be supplied from without. And during extended good times, a supply of fresh disasters is required as each one comes progressively to lose its appeal. Air pollution, rising to disaster proportions in the Club of Rome report, declines in importance but is soon succeeded by loss of the ozone layer, which will supposedly leave mankind vulnerable to the unfiltered rays of the sun and a consequent plague of, among other things, skin cancers and blindness. Continent-wide poisoning of fresh water through the eutrophication of lakes and streams from fertilizer runoff is forgotten only to be replaced by the threat of acid rain. Direct incineration of all mankind by atomic war cedes to a secondary stage of destruction by nuclear winter, and nuclear winter in turn to global warming.

This persistent and insistent imagining of disaster might be no more than a **21** sideshow were it not for its political dimension. But in the 1970's and 80's, successive waves of catastrophism followed and reflected episodes of defeat for radical political movements. The 70's wave succeeded the collapse of the New Left and engaged many of that movement's disillusioned supporters (as well, of course, as many people opposed or indifferent to the New Left). That of the 80's followed the worldwide discrediting of the economic, political, and moral record of Communism. It was as if sanguine hopes of an end to the cold war required a compensatory new fear, one that natural catastrophe alone could supply. And thus, soon after James Baker's nomination as Secretary of State, a bipartisan memorandum from members of the Senate Foreign Relations Committee called his urgent attention to the leading foreign-policy issue he would have to face, a "global problem of unprecedented magnitude." The issue was global warming.

It goes without saying that clean air and water, the retention of farmland **22** and forests, a satisfactory ozone layer, and the avoidance of nuclear war are all desirable things. But the pursuit of these goals through the rhetoric of hellfire renders more immediate political concerns mundane and secondary. Many are the societies that have been distracted from the actual dangers they faced by the allure of disasters wholly imaginary. That consideration aside, though, our obsession with distant and unprovable catastrophe is so stultifying, from both the moral and the intellectual point of view, as to constitute a cultural disaster in its own right.

FOR CLASS DISCUSSION

1. Analyze and evaluate the disagreements among these writers concerning the greenhouse effect. (Consider your own analysis on page 443. To what extent are disagreements based on uncertainties concerning "the facts of the case"? To what extent are they based on differing values, assumptions, and beliefs?

2. Choose one of the arguments for closer analysis, applying the second set of guide questions on pages 443–444.

OPTIONAL WRITING ASSIGNMENT You are the CEO of a large air conditioning manufacturer. Your company is barely hanging on in an extremely competitive market. Five thousand jobs depend on your ability to make sound decisions. You have just been asked by your board of directors to respond to significant shareholder concern about the impact of your air conditioners on the environment. The facts of the case are as follows:

- Your present air conditioners use freon, which, when leaked into the atmosphere, harms the ozone layer.

- There is an environmentally sound alternative to freon, but the alternative would raise the cost of your air conditioning system by 30 percent.

- The alternative would be less efficient and force the machines to use 15 percent more power.

- Your current air conditioners have been made more efficient and use 25 percent less freon than their predecessors.

- Your current air conditioners have been approved and commended by the EPA for their efficiency.

Using all of the above information, and drawing on the preceding essays, personal experience, and any other research you may have done, write an open letter to your shareholders announcing your company's future plans with regard to possible modifications in its air conditioners.

SYMBOLIC ACTIONS AND FREEDOM OF SPEECH: IS PUBLIC FLAG BURNING AN ACT OF FREE SPEECH PROTECTED BY THE FIRST AMENDMENT?

FORUM: FROM THE SUPREME COURT ORAL ARGUMENT IN *THE STATE OF TEXAS V. GREGORY LEE JOHNSON*

Introduction and Background by Lyle Denniston

This forum shows the members of the United States Supreme Court in lively debate with opposing attorneys over the issue of flag burning. In an introductory essay, legal commentator Lyle Denniston sketches in the background needed to understand the case.

When a case is called for oral argument, it is the only time the justices take their ongoing conversation about the law out in the open, before a public audience. It is during the oral argument that consensus building among the justices actually begins. Much of what they say and ask is actually intended to attract one another's attention — to define the issue for decision more precisely, to encourage trends in thinking, or to stir inclinations. Sometimes their questions seek to steer the lawyers' arguments, either by waving a

1

lawyer off a weak point or by buttressing a good argument—often with tough interrogation.

The case of *Texas v. Johnson* involves the burning of the American flag by 2
Gregory Lee Johnson at a political protest on August 22, 1984, during the Republican National Convention in Dallas. Johnson was arrested and charged under a Texas law forbidding the "desecration of a venerated object"— which is defined to include the American flag. Johnson was sentenced to a year in prison and fined $2,000; he appealed to the state court of appeals, which upheld his conviction. He further appealed his case to the highest state court, the Texas Court of Criminal Appeals. By a 5–4 vote, that court threw out his conviction and concluded that the Texas statute was unconstitutional. The State of Texas then appealed this result to the U.S. Supreme Court.

On the face of this case and from the way the justices frame their questions 3
to the lawyers arguing the case, the reader may too quickly conclude that a decision against Texas is inevitable. But keep in mind: The Supreme Court had no legal obligation to take this case, and in order to be placed on the docket, at least four of the nine justices had to vote to consider the issue— indicating that almost half the Court saw some potential legal merit to Texas's claim.

It is typical of the Rehnquist Court to volunteer to answer such 4
assumptions—to let it be known that it may well disturb what might appear to be settled expectations about the law, particularly in the field of civil rights. Recently the justices have taken up challenges to such settled areas of law as abortion, affirmative action, and private forms of racial discrimination. The Court is in transition, and that alone makes this a fascinating moment to examine one of the Court's most hallowed rituals.

Not long ago, it is fair to suggest, the Johnson case would have been 5
allowed to pass unreviewed, and the lower court's pro–First Amendment argument left to stand. The Warren Court took an almost "absolute" approach to the First Amendment—that is, it understood the First Amendment to protect all expressions of political dissent. The Burger Court by and large stood by those precedents. But since the arrival of Justices Sandra Day O'Connor, Antonin Scalia, and Anthony Kennedy, and the elevation of William H. Rehnquist to Chief Justice, the conservative bloc has been strengthened and emboldened. It is developing a passion to decide for itself whether and how far to adhere to precedent—especially those established by liberal-dominated Courts.

In this case, Kathi Alyce Drew's opening remarks reveal her strategy. She 6
argues that Texas has the right to protect the integrity of the flag as a symbol and that an act—such as a flag burning—which publicly degrades that symbol's value can be held illegal. Because First Amendment case law holds to a nearly absolute interpretation of protecting all language—even symbolic speech such as flag burning—Drew conspicuously avoids citing precedent.

Justice Scalia immediately puts Drew on notice that she is on weak ground with him in making the "destruction of the symbol" argument. Indeed, he argues directly with her on the point, seemingly urging her to move off of it. Rehnquist tries to shore up Drew's argument, but Scalia is relentless in his challenge.

Although still a junior justice, Scalia has become *the* dominant figure   7 during oral argument. More than any other justice, he seeks control of lawyers' arguments, either to rescue a failing effort or to undermine an apparently successful one. At times, what he does seems like teaching, at other times, badgering. Scalia, however, gives Drew no clear signal of an alternate direction he may want her to take. Sometimes he seems to urge her to take a dare, to argue for *enforced* veneration of the flag as a unique symbol. He is as aware as she is that the precedents are against her; in fact, he may well want to hear a direct assault on those precedents. But Drew declines, seeking instead to steer cautiously between them. However, Scalia's intent is opaque; he may simply be toying with Drew as a way to ridicule her weak performance.

William M. Kunstler, Johnson's lawyer, pursues a very different strategy.   8 He cites numerous precedents, calling out quotations, especially from cases the authors of which are seated before him. The justices' prior opinions are reasonably accurate predictors of their future positions, but an attorney gains no points by seeming to attach a justice's name to one side of a case. That is seen as a bid for a justice's vote by flattery. Kunstler is practically shameless in adopting this approach. Scalia makes light of it by suggesting that the quotation from him offered by Kunstler was written during Scalia's prior role as an appeals court judge.

Otherwise, Scalia keeps to the sidelines during Kunstler's argument, and   9 this may well be a concession that Kunstler cannot be expected to yield to any steering. It also may be an acknowledgment that Kunstler, a known maverick at the bar, might not be held in check were Scalia's aggressive style to ignite the lawyer emotionally. Given the Court's rather stiff notions of civility, a lawyer such as Kunstler is always perceived as a threat to the Court's decorum.

Rehnquist has a well-developed reputation for impatience with lawyers   10 who argue liberal causes, and that tendency emerges even more clearly when a lawyer has an identification, as does Kunstler, with radical leftist positions. This probably accounts for the strong signs of hostility Rehnquist displays toward Kunstler during the argument. Kunstler is less confrontational during this case than he can be, and at several points engages the Court in easy banter. He appears startled when those relaxing, and tension-relieving, moments get him into trouble with Justice Thurgood Marshall. Usually, Marshall is the one who is prepared to take an argument astray and seems to have fun while doing so. On this occasion, though, he is brusque with Kunstler for doing just that — thus displaying Marshall's seldom-seen hard edge, an edge that can cut down an attorney without ceremony.

The justice most likely to bring a discursive attorney up short is Justice   11
Byron R. White, ordinarily the Court's most aggressive interrogator. But White is remarkable in the Johnson case for his *lack* of participation. Typically, he is in the midst of most arguments, testing lawyers in a mood of utmost impatience, giving no quarter, and almost never showing a sense of humor.

There are other justices who also seem to find the entire enterprise too   12
serious an undertaking to engage in lighthearted exchanges. Justice Kennedy, the newest member of the Court, is one of them. Thus, it is a bit out of character when he makes a humorous remark about flying a flag in the rain, against the rules, because it is an "all-weather" flag. One of the strengths that Kennedy displays early in the Johnson argument is his keen sense that the Court must base its decision upon a narrowly defined, concrete principle, which can be articulated and defended. No doubt this is why he appears so skeptical about creating something as seemingly flimsy as a "flag exception" to the First Amendment. Like Lewis F. Powell Jr., the justice he replaced, Kennedy resists having the Court issue sweeping decisions.

Justice John Paul Stevens has a similar interest in keeping the Court's   13
rulings within strict bounds, but he pursues that interest by seeking out implications for cases beyond the one before the Court, and he will chase those implications through a series of hypotheticals. Here, he explores what Kunstler's argument might mean in other contexts — such as a soldier refusing to salute a flag. Stevens is the most unpredictable of the nine justices, and he does not often play off of other justices' questions; his "loner" approach often gives the impression that he would be asking the same questions if he were sitting on the bench by himself.

O'Connor, like Stevens, comes to the bench unusually well schooled in the   14
details of the cases, and they share an uncanny ability to knock a lawyer off guard with their keen attention to what sometimes seem like the smaller points of the case. O'Connor displays this tendency when she asks whether burning a copy of the Constitution might be a crime, and when she bores in on the relevance of the flag burner's motive. O'Connor shares another kind of attention to detail with Rehnquist — their easy familiarity with the precedents that bear upon the case. Both seem to get some reward from trying to shackle attorneys with relevant precedents: Rehnquist often does it with impish pleasure; O'Connor usually does it with deadpan seriousness — at times with testy impatience.

Justices William J. Brennan Jr. and Harry A. Blackmun take little part in   15
the arguments of this case, which is typical. They intervene to clarify small,

potentially significant points. Blackmun also sometimes disarms lawyers by seeking information outside the record of a case, as he does when he explores whether the flag burned by Johnson had been stolen.

Examining the oral argument for evidence of which way each justice might **16** vote is foolhardy. Last winter, a case that pitted press access to the *public* arrest and conviction records of a defense contractor against the contractor's right to privacy seemed — at oral argument — an easy victory for the press. Nevertheless, when the Court issued its opinion in March, the privacy argument prevailed by a vote of 9 – 0. Regardless of the outcome in the flag burning case, that the Court even chose to hear it reveals that the justices are willing to review cases that challenge what was once considered *settled* law about free expression. Americans can expect the Rehnquist Court to hear similar challenges to the First Amendment in the future. And, unlike most Courts — particularly the Warren Court or the Burger Court, which established reputations for creating *new* interpretations of precedents — the emerging trend of the Rehnquist Court, perhaps even its agenda, is an invitation to the legal community to challenge the abiding precedents of the Supreme Court.

The Oral Argument

[In this transcript of the Supreme Court oral argument, edited for readability, the opposing attorneys debate the issue with Supreme Court Justices. Participants are as follows: Kathi Alyce Drew, an assistant district attorney from Dallas representing the State of Texas; attorney William M. Kunstler, founder of the Center for Constitutional Rights, who is defending Gregory Lee Johnson; and various members of the Supreme Court.]

CHIEF JUSTICE WILLIAM H. REHNQUIST: We'll hear argument next in *Texas v. Gregory Lee Johnson.* Ms. Drew, you may proceed whenever you're ready.

KATHI ALYCE DREW: Thank you, Mr. Chief Justice, and may it please the Court: The issue before this Court is whether the public burning of an American flag, which occurred during the 1984 Republican National Convention in Dallas, Texas, as part of a demonstration with political overtones, is entitled to First Amendment protection. The flag was burned in front of city hall during a demonstration march through downtown Dallas in a crowd of demonstrators and onlookers. The flag burner was convicted under a Texas statute which prohibits desecration of the national flag. His punishment was one year in the county jail plus a $2,000 fine.

The Texas Court of Criminal Appeals reversed his conviction and held that the Texas statute was unconstitutional since Mr. Johnson was a political protester. Judge Campbell of that court found that flag burning constituted symbolic speech. That court also found that the interest that Texas has in regulating the act of flag burning does not outweigh a protester's First Amendment rights to expression.

For purposes of this argument today and with the Court's indulgence, the state will assume the symbolic speech standard* and proceed directly to the question of Texas's compelling interest in regulating such conduct. Texas has advanced two compelling state interests. One is the preservation of the flag as a symbol of nationhood and national unity. The second is the prevention of a breach of the peace.

I would like to address first the nationhood interest. We believe that preservation of the flag as a symbol of nationhood and national unity is a compelling and valid state interest. We feel certain that the government has the power both to adopt a national symbol and to take steps to prevent the destruction of that symbol.

JUSTICE ANTONIN SCALIA: Now, why did the defendant's actions destroy the symbol? His actions would have been useless unless the flag was a very good symbol for what he intended to show contempt for. His action does not make the flag any less a symbol.

DREW: Your Honor, we believe that if a symbol is ignored or abused over a period of time that it can, in fact, lose its symbolic effect.

SCALIA: I think not at all. I think when somebody does that to the flag, the flag becomes even *more* a symbol of the country. It seems to me you're running quite a different argument: not that he's destroying its symbolic character, but that he is showing disrespect for it. You want not just a symbol, but you want a venerated symbol. But I don't see how you can argue that he's making the flag any less of a symbol.

DREW: Your Honor, I'm forced to disagree with you. If Mr. Johnson's actions in this case do not constitute flag desecration, then I am not certain what would.

SCALIA: His actions desecrate the flag indeed, but do they *destroy* the symbol? Do they make it any less symbolic of the country? That's your argument — that we have a right to have a national symbol. And if you let the people desecrate the flag, you don't have a national symbol. I don't see how that follows. We may not have a *respected* national symbol, but that's a different argument. Now, if you want to argue that we have the right to insist upon respect for the flag, that's a different argument.

DREW: Texas is not suggesting that we can insist on respect. Rather, we have the right to preserve the physical integrity of the flag so that it can serve as a

*Under Supreme Court precedent, certain forms of speech — including acts which intend to communicate an idea — may be restricted if the state can show a "compelling interest." Drew concedes that Johnson's flag burning is a form of speech and argues that Texas has a compelling interest in restricting such activity.

symbol, because its symbolic effect is diluted by certain flagrant public acts of flag desecration.

REHNQUIST: Well, in a sense you're arguing for a minimal form of respect for the flag, aren't you? Not that the state can require you to take your hat off and salute when the flag goes by, but at least it can insist that you not destroy it?

DREW: Yes, Your Honor. To the extent that we are asking for any respect for the flag, we are asking for respect for its physical integrity. Certainly we do not demand that any individual view it with any discernible emotion, only that its physical integrity be respected. . . .

JUSTICE ANTHONY KENNEDY: Well, over the centuries the cross has been respected. I recognize one is a religious symbol and the other is a national symbol, but it's never been necessary to pass legislation to protect the cross.

DREW: That's true, Your Honor.

KENNEDY: So it may be that you can protect symbols by measures other than the imposition of criminal law.

DREW: Your Honor, I don't believe that a cross has quite the same character as the American flag, because there are many people in this nation who do not view the cross as a symbol. . . .

And this particular statute, Your Honor, would not protect that sort of a symbol. It recognizes that the flag is national property, that it belongs to all people, that all people are entitled to view it symbolically in whatever way they wish. Some people may give it great respect. Others may not. That's not what we're regulating here. We are simply trying to preserve the flag as a symbol for all people.

KENNEDY: Well, you begin by saying that it's a symbol and by acknowledging that what the defendant did was speech, is that correct?

DREW: We are assuming that standard.

KENNEDY: All right. What is the constitutional category you're asking us to adopt in order to say we can punish this kind of speech? An exception just for flags? [Editor's note: The Supreme Court has held that certain constitutional categories of speech, such as "obscenity" or "fighting words," may be restricted.]

DREW: With respect to the symbolic speech standard, we believe that there are compelling state interests that override this individual's symbolic speech rights, and that preserving the flag as a symbol is one of these. . . .

KENNEDY: This statute prohibits the desecration of a state flag as well?

DREW: Yes, it does.

KENNEDY: And if we upheld the statute in every state, each would have the same right?

DREW: Yes, Your Honor.

KENNEDY: So your category for one flag is now expanded to fifty-one. . . .

JUSTICE SANDRA DAY O'CONNOR: Could Texas prohibit the burning of copies of the Constitution, state or federal?

DREW: Not to my knowledge, Your Honor.

O'CONNOR: There wouldn't be the same interest in symbolism?

DREW: No, Your Honor.

SCALIA: Why not? What about the state flower?

DREW: There is legislation, Your Honor, that does establish the bluebonnet as the state flower.

SCALIA: I thought so.

DREW: It does not seek to protect it.

SCALIA: Well, how do you pick out what to protect? If I had to pick between the Constitution and the flag, I might well go with the Constitution. I don't know.

DREW: Your Honor, Texas has made a judgment that certain items are protected—and the statute is not limited to just the flag. But the portion in question here is limited to the flag.

SCALIA: I understand that. But we—up to now—have never allowed such an item to be declared a national symbol and to be usable symbolically in only one direction, which is essentially what you're arguing.

DREW: No, Your Honor. We're not arguing that at all. What we are arguing is that you may not publicly desecrate a flag, regardless of the motivation for your action.

SCALIA: Well, one hardly desecrates it in order to *honor* it. I mean, you only desecrate the flag in order to show your disagreement with what it stands for, isn't that right? . . .

DREW: Not necessarily.

SCALIA: Will you give me an example of somebody desecrating the flag in order to show that he agrees with the policies of the United States?

DREW: I think it is possible that an individual could burn a flag as an honor for all the individuals who died in Vietnam. This is their most prized possession. They're going to take it in front of Dallas city hall in the midst of a hundred people in the middle of the afternoon. They're going to ignite it, and they are doing this to honor the Americans who died in Vietnam. . . .

JUSTICE JOHN PAUL STEVENS: Your statute would cover that example?

DREW: Yes, it would, Your Honor, because it does not go to the motive of the actor. . . .

O'CONNOR: I thought this statute only applies if the desecration was done in a way that the actor *knows* will offend one or more persons likely to discover it.

DREW: That is correct, Your Honor. . . .

O'CONNOR: I thought that the Court had held that it's firmly settled under the Constitution that the public expression of ideas may not be prohibited merely because the ideas themselves are offensive to some of the hearers.

DREW: That's correct, Your Honor.

O'CONNOR: And this statute seems to try to achieve exactly that.

DREW: I don't believe that it does, Your Honor, because the pivotal point is *how* the act is carried out: not what an individual may be trying to say, not how onlookers perceive the action, not how the crowd reacts, but *how* it is done. If you burn the flag in your basement in the dead of night, you probably have not violated this statute, because the Texas statute is restricted to certain limited forms of flag desecration.

JUSTICE HARRY A. BLACKMUN: Ms. Drew, it's probably of no consequence, but was the flag stolen?

DREW: Yes, Your Honor. . . .

BLACKMUN: Would you be making the same argument if he owned the flag?

DREW: Yes, Your Honor, we would.

STEVENS: Was he prosecuted for stealing the flag?

DREW: No, Your Honor.

STEVENS: I wonder why not.

DREW: I believe, Your Honor, that no one actually *saw* him take it. In fact, the testimony was that others took it and gave it to him. There were so many problems with proof that prosecution was very speculative. . . .

KENNEDY: You're asking us to define a constitutional category. And from what I can see, the category is that we simply say the flag is different.

DREW: That is one possibility that we have advanced. We have also suggested that another route would be to assume the symbolic speech standard and to look at what the state's interests are in proscribing this type of behavior.

O'CONNOR: Do you suppose Patrick Henry and any of the Founding Fathers ever showed disrespect to the Union Jack?

DREW: Quite possibly, Your Honor.

O'CONNOR: Do you think that when they drafted the First Amendment they meant to make that a prosecutable offense?

DREW: Of course, Your Honor, one has no way of knowing whether they intended it or not.

SCALIA: I think your response is that they were willing to go to jail, just as they were when they signed the Declaration.

STEVENS: They were hoping they wouldn't get caught.

DREW: Yes, Your Honor. I believe the classic line is "We hang together or separately."

SCALIA: You said that this flag may be different from other symbols. You don't argue that there's something unique about this flag?

DREW: Of course there is, Your Honor. . . .

STEVENS: But you have not made an argument that there's anything unique about the flag.

DREW: Well, Your Honor, I disagree. The flag is the visible manifestation of over 200 years of history in this nation. The thirteen stripes represent the original thirteen colonies, and every state is represented on the field of blue by a star. It is unique. It is immediately recognizable to almost anyone who sees it.

JUSTICE THURGOOD MARSHALL: Suppose somebody burns an American flag with forty-eight stars.

DREW: I believe that that would be covered under this statute. That is clearly a past flag. Many people probably still own and display forty-eight-star flags.

SCALIA: But forty-seven wouldn't work because there was never a forty-seven-star flag, is that—

DREW: —that would depend, Your Honor—

SCALIA: —all you have to do is take one star out of the flag and it's okay?

DREW: That would depend, Your Honor, on how "flag" is defined. Congress itself defines the flag: "The Stars and Stripes in any number which to an individual who looks at it without deliberation may be a flag." The flag behind you looks to me to be a flag, but I cannot count fifty stars on it.

SCALIA: So you're saying forty-seven would be okay. I tend to think that's probably right.

DREW: . . . I'd like to turn briefly to the breach-of-the-peace interest. We feel that preventing a breach of the peace is a legitimate state interest. Again, the Texas legislature has made a judgment in this area that public desecration is likely to lead to violence. The record is clear that it was our good luck that a breach of the peace did not occur during this particular flag desecration. The appropriate test to be used in this area has not been decided by this Court.

There are two lines of cases. One is that public desecration of a flag is inherently inflammatory. Another is that "imminence" [of a breach of peace] must be shown. The goal is a *prevention* of a breach of the peace, not a punishment for a breach of the peace. And in analyzing this particular statute, the Texas Court of Criminal Appeals said that there was no actual breach of the peace. That's true. Individuals who were seriously offended by this conduct were not moved to violence. I believe that the reading by the Court of Criminal Appeals is too narrow. If you have to show an *actual* breach of the peace, the purpose of a flag-desecration statute is obviated. Some other statute would serve that interest, but not a flag-desecration standard, because its purpose is *prevention.*

SCALIA: If that theory alone is enough, I suppose you could have statutes for Stars of David and crosses and maybe Salman Rushdie's book. Whatever might incite people, you can prevent such desecration.

DREW: Your Honor, there are other sections of this statute where other things are protected, specifically public monuments, places of burial and worship. I don't believe that anyone would suggest that one may paint swastikas on the Alamo in San Antonio.

KENNEDY: But that's because it's public property. Unless you say that the flag is somehow the public property of us all and ignore traditional distinctions of property, your example just doesn't work.

DREW: Your Honor, I believe that it does. The brief filed on behalf of Mr. Johnson by the American Civil Liberties Union confesses that there is no First Amendment interest in protecting desecrations of either public monuments or places of worship or burial because they are — and this is a direct quote — "someone else's cherished property." I think the flag is this nation's cherished property. The government may maintain a residual interest, but so do the people. And we protect the flag because it is such an important symbol of national unity.

SCALIA: If we say so, it becomes so. But it certainly isn't self-evident. I never thought that the flag I own is your flag.

DREW: Many justices of this Court have held that the flag is national property. Unless the Court has additional questions, I would like to reserve my remaining time for rebuttal.

REHNQUIST: Very well, Ms. Drew. Mr. Kunstler?

WILLIAM M. KUNSTLER: Mr. Chief Justice, may it please the Court: I would like to suggest that this particular law singles out communicative impact [i.e., not the act of flag burning itself but the reaction onlookers might have] for punishment. Now, Ms. Drew apparently concedes that you can write out of a statute what Justice O'Connor referred to: the question of whether the actor intends that what he's doing will seriously offend one or more persons likely to observe his particular act. . . . But it's not out as far as this Court is concerned. That's what the conviction was about, that's what the argument to the jury was about, that's what the charge was about.

SCALIA: Mr. Kunstler, I think you're stretching her argument. She said that there has to be offense, but it doesn't have to be the *intention* to communicate that offense. . . .

KUNSTLER: I can understand that rationale, but the Texas brief virtually took the notion of offense out of the statute. Now, maybe I do misstate her argument slightly, but the words "a flag burning is a flag burning" are in the reply brief.

Now, Justice Scalia, in your dissent in *Community for Creative Non-Violence v. Watt,* you said, "A law *directed at* the communicative nature of conduct must, like a law directed at speech itself, be justified by the substantial showing of need that the First Amendment requires." I subscribe to that wholeheartedly.

SCALIA: I was on the court of appeals then, Mr. Kunstler.

KUNSTLER: I hope that the elevation hasn't changed your thought. In any event, we subscribe to your opinion in our argument, and to Justice O'Connor's in *Boos v. Barry** when she said, essentially, that the state's interest turned only on the content of the speech and the direct impact that speech has on its listeners.

And in [*Smith v. Goguen***] Justice White in his concurrence said that that statute made the communicative aspect of the proscribed conduct a crucial element of the violation. And that's what we have here. Everything depends on the communication that is made by the actor to the people on the street. But in this statute, Justice Scalia, it goes even further and says "likely to observe or discover," which could be in the newspapers, for example, as well as being an onlooker. Given the concession that the act is pure speech, and given the past decisions of this Court on what should happen to a law that makes communicative impact the criterion for punishment, this statute fails that test. . . .

Now, with reference to the issue of national unity, I thought *West Virginia State Board of Education v. Barnette* set that to rest. In that case Justice Robert Jackson said, "If there is any fixed star in our constitutional constellation, it is that no official, high or petty, can prescribe what shall be orthodox in politics—"

REHNQUIST: —well, the facts of *Barnette* were quite different from this. There the students were required to salute the flag.

KUNSTLER: And here, Chief Justice, people are required *not* to do something.

---

*The Court ruled that a law prohibiting picketing near a foreign embassy that intended to bring that foreign government into "public odium" or "public disrepute" was unconstitutional because it was a "content-based restriction on political speech in a public forum, which is not narrowly tailored to serve a compelling state interest."
**The Court ruled that a Massachusetts statute that prohibited contemptuous treatment of the American flag was unconstitutional.

REHNQUIST: Yes.

KUNSTLER: And I think that's a comparable situation.

REHNQUIST: Well, to me they're quite different. You say that if you can't do one, you can't do the other. But it seems to me one could easily say you can't do one but you can do the other.

KUNSTLER: Well, you know, I understand that, but in *Street v. New York,* he did exactly what we're talking about here. Street burned the flag to protest the shooting of James Meredith in Mississippi in 1966.

REHNQUIST: And what was the holding of the Court in *Street?*

KUNSTLER: The Court indicated that it couldn't tell whether it was speech or flag burning. But the Court also said that it was an illegitimate interest in *Street* to compel respect by prohibiting criticism of the flag, including flag burning. So I guess we have a little difference of opinion on the facts. Can you say you can't force them to salute the flag, but you can force them *not* to show other forms of disrespect for the flag? I think they're the same, in all due deference.

REHNQUIST: Well—

KUNSTLER: —I don't know if I've convinced you, but—

REHNQUIST: —well, you may have convinced others. But take the "Live Free or Die" case. We said that New Hampshire couldn't require the display of the motto "Live Free or Die" on a license plate. But certainly New Hampshire could have prevented you from making other statements on your license plate.

KUNSTLER: As I recall, the Jehovah's Witnesses didn't believe in that motto, so they *painted* it out.

REHNQUIST: And the Court said you couldn't require someone to make an *affirmation.* But if someone applies for a New Hampshire license plate containing foul language, that can be proscribed.

KUNSTLER: I would agree with you on that, but that's putting something *on* the license plate that is profane. But what the Jehovah's Witnesses did was to paint out the state motto. They burned the flag, in essence.

REHNQUIST: I don't think we're going to see eye to eye on this.

KUNSTLER: . . . In front of the Supreme Court, when I came by today, the flags were up in the rain, and under 36 U.S. Code, flags shall not be displayed in inclement weather.

KENNEDY: Exemption One applies to *all-weather* flags.

KUNSTLER: That could be physical mistreatment under the Texas statute.

MARSHALL: Mr. Kunstler, are you going to get back to the case at hand?

KUNSTLER: Yes, I'm getting back to the case. . . .

STEVENS: Mr. Kunstler, is there any public interest in any of these regulatory measures that say don't display the flag in the rain or don't fly it upside down?

KUNSTLER: I don't know, but I don't think it matters, because they're not criminal statutes. They are recommendations. It used to be you couldn't fly the flag at night. Now you can fly it if it's illuminated and so on.

STEVENS: Do you think the federal government has any power at all to regulate how this flag is displayed in public places?

KUNSTLER: I don't believe so. . . .

KENNEDY: Can the federal government prohibit use of the flag for commercial purposes? Advertising?

KUNSTLER: I don't know. Ever since *Halter v. Nebraska*, where there was a statute against using the flag on beer bottles or cans, I don't know whether there can be any prohibition. Barbara Bush wore a flag scarf once. There are flag bikinis, there are flag everything. There are little cocktail flags that you put in hot dogs or meatballs and then throw in the garbage pail. They're flags under the Texas statute. . . .

STEVENS: Do you think the military would have any legitimate interest in disciplining a member of the military who showed disrespect for the flag on public occasions?

KUNSTLER: You might have a case there.

STEVENS: *You* might have a case.

KUNSTLER: The flag has a more peculiar significance to people in the army. I would have problems with it. But if a soldier destroyed a flag that was the property of the army, I think that soldier would be court-martialed. I'm sure it would violate what I used to call the Articles of War, which forbid "conduct unbecoming a member of the military" and which include a refusal to salute the flag.

STEVENS: I was only suggesting that maybe there is some identifiable state interest that's involved here.

KUNSTLER: Yes. But I'm not saying — I don't want you to get the wrong impression —

STEVENS: I think you're acknowledging that there is —

KUNSTLER: I'm not saying that. I'm trying to confine it to this case.

STEVENS: You did say that.

KUNSTLER: I know I did. I guess I have too much of a First Amendment consciousness.

With reference to breach of the peace, none of the flag cases that have ever come before this Court involved a breach of the peace. The only one I found where there was any violence was what Judge Tuttle found in the *Monroe v. State Court of Fulton County* case [in which an onlooker struggled with someone burning an American flag]. And Judge Tuttle pointed out that there was no clear and present danger. [The Court has ruled that speech which poses a "clear and present danger" to public safety may be restricted.]

REHNQUIST: What about *Finer v. New York,* where that fellow was speaking at Syracuse and said President Truman is a champagne-sipping bum, whereupon they told him he had to stop speaking because of fear the crowd would attack him?

KUNSTLER: Well, I don't think that changes the position, because it's no different than *Terminiello v. City of Chicago** really.

REHNQUIST: Well, it came after *Terminiello,* and it came out the other way.

KUNSTLER: I know, but apparently the imminence there was so —

REHNQUIST: — Imminent?

KUNSTLER: Thank you. Was so imminent. But when I was reading Terminiello's remarks in the transcript, it showed he ducked several times. Apparently someone threw something during his rampage against the Jews, but this Court held that *that* wasn't enough. And there's no breach of the peace here and no imminence of the breach of the peace at all.

BLACKMUN: Well, then we come close to the Skokie cases.

KUNSTLER: Well, Skokie presents [an attempt by neo-Nazis to parade through a Jewish neighborhood]. But even there, you couldn't stop it.

BLACKMUN: That's my point.

KUNSTLER: If you're going to stop it, it has to be so imminent, as the Chief said, that it really reaches clear-and-present-danger proportions. Furthermore, the Texas statute is not limited to an imminent breach of the peace. It just says "in a way that the actor knows will seriously offend one or more persons likely to observe or discover his action." The Texas court of appeals said that this statute "is so broad that it may be used to punish protected conduct which has no propensity to result in breaches of the peace." Serious offense does not always result in a breach of the peace. The protest in this case did not lead to violence. A witness to the burning was obviously seriously offended by the defendant's conduct because he gathered the burned flag and buried it at his home. Nevertheless, however offended, this man was not moved to violence. Serious offense occurred, but there was no breach of the peace. One cannot equate serious offense with incitement to breach the peace. . . .

---

*In this case involving a near riot during an anti-Semitic speech, the Court ruled that a law restricting speech that "stirs the public to anger, invites dispute, brings about a condition of unrest, or creates a disturbance" is unconstitutional.

REHNQUIST: What was Johnson charged with when it was submitted to the jury?

KUNSTLER: Eventually he was charged only with flag burning. But initially, Chief Justice, he was charged with disorderly conduct. And then they dropped the disorderly conduct and substituted the flag desecration charge. . . .

I want to close with two remarks. One, Justice Jackson said in *Barnette*: "Those who begin coercive elimination of dissent soon find themselves eliminating dissenters. Compulsory unification of opinion achieves only the unanimity of the graveyard . . . the First Amendment to our Constitution was designed to avoid these ends by avoiding these beginnings." And in a recent article in the *New York Times* entitled "In Chicago, A Holy War Over the Flag," J. Anthony Lukas said, "Whatever pain freedom of expression may inflict, it is a principle on which we can give no ground."

I understand that this flag has serious important meanings, real meaning to real people out there. But that does not mean that it may have different meanings to others and that they may not — under the First Amendment — show their feelings by what Texas calls desecration of a venerated object. The First Amendment was designed so that the things we hate — Terminiello's remarks, burnings of flags, or what have you — can have a place in the marketplace of ideas. I submit that this Court could affirm the holding of the Texas Court of Criminal Appeals. Thank you very much.

REHNQUIST: Thank you, Mr. Kunstler. Ms. Drew?

DREW: Thank you, Your Honor. . . . I fail to see how — if I understand Mr. Kunstler's concession — if one can protect *government* flags, why one cannot protect a flag that is not necessarily the property of the government but represents the danger of a breach of the peace and the denigration of the symbol. Unless the Court has questions, that will conclude my remarks.

REHNQUIST: Thank you, Ms. Drew. The case is submitted.

EXCERPTS FROM THE DISSENTING OPINIONS IN
TEXAS V. JOHNSON

Justice John Paul Stevens
Chief Justice William H. Rehnquist

In these excerpts from their dissenting opinions in Texas v. *Johnson, Justice Stevens and Chief Justice Rehnquist set forth their arguments against flag burning as protected free speech.*

Justice John Paul Stevens

1   Even if flag burning could be considered just another species of symbolic speech under the logical application of the rules that the Court has developed in its interpretation of the First Amendment in other contexts, this case has an intangible dimension that makes those rules inapplicable.

2   A country's flag is a symbol of more than "nationhood and national unity." It also signifies the ideas that characterize the society that has chosen that emblem, as well as the special history that has animated the growth and power of those ideas. . . .

3   So it is with the American flag. It is more than a proud symbol of the courage, the determination and the gifts of nature that transformed 13 fledgling colonies into a world power. It is a symbol of freedom, of equal opportunity, of religious tolerance and of good will for other peoples who share our aspirations. . . .

4   The value of the flag as a symbol cannot be measured. Even so, I have no doubt that the interest in preserving that value for the future is both significant and legitimate. . . . The creation of a Federal right to post bulletin boards and graffiti on the Washington Monument might enlarge the market for free expression, but at a cost I would not pay.

5   Similarly, in my considered judgment, sanctioning the public desecration of the flag will tarnish its value—both for those who cherish the ideas for which it waves and for those who desire to don the robes of martyrdom by burning it. That tarnish is not justified by the trivial burden on free expression occasioned by requiring that an available, alternative mode of expression—including uttering words critical of the flag—be employed.

* * *

The ideas of liberty and equality have been an irresistible force in motivat- 6
ing leaders like Patrick Henry, Susan B. Anthony, and Abraham Lincoln,
schoolteachers like Nathan Hale and Booker T. Washington, the Philippine
Scouts who fought at Bataan, and the soldiers who scaled the bluff at Omaha
Beach. If those ideas are worth fighting for—and our history demonstrates
that they are—it cannot be true that the flag that uniquely symbolizes their
power is not itself worthy of protection from unnecessary desecration.

Chief Justice
William H. Rehnquist

In holding this Texas statute unconstitutional, the Court ignores Justice 1
Holmes's familiar aphorism that "a page of history is worth a volume of
logic." For more than 200 years, the American flag has occupied a unique
position as the symbol of our nation, a uniqueness that justifies a governmental prohibition against flag burning in the way respondent Johnson did here.

At the time of the American Revolution, the flag served to unify the 13 2
colonies at home while obtaining recognition of national sovereignty abroad.
Ralph Waldo Emerson's Concord Hymn describes the first skirmishes of the
Revolutionary War in these lines:

> "By the rude bridge that arched the flood,
> Their flag to April's breeze unfurled,
> Here once the embattled farmers stood,
> And fired the shot heard round the world."

* * *

In the First and Second World Wars, thousands of our countrymen died on 3
foreign soil fighting for the American cause. At Iwo Jima in the Second World
War, United States Marines fought hand to hand against thousands of Japanese. By the time the marines reached the top of Mount Suribachi, they raised
a piece of pipe upright and from one end fluttered a flag. That ascent had cost
nearly 6,000 American lives. . . .

* * *

The flag symbolizes the nation in peace as well as in war. It signifies our 4
national presence on battleships, airplanes, military installations and public
buildings from the United States Capitol to the thousands of county courthouses and city halls throughout the country. . . .

No other American symbol has been as universally honored as the flag. In 5
1931 Congress declared "The Star Spangled Banner" to be our national

anthem. In 1949 Congress declared June 14th to be Flag Day. In 1987 John Philip Sousa's "The Stars and Stripes Forever" was designated as the national march. Congress has also established "The Pledge of Allegiance to the Flag" and the manner of its deliverance. . . .

* * *

With the exception of Alaska and Wyoming, all of the states now have 6 statutes prohibiting the burning of the flag. . . .

* * *

The result of the Texas statute is obviously to deny one in Johnson's frame 7 of mind one of many means of "symbolic speech." Far from being a case of "one picture being worth a thousand words," flag burning is the equivalent of an inarticulate grunt or roar that, it seems fair to say, is most likely to be indulged in not to express any particular idea, but to antagonize others. . . .

The Texas statute deprived Johnson of only one rather inarticulate sym- 8 bolic form of protest—a form of protest that was profoundly offensive to many—and left him with a full panoply of other symbols and every conceivable form of verbal expression to express his deep disapproval of national policy. . . .

WAIVING THE FLAG

Robert Bork

Robert Bork, an unsuccessful Reagan nominee to the Supreme Court, argues that First Amendment defenses of flag burning are "irrelevant" insofar as the issue is not a person's ideas but a person's mode of expressing those ideas. To outlaw offensive expressions is not the same as banning ideas.

The Supreme Court's recent five-to-four decisions allowing the burning of   1
the American flag as a right protected by the First Amendment have set off an emotional debate. Yet the debate reveals that many Americans are confused about the reasoning behind the decisions and about the appropriate response to them.

The majority opinions in *Texas* v. *Johnson* and *United States* v. *Eichman,*   2
both written by Justice William J. Brennan, rest upon one central argument: "If there is a bedrock principle underlying the First Amendment, it is that the government may not prohibit the expression of an idea simply because society finds the idea itself offensive or disagreeable."

Although this statement is quite true, it is irrelevant. In both of the   3
flag-burning cases, no idea of any sort was being suppressed. The flag burners were entirely free to express their "ideas" in a thousand other ways. Gregory Johnson, for example, chanted, "America, the red, white, and blue, we spit on you," while he burned a flag in Dallas. He was not prosecuted for his verbal expression because, under the First Amendment, his right to free speech was protected. Instead, he was prosecuted for a deeply offensive act prohibited by a state and federal statute.

The First Amendment has always permitted our government to ban offen-   4
sive ways of expressing ideas — though not the ideas themselves. For instance, even after the rulings in *Johnson* and *Eichman,* one would hope that our laws can still punish a televised speech riddled with obscenities, stop a political speech made from a sound truck at 2:00 A.M., or prosecute a protest against sodomy laws where demonstrators engage in the practice in public. The Supreme Court, however, made no attempt to explain why flag burning was not a similarly offensive method of expression. The majority's ruling that flag burning is a form of free speech implies that anybody can express himself with any public behavior at any time, and the community can set no limits on these acts.

I am not alone in my disagreement with the court's conclusion. Chief   5
Justice Earl Warren and Associate Justices Hugo Black and Abe Fortas, three of the most liberal Supreme Court judges in our history, stated unequivocally

that flag burning was not protected speech and could be punished. In fact, at the time of the *Johnson* decision, the government's power to punish flag burners was so widely accepted that 48 states and the federal government had written statutes or laws prohibiting desecration of the American flag.

Some of us support a constitutional amendment that would allow state and   6
federal legislatures — if they choose — to protect the flag against defilement. Many others have opposed this view. Unfortunately, the public debate is conducted in slogans that drown out sensible discussion.

Some opponents of an amendment objected to "chipping away at the First   7
Amendment." A constitutional amendment allowing the government to protect the flag, however, would not diminish the First Amendment. Instead, it would restore the amendment to its condition before the court made its erroneous rulings.

One opponent of the amendment compared the effort to stop flag desecra-   8
tion to Romania's suppression of speech. But suppressing ideas that a dictator dislikes can hardly be compared to objecting to offensive acts of expression. Others noted that Adolf Hitler made defiling the German flag a crime, suggesting, apparently, that nothing Hitler did should ever find an analogy in any shape or form in our society. Of course, Hitler also attacked unemployment, which apparently means we must drop any social policy directed to reducing unemployment in this country.

Still others said that allowing legislatures to prevent flag desecration is   9
equal to desecrating the Constitution. Warren, Black, and Fortas must have been Constitution desecrators, not because they made up freedoms not mentioned in the Constitution — the usual charge against them — but because they recognized that somewhere there is a limit to freedom. Unlimited freedom would make all law, which by definition restricts freedom, impossible.

A final group of opponents argued that we should not set a precedent of   10
overturning Supreme Court decisions with amendments to the Constitution. The precedent, however, has already been set; in the United States, on numerous occasions, we have adopted amendments to overturn Supreme Court judgments.

Ultimately, the question is whether the nation is entitled to one symbol   11
that must remain undefiled. I think so. To say that the freedom of speech requires that no symbol remain sacrosanct is to say something demeaning about the First Amendment itself.

WAIVING THE FLAG [BACK]

Editors of *New Republic*

New Republic *editors suggest that the real issue in the flag burning case is whether government has the power to punish disrespect for the flag. Flag burning is defined as speech, and since burning the flag seriously threatened neither to disrupt the peace nor to impair the flag's ability to symbolize national unity, the editors deny that the government has any authority to intervene.*

Those of us who found George Bush's flag-waving presidential campaign a   1
bit nauseating were consoled by the knowledge that it would come to an end. He would impugn Michael Dukakis's patriotism for a few months, tug shamelessly on the nation's heartstrings, and then, come early November, it would all be over, one way or the other. We didn't expect a President Bush to convert demagoguery into legislation, by, say, proposing a law mandating rituals of respect for the flag. And we still don't. But some of the issues Bush cynically raised last fall may live on by other means. Whether coincidentally or not, the Supreme Court has decided to examine anew a question that was thought to have been virtually settled: whether the government has the power to punish disrespect for the flag—specifically, burning it.

The case derives from the presidential election before this one. On August   2
22, 1984, Gregory Lee Johnson was arrested during the Republican National Convention in Dallas for setting fire to an American flag at a rally in front of city hall. At the trial he was represented by—who else?—an ACLU lawyer. Johnson was convicted of violating an obscure Texas statute—Desecration of Venerated Object—that makes it a crime to desecrate churches, grave stones, monuments, or any state or national flag. "Desecrate" is defined as damaging the object with knowledge that someone else is likely to be seriously offended. For the crime of seriously offending a bystander, Johnson got a year in jail and a $2,000 fine. The Texas Court of Criminal Appeals held that the conviction violated the First Amendment, and the state appealed to the U.S. Supreme Court.

In the past 20 years, the Court has decided a number of flag desecration   3
cases, and has always overturned the convictions. But it has done so with narrow rulings; it has never definitively decided whether flag burning can be banned. And William Rehnquist, now chief justice, has dissented in all such cases. The decision to hear the *Johnson* case may be a sign that the Court is coming around to his view. That would be unfortunate.

It is fairly widely accepted that burning the flag is a form of speech.   4
Displaying the Red flag, wearing a swastika, wearing an arm band, taping a

peace symbol on the American flag—all have been classified by the Supreme Court as speech protected by the First Amendment. It is no wonder that, during the *Johnson* case, the government conceded that burning the flag is a form of speech, too. Indeed, the entire point of the prosecution was that Johnson had conveyed an offensive idea, contempt for the United States.

For some First Amendment absolutists, this would be enough to settle the 5 case. We don't go that far; we'll concede that even though Johnson was engaged in "speech," the government might still have been right to intervene, given a "clear and present danger" or some other conventionally accepted justification. But neither of the two justifications claimed by the government comes close to being strong enough by accepted First Amendment standards.

The government's first claim is that the statute is necessary to prevent 6 violence. The idea is that flag burning could cause a riot. Possible, but unlikely. There have, lamentably, been many flags burned since the Gulf of Tonkin Resolution, but we don't recall any major riots resulting. Besides, it's wrong in principle to allow the state to censor speech just because listeners might attack the speaker. The boundaries of free speech should not be determined by the sensibilities of the most intolerant and violent members of the community. Even in cases where a speaker has tried to incite a crowd to violence, the Court has been justifiably reluctant to allow prosecution.

Anyway, there is no evidence in the *Johnson* case that burning the flag 7 threatened the peace. So far as the record shows, the only member of the audience who reacted dramatically took a much more constructive step: he swept up the ashes, took them home, and buried them in his backyard.

Besides its interest in preventing violence, the government argues that it 8 also has an interest in "preserving the flag as a symbol of national unity." This justification has a nice sound to it, but its meaning is a bit obscure. Unlike the bald eagle, another symbol of national unity, the flag is not an endangered species, so why is it in need of preservation?

TRIVIAL ISSUES DIVERT FLOUNDERING NATION

David Broder

Although personally opposed to First Amendment protection for flag burners, Broder argues that the flag burning issue is trivial, distracting the nation from getting on with more important business.

In years to come, if any historians look back at the United States' entry into   1
the 1990s, I expect they will be very puzzled. At a time when the world was being reshaped by the collapse of the Soviet empire and the emergence of powerful new economic blocs in Europe and Asia, they will surely wonder why Americans were preoccupied by such topics as flag-burning, dirty records and government funding of offensive art.

My friend and former colleague, Michael Barone, has written a weighty   2
history of the last 60 years, "Our Country," which argues that cultural issues often have played a larger role in our politics than most scholars have recognized. If one thinks of race, religion, social status and moral values as the sources of cultural conflict, Barone certainly has a point. Debates on civil rights, abortion, foreign interventions and many other issues were driven by the cultural divisions in this republic.

But the incidents that provoked the headlined cultural controversies of   3
recent days occurred on the fringes of American society. The 2 Live Crew recording, "As Nasty as They Wanna Be," was commercially dying — until a judge in Florida gave it a huge shot of free publicity by ruling it obscene.

The paintings, sculptures and performances that have enmeshed the Na-   4
tional Endowment for the Arts in controversy represent a tiny sliver of its grants — and have a comparably small audience.

As for flag burning, if the television cameras did not compulsively cover   5
these attention-seeking protesters, most Americans would pass through their entire lives without having that offensive spectacle inflicted on them.

These are events which American society would have dismissed or ignored   6
in times past, because we had far more important fish to fry: a frontier to settle and civilize; industries, homes and schools to build; a world to save.

These cultural disputes preoccupy us now, because we are floundering.   7
No American leader in 25 years has discovered or articulated a popular goal to focus the nation's energy and attention. As we drift in our debt-financed, synthetic prosperity, we are losing confidence in our future. So we let ourselves be upset by fringe characters whose goal is simply to shake us up.

How do you suppose we managed to survive for more than 200 years in   8
this country before forcing the Supreme Court to decide, twice in 12 months, the constitutionality of statutes protecting the flag from physical abuse? The

answer is that we were too busy with matters of real importance to be distracted by such a question.

State and federal laws protecting the flag go back more than a century, 9 doing no visible damage to the First Amendment or the exercise of free speech. Violations were rare and occasioned little controversy.

A year ago, when the Supreme Court first ruled, 5–4, that the govern- 10 ment could not punish a physical abuse of the flag, I thought the decision wrong. The reaffirmation last week is no more persuasive. Speech is speech, and should be protected, no matter how offensive to majority opinion. But Chief Justice Rehnquist made the obvious point when he said that "flag burning is the equivalent of an inarticulate grunt or roar that . . . is most likely to be indulged in not to express any particular idea but to antagonize others."

Liberal judges have agreed. Former Chief Justice Earl Warren once wrote, 11 "I believe that the states and the federal government do have the power to protect the flag from acts of desecration and disgrace." The late Justice Hugo Black said, "It passes my belief that anything in the federal Constitution bars a state from making the deliberate burning of the American flag an offense."

This was a 5–4 decision, and those of us who disagree with it know it may 12 be reversed with the next change in membership of the court. Meantime, the handful of flag burners are no threat to this society — unless we inflate them into one by our preoccupation with them.

Some politicians would like to do just that. 13

The decision was no more than announced when Sen. Bob Dole (R-Kan.) 14 and others began illustrating dissenting Justice John Paul Stevens' warning against "leaders who seem to advocate compulsory worship of the flag . . . or who seem to manipulate the symbol of national purpose into a pretext for partisan disputes about meaner ends."

One Republican who is not playing that game is John Yoder, the GOP 15 candidate against Sen. Jay Rockefeller (D-W.Va.). Yoder is a former official in the Reagan administration Justice Department. He understands the appeal Rockefeller's support for a constitutional amendment to ban flag burning will have in an intensely patriotic state like West Virginia.

I do not think the constitutional amendment is as fraught with danger to 16 the Bill of Rights as Yoder and others do. But I admire his guts — and his sense of priorities. He called the controversy "a trivial issue for trivial minds." And he said that "at a time when two-thirds of West Virginia's college graduates are moving out of state to find jobs, we have far more important issues to debate."

America has far more important issues to settle. Let's not fall for the 17 politics of distraction.

KLAN CHALLENGES LAW AGAINST HOODS

Peter Applebome

Peter Applebome surveys a definitional controversy analogous to the flag burning issue: Is the wearing of Ku Klux Klan masks and hoods a constitutionally protected form of free speech?

From the founding of the Ku Klux Klan after the Civil War, its ghostly 1 white robes with peaked hoods have been indelible symbols of racial and religious hatred.

Now a Georgia Klansman is asking a court to rule that the traditional Klan 2 outfit complete with hood represents something quite different: the First Amendment right to free speech.

A motion in a criminal case against the Klansman, who is being defended 3 by the president of the Georgia American Civil Liberties Union, is challenging a 38-year-old state law that tried to stamp out the Klan by banning the wearing of masks or hoods in public.

The result is a case rife with paradox, including the Klan member's citing a 4 landmark case involving the National Association for the Advancement of Colored People. And it is raising the vexing legal issue of whether the Constitution protects the right to make public statements anonymously. If the issue makes its way into Federal courts, a ruling could affect similar laws in many states.

'Offensive' But
Needing Protection

Howard O. Hunter, dean of the Emory University School of Law here, said the 5 case involved "a fairly important definitional issue about the scope of free speech."

Michael R. Hauptman, handling the case in his private capacity and not as 6 a representative of the A.C.L.U., says the law is too broad and deprives his client of the right of anonymous free speech.

"Whatever their motives, they still have in my opinion a right to anony- 7 mous speech under our Constitution," Mr. Hauptman said. "Even though they are offensive not only to myself but to the majority of Americans, they still have a right that needs to be protected."

The state, which is represented by the solicitor's office in Gwinnett 8 County, north of Atlanta, says the Klan is still the malignant force that the

1952 law helped combat and adds that the mask law provides important protection for the public.

'Symbol of Decades
of Violence'

In a brief written on behalf of the state, David M. Fuller, chief assistant 9
solicitor for the Gwinnett County State Court, said, "The mask is a symbol of
decades of violence and terrorism."

The law, he wrote, "is not a statute that forbids the wearing of masks 10
because of undifferentiated fears of the people. The . . . statute forbids the
wearing of masks because those fears are very real."

The law does not name the Klan and includes numerous exceptions, like 11
holiday masks or masks for sports or occupational safety. But its purpose
was clear: to unmask Klan members and thus take away their ability to inflict
anonymous terror.

Osgood Williams, now a senior judge in Georgia Superior Court and one of 12
the State Senators who drew up the law in 1952, said, "I regard the unmasking of the Klan as being the beginning of its demise, and I'm proud of that."

The law faced no legal challenges until this year. On Feb. 27, a caller told 13
the Gwinnett County police that a masked Klansman would show up at the
old county courthouse in Lawrenceville the next day in violation of the law.

The next day the Klan member now at the center of the case, Shade Miller, 14
drove up in his pickup truck, put on his mask and hood and was arrested by
waiting policemen.

Mr. Miller pleaded not guilty to the misdemeanor charges, which carry a 15
maximum penalty of a $1,000 fine and a year in prison. A hearing is sched-
uled in State Court on April 19 to hear Mr. Miller's motion to dismiss the
charges on the ground that the law is unconstitutional.

Mr. Hauptman's brief says the law violates his client's rights under the 16
First Amendment and the due process clause of the 14th Amendment.

He says the law is so vague and broad that someone could be arrested for 17
wearing a ski mask in winter or a Richard Nixon mask. Furthermore, he says,
the full Klan uniform is a powerful form of symbolic speech.

To back up his assertion that anonymity can be essential to the freedom of 18
speech, Mr. Hauptman cites a landmark case, N.A.A.C.P. v. Alabama, in
which Federal courts ruled that the civil rights organization did not have to
divulge its membership rolls to the state of Alabama.

The courts ruled that members of a dissident group like the N.A.A.C.P. in 19
Alabama at the height of the civil rights movement needed anonymity to be
able to exercise its First Amendment rights. Mr. Hauptman said the same was

now true of Klan members, who risk harassment or the loss of jobs if their identity is known.

The state contends that the Klan has not proved any such risk exists for its 20 members and that the N.A.A.C.P. case, in which the government was seeking a membership list, has no relevance to the issue of wearing a mask.

It maintains that the law is not too broad because its intent is clear and 21 readily understood by people of ordinary intelligence. And state officials say the Klan's history of anonymous violence and intimidation in Georgia makes the issue not one of free speech but of terroristic activity.

History of Terrorism Is Seen

Georgia Attorney General Michael J. Bowers said: "It's a matter of historical 22 fact that people have gone out as members of the Klan for the purpose of terrorizing people, most particularly to terrorize them to keep them from exercising their constitutional rights such as voting and assembly. Our legislature said they weren't going to permit it. The First Amendment is not absolute."

But Mr. Hunter said the overall direction of the courts had been to broaden 23 the scope of free speech, even to unpopular areas such as flag burning or wearing swastikas, a trend that argued for overturning the law.

On the other hand, he said, the courts have also made it clear that 24 symbolic speech has to be viewed in context. The terroristic history of the Klan may make the hood more a form of conduct than expression and thus not protected, he said.

Iranian Case Cited

Pat Clark of the Southern Poverty Law Center in Montgomery, Ala., said that 25 rulings in Texas and California had upheld the right of Iranian students to protest in masks because of fears for their safety but that the legal unmasking of the Klan had never faced legal scrutiny.

She and others said the Georgia lawsuit was partly an attempt by the Klan 26 to get publicity. But they said such laws had been effective in combating the group and were useful for law-enforcement officers policing Klan rallies that sometimes turn violent.

"I think if we had a situation where people could go around with their 27 identity concealed we would see a lot more violent activity by some of these groups," she said. "I know the Klan groups will be watching this very, very closely."

FOR CLASS DISCUSSION

1. Analyze and evaluate the debate on flag burning by applying the first set of guide questions from pages 443–444. How do you account for the disagreements among the disputants? This is a particularly good controversy for examining arguments by analogy.

2. Choose one of the arguments for closer analysis, applying the second set of guide questions on page 444.

OPTIONAL WRITING ASSIGNMENT You are a newspaper reporter. Your editor has asked you to write an editorial on the local high school's new dress code. The school has been beset by gang rivalry that recently erupted in a school parking lot shooting. Two students were wounded in the shootout over drug territories.

At issue in the dress code is the gang members' habit of wearing red or blue garb, particularly bandanas, to distinguish themselves from their rivals. The principal has outlawed the wearing of any bandana or predominantly red or blue attire in hopes of relieving tension. Student leaders have complained that many innocent students who simply like the colors are being hurt by this decree. Other students complain that the dress code violates civil rights. One student has facetiously recommended that the U.S. flag be removed from the front of the school because of its red and blue motif.

Drawing on your reading of the preceding essays, write an editorial on the issue.

MERCY KILLING AND THE RIGHT TO DIE: CAN EUTHANASIA BE A MORAL GOOD? IF SO, WHO DECIDES WHEN A COMATOSE PATIENT HAS THE RIGHT TO DIE?

Excerpts from the Supreme Court's Ruling on
Nancy Cruzan v. State of Missouri

In these excerpts from the Supreme Court opinions in Cruzan v. Missouri, *Chief Justice Rehnquist, explaining the majority opinion, supports Missouri's right to protect life. Justices Brennan and Stevens explain their dissenting votes.*

Justice Rehnquist's Majority Opinion

The majority of states in this country have laws imposing criminal penalties 1
on one who assists another to commit suicide. . . . We do not think a State

is required to remain neutral in the face of an informed and voluntary decision by a physically able adult to starve to death.

But in the context presented here, a state has more particular interests at 2 stake. The choice between life and death is a deeply personal decision of obvious and overwhelming finality. We believe Missouri may legitimately seek to safeguard the personal element of this choice through the imposition of heightened evidentiary requirements. . . .

Not all incompetent patients will have loved ones available to serve as 3 surrogate decision-makers. And even where family members are present, "(t)here will, of course, be some unfortunate situations in which family members will not act to protect a patient." . . .

An erroneous decision not to terminate results in a maintenance of the 4 status quo; the possibility of subsequent developments such as advancements in medical science, the discovery of new evidence regarding the patient's intent, changes in the law, or simply the unexpected death of the patient despite the administration of life-sustaining treatment, at least create the potential that a wrong decision will eventually be corrected or its impact mitigated.

An erroneous decision to withdraw life-sustaining treatment, however, is 5 not susceptible of correction. . . .

No doubt is engendered by anything in this record but that Nancy Cruzan's mother and father are loving and caring parents. Close family members may have a strong feeling — a feeling not at all ignoble or unworthy, but not entirely disinterested, either that they do not wish to witness the continuation of the life of a loved one which they regard as hopeless, meaningless, and even degrading.

But there is no automatic assurance that the view of close family members 7 will necessarily be the same as the patient's would have been had she been confronted with the prospect of her situation while competent. All of the reasons previously discussed for allowing Missouri to require clear and convincing evidence of the patient's wishes lead us to conclude that the State may choose to defer only to those wishes, rather than confide the decision to close family members.

Justice Brennan's Dissent

Because I believe that Nancy Cruzan has a fundamental right to be free of 8 unwanted artificial nutrition and hydration, which right is not outweighed by any interests of the State, and because I find that the improperly biased procedural obstacles imposed by the Missouri Supreme Court impermissibly burden that right, I respectfully dissent.

Nancy Cruzan is entitled to choose to die with dignity. 9

An erroneous decision to terminate life-support is irrevocable, says the 10
majority, while an erroneous decision not to terminate "results in a maintenance of the status quo." . . .

But from the point of view of the patient, an erroneous decision in either 11
direction is irrevocable. An erroneous decision to terminate artificial nutrition
and hydration, to be sure, will lead to failure of that last remnant of physiological life, the brain stem, and result in complete brain death. An erroneous
decision not to terminate life-support, however, robs a patient of the very
qualities protected by the right to avoid unwanted medical treatment. His own
degraded existence is perpetuated; his family's suffering is protracted; the
memory he leaves behind becomes more and more distorted. . . .

The Missouri court's disdain for Nancy's statements in serious conversa- 12
tions not long before her accident, for the opinions of Nancy's family and
friends as to her values, beliefs and certain choice, and even for the opinion of
an outside objective factfinder appointed by the State evinces a disdain for
Nancy Cruzan's own right to choose.

The rules by which an incompetent person's wishes are determined must 13
represent every effort to determine those wishes. The rule that the Missouri
court adopted . . . transforms human beings into passive subjects of medical technology.

The majority justifies its position by arguing that, while close family 14
members may have a strong feeling about the question, "there is no automatic assurance that the view of close family members will necessarily be the
same as the patient's would have been had she been confronted with the
prospect of her situation while competent." I cannot quarrel with this observation.

But it leads only to another question: Is there any reason to suppose that a 15
State is more likely to make the choice that the patient would have made than
someone who knew the patient intimately? To ask this is to answer it. As the
New Jersey Supreme Court observed: "Family members are best qualified to
make substituted judgments for incompetent patients not only because of
their peculiar grasp of the patient's approach to life, but also because of their
special bonds with him or her. . . . It is . . . they who treat the patient as a
person, rather than a symbol of a cause." . . .

The State, in contrast, is a stranger to the patient. 16

Justice Stevens's Dissent

"The portion of this court's opinion that considers the merits of this case is 17
similarly unsatisfactory. It, too, fails to respect the best interests of the
patient.

"An innocent person's constitutional right to be free from unwanted 18 medical treatment is thereby categorically limited to those patients who had the foresight to make an unambiguous statement of their wishes while competent.

"Because Nancy Beth Cruzan did not have the foresight to preserve her 19 constitutional right in a living will, or some comparable 'clear and convincing' alternative, her right is gone forever and her fate is in the hands of the state Legislature instead of in those of her family."

THE STATE AS PARENT

Sandra H. Johnson

After clarifying the judicial questions at issue in Cruzan v. Missouri, *law professor Sandra Johnson argues that the right to accept or refuse medical treatment for a permanently comatose individual should belong to the family, not the state.*

I have to admit that when I first heard of the Missouri Supreme Court's   1
decision in Nancy Cruzan's case, my reaction was not a particularly "lawyerly" one. My thoughts went first to my soon-to-be-driving teenage daughter Emily. What this decision meant to me was that if Emily were severely and irreversibly injured in a car accident it would be the state of Missouri and not I who would decide what would happen to her. How could this state, whether judge or legislature, take the place of a parent who had loved and protected and known her all her life?

The court's salute to the compassion and faithfulness of the Cruzan family   2
was no comfort. It chose to look not at the real Nancy Cruzan, whose family had kept a vigil at her bedside, but at "all the Nancy Cruzans." In the name of protecting these hypothetical and symbolic Nancy Cruzans, who certainly do exist somewhere, the majority of the Supreme Court of Missouri denied to the Cruzans the authority to make a very important decision on behalf of their child. While deciding for "all the Nancy Cruzans" this court also decided for all the parents — and spouses — in Missouri.

When the Missouri Supreme Court issued its opinions in the case of Nancy   3
Cruzan, it became the first and only court to require the continued medical treatment of a formerly competent adult who was now in a persistent vegetative state (PVS). During the nearly fifteen years since the case of Karen Ann Quinlan thrust the choices presented by advancing medical technology into the consciousness of the public, state courts had developed a framework for analysis that attracted a wide consensus. These courts generally approached the cases involving formerly competent adults as requiring the court to discover what the particular individual would do if able to make the decision himself or herself. Sometimes these cases were not very persuasive. Many of the patients involved had not expressed any preferences concerning medical treatment. In those cases, it became customary for the courts to defer to the decision of family members if it was compatible with what was known about the patient. The Missouri Supreme Court in *Cruzan* defied this framework. But its holding could be dismissed cavalierly as an "odd decision from a strange state."

Or, it could be placed among the "hard" cases because it involved the   4 discontinuation of nutrition and hydration for a person who was not terminally ill. While every other court examining the issue had concluded that such treatment should be approached in the same fashion as any other medical treatment, several state legislatures, including Missouri's, had specifically excluded medically provided nutrition and hydration from the medical treatments that could be refused through a document executed by a person prior to becoming incapacitated. The major medical professional associations, including the American Medical Association and the American Academy of Neurology, had adopted the same position as had the courts, concluding that it was ethical for physicians to withdraw nutrition for patients suffering irreversible conditions such as PVS. Ethicists, including many from the Catholic faith, had reasoned that there was no moral compulsion to accept medically provided nutrition in such circumstances. Still, many disagreed and there remained a degree of discomfort with withdrawal of nutrition and hydration that didn't exist with medical interventions such as ventilators, chemotherapy, hemodialysis, or surgeries such as amputations.

The Missouri Supreme Court did not clearly confine its decision in *Cruzan* 5 to the withdrawal of medically provided nutrition. Drawing a line between medically provided nutrition and other medically provided sustenance, such as oxygen provided by a ventilator, is difficult. If withdrawing medically provided nutrition is death by starvation, then withdrawing the ventilator is death by suffocation. There are strong advocates on each side of this issue within various traditions, including the Catholic tradition. The *Cruzan* case, involving the withdrawal of nutrition, thus falls within the area of least consensus.

But the *Cruzan* case clearly involves more, as the decision by the U.S. 6 Supreme Court to accept the case for review indicates. The fact that the Court announced that it had accepted this case on the same day that it announced its decision in the abortion case (*Webster* v. *Reproductive Health Services*) only increased speculation over the justices' strategy in selecting it.

Of course, the Supreme Court will *not* be deciding what *ought* to be done 7 for Nancy Cruzan. Rather, the Court will be deciding whether the law of Missouri, as identified by the Missouri Supreme Court, is unconstitutional. A lot will depend, then, on how the U.S. Supreme Court describes what the Missouri Supreme Court did. Surprisingly enough, there are a few choices here.

The bottom line of the Missouri Supreme Court's majority opinion is quite 8 clear — neither Nancy Cruzan herself nor her family has any legal authority under Missouri law to refuse continued medical treatment. She must continue, as a matter of legal compulsion, to receive medical treatment, at least medically provided nutrition. The major justifications for the Missouri court's conclusion are the gravity of the state's interest in the preservation of life; their skepticism that any right to refuse or consent to medical treatment would survive a person's incompetency; and the absence of clear and convincing evidence of Nancy Cruzan's own decision concerning medical treatment.

The Missouri Supreme Court clearly held that the state of Missouri had an 9
interest in life that was unique among the states. The court relied on Missouri's abortion statute, which survived constitutional challenge in *Webster*, and its living will statute as evidence of an intense interest in the "sanctity" of life, which it defined as prolongation of life. The court also held that the state's interest in life outweighed Nancy Cruzan's right to refuse medical treatment, if she in fact had such a right, because the continued treatment caused no burden to her. The court concluded that Nancy Cruzan herself bore no burden because the treatment caused her no pain.

The court repeatedly described its belief that any right that a competent 10
person has to control his or her own medical treatment ends when he or she loses the physical or mental capacity to make his or her own decisions. Since the incompetent patient had no right to refuse treatment herself, that right could not be delegated to her family "absent the most rigid formalities," if at all.

Rather than decide squarely on that basis, however, the Missouri Supreme 11
Court concluded that Nancy Cruzan had left no clear and convincing evidence of her own desires concerning medical treatment in the event of a catastrophe such as the one in which she now finds herself. The court viewed her conversations with her family and friends as too informal to bear any weight in the decision now confronting the state of Missouri.

What the Cruzan case really does, if taken in its entirety, is to appropriate 12
for the state the entire responsibility of deciding the course of medical treatment for an incompetent person like Nancy Cruzan. It completely eliminates any role for the family: as guardians, according to the opinion, they are acting merely as agents for the state of Missouri. It eliminates any concern for what this individual would have desired unless that desire is expressed in the most rigid formalities. It gives to the state the sole authority for weighing the benefits and burdens of a particular medical treatment and further asserts that, for the state of Missouri, the prolongation of life will be the primary value unless achieving that goal is too painful physically.

Still, the United States Supreme Court could read *Cruzan* v. *Harmon* as a 13
case in which the state of Missouri simply requires that medical treatment must be administered to any person who is no longer capable of making his or her own decisions, unless there is clear and convincing evidence that that person would have chosen to refuse that particular treatment. Speculation over what the U.S. Supreme Court will do in any case is hazardous. The Court includes relatively new justices who are developing their own jurisprudence and making their mark on the law of the Constitution. If the question framed by the Court is whether Missouri's requirement of maintaining treat-

ment is constitutional. I would guess that the majority of the justices will say that it is.

In many ways, this is the least offensive course because it strikes a middle 14 ground. It does recognize that there is some constitutional protection for refusal of medical treatment and so does not compel medical treatment in all cases. It does allow individuals to exempt themselves from the state's requirement that they accept medical treatment, if the individual plans well enough in advance. It appears to establish merely procedural protections for vulnerable persons. Furthermore, approval of this approach of itself would not require other states to establish such rules. State courts and legislatures could choose other approaches. The question of what ought to be done would remain the prerogative of the states.

I approach the question of what ought to be done from presumptions that 15 are quite different from those implicit in the opinion of the Missouri Supreme Court. It is from these presumptions that I would criticize a requirement that treatment is to be provided unless there is clear and convincing evidence of the person's choice, especially if that standard implies mandatory judicial process.

First, I do not begin with the presumption that the very availability of 16 medical treatment creates a moral obligation to accept such treatment. Rather, the decision to undergo or refuse treatment must involve weighing the benefits and burdens of that treatment in particular circumstances. There is a surprising uniformity of consent or refusal concerning some medical treatments; for example, most people consent to blood transfusions in life-threatening situations and most at least say they would refuse life support if they were in PVS. But for most medical treatment decisions, the weighing of benefits and burdens is quite personal. While one now-incompetent individual may have firmly believed and practiced a faith that holds a vision of an everlasting life after death, another may have equally firmly and devotedly believed that the breath of life on earth is the ultimate value of human life. Allowing the decision to be made on an individual basis and taking account of the individual's values and life history is most true to the ethical nature of the medical treatment decision.

Second, most people expect that their spouses or adult children will be in 17 charge of any medical treatment decisions that must be made without their own participation. The custom of the medical profession to confer with and seek the consent of the spouse or the parent or the adult children of their incompetent patients reflects this expectation. The expectation that the family will make these decisions is grounded in trust and intimacy. It is also one that recognizes the importance of having someone that can engage the physicians in explaining the risks and benefits of recommended treatments when the very specific and very important facts of the particular situation are known.

One supposed advantage of the clear and convincing evidence approach is 18 that it would force people to confront medical treatment decisions while still capable of doing so. Perhaps. But if you are not a nurse or a physician or otherwise familiar with the great variety of medical treatments that are now available or will be available in the near future for a full range of illnesses or conditions that might rob you of your ability to make your own decisions, how will you leave clear and convincing evidence of your choice? Imagine trying to write out instructions that cover all the bases in a fashion that cannot be misinterpreted. The clear and convincing evidence standard reduces the process of medical treatment decision making to a set of directions and the family to tape recorders.

Who will be authorized to apply this standard? If a court is the only 19 authorized agent of the state, then a court must be used for every case. One need only remember the Linares tragedy in Chicago last year — when a father took his comatose child off a respirator holding the nursing staff at bay with a gun — to see the unworkability of mandated judicial proceedings. Would the Linares child have been better protected by the court? Would the court have reached a different decision? If not, what is the purpose of mandating a judicial process?

In the aftermath of *Cruzan*, it is likely that the various states will have 20 wide latitude in regulating medical treatment decision making. My expectation is that the legal system in this context will honor the medical ethical principle — first, do no harm. The law should not deny the expectations of the vast majority of citizens who believe that their spouses or parents or children are the persons who, knowing them best, should make these important and intimate decisions. Nor should the law reject so completely the tradition and custom of health-care providers in consulting with these natural surrogates. Rather, the legal system should strive to be in harmony with these expectations by giving legal authority to documents appointing health-care proxies. Of course, not all families are wonderful and not all decisions are correct. There will need to be some protection developed.

No legal procedure will resolve all the issues. Conflicts over the goals and 21 limitations of medical treatment will remain. But in a case such as that of the Cruzans, where the family was examined under a microscope by the trial court and the Missouri Supreme Court and found to be a "loving family" and where the courts found that the Cruzans' decision was supported by widely accepted medical principles, by ethical reasoning, and by their daughter's own statements, the state's order of medical treatment simply reduces itself to the assertion that the state knows best.

RISING TO THE OCCASION OF OUR DEATH

William F. May

Legalizing active euthanasia to eliminate suffering may blind us to the value of suffering. "The community . . . may need its aged and dependent, its sick and its dying, and the virtues they sometimes evince—the virtues of humility, courage, and patience—just as much as the community needs the virtues of justice and love manifest in the agents of care."

For many parents, a Volkswagen van is associated with putting children to sleep on a camping trip. Jack Kevorkian, a Detroit pathologist, has now linked the van with the veterinarian's meaning of "putting to sleep." Kevorkian conducted a dinner interview with Janet Elaine Adkins, a 54-year-old Alzheimer's patient, and her husband and then agreed to help her commit suicide in his VW van. Kevorkian pressed beyond the more generally accepted practice of passive euthanasia (allowing a patient to die by withholding or withdrawing treatment) to active euthanasia (killing for mercy). 1

Kevorkian, moreover, did not comply with the strict regulations that govern active euthanasia in, for example, the Netherlands. Holland requires that death be imminent (Adkins had beaten her son in tennis just a few days earlier); it demands a more professional review of the medical evidence and the patient's resolution than a dinner interview with a physician (who is a stranger and who does not treat patients) permits; and it calls for the final, endorsing signatures of two doctors. 2

So Kevorkian-bashing is easy. But the question remains: Should we develop a judicious, regulated social policy permitting voluntary euthanasia for the terminally ill? Some moralists argue that the distinction between allowing to die and killing for mercy is petty quibbling over technique. Since the patient in any event dies—whether by acts of omission or commission—the route to death doesn't really matter. The way modern procedures have made dying at the hands of the experts and their machines such a prolonged and painful business has further fueled the euthanasia movement, which asserts not simply the right to die but the right to be killed. 3

But other moralists believe that there is an important moral distinction between allowing to die and mercy killing. The euthanasia movement, these critics contend, wants to engineer death rather than face dying. Euthanasia would bypass dying to make one dead as quickly as possible. It aims to relieve suffering by knocking out the interval between life and death. It solves the problem of suffering by eliminating the sufferer. 4

The impulse behind the euthanasia movement is understandable in an age when dying has become such an inhumanly endless business. But the move- 5 ment may fail to appreciate our human capacity to rise to the occasion of our death. The best death is not always the sudden death. Those forewarned of death and given time to prepare for it have time to engage in acts of reconciliation. Also, advanced grieving by those about to be bereaved may ease some of their pain. Psychiatrists have observed that those who lose a loved one accidentally have a more difficult time recovering from the loss than those who have suffered through an extended period of illness before the death. Those who have lost a close relative by accident are more likely to experience what Geoffrey Gorer has called limitless grief. The community, moreover, may need its aged and dependent, its sick and its dying, and the virtues which they sometimes evince — the virtues of humility, courage, and patience — just as much as the community needs the virtues of justice and love manifest in the agents of care.

On the whole, our social policy should allow terminal patients to die but it 6 should not regularize killing for mercy. Such a policy would recognize and respect that moment in illness when it no longer makes sense to bend every effort to cure or to prolong life and when one must allow patients to do their own dying. This policy seems most consonant with the obligations of the community to care and of the patient to finish his or her course.

Advocates of active euthanasia appeal to the principle of patient 7 autonomy — as the use of the phrase "voluntary euthanasia" indicates. But emphasis on the patient's right to determine his or her destiny often harbors an extremely naïve view of the uncoerced nature of the decision. Patients who plead to be put to death hardly make unforced decisions if the terms and conditions under which they receive care already nudge them in the direction of the exit. If the elderly have stumbled around in their apartments, alone and frightened for years, or if they have spent years warehoused in geriatrics barracks, then the decision to be killed for mercy hardly reflects an uncoerced decision. The alternative may be so wretched as to push patients toward this escape. It is a huge irony and, in some cases, hypocrisy to talk suddenly about a compassionate killing when the aging and dying may have been starved for compassion for many years. To put it bluntly, a country has not earned the moral right to kill for mercy unless it has already sustained and supported life mercifully. Otherwise we kill for compassion only to reduce the demands on our compassion. This statement does not charge a given doctor or family member with impure motives. I am concerned here not with the individual case but with the cumulative impact of a social policy.

I can, to be sure, imagine rare circumstances in which I hope I would have 8 the courage to kill for mercy — when the patient is utterly beyond human care, terminal, and in excruciating pain. A neurosurgeon once showed a group of physicians and an ethicist the picture of a Vietnam casualty who had lost all four limbs in a landmine explosion. The catastrophe had reduced the soldier to a trunk with his face transfixed in horror. On the battlefield I would hope that I would have the courage to kill the sufferer with mercy.

But hard cases do not always make good laws or wise social policies. 9
Regularized mercy killings would too quickly relieve the community of its obligation to provide good care. Further, we should not always expect the law to provide us with full protection and coverage for what, in rare circumstances, we may morally need to do. Sometimes the moral life calls us out into a no-man's-land where we cannot expect total security and protection under the law. But no one said that the moral life is easy.

DEATH BY CHOICE: WHO SHOULD DECIDE?

Daniel C. Maguire

Writing before recent court decisions brought these issues to full national consciousness, Catholic theologian Daniel Maguire asks whether any decision to end life can be a moral good. Using the cases of a hydrocephalic boy and a severely deformed infant girl, Maguire argues that it can. He remains in a quandary, however, about who should decide.

Who would dare arrogate to himself the decision to impose death on a child 1 or unconscious person who is not in a position to assent or dissent to the action? What right does any person have to make decisions about life and death in a way that assumes absolute and ultimate authority over another human being? Could a doctor make such a decision? It would seem that he could not. His medical skills are one thing, the moral decision to end a life is another. How would a family feel who learned that a doctor had reached an independent decision to terminate their father's life?

Could the family make such a decision? It would seem not, for several good 2 reasons. There might be a conflict of interest arising from avarice, spite, or impatience with the illness of the patient. And even if these things were not present, the family might be emotionally traumatized when their pain of loss is complicated by the recollection of their decision. Also, the family might constitute a split and therefore a hung jury. Then what?

Could a court-appointed committee of impartial persons make the deci- 3 sion? No, it would seem not. They would not only be impartial but also uninformed about the personal realities of the patient. The decision to terminate life requires a full and intimate knowledge of all the reality-constituting circumstances of the case. Strangers would not have this.

The conclusion, therefore, would seem inescapable that there is no moral 4 way in which death could be imposed on a person who is incapable of consent because of youth or irreversible loss of consciousness.

This objection contains so much truth that my reply to it will contain 5 much agreement as well as disagreement. To begin with, it should be noted that we are discussing not the legality but the morality of terminating life without the consent of the patient. Terminating life by a deliberate act of commission in the kinds of cases here discussed is illegal in this country. By an ongoing fiction of American law it would be classified as murder in the first degree. Terminating by calculated omission is murky at best and perilous at worst under current law. Therefore, it can be presumed that any conclusion we reach here will probably be illegal. This is a morally relevant fact; it is not to be presumed morally decisive, however, since there may be good moral grounds to assume the risk of illegality. As we have stated, morality and legality are not identical.

With this said, then, let us face up to the objection. There are two parts to **6** my response. First, holding the question of who should decide in abeyance for the moment, I would suggest that there are cases where, if that difficult question could be satisfactorily answered, it would seem to be a morally good option (among other morally good options) to terminate a life. In other words, there are cases where the termination of a life could be defended as a moral good if the proper authority for making the decision could be located. Of course, if the objections raised against all those who could decide are decisive, then this otherwise morally desirable act would be immoral by reason of improper agency.

There are cases where it would appear to be arguably moral to take the **7** necessary action (or to make the necessary omission) to end a life. Dr. Ruth Russell tells this story:

> I used to annually take a class of senior students in abnormal psychology to visit the hospital ward in a training school for medical defectives. There was a little boy about 4 years old the first time we visited him in the hospital. He was a hydrocephalic with a head so immensely large that he had never been able to raise it off the pillow and he never would. He had a tiny little body with this huge head and it is very difficult to keep him from developing sores. The students asked, "Why do we keep a child like that alive?"
>
> The next year we went back with another class. This year the child's hands had been padded to keep him from hitting his head. Again the students asked, "Why do we do this?" The third year we went back and visited the same child. Now the nurses explained that he had been hitting his head so hard that in spite of the padding he was injuring it severely and they had tied his arms down to the sides of his crib.[1]

What are the defensible moral options in this kind of case? One might be to **8** keep the child alive in the way that was being done. This might show a great reverence for life and re-enforce society's commitment to weak and defective human life. It may indeed be the hallmark of advancing civilization that continuing care would be taken of this child. Termination of this child's life by omission or commission might set us on the slippery slope that has led other societies to the mass murder of physically and mentally defective persons.

All of this is possibly true but it is by no means self-evidently true to the **9** point that other alternatives are apodictically excluded. This case is a singularly drastic one. Given its special qualities, action to end life here is not

[1] See *Dilemmas of Euthanasia*, a pamphlet containing excerpts, papers and discussions from the Fourth Euthanasia Conference, held in New York on December 4, 1971; this is a publication of the Euthanasia Educational Council, Inc. [now called Concern for Dying], New York, p. 35.

necessarily going to precipitate the killing of persons in distinguishably different circumstances.

Furthermore, keeping this child alive might exemplify the materialistic 10 error interpreting the sanctity of life in merely physical terms. This interpretation, of course, is a stark oversimplification. It is just as wrong as the other side of the simplistic coin, which would say that life has no value until it attains a capacity for distinctively personal acts such as intellectual knowledge, love, and imagination. A fetus, while not yet capable of intellectual and other distinctively personal activity, is on a trajectory toward personhood and already shares in the sanctity of human life. (This does not mean that it may never be terminated when other sacred values out-weigh its claim to life in a conflict situation.)

The sanctity of life is a generic notion that does not yield a precisely 11 spelled-out code of ethics. Deciding what the sanctity of life requires in conflict situations such as the case of the hydrocephalic child described by Dr. Russell, may lead persons to contradictory judgments. To say that the sanctity of life requires keeping that child alive regardless of his condition and that all other alternatives impeach the perception of life as sacred, is both arrogant and epistemologically unsound. In this case, maintaining this child in this condition might be incompatible with its sacred human dignity. It might not meet the minimal needs of human physical existence. In different terms, the sanctity of death might here take precedence over a physicalist interpretation of the sanctity of life. There is a time when human death befits human life, when nothing is more germane to the person's current needs. This conclusion appears defensible in the case of the hydrocephalic boy.

Also, to keep this child alive to manifest and maintain society's respect for 12 life appears to be an unacceptable reduction of this child to the status of means. Society should be able to admit the value of death in this case and still maintain its respect for life. Our reverence for life should not be dependent on this sort of martyrdom.

The decision, therefore, that it is morally desirable to bring on this boy's 13 death is a defensible conclusion from the facts and prognosis of this case. (We are still holding in abeyance the question of who should make that decision.) There are two courses of action that could flow from that decision. The decision could be made to stop all special medication and treatment and limit care to nourishment, or the decision could be made in the light of all circumstances to take more direct action to induce death.

There is another case, a famous one . . . , where the life of a radically 14 deformed child was ended. This is the tragic case of Corinne van de Put, who was a victim of thalidomide, a drug that interfered with the limb buds between the sixth and eighth weeks of pregnancy. Corinne was born on May 11, 1962, with no arms or shoulder structure and with deformed feet. It would not even be possible to fit the child with artificial limbs since there was no shoulder structure, but only cartilage. Some experts said the chances for survival were one in ten and Dr. Hoet, a professor of pathological embryology at the Catholic University of Louvain, was of the opinion that the child had only a year or two to live. Eight days after the baby was born, the mother Madame Suzanne van de Put, mixed barbiturates with water and honey in the baby's bottle and thus killed her daughter.

During the trial, Madame van de Put was asked why she had not followed 15 the gynecologist's advice to put the child in a home. "I did not want it," she replied. "Absolutely not. For me, as an egoist, I could have been rid of her. But it wouldn't have given her back her arms." The president of the court pointed out that the child appeared to be mentally normal. "That was only worse," said Madame van de Put. "If she had grown up to realize the state she was in, she would never have forgiven me for letting her live."[2]

Is Madame van de Put's decision to be seen as one of the several morally 16 defensible options available in this case? I think that it is. Again, this does not say that other solutions have no moral probability. As Norman St. John-Stevas points out in his discussion of this case, there are individuals who, though terribly disadvantaged, live fruitful and apparently happy lives. He speaks of Arthur Kavanagh, who was born in 1831 without limbs. No mechanical mechanism could be devised to help him. According to St. John-Stevas, however, Kavanagh managed to achieve some mystifying successes.

> Yet throughout his life he rode and drove, traveled widely, shot and fished. From 1868 until 1880 he sat as member for Carlow and spoke in the Commons. In addition, he was a magistrate, a grand juror, a poor-law guardian, and he organized a body to defend the rights of landlords.[3]

St. John-Stevas, however, does admit that "Not everyone can be an Arthur 17 Kavanagh. . . ." Neither could everyone be a Helen Keller. The problem is that no one knows this when these decisions are made. The option to let the person live and find out is not necessarily safe. The person may not have the resources of a Kavanagh or a Keller and may rue both the day of birth and the decision to let him live. As Madame van de Put said, Corinne may "never have forgiven me for letting her live." The decision to let live is not inherently safe. It may be a decision for a personal disaster. There are persons living who have found their lives a horror, who do not think they have the moral freedom to end their lives, and who ardently wish someone had ended life for them before they reached consciousness. It is little consolation to these people to be told that they were let live on the chance that they might have been a Beethoven. The presumption that the decision to let live will have a happy

---

[2]For an account of this case and a negative judgment on Madame van de Put's action, see Norman St. John-Stevas, *The Right to Life* (New York: Holt, Rinehart & Winston, 1964), pp. 3–24.
[3]Ibid, p. 16.

moral ending is gratuitous and is not a pat solution to the moral quandary presented by such cases.

Interestingly, in the van de Put case, the defense counsel told the jury that 18 he did not think Madame van de Put's solution was the only one, but that it was not possible to condemn her for having chosen it.[4] It could have been moral also to muster all possible resources of imagination and affection and give Corrine the ability to transcend her considerable impairments and achieve fullness of life. In this very unclear situation, this could have been a defensible option. It was not, however, one without risks. It could have proved itself wrong.

The decision to end Corinne's life was also arguably moral, though, again, 19 not without risks. It could not be called immoral on the grounds that it is better to live than not to live regardless of the meaning of that life. This is again a physicalist interpretation of the sanctity of life. It also could not be called immoral on the grounds that this kind of killing is likely to spill over and be used against unwanted children, etc., since this case has its own distinguishing characteristics which make it quite exceptional. It could not be called immoral because it is direct killing since . . . the issue is not directness or indirectness, but whether there is proportionate reason.

In this case, then, as in the case of the hydrocephalic boy, we have a 20 situation where the imposition of death could seem a moral good, prescinding still from the question of who should decide. There could be other cases, too, where death could be seen as a good. Suppose someone suffers severe cerebral damage in an accident but due to continuing brainstem activity can be kept alive almost indefinitely through tubal nourishing and other supportive measures. Would it not seem a clear good if a decision could be made to withdraw support and allow death to have its final say? The spectacle of living with the breathing but depersonalized remains of a loved one could make death seem a needed blessing. In conclusion, then, there are cases where the imposition of death would seem a good. It was logically indicated to state that conclusion before going to the main thrust of the objection, the question of who could decide when the person in question can give no consent.

[4]Ibid, pp. 7-8.

FOR CLASS DISCUSSION

1. Analyze and evaluate the debate on the right to die by applying the first set of guide questions from pages 443–444. How do you account for the disagreement among the disputants?

2. Choose one of the arguments for closer analysis, applying the second set of guide questions on page 444. Also consider student writer Dao Do's essay on pages 141–142.

OPTIONAL WRITING ASSIGNMENT As a member of the state medical board, you have been asked by a local civic organization to give your thoughts on the recent controversy over "Dr. Death," the Detroit physician who designed and made available a "suicide machine" to ensure that those who are suffering from incurable diseases and who wish to kill themselves have a speedy and painless death. (For more background on the Jack Kevorkian case, see the opening of William May's essay, page 652).

Do people have the right to avail themselves of such machines? Do doctors have a right (or even an obligation) to help patients die? What's the state's role in deciding this issue? These are some of the questions the group would like you to consider in a brief (no more than four pages) speech at their weekly Wednesday luncheon. Drawing on your reading of the preceding essays, personal experience, and any other research you may have done, write your speech.

THE DISTRIBUTION OF WEALTH: WHAT RESPONSIBILITY DO THE RICH HAVE FOR THE POOR?

THE GOSPEL OF WEALTH

Andrew Carnegie

Andrew Carnegie, the late nineteenth-century industrialist and philanthropist, argues that the advancement of civilization depends on the right to private property, which leads to accumulation of vast wealth in the hands of a few highly gifted individuals. However, Carnegie argues that these wealthy individuals are obligated to return the wealth to the community in the form of carefully planned charity.

The problem of our age is the proper administration of wealth, that the ties 1
of brotherhood may still bind together the rich and poor in harmonious
relationship. The conditions of human life have not only been changed, but
revolutionized, within the past few hundred years. In former days there was
little difference between the dwelling, dress, food, and environment of the
chief and those of his retainers. The Indians are today where civilized man
then was. When visiting the Sioux, I was led to the wigwam of the chief. It
was like the others in external appearance, and even within the difference was

trifling between it and those of the poorest of his braves. The contrast between the palace of the millionaire and the cottage of the laborer with us today measures the change which has come with civilization. This change, however, is not to be deplored, but welcomed as highly beneficial. It is well, nay, essential, for the progress of the race that the houses of some should be homes for all that is highest and best in literature and the arts, and for all the refinements of civilization, rather than that none should be so. Much better this great irregularity than universal squalor. Without wealth there can be no Mæcenas. The "good old times" were not good old times. Neither master nor servant was as well situated then as today. A relapse to old conditions would be disastrous to both — not the least so to him who serves — and would sweep away civilization with it. But whether the change be for good or ill, it is upon us, beyond our power to alter, and, therefore, to be accepted and made the best of it. It is a waste of time to criticize the inevitable.

It is easy to see how the change has come. One illustration will serve for 2 almost every phase of the cause. In the manufacture of products we have the whole story. It applies to all combinations of human industry, as stimulated and enlarged by the inventions of this scientific age. Formerly, articles were manufactured at the domestic hearth, or in small shops which formed part of the household. The master and his apprentices worked side by side, the latter living with the master, and therefore subject to the same conditions. When these apprentices rose to be masters, there was little or no change in their mode of life, and they, in turn, educated succeeding apprentices in the same routine. There was, substantially, social equality, and even political equality, for those engaged in industrial pursuits had then little or no voice in the State.

The inevitable result of such a mode of manufacture was crude articles at 3 high prices. Today the world obtains commodities of excellent quality at prices which even the preceding generation would have deemed incredible. In the commercial world similar causes have produced similar results, and the race is benefited thereby. The poor enjoy what the rich could not before afford. What were the luxuries have become the necessaries of life. The laborer has now more comforts than the farmer had a few generations ago. The farmer has more luxuries than the landlord had, and is more richly clad and better housed. The landlord has books and pictures rarer and appointments more artistic than the king could then obtain.

The price we pay for this salutary change is, no doubt, great. We assemble 4 thousands of operatives in the factory, and in the mine, of whom the employer can know little or nothing, and to whom he is little better than a myth. All intercourse between them is at an end. Rigid castes are formed, and, as usual, mutual ignorance breeds mutual distrust. Each caste is without sympathy with the other, and ready to credit anything disparaging in regard to it. Under the law of competition, the employer of thousands is forced into the strictest economies, among which the rates paid to labor figure prominently, and often there is friction between the employer and the employed, between capital and labor, between rich and poor. Human society loses homogeneity.

The price which society pays for the law of competition, like the price it   5 pays for cheap comforts and luxuries, is also great; but the advantages of this law are also greater still than its cost — for it is to this law that we owe our wonderful material development, which brings improved conditions in its train. But, whether the law be benign or not, we must say of it, as we say of the change in the conditions of men to which we have referred: It is here; we cannot evade it; no substitutes for it have been found; and while the law may be sometimes hard for the individual, it is best for the race, because it insures the survival of the fittest in every department. We accept and welcome, therefore, as conditions to which we must accommodate ourselves, great inequality of environment; the concentration of business, industrial and commercial, in the hands of a few; and the law of competition between these, as being not only beneficial, but essential to the future progress of the race. Having accepted these, it follows that there must be great scope for the exercise of special ability in the merchant and in the manufacturer who has to conduct affairs upon a great scale. That this talent for organization and management is rare among men is proved by the fact that it invariably secures enormous rewards for its possessor, no matter where or under what laws or conditions. The experienced in affairs always rate the MAN whose services can be obtained as a partner as not only the first consideration, but such as render the question of his capital scarcely worth considering: for able men soon create capital; in the hands of those without the special talent required, capital soon takes wings. Such men become interested in firms or corporations using millions; and, estimating only simple interest to be made upon the capital invested, it is inevitable that their income must exceed their expenditure and that they must, therefore, accumulate wealth. Nor is there any middle ground which such men can occupy, because the great manufacturing or commercial concern which does not earn at least interest upon its capital soon becomes bankrupt. It must either go forward or fall behind; to stand still is impossible. It is a condition essential to its successful operation that it should be thus far profitable, and even that, in addition to interest on capital, it should make profit. It is a law, as certain as any of the others named, that men possessed of this peculiar talent for affairs, under the free play of economic forces must, of necessity, soon be in receipt of more revenue than can be judiciously expended upon themselves; and this law is as beneficial for the race as the others.

Objections to the foundations upon which society is based are not in order,   6 because the condition of the race is better with these than it has been with any other which has been tried. Of the effect of any new substitutes proposed we cannot we sure. The Socialist or Anarchist who seeks to overturn present conditions is to be regarded as attacking the foundation upon which civilization itself rests, for civilization took its start from the day when the capable, industrious workman said to his incompetent and lazy fellow, "If thou dost not sow, thou shalt not reap," and thus ended primitive Communism by separating the drones from the bees. One who studies this subject will soon be brought face to face with the conclusion that upon the sacredness of property civilization itself depends—the right of the laborer to his hundred dollars in the savings-bank, and equally the legal right of the millionaire to his millions. Every man must be allowed "to sit under his own vine and fig-tree, with none to make afraid," if human society is to advance, or even to remain so far advanced as it is. To those who propose to substitute Communism for this intense Individualism, the answer therefore is: The race has tried that. All progress from that barbarous day to the present time has resulted from its displacement. Not evil, but good, has come to the race from the accumulation of wealth by those who have had the ability and energy to produce it. But even if we admit for a moment that it might be better for the race to discard its present foundation, Individualism,—that it is a nobler ideal that man should labor, not for himself alone, but in and for a brotherhood of his fellows, and share with them all in common . . . even admit all this, and a sufficient answer is, This is not evolution, but revolution. It necessitates the changing of human nature itself—a work of eons, even if it were good to change it, which we cannot know.

It is not practicable in our day or in our age. Even if desirable theoretically,   7 it belongs to another and long-succeeding sociological stratum. Our duty is with what is practicable now—with the next step possible in our day and generation. It is criminal to waste our energies in endeavoring to uproot, when all we can profitably accomplish is to bend the universal tree of humanity a little in the direction most favorable to the production of good fruit under existing circumstances. We might as well urge the destruction of the highest existing type of man because he failed to reach our ideal as to favor the destruction of Individualism, Private Property, the Law of Accumulation of Wealth, and the Law of Competition; for these are the highest result of human experience, the soil in which society, so far, has produced the best fruit. Unequally or unjustly, perhaps, as these laws sometimes operate, and imperfect as they appear to the Idealist, they are, nevertheless, like the highest type of man, the best and most valuable of all that humanity has yet accomplished.

We start, then, with a condition of affairs under which the best interests of   8 the race are promoted, but which inevitably gives wealth to the few. Thus far, accepting conditions as they exist, the situation can be surveyed and pronounced good. The question then arises, — and if the foregoing be correct, it is the only question with which we have to deal, — What is the proper mode of administering wealth after the laws upon which civilization is founded have thrown it into the hands of the few? And it is of this great question that I believe I offer the true solution. It will be understood that fortunes are here spoken of, not moderate sums saved by many years of effort, the returns from which are required for the comfortable maintenance and education of families. This is not wealth, but only competence, which it should be the aim of all to acquire, and which it is for the best interests of society should be acquired.

This, then, is held to be the duty of the man of wealth: To set an example 9 of modest, unostentatious living, shunning display or extravagance; to provide moderately for the legitimate wants of those dependent upon him; and, after doing so, to consider all surplus revenues which come to him simply as trust funds, which he is called upon to administer, and strictly bound as a matter of duty to administer in the manner which, in his judgment, is best calculated to produce the most beneficial results for the community — the man of wealth thus becoming the mere trustee and agent for his poorer brethren, bringing to their service his superior wisdom, experience, and ability to administer, doing for them better than they would or could do for themselves.

. . . Those who would administer wisely must, indeed, be wise; for one of 10 the serious obstacles to the improvement of our race is indiscriminate charity. It were better for mankind that the millions of the rich were thrown into the sea than so spent as to encourage the slothful, the drunken, the unworthy. Of every thousand dollars spent in so-called charity today, it is probable that nine hundred and fifty dollars is unwisely spent — so spent, indeed, as to produce the very evils which it hopes to mitigate or cure. A well-known writer of philosophic books admitted the other day that he had given a quarter of a dollar to a man who approached him as he was coming to visit the house of his friend. He knew nothing of the habits of this beggar, knew not the use that would be made of this money, although he had every reason to suspect that it would be spent improperly. This man professed to be a disciple of Herbert Spencer; yet the quarter-dollar given that night will probably work more injury than all the money will do good which its thoughtless donor will ever be able to give in true charity. He only gratified his own feelings, saved himself from annoyance — and this was probably one of the most selfish and very worst actions of his life, for in all respects he is most worthy.

In bestowing charity, the main consideration should be to help those who 11 will help themselves; to provide part of the means by which those who desire to improve may do so; to give those who desire to rise the aids by which they may rise; to assist, but rarely or never to do all. Neither the individual nor the race is improved by almsgiving. Those worthy of assistance, except in rare cases, seldom require assistance. . . .

The best means of benefiting the community is to place within its reach the 12 ladders upon which the aspiring can rise — free libraries, parks, and means of recreation, by which men are helped in body and mind; works of art, certain to give pleasure and improve the public taste; and public institutions of various kinds, which will improve the general condition of the people; in this manner returning their surplus wealth to the mass of their fellows in the forms best calculated to do them lasting good.

Thus is the problem of rich and poor to be solved. The laws of accumulation will be left free, the laws of distribution free. Individualism will continue, but the millionaire will be but a trustee for the poor, entrusted for a season with a great part of the increased wealth of the community, but administering it for the community far better than it could or would have done for itself. The best minds will thus have reached a stage in the development of the race in which it is clearly seen that there is no mode of disposing of surplus wealth creditable to thoughtful and earnest men into whose hands it flows, save by using it year by year for the general good. This day already dawns. Men may die without incurring the pity of their fellows, still sharers in great business enterprises from which their capital cannot be or has not been withdrawn, and which is left chiefly at death for public uses; yet the day is not far distant when the man who dies leaving behind him millions of available wealth, which was free to him to administer during life, will pass away "unwept, unhonored, and unsung," no matter to what uses he leaves the dross which he cannot take with him. Of such as these the public verdict will then be: "The man who dies thus rich dies disgraced."

Such, in my opinion is the true gospel concerning wealth, obedience to which is destined some day to solve the problem of the rich and the poor, and to bring "Peace on earth, among men good will."

RICH AND POOR

Peter Singer

We have a moral obligation to help those living in "absolute poverty." "Helping is not, as conventionally thought, a charitable act that is praiseworthy to do, but not wrong to omit; it is something that everyone ought to do."

Consider these facts: by the most cautious estimates, 400 million people   1
lack the calories, protein, vitamins and minerals needed for a normally healthy life. Millions are constantly hungry; others suffer from deficiency diseases and from infections they would be able to resist on a better diet. Children are worst affected. According to one estimate, 15 million children under five die every year from the combined effects of malnutrition and infection. In some areas, half the children born can be expected to die before their fifth birthday.

Nor is lack of food the only hardship of the poor. To give a broader   2
picture, Robert McNamara, President of the World Bank, has suggested the term 'absolute poverty.' The poverty we are familiar with in industrialized nations is relative poverty—meaning that some citizens are poor, relative to the wealth enjoyed by their neighbours. People living in relative poverty in Australia might be quite comfortably off by comparison with old-age pensioners in Britain, and British old-age pensioners are not poor in comparison with the poverty that exists in Mali or Ethiopia. Absolute poverty, on the other hand, is poverty by any standard. In McNamara's words:

Poverty at the absolute level . . . is life at the very margin of existence.

The absolute poor are severely deprived human beings struggling to survive in a set of squalid and degraded circumstances almost beyond the power of our sophisticated imaginations and privileged circumstances to conceive.

Compared to those fortunate enough to live in developed countries, individuals in the poorest nations have:

An infant mortality rate eight times higher

A life expectancy one-third lower

An adult literacy rate 60% less

A nutritional level, for one out of every two in the population, below acceptable standards; and for millions of infants, less protein than is sufficient to permit optimum development of the brain.

Absolute poverty is, as McNamara has said, responsible for the loss of   3
countless lives, especially among infants and young children. When absolute poverty does not cause death it still causes misery of a kind not often seen in

Source: Peter Singer, "Rich and Poor," *Practical Ethics* (New York: Cambridge University Press, 1979).

the affluent nations. Malnutrition in young children stunts both physical and mental development. It has been estimated that the health, growth and learning capacity of nearly half the young children in developing countries are affected by malnutrition. Millions of people on poor diets suffer from deficiency diseases, like goitre, or blindness caused by a lack of vitamin A. The food value of what the poor eat is further reduced by parasites such as hookworm and ringworm, which are endemic in conditions of poor sanitation and health education.

Death and disease apart, absolute poverty remains a miserable condition of   4
life, with inadequate food, shelter, clothing, sanitation, health services and education. According to World Bank estimates which define absolute poverty in terms of income levels insufficient to provide adequate nutrition, something like 800 million people — almost 40% of the people of developing countries — live in absolute poverty. Absolute poverty is probably the principal cause of human misery today. . . .

The problem is not that the world cannot produce enough to feed and   5
shelter its people. People in the poor countries consume, on average, 400 lbs of grain a year, while North Americans average more than 2000 lbs. The difference is caused by the fact that in the rich countries we feed most of our grain to animals, converting it into meat, milk and eggs. Because this is an inefficient process, wasting up to 95% of the food value of the animal feed, people in rich countries are responsible for the consumption of far more food than those in poor countries who eat few animal products. If we stopped feeding animals on grains, soybeans and fishmeal the amount of food saved would — if distributed to those who need it — be more than enough to end hunger throughout the world.

These facts about animal food do not mean that we can easily solve the   6
world food problem by cutting down on animal products, but they show that the problem is essentially one of distribution rather than production. The world does produce enough food. Moreover the poorer nations themselves could produce far more if they made more use of improved agricultural techniques.

So why are people hungry? Poor people cannot afford to buy grain grown   7
by American farmers. Poor farmers cannot afford to buy improved seeds, or fertilizers, or the machinery needed for drilling wells and pumping water. Only by transferring some of the wealth of the developed nations to the poor of the undeveloped nations can the situation be changed.

That this wealth exists is clear. Against the picture of absolute poverty   8
that McNamara has painted, one might pose a picture of 'absolute affluence.' Those who are absolutely affluent are not necessarily affluent by comparison with their neighbours, but they are affluent by any reasonable definition of human needs. This means that they have more income than they need to provide themselves adequately with all the basic necessities of life. After

buying food, shelter, clothing, necessary health services and education, the absolutely affluent are still able to spend money on luxuries. The absolutely affluent choose their food for the pleasures of the palate, not to stop hunger; they buy new clothes to look fashionable, not to keep warm; they move house to be in a better neighbourhood or have a play room for the children, not to keep out the rain; and after all this there is still money to spend on books and records, colour television, and overseas holidays.

At this stage I am making no ethical judgments about absolute affluence, merely pointing out that it exists. Its defining characteristic is a significant amount of income above the level necessary to provide for the basic human needs of oneself and one's dependents. By this standard Western Europe, North America, Japan, Australia, New Zealand and the oil-rich Middle Eastern states are all absolutely affluent, and so are many, if not all, of their citizens. The USSR and Eastern Europe might also be included on this list. To quote McNamara once more: 9

> The average citizen of a developed country enjoys wealth beyond the wildest dreams of the one billion people in countries with per capita incomes under $200. . . .

These, therefore, are the countries — and individuals — who have wealth which they could, without threatening their own basic welfare, transfer to the absolutely poor.

At present, very little is being transferred. Members of the Organization of Petroleum Exporting Countries lead the way, giving an average of 2.1% of their Gross National Product. Apart from them, only Sweden, The Netherlands and Norway have reached the modest UN target of 0.7% of GNP. Britain gives 0.38% of its GNP in official development assistance and a small amount in unofficial aid from voluntary organizations. The total comes to less than £1 per month per person, and compares with 5.5% of GNP spent on alcohol, and 3% on tobacco. Other, even wealthier nations, give still less: Germany gives 0.27%, the United States 0.22% and Japan 0.21%.   10

The obligation to assist. The path from the library at my university to the Humanities lecture theatre passes a shallow ornamental pond. Suppose that on my way to give a lecture I notice that a small child has fallen in and is in danger of drowning. Would anyone deny that I ought to wade in and pull the child out? This will mean getting my clothes muddy, and either cancelling my lecture or delaying it until I can find something dry to change into; but compared with the avoidable death of a child this is insignificant.   11

A plausible principle that would support the judgment that I ought to pull the child out is this: if it is in our power to prevent something very bad happening, without thereby sacrificing anything of comparable moral significance, we ought to do it. This principle seems uncontroversial. It will ob-   12 viously win the assent of consequentialists; but non-consequentialists should accept it too, because the injunction to prevent what is bad applies only when nothing comparably significant is at stake. Thus the principle cannot lead to the kinds of actions of which non-consequentialists strongly disapprove— serious violations of individual rights, injustice, broken promises, and so on. If a non-consequentialist regards any of these as comparable in moral significance to the bad thing that is to be prevented, he will automatically regard the principle as not applying in those cases in which the bad thing can only be prevented by violating rights, doing injustice, breaking promises, or whatever else is at stake. Most non-consequentialists hold that we ought to prevent what is bad and promote what is good. Their dispute with consequentialists lies in their insistence that this is not the sole ultimate ethical principle: that it is *an* ethical principle is not denied by any plausible ethical theory.

Nevertheless the uncontroversial appearance of the principle that we 13 ought to prevent what is bad when we can do so without sacrificing anything of comparable moral significance is deceptive. If it were taken seriously and acted upon, our lives and our world would be fundamentally changed. For the principle applies, not just to rare situations in which one can save a child from a pond, but to the everyday situation in which we can assist those living in absolute poverty. In saying this I assume that absolute poverty, with its hunger and malnutrition, lack of shelter, illiteracy, disease, high infant mortality and low life expectancy, is a bad thing. And I assume that it is within the power of the affluent to reduce absolute poverty, without sacrificing anything of comparable moral significance. If these two assumptions and the principle we have been discussing are correct, we have an obligation to help those in absolute poverty which is no less strong than our obligation to rescue a drowning child from a pond. Not to help would be wrong, whether or not it is intrinsically equivalent to killing. Helping is not, as conventionally thought, a charitable act which it is praiseworthy to do, but not wrong to omit; it is something that everyone ought to do.

This is the argument for an obligation to assist. Set out more formally, it 14 would look like this:

First premise: If we can prevent something bad without sacrificing anything of comparable significance, we ought to do it.

Second premise: Absolute poverty is bad.

Third premise: There is some absolute poverty we can prevent without sacrificing anything of comparable moral significance.

Conclusion: We ought to prevent some absolute poverty.

The first premise is the substantive moral premise on which the argument 15 rests, and I have tried to show that it can be accepted by people who hold a variety of ethical positions.

The second premise is unlikely to be challenged. Absolute poverty is, as 16
McNamara put it, 'beneath any reasonable definition of human decency' and it
would be hard to find a plausible ethical view which did not regard it as a bad
thing.

The third premise is more controversial, even though it is cautiously 17
framed. It claims only that some absolute poverty can be prevented without
the sacrifice of anything of comparable moral significance. It thus avoids the
objection that any aid I can give is just 'drops in the ocean' for the point is not
whether my personal contribution will make any noticeable impression on
world poverty as a whole (of course it won't) but whether it will prevent some
poverty. This is all the argument needs to sustain its conclusion, since the
second premise says that any absolute poverty is bad, and not merely the total
amount of absolute poverty. If without sacrificing anything of comparable
moral significance we can provide just one family with the means to raise
itself out of absolute poverty, the third premise is vindicated.

I have left the notion of moral significance unexamined in order to show 18
that the argument does not depend on any specific values or ethical principles. I think the third premise is true for most people living in industrialized
nations, on any defensible view of what is morally significant. Our affluence
means that we have income we can dispose of without giving up the basic
necessities of life, and we can use this income to reduce absolute poverty. Just
how much we will think ourselves obliged to give up will depend on what we
consider to be of comparable moral significance to the poverty we could
prevent: colour television, stylish clothes, expensive dinners, a sophisticated
stereo system, overseas holidays, a (second?) car, a larger house, private
schools for our children. . . . For a utilitarian, none of these is likely to be of
comparable significance to the reduction of absolute poverty; and those who
are not utilitarians surely must, if they subscribe to the principle of universa-
lizability, accept that at least *some* of these things are of far less moral
significance than the absolute poverty that could be prevented by the money
they cost. So the third premise seems to be true on any plausible ethical
view — although the precise amount of absolute poverty that can be prevented before anything of moral significance is sacrificed will vary according
to the ethical view one accepts.

Taking care of our own. Anyone who has worked to increase overseas aid 19
will have come across the argument that we should look after those near us,
our families and then the poor in our own country, before we think about
poverty in distant places.

No doubt we do instinctively prefer to help those who are close to us. 20
Few could stand by and watch a child drown; many can ignore a famine in
Africa. But the question is not what we usually do, but what we ought to do,
and it is difficult to see any sound moral justification for the view that

distance, or community membership, makes a crucial difference to our obligations.

Consider, for instance, racial affinities. Should whites help poor whites 21 before helping poor blacks? Most of us would reject such a suggestion out of hand: people's need for food has nothing to do with their race, and if blacks need food more than whites, it would be a violation of the principle of equal consideration to give preference to whites.

The same point applies to citizenship or nationhood. Every affluent nation 22 has some relatively poor citizens, but absolute poverty is limited largely to the poor nations. Those living on the streets of Calcutta, or in a drought stricken region of the Sahel, are experiencing poverty unknown in the West. Under these circumstances it would be wrong to decide that only those fortunate enough to be citizens of our own community will share our abundance. . . .

The element of truth in the view that we should first take care of our own, 23 lies in the advantage of a recognized system of responsibilities. When families and local communities look after their own poorer members, ties of affection and personal relationships achieve ends that would otherwise require a large, impersonal bureaucracy. Hence it would be absurd to propose that from now on we all regard ourselves as equally responsible for the welfare of everyone in the world; but the argument for an obligation to assist does not propose that. It applies only when some are in absolute poverty, and others can help without sacrificing anything of comparable moral significance. To allow one's own kin to sink into absolute poverty would be to sacrifice something of comparable significance; and before that point had been reached, the breakdown of the system of family and community responsibility would be a factor to weigh the balance in favour of a small degree of preference for family and community. This small degree of preference is, however, decisively outweighed by existing discrepancies in wealth and property.

Property rights. Do people have a right to private property, a right which 24 contradicts the view that they are under an obligation to give some of their wealth away to those in absolute poverty? According to some theories of rights (for instance, Robert Nozick's)* provided one has acquired one's property without the use of unjust means like force and fraud, one may be entitled to enormous wealth while others starve. This individualistic conception of rights is in contrast to other views, like the early Christian doctrine to be found in the works of Thomas Aquinas, which holds that since property exists for the satisfaction of human needs, 'whatever a man has in superabundance is owed, of natural right, to the poor for their sustenance.' A socialist would also, of course, see wealth as belonging to the community rather than the individual, while utilitarians, whether socialist or not, would be prepared to override property rights to prevent great evils. . . .

*Robert Nozick, *Anarchy, State and Utopia* (New York, Basic Books, 1974).

However, I do not think we should accept such an individualistic theory. It 25
leaves too much to chance to be an acceptable ethical view. For instance,
those whose forefathers happened to inhabit some sandy wastes around the
Persian Gulf are now fabulously wealthy, because oil lay under those sands;
while those whose forefathers settled on better land south of the Sahara live
in absolute poverty, because of drought and bad harvests. Can this distribution be acceptable from an impartial point of view? If we imagine ourselves
about to begin life as a citizen of either Kuwait or Chad—but we do not
know which—would we accept the principle that citizens of Kuwait are
under no obligation to assist people living in Chad?

Population and the ethics of triage. Perhaps the most serious objection to 26
the argument that we have an obligation to assist is that since the major
cause of absolute poverty is overpopulation, helping those now in poverty
will only ensure that yet more people are born to live in poverty in the
future.

In its most extreme form, this objection is taken to show that we should 27
adopt a policy of 'triage.' The term comes from medical policies adopted in
wartime. With too few doctors to cope with all the casualties, the wounded
were divided into three categories: those who would probably survive without
medical assistance, those who might survive if they received assistance, but
otherwise probably would not, and those who even with medical assistance
probably would not survive. Only those in the middle category were given
medical assistance. The idea, of course, was to use limited medical resources
as effectively as possible. For those in the first category, medical treatment
was not strictly necessary; for those in the third category, it was likely to be
useless. It has been suggested that we should apply the same policies to
countries, according to their prospects of becoming self-sustaining. We
would not aid countries which even without our help will soon be able to feed
their populations. We would not aid countries which, even with our help, will
not be able to limit their population to a level they can feed. We would aid
those countries where our help might make the difference between success
and failure in bringing food and population into balance.

Advocates of this theory are understandably reluctant to give a complete 28
list of the countries they would place into the 'hopeless' category; but
Bangladesh is often cited as an example. Adopting the policy of triage would,
then, mean cutting off assistance to Bangladesh and allowing famine, disease
and natural disasters to reduce the population of that country (now around
80 million) to the level at which it can provide adequately for all.

In support of this view Garrett Hardin has offered a metaphor: we in the 29
rich nations are like the occupants of a crowded lifeboat adrift in a sea full of
drowning people. If we try to save the drowning by bringing them aboard our
boat will be overloaded and we shall all drown. Since it is better that some
survive than none, we should leave the others to drown. In the world today,

according to Hardin, 'lifeboat ethics' apply. The rich should leave the poor to starve, for otherwise the poor will drag the rich down with them. . . .

The consequences of triage on this scale are so horrible that we are 30 inclined to reject it without further argument. How could we sit by our television sets, watching millions starve while we do nothing? Would not that (far more than the proposals for legalizing euthanasia) be the end of all notions of human equality and respect for human life? Don't people have a right to our assistance, irrespective of the consequences?

Anyone whose initial reaction to triage was not one of repugnance would 31 be an unpleasant sort of person. Yet initial reactions based on strong feelings are not always reliable guides. Advocates of triage are rightly concerned with the long-term consequences of our actions. They say that helping the poor and starving now merely ensures more poor and starving in the future. When our capacity to help is finally unable to cope — as one day it must be — the suffering will be greater than it would be if we stopped helping now. If this is correct, there is nothing we can do to prevent absolute starvation and poverty, in the long run, and so we have no obligation to assist. Nor does it seem reasonable to hold that under these circumstances people have a right to our assistance. If we do accept such a right, irrespective of the consequences, we are saying that, in Hardin's metaphor, we would continue to haul the drowning into our lifeboat until the boat sank and we all drowned.

If triage is to be rejected it must be tackled on its own ground, within the 32 framework of consequentialist ethics. Here it is vulnerable. Any consequentialist ethics must take probability of outcome into account. A course of action that will certainly produce some benefit is to be preferred to an alternative course that may lead to a slightly larger benefit, but is equally likely to result in no benefit at all. Only if the greater magnitude of the uncertain benefit outweighs its uncertainty should we choose it. Better one certain unit of benefit than a 10% chance of 5 units; but better a 50% chance of 3 units than a single certain unit. The same principle applies when we are trying to avoid evils.

The policy of triage involves a certain, very great evil: population control 33 by famine and disease. Tens of millions would die slowly. Hundreds of millions would continue to live in absolute poverty, at the very margin of existence. Against this prospect, advocates of the policy place a possible evil which is greater still: the same process of famine and disease, taking place in, say, fifty years time, when the world's population may be three times its present level, and the number who will die from famine, or struggle on in absolute poverty, will be that much greater. The question is: how probable is this forecast that continued assistance now will lead to greater disasters in the future?

Forecasts of population growth are notoriously fallible, and theories about 34 the factors which affect it remain speculative. One theory, at least as plausible as any other, is that countries pass through a 'demographic transition' as their standard of living rises. When people are very poor and have no access to modern medicine their fertility is high, but population is kept in check by high death rates. The introduction of sanitation, modern medical techniques and other improvements reduces the death rate, but initially has little effect on the birth rate. Then population grows rapidly. Most poor countries are now in this phase. If standards of living continue to rise, however, couples begin to realize that to have the same number of children surviving to maturity as in the past, they do not need to give birth to as many children as their parents did. The need for children to provide economic support in old age diminishes. Improved education and the emancipation and employment of women also reduce the birthrate, and so population growth begins to level off. Most rich nations have reached this stage, and their populations are growing only very slowly.

If this theory is right, there is an alternative to the disasters accepted as 35 inevitable by supporters of triage. We can assist poor countries to raise the living standards of the poorest members of their population. We can encourage the governments of these countries to enact land reform measures, improve education, and liberate women from a purely child-bearing role. We can also help other countries to make contraception and sterilization widely available. There is a fair chance that these measures will hasten the onset of the demographic transition and bring population growth down to a manageable level. Success cannot be guaranteed; but the evidence that improved economic security and education reduce population growth is strong enough to make triage ethically unacceptable. We cannot allow millions to die from starvation and disease when there is a reasonable probability that population can be brought under control without such horrors.

LIFEBOAT ETHICS: THE CASE AGAINST HELPING THE POOR

Garrett Hardin

Hardin argues that rich nations are like lifeboats and that impoverished people are like swimmers in the sea clamoring to climb aboard the lifeboat. If we allow all the swimmers to come aboard, the lifeboat sinks. "Complete justice; complete catastrophe."

Environmentalists use the metaphor of the earth as a "spaceship" in trying 1
to persuade countries, industries and people to stop wasting and polluting our natural resources. Since we all share life on this planet, they argue, no single person or institution has the right to destroy, waste or use more than a fair share of its resources.

But does everyone on earth have an equal right to an equal share of its 2
resources? The spaceship metaphor can be dangerous when used by misguided idealists to justify suicidal policies for sharing our resources through uncontrolled immigration and foreign aid. In their enthusiastic but unrealistic generosity, they confuse the ethics of a spaceship with those of a lifeboat.

A true spaceship would have to be under the control of a captain, since no 3
ship could possibly survive if its course were determined by committee. Spaceship Earth certainly has no captain; the United Nations is merely a toothless tiger, with little power to enforce any policy upon its bickering members.

If we divide the world crudely into rich nations and poor nations, two 4
thirds of them are desperately poor, and only one third comparatively rich, with the United States the wealthiest of all. Metaphorically each nation can be seen as a lifeboat full of comparatively rich people. In the ocean outside each lifeboat swim the poor of the world, who would like to get in, or at least to share some of the wealth. What should the lifeboat passengers do?

First, we must recognize the limited capacity of any lifeboat. For example, 5
a nation's land has a limited capacity to support a population and as the current energy crisis has shown us, in some ways we have already exceeded the carrying capacity of our land.

Adrift in a Moral Sea

So here we sit, say fifty people in our lifeboat. To be generous, let us assume 6
it has room for ten more, making a total capacity of sixty. Suppose the fifty of us in the lifeboat see 100 others swimming in the water outside, begging for admission to our boat or for handouts. We have several options: We may be tempted to try to live by the Christian ideal of being "our brother's keeper,"

or by the Marxist ideal of "to each according to his needs." Since the needs of all in the water are the same, and since they can all be seen as "our brothers," we could take them all into our boat, making a total of 150 in a boat designed for sixty. The boat swamps, everyone drowns. Complete justice, complete catastrophe.

Since the boat has an unused excess capacity of ten more passengers, we 7 could admit just ten more to it. But which ten do we let in? How do we choose? Do we pick the best ten, the neediest ten, "first come, first served"? And what do we say to the ninety we exclude? If we do let an extra ten into our lifeboat, we will have lost our "safety factor," an engineering principle of critical importance. For example, if we don't leave room for excess capacity as a safety factor in our country's agriculture, a new plant disease or a bad change in the weather could have disastrous consequences.

Suppose we decide to preserve our small safety factor and admit no more 8 to the lifeboat. Our survival is then possible, although we shall have to be constantly on guard against boarding parties.

While this last solution clearly offers the only means of our survival, it is 9 morally abhorrent to many people. Some say they feel guilty about their good luck. My reply is simple: "Get out and yield your place to others." This may solve the problem of the guilt-ridden person's conscience, but it does not change the ethics of the lifeboat. The needy person to whom the guilt-ridden person yields his place will not himself feel guilty about his good luck. If he did, he would not climb aboard. The net result of conscience-stricken people giving up their unjustly held seats is the elimination of that sort of conscience from the lifeboat.

This is the basic metaphor within which we must work out our solutions. 10 Let us now enrich the image, step by step, with substantive additions from the real world, a world that must solve real and pressing problems of overpopulation and hunger.

The harsh ethics of the lifeboat become even harsher when we consider the 11 reproductive differences between the rich nations and the poor nations. The people inside the lifeboats are doubling in numbers every eighty-seven years; those swimming around outside are doubling, on the average, every thirty-five years, more than twice as fast as the rich. And since the world's resources are dwindling, the difference in prosperity between the rich and the poor can only increase.

As of 1973, the U.S. had a population of 210 million people, who were 12 increasing by 0.8 percent per year. Outside our lifeboat, let us imagine another 210 million people (say the combined populations of Colombia, Ecuador, Venezuela, Morocco, Pakistan, Thailand and the Philippines), who are increasing at a rate of 3.3 percent per year. Put differently, the doubling time for this aggregate population is twenty-one years, compared to eighty-seven years for the U.S.

Multiplying the Rich and the Poor

Now suppose the U.S. agreed to pool its resources with those seven coun-   13
tries, with everyone receiving an equal share. Initially the ratio of Americans
to non-Americans in this model would be one-to-one. But consider what the
ratio would be after eighty-seven years, by which time the Americans would
have doubled to a population of 420 million. By then, doubling every twenty-
one years, the other group would have swollen to 354 billion. Each American
would have to share the available resource with more than eight people.

But, one could argue, this discussion assumes that current population   14
trends will continue, and they may not. Quite so. Most likely the rate of
population increase will decline much faster in the U.S. than it will in the
other countries, and there does not seem to be much we can do about it. In
sharing with "each according to his needs," we must recognize that needs are
determined by population size, which is determined by the rate of reproduction, which at present is regarded as a sovereign right of every nation, poor or
not. This being so, the philanthropic load created by the sharing ethic of the
spaceship can only increase.

The Tragedy of the Commons

The fundamental error of spaceship ethics, and the sharing it requires, is that   15
it leads to what I call "the tragedy of the commons." Under a system of
private property, the men who own property recognize their responsibility to
care for it, for if they don't they will eventually suffer. A farmer, for instance,
will allow no more cattle in a pasture than its carrying capacity justifies. If he
overloads it, erosion sets in, weeds take over, and he loses the use of the
pasture.

If a pasture becomes a commons open to all, the right of each to use it may   16
not be matched by a corresponding responsibility to protect it. Asking everyone to use it with discretion will hardly do, for the considerate herdsman who
refrains from overloading the commons suffers more than a selfish one who
says his needs are greater. If everyone would restrain himself, all would be
well; but it takes only one less than everyone to ruin a system of voluntary
restraint. In a crowded world of less than perfect human beings, mutual ruin
is inevitable if there are no controls. This is the tragedy of the commons.

One of the major tasks of education today should be the creation of such   17
an acute awareness of the dangers of the commons that people will recognize
its many varieties. For example, the air and water have become polluted
because they are treated as commons. Further growth in the population or
per-capita conversion of natural resources into pollutants will only make the
problem worse. The same holds true for the fish of the oceans. Fishing fleets
have nearly disappeared in many parts of the world, technological improve-

ments in the art of fishing are hastening the day of complete ruin. Only the replacement of the system of the commons with a responsible system of control will save the land, air, water and oceanic fisheries.

The World Food Bank

In recent years there has been a push to create a new commons called a World 18
Food Bank, an international depository of food reserves to which nations would contribute according to their abilities and from which they would draw according to their needs. This humanitarian proposal has received support from many liberal international groups, and from such prominent citizens as Margaret Mead, U.N. Secretary General Kurt Waldheim, and Senators Edward Kennedy and George McGovern.

A world food bank appeals powerfully to our humanitarian impulses. But 19
before we rush ahead with such a plan, let us recognize where the greatest political push comes from, lest we be disillusioned later. Our experience with the "Food for Peace program," or Public Law 480, gives us the answer. This program moved billions of dollars' worth of U.S. surplus grain to food-short, population-long countries during the past two decades. But when P.L. 480 first became law, a headline in the business magazine *Forbes* revealed the real power behind it: "Feeding the World's Hungry Millions: How It Will Mean Billions for U.S. Business."

And indeed it did. In the years 1960 to 1970, U.S. taxpayers spent a total 20
of $7.9 billion on the Food for Peace program. Between 1948 and 1970, they also paid an additional $50 billion for other economic-aid programs, some of which went for food and food-producing machinery and technology. Though all U.S. taxpayers were forced to contribute to the cost of P.L. 480, certain special interest groups gained handsomely under the program. Farmers did not have to contribute the grain; the Government, or rather the taxpayers, bought it from them at full market prices. The increased demand raised prices of farm products generally. The manufacturers of farm machinery, fertilizers and pesticides benefited by the farmers' extra efforts to grow more food. Grain elevators profited from storing the surplus until it could be shipped. Railroads made money hauling it to ports, and shipping lines profited from carrying it overseas. The implementation of P.L. 480 required the creation of a vast Government bureaucracy, which then acquired its own vested interest in continuing the program regardless of its merits.

Extracting Dollars

Those who proposed and defended the Food for Peace program in public 21
rarely mentioned its importance to any of these special interests. The public

emphasis was always on its humanitarian effects. The combination of silent selfish interests and highly vocal humanitarian apologists made a powerful and successful lobby for extracting money from taxpayers. We can expect the same lobby to push now for the creation of a World Food Bank.

However great the potential benefit to selfish interests, it should not be a 22 decisive argument against a truly humanitarian program. We must ask if such a program would actually do more good than harm, not only momentarily but also in the long run. Those who propose the food bank usually refer to a current "emergency" or "crisis" in terms of world food supply. But what is an emergency? Although they may be infrequent and sudden, everyone knows that emergencies will occur from time to time. A well-run family, company, organization or country prepares for the likelihood of accidents and emergencies. It expects them, it budgets for them, it saves for them.

Learning the Hard Way

What happens if some organizations or countries budget for accidents and 23 others do not? If each country is solely responsible for its own well-being, poorly managed ones will suffer. But they can learn from experience. They may mend their ways, and learn to budget for infrequent but certain emergencies. For example, the weather varies from year to year, and periodic crop failures are certain. A wise and competent government saves out of the production of the good years in anticipation of bad years to come. Joseph taught this policy to Pharaoh in Egypt more than 2,000 years ago. Yet the great majority of the governments in the world today do not follow such a policy. They lack either the wisdom or the competence, or both. Should those nations that do manage to put something aside be forced to come to the rescue each time an emergency occurs among the poor nations?

"But it isn't their fault!" some kindhearted liberals argue. "How can we 24 blame the poor people who are caught in an emergency? Why must they suffer for the sins of their governments?" The concept of blame is simply not relevant here. The real question is, what are the operational consequences of establishing a world food bank? If it is open to every country every time a need develops, slovenly rulers will not be motivated to take Joseph's advice. Someone will always come to their aid. Some countries will deposit food in the world food bank, and others will withdraw it. There will be almost no overlap. As a result of such solutions to food shortage emergencies, the poor countries will not learn to mend their ways, and will suffer progressively greater emergencies as their populations grow.

Population Control the Crude Way

On the average, poor countries undergo a 2.5 percent increase in population **25**
each year; rich countries, about 0.8 percent. Only rich countries have anything in the way of food reserves set aside, and even they do not have as much
as they should. Poor countries have none. If poor countries received no food
from the outside, the rate of their population growth would be periodically
checked by crop failures and famines. But if they can always draw on a world
food bank in time of need, their populations can continue to grow unchecked,
and so will their "need" for aid. In the short run, a world food bank may
diminish that need, but in the long run it actually increases the need without
limit.

Without some system of worldwide food sharing, the proportion of people **26**
in the rich and poor nations might eventually stabilize. The overpopulated
poor countries would decrease in numbers, while the rich countries that had
room for more people would increase. But with a well-meaning system of
sharing, such as a world food bank, the growth differential between the rich
and the poor countries will not only persist, it will increase. Because of the
higher rate of population growth in the poor countries of the world, 88
percent of today's children are born poor, and only 12 percent rich. Year by
year the ratio becomes worse, as the fast-reproducing poor outnumber the
slow-reproducing rich.

A world food bank is thus a commons in disguise. People will have more **27**
motivation to draw from it than to add to any common store. The less
provident and less able will multiply at the expense of the abler and more
provident, bringing eventual ruin upon all who share in the commons. Besides, any system of "sharing" that amounts to foreign aid from the rich
nations to the poor nations will carry the taint of charity, which will contribute little to the world peace so devoutly desired by those who support the idea
of a world food bank.

As past U.S. foreign-aid programs have amply and depressingly demon- **28**
strated, international charity frequently inspires mistrust and antagonism
rather than gratitude on the part of the recipient nation.

Chinese Fish and Miracle Rice

The modern approach to foreign aid stresses the export of technology and **29**
advice, rather than money and food. As an ancient Chinese proverb goes:
"Give a man a fish and he will eat for a day; teach him how to fish and he will
eat for the rest of his days." Acting on this advice, the Rockefeller and Ford
Foundations have financed a number of programs for improving agriculture
in the hungry nations. Known as the "Green Revolution," these programs
have led to the development of "miracle rice" and "miracle wheat," new

strains that offer bigger harvests and greater resistance to crop damage. Norman Borlaug, the Nobel Prize winning agronomist who, supported by the Rockefeller Foundation, developed "miracle wheat," is one of the most prominent advocates of a world food bank.

Whether or not the Green Revolution can increase food production as   30 much as its champions claim is a debatable but possibly irrelevant point. Those who support this well-intended humanitarian effort should first consider some of the fundamentals of human ecology. Ironically, one man who did was the late Alan Gregg, a vice president of the Rockefeller Foundation. Two decades ago he expressed strong doubts about the wisdom of such attempts to increase food production. He likened the growth and spread of humanity over the surface of the earth to the spread of cancer in the human body, remarking that "cancerous growths demand food; but, as far as I know, they have never been cured by getting it."

Overloading the Environment

Every human born constitutes a draft on all aspects of the environment: food,   31 air, water, forests, beaches, wildlife, scenery and solitude. Food can, perhaps, be significantly increased to meet a growing demand. But what about clean beaches, unspoiled forests, and solitude? If we satisfy a growing population's need for food, we necessarily decrease its per-capita supply of the other resources needed by men.

India, for example, now has a population of 600 million, which increases   32 by 15 million each year. This population already puts a huge load on a relatively impoverished environment. The country's forests are now only a small fraction of what they were three centuries ago, and floods and erosion continually destroy the insufficient farmland that remains. Every one of the 15 million new lives added to India's population puts an additional burden on the environment, and increases the economic and social costs of crowding. However humanitarian our intent, every Indian life saved through medical or nutritional assistance from abroad diminishes the quality of life for those who remain, and for subsequent generations. If rich countries make it possible, through foreign aid, for 600 million Indians to swell to 1.2 billion in a mere twenty-eight years, as their current growth rate threatens, will future generations of Indians thank us for hastening the destruction of their environment? Will our good intentions be sufficient excuse for the consequences of our actions?

My final example of a commons in action is one for which the public has   33 the least desire for rational discussion — immigration. Anyone who publicly questions the wisdom of current U.S. immigration policy is promptly charged with bigotry, prejudice, ethnocentrism, chauvinism, isolationism or selfishness. Rather than encounter such accusations, one would rather talk about other matters, leaving immigration policy to wallow in the crosscurrents of special interests that take no account of the good of the whole, or the interest of posterity.

Perhaps we still feel guilty about things we said in the past. Two genera- 34 tions ago the popular press frequently referred to Dagos, Wops, Polacks, Chinks and Krauts, in articles about how America was being "overrun" by foreigners of supposedly inferior genetic stock. But because the implied inferiority of foreigners was used then as justification for keeping them out, people now assume that restrictive policies could only be based on such misguided notions. There are no other grounds.

A Nation of Immigrants

Just consider the numbers involved. Our Government acknowledges a net 35 inflow of 400,000 immigrants a year. While we have no hard data on the extent of illegal entries, educated guesses put the figure at about 600,000 a year. Since the natural increase (excess of births over deaths) of the resident population now runs about 1.7 million per year, the yearly gain from immigration amounts to at least 19 percent of the total annual increase, and may be as much as 37 percent if we include the estimate for illegal immigrants. Considering the growing use of birth-control devices, the potential effect of educational campaigns by such organizations as Planned Parenthood Federation of America and Zero Population Growth, and the influence of inflation and the housing shortage, the fertility rate of American women may decline so much that immigration could account for all the yearly increase in population. Should we not at least ask if that is what we want?

For the sake of those who worry about whether the "quality" of the 36 average immigrant compares favorably with the quality of the average resident, let us assume that immigrants and nativeborn citizens are of exactly equal quality, however one defines that term. We will focus here only on quantity; and since our conclusions will depend on nothing else, all charges of bigotry and chauvinism become irrelevant.

Immigration vs. Food Supply

World food banks *move food to the people*, hastening the exhaustion of the 37 environment of the poor countries. Unrestricted immigration, on the other hand, *moves people to the food*, thus speeding up the destruction of the environment of the rich countries. We can easily understand why poor people should want to make this latter transfer, but why should rich hosts encourage it?

As in the case of foreign-aid programs, immigration receives support from 38
selfish interests and humanitarian impulses. The primary selfish interest in
unimpeded immigration is the desire of employers for cheap labor, particularly in industries and trades that offer degrading work. In the past, one wave
of foreigners after another was brought into the U.S. to work at wretched
jobs for wretched wages. In recent years, the Cubans, Puerto Ricans and
Mexicans have had this dubious honor. The interests of the employers of
cheap labor mesh well with the guilty silence of the country's liberal intelli-
gentsia. White Anglo-Saxon Protestants are particularly reluctant to call for
a closing of the doors to immigration for fear of being called bigots.

But not all countries have such reluctant leadership. Most educated 39
Hawaiians, for example, are keenly aware of the limits of their environment,
particularly in terms of population growth. There is only so much room on
the islands, and the islanders know it. To Hawaiians, immigrants from the
other forty-nine states present as great a threat as those from other nations.
At a recent meeting of Hawaiian government officials in Honolulu, I had the
ironic delight of hearing a speaker, who like most of his audience was of
Japanese ancestry, ask how the country might practically and constitutionally
close its doors to further immigration. One member of the audience coun-
tered: "How can we shut the doors now? We have many friends and relatives
in Japan that we'd like to bring here some day so that they can enjoy Hawaii
too." The Japanese-American speaker smiled sympathetically and answered:
"Yes, but we have children now, and someday we'll have grandchildren too.
We can bring more people here from Japan only by giving away some of the
land that we hope to pass on to our grandchildren some day. What right do
we have to do that?"

At this point, I can hear U.S. liberals asking: "How can you justify 40
slamming the door once you're inside? You say that immigrants should be
kept out. But aren't we all immigrants, or the descendants of immigrants? If
we insist on staying, must we not admit all others?" Our craving for intellectual order leads us to seek and prefer symmetrical rules and morals: a single
rule for me and everybody else; the same rule yesterday, today, and tomorrow.
Justice, we feel, should not change with time and place.

We Americans of non-Indian ancestry can look upon ourselves as the 41
descendants of thieves who are guilty morally, if not legally, of stealing this
land from its Indian owners. Should we then give back the land to the now
living American descendants of those Indians? However morally or logically
sound this proposal may be, I, for one, am unwilling to live by it and I know
no one else who is. Besides, the logical consequence would be absurd.
Suppose that, intoxicated with a sense of pure justice, we should decide to
turn our land over to the Indians. Since all our wealth has also been derived
from the land, wouldn't we be morally obliged to give that back to the Indians
too?

Pure Justice vs. Reality

Clearly, the concept of pure justice produces an infinite regression to absur- **42** dity. Centuries ago, wise men invented statutes of limitations to justify the rejection of such pure justice, in the interest of preventing continual disorder. The law zealously defends property rights, but only relatively recent property rights. Drawing a line after an arbitrary time has elapsed may be unjust, but the alternatives are worse.

We are all descendants of thieves, and the world's resources are inequit- **43** ably distributed. But we must begin the journey to tomorrow from the point where we are today. We cannot remake the past. We cannot safely divide the wealth equitably among all peoples so long as people reproduce at different rates. To do so would guarantee that our grandchildren, and everyone else's grandchildren, would have only a ruined world to inhabit.

To be generous with one's own possessions is quite different from being **44** generous with those of posterity. We should call this point to the attention of those who, from a commendable love of justice and equality, would institute a system of the commons, either in the form of a world food bank, or of unrestricted immigration. We must convince them if we wish to save at least some parts of the world from environmental ruin.

Without a true world government to control reproduction and the use of **45** available resources, the sharing ethic of the spaceship is impossible. For the foreseeable future, our survival demands that we govern our actions by the ethics of a lifeboat, harsh though they may be. Posterity will be satisfied with nothing less.

FOR CLASS DISCUSSION

1. Analyze and evaluate the controversy over the obligation of the rich to help the poor by applying the first set of guide questions from pages 443–444. How do you account for the disagreement between Hardin, on the one hand, and Singer or Carnegie on the other?

2. Choose one of the arguments for closer analysis, applying the second set of guide questions on page 444.

OPTIONAL WRITING ASSIGNMENT   At last, you've won the lottery. You'll be receiving $250,000 per year for the next 20 years. Ever since you got the news, your phone's been ringing off the hook. Your older brother, Fast Eddie, has called urging you to buy a big house and a fast car and to consider putting a couple of big ones on the Blue Jays for the American League pennant. Your younger sister, Sensible Sarah, has outlined a comprehensive investment strategy for you that will put you into CD's, zero coupon bonds, and a few blue chippers. Then Aunt Teresa calls. "What are your plans for charitable giving?" she wants to know.

"I'm looking into that," you lie. "I have a plan," you lie further.

"Good," she responds. "Send it to me next week in my birthday card."

Your time is running out. What will you tell Aunt Teresa? Just what are your obligations? Some? None? All? Drawing on ideas from the preceding essays, personal experience, and any other research you may have done, write a letter to her justifying your decision.

AFFIRMATIVE ACTION AND REVERSE DISCRIMINATION: WHAT DOES THE PRESENT OWE TO THE PAST?

AFFIRMATIVE ACTION, QUOTAS AND MERIT

Jack Greenberg

An officer and administrator for the NAACP, writer Jack Greenberg defends affirmative action on the basis of analogy to other cases in the free market, where certain groups are given preferences not related to merit.

The moral legitimacy of affirmative action and quotas favoring racial   1
minorities must be assessed in a social and historical context, in the light of
the many conflicting values that our society holds.

Traditionally, we profess reliance upon grades, scores and experience as   2
bases upon which to assign jobs or admit to schools those who by these
prevailing measures of competence are said to be most qualified.

Recently, as a result of litigation, we have found that these criteria often   3
fail to select the best candidates or are not job-related. But when it works, the
merit standard often picks those who do in fact perform better, and by
offering incentive probably makes society more productive.

However, many dissimilar, widely accepted or barely tolerated criteria that   4
serve other values often are designed to select persons other than those best
qualified.

A tenured professor will hold his position in spite of competition from   5
younger, better, more vigorous scholars. Tenure is thought, however, to
serve the important societal interest in academic freedom by enabling teachers
to take controversial positions without fear and by shielding them against
petty politics.

Seniority rights advance individual security, worker satisfaction and job   6
loyalty by promoting older workers although younger persons may be objectively more qualified, while, paradoxically, compulsory retirement favors
younger persons over older, experienced, and perhaps more competent
workers.

The union shop favors a union member against a superior outside competi-   7
tor in the belief that a strong labor movement is more important than the
employers' right to hire and fire on the basis of whim, or merit.

Hiring and promotional preferences granted to veterans express national   8
gratitude for military sacrifice and expressly subordinate claims of superior
persons without military experience.

Even the most prestigious schools consider more than marks as criteria for   9
admission — to obtain a geographically and otherwise diverse student body
and thereby enhance the educational experience of all. Some admissions
officers contend that if "all other things are equal" they will favor a great
industrial or financial family by admitting one of its children. Perhaps this
helps raise funds.

There are not many in positions of influence who have not been asked to   10
help a relative or friend get a job or be admitted to a school. This is called
word-of-mouth recruitment, "old boy network," or "pull." It is natural to
assist friends and useful to have additional information about candidates. But
persons not plugged into the network do not have the same access.

One would imagine, to pick only names from the past, that Carnegies and   11
Morgans did not travel a rough road in getting an education and obtaining employment. Inheritability of wealth is an economic incentive, and
strengthens the family, although some see unfairness in benefiting those who
played no part in creating the wealth.

The general, sometimes grudging, sometimes comfortable acceptance of   12
antimerit preferences requires close scrutiny of arguments that affirmative
action for blacks violates America's merit ethic.

Even the most conservative must agree that the historic injustices that   13
America has heaped upon its black citizens are beyond calculation.

After the abolition of the inhumane institution of slavery, racial segrega-   14
tion and discrimination persisted in virtually the same form, almost unchecked for generations.

In our lifetime, Washington, D.C., as well as other portions of our nation,   15
compared with Capetown, South Africa, in the entrenchment of apartheid,
and lynchings were frequent.

Black unemployment remains about double white unemployment, and 16
health, housing and other inequities persist.

America's historic public and private racial discrimination has left a legacy 17
of inequality and inopportunity, and infuses virtually every major social
problem: unemployment, poverty, crime, welfare, slum housing.

The mere assertion of new policy with respect to black citizens has not 18
adequately changed the social situation. To select someone for employment
or school on the basis of race, as a means of breaking the cycle of inferior
education, poverty, unemployment, and damaged families, has at least as
great moral justification as the many criteria we use other than so-called
merit.

SURVIVING AFFIRMATIVE ACTION (MORE OR LESS)

Frederick Lynch

Sociologist Frederick Lynch, who specializes in the study of reverse discrimination, combines academic research and personal experience in a scathing attack on reverse discrimination practices.

In the mid-1970's, I became increasingly interested in what I assumed were   1
two sociologically compelling questions: (1) how did white males (and their
families, co-workers, and friends) respond to reverse discrimination?; and (2)
how were the media portraying affirmative action? I conducted the research
and later published the results while teaching in temporary faculty positions
on the Los Angeles and San Bernardino campuses of the California State
University (CSU) system.

Throughout this period, the nineteen-campus CSU empire became caught   2
up in an intensifying affirmative-action crusade involving blatant race, ethnic,
and gender preferences in recruiting faculty, staff, and students. Thus, I was
engaging in critical studies of policies championed by my own employer (and
most alternative academic employers). This was risky business. Scattered
reports from critics of affirmative action made it obvious that academic
freedom on the topic was fragile even for tenured scholars, and the tight job
market for sociologists rendered the kind of research I was doing doubly
dangerous. Nevertheless, curiosity ultimately prevailed over fear and anxiety.

For me this research saga illuminated the powerful taboos which have   3
dominated the American intellectual landscape for more than twenty years,
and I learned a great deal from the experience. I would, however, never do
such a thing again. My career has been badly damaged. Worse, I have
watched a political steamroller flatten civil liberties and due process as it has
moved through institutions designed to be bastions of traditionally liberal
values and forums for the free discussion and rational analysis of ideas. The
academic and intellectual communities which once embraced Martin Luther
King's call to judge an individual by the content of his character, not the
color of his skin, now do precisely the opposite. They bow reverentially to the
gods of tribalism, while also doing almost everything possible to suppress any
challenge to their current orthodoxies.

My interest in affirmative action was whetted in the early 1970's when I   4
began hearing anecdotes about reverse discrimination. Watching for television and newspaper reports on this remarkable policy, I came upon very few.
With the exception of some polemical essays, sociologists also paid relatively
little attention to the topic. Throughout the 1970's, the anecdotes continued

to increase as affirmative-action rhetoric became more strident. Certainly this was the case in the CSU system, where I started teaching as a temporary member of the sociology faculty in 1977.

Like most American colleges and universities, the CSU campuses devel- 5
oped affirmative-action plans, hired affirmative-action officers, and billed themselves as "affirmative-action/equal-opportunity employers." (It was not until the mid-to-late 1980's that the term "equality" was eclipsed by the more hard-line vocabulary of "equity," "diversity," and "access.")

In spite of all this, few of my colleagues in the CSU knew much about 6
affirmative-action programs on their own campuses or in the wider society. One reason was that these programs — in the CSU as elsewhere — had been formulated and implemented quietly. Legal ambiguities wrought by Supreme Court vacillation promoted the use of informal pressures and "discretion" rather than codified or systematic measures.

A second reason for lack of concern among my fellow sociologists with 7
affirmative action was the slowdown in hiring that set in during the mid-1970's. Sociology, the most popular major of the 1960's, was by now becoming one of the least popular. Indeed, the CSU system lost nearly 90 percent of its sociology majors from the mid-1970's to the mid-1980's. In combination with the cuts forced by Proposition 13, the inevitable result was a hiring freeze.

For most of my colleagues, the hiring freeze meant that no white male they 8
personally knew had been denied a job because of his race or gender. If they spoke of affirmative action at all, they did so in vague, simplistic terms. They talked of the policy as the "ideal situation" of an equally qualified white male competing for a position with an equally qualified female or minority candidate — in which case the latter candidate should be given the job. That the realities of affirmative action might involve outright preference of less qualified (or unqualified) women or minorities was dismissed. Nor could these Ph.D.'s in sociology grasp the elementary economic fact that, in a tight labor market, affirmative action must necessarily operate in a zero-sum context: when one person was hired because of race, ethnicity, or gender, others were thereby excluded on the same discriminatory grounds.

Yet to recognize that affirmative action could not help without hurting ran 9
up against an absolute dictum of the Marxist/feminist orthodoxy which had crept into the everyday academic world view of the 1970's and 1980's: the idea that only certified minorities — especially blacks and women — could be victims. To suggest that white males were being injured by affirmative action invited righteous scorn and contempt — even among white males themselves.

The question that intrigued me was how these same (or similar) white 10
males would respond when and if they themselves encountered reverse discrimination. Would they protest? Would they accord one another support and understanding?

In 1984, I obtained a small grant from the Institute for Educational Affairs 11 which enabled me to hire two research assistants. In the ensuing months we found our way to 34 white males in a variety of occupations who had good reason to believe that they had been the victims of reverse discrimination in seeking jobs or promotions. After dropping two of the 34 because it was not clear that affirmative action had been a decisive factor in their cases, we wound up with 32 subjects. The data we got from them were supplemented by background interviews with a dozen personnel or affirmative-action officers, employment counselors, and corporate executives. Many informal interviews with others who learned of the research and wanted to talk added to our sense of what was happening.

By coincidence, our 32 formal interviews equaled the number of college- 12 student participants in a laboratory experiment which had been conducted in 1980 by a sociologist named Stephen Johnson. Johnson discovered that white male students who had lost a puzzle-solving exercise to a fictitious competitor expressed more hostility toward the victor when told that he was black and had been given a bonus score by the experimenter to compensate for his cultural disadvantages. The student subjects, however, expressed less hostility toward black victors than toward white ones when told that they had lost because of the competitor's superior performance.

Suggestive though they were, Johnson's laboratory results were simply 13 too limited to predict the real-world effects of reverse discrimination. Practically no one could truly guess at the responses we would find "out there." Using a semi-structured interview format — which let the subjects discuss their experiences in their own words — we discovered a wide and deep spectrum of responses ranging from acquiescence to anger to protest.

The vast majority — 20 out of 32 — simply endured reverse discrimination 14 without protest, though many were quietly angry. Among the other twelve, six quit the jobs in which they encountered discrimination; four protested, including three who took legal action — to no avail; and two circumvented barriers through other organizational means.

Our subjects were not angry white racists eager to take to the streets. On 15 the contrary, the mostly middle-class males we interviewed felt bewildered and isolated by what had happened to them. Hardly a one of them was willing to voice any open antagonism toward affirmative action. Why?

First, they feared being labeled "racist" if they complained about pro- 16 grams that purportedly redressed past discrimination. In fact, almost to a man they took pains to explain to the interviewers that they understood and deplored the history of racism in America. Yet many had sustained real career injuries and felt betrayed by the system. Said a middle-management state worker: "A lot of us were sold a bill of goods. We were told if you went to college, you could write your own ticket. . . . But . . . affirmative action has lowered standards to the point where education almost counts against you. . . ."

Unlike minority or female victims of discrimination, white males could not   17
necessarily count on in-group support. Wives aside ("My wife is mad as hell;
she's angrier than I am"), only half reported any such support from friends
and co-workers.

This seems to be why teachers selected by computer for transfer in a   18
massive racial-balancing plan by the Los Angeles Unified School district were
especially bitter. Commented one: "You found out who your friends were. I
found I didn't have as many as I thought." Said another: "My friends and
co-workers didn't know how to handle this. They wanted to empathize but [as
political liberals] felt cognitive dissonance." A third stated dryly, "People
don't like victims."

Deeply ingrained norms regarding silent, "manly" behavior and individual   19
responsibility have crushed any sort of collective awareness and class action
by white males. "When it hits you," a community-college instructor stated,
"you don't want to admit it at first. Instead, you think it must be something
in you. You doubt yourself. You repress it, try to forget it." No one wanted to
be accused of "alibiing."

A Ph.D. in political science and a once aspiring university professor (now a   20
government worker) articulated a common concern: "Why didn't I say anything about it? . . . Pride, I guess. I didn't want to make excuses." Many
others feared for the future of their careers if they vented their objections.
They felt that if they did not "rock the boat," things would work out later.

Another key factor in keeping silent was the fear of not being believed.   21
Reverse discrimination simply sounded too outlandish and incredible without
external validation by the mass media — and the mass media were not providing such validation.

This neglect by the news and entertainment industry — especially in the   22
1970's — was quickly confirmed even before we began interviewing. I simply
counted the number of articles on affirmative action indexed in the *Reader's
Guide to Periodical Literature* from 1968 to 1980, and the number of
minutes on the network newscasts as tabulated in the *Vanderbilt Television
News Index and Abstracts* (from its inception in 1972 through 1980). What I
discovered was that, until the *Bakke* case moved to the U.S. Supreme Court
in 1977, there was about one article per year in each of the major newsweek-
lies and about twelve to fifteen minutes per year (and sometimes much less)
on the networks on topics related to affirmative action. There was a slight
fall-off after *Bakke.*

Qualitative evidence reinforced quantitative data. In comparison with other   23
race-related issues, especially the school-busing battles, affirmative action
was not box-office. It was treated as a non-issue and rarely, if ever, mentioned
in press coverage of the 1980, 1984, and 1988 presidential campaigns, not
even in cover stories by major news magazines about Jesse Jackson. As for
commercial television, on those few occasions when affirmative action was

dealt with—such as a 1975 episode of *All in the Family*—it was portrayed in its "ideal" form and in highly sympathetic terms.

There were also several issues to which affirmative action seemed "natu- 24 rally" related, but where it remained the other shoe that never dropped. For example, very few reporters or commentators noted the clash between the egalitarian thrust of affirmative action and the drive for higher standards in education and business. And, until the late 1980's, few journalists ever pointed to the role of affirmative action in promoting discord in the Democratic party.

Yet by the mid-1980's, the emergence of blue-collar, white, male "Reagan 25 Democrats" compelled the guarded attention of political analysts and pollsters. Thus, after the 1984 Reagan landslide, Michigan Democrats commissioned Stanley Greenberg to study "Democratic defection" in their state. Greenberg and his associates gathered discussion groups of white, working-class Democrats and posed a series of questions designed to assess their political mood. Asked, "Who do you think gets the raw deal?" they responded:

> "We do."
> "The middle-class white guy."
> "The working middle class."
> "Cause women get advantages, the Hispanics get advantages, Orientals get advantages. Everybody but the white male race gets advantages now."

and:

> "I have been here all my life working, paying taxes and the whole shot, and I can't start my own business unless I have 30 percent down on whatever I want to buy. I have the experience on the job, I have put in for openings, and they have come right out and told me in personnel that the government has come down and said that I can't have the job because they have to give it to the minorities."

Greenberg and his sponsors were stunned and chagrined by this fury over 26 affirmative action among working-class whites. Clearly preferential treatment had poisoned traditional Democratic appeals to "fairness" and "justice," and it also seemed that racial preferences were turning white working-class males against government programs in general. Similar data were obtained in a 1985 "Democrats Listening to America" poll of 5,500 voters, as well as in a replication of the Michigan study in 1987.

The response of the Democratic party to findings such as Greenberg's was 27 instructive: it tried to suppress the reports. As the social critic Charles Murray observed of the ill effects of affirmative action: "Hardly a policy-maker or academic anywhere wants to examine these results and fewer still want to speak of them."

In discussing the hostile reception accorded in the 1970's to his work on 28 school busing (which demonstrated that it was causing white flight and other problems), the eminent sociologist James Coleman suggested that when senior scholars act as a lightning rod for controversial research, it makes the world safer for their less secure juniors laboring in the same field. As I have good reason to know, Coleman was right. For it took a number of books and articles by well-known scholars to pave the way for my own work.

Nathan Glazer was the first important sociologist to break the ice, with **29** *Affirmative Discrimination* in 1975. Nearly a decade later came Charles Murray's *Losing Ground*, which appeared just as I was launching my interviews. During these same years, articles criticizing affirmative action also began to appear here and there, making it easier for me to publish two of my own articles and to edit a special issue of *The American Behavioral Scientist* on the subject.

But then, in a deeply ironic twist, I began discovering that I myself had **30** joined the subjects of my own study as a victim of reverse discrimination. Which is to say that while my résumé continued to grow with more publications and references, I was unable to move beyond temporary faculty status to a tenure-track position.

No doubt my career struggles were in part linked to the huge surplus of **31** baby-boomer Ph.D.'s. Furthermore, I had a Ph.D. from the University of California at Riverside, not the more prestigious UC-Berkeley. And I was growing older. But there could be little doubt that reverse discrimination was a major cause of my stalled career.

Once, for example, I was informed by a plainly discomfited chairman that I **32** had lost a position at Sweet Briar College strictly because I was male. On another occasion the department chairman at Pomona College told me that the only sociologist he could hire was a black. On yet a third occasion, Occidental College abruptly canceled an interview, later notifying me (and several other candidates) that it had hired a female "native of Jamaica."

Making matters even worse, there was my research on affirmative action. **33** Job nibbles usually ceased the moment I mentioned it. When I was interviewed at a seven-sisters college in the early 1980's, the chairman pleaded with me: "Please, I want you to get this job. Don't talk about your affirmative-action research." A scheduled interview at a Southwestern university was suddenly canceled in 1987 after the dean learned of the topic of my research. In 1990, the political implications of my research sabotaged an otherwise successful interview at a large Midwestern state university.

To keep my research afloat, I needed financial support, but initial queries **34** to such major foundations as Ford, Rockefeller, and Carnegie met with bewilderment or contempt. Fortunately, smaller, less ideologically orthodox foundations like Earhart and Sarah Scaife were more responsive. Help from Earhart made it possible for me to complete the project and analyze its results in a book, *Invisible Victims: White Males and the Crisis of Affirmative*

Action. The editors at Greenwood Press were more willing to take a risk with such a manuscript than several larger publishers who hinted or admitted outright that their firms subscribed to a "party line" on this issue.

At first, my colleagues treated my complaints about reverse discrimination 35 exactly as the few complaints made by the subjects of my research project were treated by the people around them: as a form of "alibiing." But by the late 1980's, acknowledgment of race-and-gender pressures became more explicit. Universities openly began to advertise "targets of diversity" and other set-aside positions for minorities and women.

Then, in the late 1980's, limited hiring began again in sociology and 36 related fields at both CSU Los Angeles and San Bernardino. Suddenly, colleagues who had once dismissed complaints about reverse discrimination were now instructed to implement such practices.

In 1986, 19.2 percent of newly-hired, tenure-track CSU faculty were 37 minorities and 34.8 percent were women. By 1988, 23.4 percent of new hires were minorities and 38.4 percent were women. Since there have been few female, black, or Hispanic Ph.D.'s in the high-demand fields of physical science, business, engineering, and math, most female, non-Asian minority faculty were likely to be hired in education and in the glutted, low-demand humanities and social sciences. It is reasonable to assume that administrative prompting to hire females and minorities created pressures — however subtle — against hiring white males.

Less subtle were pools of set-aside faculty positions reserved for minorities 38 and females established at San Bernardino and some other CSU campuses. In 1989, a black female (*sans* Ph.D.) was hired by the sociology department to fill such a set-aside position, with a high salary and reduced teaching load which included classes I had taught for several years. Since I was directly affected, I was able to check out the futility of legal redress as reported by some of my interview subjects. Their accounts were grimly confirmed. The representative of the State Fair Housing and Employment Commission ratio-nalized the CSU set-asides as a legally acceptable attempt to bring its work force into "balance" and I was informed by the Equal Employment Opportu-nity Commission that Cal State's use of set-asides was "voluntary affirmative action." Unless I had direct, "smoking-gun" evidence that I had been denied employment because I was a white male, nothing could be done.

Interestingly, both of these defenses of CSU's set-asides were offered *after* 39 the Supreme Court, in *Richmond* v. *Croson*, specifically limited the use of voluntary set-asides by state or local government agencies. No wonder, then, that Cal State Northridge saw no risk in running a large ad in the *Chronicle of Higher Education* announcing that it was "setting aside a pool of faculty positions to allocate to those departments that identify well-qualified minority candidates for either full-time tenure track or lecturer appointments." The

CSU system has also provided 200 minority and female Ph.D. aspirants with up to $30,000 each through a set-aside forgivable loan program.

My subjects' accounts of union paralysis on reverse discrimination were **40** also confirmed by my own experience. Our fledgling faculty union was even more strident than the CSU in its calls for "diversity, equity, and affirmative action." The union was content that the CSU's programs be merely "legally defensible." Publicly, it would take no stand on reverse discrimination; privately, there was recognition of the problem, a little anguish, and no action.

"People still can't deal with this issue," a UCLA sociologist recently told **41** me, "they don't want to be critical." Indeed they don't, as I and so many others have learned from bitter personal experience.

COLOR BLINDERS

Julian Bond

Civil rights activist Julian Bond supports the 1990 Civil Rights Act [subsequently vetoed by George Bush] on the grounds that it will offer clearer guidance to the courts without leading to quotas.

Should racial minorities and women have the same legal rights — and   1
remedies — as old white men? Supporters of the Civil Rights Act of 1990 say
yes. Its opponents, mostly old white men, say no.

Lining up behind the legislation, intended to overturn five 1989 Supreme   2
Court decisions that weakened civil rights protections, is a broad range of
civil rights groups. In opposition, besides the usual bigots and neo-Bourbons,
is the Bush Administration, led by its biggest quota-baiter, Attorney General
Dick Thornburgh.

White House civil rights strategy since the early days of the Reagan   3
Administration has been to associate any progressive measure affecting
blacks with hated quotas; the kinder, gentler Bush is carrying on the tradition. The new bill would strengthen guarantees against discrimination in
employment and, by restoring a "business necessity" rule that had been in
effect from 1971 to 1989, would make it easier for victims to prove discrimination. Opponents of the bill argue that if plaintiffs can invoke statistical
disparities, thus forcing companies to prove that such disparities result from
a business necessity, then employers will impose quotas on themselves as a
pre-emptive measure. Unable to find qualified women or minorities, these
businesses apparently would just hire incompetents.

But "business necessity" is a standard developed not by quota-loving   4
Kennedyites but by former Supreme Court Chief Justice Warren Burger, a
Nixon appointee who wrote in *Griggs v. Duke Power Company* in 1971 that
it was the "touchstone" for determining the validity of employment practices
that result in a work force that does not reflect the makeup of the available
labor pool. Senate Republicans said the 1990 bill would be a "litigation
bonanza" because of the "necessity" rule, but couldn't explain how it had
been in effect for eighteen years without that result. Likewise, Thornburgh
was unable to tell a *Washington Post* reporter how restoring the rule would
create quotas in the future when none had been created in the past.

When Edward Kennedy, the bill's chief Senate sponsor, offered compro-   5
mise language prohibiting quotas, White House Chief of Staff John Sununu
said no. Such language was nevertheless included in the bill that passed on
July 18 by 65 to 34, two votes less than required to overturn a veto, which
President Bush continues to threaten.

So far, Bush has had it both ways—for civil rights and against quotas. 6
But the bill the House is now considering takes both positions into account,
and Bush may have painted himself into a corner by condemning the legislation as a "quota bill."

The opposition also includes many major American corporations, such as 7
A.T.&T., Bank of America, Dow Chemical, Exxon, I.B.M., K Mart and Tex-
aco. Their opposition stems largely from the fact that the bill would, for the
first time, allow damages to successful plaintiffs under Title VII of the 1964
Civil Rights Act. This would give Latinos, blacks and women equal footing in
discrimination suits with that of white men over 40.

Under the Age Discrimination in Employment Act of 1967 plaintiffs who 8
prove age discrimination have been able to collect punitive damages. At best,
a plaintiff who proves sexual or racial bias in the workplace under Title VII
can get no more than two years' back pay. Now, a majority of discrimination
complaints before the Equal Employment Opportunity Commission charge
age bias, and 83 percent of claims under the age discrimination act are filed
by white men. A study by the Syracuse University School of Management
found that the act primarily protects white male executives in their late 50s
who have lost their jobs.

All but two of America's 100 senators are white men; the average age in 9
the Senate is 55.6. Twenty-four of the 435 Representatives are black;
twenty-eight are women; twelve are Latinos. The average age in the House is
51.3. A Congress dominated by older white men—the average ages were
even higher when the age discrimination act was passed—extended maximum protections to people like themselves and the people they would become. The 1990 Civil Rights Act would finally give women and minorities
damages if they prove willful discrimination.

Earlier this year the Disabilities Act breezed through Congress as member 10
after member rose to tell colleagues of a sightless brother or a cousin in a
wheelchair or other disabled relatives whose rights would be protected by the
law. No member of Congress claimed kinship to old white men when the age
discrimination act passed with punitive damages included; none had to.

Sadly, few in the Bush Administration or corporate America have black 11
relatives, and apparently few have any female relatives—sisters, daughters,
wives or mothers—whose rights need the same protection as aged, and
aging, white men.

AN ECONOMIC DEFENSE OF AFFIRMATIVE ACTION

Bernard Anderson

Economist Anderson's article, which first appeared in the May, 1982, issue of Black Enterprise, *argues that affirmative action has been very effective in changing the color and gender of the workplace and that it is still necessary to the well-being of blacks and females.*

Is affirmative action still necessary? Many critics argue that attitudes 1 toward race relations have improved to a substantial degree and that discrimination is no longer a major factor in explaining employment and earnings disparities among minorities and others. According to these critics, economic growth and the expansion of jobs through unregulated, free market processes is all that is required to improve the economic status of minorities.

However, the available evidence suggests that just the reverse is true. 2 Much of the progress achieved by minorities and women in some occupations and industries was either the direct result of or was substantially influenced by affirmative action remedies to employment discrimination.

Affirmative Action Is Necessary

The position of blacks and other minorities in the economy is like that of the 3 caboose on a train. When the train speeds up, the caboose moves faster; when the train slows down, so does the caboose. No matter how fast the train goes, the caboose will never catch up with the engine unless special arrangements are made to change its position. So it is with minorities and the economy: Even during the best of times, there will be no change in the relative position of minorities unless affirmative action or other special measures are taken.

Policies designed to improve the relative position of minorities are justified 4 by the continuing evidence of racial inequality in American economic life. In 1980, black unemployment was more than twice that of whites (13.2 percent vs. 6.3 percent). Unemployment among black teenagers, now officially reported at close to 50 percent, has been greater than 30 percent throughout the past decade, but has not reached that level among white youths in any year. Further, the employment/population ratio — for some purposes a more instructive measure of labor market participation than the unemployment rate — has steadily declined among black youths while increasing among whites. About 25 out of every 100 black youths had jobs in 1980, compared with 50 of every 100 whites.

Comparative income data also show continuing evidence of economic   5
disparity between blacks and others. In 1979, the average black family had only $57 for every $100 enjoyed by whites. Even in families headed by persons fortunate enough to work year round, blacks have failed to achieve parity, earning only 77 percent of the income of comparable white families.

Effects of Past Discrimination

It would be incorrect to say that the continuing presence of such economic   6
inequality is entirely the result of overt or systemic discrimination or that affirmative action alone would improve the economic position of minorities. But there is no question that much of the income and employment disadvantage of blacks and other minorities reflects the accumulated impact of past discrimination. The continuing presence of many seemingly objective policies in the workplace has also had disproportionately unfavorable effects on the hiring, training and upgrading of minority-group workers. Affirmative action has an important role to play in correcting inequities.

In 1969, black workers represented 6.7 percent of the nearly 600,000   7
employees in the Bell System, mostly black women employed as telephone operators. Only 12 percent of Bell's black employees were in management (compared with 24 percent of whites), 7.2 percent were skilled craftsmen (compared with 26 percent of whites), and less than one percent were in professional jobs (compared with 8 percent of whites).

In 1971, the Equal Employment Opportunity Commission (EEOC) charged   8
AT&T and its affiliates with discrimination against minorities and women. In 1975, after prolonged litigation and negotiations, EEOC and AT&T signed a consent decree designed to correct the inequities in the company's employment practices, and to provide back pay to many minority and female employees who had not enjoyed full equal opportunity in the past. In 1979, blacks and other minorities accounted for 14.4 percent of the Bell System's managerial employees, 18.7 percent of the outside craftsmen, 19.1 percent of the inside craftsmen, and 23.3 percent of the sales workers.

The consent decree was the catalyst necessary to spur the company toward   9
many positive changes in personnel policies that top management today lauds as beneficial to the firm. The more efficient and equitable personnel selection and assessment system adopted by AT&T and its Bell operating affiliates puts the telephone company in a much stronger position to compete with other firms in the increasingly difficult and complex information systems markets.

The experience of AT&T, and other firms specifically identified as subjects for affirmative action enforcement, is instructive for understanding the potential impact of affirmative action on the occupational status of minorities. For purposes of public policy formulation, such evidence may be more useful than inconclusive studies that attempt to show the relationship between affirmative action and minority employment opportunities.

IN IVORY TOWERS

Roger Wilkins

Wilkins, himself black, argues from personal experience that businesses that make affirmative action hires are better for having done so and that beneficiaries of affirmative action policies need feel no guilt about their "advantages."

Blacks are among those expressing second thoughts about affirmative   1
action in college and university life these days. The first concern is expressed by a brilliant young black friend, who laments that despite his formidable intellectual accomplishments, peopl^ still judge him not as a splendid scholar, but only as a smart black. The second is a concern expressed by some black educators that students admitted under affirmative action programs may come to doubt their own capacities as a result.

These complaints proceed from the same idea: that the main thing to think   2
about when considering affirmative action is the damage it does to black self-esteem—either because whites will doubt blacks' capacities, or because the remedy itself makes blacks doubt their own capacities. I understand this burden, having carried part of it all my adult life, but the simple colloquial response I give to black faculty members and black students who express similar concerns to me is: "You're upset because you think *affirmative action* makes white folks look at you funny. Hell, white folks were looking at black folks funny long before affirmative action was invented. They been lookin' at black folks funny since 1619."

The founding tenet of racism is that blacks are inferior, particularly when   3
it comes to intellectual capability. And an underpinning of racism has been an all-out cultural onslaught on the self-esteem of blacks, to transform them from assertive and self-sufficient human beings into dependents, mere extensions of the will of the whites who choose to use them.

Affirmative action, even weakly and spottily deployed, opens doors of   4
opportunity that would otherwise be slammed tight. As a result, the country is better and stronger. It surely is one of the most effective antidotes to the widespread habit of undervaluing the capacities of minorities and women. It also serves as a counterbalance to the tendency to overvalue, as a recruitment tool, the effectiveness and fairness of old-boy networks.

But affirmative action did not magically erase racism. It simply pushed   5
back the boundaries of the struggle a little bit, giving some of us better opportunities to fulfill our capacities, and higher perches from which to conduct our battles. Anyone who thinks there are no more battles to be fought, even on the highest battlements of the ivoriest of the ivory towers, simply doesn't understand America.

Whatever confusion I've had about such things was knocked out of me a   6
long time ago. Almost everything that has happened to me since I was
twenty-one has resulted from one sort of affirmative action or another.
Thirty-seven years as the object of affirmative action in such places as the
Department of Justice, the Ford Foundation, the *Washington Post* and the
New York Times have given me a rich understanding of the endurance of U.S.
racism. I have done battle and emerged with enough self-confidence to assert
that all of the places that hired me because of affirmative action were better
for having done so.

Nevertheless, I am sympathetic to the desire of my young black friend for   7
the excellence of his mind to wash the color off his accomplishments. Unfortunately, even in 1990, color is not irrelevant in the United States at any
level — and perhaps that is fortunate, for it maintains some fragmentary bond
between my friend and poor black people who need his concern and strength.
I am reminded, in this regard, of the wisdom embedded in an old joke that
comes from deep in African-American culture. In this story, two old white
men are rocking on a porch in a Southern town. Says the first, "Zeke, what
do you call a black man with a Ph.D. who has just won the Nobel Prize in
physics?" Replies Zeke, after a long pause and much contemplative rocking,
"I calls him nigger."

Not all white people are as deeply racist as Zeke, of course, but enough are   8
to make it wise for young black people to follow what our mothers and
fathers have taught us over the generations: that white people's judgments of
us are to be viewed with great skepticism, and that accepting those judgments whole is apt to be hazardous to our mental health. Thus, mental
toughness and an independent sense of our own worth are elements as
essential to the black survival kit in 1990 as they ever were.

Not only do black professors need to know this, but black students   9
entering predominantly white campuses have to be taught it, as well. Such
campuses are products of white-American culture, and most black youngsters, particularly those from the inner cities, find them to be alien places.
Moreover, they sometimes get mixed messages. Often recruited assiduously,
they frequently find pockets of hostility and seas of indifference.

That is not a reason for less affirmative action, but for more — at the   10
faculty, staff level. There should be many black adults on those campuses to
make them feel less foreign to black students and more like places of
opportunity, full of challenges that can be overcome with excellence and
effort. If the number of knowledgeable and sympathetic adults is minuscule,
the youngsters will see that the commitment to an atmosphere where everyone can learn is crimped and limited.

In this imperfect world, racism remains a major affliction that burdens all   11
Americans — and it hits black Americans right in the self-esteem. But it must
surely be easier to firm up your self-regard when you are employed with

tenure than when working as an itinerant researcher. Similarly, the task is undoubtedly easier for a college graduate—even one who had to struggle with self-doubt during college years because of affirmative action—than for someone who has never gone to college.

It would be nice to think that in the academy we could escape cultural 12 habits wrought during more than three centuries of legal racial oppression. But that won't happen in this century. So black people—even those who are privileged—just have to suck it in and keep on pushing, breaking their own paths and making a way for those still struggling behind.

WOUNDS OF RACE

Hendrick Hertzberg

The author chides Supreme Court justices for their extremely narrow and technical rulings on affirmative action cases and questions whether they understand the spirit as well as the letter of civil rights law. Hertzberg characterizes affirmative action as a sacrifice by this generation for future generations but worries that it will have little effect on the vast black "underclass."

I have yet to meet a well-informed, unbigoted black American who would   1
not firmly endorse the following statement: If you're black, you have to be twice as good to travel the same socioeconomic distance as a white person in this country—twice as talented, twice as ambitious, twice as determined.

To this, the average well-informed, unbigoted white American will reply: 2
Nonsense. Sure, that was true years ago, but today if you're black and minimally qualified all you have to do is show up, and bang—you're in college, you're in law school, you've got the job.

The gap between these two honest perceptions is a measure of the passion   3
and pain of race in America. Race is the wound that will not heal, and the Supreme Court has just rubbed fresh salt in that wound with a series of decisions truncating the equal employment provisions of the Civil Rights Act of 1964—which, as of July 2, will have been the law for exactly 25 years. What a dismal anniversary present.

To read these decisions is to become aware of the dizzying moral fall from   4
the Warren Court, a product of Eisenhower Republicanism, to the Rehnquist Court, a product of Reagan Republicanism. When the Warren Court took up this most divisive of American perplexities, it was careful to seek unanimity among its own members: *Brown* v. *Board of Education* was a 9-0 decision. The Rehnquist Court hacks away at settled precedent by repeated votes of 5 to 4. The Warren Court looked to the grandeur of the Constitution for guidance. The Rehnquist Court draws its arguments from abstruse (and questionable) points of contract law. The Warren Court took history (not just "legislative history") into account, and considered the building of social justice to be part of its writ. The Rehnquist Court renders its decisions in highly technical, almost impenetrable language wholly free of any hint of the suffering, the bitterness, and all the other human realities that inform the cases it decides.

"The linchpin of the 'impermissible collateral attack' doctrine—the attri-   5
bution of preclusive effect to a failure to intervene—is therefore quite inconsistent with Rule 19 and Rule 24," writes Chief Justice Rehnquist in a typical passage of *Martin* v. *Wilks*—and that's about as exalted as his

language gets. In that particular case, the Court, by the usual 5–4 majority, opened the way for endless legal assaults on an affirmative action program, the product of seven years of painful negotiations and lawsuits, that since 1981 has peacefully and effectively brought a measure of racial integration to the previously all-white fire department of Birmingham, Alabama.

After reading the decisions, I ended up sharing the dismay of Justice 6 Blackmun, who wrote in dissent, "One wonders whether the majority still believes that race discrimination — or, more accurately, race discrimination against non-whites — is a problem in our society, or even remembers that it ever was." But the cases themselves are less important than the larger questions about race (and about affirmative action) they raise.

The affirmative action debate takes place in a context shaped by the 7 success of civil rights and the failure of social policy. The triumphant destruction of institutionalized segregation broke apart the old black communities in which people of all classes and levels of accomplishment lived together in oppression. The most ambitious, lucky, and talented were — and are — boiled off into the larger society. As an unintended consequence, those left behind have been distilled into an increasingly isolated, increasingly pathological, increasingly self-destructive subculture, the urban black underclass. Social programs designed to alleviate its condition have either proved unworkable or been starved. Reaganism's upward redistribution of income has sharpened the pain. But the failure is general. "Conservatives have ignored the problem, left the solution to 'market forces' or, worse, to social Darwinism," writes Joe Klein in a brilliant essay in the May 29 *New York* magazine. "Liberals seem to have abandoned critical thought entirely, allowing militants to dictate their agenda, scorning most efforts to impose sanctions on anti-social behavior by underclass blacks."

Affirmative action is a kind of homeopathic medicine, an effort to correct 8 an immense historic injustice with small doses of "injustice" in the present. It is an effort to lift some blacks by main force into the middle class. It should properly be seen not as a sacrifice by whites for the benefit of blacks, but rather as a sacrifice by the present generation for the benefit of the next. The cost is paid today — by the whites shunted aside, and, more subtly, by the blacks obliged to doubt that their advancement is personally deserved. ("Social victims may be collectively entitled, but they are all too often individually demoralized," writes the black essayist Shelby Steele, quoted by Klein.) The payoff will come tomorrow, when a new generation of black children is born into the middle class — there to share, presumably, the un-self-conscious advantages and complexes of a bourgeois upbringing.

The psychic cost of affirmative action to its purported "real-time" benefi- 9 ciaries is very high. In the post-slavery century of segregated oppression, few members of what W. E. B. DuBois called "the talented tenth" were troubled by lack of self-esteem. They *knew* that whatever they had they had more than earned, because there was no other way to get it. Their affirmative action counterparts of today cannot be so sure. Yes, the jobs are easier to get — and in this sense the white perception is correct. But the *respect* that is supposed to come with the job — that comes with it more or less automatically for whites — does not come automatically for blacks. It cannot be "demanded," Jesse Jackson notwithstanding. It must be struggled for and earned. This applies to self-respect as well as to the respect of others. "You're not here because you're smart or because you worked hard, you're here because there's a program for hiring black people." That's a natural enough thought for whites to have, and they don't have to be "racist" in any classic way to have it. It's a thought, moreover, that on some level the black beneficiaries of affirmative action are obliged to share. That is a high hurdle to overcome — as high, psychologically, as segregation was. The fact that the hurdle is subjective and invisible, that it cannot be measured by outward signs, does not make it any the less real. That is why, when blacks insist they must be "twice as good," they are merely reporting the existential truth of their own experience.

In any event, affirmative action can work only at the margins. It can pull 10 up only those who are ready to be pulled up. It can do little or nothing for the mind-numbingly dreadful problems of the underclass — the powerful, self-reinforcing nexus of crime, drugs, children bearing children, family atomization, despair, peer pressure to fail in school, and all the fearful rest.

Against those problems — the real problems — affirmative action is help- 11 less; and, in isolation, it fosters a cycle of mutual racial resentment destructive to the political will that is needed. There is no sign of that political will. President Bush and the Republicans have absolutely nothing to say about it. Black nationalism is a dead end, as many observers, black and white, have noted. But so is what might be called white nationalism. And in this connection the tragic elements of American history hang heavy — not because they are acknowledged but because they are ignored. Many of our reigning national myths, important parts of America's civil religion, simply exclude black people. I have been trying to imagine what it's like for a black person to listen to a speech about how America is a "nation of immigrants" and the "land of opportunity." The truth is that this is *not* a nation of immigrants. It is a nation of immigrants and slaves. Our ancestors did *not* come here full of hope, seeking freedom and a better life. They came seeking freedom and they came in chains.

The speeches of politicians and other national leaders seldom take this into 12 account. In their anxiety to draw happy, uncomplicated morals, they seldom tell the full American story. No wonder black people — whose roots in this country, on average, go back further than those of white people — are alienated.

Consider a couple of exceptions, drawn from the two greatest speeches 13
ever delivered by Americans.

"Fondly do we hope — fervently do we pray — that this mighty scourge of 14
war may speedily pass away. Yet, if God wills that it continue, until all the
wealth piled by the bondman's two hundred and fifty years of unrequited toil
shall be sunk, and until every drop of blood drawn with the lash, shall be paid
by another drawn with the sword, as was said three thousand years ago, so
still it must be said 'the judgments of the Lord, are true and righteous
altogether.'"

"I still have a dream. It is a dream deeply rooted in the American dream. I 15
have a dream that one day on the red hills of Georgia the sons of former
slaves and the sons of former slaveowners will be able to sit down together at
the table of brotherhood."

Abraham Lincoln and Martin Luther King Jr. told the whole truth about 16
America, and that is one reason they are deified in the American memory. Few
of their contemporary successors emulate them. Yet what is needed, as the
spiritual precondition to a material commitment, is a refurbished national
mythology that takes account of the historical experience of all Americans.
That is something politicians can begin to provide without spending a dime.
The dilemma is not a black dilemma (or a white one) but an American
dilemma. The answer is not "black history" but American history, not "black
pride" (or white guilt) but American determination.

MISQUOTA: SCHOLARSHIPS SHOULD BE BASED ON NEED

Thomas Sowell

Hoover Institution economist Thomas Sowell argues against minority scholarships because most minority students qualify for aid based on need and because minority-only scholarships fuel the fires of "racial backlash."

What is the Bush administration's position on racial quotas? If you know 1 the answer to that one, then you know more than the Bush administration itself knows.

Not so long ago, the president vetoed the Civil Rights Act of 1990 on 2 grounds that it would lead to racial quotas in employment. But just last week President Bush decided that scholarships set aside for blacks and other minorities were all right, so long as federal money was not used.

That decision pulled the rug out from under a black official of his own 3 administration, who had ruled that race-based scholarships were illegal.

Does this mean that racial quotas are wrong in employment but right when 4 it comes to scholarships? Or does it mean only that the Bush administration was being politically "pragmatic" once again?

In the long run, unbridled pragmatism can turn out to be very impractical, 5 even in political terms. Once friend and foe alike see you as following no principle, it will be hard to maintain the respect of either.

Voters have already shown that they will accept either pro-abortion or 6 anti-abortion candidates better than they will accept candidates who waffle on the issue. Being totally pragmatic can be a real handicap.

When 1992 rolls around, the Bush administration is certain to be attacked 7 for vetoing the Civil Rights Act of 1990 and for putting even limited restrictions on race-based scholarships. What principle can they cite and still be believable?

Like so many political controversies, the issue of race-based scholarships 8 was blown out of all proportion in the media. Most black students in college receive financial aid, but very little of it is set aside by race. They get financial aid because they come from low-income families — and this fact doesn't change, regardless of what the official ruling may be on race-based scholarships.

A 1985 study showed that more than half of all black students who took 9 the Scholastic Aptitude Test for college entrance came from families with incomes under $18,000. Meanwhile, more than half of all the white students who took the same test came from families with incomes of $30,000 or more.

What low-income students need is money — not a racial label on that 10 money. What high-income students need to do is pay their own way, regardless of what color they are. If the president had said that plainly, he would have won the respect of blacks and whites alike.

More important, putting a stop to racial preferences and quotas would 11 defuse the dangers of a growing racial backlash in this country—a backlash that has torn other countries apart.

Preferential policies in India have led to caste riots there that make race 12 riots in the United States look tame by comparison. An incident like Howard Beach would scarcely be noticed amid the group carnage in India. Preferential policies in Sri Lanka have led to a civil war filled with atrocities—and with no end in sight.

These countries have had widespread group preferences and quotas about 13 twice as long as the United States has. How far do we want to follow in their footsteps?

Anyone who believes that racial preferences help minorities should think 14 about the fact that the first minority hiring preferences in this country appeared in 1834—giving American Indians preferences in employment by the Bureau of Indian Affairs. What has a century and a half of various government "help" done for the American Indians? They are today one of the few groups with lower incomes than blacks.

Government handouts benefit a small class of political activists, care- 15 takers, and hustlers. The atmosphere and attitudes generated by this small but vocal class of "leaders" can then disorient millions of others, who are taught to think of their salvation as being in other people's hands.

How much some people ought to do to help others is a philosophical 16 question. But, as a practical matter, what others are likely to do to help is usually trivial compared to what people can do for themselves.

Sometimes a small amount of help at a strategic point—financial aid in 17 college, for example—can be very important in creating a self-supporting, educated class. The ban on race-based scholarships would have had no real impact on needy students.

If a few upper-income minority students had to pay their own way, that 18 would be a small price to pay to defuse a dangerous polarization over preferences and quotas.

A DEFENSE OF QUOTAS

Charles Krauthammer

The often conservative columnist Charles Krauthammer here takes a surprisingly liberal position in support of affirmative action quotas. Krauthammer argues that quotas work and that it is more important to redress historical and class injustices than to protect the rights of "blameless individuals."

As recently as three years ago Nathan Glazer noted with dismay the 1
inability, or unwillingness, of the most conservative American administration in 50 years to do anything about the growing entrenchment, in law and in practice, of racial quotas. It seemed that officially sanctioned race consciousness was becoming irrevocably woven into American life.

Glazer's pessimism was premature. In the last two years a revolution has 2
been brewing on the issue of affirmative action. It is marked not by the pronouncements of Clarence Pendleton, or the change in composition and ideology of the United States Commission on Civil Rights. That is for show. It is marked by a series of court rulings and administration actions that, step by step, will define affirmative action out of existence.

How far this process had gone was dramatized by the leak of a draft 3
executive order that would outlaw in federal government contracting not only quotas and statistical measures but any "preference . . . on the basis of race, color, religion, sex or national origin . . . with respect to any aspect of employment." Although this appeared as a bolt from a blue August sky, it was, in fact, the culmination of a process that has been building over the last several years. It amounts to a counterrevolution in stages on the issue of race-conscious social policy.

The counterrevolution has occurred in what is probably the most crucial 4
domain of affirmative action: employment. Classic affirmative action mandates preference for blacks (and women and other favored groups) at all four steps in the employment process: recruitment, hiring, promotion, and firing. The counterrevolution has attacked such preferences at each step of the way, beginning at the end.

The first major breach in the edifice of affirmative action was the Supreme 5
Court's Memphis fire fighters decision of June 1984. The City of Memphis had been under a court-ordered consent decree to increase the number of blacks in the fire department. When layoffs came in 1981, a U.S. District Court ruled that last-hired blacks could not be the first fired, as the seniority system dictated. Three whites were laid off instead. The Supreme Court reversed that decision. It ruled that in a clash between a bona fide seniority system and affirmative action, seniority prevails.

You cannot fire by race. But can you promote? Can you hire? The next,   6
more tentative, step in the counterrevolution occurred this past spring in the
District of Columbia. A suit originally filed in the waning days of the Carter
administration had resulted in mandated preferential hiring and promotions
for minorities in the city's fire departments. In March the D.C. fire chief,
according to one of the judge's directives in the case, ordered that five black
fire fighters be promoted over whites who had scored higher than they had.

The union immediately filed suit to block the promotions. And the Justice   7
Department joined the suit on the union's side. The judge in the case then
rendered a Solomonic decision prohibiting race consciousness in promotion,
but permitting it in hiring.

The case is under appeal and no one knows how it will come out. The   8
reason is that no one knows how to interpret *Memphis*. Did this ruling apply
only to layoffs, as suggested to civil rights groups trying to limit their losses?
Or did it apply also to hiring and/or promotion, the other crucial career
choke points? You can read *Memphis* either way, and everyone is waiting for
the Court to say.

Everyone, that is, except William Bradford Reynolds, head of the Justice   9
Department's Civil Rights Division, and leading *contra*. Reynolds is a conservative in a hurry. Invoking *Memphis* as his authority, he ordered 51
jurisdictions from New York to Los Angeles to cleanse existing consent
decrees (which mandated goals — quotas — in hiring) of any hint of group or
racial preference. Not only would preferences be outlawed from now on, but
existing decrees would have to be revised to reflect the new dispensation.

Reynolds's target is to root out race consciousness in toto, from firing to   10
promotion to hiring. Everything, it seems, except recruitment. Last June, at
the start of Reynolds's confirmation hearings for the number three job at
Justice (he was eventually turned down), he sent a letter to Senator Edward
Kennedy stating that he favored affirmative action in recruitment. He argued
that it is the only permissible affirmative action; in fact, it is how you
determine its success. Its success could be "measured," he wrote, "in the
number of persons who are recruited to apply."

Recruiting, it seems, would be the last refuge for affirmative action. Or so   11
it seemed, until the final step: draft executive order 11246 revising the
affirmative action order that since 1968 has mandated race consciousness and
statistical norms (quotas) in employment for government contractors. The
draft executive order would repeal it all: goals, timetables, statistical norms,
and other forms of racial preference.

It appears to do so even for Reynolds's cherished exception, recruitment.   12
Hard to tell, though. The first section of the draft order seems to define
affirmative action, as Reynolds likes to, as exclusively applicable to recruitment. "Each government contractor . . . shall engage in affirmative re-

cruitment . . . to . . . expand[ing] the number of qualified minorities and women who receive full consideration for hiring and promotion." But the very next section continues: "Nothing in this executive order shall be interpreted to require . . . any preference . . . on the basis of race . . . with respect to any aspect of employment, including . . . recruitment. . . ."

Either the drafters are exceedingly careless, or the internal administration 13 debate over whether to go the very last mile in eradicating race consciousness has yet to be decided. In either case, recruitment poses a logical problem for Reynolds & Company (if race consciousness is in principle unjust, how can it be O.K. for recruitment?). But it is not, in practice, a serious issue. If preferential treatment is outlawed for firing, promotion, and hiring, then recruitment really is the last mile: affirmative action expires long before it is reached. The administration and its civil rights opponents seem to agree that if this program — renegotiating the consent decrees and draft executive order 11246 — is enacted, recruitment or not, race-conscious affirmative action is dead.

They disagree about whether that would be a good thing. Is race- 14 conscious affirmative action worth saving?

There are three arguments in favor. The first, marshaled principally 15 against Reynolds's revisionist consent decree is profoundly conservative. It says that at this late date, things are working out well, whatever the merits. Let well enough alone. The Justice Department would "disturb the acquiescence of the community in the new systems established after much travail and effort under the consent decrees," charged the NAACP. It will "threaten social peace for the sake of ideology," said *The Washington Post.* "Don't stick your nose in cases that have already been resolved," said Representative Don Edwards, one of five representatives who wrote to the attorney general asking him to cease and desist.

The irony here, of course, is that the NAACP is relatively new to the cause 16 of "settledness." Not always has it argued that justice should be deferred so as not to "disturb the acquiescence of the community" in existing social arrangements. That was the segregationist case. And in that case, it was argued, correctly, that although settledness and social peace have some claims to make, they cannot prevail over the claims of justice.

It works, argues William H. Hudnut, the Republican mayor of Indianapo- 17 lis, of his city's consent decree setting aside a quarter of its police and fire fighting slots for minorities. Why fix what ain't broke?

Because justice is not interested in what's broke and what's not; it is 18 interested in justice. Hence the second argument for affirmative action, the familiar argument that while color blindness may be a value, remedying centuries of discrimination through (temporary) race consciousness is a higher value.

Does the right of the disadvantaged to redress (through preferential treat-   19
ment) override the right of individuals to equal treatment? *Memphis* and the
D.C. fire fighters decision begin to parse the issue. The logic of these
decisions is that in layoffs and promotion the aggrieved whites have, by dint
of service, acquired *additional* individual claims that outweigh the historical
claims of blacks. But what about unadorned individual claims? When hired
you bring your citizenship with you and nothing else. Shouldn't that be
enough to entitle you to equal, colorblind treatment?

It is not clear how to adjudicate the competing claims, that of a historically   20
oppressed community for redress, and of the blameless individual for equal
treatment. One side claims the mantle of—indeed, it defines itself as the side
of—civil rights. But that is surely a semantic claim. The movement began, of
course, as a civil rights movement. But when, for example, the D.C. Office of
Human Rights declares that its primary mission is to ensure that blacks end
up in city jobs in proportion "equal to their group representation in the
available work force," the issue has ceased to be rights. It is group advancement.

The other side claims the mantle of individual rights and equal treatment.   21
That is not a semantic claim. But it is not an absolute one either. After all,
either by design or default, we constantly enact social policies that favor
certain groups at the expense of others, the individuals in neither group
having done anything to deserve their fate. One routine, and devastating,
exercise in social engineering is the government-induced recession, periodically applied to the economy to curb inflation. The inevitable result is suffering, suffering that we know well in advance will be borne disproportionately
by the poor and working class.

Is this discrimination by class? Certainly. It is not admitted to be so, and it   22
is certainly not the primary effect. But it is an inevitable and predictable side
effect. Yet in the face of an overriding national priority—saving the
currency—we adopt policies that disproportionately injure a recognized
class of blameless individuals. (Similarly, the draft discriminates by age, the
placement of toxic waste dumps by geography, etc. We continually ask one
group or another to bear special burdens for the sake of the community as a
whole.)

If controlling inflation is a social goal urgent and worthy enough to   23
warrant disproportionate injury to a recognized class of blameless individuals, is not the goal of helping blacks rapidly gain the mainstream of American life? Which suggests a third, and to my mind most convincing, line of
defense for affirmative action. It admits that the issue is not decidable on the
grounds of justice. It argues instead a more humble question of policy: that
the rapid integration of blacks into American life is an overriding national
goal, and that affirmative action is the means to that goal.

To be sure, affirmative action has myriad effects. They even include such 24
subtle negative psychological effects on blacks as the "rumors of inferiority"
studied by Jeff Howard and Ray Hammond (TNR, September 9). The calculation is complex. But, it is hard to credit the argument that on balance
affirmative action actually harms blacks. Usually advanced by opponents of
affirmative action, this argument is about as ingenuous as Jerry Falwell's
support of the Botha regime out of concern for South African blacks. One
needs a willing suspension of disbelief to maintain that a policy whose essence
is to favor blacks hurts them. Even the Reagan administration admits (in a
report sent to Congress in February) that executive order 11246 has helped
skilled black men.

The Reagan counterrevolutionaries want to end the breach of justice that 25
is affirmative action. A breach it is, and must be admitted to be. It is not clear,
however, that correcting this breach is any more morally compelling than
redressing the historic injustice done to blacks. In the absence of a compelling moral case, then, the Reagan counterrevolution would retard a valuable
social goal: rapid black advancement and integration. Justice would perhaps
score a narrow, ambiguous victory. American society would suffer a wide and
deepening loss.

FOR CLASS DISCUSSION

1. Analyze and evaluate the controversy over affirmative action by applying the first set of guide questions from pages 443–444. Students are often surprised to learn that a black scholar and economist like Thomas Sowell should be opposed to racial quotas while a normally conservative white male such as Charles Krauthammer should support them. Why do these two writers disagree?

2. Choose one of the arguments for closer analysis, applying the second set of guide questions on page 444.

OPTIONAL WRITING ASSIGNMENT   You are the editor of your school's newspaper. In the past year, students at your school have become increasingly angered by the lack of minority professors on campus. Although people of color make up nearly 30 percent of your student body, there are currently only three minority professors on a faculty of more than 120 persons. The administration, in an effort to redress this situation, has decided to open several new positions identified as "minority hires." Because the demand for minority professors across the country is so high, such professors command starting salaries that are 20 to 30 percent higher than the salaries of white male or female professors with equivalent experience. Therefore the administration has decided to increase the starting salary for these minority positions in order to attract candidates.

Suddenly your paper is inundated with letters to the editor complaining about the "racist" implications of a policy that selects faculty on the basis of skin color and then pays them more. Write an editorial either supporting or opposing the administration's decision to actively seek people of color to fill new faculty positions.

LOGICAL FALLACIES

In this appendix, we look at ways of testing the legitimacy of an argument. Sometimes, there are fatal logical flaws hiding in the heart of a perfectly respectable looking argument, and if we miss them, we may find ourselves vainly defending the indefensible. Take, for example, the following cases. Do they seem persuasive to you?

Creationism must be a science because hundreds of scientists believe in it.

I voted for the recent California environmental bond issue because Ted Danson supported it and "Sam Malone" would never lie.

Smoking must cause cancer because a higher percentage of smokers get cancer than do nonsmokers.

Smoking doesn't cause cancer because my grandfather smoked two packs per day for fifty years and died in his sleep at age ninety.

An abnormal percentage of veterans who were marched to ground zero during atomic tests in Nevada died of leukemia and lung cancer. Surely their deaths were caused by the inhalation of radioactive isotopes.

THE PROBLEM OF CONCLUSIVENESS IN AN ARGUMENT

Although it may distress us to think so, none of the above arguments is conclusive. But that doesn't mean they're all false either. So what are they? Well, they are, to various degrees, "persuasive" or "unpersuasive." The problem is that some people will mistake arguments such as those above for "conclusive" or airtight arguments. A person may rest an entire argument on them and then fall right through the holes that observant logicians open in them. Although few people will mistake an airtight case for a fallacious one, lots of people mistake logically unsound arguments for airtight cases. So let's see how to avoid falling into specious reasoning.

Some arguments are flawed because they fail to observe certain formal logical rules. In constructing syllogisms, for example, there are certain formal laws that must be followed if we are to have a valid syllogism. The following argument is beyond doubt invalid and inconclusive:

No Greeks are bald.

No Lithuanians are Greek.

Therefore, all Lithuanians are bald.

But to say the argument is invalid isn't to say that its conclusion is necessarily untrue. Perhaps all Lithuanians really are bald. The point is, if the conclusion were true, it would be by coincidence, not design, because the above argument is invalid. All invalid arguments are inconclusive. And, by the same token, a perfectly valid syllogism may be untrue. Just because the premises follow the formal laws of logic doesn't mean that what they say is true. For a syllogistic argument to be absolutely conclusive, its form must be valid and its premises must be true. A perfectly conclusive argument would therefore yield a noncontroversial truth—a statement that no one would dispute.

This is a long way around to reach our point: The reason we argue about issues is that none of the arguments on any side of an issue is absolutely conclusive; there is always room to doubt the argument, to develop a counterargument. We can only create more or less persuasive arguments, never conclusive ones.

We have examined some of these problems already. In Chapter 12 on causal arguments we discussed the problem of correlation versus causation. We know, for example, that smoking and cancer are correlated but that further arguments are needed in order to increase the conclusiveness of the claim that smoking *causes* cancer.

In this appendix we explore the problem of conclusiveness in various kinds of arguments. In particular, we use the "informal" fallacies of logic to explain how inconclusive arguments can fool us into thinking they are conclusive.

AN OVERVIEW OF INFORMAL FALLACIES

The study of informal fallacies remains the murkiest of all logical endeavors. It's murky in the sense that informal fallacies are as unsystematic as formal fallacies are rigid and systematized. Whereas formal fallacies of logic have the force of laws, informal fallacies have little more than explanatory power. Informal fallacies are quirky; they identify classes of less conclusive arguments that recur with some frequency, but they do not contain formal flaws that make their conclusions illegitimate no matter what the terms may say. Informal fallacies require us to look at the meaning of the terms to determine how much we should trust or distrust the conclusion. The most common mistake one can make with informal fallacies is to assume that they have the force of laws like formal fallacies. They don't. In evaluating arguments with informal fallacies, we usually find that arguments are "more or less" fallacious, and determining the degree of fallaciousness is a matter of judgment.

Knowledge of informal fallacies is most useful when we run across arguments that we "know" are wrong, but we can't quite say why. They just don't "sound right." They look reasonable enough, but they remain unacceptable to us. Informal fallacies are a sort of compendium of symptoms for arguments flawed in this way. We must be careful, however, to make sure that the particular case before us "fits" the descriptors for the fallacy that seems to explain its problem. It's much easier, for example, to find informal fallacies in a hostile argument than in a friendly one simply because we are more likely to expand the limits of the fallacy to make the disputed case fit.

Not everyone agrees about what to include under the heading of informal fallacies. In selecting the following set of fallacies, we left out far more candidates than we included. Since Aristotle first developed his list of thirteen elenchi (refutations) down to the present day, there have been literally dozens of different systems of informal fallacy put forward. Although there is a good deal of overlap among these lists, the terms are invariably different, and the definition of fallacy itself shifts from age to age. In selecting the following set of fallacies, we left out a number of other candidates. We chose the following because they seemed to us to be the most commonly encountered.

In arranging the fallacies we have, for convenience, put them into three categories derived from classical rhetoric: *pathos, ethos,* and *logos.* Fallacies of *pathos* rest on a flawed relationship between what is argued and the audience for the argument. Fallacies of *ethos* rest on a flawed relationship between the argument and the character of those involved in the argument. Fallacies of *logos* rest on flaws in the relationship among statements of an argument.

Fallacies of *Pathos*

ARGUMENT TO THE PEOPLE (APPEAL TO STIRRING SYMBOLS)

This is perhaps the most generic possible example of a *pathos* fallacy. Argument to the people appeals to the fundamental beliefs, biases, and prejudices of the audience in order to sway opinion through a feeling of solidarity among those of the group. For example, when a politician says, "My fellow Americans. I stand here, draped in this flag from head to foot, to indicate my fundamental dedication to the values and principles of these sovereign United States," he's redirecting to his own person our allegiance to nationalistic values by linking himself with the prime symbol of those values, the flag. The linkage is not rational, it's associative. It's also extremely powerful—which is why arguments to the people crop up so frequently.

APPEAL TO IGNORANCE (PRESENTING EVIDENCE THE AUDIENCE CAN'T EXAMINE)

Those who commit this fallacy present assumptions, assertions, or evidence that the audience is incapable of judging or examining. If, for example, a critic were to praise the novel *Clarissa* for its dullness on the grounds that this dullness was the intentional effect of the author, we would be unable to respond because we have no idea what was in the author's mind when he created the work.

APPEAL TO IRRATIONAL PREMISES (APPEALING TO REASONS THAT MAY HAVE NO BASIS IN LOGIC)

This particular mode of short-circuiting reason may take one of three forms:

1. Appeal to common practice. (It's all right to do X because everyone else does it.)
2. Appeal to traditional wisdom. (It's all right because we've always done it this way.)
3. Appeal to popularity—the bandwagon appeal. (It's all right because lots of people like it.)

In all three cases, we've moved from saying something is popular, common, or persistent to saying it is right, good, or necessary. You have a better chance of rocketing across the Grand Canyon on a motorcycle than you have of going from "is" to "ought" on a because clause. Some examples of this fallacy would include (1) "Of course I borrowed money from the company slush fund. Everyone on this floor has done the same in the last eighteen months"; (2) "We've got to require everyone to read *Hamlet* because we've always required everyone to read it"; and (3) "I'm buying a Ford Escort because it's the best-selling car in the world."

PROVINCIALISM (APPEALING TO THE BELIEF THAT THE KNOWN IS ALWAYS BETTER THAN THE UNKNOWN)

Here is an example from the 1960s: "You can't sell small cars in America. In American culture, automobiles symbolize prestige and personal freedom. Those cramped little Japanese tin boxes will never win the hearts of American consumers." Although we may inevitably feel more comfortable with familiar things, ideas, and beliefs, we are not necessarily better off for sticking with them.

RED HERRING (SHIFTING THE AUDIENCE'S ATTENTION FROM A CRUCIAL ISSUE TO AN IRRELEVANT ONE)

A good example of a red herring showed up in a statement by Secretary of State James Baker that was reported in the 10 November 1990 *New York Times*. In response to a question about the appropriateness of using American soldiers to defend wealthy, insulated (and by implication, corrupt) Kuwaiti royalty, Baker told an anecdote about an isolated encounter he had with four Kuwaitis who had suffered; he then made a lengthy statement on America's interests in the Gulf. Although no one would argue that America is unaffected by events in the Middle East, the question of why others with even greater interests at stake had not contributed more troops and resources went unanswered.

Fallacies of *Ethos*

APPEAL TO FALSE AUTHORITY (APPEALING TO THE AUTHORITY OF A POPULAR PERSON RATHER THAN A KNOWLEDGEABLE ONE)

Appeals to false authority involve relying on testimony given by a person incompetent in the field from which the claims under question emerge. Most commercial advertisements are based on this fallacy. Cultural heroes are paid generously to associate themselves with a product without demonstrating any real expertise in evaluating that product. In at least one case, consumers who fell victim to such a fallacy made a legal case out of it. People bilked out of their life savings by a Michigan mortgage company sued the actors who represented the company on TV. Are people fooled by such appeals to false authority entitled to recover assets lost as a result?

The court answered no. The judge ruled that people gullible enough to believe that George Hamilton's capped-tooth smile and mahogany tan qualify him as a real estate consultant deserve what they get. Their advice to consumers?—"Buyers beware," because even though sellers can't legally lie, they can legally use fallacious arguments—all the more reason to know your fallacies.

Keep in mind, however, that occasionally the distinction between a false authority fallacy and an appeal to legitimate authority can blur. Suppose that Arnold Palmer were to praise a particular company's golf club. Because he is an expert on golf, it is possible that Palmer actually speaks from authority and that the golf club he praises is superior. But it might also be that he is being paid to advertise the golf club and is endorsing a brand that is no better than its competitors'. The only way we could make even a partial determination of Palmer's motives would be if he presented an *ad rem* ("to the thing") argument showing us scientifically why the golf club in question is superior. In short, appeals to authority are legitimate when the authority knows the field and when her motive is to inform others rather than profit herself.

APPEAL TO THE PERSON/*AD HOMINEM* (ATTACKING THE CHARACTER OF THE ARGUER RATHER THAN THE ARGUMENT ITSELF)

Literally, *ad hominem* means "to the man or person." Any argument that focuses on the character of the person making the argument rather than the quality of the reasoning qualifies as an *ad hominem* argument. Ideally, arguments are supposed to be *ad rem*, or "to the thing," that is, addressed to the specifics of the case itself. Thus an *ad rem* critique of a politician would focus on her voting record, the consistency and cogency of her public statements, her responsiveness to constituents, and so forth. An *ad hominem* argument would shift attention from her record to irrelevant features of her personality or personal life. Perhaps an *ad hominem* argument would suggest that she had a less than stellar undergraduate academic record.

But not all *ad hominem* arguments are *ad hominem* fallacies. It's not always fallacious to address your argument to the arguer. There are indeed times when the credibility of the person making an opposing argument is at issue. Lawyers, for example, when questioning expert witnesses who give damaging testimony, will often make an issue of their credibility, and rightfully so. And certainly it's not that clear, for instance, that an all-male research team of social scientists would observe and interpret data in the same way as a mixed-gender research group. An *ad hominem* attack on an opponent's argument is not fallacious so long as (1) personal authority is what gives the opposing argument much of its weight, and (2) the critique of the person's credibility is fairly presented.

An interesting recent example of an *ad hominem* argument occurred in the context of the Star Wars debate. Many important physicists around the country signed a statement in which they declared their opposition to Star Wars research. Another group of physicists supportive of that research condemned them on the grounds that none of the protesting physicists stood to get any Star Wars research funds anyway.

This attack shifted attention away from the reasons given by the protesting physicists for their convictions and put it instead on the physicists' motives. To some extent, of course, credibility is an issue here, because many of the key issues raised in the debate required some degree of expertise to resolve. Hence, the charges meet the first test for nonfallacious reasoning directed to the arguer.

But we must also ask ourselves if the charges being made are fair. If you'll recall from earlier discussions of fairness, we said that fairness requires similar treatment of similar classes of things. Applying this rule to this situation, we can simply reverse the charge being levied against the anti-SDI group and say of the pro-SDI group: "Because you stand to gain a good deal of research money from this project, we can't take your support of the SDI initiatives seriously." The Star Wars supporters would thus become victims of their own logic. *Ad hominem* attacks are often of this nature: The charges are perfectly reversible. (E.g., "Of course you support abortion; all your friends are feminists." "Of course you oppose abortion; you've been a Catholic all your life.") *Ad hominem* debates resemble nothing so much as mental quick-draw contests. Whoever shoots first wins because the first accuser puts the burden of proof on the opposition.

It's important to see here that an *ad hominem* argument, even if not fallacious, can never be definitive. Like analogies, they are simply suggestive; they raise doubts and focus our attention. Catholic writers can produce reasonable arguments against abortion, and feminists can produce reasonable ones for it. *Ad hominem* attacks don't allow us to discount arguments; but they do alert us to possible biases, possible ways the reasoned arguments themselves are vulnerable.

Several subcategories of the *ad hominem* argument that are almost never persuasive include:

1. name-calling (referring to a disputant by unsavory names)
2. appeal to prejudice (applying ethnic, racial, gender, or religious slurs to an opponent)
3. guilt by association (linking the opposition to extremely unpopular groups or causes)

Name-calling is found far more often in transcripts of oral encounters than in books or essays. In the heat of the moment, speakers are more likely to lapse into verbal abuse than are writers who have time to contemplate their words. The Congressional Record is a rich source for name-calling. Here, for example, one finds a duly elected representative of the electorate referring to another duly elected representative as "a pimp for the Eastern establishment environmentalists." One of the biggest problems with such a charge is that it's unlikely to beget much in the way of reasoned response. It's far easier to respond in kind than it is to persuade people rationally that one is not a jackass of *that* particular sort.

When name-calling is "elevated" to include slighting reference to the opponent's religion, gender, race, or ethnic background, we have encountered an appeal to prejudice. When it involves lumping an opponent with unsavory, terminally dumb, or extremely unpopular causes and characters, it constitutes guilt by association.

STRAWPERSON (GREATLY OVERSIMPLIFYING AN OPPONENT'S ARGUMENT TO MAKE IT EASIER TO REFUTE OR RIDICULE)

Although typically less inflammatory than the above sorts of *ethos* fallacies, the strawperson fallacy changes the character of the opposition in order to suit its own needs. In committing a strawperson fallacy, you basically make up the argument you *wish* your opponents had made and attribute it to them because it's so much easier to refute than the argument they actually made. Some political debates consist almost entirely of strawperson exchanges such as: "You may think that levying confiscatory taxes on homeless people's cardboard dwellings is the surest way out of recession, but I don't." Or: "While my opponent would like to empty our prisons of serial killers and coddle kidnappers, I hold to the sacred principles of compensatory justice."

Fallacies of *Logos*

Logos fallacies comprise flaws in the relationships among the statements of an argument. Thus, to borrow momentarily from the language of the Toulmin schema discussed earlier, you can think of *logos* fallacies as breakdowns between argument's warrants and their claims, between their warrants and their backing, or between their claims and their grounds.

BEGGING THE QUESTION (SUPPORTING A CLAIM WITH A REASON THAT IS REALLY A RESTATEMENT OF THE CLAIM IN DIFFERENT WORDS)

Question begging is probably the most obvious example of a *logos* fallacy in that it involves stating a claim as though it were a warrant for itself. For example, the statement "Abortion is murder because it involves the intentional killing of an unborn human being" is tantamount to saying "Abortion is murder because it's murder." The warrant "If something is the intentional killing of a human life, it is murder" simply repeats the claim; murder is *by definition* the intentional killing of another human being. Logically, the statement is akin to a statement like "That fellow is fat because he's considerably overweight." The crucial issue in the abortion debate is whether or not a fetus is a human being in the legal sense; this crucial issue is avoided in the argument, which begins by assuming that the fetus is a legal human being. Hence the argument goes in an endless circle from claim to warrant and back again.

Or consider the following argument: "How can you say Minnie Minoso belongs in the Hall of Fame? He's been eligible for over a decade and the Selection Committee turned him down every year. If he belonged in the Hall of Fame, the Committee would already have chosen him." Because the point at issue is whether or not the Hall of Fame Selection Committee *should* elect Minnie Minoso (and they should), the use of their vote as proof of the contention that they should not elect him is wholly circular and begs the question.

In distinguishing valid syllogistic reasoning from fallacious examples of question begging, some philosophers say that the question has been begged when the premises of an argument are at least as uncertain as the claim. In such cases, we are not making any movement from some known general principle toward some new particular conclusion; we are simply asserting an uncertain premise in order to give the appearance of certainty to a shaky claim.

To illustrate the preceding observation, consider the controversy that arose in the late eighties over whether or not to impose economic sanctions against South Africa in order to pressure the South Africans into changing their racial policies. One argument against economic sanctions went like this: "We should not approve economic sanctions against South Africa (claim) because economic sanctions will hurt blacks as much as whites" (premise or stated reason). The claim ("We should not impose economic sanctions") is only as certain as the premise from which it was derived ("because blacks will suffer as much as whites"), but many people argued that that premise was extremely uncertain. They thought that whites would suffer the most under sanctions and that blacks would ultimately benefit. The question would no longer be begged if the person included a documented defense of the premise. But without such a defense, the arguer's claim is grounded on a shaky premise that sounds more certain than it is.

COMPLEX QUESTION (CONFRONTING THE OPPONENT WITH A QUESTION THAT WILL PUT HER IN A BAD LIGHT NO MATTER HOW SHE RESPONDS)

A complex question is one that requires, in legal terms, a self-incriminating response. For example, the question "When did you stop abusing alcohol?"

requires the admission of alcohol abuse. Hence the claim that a person has abused alcohol is silently turned into an assumption.

FALSE DILEMMA/EITHER-OR (OVERSIMPLIFYING A COMPLEX ISSUE SO THAT ONLY TWO CHOICES APPEAR POSSIBLE)

A good extended analysis of this fallacy is found in sociologist Kai Erickson's essay on the decision to drop the A-bomb on Hiroshima (pages 461–471). His analysis suggests that the Truman administration prematurely reduced numerous options to just two: Either drop the bomb on a major city or sustain unacceptable losses in a land invasion of Japan. Typically, we encounter false dilemma arguments when people are trying to justify a questionable action by creating a false sense of necessity, forcing us to choose between two options, one of which is clearly unacceptable. Hence, when someone orders us to do it "My way or hit the highway," or to "Love it or leave it," it's probably in response to some criticism we made about the "way" we're supposed to do it or the "it" we're supposed to love.

But of course not all dilemmas are false. People who reject all binary oppositions (that is, thinking in terms of pairs of opposites) are themselves guilty of a false dilemma. There are times when we might determine through a rational process of elimination that only two possible choices exist. Deciding whether a dilemma is truly a dilemma or only an evasion of complexity often requires a difficult judgment. Although we should initially suspect any attempt to convert a complex problem into an either/or choice, we may legitimately arrive at such a choice through thoughtful deliberation.

EQUIVOCATION (USING TO YOUR ADVANTAGE AT LEAST TWO DIFFERENT DEFINITIONS OF THE SAME TERM IN THE SAME ARGUMENT)

For example, if we're told that people can't "flourish" unless they are culturally literate, we must know which of the several possible senses of *flourish* are being used before we can test the persuasiveness of the claim. If by *flourishing* the author means acquiring great wealth, we'll look at a different set of grounds than if *flourishing* is synonymous with moral probity, recognition in a profession, or simple contentment. To the extent that we're not told what it means to flourish, the relationship between the claim and the grounds and between the claim and the warrant remains ambiguous and unassailable.

CONFUSING CORRELATION FOR CAUSE/ *POST HOC, ERGO PROPTER HOC* (AFTER THIS, THEREFORE BECAUSE OF THIS) (ASSUMING THAT EVENT X CAUSES EVENT Y BECAUSE EVENT X PRECEDED EVENT Y)

Here are two examples in which this fallacy may be at work:

> Cramming for a test really helps. Last week I crammed for a psychology test and I got an A on it.

> I am allergic to the sound of a lawn mower because every time I mow the lawn I start to sneeze.

We've already discussed this fallacy in our chapter on causal arguments, particularly in our discussion of the difference between correlation and causation. This fallacy occurs when a sequential relationship is mistaken for a causal relationship. To be sure, when two events occur frequently in conjunction with each other in a particular sequence, we've got a good case for a causal relationship. But until we can show how one causes the other, we cannot be certain that a causal relationship is occurring. The conjunction may simply be a matter of chance, or it may be attributable to some as-yet-unrecognized other factor. For example, your A on the psych test may be caused by something other than your cramming. Maybe the exam was easier, or perhaps you were luckier or more mentally alert.

Just when an erroneous causal argument becomes an example of the *post hoc* fallacy, however, is not cut and dried. Many reasonable arguments of causality later turn out to have been mistaken. We are guilty of the *post hoc* fallacy only when our claim of causality seems naively arrived at, without reflection or consideration of alternative hypotheses. Thus in our lawn mower argument, it is not the sound that creates the speaker's sneezing, but all the pollen stirred up by the spinning blades.

We arrived at this more certain argument by applying a tool known as Occam's Razor — the principle that "what can be explained on fewer principles is explained needlessly by more," or "between two hypotheses, both of which will account for a given fact, prefer the simpler." If we posit that sound is the cause of our sneezing, all sorts of intermediate causes are going to have to be fetched from afar to make the explanation persuasive. But the blades stirring up the pollen will cause the sneezing more directly. So, until science connects lawn mower noises to human eardrums to sneezing, the simpler explanation is preferred.

SLIPPERY SLOPE

The slippery slope fallacy is based on the fear that once we take a first step in a direction we don't like we will have to keep going.

We don't dare send weapons to guerrillas in Central America. If we do so, we will next send in military advisers, then a special forces battalion, and then large numbers of troops. Finally, we will be in all-out war.

Look, Blotnik, no one feels worse about your need for open-heart surgery than I do. But I still can't let you turn this paper in late. If I were to let you do it, then I'd have to let everyone turn in papers late.

We run into slippery slope arguments all the time, especially when person A opposes person B's proposal. Those opposed to a particular proposal will often foresee an inevitable and catastrophic chain of events that would follow from taking a first, apparently harmless step. In other words, once we put a foot on that slippery slope, we're doomed to slide right out of sight. Often, such arguments are fallacious insofar as what is seen as an inevitable effect is in fact dependent on some intervening cause or chain of causes to bring it about. Will smoking cigarettes lead inevitably to heroin addiction? Overwhelming statistical evidence would suggest that it doesn't. A slippery slope argument would, however, lovingly trace the inevitable descent from a clandestine puff on the schoolground through the smoking of various controlled substances to a degenerate end in some Needle Park somewhere. The power of the slippery slope argument lies as much as anything in its compelling narrative structure. It pulls us along irresistibly from one plausible event to the next, making us forget that it's a long jump from plausibility to necessity.

One other common place to find slippery slope arguments is in confrontations between individuals and bureaucracies or other systems of rules and laws. Whenever individuals ask to have some sort of exception made for them, they risk the slippery slope reply. "Sorry, Ms. Jones, if we rush your order, then we will have to rush everyone else's order also."

The problem, of course, is that not every slippery slope argument is an instance of the slippery slope fallacy. We all know that some slopes are slippery and that we sometimes have to draw the line, saying "to here, but no farther." And it is true also that making exceptions to rules is dangerous; the exceptions soon get established as regular procedures. The slippery slope becomes a fallacy, however, when we forget that some slopes don't *have* to be slippery unless we let them be slippery. Often we do better to imagine a staircase with stopping places all along the way. The assumption that we have no control over our descent once we take the first step makes us unnecessarily rigid.

HASTY GENERALIZATION (MAKING A BROAD GENERALIZATION ON THE BASIS OF TOO LITTLE EVIDENCE)

Typically, a hasty generalization occurs when someone reaches a conclusion on the basis of insufficient evidence. But what constitutes "sufficient" evidence? No generalization arrived at through empirical evidence would meet a logician's strict standard of certainty. And generally acceptable standards of proof in any given field are difficult to determine.

The Food and Drug Administration (FDA), for example, generally proceeds very cautiously before certifying a drug as "safe." However, whenever doubts arise about the safety of an FDA-approved drug, critics accuse the FDA of having made a hasty generalization. At the same time, patients eager to have access to a new drug and manufacturers eager to sell a new product may lobby the FDA to "quit dragging its feet" and get the drug to market. Hence, the point at which a hasty generalization about drug safety passes over into the realm of a prudent generalization is nearly always uncertain and contested.

A couple of variants of hasty generalization that deserve mention are

1. Pars pro toto/*Mistaking the part for the whole (assuming that what is true for a part will be true for the whole). Pars pro toto* arguments often appear in the critiques of the status quo. If, say, someone wanted to get rid of the National Endowment for the Arts, they might focus on several controversial grants they've made over the past few years and use them as justification for wiping out all NEA programs.

2. *Suppressed evidence (withholding contradictory or unsupportive evidence so that only favorable evidence is presented to an audience).* The flip side of *pars pro toto* is suppressed evidence. If the administrator of the NEA were to go before Congress seeking more money and conveniently forgot about those controversial grants, he would be suppressing damaging but relevant evidence.

FAULTY ANALOGY (CLAIMING THAT BECAUSE X RESEMBLES Y IN ONE REGARD, X WILL RESEMBLE Y IN ALL REGARDS)

Faulty analogies occur whenever a relationship of resemblance is turned into a relationship of identity. For example, the psychologist Carl Rogers uses a questionable analogy in his argument that political leaders should make use of discoveries about human communication derived from research in the social sciences. "During the war when a test-tube solution was found to the problem of synthetic rubber, millions of dollars and an army of talent was turned loose on the problem of using that finding. . . . But in the social science realm, if a way is found of facilitating communication and mutual understanding in small groups, there is no guarantee that the finding will be utilized."

Although Rogers is undoubtedly right that we need to listen more carefully to social scientists, his analogy between the movement from scientific discovery to product development and the movement from insights into small group functioning to political change is strained. The laws of cause and effect at work in a test tube are much more reliable and generalizable than the laws of cause and effect observed in small human groups. Whereas lab results can be readily replicated in different times and places, small group dynamics are altered by a whole host of factors, including the cultural background, gender, age of participants, and so forth. The warrant that licenses you to move from grounds to claim in the realm of science runs up against a statute of limitation when it tries to include the realm of social science.

FOR CLASS DISCUSSION

Working individually or in small groups, determine the potential persuasiveness of each argument. If the arguments are nonpersuasive because of one or more of the fallacies discussed in this appendix, identify the fallacies and explain how they render the argument nonpersuasive.

1. a. All wars are not wrong. The people who say so are cowards.

   b. Either we legalize marijuana or we watch a steady increase in the number of our citizens who break the law.

   c. The Bible is true because it is the inspired word of God.

   d. Mandatory registration of handguns will eventually lead to the confiscation of hunting rifles.

   e. All these tornadoes started happening right after they tested the A-bombs. The A-bomb testing has changed our weather.

   f. Most other progressive nations have adopted a program of government-provided health care. Therefore, it is time the United States abandoned its outdated practice of private medicine.

   g. The number of Hollywood movie stars who support liberal policies convinces me that liberalism is the best policy. After all, they are rich and will not benefit from better social services.

   h. Society has an obligation to provide housing for the homeless because people without adequate shelter have a right to the resources of the community.

   i. I have observed the way the two renters in our neighborhood take care of their rental houses and have compared that to the way homeowners take care of their houses. I have concluded that people who own their own homes take better care of them than those who rent. [This argument goes on to provide detailed evidence about the housecaring practices of the two renters and of the homeowners in the neighborhood.]

   j. Since the universe couldn't have been created out of nothing, it must have been created by a divine being.

2. Consider the following statements. Note places where you think the logic is flawed. If you were asked by writers or speakers to respond to their statements, what advice would you give to those who wrote or said them to rescue them from charges of fallaciousness? What would each of these speakers/writers have to show, in addition to what's given, to render the statements cogent and persuasive?

a. "America has had the luxury throughout its history of not having its national existence directly threatened by a foreign enemy. Yet we have gone to war. Why?

"The United States of America is not a piece of dirt stretching mainly from the Atlantic to the Pacific. More than anything else, America is a set of principles, and the historical fact is that those principles have not only served us well, but have also become a magnet for the rest of the world, a large chunk of which decided to change course last year.

"Those principles are not mere aesthetic ideas. Those principles are in fact the distillation of 10,000 years of human social evolution. We have settled on them not because they are pretty; we settled on them because they are the only things that work. If you have trouble believing that, ask a Pole." (novelist Tom Clancy)

b. "What particularly irritated Mr. Young [Republican Congressman from Alaska] was the fact that the measure [to prohibit logging in Alaska's Tongass National Forest] was initiated by . . . Robert Mrazek, a Democrat from Long Island. 'Bob Mrazek never saw a tree in his entire life until he went to Alaska' said Mr. Young. . . ." (*New York Times*, 11/10/90)

c. "When Senator Tim Wirth . . . was in Brazil earlier this year on behalf of an effort to save the tropical rain forest of the Amazon basin, the first thing Brazilian President Jose Sarney asked him was, 'What about the Tongass?'" (*New York Times*, 11/10/90)

STATISTICAL TRAPS IN ARGUMENTS

According to one thinker, "There are three kinds of lies: lies, damned lies, and statistics." Somehow arguments seem especially persuasive when they are decked out in percentages and ratios, and buttressed with charts, graphs, and tables. But much fallacious reasoning can be masked by statistics. Consequently, we are here devoting some special attention to the use of numbers in argument.

The heavy reliance on and belief in numbers is unique to modern argumentation. Whereas in ancient times speakers relied primarily on logical proof and the invocation of shared principles to convince an audience to accept their point of view, writers and speakers today rely more on statistics and various other manifestations of numbers to make their points. An opponent of abortion in older times might simply invoke the principle "Thou shalt not kill" and then amplify that principle by citing horrors that occurred in the lives of women who aborted their offspring; however, a latter-day opponent of abortion will have to confront statistical or quantitative issues such as biological data about the day-by-day development of the fetus, the percentage of abortions that result in death for the mother, the comparative death rates for mothers who legally or illegally abort offspring, the economic costs associated with aborting or not aborting an offspring, the increase or decrease in unwanted pregnancy that follows changes in abortion laws, and so on. Although one may argue with the appropriateness of statistical arguments, one cannot argue with the pervasiveness of data in argumentation.

Before moving on to a discussion of arguments based on data, we need to say a word about our infatuation with numbers themselves. We speak of "hard" data — usually data expressed in numbers — as though they were eternal and unquestionable truths and contrast them sneeringly with the "soft data" that fuzzy thinkers derive from poorly constructed questionnaires. Whereas hard data often seem factual, soft data seem one step removed from opinion.

But how "factual" are hard data? One could, for instance, ask a hundred students to rank professors A and B on "overall effectiveness as a teacher" (on a scale, say, of 1 to 10 with 10 the highest) and find that A scored 8.2 whereas B scored 5.8. What do these "hard" data mean? Do they mean that A is a better teacher than B? Do they necessarily even mean that students think that A is a better teacher than B? Do we have any certainty of what criteria students are using when they evaluate "effectiveness"? Are they all using about the same criteria? What if A teaches consistently through lecture and multiple choice exams and B teaches through small-group discussion interspersed with lots of writing assignments? Do the "hard" data mean that students think A is a better teacher than B or that lecturing is a better teaching method than small-group discussions? What if every student ranked A as either 8 or 9 on the scale, whereas 50 percent of all students ranked B as 10 and the other 50 percent ranked B between 1 and 4?

The point being made is that although some data can be considered more trustworthy than other data, no data are "hard" in quite the way that word suggests. In some sense, all numbers are "soft." You can't pick them up or eat them or build houses out of them. Any number system is "made up" and is meaningful only in relation to other numbers. All that "2" means is twice as many as "1" and half as much as "4." Although numbers can be applied to almost anything in the world, none of them refers directly to anything outside the system of numbers. What all this means is that numbers must be made meaningful by viewing them in the context of other numbers. Hence, a billion is a big number if you're talking about people, but a small number if you're talking about atoms. Numbers alone, then, won't settle arguments, and one of the greatest dangers people fall prey to is to rely too much on numbers and not enough on analysis to make numbers significant.

Numbers, in abundance, can also be extremely boring to the general audience unless you have created a context to make them meaningful— thus the unpersuasiveness of long strings of figures that roll unheeded past the glazed eyes of the reader. Numbers have to be grounded in whatever it is that they describe and the numerical system appropriate to that reality before anyone can know what to make of them.

MAKING NUMBERS MEANINGFUL: CHARTS, TABLES, AND GRAPHS

One of the most common ways of making numbers meaningful is to "picture" them in graphs, charts, or tables. A chart is quite literally a picture of numerical values. A pie chart, for example, gives you an immediate sense of how big a portion of the whole each part claims. Figure AP2-1, for example, shows two pie charts indicating how big a piece of the "personal consumption expenditure" pie Americans spend on recreation and, in turn, how the recreation pie is divided up among various areas. In a table, numerical data can be expressed much more complexly than in a pie chart, but their significance in relation to other numbers is not so visually immediate. A graph, on the other hand, is somewhere between a chart and a table. In a graph, the numbers can be taken from a table and "pictured" either in

Personal Consumption Expenditures (PCE) for Recreation: 1984

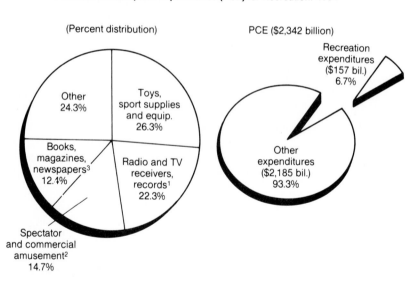

[1] Includes musical instruments and radio and TV repair.
[2] Includes admissions to spectator amusements, commercial participant amusements and parimutuel net receipts.
[3] Includes maps and sheet music.
Source: Chart prepared by U.S. Bureau of the Census.

FIGURE AP2-1. Examples of Pie Charts

the form of lines drawn on a grid of squares called "scale units" or else in the form of bars drawn out from the vertical or horizontal axis of the graph. "Line" graphs show how one quantity changes as a function of changes in another quantity. Because graphs are the most common — and most commonly misunderstood — form of data presentation, we'll now take a closer look at them.

Interpreting Graphs

In reading a line graph, as in reading a table, we read from the "outside in." We look for a title to the graph which tells us what two values are being related. We then look to see which value is represented on the vertical axis and which is represented on the horizontal axis. We check to see what quantity each scale unit represents for each of the two values. Then we look at the line to see what it tells us about the relationship between the two values.

When the graph line goes in one direction, we know the relationship between the two values is continuous. This means either that every increase in one value is reflected by an increase in the other value, or that every increase in one value is reflected in a decrease in the other value. Squiggly lines that go up and down indicate a variable relationship between the two values.

But graphs can be deceiving. Let's take a look at a graph more closely to see how they are made and what sorts of things one should be careful of in interpreting them. Arranged in tabular form, Table AP2−1 shows some data on the profitability of Bicker Pen Company, manufacturers of cheap ballpoint pens.

TABLE AP2−1. Monthly Net
Profits for Bicker Pen Company,
1987 — First Three Quarters

Month	Net Profits (in thousands of $)
Jan.	1.0
Feb.	2.0
Mar.	3.0
Apr.	4.0
May	4.0
June	5.0
July	6.0
Aug.	8.0
Sept.	12.0

One can, by looking at the table, get a general sense of Bicker's profit pattern, but it takes a while and the impact is thus diminished. Now let's take a look at a graphic display of the information as compiled by Bernie Bicker, president of the firm (see Figure AP2–2).

Looking at this graph, one might well conclude that Bicker Pen is headed for the stars. Just look at that line, taking off like an Airwolf. But before you grab your checkbook and ring up your broker, let's analyze the graph a bit more closely. One of the trickiest features of graphs is that they often suggest more about relationships than we have any cause to infer. It would appear from looking at this graph that as time passes on the horizontal axis, profitability increases on the vertical axis. Our tendency is to say that the passage of time "results in" an increase in profit. In fact, all we can say is that during the time period depicted in the graph, profits did increase. We cannot legitimately infer that profits will continue to increase over time. No permanent or necessary relationship between the two values has been

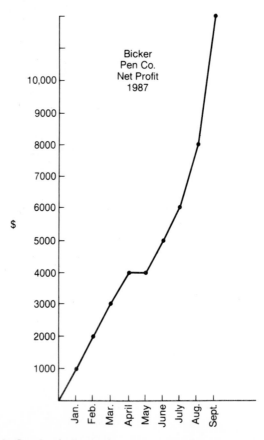

FIGURE **AP2–2.** Graph of Net Profits, Bicker Pen Company, 1987 (Example 1)

established, though the picture presented by the graph tends to "fix" that relationship and make it appear permanent.

The graph presents "a" picture of Bicker's profitability, but not "the" picture. The graph is a snapshot of a moving object. To fully understand this graph, we need to have a sense of the larger picture, of other numbers and other graphs. The assumption we made above was that this particular picture of Bicker's profits was "typical" or "representative" of the larger picture. But the smaller the particular picture we look at in a graph, the more risky it is to make inferences about the bigger picture. If, for example, we looked at a graph that represented Bicker's profits over the life of the company, our steeply rising line might turn out to be a mere blip upward in an inexorably descending line. If we looked at profits for the last quarter of 1986 we might see a precipitous drop. If we looked at the same graphs for 1984 and 1985, we might see the same pattern, which would indicate that the apparent steady ascent is merely part of a cyclic pattern of rises and falls, with every January being a low-sale month (after shoppers have bought their Christmas stocking stuffers) and every September being a high-sale month (when students return to school).

Another important consideration to keep in mind when interpreting graphs is the quantity assigned to each square. However truthful one must be in picturing the correct quantities graphically, the proportion represented by each square is usually a matter of choice and can profoundly influence a reader's perception of the relationship being pictured in the graph. If Bicker, for example, had chosen, instead of $1000, a larger increment for each square on the vertical axis, his company's rise in profitability might not look quite so astonishing. If each of the squares instead represented $5,000, it would appear to be a less remarkable change, barely creeping up to the second square (see Figure AP2–3). Hence one can easily distort or overstate

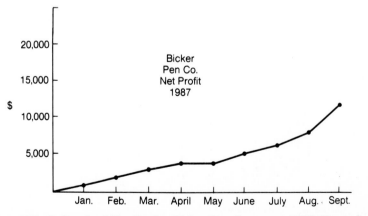

FIGURE **AP2-3.** Graph of Net Profits, Bicker Pen Company, 1987 (Example 2)

a rate of change on a graph by consciously selecting the quantities one assigns to each scale unit on either the horizontal or the vertical axis. The only guideline we have is the standard practice for graphing phenomena of the type frequently depicted. Thus, Bicker Pen should use the same sort of graph used by other companies of its type and size to depict profitability, thus allowing us to compare the graphs.

Bar graphs are an especially effective way of representing differing quantities. For example, Figure AP2-4 dramatically illustrates both the growth of the cable TV industry over a fifteen-year period, as measured by numbers of subscribers and revenues, and the relatively small increase in cost to the consumer. Because they are generally easier to understand than line graphs, bar graphs are a more effective way of communicating with technically unsophisticated audiences.

NUMBER TRAPS TO BEWARE OF

In addition to these basic sorts of questions about tables, charts, and graphs, one should always be on the lookout for common number traps. For

Cable TV — Average Subscribers, Average Monthly Rate and Revenue: 1970 to 1984

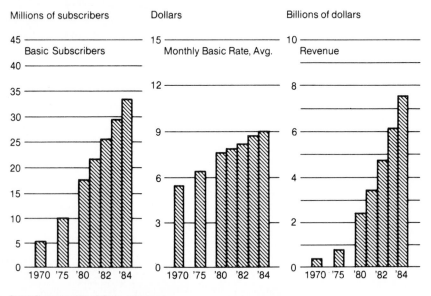

Source: Chart prepared by U.S. Bureau of the Census.

FIGURE **AP2-4.** Example of a Bar Graph

example, beware of "hidden factors," things that influence the picture you're seeing but that aren't mentioned explicitly when a series of numbers is displayed. The discovery of hidden factors requires that you know something about the phenomenon being shown in a chart, table, or graph. First, you need to know how the values being related on a graph were derived. In the case of Bicker, for instance, you might want to question why the graph depicts only the first three quarters and ends in September, a month that's bound to be a fat one for a cheap-pen company. You might also want to know how net profit was computed, since there are various bookkeeping procedures that allow companies to hide losses or understate gains. (For example, you need to know whether or not net profit includes sale of land or equipment, or a tax write-off.) Or what about inflation, a major hidden factor in many economic pictures of the mid-1970s through the early 1980s? If inflation was running at a high rate during 1986, so that Bicker felt justified in doubling the price of his pens in July, then Bicker's profit picture might have to be reevaluated.

Also, you need to be especially careful in interpreting data that might be reported either as raw numbers or as percentages. Bicker's profit picture becomes a good deal more meaningful, for example, if we could see it expressed as a percentage of the company's assets. We would then know how good a return on the investment Bicker was providing to its shareholders — which is the point of profit. Turning to the political scene, politicians who enthusiastically report that more Americans are working than ever before may be conveniently forgetting to mention that the percentage of unemployment is higher than it was during the Depression. In other words, we may have more employed persons because the population has grown, not because the economy is better. Similarly, the increase in the size of the defense budget can be made to sound huge if raw numbers are displayed, but much more moderate if the defense budget is displayed as a percentage of the gross national product. Thus, in order to comprehend the significance of absolute numbers, you often need to see them both in relation to other absolute numbers and in relation to percentages. For example, "40 percent of the American population would survive nuclear war," doesn't have quite the same ring as "130 million Americans would die in a nuclear war." You need to see the numbers both ways to get a comprehensible picture.

In sum, arguments relying on data, and visual displays of data, demand a knowledge of the sources of those numbers and the context within which those numbers are meaningful. You can always choose to express the same data in a number of ways, and how you say it with numbers is as important as what you say. Whenever you are given numerical evidence of any kind, ask yourself the following questions: "Where did the numbers come from?" "What phenomena do they describe?" "How were they gathered?" "By whom?" and "In relation to what other numbers are these numbers significant?"

FOR CLASS DISCUSSION

Look at the following table presented in evidence during a discrimination suit brought by a black teacher. The teacher charged that her salary was artificially low. Looking over the data for her school district, could you infer that a pattern of discrimination against black teachers is indeed apparent? What other information would you require to conclude with certainty that black teachers were being discriminated against?

TABLE AP2-2. Salary Comparison of Black and White Teachers

Salary Categories	Black Teachers		White Teachers	
	Number	Percentage	Number	Percentage
$4,001-4,500	10	77	3	15
$4,501-5,000	2	15	1	5
$5,001-5,500	1	8	2	10
$5,501-6,000	0	0	9	45
$6,001-6,500	0	0	3	15
$6,501-7,000	0	0	1	5
$7,001-7,500	0	0	0	0
$7,500 and above	0	0	1	5
Total	13	100	20	100

Source: Reprinted from *Statistical Proof of Discrimination* by David C. Baldus and James W. L. Cole, copyright 1980 by McGraw-Hill, Inc. Reprinted by permission of Shepard's/McGraw-Hill, Inc. Further reproduction is strictly prohibited.

3

THE WRITING COMMUNITY: WORKING IN GROUPS

In Chapter 1 we stressed that today truth is typically seen as a product of discussion and persuasion by members of a given community. Instead of seeing "truth" as grounded in some absolute and timeless realm such as Plato's forms or the unchanging laws of logic, many modern thinkers assert that truth is the product of a consensus among a group of knowledgeable peers. Our own belief in the special importance of argumentation in contemporary life follows from our assumption that truth arises out of discussion and debate rather than dogma or pure reason.

In this appendix, we extend that assumption to the classroom itself. We introduce you to a mode of learning often called collaborative learning. It involves a combination of learning from an instructor, learning independently, and learning from peers. Mostly it involves a certain spirit—the same sort of inquiring attitude that's required of a good arguer.

FROM CONFLICT TO CONSENSUS: HOW TO GET THE MOST OUT OF THE WRITING COMMUNITY

Behind the notion of the writing community lies the notion that thinking and writing are social acts. At first, this notion may contradict certain widely accepted stereotypes of writers and thinkers as solitary souls who

743

retreat to cork-lined studies where they conjure great thoughts and works. But although we agree that every writer at some point in the process requires solitude, we would point out that most writers and thinkers also require periods of talk and social interchange before they retreat to solitude. Poets, novelists, scientists, philosophers, and technological innovators tend to belong to communities of peers with whom they share their ideas, theories, and work. In this section, we try to provide you with some practical advice on how to get the most out of these sorts of communities in developing your writing skills.

Avoiding Bad Habits of Group Behavior

Over the years, most of us have developed certain bad habits that get in the way of efficient group work. Although we use groups all the time to study and accomplish demanding tasks, we tend to do so spontaneously and unreflectively without asking why some groups work and others don't. Many of us, for example, have worked on committees that just didn't get the job done and wasted our time, or else got the job done because one or two tyrannical people dominated the group. Just a couple of bad committee experiences can give us a healthy skepticism about the utility of groups in general. "A committee," according to some people, "is a sort of centipede. It has too many legs, no brain, and moves very slowly."

At their worst, this is indeed how groups function. In particular, they have a tendency to fail in two opposite directions, failures that can be avoided only by conscious effort. Groups can lapse into "clonethink" and produce a safe, superficial consensus whereby everyone agrees with the first opinion expressed in order to avoid conflict or to get on to something more interesting. At the other extreme is a phenomenon we'll call "egothink." In egothink, all members of the group go their own way and produce a collection of minority views that have nothing to do with each other and would be impossible to act on. Clonethinkers view their task as conformity to a norm; egothinkers see their task as safeguarding the autonomy of individual group members. Both fail to take other people and other ideas seriously.

Successful groups avoid both extremes and achieve unity out of diversity. This means that any successful community of learners must be willing to endure creative conflict. Creative conflict results from an initial agreement to disagree respectfully with each other and to focus that disagreement on ideas, not people. For this reason, we say that the relationship among the members of a learning community is not so much interpersonal or impersonal as transpersonal or "beyond the personal." Each member is personally committed to the development of ideas and does whatever is necessary to achieve that development.

The Value of Group
Work for Writers

Because we are basically social animals, we find it natural, pleasurable even, to deal with problems in groups. Proof of this fact can be found on any given morning in any given student union in the country. Around the room you will find many students working in groups. Math, engineering, and business majors will be solving problems together, comparing solutions and their ways of arriving at solutions. Others will be comparing their class notes and testing their understanding of concepts and terms by explaining them to each other and comparing their explanations. To be sure, their discussions will occasionally drift off the topic to encompass pressing social issues such as what they're going to do next weekend, or why they like or dislike the class they're working on, but much of the work of college students seems to get done in convivial conversation over morning coffee or late-night popcorn. Why not ease into the rigors of writing in a similar fashion?

A second major advantage of working on writing in a group is that it provides a real and immediate audience for people's work. Too often, when students write in a school setting they get caught up in the writing-for-teacher racket, which may distort their notion of audience. Argumentative writing is best aimed either at opponents or at a neutral "jury" who will be weighing both sides of a controversy. A group of peers gives you a better sense of a real-world audience "out there" than does a single teacher.

There's danger, of course, in having several audiences consider your writing. Your peer audience well might respond differently to your writing than your instructor. You may feel misled if you are praised for something by a peer and then criticized for the same thing by your instructor. These things can and will happen, no matter how much time you spend developing universally accepted criteria for writing. Grades are not facts but judgments, and all judgments involve uncertainty. Students who are still learning the criteria for making judgments will sometimes apply those criteria differently than an instructor who has been working with them for years. But you should know too that two or more instructors might give you conflicting advice also, just as two or more doctors might give you different advice on what to do about the torn ligaments in your knee. In our view, the risks of misunderstanding are more than made up for by gains in understanding of the writing process, an understanding that comes from working in writing communities where everyone functions both as a writer and a writing critic.

A third advantage to working in writing communities is closely related to the second advantage. The act of sharing your writing with other people helps you get beyond the bounds of egocentrism that limit all writers. By egocentrism, we don't mean pride or stuck-upness; we mean the failure to consider the needs of your readers. Unless you share your writing with another person, your audience is always a "mythical group," a fiction or a theory that exists only in your head. You must always try to anticipate the problems others will have in reading your work, but until others actually read it and share their reactions to it with you, you can never be fully sure you have understood your audience's point of view. Until another reads your writing critically, you can't be sure you aren't talking to yourself.

FORMING WRITING COMMUNITIES: SKILLS AND ROLES

Given that there are advantages to working in groups, just how do we go about forming writing communities in the classroom? We first have to decide how big to make the groups. From our experience, the best groups consist of either five to seven people or simply two people. Groups of three to four tend to polarize and become divisive, and larger groups tend to be unmanageable. Because working in five- to seven-person groups is quite different from working in pairs, we discussed each of these different-sized groups in turn.

Working in Groups of Five to Seven People

The trick to successful group work is to consider the maximum number of viewpoints and concerns without losing focus. Because these two basic goals frequently conflict, you need some mechanisms for monitoring your progress. In particular, it's important that each group member is assigned to perform those tasks necessary to effective group functioning. (Some teachers assign "roles" to individual students, shifting the roles from day to day; other teachers let the groups themselves determine the roles of individuals.) That is, the group must recognize that it has two objectives at all times: the stated objectives of a given task and the objective of making the group work well. It is very easy to get so involved with the given task that you overlook the second objective, generally known as "group maintenance."

The first role is group leader. We hesitate to call persons who fill this role "leaders" because we tend sometimes to think of leaders as know-it-alls who "take charge" and order people about. In classroom group work, however, being a group leader is a role you play, not a fixed part of your identity. The leader, above all else, keeps the groups focused on agreed-on ends and protects the right of every group member to be heard. It's an important function, and group members should share the responsibility from task to task. Here is a list of things for the leader to do during a group discussion:

1. Ensure that everyone understands and agrees on the objectives of any given task and on what sort of final product is expected of the group (for example, a list of criteria, a brief written statement, oral response to a question, and so forth).

2. Ask that the group set an agenda for completing the task and have some sense of how much time they will spend at each stage. (Your instructor should always make clear what time limits you have to operate within and when he or she expects your task to be completed. If a time limit isn't specified, you should request a reasonable estimate.)

3. Look for signs of getting off the track and ask individual group members to clarify how their statements relate to agreed-on objectives.

4. Actively solicit everyone's contributions and take care that all viewpoints are listened to and that the group does not rush to incomplete judgment.

5. Try to determine when the task has been adequately accomplished.

In performing each of these functions, the leader must be concerned to turn criticisms and observations into questions. Instead of saying to one silent and bored-looking member of the group, "Hey, Gormley, you haven't said didley squat here so far; say something relevant or take a hike," the leader might ask, "Irwin, do you agree with what Beth just said about this paper being disorganized?" Remember, every action in nature is met with an equal and opposite reaction—commands tend to be met with resistance, questions with answers.

A second crucial role for well-functioning groups is that of recorder. The recorder's function is to provide the group with a record of their deliberations so they can measure their progress. It is particularly important that the recorder write down the agenda and the solution to the problem in precise form. Because the recorder must summarize the deliberations fairly precisely, he must ask for clarifications. In doing this, he ensures that group members don't fall into the "ya know?" syndrome (a subset of clonethink) in which people assent to statements that are in fact cloudy to them. (Ya know?) At the completion of the task, the recorder should also ask if there are any significant remaining disagreements or unanswered questions. Finally, the recorder is responsible for reporting the group's solutions to the class as a whole.*

If these two roles are conscientiously filled, the group should be able to identify and solve problems that temporarily keep it from functioning effectively. Maybe you are thinking that this sounds dumb. Whenever you've been in a group everyone has known if there were problems or not without leaders or recorders. Too often, however, a troubled group may sense that there is a problem without being perfectly clear about the nature of the problem or the solution. Let's say you are in a group with Elwood Lunt, Jr., who is very opinionated and dominates the discussions. (For a sample of Elwood's cognitive style, see his essay in Task 2 at the end of this Appendix.) Group members may represent their problem privately to themselves with a statement such as "Lunt's such a jerk nobody can work with him. He talks constantly and none of the rest of us can get a word in." The group may devote all of its energies to punishing Lunt with ridicule or silence rather than trying to solve the problem. Although this may make you feel better for a short time, Lunt is unlikely to get any better and the group is unlikely to get much done.

If Lunt is indeed bogging the group down by airing his opinions at great length, it is the leader's job to limit his dominance without excluding him. Because group members all realize that it is the group leader's role to handle such problems, the leader has a sort of license that allows her or him to deal directly with Lunt. Moreover, the leader also has the explicit responsibility to do so, so that each member is not forced to sit, silently seething and waiting for someone to do something.

The leader might control Lunt in one of several ways: (1) by keeping to the agenda ("Thanks Elwood, hate to interrupt, but we're a bit behind schedule and we haven't heard from everyone on this point yet. Jack, shall we move on to you?"); (2) by simply asking Lunt to demonstrate how his remarks are relevant to the topic at hand ("That's real interesting, Elwood, that you got to see Sid Vicious in his last performance, but can you tell us how you see that relating to Melissa's point that a sense of humor is crucial to good teaching?"); or (3) by introducing more formal procedures such as asking group members to raise their hands and be called on by the chair. These procedures might not satisfy your blood lust, your secrete desire to stuff Lunt into a dumpster; however, they are more likely to let the group get its work done and perhaps, just maybe, to help Lunt become a better listener and participant.

The rest of the group, though they have no formally defined roles, have an equally important obligation to participate fully. To ensure full participation, group members can do several things. They can make sure that they

---

*There is a debate among experts who study small group communications whether or not the roles of leader and recorder can be collapsed into one job. Your group may need to experiment until it discovers the structure that works best for bringing out the most productive discussions.

know all the other group members by their first names and speak to them in a friendly manner. They can practice listening procedures wherein they try not to dissent or disagree without first charitably summarizing the view with which they are taking issue. Most importantly, they can bring to the group as much information and as many alternative points of view as they can muster. The primary intellectual strength of group work is the ability to generate a more complex view of a subject. But this more complex view cannot emerge unless all individuals contribute their perspectives.

One collaborative task for writers that requires no elaborate procedures or any role playing is reading your essays aloud within the group. A good rule for this procedure is that no one responds to any one essay until all have been read. This is often an effective last step before handing in any essay. It's a chance to share the fruits of your labor with others and to hear finished essays that you may have seen in the draft stages. Hearing everyone else's final draft can also help you get a clearer perspective on how your own work is progressing. Listening to the essays read can both reassure you that your work is on a par with other people's and challenge you to write up to the level of the best student writing in your group.

Many of you may find this process a bit frightening at first. But the cause of your fright is precisely the source of the activity's value. In reading your work aloud, you are taking responsibility for that work in a special way. Writing specialist Kenneth Bruffee, whose work on collaborative learning introduced us to many of the ideas in this chapter, likens the reading of papers aloud to reciting a vow, of saying "I do" in a marriage ceremony. You are taking public responsibility for your words, and there's no turning back. The word has become deed. If you aren't at least a little nervous about reading an essay aloud, you probably haven't invested much in your words. Knowing that you will take public responsibility for your words is an incentive to make that investment—a more real and immediate incentive than a grade.

Working in Pairs

Working in pairs is another effective form of community learning. In our classes we use pairs at both the early-draft and the late-draft stages of writing. At the early-draft stage, it serves the very practical purpose of clarifying a student's ideas and sense of direction at the beginning of a new writing project. The interaction best takes place in the form of pair interviews. When you first sit down to interview each other, each of you should have done a fair amount of exploratory writing and thinking about what you want to say in your essay and how you're going to say it. Here is a checklist of questions you can use to guide your interview:

1. "What is your issue?" Your goal here is to help the writer focus an issue by formulating a question with clearly opposing answers.

2. "What is your position on the issue and what are alternative positions?" After you have helped your interviewee formulate the issue question, help her clarify this issue by stating her own position and showing how that position differs from opposing ones. Your interviewee might say, for example, that "many of my friends are opposed to building more nuclear power plants, but I think we need to build more of them."

3. "Can you walk me through your argument step by step?" Once you know your interviewee's issue question and intended position, you can best help her by having her walk you through her argument talking out loud. You can ask prompting questions such as "What are you going to say first?" "What next?" and so on. At this stage your interviewee will probably still be struggling to discover the best way to support the point. You can best help by brainstorming along with her, both of you taking notes on your ideas. Often at this stage you can begin making a schematic plan for the essay and formulating supporting reasons as because clauses. Along the way give your interviewee any information or ideas you have on the issue. It is particularly helpful at this stage if you can provide counterarguments and opposing views.

The interview strategy is useful before writers begin their rough drafts. After the first drafts have been written, there are a number of different ways of using pairs to evaluate drafts. One practice that we've found helpful is simply to have writers write a one-paragraph summary of their own drafts and of their partner's. In comparing summaries, writers can often discover which, if any, of their essential ideas are simply not getting across. If a major idea is not in the reader's summary, writer and reader need to decide if it's due to a careless reading or to problems within the draft. The nice thing about this method is that the criticism is given indirectly and hence isn't as threatening to either party. At other times, your instructor might also devise a checklist of features for you to consider, based on the criteria you have established for the assignment.

FOR CLASS DISCUSSION

1. As a group, consider the following quotation and then respond to the questions that follow: "In most college classrooms there is a reluctance to assume leadership. The norm for college students is to defer to someone else, to refuse to accept the position even if it is offered. There is actually a competition in humility and the most humble person usually ends up as the leader."*

a. Do you think this statement is true?

b. On what evidence do you base your judgment of its truthfulness?

*Philips, Gerald; Pederson, Douglas; and Wood, Julia. *Group Discussion: A Practical Guide to Participant Leadership.* Boston: Houghton Mifflin, 1979.

c. As a group, prepare an opening sentence for a paragraph that would report your group's reaction to this quotation.

2. Read the following statements about group interaction and decide as a group whether these statements are true or false.

   a. Women are less self-assertive and less competitive in groups than are men.

   b. There is a slight tendency for physically superior individuals to become leaders in a group.

   c. Leaders are usually more intelligent than nonleaders.

   d. Females conform to majority opinion more than males in reaching group decisions.

   e. An unconventional group member inhibits group functioning.

   f. An anxious group member inhibits group functioning.

   g. Group members with more power are usually better liked than low-power group members.

   h. Groups usually produce more and better solutions to problems than do individuals working alone.

With the assistance of the group, the recorder should write a four- to five-sentence description of the process your group used to reach agreement on the true/false statements. Was there discussion? Disagreement? Did you vote? Did every person give an opinion on each question? Were there any difficulties?

A SEVERAL-DAYS' GROUP PROJECT: DEFINING "GOOD ARGUMENTATIVE WRITING"

The problem we want you to address in this sequence of tasks is how to define and identify "good argumentative writing." This is a particularly crucial problem for developing writers insofar as you can't begin to measure your growth as a writer until you have some notion of what you're aiming for. To be sure, it's no easy task defining good argumentative writing. In order for even experienced teachers to reach agreement on this subject, some preliminary discussions and no small amount of compromise are necessary. By the end of this task you will most certainly not have reached a universally acceptable description of good argumentative writing. (Such a description doesn't exist.) But you will have begun a dialogue with each other and your instructor on the subject. Moreover, you will have developed a vocabulary for sharing your views on writing with each other.

For this exercise, we give you a sequence of four tasks, some being homework and others being in-class group tasks. Please do the tasks in sequence.

TASK 1 (HOMEWORK): PREPARING FOR THE GROUP DISCUSSION

Freewrite for five minutes on the question:

"What is good argumentation writing?"

After finishing your freewrite, read fictional student Lunt's argument below and, based on the principles that Lunt seems to break, develop a tentative list of criteria for good argumentative writing.

EXPLANATION   Before you come together with a group of people to advance your understanding and knowledge collectively, you first need to explore your own thoughts on the matter. Too often, groups collapse not because the members lack goodwill, but because they lack preparation. In order to discharge your responsibility as a good group member, you must therefore begin by doing your homework. By using a freewriting exercise, you focus your thinking on the topic, explore what you already know or feel about it, and begin framing questions and problems.

To help you establish a standard for good argumentative writing, we've produced a model of bad arguing by a fictional student, one Elwood P. Lunt, Jr. If you can figure out what's bad about Lunt's argument, then you can formulate the principles of good argument that he violates. Of course, no student of our acquaintance has ever written anything as bad as Lunt's essay. That's the virtue of this contrived piece. It's an easy target. In going over it critically, you may well find that Lunt violates principles of good writing you hadn't thought of in your freewrite. (We tried to ensure that he violated as many as possible.) Thus, you should be sure to go back and modify your ideas from your freewrite accordingly.

A couple of important points to keep in mind here as you prepare to critique another person s work: (1) Remember the principle of charity. Try to look past the muddied prose to a point or intention that might be lurking in the background. Your critique should speak as much as possible to Lunt's failure to realize this intent. (2) Direct your critique to the prose, not the writer. Don't settle for "He just doesn't make sense" or "He's a dimwit." Ask yourself why he doesn't make sense and point to particular places where he doesn't make sense. In sum, give Lunt the same sort of reading you would like to get: compassionate and specific.

GOOD WRITING AND COMPUTERS FOR TODAY'S MODERN AMERICAN YOUTH OF AMERICA

(A partial fulfillment of writing an argument in the
course in which I am attending)

In todays modern fast paced world computers make living a piece of cake. **1**
You can do a lot with computers which in former times took a lot of time and
doing a lot of work. Learning to fly airplanes, for example. But there are no
such things as a free lunch. People who think computers will do all the work
for you need to go to the Iron Curtain and take a look around, that's the
place for people who think they can be replaced by computers. The precious
computer which people think is the dawn of a new civilization but which is in
all reality a pig in a poke makes you into a number but can't even add right!
So don't buy computers for two reasons.

The first reason you shouldn't buy a computer is writing. So what makes **2**
people think that they won't have to write just because they have a computer
on his desk. "Garbage in and garbage out one philosopher said." Do you
want to sound like garbage? I don't. That's why modern American fast paced
youth must conquer this affiar with computers and writing by ourselves is the
answer to our dreams and not just by using a computer for that aforemen-
tioned writing. A computer won't make you think better and thats the
problem because people think a computer will do your thinking for you. No
way, Jose.

Another thing is grammar. My Dad Elwood P. Lunt Sr. hit the nail on the **3**
head; when he said bad grammar can make you sound like a jerk. Right on
Dad. He would be so upset to think of all the jerks out there who wasted their
money on a computer so that the computer could write for them. But do
computers know grammar? So get on the bandwagon and write good and get
rich with computers. Which can make you write right. You think any computer could catch the errors I just made? Oh, sure you do. Jerk. And
according to our handbook on writing writing takes intelligence which computers don't have. Now I'm not against computers. I am just saying that
computers have there place.

In conclusion there are two reasons why you shouldn't buy a computer. **4**
But if you want to buy one that is all right as long as you understand that it
isn't as smart as you think.

TASK 2 (IN-CLASS GROUP WORK): DEVELOPING A MASTER LIST OF CRITERIA

As a group, reach a consensus on at least six or seven major problems with
Lunt's argumentative essay. Then use that list to prepare a parallel list of
criteria for a good written argument. Please have your list ready in thirty
minutes.

EXPLANATION Your goal for this task is to reach consensus about what's wrong with Lunt's argument. As opposed to a "majority decision," in which more people agree than disagree, a "consensus" entails a solution that is generally acceptable to all members of the group. In deciding what is the matter with Lunt's essay, you should be able to reach consensus also on the criteria for a good argument. After each group has completed its list, recorders should report each group's consensus to the class as a whole. Your instructor will facilitate a discussion leading to the class's "master list" of criteria.

TASK 3 (HOMEWORK): APPLYING CRITERIA TO STUDENT ESSAYS

At home, consider the following five samples of student writing. (This time they're real examples.) Rank the essays "1" through "5," with 1 being the best and 5 the worst. Once you've done this, develop a brief rationale for your ranking. This rationale should force you to decide which criteria you rank highest and which lowest. For example, does "quality of reasons" rank higher than "organization and development"? Does "colorful, descriptive style" rank high or low in your ranking system?

EXPLANATION The essays reprinted below were all written in response to Option 6, page 139, in "Writing Assignments for Part II." Before judging the arguments, read over that assignment so you know what students were asked to do. Judge the essays on the basis of the criteria established in class.

BLOODY ICE

It is March in Alaska. The ocean-side environment is full of life and death.   1
Man and animal share this domain but not in peace. The surrounding icefloes, instead of being cold and white, are steaming from the remains of gutted carcasses and stained red. The men are hunters and the animals are barely six weeks old. A slaughter has just taken place. Thousands of baby Harp seals lay dead on the ice and thousands more of adult mothers lay groaning over the death of their babies. Every year a total limit of 180,000 seals set by the U.S. Seal Protection Act is filled in a terrifying bloodbath. But Alaska with its limit of 30,000 is not alone. Canadians who hunt seals off the coast of Northern Newfoundland and Quebec are allowed 150,000 seals. The Norwegians are allowed 20,000 and native Eskimos of Canada and Greenland are allowed 10,000 seals per year. Although this act appears heartless and cruel, the men who hunt have done this for 200 years as a tradition for survival. They make many good arguments supporting their traditions. They feel the

seals are in no immediate danger of extinction. Also seal furs can be used to line boots and gloves or merely traded for money and turned into robes or fur coats. Sometimes the meat is even used for food in the off hunting months when money is scarce. But are these valid justifications for the unmerciful killings? No, the present limit on Harp seal killings should be better regulated because the continued hunting of the seals will lead to eventual extinction and because the method of slaughter is so cruel and inhumane.

The Harp seal killing should be better regulated first because eventual **2** extinction is inevitable. According to *Oceans* magazine, before the limit of 180,000 seals was established in 1950, the number of seals had dwindled from 3,300,000 to 1,250,000. Without these limitations hundreds of thousands were killed within weeks of birth. Now, even with this allotment, the seals are being killed off at an almost greater rate than they can remultiply. Adult female seals give birth once every year but due to pollution, disease, predation, whelping success and malnutrition they are already slowly dying on their own without being hunted. Eighty percent of the seals slaughtered are pups and the remaining twenty percent are adult seals and even sometimes mothers who try attacking the hunters after seeing their babies killed. The hunters, according to the Seal Protection Act, have this right.

Second, I feel the killings should be better regulated because of the **3** inhumane method used. In order to protect the fur value of the seals, guns are not used. Instead, the sealers use metal clubs to bludgen the seal to death. Almost immediately after being delivered a direct blow, the seals are gutted open and skinned. Although at this stage of life the seal's skull is very fragile, sometimes the seals are not killed by the blows but merely stunned; thus hundreds are skinned alive. Still others are caught in nets and drowned, which according to *America* magazine, the Canadian government continues to deny. But the worst of the methods used is when a hunter gets tired of swinging his club and uses the heel of his boot to kick the seal's skull in. Better regulation is the only way to solve this problem because other attempts seem futile. For example, volunteers who have traveled to hunting sites trying to dye the seals to ruin their fur value have been caught and fined heavily.

The plight of the Harp seals has been long and controversial. With the **4** Canadian hunters feeling they have the right to kill the seals because it has been their industry for over two centuries, and on the other hand with humane organizations fearing extinction and strongly opposing the method of slaughter, a compromise must be met among both sides. As I see it, the solution to the problem is simple. Since the Canadians do occasionally use the whole seal and have been sealing for so long they could be allowed to continue but at a more heavily regulated rate. Instead of filling the limit of 180,000 every year and letting the numbers of seals decrease, Canadians could learn to ranch the seals as Montanans do cattle or sheep. The United

States has also offered to help them begin farming their land for a new livelihood. The land is adequate for crops and would provide work all year round instead of only once a month every year. As a result of farming, the number of seals killed would be drastically cut down because Canadians would not be so dependent on the seal industry as before. This would in turn lead back to the ranching aspect of sealing and allow the numbers to grow back and keeping the tradition alive for future generations and one more of natures's creatures to enjoy.

RSS SHOULD NOT PROVIDE DORM ROOM CARPETS

Tricia, a University student, came home exhausted from her work-study job. She took a blueberry pie from the refrigerator to satisfy her hunger and a tall glass of milk to quench her thirst. While trying to get comfortable on her bed, she tipped her snack over onto the floor. She cleaned the mess, but the blueberry and milk stains on her brand new carpet could not be removed. She didn't realize that maintaining a clean carpet would be difficult and costly. Tricia bought her own carpet. Some students living in dorm rooms want carpeted rooms provided for them at the expense of the University. They insist that since they pay to live on campus, the rooms should reflect a comfortable home atmosphere. However, Resident Student Services (RSS) should not be required to furnish the carpet because other students do not want carpets. Furthermore, carpeting all the rooms totals into a very expensive project. And lastly, RSS should not have to provide the carpet because many students show lack of respect and responsibility for school property. 1

Although RSS considers the carpeting of all rooms a strong possibility, students like Tricia oppose the idea. They feel the students should buy their own carpets. Others claim the permanent carpeting would make dorm life more comfortable. The carpet will act as insulation and as a sound proofing system. These are valid arguments, but they should not be the basis for changing the entire residence hall structure. Those students with "cold feet" can purchase house footwear, which cost less than carpet. Unfortunately carpeting doesn't muffle all the noise; therefore, some students will be disturbed. Reasonable quietness should be a matter of respect for other students' privacy and comfort. Those opposed to the idea reason out the fact that students constantly change rooms or move out. The next person may not want carpet. Also, if RSS carpets the rooms, the students will lose the privilege they have of painting their rooms any color. Paint stains cannot be removed. Some students can't afford to replace the carpet. Still another factor, carpet color may not please everyone. RSS would provide a neutral color like brown or gray. With tile floors, the students can choose and purchase their own carpets to match their taste. 2

Finally, another reason not to have carpet exists in the fact that the project 3 can be expensive due to material costs, installation cost, and the maintenance cost caused mainly by the irresponsibility of many students. According to Rick Jones, Asst. Director of Housing Services, the cost will be $300 per room for the carpet and installation. RSS would also have to purchase more vacuum cleaners for the students use. RSS will incur more expense in order to maintain the vacuums. Also, he claims that many accidents resulting from shaving cream fights, food fights, beverage parties, and smoking may damage the carpet permanently. With floor tiles, accidents such as food spills can be cleaned up easier than carpet. The student's behavior plays an important role in deciding against carpeting. Many students don't follow the rules of maintaining their rooms. They drill holes into the walls, break mirrors, beds, and closet doors, and leave their food trays all over the floor. How could they be trusted to take care of school carpet when they violate the current rules? Many students feel they have the "right" to do as they please. This irresponsible and disrespectful behavior reflects their future attitude about carpet care.

In conclusion, the university may be able to afford to supply the carpets in 4 each room, but maintaining them would be difficult. If the students want carpets, they should pay and care for the carpets themselves. Hopefully, they will be more cautious and value it more. They should take the initiative to fundraise or find other financial means of providing this "luxury". They should not rely on the school to provide unnecessary room fixtures such as carpets. Also, they must remember that if RSS provides the carpet and they don't pay for the damages, they and future students will endure the consequences. What will happen???? Room rates will skyrocket!!!!!

STERLING HALL DORM FOOD

The quality of Sterling Hall dorm food does not meet the standard needed 1 to justify the high prices University students pay. As I watched a tall, medium-built University student pick up his Mexican burrito from the counter it didn't surprise me to see him turn up his nose. Johnny, our typical University student, waited five minutes before he managed to make it through the line. After he received his bill of $4.50 he turned his back to the cash register and walked away displeased with his meal.

As our neatly groomed University student placed his validine eating card 2 back into his Giorgio wallet, he thought back to the balance left on his account. Johnny had $24 left on his account and six more weeks left of school. He had been eating the cheapest meals he could and still receive a balanced meal, but the money just seemed to disappear. No student, not even a thrifty boy like Johnny could possibly afford to live healthfully according to the University meal plan system.

Johnny then sat down at a dirty table to find his burrito only half way   3 cooked. Thinking back to the long-haired cook who served him the burrito, he bit into the burrito and noticed a long hair dangling from his lips. He realized the cook's lack of preparation when preparing his burrito.

Since the food costs so much, yet the quality of the food remains low,   4 University students do not get the quality they deserve. From the information stated I can conclude that using the validine service system University students would be jeopardizing their health and wasting their hard-earned money. University students deserve something more than what they have now.

ROTC COURSES SHOULD NOT GET COLLEGE CREDIT

One of the most lucrative scholarships a student can receive is a four-year   1 R.O.T.C. scholarship that pays tuition and books along with a living allowance. It was such a scholarship that allowed me to attend an expensive liberal arts college and to pursue the kind of well rounded education that matters to me. Of course, I am obligated to spend four years on active duty — an obligation that I accept and look forward to. What I am disappointed in, however, is the necessity to enroll in Military Science classes. Strong ROTC advocates argue that Military Science classes are essential because they produce good citizens, teach leadership skills, and provide practical experience for young cadets. Maybe so. But we could get the same benefits without having to take these courses for credit. Colleges should make ROTC training an extracurricular activity, not a series of academic courses taken for academic credit.

First of all, ROTC courses, unlike other college courses, do not stress   2 inquiry and true questioning. The ROTC program has as its objective the preparation of future officers committed to the ideals and structure of the military. The structure of the military is based upon obediently following the orders of military superiors. Whereas all my other teachers stress critical thinking and doing independent analysis, my ROTC instructors avoid political or social questions saying it is the job of civilian leaders to debate policies and the job of the military to carry them out. We don't even debate what role the military should play in our country. My uncle, who was an ROTC cadet during the Vietnam war, remembers that not only did ROTC classes never discuss the ethics of the war but that cadets were not allowed to protest the war outside of their ROTC courses. This same obedience is demanded in my own ROTC courses, where we are not able to question administration policies and examine openly the complexity of the situation in Iraq and Kuwait.

A second reason that Army ROTC courses do not deserve academic credit   3 is that the classes are not academically strenuous, thus giving cadets a higher G.P.A. and an unfair advantage over their peers. Much of what a cadet does for academic credit involves non-academic activities such as physical training for an hour three days a week so that at least some of a cadet's grade is based on physical activity, not mental activity. In conducting an informal survey of 10 upper-classmen, I found out that none of them has ever gotten anything lower than an A in a Military Science class and they do not know of anyone who got anything lower than an A. One third-year cadet stated that "the classes are basic. A monkey coming out of the zoo could get college credit for a Military Science class." He went on to say that most of the information given in his current class is a brush-up to 8th grade U.S. history. In contrast, a typical liberal arts college class requires much thought, questioning, and analysis. The ROTC Military Science class is taught on the basis of "regurgitated knowledge," meaning that once you are given a piece of information you are required to know it and reproduce it at any time without thought or question. A good example is in my class Basic Officership. Our first assignment is to memorize and recite in front of the class the Preamble to the Constitution of the United States. The purpose of doing so doesn't seem to be to understand or analyze the constitution because we never talk about that. In fact, I don't know what the purpose is. I just do it because I am told to. Because the "A" is so easy to get in my ROTC class, I spend all my time studying for my other classes. I am a step ahead of my peers in the competition for a high GPA, even though I am not getting as good an education.

Finally, having to take ROTC classes means that I can't take other liberal   4 arts courses which would be more valuable. One of the main purposes for ROTC is to give potential officers a liberal education. Many cadets have the credentials to get into an armed forces academy, but they chose ROTC programs because they could combine military training with a well-rounded curriculum. Unfortunately, by taking Military Science classes each quarter, cadets find that their electives are all but eaten up by the time they are seniors. If ROTC classes were valuable in themselves, I wouldn't complain. But they aren't, and they keep me from taking upper division electives in philosophy, literature, and the humanities.

All of these reasons lead me to believe that Army ROTC cadets are getting   5 short-changed when they enroll for Military Science classes. Because cadets receive a lucrative scholarship, they should have to take the required military science courses. But these courses should be treated as extra-curricular activities, like a work-study job or like athletics. Just as a student on a full-ride athletic scholarship does not receive academic credit for football practices and games, so should a student on a full-ride R.O.T.C. scholarship have to participate in the military education program without getting academic credit. By treating R.O.T.C. courses as a type of extra-curricular activity like athletics, students can take more elective credits that will expand their minds, better enabling them to have the knowledge to make moral decisions and to enjoy their world more fully.

LEGALIZATION OF PROSTITUTION?

Prostitution . . . it is the world's oldest profession. It is by definition the 1 act of offering or soliciting sex for payment. It is, to some, evil. Yet, the fact is it exists.

Arguments are not necessary to prove the existence of prostitution. 2 Rather, the argument arises when trying to prove something must be done to reduce the problems of this profession. The problems which exist are in the area of crime, of health, and of environment. Crime rates are soaring, diseases are spreading wildly, and the environment on the streets is rapidly decaying. Still, it has been generally conceded that these problems cannot be suppressed. However they can be reduced. Prostitution should be legalized because it would reduce the wave of epidemics, decrease high crime rates, provide good revenue by treating it like other businesses, and get girls off the streets where sexual crimes often occur.

Of course, there are those who would oppose the legalization of prostitu- 3 tion stating that it is one of the main causes for the spread of venereal diseases. Many argue that it is inter-related with drug-trafficking and other organized crimes. And probably the most controversial is the moral aspect of the subject; it is morally wrong, and legalizing it would be enforcing, or even justifying, such an existence.

These points propose good arguments, but I shall counter each point and 4 explain the benefits and advantages of legalizing prostitution. In the case of prostitution being the main cause for the spread of epidemics, I disagree. By legalizing it, houses would be set up which would solve the problem of girls working on the streets and being victims of sexual crimes. It would also provide regular health checks, as is successfully done in Nevada, Germany, and other parts of the U.S. and Europe, which will therefore cut down on diseases spreading unknowingly.

As for the increase of organized crime if prostitution is legalized, I disagree 5 again. Firstly, by treating it like businesses, then that would make good state revenue. Secondly, like all businesses have regulations, so shall these houses. That would put closer and better control in policing the profession, which is presently a problem. Obviously, if the business of prostitution is more closely supervised, that would decrease the crime rates.

Now, I come to one of the most arguable aspects of legalizing prostitution: 6 the moral issue. Is it morally wrong to legalize prostitution? That is up to the individual. To determine whether anything is "right or wrong" in our society is nearly impossible to do since there are various opinions. If a person were to say that prostitution is the root of all evil, that will not make it go away. It exists. Society must begin to realize that fear or denial will not make the "ugliness' disappear. It still exists.

Prostitution can no longer go ignored because of our societal attitudes. 7 Legalizing it is beneficial to our society, and I feel in time people may begin to form an accepting attitude. It would be the beginning of a more open-minded view of what is reality. Prostitution . . . it is the world's oldest profession. It exists. It is a reality.

TASK 4 (IN-CLASS GROUP WORK): REACHING CONSENSUS ON RANKING OF ESSAYS

Working again in small groups, reach consensus on your ranking of the five essays. Groups should report both their rankings and their justification for the rankings based on the criteria established in Task 2 or as currently modified by your group.

EXPLANATION You are now to reach consensus on how you rank the papers and why you rank them the way you do. Feel free to change the criteria you established earlier if they seem to need modification. Be careful in your discussions to distinguish between evaluation of the writer's written product and your own personal position on the writer's issue. In other words, there is a crucial difference between saying "I don't like Pete's essay because I disagree with his ideas" and "I don't like Pete's essay because he didn't provide adequate support for his ideas." As each group reports back the results of their deliberations to the class as a whole, the instructor will highlight discrepancies among the groups' decisions and collate the criteria as they emerge. If the instructor disagrees with the class consensus or wants to add items to the criteria, he or she might choose to make these things known now. By the end of this stage, everyone should have a list of criteria for good argumentative writing established by the class.

A CLASSROOM DEBATE

In this exercise, you have an opportunity to engage in a variant of a formal debate. Although debates of this nature don't always lead to truth for its own sake, they are excellent forums for the development of analytical and organizational skills. The format for the debate is as follows.

FIRST HOUR   Groups will identify and reach consensus on "the most serious impediment to learning at this institution." Participants should have come to class prepared with their own individual lists of at least three problems. Once the class has reached consensus on the single most serious impediment to learning on your campus, your instructor will write it out as a formal statement. This statement constitutes the preliminary topic, which will eventually result in a proposition for your debate.

The instructor will then divide the class into an equal number of Affirmative and Negative teams (three to five members per team). Homework for all the Affirmative team members is to identify proposals for solving the problem identified by the class. Negative team members, meanwhile, will concentrate on reasons that the problem is not particularly serious and/or that the problem is "in the nature of things" and simply not soluble by any sort of proposal.

SECOND HOUR   At the beginning of the period, the instructor will pair up each Affirmative team with a Negative team. The teams will be opponents during the actual debate, and there will be as many debates as there are paired teams. Each Affirmative team will now work on choosing the best proposal for solving the problem, while the Negative team pools its resources and builds its case against the seriousness and solubility of the problem. At the end of the period, each Affirmative team will share its proposal with its corresponding Negative team. The actual topic for each of the debates is now set: "Resolved: Our campus should institute Z (the Affirmative team's proposal) in order to solve problem X (the class's original problem statement)."

Homework for the next class is for each team to conduct research (interviewing students, gathering personal examples, polling students, finding data or expert testimony from the library, and so forth) to support its case. Each Affirmative team's research will be aimed at showing that the problem is serious and that the solution is workable. Each Negative team will try to show that the proposal won't work or that the problem isn't worth solving.

THIRD HOUR   At this point each Affirmative team and each Negative team will select two speakers to represent their sides. During this hour each team will pool its ideas and resources to help the speakers make the best possible cases. Each team should prepare an outline for a speech supporting its side of the debate. Team members should then anticipate the arguments of the opposition and prepare a rebuttal.

FOURTH (AND FIFTH) HOUR(S)   The actual debates. (There will be as many debates as there are paired Affirmative and Negative teams.) Each team will present two speakers. Each speaker is limited to five minutes. The order of speaking is as follows:

First Affirmative: Presents best case for the proposal

First Negative: Presents best case against the proposal

Second Negative: Rebuts argument of First Affirmative

Second Affirmative: Rebuts argument of First Negative

Those team members who do not speak will be designated observers. Their task is to take notes on the debate, paying special attention to the quality of support for each argument and to those parts of the argument that are not rebutted by the opposition. By the next class period (fifth or sixth), they will have prepared a brief, informal analysis titled "Why Our Side Won the Debate."

FIFTH OR SIXTH HOUR   The observers will report to the class on their perceptions of the debates by using their prepared analysis as the basis of the discussion. The instructor will attempt to synthesize the main points of the debates and the most telling arguments for either side. At this point, your instructor may ask each of you to write an argument on the debate topic, allowing you to argue for or against any of the proposals presented.

ACKNOWLEDGMENTS

Charles Krauthammer, "Censorship Is a Matter of Classification," © 1990, Washington Post Writers Group. Reprinted with permission.

Charles Krauthammer, "A Defense of Quotas," *The New Republic*, September 16/23, 1985. Reprinted by permission of *The New Republic*, © 1987, The New Republic, Inc.

Charles Krauthammer, "School Birth-Control Clinics: Necessary Evil," © 1991, Washington Post Writers Group. Reprinted with permission.

Charles Krauthammer, "Why Lithuania Is Not Like South Carolina," *Time*, April 16, 1990. Copyright © 1990 The Time Inc. Magazine Company. Reprinted by permission.

"Pornography, Obscenity and the Case for Censorship" from *Reflections of a Neo-Conservative* by Irving Kristol. Copyright © 1983 by Basic Books Inc. Reprinted by permission of Basic Books, a division of HarperCollins Publishers, Inc.

"Global Climatic Trends" by H. E. Landsberg, from *The Resourceful Earth*, edited by J. L. Simon. Reprinted by permission of Blackwell Publishers.

"The Ones Who Walk Away from Omelas," by Ursula Le Guin. Copyright © 1973, 1975 by Ursula K. Le Guin; reprinted by permission of the author and the author's agent, Virginia Kidd.

Michael Levin, "The Case for Torture," *Newsweek*, June 7, 1982. Reprinted by permission of the author.

Frederick R. Lynch, "Surviving Affirmative Action (More or Less)," *Commentary*, August 1990. Reprinted from *Commentary*, August 1990, by permission; all rights reserved. Frederick R. Lynch is author of *Invisible Victims: White Males and the Crisis of Affirmative Action* (Westport, CT: Praeger Paperbacks, Greenwood Publishing Group, 1991).

"Death by Choice: Who Should Decide?" from *Death by Choice* by Daniel C. Maguire. Copyright © 1973, 1974 by Daniel C. Maguire. Used by permission of Doubleday, a division of Bantam Doubleday Dell Publishing Group, Inc.

William F. May, "Rising to the Occasion of our Death," *The Christian Century*, July 11–18, 1990. Copyright © 1990, Christian Century Foundation. Reprinted by permission from the July 11–18, 1990 issue of *The Christian Century*.

Walter S. Minot, "Students Who Push Burgers," *The Christian Science Monitor*, November 22, 1988. Reprinted by permission of the author.

Eli M. Oboler, "Defending Intellectual Freedom," *Newsletter on Intellectual Freedom*, January 1972. Reprinted by permission of the American Library Association.

Ronald J. Ostrow, "U.S. Cocaine Use Plunges, Survey Shows," *Seattle Times*, December 20, 1990. Reprinted by permission of Los Angeles Times Syndicate.

Dr. Richard A. Peters, "Yes: It Saves Lives and Lowers Prices," and Uwe Reinhart, "No: Their Motives Are Purely Economic," Scripps-Howard News Service. Reprinted by permission of Scripps-Howard News Service.

Dixy Lee Ray, "The Greenhouse Blues: Keep Cool about Global Warming," *Policy Review*, Summer 1989. Reprinted with permission from the Summer 1989 issue of *Policy Review*, the flagship publication of the Heritage Foundation, Massachusetts Ave., NE, Washington, DC.

Andrew C. Revkin, "Endless Summer: Living with the Greenhouse Effect," *Discover* Magazine, October 1988. Andrew C. Revkin/ © 1988 Discover Publications.

Mike Royko, "Drug War Is Lost; Here's What To Do Now." Reprinted by permission of Sterling Lord Literistic, Inc. Copyright © 1989.

Carl Sagan, "The Warming of the World," was first published in *Parade*, February 3, 1985. Copyright © 1985. All rights reserved. Reprinted by permission of the author.

David G. Savage, "Studies Show Drug Problems Persist," *Seattle Times*, December 21, 1990. Reprinted by permission of Los Angeles Times Syndicate.

768 ACKNOWLEDGMENTS

Peter Shaw, "Apocalypse Again," *Commentary*, April 1989. Reprinted from *Commentary*, April 1989, by permission; all rights reserved.

Peter Singer, "A Review of Animals, Men and Morals," April 15, 1973, *New York Review of Books*. Reprinted by permission of the author.

"Rich and Poor" from *Practical Ethics* by Peter Singer. Copyright © 1979, Cambridge University Press. Reprinted with permission of Cambridge University Press and the author.

Thomas Sowell, "Misquotas: Scholarships Should Be Based on Need," *Tempe Tribune*, December 29, 1990. Copyright © 1990 by Thomas Sowell. First appeared in *Tempe Tribune*. Reprinted by permission of Georges Borchardt, Inc. for the author.

Bruce Sterling, "Drugs an Essential Part of Modern Life," *Seattle Times*, September 7, 1989. Reprinted by permission of Writers House Inc. and the author.

James R. Udall, "Global Warming: Diplomacy's Next Great Challenge," *Phi Kappa Phi Journal*, Winter 1990. Reprinted from the Winter 1990 issue of *National Forum: The Phi Kappa Phi Journal*.

"U.S. Should Take Immediate Measures To Combat Global Warming" (Editorial), *USA Today* magazine, June 1986. Reprinted from *USA Today* magazine, copyright © 1986 by the Society for the Advancement of Education.

Roger Wilkins, "In Ivory Towers," *Mother Jones*, July/August 1990. Reprinted with permission from *Mother Jones* magazine, © 1990, Foundation for National Progress.

James Q. Wilson, "Against the Legalization of Drugs," *Commentary*, February 1990. Reprinted from *Commentary*, February 1990, by permission; all rights reserved.

INDEX